A Companion to the Works of Hermann Hesse

Studies in German Literature, Linguistics, and Culture

Camden House Companion Volumes

The Camden House Companions provide well-informed and up-to-date critical commentary on the most significant aspects of major works, periods, or literary figures. The Companions may be read profitably by the reader with a general interest in the subject. For the benefit of student and scholar, quotations are provided in the original language.

A Companion to the Works of
Hermann Hesse

Edited by
Ingo Cornils

CAMDEN HOUSE
Rochester, New York

First published 2009
by Camden House

Camden House is an imprint of Boydell & Brewer Inc.
668 Mt. Hope Avenue, Rochester, NY 14620, USA
www.camden-house.com
and of Boydell & Brewer Limited
PO Box 9, Woodbridge, Suffolk IP12 3DF, UK
www.boydellandbrewer.com

ISBN-13: 978-1-57113-330-4
ISBN-10: 1-57113-330-5

Library of Congress Cataloging-in-Publication Data

A companion to the works of Hermann Hesse / edited by Ingo Cornils.
    p. cm.
Includes bibliographical references and index.
ISBN-13: 978-1-57113-330-4 (hardcover: alk. paper)
ISBN-10: 1-57113-330-5 (hardcover: alk. paper)
    1. Hesse, Hermann, 1877–1962 — Criticism and interpretation.
I. Cornils, Ingo.

PT2617.E85Z6754 2009
838'.91209—dc22

2009035701

A catalogue record for this title is available from the British Library.

This publication is printed on acid-free paper.
Printed in the United States of America.

Contents

Acknowledgments   vii

Introduction: From Outsider to Global Player — Hermann
    Hesse in the Twenty-First Century   1
    Ingo Cornils

1:   Novel Ideas: Notes toward a New Reading of Hesse's
    Unterm Rad   17
    Jefford Vahlbusch

2:   *Roßhalde* (1914): A Portrait of the Artist as a Husband
    and Father   57
    Osman Durrani

3:   The Aesthetics of Ritual: Pollution, Magic, and
    Sentimentality in Hesse's *Demian* (1919)   81
    Andreas Solbach

4:   *Klein und Wagner*   117
    Stefan Höppner

5:   *Klingsors letzter Sommer* and the Transformation
    of Crisis   139
    Ralph Freedman

6:   *Siddhartha*   149
    Adrian Hsia

7:   *Der Steppenwolf*   171
    Martin Swales

8:   Hermann Hesse's *Narziss und Goldmund:* Medieval
    Imaginaries of (Post-)Modern Realities   187
    Frederick Lubich

9: Beads of Glass, Shards of Culture, and the Art of Life:
Hesse's *Das Glasperlenspiel*
Paul Bishop   215

10: Hesse's Poetry   241
Olaf Berwald

11: *"Ob die Weiber Menschen seyn?"* Hesse, Women,
and Homoeroticism   263
Kamakshi P. Murti

12: Hermann Hesse's Politics   301
Marco Schickling

13: Hermann Hesse and Psychoanalysis   323
Volker Michels

14: On the Relationship between Hesse's Painting and
Writing: *Wanderung, Klingsors letzter Sommer,*
Gedichte des Malers and *Piktors Verwandlungen*   345
Godela Weiss-Sussex

15: Hermann Hesse and Music   373
C. Immo Schneider

16: Hermann Hesse's Goethe   395
Hans-Joachim Hahn

List of English Translations   421

Select Bibliography   423

Notes on the Contributors   427

Index   431

Acknowledgments

I would like to thank the following:

Jim Walker, Editorial Director of Camden House, for suggesting the project and supporting it with unfailing enthusiasm, knowledgeable comments, and infinite patience.

The contributors, for their willingness to share their expertise and to engage in often lengthy correspondences with the editor.

Michael M. Metzger, for his skillful translations of four chapters from German.

Jayantha Gomes, for kind permission to use his illustration on the back cover.

Volker Michels, spiritus rector of all things Hesse, for saving this extraordinary writer from the nay-sayers.

My wife Liza, for being there.

I.C.
Leeds, September 2009

Introduction: From Outsider to Global Player: Hermann Hesse in the Twenty-First Century

Ingo Cornils

MORE THAN THIRTY YEARS have passed since the last *Hesse Companion*, edited by Anna Otten, was published.[1] The book was a response to Hesse's phenomenal popularity in the United States following his discovery by the hippie generation in the 1960s.[2] The world has changed beyond recognition since those heady days when self-discovery had become the ultimate goal for a generation "born to be wild."[3] Today, the young men and women who found inspiration in Hesse's works are reaching retirement age. Their idealism has become jaded, their legacy uncertain.[4] But what about their "guru"? Is Hesse a writer for aging hippies or is he still relevant for a new generation of readers? These are the questions that this new Hesse Companion sets out to answer.

There is no doubt that the works of Hermann Hesse continue to be immensely popular. With more than 100 million copies of his books sold worldwide, he is one of the best selling German-language authors, and, more significantly, *the* most widely translated German-language author. His major texts *Demian, Siddhartha, Der Steppenwolf, Narziß und Goldmund,* and *Das Glasperlenspiel* have been translated into more than sixty languages. There are Hesse societies in Korea and Hungary, Hesse museums, regular events such as the Hesse Colloquium in Calw and the Hesse Tage in Sils-Maria, a Hesse yearbook and several Web sites. Among his dedicated followers, he enjoys fierce loyalty. However, because of his great popular appeal and his message "Werde du selbst" [Become yourself], Hermann Hesse provokes strong reactions. Academics and literary critics in his birth country were long ill at ease with him, and some have remained so well into the new millennium, though more of them have been willing to treat him as a serious writer in recent years. Self-effacing and private by nature, Hesse was certainly not considered to be in the same league as his contemporary Thomas Mann. Both won the Nobel Prize for Literature and had equally appreciative audiences, but it was Mann who insisted "Wo ich bin, ist Deutschland" and cultivated his celebrity status, while Hesse spent the latter half of his long life in Ticino, the Italian-speaking part of Switzerland, carefully avoiding both the media and any association with "official" Germany.

The view that Hesse is somehow not worthy of "serious" literary engagement is rapidly changing, as a new critical edition of his works, a reevaluation of his political thought in the context of global environmental developments, and an appreciation of his seemingly simple yet profound message give rise to new research around the world. This volume presents the latest thinking on Hesse by leading scholars in the field, provides critical new readings, and demonstrates that his writings are eminently suited to literary study: they offer moments of sublime beauty and important clues for the understanding of the human psyche.

Romantic Outsider

Hermann Hesse was born on 2 July 1877 in the small town of Calw in the Black Forest near Stuttgart. His parents, Johannes Hesse and Marie Hesse (née Gundert) worked in his grandfather's missionary publishing house. Most biographies stress that he spent his first years of life surrounded by the spirit of Swabian piety.[5] Prayer, the daily reading of exemplary lives, introspection, and the development of a strong awareness of right and wrong, of transgression and atonement, certainly permeated Hesse's childhood in Calw and, from 1881 to 1886, in Basel, Switzerland. Equally important, though, is an atmosphere of learning, an awareness of exotic places and cultures (both his parents had worked for a Basel Mission to India, and his grandfather, Hermann Gundert, was the author of a Malay-English dictionary and the owner of a vast library to which the young Hermann had free access), and a sense that he was destined for higher things.

Unfortunately, Hermann's early determination "ein Dichter zu werden, oder gar nichts" set him in direct confrontation with his parents, who expected him to attend the Evangelical Theological Seminary and follow in their footsteps. Ninon Hesse, his third wife, collected the extensive correspondence of this period, during which young Hermann clashed with his parents, fled from the seminary, attempted suicide, was sent to a "healer" who was supposed to break his rebellious spirit, and was briefly committed to a mental institution. The problem was an existential one, as far as young Hermann was concerned. His parents had put him under intense moral pressure to conform to their wishes and values, which part of him wanted to comply with, while another part of him yearned for independence. Various attempts by his parents to find a suitable occupation for him failed (including an apprenticeship at a metal workshop) and he only found relative peace of mind and some emotional distance from his parents in an apprenticeship as a bookseller in Tübingen. Here, in spite of demanding twelve-hour days packing and cataloguing books, he could follow his own interests, exploring German literature, especially the Romantics. At the same time, the university town of Tübingen allowed him to mix with students destined for "respectable" careers, fueling his desire to prove himself as a writer.

Following two unsuccessful volumes of poetry and short prose pieces (*Romantische Lieder,* 1898, and *Eine Stunde hinter Mitternacht,* 1899), he moved to Basel in 1899 to work in a well-known antique bookshop and experienced the cultural and intellectual stimulation that he had clearly lacked in Calw and Tübingen. He read voraciously, especially Nietzsche and the works of the cultural historian Jacob Burckhardt. He also developed a keen interest in art — for example he was intrigued by the local painter Arnold Böcklin — and developed his appreciation for classical music. In his spare time Hesse would go for long walks in the country or on climbing trips, alone or with friends. Images of these trips, and also of his observations of the Basel art scene, made their way into his first novel, *Peter Camenzind,* which was published by S. Fischer in 1904. The book powerfully expresses Hesse's skepticism of modernity and contrasts the refined tastes of the city with the experience of nature.

With the proceeds of the book, Hesse could afford to set himself up as an independent writer. He married Maria Bernoulli, a photographer nine years his senior, and settled in the small village of Gaienhofen on the German side of Lake Constance. Here, he wrote *Unterm Rad* (Beneath the Wheel, 1905) his celebrated novel of a doomed childhood, and attempted to balance the life of a creative artist with the respectable bourgeois life of a successful storyteller, husband, and father of his three sons. His idyll soon became a burden to him and he escaped on several walking tours to Italy and, in 1911, on a sea-journey to Sri Lanka (then Ceylon) and Indonesia. His marriage had become problematic, first signs of which can be seen in his 1910 novel *Gertrude.* Following the family's move to Bern in 1912, the theme of a failed marriage also became the topic of his novel *Roßhalde,* which appeared in 1914. By this time Hesse had reached a new level of mastery in his writing[6] but felt that something vital was missing. He had outgrown his role as established *Heimatdichter,* but could not see a way forward. It took a world war, a painful separation from his family, and serious self-scrutiny to reinvent himself.

The inexorable pull of a *Zeitenwende,* a turning point in history, was acutely felt in the decade before the First World War. Even in his isolated existence Hesse was aware that the Second German Empire with its certainties was coming to an end. The saber-rattling policies of Emperor Wilhelm II and his Prussian generals, as well as the clamoring of the new elites of industry and culture who propagated the idea that Germany should become a world power, augured a leap into the unknown that was, in the confused and heated debates of the day, seen as preferable to any diplomatic solution to the mounting tensions between the European powers.[7] Hesse initially greeted the outbreak of the First World War with some enthusiasm, registering as a volunteer like so many other idealistic men, but was exempted due to poor eyesight and his recurring migraines. Throughout the war he worked tirelessly for the care of prisoners of war, raising funds and providing thousands of wounded, demoralized and shell-shocked soldiers with books and a sense that they were not forgotten.

Politically, Hesse soon realized that any voice of sanity and calm was unwanted during the nationalist fervor that had been whipped up by the German government and the media. When he published a plea for a civil tone among intellectuals (*O Freunde, nicht diese Töne*, Neue Zürcher Zeitung, 3 Nov. 1914),[8] he was attacked by all quarters of the German press. With his father's death in 1916, his own son's serious illness and his wife's worsening schizophrenia, Hesse himself was plunged into a deep personal crisis. Following a series of psychotherapy sessions with the analyst Josef Bernhard Lang, a colleague and student of Carl Gustav Jung, in which he began to confront the demons that had plagued him since his youth, he wrote the novel *Demian*. Initially published in 1919 under the pseudonym of "Emil Sinclair," it quickly became a bestseller, especially among young Germans. In the aftermath of the war Hesse rejected offers to participate in the short-lived socialist revolution in Munich and focused his energies on reaching his disillusioned German readers through essays such as *Zarathustras Wiederkehr* and through the journal *Vivos voco* (I Call Upon the Living), which he co-founded.

The year 1919 brought many changes for Hesse: he left his wife and rented a flat in the Casa Camuzzi in Montagnola, a village in the Italian-speaking part of Switzerland. Here, he experienced an intense period of creativity, discovered the therapeutic power of painting, and wrote three short texts in succession that would later be published together under the title *Der Weg nach Innen* (The Interior Journey): *Klingsors letzter Sommer, Klein und Wagner,* and *Siddhartha*. He also fell in love again and, following the divorce from his first wife (his sons were meanwhile placed in the care of friends) and very much against his own better judgment, married his second wife, the young singer Ruth Wenger. Their marriage only lasted three years but had a profound influence on Hesse, as can be seen in his *Krisis* poems and his most famous novel *Der Steppenwolf*. In the image of the "half-tame" Harry Haller, who is attracted by the lights and the cultural delights of the city but also desires to follow his wild instincts, Hesse had found a central metaphor for the fragmentation of the individual in the period of the Weimar Republic.

Der Steppenwolf was enthusiastically received by literary critics and Hesse's fellow writers, but his reading public clamored for something less tortured and challenging. Hesse obliged with *Narziß und Goldmund* (1930), a romantic medieval tale that scandalized some and fascinated others with its gentle and glorious depiction of its hero's discovery and pursuit of physical pleasure. In 1931, Hesse married his third wife, Ninon Dolbin (née Ausländer) and moved into a large house near Montagnola that one of his patrons had built for them to their specifications, and where he would live for the rest of his life.

When the Nazis seized power in 1933, Hesse was faced with a dilemma. He was tempted to make a clear statement denouncing Hitler, which would have meant that his books would have disappeared from German bookshops and libraries. Instead, he chose silence in order to continue to reach his readers. He was severely criticized by many emigrant writers for what they saw as his having given the Nazis a mantle of respectability. Yet he helped many emigrants to leave Germany, and continued to write reviews about books by Jewish and foreign writers for German newspapers and journals when all other writers had been silenced.[9] Will Vesper, the Nazi's "poet laureate" openly attacked Hesse for his "pacifism," "internationalism," and "support of Jewish writers," a clear sign that the regime knew full well that Hesse's moral influence continued to work against Nazi propaganda.

Hesse had long foreseen the weakness of the Weimar Republic and its ultimate collapse in the face of totalitarian ideologies. By 1932 he started to conceive a utopian alternative world that would become his spiritual refuge for the next years: the province of Castalia with its monastic order of highly skilled educators who have a civilizing influence on a future society. *Das Glasperlenspiel,* Hesse's magnum opus, went through many revisions and was not published until 1943, and then only in Switzerland. It is dedicated to the "Morgenlandfahrer," a reference to Hesse's magical narrative *Die Morgenlandfahrt* (Journey to the East, 1932), which depicts a "League" of like-minded travelers in time and space who pursue their common ideals in a Romantic quest that is constantly in danger of failure due to self-doubt, lack of courage, and worldly distractions. The juxtaposition of historical figures and thinly disguised portraits of his artist friends may initially confuse the reader, but the notion that one might believe in a different reality, and by writing about it, bring it one step closer to coming true, was to figure as the motto of the Glass Bead Game.

Hesse began the first version of *Das Glasperlenspiel* with a thinly veiled criticism of the fascist barbarians who, in his view, were the consequence of the collective madness of a society that had chosen to abandon all moral, ethical and cultural values in favor of an inhuman ideology that allowed the individual to abdicate his or her responsibilities to a ruthless regime. He was well informed about what was going on in Germany through letters, eyewitness accounts from visitors,[10] and the plight of the refugees, including Ninon's Jewish relatives, many of whom later died in the Holocaust.

Hesse was almost seventy at the end of the war. He viewed his now rising fame with deep suspicion. He was awarded the Goethe Prize of the city of Frankfurt and the Nobel Prize in 1946, while his books became standard texts in German schools. He also refused to speak out in favor of either of the two emerging German states. He kept faith with his publisher Peter Suhrkamp, who had managed his affairs during the Third Reich and suffered cruelly for his loyalty in a concentration camp. His works would become the foundation of the Suhrkamp Verlag, one of Germany's leading publishing houses to this day. Even in old age, Hesse continued to handle a huge correspondence with his readers — he received about 35,000 letters in his lifetime. He died on 9 August 1962, peacefully in his sleep.

Critical Voices

Hesse the person and Hesse the writer continue to divide opinions. There is a growing, if grudging, recognition among German academics that he has the ability to present existential themes and abstract philosophical thought in a way that can be generally understood. However, deep suspicions arise among literary scholars when devoted readers proclaim that we need to "heed his words, not interpret them." In other words, his success, his broad appeal, and his apparent escapist message stand in the way of objective analysis. Given such reluctant acceptance, it is no surprise that his stock fluctuated in the second half of the twentieth century. While he was held in high regard after the war by everyone from contrite individuals hoping for a moral renewal all the way to West Germany's first president, Theodor Heuss, who represented the political new start, changing literary fashions (such as the *Gruppe 47*) and a general desire to appear "modern" meant that his star began to wane. One particularly vitriolic title story in the news magazine *Der Spiegel* in 1958[11] that ridiculed Hesse as an old man tending his vegetable patch is indicative of the new mood. It is worth looking at this polemic in some detail, since it contains the key elements of all future attacks on Hesse.

The anonymous author argues that Hesse's "Abwendung" (detachment) is "ein Wesenszug deutscher Dichtung" (a characteristic of German literature) that prevents his work from playing a role in world literature (ironically, a decade later Hesse would be widely read both in the Americas and in Asia). The author also accuses Hesse of not getting involved politically in questions like the division of Germany into two separate states, of being lightweight, and that his success is based on a pietist "Neigung, Trost zu spenden" (inclination to give comfort to others). He regards *Peter Camenzind* as the beginning of Hesse's reluctance to face the challenges of life, while *Demian* is denounced as formulaic and "knabenhaft" (boyish). The author criticizes Hesse for not accepting realities: presumably referring to the collective belief at the time that Germans under Hitler had no choice but to conform. He also challenges Hesse's views on "deutsche Schuld" (German guilt),[12] which was a taboo subject in the 1950s, and not publicly debated until the advent of the rebellious '68ers, who, like their American counterparts, held Hesse in high regard.

While the *Spiegel* article can be read as an attempt by a young generation to emancipate itself from an *Übervater,* the attack also demonstrates a deep uneasiness with an author who not only criticized the newly confident Federal Republic for its decision to arm itself again,[13] but around whom a circle of admirers (especially of his earlier works) had formed that appeared to discourage critical inquiry. This unease with a writer who attracts a large and allegedly uncritical readership continues to this day in influential quarters in Germany. The "Literaturpapst" Marcel Reich-Ranicki, final arbiter on literary matters, describes in his autobiography how his youthful adoration of Hesse's works turned into rejection:

> The somewhat overpowering mixture of German Romantic tradition and dreamy inwardness, of gentle sentimentality and angry contempt of modernity, all this became unbearable to me.[14]

Many readers have testified to a similar experience: they discovered and valued Hesse's *Identifikationsangebote* (models one can identify with) on their personal journey to adulthood, but later found them embarrassing.[15] Klaus-Peter Philippi, Professor of German at Tübingen University, recently argued that one could not take Hesse seriously because his books were marketed as "self-help," "alternative therapy," and "guides to self discovery."[16] While this may not be Hesse's fault but that of the admittedly highly successful marketing strategists in his publishing house,[17] Philippi's critique goes deeper.

Philippi claims that Hesse does not fit easily into literary epochs, that he didn't become part of a new artistic movement, and that he had never been involved in any of the theoretical debates that paved the way for modern literature. Ultimately, he criticizes Hesse for resisting modernity.[18] By this he means that stylistically, Hesse does not produce sophisticated structures but focuses on content and message, much to the satisfaction of uncritical young readers who do not know any better. Furthermore, he believes that Hesse's novels remain "narzißtische Selbstdarstellung" (narcissistic self-representation), in which the protagonists become stylized as guides on the path to self-discovery, in the hope of creating an elite of "neue[r] Menschen" that is set apart from the masses so despised by Nietzsche.[19]

In summary, there is a suspicion that Hesse's loyal readers, believing that they have become part of a select group with superior insight, are in fact simply "the herd" who want to "follow" their guru. This reservation is widespread in academic circles:

The "Hesse problem" [. . .] really boils down to his *readers,* who allow themselves to be trapped by becoming a community of followers, and who, by doing so, surrender their capacity for independent thought at the entrance to the magical narrative theater, unless, even worse, they happen to be unwitting supporters of an event culture that is promoted by business interests.[20]

In Hesse's defense, this kind of criticism is aimed at his readership and his publisher, not the author and his work. Secondly, almost half a century after the author's death, one could welcome this criticism as evidence of a lively academic discussion: some would say that the debate is just beginning. Furthermore, given that these criticisms are made in a tone that indicates a certain disappointment, one could argue that these critics did indeed find Hesse stimulating — a point that Reich-Ranicki acknowledges when he ironically describes Hesse's books as "Seelenspeise" (food for the soul).

The reason for this *Berührungsangst,* or reluctance to engage with Hesse for fear of contamination, can be traced back to the fact that Hesse himself characterized his works as *Seelenbiographien,* literally "biographies of the soul." However, one must be clear about the term. His texts are not externalized carbon copies of his own psyche. Rather, Hesse explored his innermost thoughts and feelings as a starting point for constructing characters that serve as case studies both for the narrator and for the reader, who might or might not sense an affinity with them. In his groundbreaking study of Hesse's novels, Reso Karalaschwili clearly understood the significance of this difference:

A biography of the soul, then, is an epic form in which the hero experiences a specific inner development which leads to a rebirth. Consequently, it requires the existence of two distinct biographical moments between which the spiritual adventure of the protagonist and his inner metamorphosis take place.[21]

Karalaschwili cautions against taking the documentary/biographical element of Hesse's stories at face value. In order to create his works, Hesse had to re-function many of its components and set them into a new relation to each other in order to provide his readers with a model of the world that bears some similarity with universal laws.[22]

As such, Hesse's heroes experience a similar development as do those of the traditional *Bildungsroman,* with the vital difference that instead of going through a number of stages that educate them and allow them to find their places in society, they go on an "interior journey" that brings them face to face with their "true" selves. Unfortunately, distinguished scholars continue to read Hesse's work rather sweepingly as "self-therapy"[23] and "transposed life history,"[24] to the detriment of a better understanding of the texts themselves. If we assume that all he did was write about himself, we neglect the fact that Hesse cleansed his works of all specific personal references (i.e. the mundane, the accidental) and came up with a modus of narration that focuses both on the individual (taking a single consciousness seriously), and at the same time the trans-individual (in that what is presented is understood and applicable to the life-experience of many readers). Given that so many — and very different — readers testify to have recognized themselves in Hesse's *literary* self, the method seems to have been successful.[25]

A further, and perhaps more serious, point of criticism that continues to be leveled at Hesse is his attitude toward "consensus reality": the assumption that the headlong rush of scientific and industrial "progress" following Germany's belated industrialization had to be welcomed without question and that traditional values and certainties had no place in a modern world. Helga Esselborn-Krumbiegel correctly locates Hesse at the intersection of competing political, social, and cultural trends during his formative years: trends such as a late-Romantic veneration of nature as well as a vehement rejection of technological progress and modern civilization which sympathized with the pessimistic view of "civilization" associated with Friedrich Nietzsche and Oswald Spengler.[26] However, we should not assume that Hesse was a cultural conservative and technophobe, but rather that he felt that the need for certainties and joys was not being satisfied by modern life:

> Dem innerhalb weniger Jahrzehnte vollkommen verwandelten und umgestalteten Bild der Erdoberfläche, den ungeheuren Veränderungen, welche jede Stadt, jede Landschaft der Welt seit der vollzogenen Industrialisierung aufweist, entspricht ein gleicher Umschwung in den Seelen und im Denken der Menschen. Die Jahre seit dem Ausbruch des Weltkrieges haben diese Entwicklung beschleunigt, so daß man ohne Übertreibung schon heute den Tod und Abbau jener Kultur feststellen kann, in welcher wir Älteren einst als Kinder hinein erzogen wurden und die uns damals ewig und unzerstörbar erschien. Hat auch der Mensch selbst sich nicht verändert [. . .], so haben doch die Ideale und Fiktionen, die Wunsch- und Traumbilder, die Mythologien und Theorien, unter deren Herrschaft unser geistiges Leben steht, sich in dieser Zeit ganz und gar verändert. Unersetzliches ist verlorengegangen und für immer zerstört, unerhört Neues wird an dessen Stelle geträumt. Zerstört und verlorengegangen sind für den größeren Teil der zivilisierten Welt vor allem die beiden Fundamente aller Lebensordnung, Kultur und Sittlichkeit: die Religion und die Sitte.[27]

> [The new image of the earth's surface, completely transformed and recast in just a few decades, and the enormous changes manifest in every city and every landscape of the world since industrialization, correspond to an upheaval in the human mind and soul. This develop-

ment has so accelerated in the years since the outbreak of the world war that one can already, without exaggeration, identify the death and dismantling of the culture into which the elder among us were raised as children and which then seemed to us eternal and indestructible. If the individual has not himself changed [. . .], then at least the ideals and fictions, the wishes and dreams, and the mythologies and theories that rule our intellectual life have; they have changed utterly and completely. Irreplaceable things have been lost and destroyed forever; new, unheard-of things are being imagined in their place. Destroyed and lost for the greater part of the civilized world are, beyond all else, the two universal foundations of life, culture, and morality: religion and customary morals.]

Hesse attempted to show in his works that the search for such foundations was not pointless, even though it might be out of fashion. And if "reality" was no longer the right place for any search for meaning, then maybe reality needed to be altered. A good example of this conviction can be found in his *Kurzgefaßter Lebenslauf* (Brief Curriculum Vitae, 1924), which begins realistically enough, describing his upbringing, his "awakening" during the First World War when he was ostracized for his pacifist views, and his increasing estrangement from modern life. Eventually, the authorities arrest him and put him in jail, but he paints a landscape onto his prison wall and magically disappears into it, leaving his jailers scratching their heads. In a passage that sounds like a pledge of allegiance to the Romantics, he writes:

Ich finde, die Wirklichkeit ist das, worum man sich am allerwenigsten zu kümmern braucht, denn sie ist, lästig genug, ja immerzu vorhanden, während schönere und nötigere Dinge unsere Aufmerksamkeit und Sorge fordern. Die Wirklichkeit ist das, womit man unter gar keinen Umständen zufrieden sein, was man unter gar keinen Umständen anbeten und verehren darf, denn sie ist der Zufall, der Abfall des Lebens. Und sie ist, diese schäbige, stets enttäuschende und öde Wirklichkeit, auf keine andre Weise zu ändern, als indem wir sie leugnen, indem wir zeigen, daß wir stärker sind als sie.[28]

[I believe that reality is that which we least need to concern ourselves with. After all, it is, bothersome enough, constantly present, while more beautiful and more urgent matters demand our attention and care. Reality is that which one must under no circumstances be content with, what one must not idolize or adore, for it is pure chance, life's waste. This cheap, forever disappointing and bleak reality can only be altered if we deny it, by proving that we are stronger than it.]

Ultimately, it is Hesse's belief that "reality" is wanting, that it is the duty of each and every one of us to transcend it, that divides readers and critics. It should be noted, though, that nowhere in this passage does Hesse advocate an "escapist" position that leaves the rest of the world to its own devices. That may have been his position before the First World War, but it was never his position after that disastrous war. He does not deny that "reality" has to be changed, but — in contrast to the popular ideologies of the time — came to believe that reality could only be changed if the individual changed him- or herself first. In the words of Josef Knecht: "Wir sind selbst Geschichte und sind an der Weltgeschichte und unserer Stellung in ihr mitverantwortlich"[29] (We ourselves are history, and we share responsibility for world history and our own place within it).

Hesse's Global Relevance

It is now time to look at the reasons for Hesse's phenomenal success and popularity. The first thing that ought to be stressed is that outside Germany, Hesse's standing as a figure of world literature has never been in question. In the United States, Lewis W. Tusken has continued a long and influential tradition of Hesse scholarship — which had been established there by the likes of Joseph Mileck, Mark Boulby, Theodore Ziolkowski, and Ralph Freedman — with a wide-ranging and perceptive study focusing on the narrative content of Hesse's novels, his use of subtle variation of motif and metaphor, and the religious implications of Hesse's works.[30]

In 2000, an exhibition and conference in Solothurn, Switzerland, asked the provocative question: "Hermann Hesse: Außenseiter oder Global Player?"[31] While the writer and critic Adolf Muschg tended towards the former and argued that the *Glass Bead Game* was best understood as "ein datierbares Stück Innere Emigration" (a datable piece of inner emigration),[32] the American Hesse scholar Günther Gottschalk, founder of the Hermann Hesse Homepage,[33] clearly supported the latter and wondered whether the author had in fact anticipated our modern Internet culture.[34] Both terms can be justified. The "outsider" thesis, first developed by Colin Wilson in 1956,[35] can easily be supported by Hesse's self-created image of the "Aussteiger" (one who has dropped out of the "rat race") at Lake Constance, his exploration of an alternative lifestyle on Monte Verita, his courageous stance against the political and cultural elites in the Kaiserreich, his metamorphosis into the lone Steppenwolf, and his opposition to the populist movements of the Weimar Republic. Proponents of the "global player" thesis have equally good arguments on their side: Hesse's phenomenal and continuing popularity around the world (not only in Europe, but also the United States, South America, India, Korea, and China), his timeless metaphor of the Glass Bead Game as a key to the attainment of serenity or enlightenment, and his cult status on the Internet.

In 2002, the 125th anniversary celebrations of Hesse's birth gave rise to two academic conferences that confirmed his status as one of the key writers on the threshold of modernity. The Mainz conference Hesse und die Modernität was especially significant given that it was the first time an academic conference on Hesse took place in Germany, that it was supported by the Deutsche Forschungsgesellschaft (German Research Council), and that it was conceived with the express aim of confronting existing reservations about his status.[36]

In his contribution to the Mainz conference volume, Siegfried Unseld, who had followed in the footsteps of Peter Suhrkamp as head of the Suhrkamp Verlag, pinpointed one of the reasons for Hesse's continuing relevance: by focusing on the process of individuation, the author provides a counterweight to the process of socialization that strips away a person's unique gifts and characteristics. This aspect is perhaps the most crucial element of Hesse's appeal. Born out of painful personal experiences (e.g. his childhood and schooling, the First World War, a stifling marriage), and confirmed whenever he followed his *Eigensinn* (self-will), Hesse advocated in his writings a sense of responsibility to one's own potential that resonates with readers who feel encouraged to know that someone is on their side when they are "the odd one out." Hesse proves particularly popular in authoritarian societies and among the young, while his works tend to drop out of view when the majority is happy with the status quo. This was also the general conclusion at the international conference Hermann Hesse Today in London in November 2002, which underlined that Hesse continues to be held in high esteem around the world.[37]

The most important indicators of Hesse's continued relevance can be found in three recent publishing projects that will attract a new generation of scholars: Volker Michels's landmark publication of Hesse's *Sämtliche Werke* (20 volumes plus index) has for the first time brought together all of Hesse's prose and poetry, his literary reviews, and his political and literary essays. Sikander Singh's recent study offers a broad overview with up-to-date references,[38] while Jürgen Below's new bibliography of secondary literature on Hermann Hesse enables scholars to access a wealth of hitherto unknown sources.[39] Together with the projected 10-volume edition of Hesse's letters, these resources bring the critical apparatus on a par with what is currently available on Thomas Mann, Heinrich Böll, or Günter Grass.

Hesse's relationship with Thomas Mann continues to intrigue scholars,[40] whose findings have led to a renewed appreciation of their merits and a re-evaluation of their respective legacies. Each writer had a unique voice, but both were well aware that together they represented the final chapter in the history of German "high" culture and hoped that their works would be viewed, perhaps after a period of obscurity, as worthy successors of the classics.[41] In the introduction to his collection of critical essays on Hesse, Harold Bloom wryly comments that the best works of Hesse and Mann transcend time, and yet may well be soon forgotten by all but an elite that has resisted the all-pervasive dumbing-down of modern culture. This would indeed be a profound loss, given that both authors saw themselves not only as part of the cultural elite, but also as proponents of a new worldview, a view described by Theodore Ziolkowski as "a humanism predicated upon belief in the integrity of the individual. This humanism, rather than blindly ignoring or rejecting certain basic traits of human nature, acknowledges all aspects of the personality."[42]

This is what makes Hermann Hesse relevant for the twenty-first century. His holistic view of a human being as an evolving, struggling, ever-changing individual chimes with modern experience. He confronts us with uncomfortable truths about human nature but encourages us to face them to discover what lies beneath. Because he knows about the awkward moments of adolescence and the pressures those around us exert on us to conform, his books continue to hold a special appeal for young readers. However, his books are equally useful for older readers, as he writes about the torment of a psyche in despair or our fear of the unknown. All these experiences are explored from the perspective of the individual self, in Hesse's eyes the repository of the divine and the only institution we are accountable to.

The Chapters

This volume is intended as a companion, not a primer. It offers new interpretations and current scholarship to those who have read Hesse's works and want to explore them further with the guidance of sixteen experts, each of them on his or her own journey to discover the author anew, each with his or her own approach and unique voice. The reader is encouraged to see this as an advantage, as it offers multiple pathways and illustrates the many ways in which Hesse can be read. Some contributors use their own personal experiences as the starting point of their analyses, putting their own biographical background and personal reception into the equation. Others choose a more distanced form of analysis. Some contributors align their essays in a symbiotic way with their subject: this may be an impressionistic response that mirrors the text, or an attempt at enlightenment to match Hesse's elusive wisdom. Such essays echo the tone and message of the works they describe. The volume intentionally offers essays on some of Hesse's less well-known but nevertheless brilliant texts, for instance *Roßhalde, Klingsors letzter Sommer, Klein und Wagner,* and his poetry. In addition, it contains six essays on key themes such as Hesse's interest in psychoanalysis or the development of his political views, areas in which new sources and findings have led us to a more nuanced understanding of the author. As editor, I believe that such variety in approach, tone, method, and scope is commensurate with the multifaceted work of Hesse and the expectations of a broad readership that this volume presupposes. The results speak for themselves: Hesse emerges as a writer whose works are more subtle and complex than previously acknowledged. His works are easily accessible for most readers, yet they challenge our intellect and spirit to the utmost. They deserve to be read carefully and with an open mind. If we can do that, then we will be rewarded with the prose of a master storyteller who does not need to show off, with protagonists who experience conflicts that matter, and with themes that transcend national cultures and fixations.

Notes

[1] *Hesse Companion*, ed. Anna Otten (Albuquerque: U of New Mexico P, 1977).

[2] See Jeff Vahlbusch, "Toward the Legend of Hermann Hesse in the USA," in *Hermann Hesse Today / Hermann Hesse heute*, ed. Ingo Cornils and Osman Durrani, Amsterdamer Beiträge zur Neueren Germanistik 58 (Amsterdam: Rodopi, 2005), 133–46.

[3] The song "Born to Be Wild" was recorded by the band *Steppenwolf* in 1968.

[4] See Gerard DeGroot, *The Sixties Unplugged* (Cambridge, MA: Harvard UP, 2008).

[5] See Barry Stephenson, *Veneration and Revolt: Hermann Hesse and Swabian Pietism* (Waterloo: Wilfried Laurier UP 2009).

[6] In his review of *Roßhalde*, the German literary critic Kurt Tucholsky described Hesse's powers as a storyteller in glowing terms: "Er kann, was nur wenige können. Er kann einen Sommerabend und ein erfrischendes Schwimmbad und die schlaffe Müdigkeit nach körperlicher Anstrengung nicht nur schildern — das wäre nicht schwer. Aber er kann machen, daß uns heiß und kühl und müde ums Herz wird" (He can do what few others are capable of. Not only can he describe a summer's evening, a refreshing swim or the limp fatigue after physical exertion — that would not be hard. But he can make us feel hot and cool and tired, right to the core).

[7] See Fred Bridgham, ed., *The First World War as a Clash of Cultures* (Rochester, NY: Camden House, 2006).

[8] "O Freunde, nicht diese Töne," *Neue Zürcher Zeitung*, 3 Nov. 1914.

[9] See Marco Schickling, *Hermann Hesse als Literaturkritiker* (Heidelberg: Winter, 2005).

[10] Thomas Mann, Bertolt Brecht, and Peter Weiss were among those who stopped in Montagnola on their way into exile.

[11] "Im Gemüsegarten," *Der Spiegel*, 9 July 1958, 42–48.

[12] Hesse reacted angrily to all suggestions that "the average German" held no responsibility for the atrocities committed by the Nazis. See "Ein Brief nach Deutschland," *SW* 15:633–40.

[13] See "Antwort auf Briefe aus Deutschland" from October 1950, *SW* 15:721–23.

[14] Marcel Reich-Ranicki, *Mein Leben* (Munich: dtv 2001), 134.

[15] See Jörg Drews, "'. . . bewundert viel und viel gescholten . . .': Hermann Hesses Werk zwischen Erfolg und Mißachtung bei Publikum und Literaturkritik," in *Hermann Hesse Today,* ed. Cornils and Durrani, 21–31.

[16] Klaus-Peter Philippi, "Hesse und die heutige Germanistik in Deutschland," in *Hermann Hesse Jahrbuch,* vol. 2, ed. Mauro Ponzi (Tübingen: Niemeyer, 2005), 19–33.

[17] 4 million copies of Hesse's works were sold during his lifetime, and more than 22 million have been sold in German-speaking countries alone since 1970. See Roman Bucheli, "Steppenwolfs Ambulatorium," *Neue Zürcher Zeitung,* 19 March 2007.

[18] Philippi, "Hesse und die heutige Germanistik," 21.

[19] Philippi, "Hesse und die heutige Germanistik," 27–28. See also my "Hermann Hesse und die Elite(n)," in *"Die gefährliche Lust, unerschrocken zu denken": Das Menschenbild bei Hermann Hesse,* ed. Michael Limbach (Stuttgart: Klett 2008), 71–90.

[20] Cornelia Blasberg, ed., *Hermann Hesse: 1877–1962–2002* (Tübingen: Attempto Verlag, 2003), 146.

[21] Reso Karalaschwili, *Hermann Hesses Romanwelt* (Cologne: Böhlau, 1986), 10.

[22] Karalaschwili, *Hermann Hesses Romanwelt,* 13.

[23] Ritchie Robertson, "Gender Anxiety and the Shaping of the Self," in *The Cambridge Companion to the Modern German Novel,* ed. Graham Bartram (Cambridge: CUP, 2004), 53.

[24] Harold Bloom, ed., *Hermann Hesse,* Bloom's Modern Critical Views (Philadelphia: Chelsea House, 2003), vii.

[25] See Volker Michels, ed., *Über Hermann Hesse,* 2 vols. (Frankfurt: Suhrkamp, 1976–1977).

[26] Helga Esselborn-Krumbiegel, *Hermann Hesse: Literaturwissen für Schüler* (Stuttgart: Reclam, 1996), 13–14.

[27] Hermann Hesse, "Die Sehnsucht unserer Zeit nach einer Weltanschauung" (The Longing of Our Time for a Worldview), first published in *Uhu* 2 (1926): 3–14, reprinted in Hesse, *Sämtliche Werke,* ed. Volker Michels, vol. 13: *Betrachtungen und Berichte I: 1899–1926* (Frankfurt am Main: Suhrkamp, 2003), 479. Subsequent references to this volume will be cited as *SW* and volume and page number.

[28] Hermann Hesse, *Kurzgefaßter Lebenslauf,* in Hesse, *Sämtliche Werke,* ed. Volker Michels, vol. 12: *Autobiographische Schriften II. Selbstzeugnisse. Erinnerungen. Gedenkblätter und Rundbriefe* (Frankfurt am Main: Suhrkamp, 2003), 57–58. Subsequent references to this volume will be indicated by *SW* and volume and page numbers.

[29] Hermann Hesse, *Das Glasperlenspiel*, in *Sämtliche Werke*, ed. Volker Michels, vol. 5: *Die Romane: Das Glasperlenspiel* (Frankfurt am Main: Suhrkamp, 2001), 323. Subsequent references to this volume will be indicated by *SW* and volume and page numbers.

[30] Lewis W. Tusken, *Understanding Hermann Hesse: The Man, His Myth, His Metaphor* (Columbia: U of South Carolina P, 1998).

[31] Selected papers from this conference were published as Eva Zimmermann, ed., *"Der Dichter sucht Verständnis und Erkanntwerden": Neue Arbeiten zu Hermann Hesse und seinem Roman Das Glasperlenspiel* (Bern: Peter Lang, 2002).

[32] Zimmermann, ed., *"Der Dichter sucht Verständnis und Erkanntwerden,"* 138.

[33] The Hermann Hesse Homepage (HHP) is hosted by the University of California, Santa Barbara, and is located at http://www.gss.ucsb.edu/projects/hesse/.

[34] Zimmermann, ed., *"Der Dichter sucht Verständnis und Erkanntwerden,"* 154. See also Ingo Cornils, "Ein Glasperlenspiel im Internet. Hesse lesen im globalen Zeitalter," in *Hermann Hesse und die literarische Moderne,* ed. Andreas Solbach, 399–413 (Frankfurt am Main: Suhrkamp, 2004).

[35] Colin Wilson, *The Outsider* (London: Gollancz, 1956), esp. chapter 3.

[36] Andreas Solbach, ed., *Hermann Hesse und die literarische Moderne* (Frankfurt am Main: Suhrkamp, 2004), 9.

[37] The papers derived from this conference have been published as Ingo Cornils and Osman Durrani, eds., *Hermann Hesse Today / Hermann Hesse Heute*, Amsterdamer Beiträge zur Neueren Germanistik 58 (Amsterdam/New York: Rodopi, 2005).

[38] Sikander Singh, *Hermann Hesse* (Stuttgart: Reclam, 2006).

[39] See my review in *Colloquia Germania,* no.2 (2007).

[40] Most recently Günter Baumann, "Thomas Mann und Hermann Hesse. Aspekte einer literarischen Freundschaft," HHP, 2006, http://www.gss.ucsb.edu/projects/hesse/papers/Baumann-Lecture-2006.pdf.

[41] Letter by Hermann Hesse to Thomas Mann from January 1953, in *The Hesse/Mann Letters: The Correspondence of Hermann Hesse and Thomas Mann 1910–1955,* ed. Anni Carlsson and Volker Michels (London: Peter Owen, 1975), 154.

[42] Theodore Ziolkowski, introduction to *The Hesse / Mann Letters,* ed. Carlsson and Michels, xv.

1: Novel Ideas: Notes toward a New Reading of Hesse's *Unterm Rad*

Jefford Vahlbusch

Allegory

IN SEPTEMBER 1968, AS U.S. INTEREST in Hesse was beginning to surge, British poet and critic D. J. Enright, writing in the *New York Review of Books*, posed two provocative rhetorical questions on *Unterm Rad* (1906; *Beneath the Wheel,* 1968). After providing a laconic plot summary — "the story of a gifted boy of humble birth who is sent from his village to a theological academy, sinks to the bottom of the class, breaks down, goes home, and dies" — Enright asks: "[B]ut why must Hans die? Surely not that Hermann may live?"[1]

"Hans" is the Swabian schoolboy Hans Giebenrath, the main character in *Unterm Rad.*[2] "Hermann" is Hermann Heilner, Hans Giebenrath's friend. But Enright's "Hermann" is also Hermann Hesse himself. Enright pokes serious fun at all the aitches and aitch-aitches in the Hesse novels he discusses — Harry Haller, Hermann Heilner, Hermine, and H.H., the narrator in *The Journey to the East* — and confesses to having learned of Hesse's tiresome penchant for such formulae in Theodore Ziolkowski's 1965 monograph, *The Novels of Hermann Hesse.*[3] Without Ziolkowski, Enright tells us, he would have read *Unterm Rad* as "simply a straight-forward warning, touching and telling, against the evils of subjecting a boy to the academic grindstone at a time when he should be giving himself up to the beneficent sway of nature" (6). Enright's implication is that Hesse might have killed off Hans Giebenrath in order to set not only Hermann Heilner but also himself, Hermann Hesse himself, somehow free. And as Enright's indignant tone suggests, he finds this notion — character assassination as authorial liberation — particularly unpalatable.

Enright here calls wittily into question the most sacred commonplace of criticism on *Unterm Rad,* the interpretive surmise on which nearly all readings of the novel have been based. The idea was mooted in 1927 by Hugo Ball, Hesse's first biographer:

> The portrayal of the state examination and of Hesse's time as a semi-nary student in *Beneath the Wheel* is true to life [. . .]. Only the experi-

ence is divided up, through a kind of splitting of Hesse's personality, between two characters and friends. Hermann Heilner's flight from Maulbronn is Hesse's own flight from the seminary. But the emotional confusion and sufferings of Hans Giebenrath, who remains behind, are also Hesse's.[4]

In 1971, Heinz Stolte named this interpretive assumption, rather grandly, "das Prinzip der polarischen Spaltung" (the principle of polarization) and explained it in detail:

> What Hesse perceived within himself as a tense contradiction, as a polarity within a single character, is divided up in the literary work between two characters, who simultaneously contradict and complete each other.[5]

According to Stolte, Giebenrath "embodies" one part of Hesse's nature: "everything that is pathological, vulnerable, or overly sensitive in Hesse, and everything that could be shattered by the world's — and by his fellow human beings' — lack of understanding" (44). Heilner "[embodies] the other, the real Hermann Hesse [. . .], the person called to be a poet, and [Heilner's first] name 'Hermann' points unmistakeably to this identity" (44). In 1978, Joseph Mileck began to make the notion of character assassination explicit:

> Giebenrath [. . .] is what Hesse was, and Heilner is the person he had to become if he was to make anything of his life. The former's demise and the latter's survival were Hesse's symbolic depiction of an actual change in his life. The hopeless Giebenrath in him died with Hans's suicide and the promising Heilner in him emerged and went his independent way.[6]

In 1982, Volker Michels, Hesse's longtime editor at Suhrkamp Verlag, lent his authoritative support to this line of argument:

> In reality, Hans Giebenrath and Hermann Heilner [embody], not two different people, but contradictory elements in Hesse himself [. . .]. There is much to say for the assumption that Hesse had to "permit" the Hans Giebenrath in himself "to die" so that he [Hesse] could follow Heilner's more unconventional path.[7]

In such readings, as D. J. Enright's questions suggest, Giebenrath and Heilner are no longer literary characters in any meaningful — interpretable — sense, but merely allegories of the authorial self. *Unterm Rad* thus becomes not so much a novel as a therapeutic encoding of Hesse's alleged psychological and artistic development, easily decipherable by anyone with the key. In such readings, it turns out, Giebenrath and Heilner can signify whatever each critic needs them to signify in a given argument; explication of the text and analysis of character seem not to be necessary. The only constants: Heilner always emerges as somehow positive because he escapes and lives, Giebenrath as somehow negative, because he doesn't.

Faced with such ubiquitous allegories, critics can do little more than restate the allegorical obvious and thus reconfirm Hesse as the hero of his own work and life.[8] Small wonder that Enright, whose irritation suggests that he felt duped for initially thinking that, in *Unterm Rad*, he was reading an actual novel, consigned both Hesse and his readers to second-class status:

> It is not so much that Hesse dramatizes or even popularizes ideas as that he takes the stiffening out of them, sandpapers the sharper edges away, and hands them over to his readers to play with as they will. A highly cultivated person, he is the ideal second-order writer for the sort of serious-minded reader desirous to believe that he is grappling successfully with intellectual and artistic profundities of the first order. (1968, n.p.)

A month later, in the *Christian Science Monitor*, novelist and comparative literature professor Donald Heiney voiced similar complaints:

> In reading this novel we see what is really wrong with all of Hesse's fiction, even the better novels like *Demian*. He is not really interested in the novelistic texture at all — in the page-by-page depiction of characters, scenes, incidents, hard concrete objects — but in the "half-asleep dream of a higher life" for which the novel is only a vehicle.
>
> Scenes fail to come alive. There are no concretions, no vivid sensations, only vague references to setting and old-fashioned nature descriptions. Most serious of all, there are no real characters, only walking puppets who embody certain fairly obvious allegorical forces. [. . .].
>
> We don't *see* these people, they do not come to life for us in any palpable way, and so we can't really sympathize with their griefs and struggles, or even comprehend them. We understand that Hans is sensitive and that the school is cruel. But just how is he destroyed? What is the mechanism and process of his neurosis? This is what a novel should tell us, and "Under the Wheel" [*sic*] never does [. . .].[9]

In fact, Heiney is mostly wrong, here, at least about *Unterm Rad*. When it is read as a novel in which character, plot, language, and structure are taken seriously, Heiney's complaints largely disappear. We do learn, or can, how Hans is "destroyed," and we can come closer to identifying "the mechanism and process of his neurosis." Still, Heiney's and Enright's critical reactions are invaluable. They demonstrate that the allegorical approach has undermined critics' abilities to understand and appreciate the novel.

Autobiography

Heribert Kuhn noted recently that scholarship on *Unterm Rad* has focused primarily on "the splitting of the author into two protagonists" and "the correspondences between events in Hesse's life and the plot of the novel."[10]

In 2003, Klaus Johann identified some of the problems caused by the latter approach:

> Many critics [. . .] have been content to point out correspondences or differences between Hesse's biography [and *Unterm Rad*] by citing Hesse's own statements and other documents; thereafter they try to set down their opinions about Hesse's presumed authorial intentions. [. . .] In addition, it seems that no new source documents remain to be discovered. This has resulted in a stagnation of research that becomes manifest in the documents cited: they are always the same ones.[11]

As it happens, Johann was wrong about the "source documents." In July 2008 Suhrkamp Verlag published "*Unterm Rad*": *Entstehungsgeschichte in Selbstzeugnissen des Autors* (Beneath the Wheel: The Story of Its Creation in the Words of Its Author), which claims to capture, for the first time, "the documentable background" of the novel "in *all* surviving biographical records."[12] According to Kuhn, this anthology includes significant new discoveries, among them a report based on "interrogations" ("Verhöre") of Hesse conducted by August Palm, *Ephorus* (director) of the Maulbronn school during Hesse's attendance there — a report that records Hesse's apparent reasons for fleeing Maulbronn (Kuhn, 223–24). The book also includes a poem apparently composed by Hesse on 6 March 1892, the very day before his "flight":

> Ich steh allein auf dem Berge,
> Allein mit all meinem Weh
> Und schaue hinab in die Weiten,
> Hinein in den ruhigen See.
>
> Der See ist so blau wie der Himmel;
> Da wird mir so eigen zumut,
> Als sollt' ich hinein in die Fluten
> als wäre dann alles gut. (quoted as in Kuhn, 225)
>
> [I stand alone on the mountain,
> Alone with all of my pain,
> And peer down into the distance,
> Down into the peaceful lake.
>
> The lake is as blue as the heavens;
> And I begin to feel quite odd.
> As if I should enter the waters,
> As if that would make everything good.]

But Johann was correct about the "stagnation of research" on *Unterm Rad*. Fascinating biographical documents such as those recently discovered, and those gathered in the invaluable *Kindheit und Jugend vor Neunzehnhundert*, may indeed help us to understand Hesse, but they do not help us much with the novel or its genesis.[13] Hesse may have been entertaining thoughts of suicide and making poetry of them on the evening before his "flight." Or he may have been playing at "Weltschmerz," imitating Heinrich Heine's disarmingly simple verse, or both. If the poem attests to feelings that led to Hesse's flight the next day, then it is of great biographical significance. But the poem is not useful as an explanation of or commentary on Hermann Heilner's fictional flight from Maulbronn. In Heilner, there is not a bit of "Weh" (pain) or "Weltschmerz" even hinted at as a reason for his flight, and no ogling with death or drowning as a solution. Heilner flees Maulbronn in a very different mood and for very different reasons:

> Um dieselben Stunden lag Heilner ein paar Meilen entfernt in einem Gehölz. Er fror und konnte nicht schlafen, doch atmete er in einem tiefen Freiheitsgefühl mächtig auf und streckte die Glieder, als wäre er aus einem engen Käfig entronnen. Er war seit Mittag gelaufen, hatte in Knittlingen Brot gekauft und nahm nun zuweilen ein Bissen davon, während er durch das noch frühlinghaft lichte Gezweige Nachtschwärze, Sterne und schnellsegelnde Wolken beschaute. Wohin er schließlich käme, war ihm einerlei; wenigstens war er nun dem verhaßten Kloster entsprungen und hatte dem Ephorus gezeigt, daß sein Wille stärker war als Befehle und Verbote. (226–27)

> [During these same hours Heilner lay a few miles away in a wood. He was freezing cold and couldn't sleep, but he heaved a powerful sigh of relief in a profound feeling of freedom and stretched his limbs as if he had just escaped from a tight cage. He had been running since midday, had bought bread in Knittlingen and now took an occasional bite thereof while he peered through the still-bare branches (it was early spring) at the night's blackness, at the stars and at the fast-sailing clouds. He didn't care where he landed; at least he had escaped from the hated cloister and had shown the Ephorus that his will was stronger than any commands and prohibitions.]

Ephorus Palm's interrogation report makes clear the vast differences between Heilner's and Hesse's motivations. Heilner's flight — in his own mind at least — is a triumphant escape, a victory of will over the Ephorus, and Heilner's resulting exultant mood finds expression in his poetic and pugnacious interior monologue. In Palm's account, Hesse's flight appears as a half-willed capitulation to vaguely sensed trouble in his psyche and a tentative, perhaps only partly understood, step toward death. As Palm reported:

> The interrogations of Hesse revealed without a doubt that this case was not about willfulness and defiance, but rather that an immature, sentimental world-weariness — which he had been cultivating for a long time — had gradually overcome his intellect & will and had caused him to want to flee his present circumstances, because he associated the

vague idea that by doing so his life would also come to an end. (quoted as in Kuhn, 224–25)

Heilner's actual and Hesse's apparent reasons for fleeing are incompatible. If Hesse's poem or Ephorus Palm's report is true to Hesse's own experience, then Hugo Ball's influential contention that "Hermann Heilner's flight from Maulbronn is Hesse's own flight from the seminary" cannot be true. Author and character both flee, but their flights are not the same. As Hesse himself admitted in 1908, he and Heilner are not one:

> Ihre Frage wegen des Heilner kann ich im großen Ganzen mit Ja beant-worten, wenn auch hier wie überall zwischen erlebter Wirklichkeit und Dichtung manche Unterschiede, ja Gegensätze bestehen. *Unterm Rad* enthält viel Erlebtes, doch sind die einzelen Erlebnisse teils verändert, teils auf verschiedene Figuren verteilt. So ist es auch mit Heilner, *der zwar kein Jugendporträt ist,* doch aber manche Züge meines damaligen Wesens bekommen hat. (Michels 1982, 214, my emphasis.)

> [For the most part, I can answer your question about Heilner with a "yes," even though there are, in this novel and everywhere, various dif-ferences, even contradictions, between lived reality and fiction. *Beneath the Wheel* contains much that I myself experienced, but the individual experiences are sometimes altered and sometimes distributed among different characters. This is the case with Heilner, *who is no portrait of my youth,* but who was given some features of the person I was back then. (My emphasis)]

At different times in the novel, of course, Hermann Heilner *does* evince "willfulness & defiance" and an impressively "immature, sentimental world-weariness" — but the latter plays no role in his flight. It is also worth noting that neither Hesse's poem nor Ephorus Palm's report provides trustworthy explanations. Despite the new source documents, Richard Helt's conclusion is still correct: "The exact motivation for Hesse's flight is uncertain."[14]

Hesse's fictionalizing of aspects of his own lived experience in *Unterm Rad* is clearly far less straightforward than the nearly universal equations be-tween life and novel have assumed. It is simply wrong to assert, with Joseph Mileck and others, that "Giebenrath and [. . .] Heilner together tell Hesse's story of 1891 to 1895" (1978, 36). *Unterm Rad* is not Hesse's life or psy-che writ large, but a complex creative work in which every detail must be read and evaluated as fiction.[15]

Self-Criticism

Nearly all of Hesse's published comments on *Unterm Rad* include self-criticisms. In retrospect, Hesse clearly thought the novel seriously flawed. In a well-known 1904 letter to his half brother Karl Isenberg, Hesse attempts to justify the novel's attacks on schools and teachers:

Unterm Rad wird nächstes Jahr als Buch erscheinen, in Kleinigkeiten gemildert. Hoffentlich nimmst Du an den paar salzigen Stellen nicht zu sehr Anstoß. Die Schule ist die einzige moderne Kulturfrage, die ich ernst nehme und die mich gelegentlich aufregt. An mir hat die Schule viel kaputtgemacht und ich kenne wenig bedeutende Persönlichkeiten, denen es nicht ähnlich ging. Gelernt habe ich dort nur Latein und Lügen, denn ungelogen kam man in Calw und im Gymnasium nicht durch — wie unser Hans beweist, den sie ja in Calw, weil er ehrlich war, fast umbrachten. Der ist auch, seit sie ihm in der Schule das Rückgrat gebrochen haben, immer unterm Rad geblieben.

Na, nichts mehr davon, ich meine es nicht bös.[16]

[*Beneath the Wheel* will be published as a book next year, toned down in minor ways. I hope you won't take too much offense at the few salty passages. School is the only question of modern culture that I take seriously and that occasionally upsets me. School did me a lot of damage, and I know few important people for whom it was any different. In school I learned only Latin and lying, because without lying you couldn't survive in Calw and in the Gymnasium [high school] — as is shown by our [brother] Hans, whom of course they almost killed in Calw because he was honest. And ever since they broke his resistance [literally, "his backbone"] in school, Hans has always remained beneath the wheel.

Well, no more of this. I don't mean to give offense.]

Eight years older than Hesse, Karl Isenberg was, in 1904, already a member of Swabia's educational establishment. He had taught in Ulm and Heilbronn, and eventually took a teaching position at Stuttgart's *Karlsgymnasium*. In Hesse's hope that his half brother not take "too much offense" at the novel's "salty" — that is, aggressively critical — passages, we surely can see Hesse's acknowledgment of Isenberg's vocation and highly pertinent educational biography, both of which *Unterm Rad* calls radically and mercilessly into question. Hesse could of course assume that, as a teacher, Isenberg would take *some* offense at the novel's critical passages; the humorous euphemism "salty" seems intended to minimize the importance or at least to make light of the novel's bitter critiques. As Hesse knew, Isenberg had preceded him on the exact educational path that Hesse himself had taken, initially succeeded on, dramatically abandoned with his "flight" from Maulbronn, and later transformed into fiction — and spectacular polemics — in *Unterm Rad*. Like Hesse, Isenberg had studied at Calw's "Latin School" (actually the *Reallyceum*), where he, unlike Hesse, was a star pupil. Like Hesse, Isenberg had prepared under the respected Rector Bauer at the Latin School in Göppingen for the Swabian *Landexamen* (the state examination) and had, like Hesse, passed it and thereby earned a prestigious place at Maulbronn and the chance to become a clergyman or an academic. Unlike Hesse, Isenberg had thrived at Maulbronn, been graduated (in 1883), and gone on to study at Tübingen, completing his university degree in 1893 and thereafter passing the examination for "higher school" employment.[17]

In the 1904 letter, Hesse justifies his novel's "salty" critiques as the understandable result of his own and his brother Hans's school experiences, here set down as radically different from Isenberg's own. It is fascinating that the passage's final line — "Na, nichts mehr davon, ich meine es nicht bös" (Well, no more of this. I don't mean to give offense) — is nearly always left out when this letter is quoted in the literature. This line concludes Hesse's discussion of *Unterm Rad* by seeking to reassure Isenberg that the novel's angry criticisms were not penned with malicious personal intent. Rhetorically, the line also undercuts what has become a mainstay of the literature on *Unterm Rad* — the emotional force of Hesse's exaggerated assessment of his younger brother Hans's difficulties in school:

> wie unser Hans beweist, den sie ja in Calw, weil er ehrlich war, fast umbrachten. Der ist auch, seit sie ihm in der Schule das Rückgrat gebrochen haben, immer unterm Rad geblieben.[18]

> [as is shown by our [brother] Hans, whom of course they almost killed in Calw because he was honest. And ever since they broke his resistance [literally, "his backbone"] in school Hans has always remained beneath the wheel.]

The passage's final line also undercuts the earnest solemnity of perhaps the most frequently quoted Hesse dictum in *Unterm Rad* criticism: "School is the only question of modern culture that I take seriously and that occasionally upsets me." On reflection, this is a surprising and embarrassing admission for a 27-year-old fiction writer and budding public intellectual to make, and it is even odder for Hesse scholars to point to it repeatedly with obvious pride. I suspect that, by identifying "school" as "the *only* question of modern culture" he takes seriously, Hesse is exaggerating to make clear to Isenberg how very emotionally involved and retrospectively upset he was while writing the novel. Such exaggerations help him make his case to his half brother.[19]

But this letter cannot be understood fully without the explication of another. On 13 May 1907, Hesse wrote again to Isenberg about *Unterm Rad:*

> Damit, daß Du das Fehlen jeder Tendenz in "Diesseits" als einen Vorzug empfindest, hast Du gewiß recht. Zwar ist *Unterm Rad* seinerzeit rein nur aus dem Bedürfnis entstanden, mir ein wichtiges Stück der eigenen Jugendzeit konzentriert vorzustellen, und das Tendenziöse kam erst während der Ausführung, absichtslos und nur aus bitteren Erinnerungen erwachsen, hinein. Aber auch das war unnötig. Künftig denke ich zwar noch öfter ein wenig zu predigen, aber nicht mehr so negativ kritisierend, sondern mehr, indem ich eigene Erfahrung und eigenes Ideal, also Positiveres, hinstelle. (*GB* 1:139–40)

[You are certainly right to see the absence of any tendentiousness in *Diesseits* as a virtue. [*This Life, a* collection of stories (1907)]. *Beneath the Wheel* really came into being only because of my need to imagine an important period of my own youth in a focused way, and the tendentiousness only entered into it during the writing phase, unintentionally and only because of my bitter memories. But that, too, was unnecessary. In the future, I'm thinking that I will still often preach a little, but not in such a negatively critical way. Instead, I'll do it more positively, by setting out my own experiences and my own ideals.]

Of great significance here is Hesse's matter-of-fact admission that, in *Unterm Rad*, he had indeed crossed the line into tendentiousness and bitter, negative criticism. Of equal importance is Hesse's explanation of the novel's genesis. Despite *Unterm Rad's* current canonical status as an uncompromising *Schulroman* (novel critical of schooling practices) or an admirable *Tendenzwerk* (a tendentious work), Hesse claims here that he set out to write neither, intending instead only to "imagine an important period of [his] own youth." Hesse then admits that the tendentious critical passages were only opportunistic and secondary ("kam erst während der Ausführung [. . .] hinein"); without a larger purpose or agenda ("absichtslos"); emotional and subjective ("nur aus bitteren Erinnerungen erwachsen"); and — at least with the benefit of hindsight — unnecessary ("unnötig"). Rhetorical concessions to Isenberg or not, these points add up to a major critique of the novel.

Almost thirty years later, in his 1936 essay "Erinnerungen an Hans" (Memories of Hans), Hesse invokes his lasting "embitterment" about his and Hans's suffering in school, and now admits that he used *Unterm Rad* to try to "settle accounts" or "get even with" "such schools." New here is also the implication that Hesse did this because he was young:

> Die Lateinschule, welche auch mir viele Konflikte gebracht hatte, wurde für [Hans] mit der Zeit zur Tragödie, auf andere Weise und aus anderen Gründen als für mich, und wenn ich später als junger Schriftsteller in der Erzählung *Unterm Rad* nicht ohne Erbitterung mit der Art von Schulen abrechnete, so war das leidensschwere Schülertum meines Bruders dazu beinah ebensosehr Ursache wie mein eigenes. (342)

> [The Latin School, which also brought me many conflicts, became in time a tragedy for Hans, in a different way and for different reasons than it did for me. And when I later, as a young writer and not without embitterment, settled accounts with that sort of school in the story *Unterm Rad*, my brother's heavy suffering as a schoolboy was almost as great a motivation for me as my own.]

Fifty years after writing the novel, in "Begegnungen mit Vergangenem" (Meetings with Past Things, 1953), Hesse declares himself proud of its essence — "das Buch enthielt doch ein Stück wirklich erlebten und erlittenen Lebens" (and yet the book did contain a chunk of life truly lived and suffered through).[20] He again plays down the novel's vitriolic asides, but also intensifies his earlier self-criticisms and multiplies their force by repetition:

> Es war die Zeit, die ich, auch da noch unsicher genug und weit vom wirklichen Verstehen und Überwundenhaben entfernt, zehn Jahre später in der Erzählung *Unterm Rad* zum erstenmal zu beschwören versucht habe. In der Geschichte und Gestalt des kleinen Hans Giebenrath, zu dem als Mit- und Gegenspieler sein Freund Heilner gehört, wollte ich die Krise jener Entwicklungsjahre darstellen und mich von der Erinnerung an sie befreien, und um bei diesem Versuche das, was mir an Überlegenheit und Reife fehlte, zu ersetzen, spielte ich ein wenig [!] den Ankläger und Kritiker jenen Mächten gegenüber, denen Giebenrath erliegt und denen einst ich selber beinahe erlegen wäre: der Schule, der Theologie, der Tradition und Autorität.
>
> Wie gesagt, es war ein verfrühtes Unternehmen, auf das ich mich mit meinem Schülerroman einließ, und es ist denn auch nur sehr teilweise geglückt. [. . .]. (571–72)

> [It was the period of time that I — still quite unsure of myself and very far from any true understanding and overcoming — tried to conjure up ten years later in the story *Beneath the Wheel*. In the tale and figure of little Hans Giebenrath, to whom his friend Heilner belongs as comrade and antagonist, I wanted to depict the crisis of those years of my development and to free myself from my memory of them. And to compensate for what I lacked in mastery and maturity, I thereby played a little bit [!] of the prosecutor and critic toward those powers to which Giebenrath succumbs and to which I had once almost succumbed myself: school, theology, tradition, and authority.
>
> But as I said: it was a premature undertaking that I got into with my schoolboy novel, and [the book] turned out to be good only in very limited ways [. . .].]

Tendentiousness

Unterm Rad exists in three German versions. It was published first in the *Neue Zürcher Zeitung* in 1904. Hesse then reworked the novel for the original book publication in late 1905 (inexplicably dated 1906); this version was used for all editions until Hesse reworked the text again for the post-war republishing of his works that began in 1951 (Michels 1982, 208–9). Even though all three versions are still available, no comparative account exists and knowledge of their differences is rare in the secondary literature. Volker Michels is certainly correct to find "the original version in many places clearly more pointed, more uncompromising, and more political" than the 1951 version, but I would not agree with him that "the contents and intent of this *first* version [are] *completely* identical with Hesse's final reworking from 1951" (208–9; my emphases). There are significant differences in the ways Hesse reworked the original newspaper version as a relatively young man in 1904/5 and the ways he revised it in 1950/51 as a 73-year-old. It turns out that Hesse was being honest with Isenberg when he claimed that the 1905 book would appear "toned down" only "in minor ways." For the 1905 version, in fact, Hesse excised none of the important criticisms of the state and only one of his tendentious asides on pedagogical matters. For the 1951 edition, Hesse produced a text that, on the surface at least, appears more responsible and believable. He made crucial passages less caustic, less gratuitously critical, and less offensive.

The most ferocious of the passages in *Unterm Rad's* so-called "original version" (from the *Neue Zürcher Zeitung*), and the passage mined most frequently in the secondary literature for key quotations on the novel's meaning from *any* of its three versions, is the narrator's long diatribe at the beginning of chapter 5. I quote here from the "original" 1904 version while marking Hesse's later cuts. The 1905 cuts are indicated by underlining, the 1951 cuts by boldface type. Square brackets show replacement words, with dates of insertion:

> Alle diese ihrer Pflicht beflissenen **Lenker** [1951: Lehrer] der Jugend, vom Ephorus bis auf den Papa Giebenrath, Professoren und Repetenten, sahen in Hans ein böses Element, ein Hindernis ihrer Wünsche, etwas Verstocktes und Träges, das man zwingen und auf gute Wege zurück-bringen müsse. Keiner, außer vielleicht jenem mitleidigen Repetenten, sah hinter dem hilflosen Lächeln des schmalen Knabengesichtes eine un-tergehende Seele leiden und im Ertrinken angstvoll und verweilend [1905: verzweifelnd] um sich blicken. Und keiner dachte etwa daran, daß die Schule und der barbarische Ehrgeiz eines Vaters und einiger Lehrer dieses gebrechliche Wesen soweit gebracht hatten, **indem sie in der unschuldig vor ihnen ausgebreiteten Seele des zarten Kindes ohne Rücksicht wüteten.** Warum hatte er in den empfindlichsten und gefähr-lichsten Knabenjahren täglich bis in die Nacht hinein arbeiten müssen? Warum hatte man ihm seine Kaninchen weggenommen, ihn den Ka-meraden in der Lateinschule mit Absicht entfremdet, ihm Angeln und Bummeln verboten und ihm das hohle, gemeine Ideal eines schäbigen, aufreibenden Ehrgeizes eingeimpft? Warum hatte man ihm selbst nach dem Examen die wohlverdienten Ferien nicht gegönnt?
>
> Nun lag das überhetzte Rößlein am Weg und war nicht mehr zu brauchen [1905: **nimmer zu brauchen**] [1951: nicht mehr zu brauchen]. Die Lehrer würden ohne Zweifel gelacht haben, wenn jemand sie so gefragt hätte. Hatten so und so viele andere nicht auch denselben Drill

ausgehalten? Wer konnte von ihnen verlangen, daß sie für das ungewöhnlich feine Nervenwesen eines solchen Knaben Witterung und Empfinden und Schonung hatten? Oder daß sie wenigstens das natürliche
Zartgefühl der Liebe besaßen?

Was hat das mit der Schule zu tun? Nein, sie hatten ihre Pflicht an
Hans redlich getan.[21]

[All of these duty-conscious **leaders** [1951: teachers] of youth, from the
Ephorus down to Papa Giebenrath, professors and lecturers, saw in Hans
an evil element, an obstacle to their desires, something stubborn and
sluggish that had to be compelled and brought back onto the proper
path. No one, except perhaps that one compassionate lecturer, saw behind the helpless smiles on the little boy's slender face a drowning soul
suffering and in its drowning fearfully and lingeringly [1905: despair-
ingly] looking around for help. And no one recognized that the school
and the barbaric ambition of a father and of a few teachers had brought
this fragile being to this point — **by recklessly ravaging around in the
soul of this delicate child, which was so innocently spread out before
them.** Why, during the most sensitive and vulnerable boyhood years, did
he have to study well into the night every day? Why did they take away
his rabbits, intentionally alienate him from his comrades in the Latin
School, forbid him to go fishing and to go for walks, and inject him with
the hollow, common ideal of a wretched, enervating ambition? Why,
even after he passed his examination, had they not granted him his well-
earned summer vacation?

Now the overstressed little horse lay at the side of the road and was
no longer of use [1905: **no longer of any use**] [1951: no longer of use].

Without a doubt, the teachers would have laughed if someone had
asked them such questions. Hadn't so many others survived the same
regimen? Who could demand that they be able to detect such a boy's
unusually delicate nervous system and that they therefore should have
spared him? Or that they at least possess the natural tender feeling of love?

What does all this have to do with school? No, they had honorably
fulfilled their duty to Hans.]

There is impressive support in this passage for the probable truth of
Hesse's 1907 claim that "das Tendenziöse kam erst während der Ausführung, absichtslos und nur aus bitteren Erinnerungen erwachsen, hinein" (the
tendentiousness only entered into it during the writing phase, unintentionally and only because of my bitter memories). A comparison of this passage
with what is described or reported in the novel reveals a surprising fact: the
narrator's prosecutorial accusations radically misrepresent what the novel
actually shows. The narrator here makes the school and the "barbaric ambition of a father and of a few teachers" exclusively responsible for bringing
Hans to the point of mental and physical dissolution. The narrator also
describes *how* Hans's father and teachers went about doing this: "indem sie

in der unschuldig vor ihnen ausgebreiteten Seele des zarten Kindes ohne Rücksicht wüteten" (by recklessly ravaging around in the soul of this delicate child, which was so innocently spread out before them). This terrible metaphor — not cut until 1951 — declares categorically that father and teachers collaborated in the psychological violation or psychological gang rape of an utterly vulnerable and innocent Hans Giebenrath. And: "ohne Rücksicht" — "recklessly," or "without second thoughts." This is so far from a just description of what Hans's father and teachers actually *do* in the novel that it should leave us aghast. That Hesse intended the rape imagery comes clear a few pages later as Hans, having been sent home from Maulbronn, begins to experience "eine unwirkliche zweite Kinderzeit" (237; an unreal second childhood). In all of the novel's three versions — 1904, 1905, 1951 — we read: "die betrogene und *vergewaltigte* Kindheit brach wie eine lang gehemmte Quelle in ihm auf" (237, my emphasis; His betrayed and *raped* [or violated] childhood broke open in him like a long-blocked subterranean spring). Obviously, all these allegations must be tested carefully.

School. There are two schools in *Unterm Rad*, the Latin School in Hans's hometown and the *Klosterschule* (monastery school) at Maulbronn. Oddly, despite the narrator's assertion that "school" had brought Hans to the point of mental and physical breakdown and despite Hesse's retrospective claim that, in writing the novel, he had sought to "get even with this sort of school," *Unterm Rad* neither depicts nor negatively evaluates Hans's Latin School nor *any* of his education therein. Instead, the novel focuses on two periods of supplementary tutoring by some of Hans's Latin School teachers and by the *Stadtpfarrer*, the head pastor in the city's main church. In this sense, *Unterm Rad* is not a "school novel" at all, but a novel about supplemental tutoring in preparation for a specific prestigious and very competitive state examination. All of Hans's tutors but one are volunteers; his mathematics teacher seems to have been paid for the second tutoring period (175). Hans's participation in the extra sessions is also clearly voluntary.

The narrator emphasizes Hans's workload during the year-long first tutoring period, and rightly so. Daily, it includes one extra hour of Latin and Religion, one or two hours of Greek; one hour of confirmation instruction and two extra hours per week of mathematics instruction (139). For Sundays and "für etwaige Mußestunden [. . .] war die Lektüre einiger in der Schule nicht gelesener Autoren und Repetieren der Grammatik dringend empfohlen" (140; for any leisure hours, the reading of a few authors not included in the school curriculum and a review of grammar were strongly recommended). We don't learn whether Hans follows these recommendations.[22] The second tutoring period is shorter and much less intense. During his seven-week summer vacation before leaving for Maulbronn, Hans works daily with the town's pastor on New Testament Greek (one hour) and with the Rector of the Latin School on Homeric Greek (two hours). The mathematics teacher gives him four hours per week on algebra (177). On the question of homework, the novel is remarkably neutral. During the first tutoring period, Hans studies at home "dienstags und samstags gewöhnlich bis zehn Uhr, sonst aber bis elf, bis zwölf und gelegentlich noch darüber" (140; Tuesdays and Saturdays usually until 10:00 PM, otherwise until 11:00 or 12:00 and occasionally even later), presumably six days a week. We aren't told if Hans works this long and late because he somehow must or because he wants to. In the summer before he enrolls at Maulbronn, however, his desire to work independently is clear. After his first-ever hour of instruction in New Testament Greek, Hans went home

> und arbeitete daheim *noch den ganzen Abend weiter.* Nun spürte er, über wieviel Berge von Arbeit und Wissen der Weg zur wahren Forschung führe, und er war bereit, sich hindurchzuschlagen und nichts am Wege liegen zu lassen. (171, my emphasis)

> [and continued working there *for the rest of the evening.* Now he was able to sense how many mountains of studying and knowledge had to be gotten over before he could do genuine research, and he was prepared to fight his way through them and to leave nothing undone behind him.]

Despite the narrator's claims, at no time during either period of tutoring do Hans's tutors maltreat him in any way. It is true that someone (presumably Hans's father) does take away his rabbits and forbid him to go fishing during his year of preparation for the state examination. But, oddly, the novel's narrator is flat wrong about two other accusations: there is no evidence that anyone also forbade Hans to take walks — "Bummeln" — and no evidence that anyone sought to "alienate Hans intentionally from his comrades at the Latin School" (229). In the novel, neither event occurs.

Unterm Rad does describe the negative effects of the extra studying. Hans "lief still und verscheucht mit übernächtigtem Gesicht und blaurandigen, müden Augen herum" (141; Hans walked around quietly and timidly with a face that looked tired from lack of sleep and with tired eyes ringed with dark circles). Flaig, the town's master cobbler, describes Hans at the end of chapter 2 as "lauter Haut und Knochen" (177; just skin and bones). Most significantly, Hans suffers from chronic headaches, which seem to him and to others clearly to be connected to his studying and extra mental exertions:

> Hier [in his room at home] hatte er im Kampf mit Ermüdung, Schlaf und Kopfweh lange Abendstunden über Cäsar, Xenophon, Grammatiken, Wörterbüchern und mathematischen Arbeiten verbrütet, zäh, trotzig und ehrgeizig, oft auch der Verzweiflung nah. (146)

> [Here [in his room at home], fighting fatigue, the urge to sleep, and his headaches, he had spent long evening hours brooding over Caesar,

Xenophon, grammars, dictionaries and math exercises — tough, de-
fiant, and full of ambition, and often also near despair.]

In the run-up to the state examination, Hans once mentions "daß er in
letzter Zeit [. . . oft] seine Gedanken untereinander brachte" (143; that he
had lately often gotten his thoughts mixed up); once he becomes inexplicably tired during a walk in the woods and finds this puzzling (169); and
once he describes "das eigentümliche Gefühl im Kopf" (the peculiar feeling
in his head) that he had felt "so often" "in the past few months" (172):

> Kein Schmerz, sondern ein hastig triumphierendes Treiben beschleunig-
> ter Pulse und heftig aufgeregter Kräfte, ein eilig ungestümes Vorwärts-
> begehren. Nachher kam freilich das Kopfweh, aber solange jenes feine
> Fieber dauerte, rückte Lektüre und Arbeit stürmisch voran [. . .]. (172)

> [No pain, but rather a hurried, triumphant surging of quickened pulses
> and strongly excited mental powers, an urgent, impetuous craving to
> make progress. Afterwards, of course, came the headaches, but as long
> as that fine fever lasted, his reading and his other work proceeded
> rapidly [. . .].]

At the same time, Hans also experienced "der leichte, oft unterbrochene
Schlaf mit sonderbar klaren Träumen" (172; a light, oft-interrupted sleep
with oddly clear dreams). Toward the end of summer, Hans again had "viel
Kopfweh" (176; many headaches) and fished "ohne rechte Aufmerksamkeit"
(176; without paying much attention).

Surprisingly, given the narrator's accusations, this is the sum of Hans's
reactions, both physical and psychological, to his supplemental academic
exertions. None of these reactions, nor any critique advanced by the narrator
prior to the start of chapter 5, prepare us for Hans's later mental disintegration — not even the headaches. Although Hans's headaches rightly
trouble Flaig (177), they are neither debilitating nor obviously dangerous;
Hans literally works through them on his own, without treatment. At the
end of chapter 3, we learn with Hans that the pastor, himself a veteran of the
state examination and a Maulbronn graduate, had also suffered from headaches "in jüngeren Jahren" (in his younger years). The narrator adds: "und
somit war alles gut" (205; and thus all was well).

Even once Hans arrives at Maulbronn, none of his teachers do anything
unprofessional or untoward until well after his mental acuity and academic
performance begin to slip. Even then, there is nothing in their behavior that
could have brought Hans to the point of mental and physical collapse. After
Hans's academic decline begins, the Ephorus speaks to him first "mit ernster
Milde" (seriously, but with kindness) and then somewhat harshly (214–15).
Hans's professor in the class on Livy yells at him and makes a mocking comment, but then is sobered by a strangeness in Hans's eyes and arranges for
him to consult the *Oberamtsarzt* (220–22; the chief physician in the dis-

trict). When Hans's academic performance continues to decline, the teachers do begin "böse Gesichter zu schneiden und sonderbare Blicke zu schiessen" (225; to make mean faces and exchange strange glances). But none of this adds up to psychological violation or rape; none of it makes Hans a victim.

Barbaric Ambition. At the start of chapter 5, the narrator also blames "der barbarische Ehrgeiz eines Vaters und einiger Lehrer" (the barbaric ambition of a father and of a few teachers) for bringing Hans to the point of mental disintegration (229). Given the force of this claim, it is astonishing that the novel does not make more of it. In fact, neither the Rector, the *Klassenlehrer* (Hans's classroom teacher), the person conducting Hans's confirmation instruction, the mathematics teacher, nor any of Hans's professors or lecturers at Maulbronn — including the Ephorus — reveal any ambition at all. Only the *Stadtpfarrer* admits to a mild case tied directly to Hans:

> Der Stadtpfarrer [. . .] sagte aber beim Frühstück zu seiner Frau: Jetzt geht der Giebenrathle ins Examen. Aus dem wird noch was Besonderes; man wird schon auf ihn aufmerksam werden, und dann schadet es nichts, daß ich ihm mit den Lateinstunden beigesprungen bin. (149–50)

> [But the pastor [. . .] said to his wife over breakfast: right now little Giebenrath is beginning his state examination. He is going to become someone special; people will take note of him. It won't hurt that I helped tutor him in Latin.]

And Hans's father? The novel addresses his ambition, such as it is, in one passage. When Hans returns to studying *after* he has passed the state examination with the second highest grade, we read:

> Vater Giebenrath sah diesen Fleiß mit Stolz. In seinem schwerfälligen Kopf lebte dunkel das Ideal so vieler beschränkter **und unbedeutender** Leute, aus seinem Stamme einen Zweig über sich in eine Höhe wachsen zu sehen, die er mit dumpfem Respekt verehrte. (176; words in bold cut in 1951)

> [Father Giebenrath looked upon this hard work with pride. Somewhere in his sluggish head there lived an ideal held by so many narrow-minded **and insignificant** people: to see a branch grow up out of his family tree and attain a great height — a height that he venerated with vague respect. (words in bold cut in 1951)]

Despite the narrator's claims, there is no ambition to speak of, and certainly no "*barbaric* ambition" (my emphasis), to be found in any of Hans's tutors, teachers, professors, or his father. "Ambition" is not shown as motivation for any of them except the pastor, and his is laughably gentle and normal. In Hans's father, ambition takes the form of a common hope — understandable and unspectacular, despite the narrator's elitist commentary — that his child might rise into a higher social and probably economic sphere. Again, this is no violation or "rape" of Hans.[23]

The narrator's final accusation centers on Hans's own ambition: "Warum hatte man [. . .] ihm das hohle, gemeine Ideal eines schäbigen, aufreibenden Ehrgeizes *eingeimpft* [. . .]?" (149, my emphasis; Why had they [. . .] *injected* him with the hollow, common ideal of a wretched, enervating ambition?). Strangely, "einimpfen" (inject, inoculate, instill with, indoctrinate with) suggests that such ambition can be inserted into the will of another. Not surprisingly, this is nowhere shown in the novel. But *Unterm Rad* does offer two separate explanations for Hans's ambition. The Rector chooses a metaphor appropriate to the pedagogic enterprise: that of "waking up" someone's (pre-existing) ambition and then guiding its growth. His pleasure at the development of Hans's ambition is mocked in memorable and overblown sarcasm by the narrator:

> Dem Rektor war es ein inniges Vergnügen gewesen, diesen von ihm geweckten, schönen Ehrgeiz zu leiten und wachsen zu sehen. Man sage nicht, Schulmeister haben kein Herz und seien verknöcherte und entseelte Pedanten! O nein, wenn ein Lehrer sieht, wie eines Kindes lange erfolglos gereiztes Talent hervorbricht, wie ein Knabe Holzsäbel und Schleuder und Bogen und die anderen kindischen Spielereien ablegt, wie er vorwärts zu streben beginnt, wie der Ernst der Arbeit aus einem rauhen Pausback einen feinen, ernsten und fast asketischen Knaben macht, wie sein Gesicht älter und geistiger, sein Blick tiefer und zielbewusster, seine Hand weißer und stiller wird, dann lacht ihm die Seele vor Freude und Stolz. (172)

> [For the Rector it was a deep pleasure to guide this lovely ambition, which he himself had awakened, and to watch it grow. Let no one say that schoolmasters have no hearts, or that they are fossilized, soulless pedants! Oh, no: when a teacher sees a child's talent finally break forth after much unsuccessful prodding; when he sees a boy put aside his wooden sword, slingshot, bow and other childish toys; when he sees him begin to strive to make progress in his studies; sees serious work turn a chubby-cheeked little tot into a fine, earnest, and almost ascetic boy; sees how the boy's face becomes older and more intellectual, the eyes deeper and more goal-centered, the hands more pale and more calm — then the teacher's soul laughs with joy and pride.]

A week into the summer vacation, the Rector asks Hans if he has "Lust, nebenher noch zu lernen" (if he "would like to do some extra studying"):

> "O doch, Herr Rektor, natürlich."
> "Ich möchte dir nichts aufzwingen, wozu du nicht selber Lust hast."
> "Freilich habe ich Lust." (174)

> ["Oh yes, Rector, certainly."
> "I don't want to force anything on you that you don't want to do."
> "Of course I want to."]

Only then does the Rector play on Hans's sense of competitiveness to make his case for reading Homer together. The Rector's lines are also overblown and quite possibly insincere, but they are hardly a violation of Hans. And like the Rector, Hans Giebenrath also locates his ambition squarely within himself. Hans has come to like and to need to be first:

> Denn das wusste er wohl, daß er im Seminar noch ehrgeiziger und zäher arbeiten müsse, wenn er auch dort die Kameraden hinter sich lassen wollte. Und das wollte er entschieden. Warum eigentlich? Das wusste er selber nicht. Seit drei Jahren war man auf ihn aufmerksam, hatten die Lehrer, der Stadtpfarrer, der Vater und namentlich der Rektor ihn angespornt und gestachelt und in Atem gehalten. Die ganze lange Zeit, von Klasse zu Klasse, war er unbestrittener Primus gewesen. Und nun hatte er allmählich selber seinen Stolz darein gesetzt, obenan zu sein und keinen neben sich zu dulden. (168)

> [For he knew that he would have to work even harder and even more ambitiously at the seminary school if he wanted to leave his classmates behind him as he had done at his earlier school. And he did want to do that, absolutely. And why? He didn't know. For the past three years people had taken note of him; the teachers, the city pastor, his father, and especially the Rector had all spurred him on and kept him on his toes. For that whole time, from grade level to grade level, he had been uncontestably first [*Primus*] — the best student. And gradually he had made it a matter of his own pride to stay on top and to tolerate no one next to him.]

The narrator's allegation of "einimpfen" (injecting ambition) is decidedly strange. Hesse can hardly be expecting parents, teachers, and city elders not to "notice," encourage, "spur on," or seek to motivate promising students.

Like many of the critical "asides" in *Unterm Rad*, the narrator's spectacular claims about Hans as a victim of his school, his father, and his teachers turn out, upon close evaluation, to be simply wrong, unsupported by the story. It's as if these accusations were composed for a different novel and then forcibly grafted onto this one at a later date. For this reason, Hesse's 1907 admission to Isenberg about the genesis of the novel's "tendentiousness" makes good sense. The narrator's tendentious asides force *Unterm Rad* to serve a more dramatic, sweeping, and abstract critical purpose than the story actually permits. Oddly, Hesse thereby creates, not an unreliable narrator, but an intermittently ignorant one, a narrator who sometimes seems not to know or not to understand the tale he is telling and commenting on. This narrator attributes particular key actions and motivations to characters who nowhere perform them; asserts that events which didn't happen in the novel actually did happen; and utterly neglects to mention, as we shall see below, the key role played in Hans's decline by Hermann Heilner. While the narrator's accusations surely attest to Hesse's admirable concerns about "the school question" and *Schulüberbürdung* (the "overburdening of schoolchildren") and to Hesse's desire to get even with "such schools" — they also prevent us from seeing what actually happens in the novel. Others since 1905 have also been troubled by this. Hugo Ball identified the problem in 1927:

> But the whole tragedy is blamed on the teachers, and it is not really clear why the schoolboy [Hans] passed the state examination with one of the best grades and then suddenly couldn't measure up. (58)

In the *Blätter für die deutsche Erziehung* in 1905, Fr. Steudel characterized *Unterm Rad,* with impressive critical insight and an obvious deep appreciation for its author, as a failed *Tendenzroman* (tendentious novel):

> Hesse wanted to write a tendentious novel. This is shown in the few commentaries [in the novel] that almost evince a personal bitterness. But he did not succeed in writing a tendentious novel that equaled the others in that well-known genre. He indicts the school without being able to undermine its system or structure. This is because his line of argument has too many questionable points, which gradually all break down — to the benefit of the actual poetic work, which gains in literary stature the more the angry tendentiousness recedes. After all, Hesse is a poet and not a prosecutor.[24]

I suspect that much of the ongoing popularity of *Unterm Rad* is due, not to the widespread assertion that the novel so effectively portrays abusive or exploitative turn-of-the-century schooling practices, but to the fact that it does not portray them at all. The narrator — who is everywhere assumed, without analysis or argument, to speak with Hesse's voice and authority — claims dramatically and quotably that Hans's father and teachers have perpetrated horrible acts against him and thus caused his psychological breakdown and perhaps even his death. Elsewhere the narrator assures us that "state and school" are always "atemlos bemüht, die alljährlich auftauchenden paar tieferen und wertvolleren Geister an der Wurzel zu knicken" (213; breathlessly trying to snap off at the roots the few more profound and more valuable intellects that surface each school year). But the novel nowhere shows or reports such acts, nor does it usefully describe or critically analyze the allegedly repressive (or even just outmoded) pedagogies of the day.[25] As Franz Servaes saw in his review of the novel in 1905, "The school really bears no guilt or responsibility [for Hans's fate], or rather a guilt so subtle that it could only be explicated at a conference of psychologists."[26]

Within its glittering polemical shell, therefore, *Unterm Rad* has a largely unnoticed empty center waiting to be filled — with readers' own painful school-centered memories and resentments, certainly, but also with Hesse scholars' retrospective hopes for a socially critical, reform-minded Hesse novel. With this empty center, *Unterm Rad* is perennially useful as a talisman for the defense of children beleaguered in any way at school or, by easy extension, for the defense of anyone weak against anyone seen as powerful or tyrannical. In a passage chosen by Suhrkamp publishing company for the dust jacket of Hesse's new *Sämtliche Werke*, volume 2, the writer Gabriele Wohmann found the novel especially helpful against what she called her "Nazi-collaborationist teachers":

> I must have recognized my dull-witted Nazi-collaborationist teachers in Hans Giebenrath's tormentors and thus discovered solidarity in literature. I very readily took up Hesse's novel as a mocking and hate-filled retaliation against the injustice done to children by incompetent teachers.[27]

But Wohmann's morally understandable if textually unsupportable reading of Hans's teachers as "incompetent" and as "tormentors" ("Peiniger"), and her breathtaking insistence that Hans's death is actually a "murder [. . .] caused by gradual poisoning" (86), suggest that she, like most of the novel's modern commentators, has mistaken the narrator's polemical accusations — and her perception of Hesse's best intentions — for the novel itself. The cumulative effect of such empathetic misreadings can be measured in Sikander Singh's important recent introduction to Hesse:

> The psychic and physical violence that [. . .] determines Hans Giebenrath's young life, and that is characteristic of the educational system of Wilhelmine Germany, has been interpreted by Alexander Mitscherlich as one of the preconditions for the genesis of fascist ideology. By telling the story of a quiet, clever, growing boy who is destroyed by an authoritarian, unjust, and inhumane educational system, *Beneath the Wheel* anticipates the experiences of a whole generation that was socialized in a system of implicit and explicit violence and that therefore compensated by permitting these experiences, which extinguished the individuality and uniqueness of the individual human being, to culminate in the excesses of violence that characterized National Socialism.[28]

This is a long way from *Unterm Rad's* Hans Giebenrath. This passage describes a novel that, in retrospect, we may indeed wish that Hesse had written. It is not the novel that Hesse wrote.

Title

The novel's title varies a phrase used by the Ephorus during his "ungeschickten Rettungsversuch" (213; inept attempt to save Hans). He notes that Hans's "Leistungen [haben] in letzter Zeit etwas nachgelassen [. . .]" (214; academic performance has declined somewhat recently), and then asks:

> "[. . .] Willst du mir versprechen, dir ordentlich Mühe zu geben?"
> Hans legte seine Hand in die ausgestreckte Rechte des Gewaltigen, der ihn mit ernster Milde anblickte.

"So ist's gut, so ist's recht, mein Lieber. Nur nicht matt werden, sonst kommt man *unters Rad*."

Er drückte Hans die Hand, und dieser ging aufatmend zur Türe. [. . .] (214–15, my emphasis)

["[. . .] Will you promise me to give it your best effort?"

Hans placed his hand on the outstretched right hand of the mighty Rector, who looked at Hans seriously, but also with kindness.

"That's good, that's right, my man. Don't give in, or you'll fall *beneath the wheel*."

He pressed Hans's hand, and Hans went to the door, relieved.]

Despite the Ephorus's unusual choice of the singular — the phrase *unters Rad* typically appeared, then as now, as the plural form *unter die Räder* (beneath the wheels) — the general meaning of the phrase should not be in doubt. Klaus Johann recently stated the following:

At the time the novel was being written, this figure of speech, especially in its plural form [. . .], was still relatively young. It is attested starting in 1850 as an expression that meant "to go off the straight and narrow"; "to sink low morally" or "to fall in a moral sense; to decline morally or economically; to become poor; to get drunk frequently," and it is "taken from accidents occurring under the wheels of a vehicle." (184–85)

Modern dictionaries confirm and extend Johann's findings. "Unter die Räder kommen / geraten" (to fall beneath the wheels) is a colloquial expression that can mean "to sink low morally or socially";[29] "go off the rails," "come down in the world," "go to the dogs," "go to seed," "waste one's time," "run things into the ground" [. . .], "lose one's way";[30] "completely come down in the world," "be ruined morally and economically," "lose one's moral compass," "fall in a moral sense," "fall into bad company."[31]

Some Hesse scholars have stayed within this broad range of established meanings in explaining the novel's title. Michael Müller notes in passing that the phrase means "aus der Bahn [werfen]" — "throwing someone off his or her track" or "leaving someone floundering."[32] Fritz Böttger calls the Ephorus's advice to Hans "a symbolic figure of speech"

that countless fathers repeated to their sons as they made their ways into the world [. . .]: "don't fall beneath the wheels!" — that meant, more or less: "don't fail in the character formation process that Wilhelmine Germany has ready for you, or you'll find yourself staring ruin in the face."[33]

But many scholars have opted to promote readings that push Hesse's title further, toward harshness and horror. For these critics, the phrase "beneath the wheel" denotes or connotes dying or being killed, often at the hands of evil others. In his *Hesse-Kommentar*, Martin Pfeifer notes without explanation or source that "to come 'beneath the wheels' means more or less 'to come to grief; perish.'"[34] Singh defines it as "failing or being ruined, not for something you did, but because of demands made on you by others" (85), and claims that the educational system in the novel destroys or even kills Hans ("zu Grunde richten"; 87). Helga Esselborn-Krumbiegel states (also without source or explanation) that "to come 'beneath the wheel' means 'to be destroyed or killed' — by an external or internal force"). In another work, she explains that the title "plays on the notion of being run over and on the notion of being destroyed by an external force."[35] And in Heribert Kuhn's recent commentary, we read the following unsourced gloss:

> *Beneath the Wheel.* Its form, which knows neither beginning nor end and is capable of representing an image of "eternal" motion, establishes the meaning of the wheel in mythology and folk custom: the physical representation and symbolizing of the celestial movement of the sun in the wheel of the sun. In Buddhism, whose world of symbols the young Hesse had access to through his parents, the Wheel of Doctrine ("dharma tschakra") stands alongside the Wheel of Life ("bhava tschakra"). All this may be thought of as part of the background to the novel's title; primarily the title alludes to the crushing effects [*zermalmende Wirkung*] of wheels during accidents and to the pre-modern penal technique of breaking someone "on the wheel." (251)

Four things must be noted here. First, Kuhn's references to "mythology," "folk custom," and "the wheel of the sun" add nothing but allusional length and luster; no connections to the novel are adduced. Similarly, there is no reason to think that Hesse — or his fictional character the Ephorus, who actually utters the phrase "unters Rad" — had reason, in this novel and this context, to invoke these particular Buddhist wheels. Third, in the dictionary definitions cited above as in the novel itself, there is no justification for the violence of Kuhn's word "zermalmend" (to crush to bits or pieces); Hans is nowhere crushed in this way, neither actually nor metaphorically.[36] Finally, there is no justification for claiming an allusion in the title to the practice of torture or execution by means of the wheel — a common assertion or assumption in *Unterm Rad* criticism. In part, it's a matter of prepositions. For such punishment to be carried out, the victim must be "on" the wheel and bound "to" the wheel. To be "under" the wheel would in fact mean that the wheel could not properly be used to perform its terrible work. In the historical references to such practices collected in the Grimms' *Deutsches Wörterbuch*, for example, the preposition used to describe the body position of the wheel's victim is always "auf" (that is, "on"): "auf dem rad [halten]"; "auf galgen und rad"; "einen aufs rad setzen"; "auf ein rad [legen]" or "flechten"; "auf dem rade liegen, sitzen, aufs rad kommen"[37] (English: "[to hold] on the wheel"; "on the gallows and the wheel"; "to set someone on the wheel"; "to place someone on the wheel"; "to break someone on the wheel"; "to lie or sit on the wheel"; "to be placed onto the wheel"). Hesse could easily have named his novel "Auf dem Rad" — "On the Wheel" — but he didn't. Far more significantly, the novel's prosecutorial narrator uses no torture or execution metaphors and no metaphors of "crushing" or "running over" someone to characterize the actions of Hans's father, teachers, tutors, professors, lecturers, the Ephorus, the school, or the state.[38]

Happily, Hesse's 1904 letter to his half brother Karl Isenberg provides contemporary guidance on how Hesse probably intended his title to be understood: "Hans [. . .] ist auch, seit sie ihm in der Schule das Rückgrat gebrochen haben, *immer unterm Rad geblieben*" (130–31, my emphasis; And ever since they broke his resistance [literally, "his backbone"] in school, Hans *has always remained beneath the wheel*). For Hesse, here, to be "beneath the wheel" is clearly to be living — not dead, not being tortured or killed or threatened with either — but living in a weakened (and likely miserable) state. *Wahrig Deutsches Wörterbuch* defines "breaking someone's resistance [or backbone]" as "ruining someone economically, morally, or psychologically" — meanings that cohere perfectly with many of the dictionary definitions cited above. For Hesse, being "beneath the wheel" must therefore mean living what life one can after such economic, moral, or psychological "ruination" has taken place. In Hans Giebenrath's case, therefore, as Michael Müller has recently implied in passing, the phrase "beneath the wheel" must logically refer to the period of Hans's life *after* his mental breakdown, the time described in the novel's chapters 5 through 7: "That Giebenrath finally falls 'beneath the wheel' is [. . .] due to [. . .] a psychological breakdown that [. . .] the school physicians cannot fully explain."[39] By itself, finally, the phrase "beneath the wheel" does not connote "destruction" by others.

Ambition and Arrogance

Most readings of *Unterm Rad* take the narrator's chapter 5 diatribe at face value. As Paul Mog sees it:

> Since Hesse does not let his story speak for itself and inserts countless accusatory commentaries by the narrator, we know unmistakably what the author wants us to think.[40]

Not surprisingly, such readings emphasize details from the text that seem to confirm Hans Giebenrath as victim. This approach may strengthen readers' sympathy for Hans, but it can also divert attention from other important aspects of his character.

An essential part of Giebenrath is his desire to be first in his class — "Primus." This ambition not only keeps him "on task" even late at night; it also has curious power over him: "Der in der Angst und im Triumph des

Examens untergetauchte Ehrgeiz [. . .] *ließ ihn keine Ruhe*" (172, my emphasis; His ambition, which had disappeared in the anxiety and triumph surrounding the state examination [. . .] *now would not leave him in peace*). As we have seen, the critique of "ambition" is a key part of the novel: the narrator identifies the force allegedly "injected" into Hans as "das hohle, gemeine Ideal eines schäbigen, aufreibenden Ehrgeizes" (229; the hollow, common ideal of a wretched, enervating ambition) and also deems it "barbaric" (229). The narrator's criticism of Hans is augmented by that of Hans's friend Hermann Heilner, who asserts — probably disingenuously — that Hans's ambition comes only from fear:

> "Das ist Taglöhnerei," hieß es, "du tust all die Arbeit ja doch nicht gern und freiwillig, sondern lediglich aus Angst vor deinen Lehrern oder vor deinem Alten. Was hast du davon, wenn du Erster oder Zweiter wirst? Ich bin Zwanzigster und darum doch nicht dümmer als ihr Streber." (198)

> ["That's just forced labor," he said. "You're not doing all that work happily, of your own free will, but only because you're afraid of your teachers or your old man. What do *you* get if you're first or second in the class? I'm twentieth, but I'm not any more stupid than you brown-nosers."]

But Hans's ambition and the academic work that it leads to are also shown to be salutary. Hans wasn't like his fellow student Emil Lucius, we are told; on the contrary, "ihm [Hans] war es wirklich um Erkenntnis zu tun" (190; [Hans] really was searching for knowledge and insight). And we note the many passages both before and after Hans enters Maulbronn in which his desire for knowledge and discovery are expressed beautifully and without apparent irony. We learn of Hans's enthusiasm for Xenophon (151–52); his great liking for learning algebra and Latin (175–76); his evolving delight and need, under the Rector's introductory tutelage, to figure out the next tough verse in Homer (176); and his wonder at the pastor's ability, in a "single hour," to give him "einen ganz neuen Begriff von Lernen und Lesen" (171; a completely new understanding of learning and reading).

But manifestations of Hans's ambition are often accompanied by evidence of a trait that makes it difficult to sustain full sympathy for him: "ein stolzes Selbstgefühl" (172; literally: a proud feeling of self-esteem). Of course, talented adolescents often manifest arrogance unwittingly. Not Hans. He recognizes his arrogance as a problem and actively works *not* to solve it:

> Außerdem hatte [Hans] sich seiner Feigheit zu schämen, denn seit einer gewissen Zeit mied er den Schuster [Master Flaig] fast ängstlich, seiner scharfen Fragen wegen. Seit er der Stolz seiner Lehrer war und selber ein wenig hochmütig geworden war, hatte der Meister Flaig ihn so komisch angesehen und zu demütigen versucht. (173)

[Hans also had to feel ashamed of his own cowardice, because for some time he had been avoiding the shoemaker [Master Flaig] almost fearfully, on account of Flaig's pointed questions. Since Hans had become the pride of his teachers and had himself become a little arrogant, Master Flaig had started to look at him quite strangely and had tried to humble him.]

Hesse's masterful use of interior monologue leaves no doubt that Hans knows exactly how disturbing his arrogance actually is. "Ein wenig hochmütig" (a little arrogant) turns out to be quite the understatement:

Die andern saßen jetzt in der Schule und hatten Geographie, nur er allein war frei und entlassen. Er hatte sie überholt, sie standen jetzt unter ihm. Sie hatten ihn genug geplagt, weil er ausser August keine Freundschaften und an ihren Raufereien und Spielen keine rechte Freude gehabt hatte. So, nun konnten sie ihm nachsehen, die Dackel, die Dickköpfe. Er verachtete sie so sehr [. . .]. (163)

[The other pupils were now in school, in geography class, and only he was free, only he had been given leave to go. He had surpassed them; they were all beneath him now. They had tormented him enough because he made no friends besides August and because he didn't really like their roughhousing and their games. So now they could admire him from below, those stupid idiots. He despised them so much [. . .].]

The novel makes it impossible to dismiss Hans's arrogance as a mere aspect of his ambition. Hans's contempt for all schoolmates except August is rooted in his most essential fear. As we learn in the conversation with his father about the "Gymnasium" (high school) — "ob ich aufs Gymnasium darf, wenn ich durchfalle" (156; whether I may go to a proper high school if I fail the state examination) — preparing for and passing the state examination has not been merely a question of ambition. For Hans, success on the *Landexamen* is a question of life and death:

Herr Giebenrath war sprachlos.
    "Was? Gymnasium?" brach er dann los. "Du auf's Gymnasium? Wer hat dir das in den Kopf gesetzt?"
    "Niemand. Ich meine nur so."
    Die Todesangst stand ihm im Gesicht zu lesen. (156)

[Mr. Giebenrath was speechless.
    "What? *Gymnasium?*" he exploded. "You go to *Gymnasium?* Who put that in your head?"
    "No one. I just wondered."
    You could see the fear of death in his face.]

Hans's ambition and arrogance are bound up together in the center of his character, in his deep need to become someone different than he is. Hans's "fear of death" is his intense fear of staying common; of being unable to rise above his lot; of having to become an apprentice and live out his life in an office or shop:

> Hans [. . .] versuchte sich vorzustellen, wie das sein würde, wenn es nun wirklich mit Seminar und Gymnasium und Studieren nichts wäre. Man würde ihn als Lehrling in einen Käsladen oder auf ein Bureau tun, und er würde zeitlebens einer von den gewöhnlichen armseligen Leuten sein, die er verachtete und über die er absolut hinaus wollte. (156–57)

> [Hans [. . .] tried to imagine what would happen if he couldn't go to the seminary school or Gymnasium and thereafter to university. They would make him an apprentice in some cheese shop or office, and for his whole life he would be one of the common, pathetic people whom he despised and whom he absolutely wanted to surpass.]

Hans therefore desperately wants what the *Landexamen* is designed, by state and church, to give him (139). His ambition and supererogatory diligence are the means to gratify his desires for high social position, power over his classmates, and the tangible and visible proof that he is different — better — than they. This is not the behavior, nor are these the dreams and desires, of an innocent or "violated" victim.

Illness

In his stimulating recent "modernising reading" of *Unterm Rad*, Andreas Solbach acknowledged the scholars who have revised what he called "the single-minded reading of the novel as a satirical critique of contemporary pedagogy." As Solbach sees it, they accomplished this revision largely by showing "the neurasthenic hero [= Hans Giebenrath] as at least partly responsible for his own fate."[41] In re-assessing Giebenrath in this light, Solbach writes: "the narrator depicts Hans as someone who strives for academic success out of personal arrogance and a feeling of intellectual superiority. This depiction is designed to influence our assessment of the protagonist in a negative way" (72). But Solbach's use of the word "neurasthenic" also invokes the fundamental question of Hans Giebenrath's health. Ever since the novel appeared, some critics have seen Giebenrath as a person uniquely fragile and vulnerable, and noted that this fact undermines Hesse's declared polemical intentions. Fr. Steudel put it this way in 1905:

> The main problem with this bill of indictment [= the novel] is this: the unfortunate consequences of the intensive studying portrayed in the novel are strictly individual, not typical, and they eventually become a catastrophe for Hans Giebenrath: but he is not an average pupil. He is a delicate, very fragile creature, predestined to fall under the wheel of life. [. . .] He is destroyed by a burden that his classmates were able to

bear — able to add to all the other burdens of their school years — without apparent damage. (179)

In 1928 Hans Rudolf Schmid wrote:

> Giebenrath suffers from a constitutional weakness of the nerves. The novel does not fulfill what it promises, and the author's secret intention of writing a novel that criticizes contemporary schooling practices is invalidated the moment he admits that his hero is neurasthenic.[42]

In his thoughtful and thorough 1967 analysis of the novel, Mark Boulby put it bluntly: "Hans's fate is no more than the story of a neurasthenic, a decadent, whose vitality is grossly impaired" (49).

Despite these voices, little attention has been paid to Giebenrath's health. Some Hesse scholars mention neurasthenia or decadence; and some, like Boulby and Solbach, properly link the terms. But none have read the novel through a detailed case history of Hans. None have examined the role of neurasthenia in the so-called *Schulüberbürdungsdebatte* ("the debate about overburdening in schools") during the second half of the nineteenth century, one of the novel's obvious historical contexts. And none have tried to explore Hesse's knowledge of neurasthenia or determine his sources for Hans's symptoms. As a single sentence from the literature makes clear, these are among the most promising areas of future inquiry on *Unterm Rad*:

> Around 1900, German, then Dutch pedagogues adopted neurasthenia to construct a diagnosis for children with problematic behaviour associated with mental overburdening, thus medicalizing a condition formerly located within a framework of sin and guilt.[43]

At least three medical scholars have commented on Giebenrath's "case." Significantly, all of them identify in Hans what today are called "pre-existing conditions." In a 1910 lecture entitled "General Etiology and Prophylaxis of Nervousness in Children," Dr. Wilhelm Strohmayer — professor at Jena, M.D., and specialist in neurology — first warns against the often facile diagnosis of "school overburdening" in words that may well have been aimed at Hesse's narrator in *Unterm Rad*, who is always quick to blame the state:

> Mit dem Schlagworte der Schulüberbürdung, die man so häufig für die Nervosität verantwortlich macht, muß man m. E. vorsichtig umgehen und nicht alles dem Regime zur Last legen, was der minderwertigen Konstitution des Schülermaterials zuzuschreiben ist.[44]

> [We must be careful how we use the buzzword "overburdening," which is so frequently identified as the cause of nervousness, and we shouldn't always blame the regime for things that are attributable to the poor-quality constitutions of the pupils.]

Just two pages later, Strohmayer holds up Hans Giebenrath himself as a prime example of "a genuine young neurasthenic." Correcting Hesse's narrator's claim that Hans's teachers and father somehow violated him to serve their own ambitions, Strohmayer describes Giebenrath unspectacularly as "an exemplar of those young boys whose delicate nervous systems [. . .] collapse under the senseless but 'well-meant' pressure of parents and teachers" (32). Strohmayer's detailed description of "die rasch ermüdbaren und schwer sich erholenden Schwächlinge" (the weaklings who quickly tire and have difficulty recovering) reads like a description of Hans:

> Physically and intellectually delicate, instantly recognizable for their unhealthy, quickly-changing facial coloring, either fidgety and agitated or fearful and timid, they are candidates for neurasthenia from the start. Quite early they begin complaining after school about fatigue, feelings of tension, and pressure in their heads. In these cases, when rest periods are kept too few and too short, the gradual accumulation of fatigue residuals, which cannot properly be offset or made up for because of the pupils' deficient circulation and blood characteristics, or because of their uneasy and dream-tormented sleep, leads to a state of perpetual exhaustion and finally to the complete collapse of their intellectual abilities. (32)

In 1968, Rolf Meister wrote a doctoral dissertation on literary portrayals of psychosis.[45] Meister praises Hesse's *Unterm Rad* as a "realistic depiction" and "exacting and detailed portrayal" of the "outbreak and development of *hebephrenia* in a schoolboy" (21, my emphasis). After detailing over seven pages "the pathological high points and milestones" of the plot, Meister concludes that "Hesse's depiction requires neither correction nor supplement by psychiatry. All details given add up to a true-to-life picture of schizophrenia in a young boy" (27). Meister finds "neurasthenic harbingers of psychosis" in Hans's recurring headaches; in the typical "discrepancy [. . .] between the pupil's psychotic reality and the lack of understanding on the part of the psychologically uninformed teachers"; in the "hallucinations" that occur but always with Hans "well-oriented"; and in Hans's increasingly frequent entry into "an autistic world" in which he experiences a rich imaginative life and develops impressive "eidetic abilities." Amusingly, Meister reads Hans's death by drowning as a Deus ex machina that saves author Hesse from having to depict "the predictable final stage of mental and psychological emptiness" (29). Significantly, Meister also rejects the notion that "mental overburdening" caused Hans's illness:

> The coincidence of a weak constitution and overburdening does not give rise to schizophrenia. Rather, the inclination to a schizophrenic development must first be present [in the patient]. Only then may such factors play contributory roles. (30)

In 1970, Dr. Adolf Schweckendiek published a literature-based guide to help parents and others recognize neuroses.[46] In assessing *Unterm Rad*, Schweckendiek rejects the narrator's claim that "the barbaric ambition of a father and of a few teachers" caused Hans's problems and eventually his premature death. He also rejects the narrator's notion that ambition can be "injected" into people. Hans "doesn't need to be 'injected' with anything; he already possesses a pathological predisposition to excessive ambition and excessive studying" (67). A detailed case history follows, analyzing significant events in Hans's development and identifying the various neuroses that cause or accompany them. For Schweckendiek, Hans's most deleterious neurosis is an "anxiety neurosis":

> The upsurging anxiety of the child who has still not crossed the threshold to adulthood, and who still trembles at the thought of being punished, drives him toward his death. In his excessive fear of those with power in the world, Hans fails the normal, healthy tests of his manhood and virility — vis-à-vis his teachers at the seminary school, the girl he loves, and the switch that his father has made ready to thrash him with. (80–81)

Friendship

As we have seen, scholars who take the allegorical-autobiographical approach to *Unterm Rad* know who Hermann Heilner is and how to read him: For Tusken, Heilner is "the secret hero of the novel" (57). For Hahn, Heilner is "the actual hero of the novel" (163). For Stolte, Hermann Heilner

> embodies the other Hermann Hesse, the real Hermann Hesse, the person called to be a poet, and the name "Hermann" points unmistakably to this identity, just as the family name "Heilner" expresses his healing, helping, saving nature. (44)

In fact, despite the narrator's insistence on the guilt of Hans's father and teachers, and despite Heilner's obviously meaning-laden names, Hermann Heilner turns out to be the novel's villain. Hesse himself indicates this possibility in "Begegnung mit Vergangenem" (Meeting with Past Things), calling Hermann Heilner Giebenrath's "Mit- und Gegenspieler": his friend and collaborator, but also his antagonist and opponent.[47] Far from being a "helper" or representing a true chance at healing for Hans ("heilen" means "to heal"), Heilner is, ironically, the one character in the novel who makes Hans sick — far more obviously and demonstrably than Hans's teachers, tutors, father, or the state. Interestingly: for critics blissfully ignorant of Stolte's "principle of polarization" — like D. J. Enright — Heilner's guilt, and his indifference to Hans's suffering, are simply obvious. The *Kirkus Reviews* in 1968 described "the wild and Byronic Heilner who, unwittingly if indifferently, brings about [Hans's] fall from grace."[48] Edward M. Potoker concluded in the *Saturday Review* that "Heilner is no hero to Hesse"; "Hans Giebenrath is as much a victim of Hermann Heilner [. . .] as he is of the system of Maulbronn."[49]

Hans Giebenrath arrives at Maulbronn almost certainly neurasthenic, perhaps severely neurotic, and at least potentially in the early stages of hebephrenia. In the novel's terms, Hans is a "gebrechliches Wesen"; a "zartes Kind" with an "ungewöhnlich feine[s] Nervenwesen" (original version 118: a fragile being, a delicate child with an uncommonly delicate nervous system); an unusual history of headaches, and a worrying new tendency to become fatigued. Hans's obvious intelligence, according to the narrator, may well be a "Symptom einer einsetzenden Degeneration" in his family (138; symptom of nascent degeneration). Hans's past year has been filled with always difficult and sometimes rewarding academic work that has enabled him to achieve the first step toward his fierce dream of studying at university. This has energized but also clearly enervated him. As Joachim Noob has brilliantly seen, Hans's headaches are the "zuverlässige Meßeinheit für Hans' Befinden" (195), the novel's way of measuring and tracking Hans's health for the reader.

Hans brings ambition, diligence, arrogance, talent, and sundry anxieties and weaknesses with him to Maulbronn. On arrival, he dedicates himself to studying and "suchte sich alles fernzuhalten, was ihn der Arbeit entziehen konnte" (190–91; sought to avoid everything that could pull him away from his work). His "ideal," as he later assures himself, "war [. . .] vorwärts zu kommen, berühmte Examina zu machen und eine Rolle zu spielen, aber keine romantische und gefährliche [. . .]" (202; [. . .] to advance himself, to write celebrated examinations, and to play an important role — but not a romantic or dangerous one [. . .]"). And he succeeds: worlds of wonder open up for him in the *New Testament* and the *Odyssey* (197–98); he becomes Maulbronn's "fleißigste[r]" (213) and "vielleicht bester Hebräer" (214; hardest-working and perhaps best student of Hebrew); and he later admits to Heilner that "es war mein fester Vorsatz, im Seminar obenan zu bleiben und womöglich vollends Erster zu werden" (211; I was firmly resolved to stay at the top of the class and, if at all possible, to be first). Nothing in the novel's early Maulbronn pages suggests that Hans could not have done just that.

One key fact has gone unnoticed in the literature. During his first weeks at Maulbronn, Hans Giebenrath does not suffer from headaches. They disappear. Despite his year of preparation for the *Landexamen*; the sacrifice of his rabbits, his fishing, and part of his summer vacation; his heavier workload at Maulbronn; his continuing need and desire to study late into the night — Hans experiences no headaches and no other physical or psychological troubles. His increased work regimen and his life as a Maulbronn "brown-noser" ("Streber": Heilner's word) appear to agree with him (189). The headaches are last mentioned at the end of chapter 2 (177) and not again until near the end of chapter 3 (200) — probably a period of between six and eight weeks.[50] And the narrator is careful to emphasize that, in the meantime, Hans's headaches have been absent: "Daß das *alte* Kopfweh *wie*-

derkam, wunderte [Hans] nicht weiter [. . .]" (200, my emphases; That the *old* headaches *returned* came as no surprise to Hans [. . .]).

Although the narrator fails to blame Hermann Heilner in the chapter 5 diatribe, he does so repeatedly in chapter 4. In fact, the narrator, Hans himself, and the Ephorus all identify Heilner as the main cause of the major troubles that now begin for Hans. As we have seen, Michael Müller has recently argued the following:

> That Giebenrath finally comes "beneath the wheel" is not due to his friend's [Heilner's] influence, but to a psychological breakdown that — exactly as in Hesse's own case — the school physicians cannot fully explain. (22)

But chapter 4 shows clearly that Hermann Heilner undermines Hans's academic success, brings back his headaches, and overstresses him academically, emotionally, and physically to the point that Hans's "psychological breakdown" can happen.

Heilner accompanies his "theoretical" combat against Hans's "hard work" (198) with daily practical warfare: interrupting Hans's studying, taking possession of his free time, creating serious anxiety and stress. For Hans, Heilner's friendship — "ein mit Stolz gehüteter Schatz" (a proudly protected treasure) — therefore also quickly becomes "eine große, schwer zu tragende Last" (198; a heavy burden that is difficult to bear):

> Bisher hatte Hans die Abendstunden stets zur Arbeit benutzt. Jetzt kam es fast alle Tage vor, daß Hermann, wenn er das Büffeln satt hatte, zu ihm herüberkam, ihm das Buch wegzog und ihn in Anspruch nahm. Schließlich zitterte Hans, so lieb der Freund ihm war, vor seinem Kommen und arbeitete in den obligatorischen Arbeitsstunden doppelt eifrig und eilig, um nichts zu versäumen. (198)

> [Up till now, Hans had always used his free evening hours for studying. But now it happened that almost every evening Hermann, when he was sick of cramming, came over to Hans's desk, pulled his book away and demanded that he be attended to. Eventually Hans began to fear Hermann's visits and to work twice as hard and twice as hurriedly in the obligatory study periods so that he wouldn't leave anything undone.]

Significantly, as this practice of stressing Hans continues, the novel's narrator finally does use verbs of torment, torture, and pressure to describe the dangerous effects on Hans, not of demands placed on him by his father or his teachers, but of particular actions by his friend Hermann Heilner, especially those accompanied by Heilner's incessant Weltschmerz-laced outpourings of moon and mood (199–200). Hans's headaches return at this point; the worrying "tatlose, müde Stunden" (hours of fatigue and idleness) are new. Hans begins to understand here that Heilner's friendship is making him sick:

Von [Heilners] Leidensszenen *bedrückt und gepeinigt*, stürzte sich [Hans] in den ihm übriggebliebenen Stunden mit hastigem Eifer in die Arbeit, die ihm doch immer schwerer viel. Das das alte Kopfweh wiederkam, wunderte ihn nicht weiter; aber daß er immer häufiger tat-lose, müde Stunden hatte und sich stacheln mußte, um nur das Not-wendige zu leisten, das machte ihm schwere Sorge. [. . .] [Er] *fühlte [. . .] dunkel, daß die Freundschaft mit dem Sonderling [Heilner] ihn erschöpfte und irgendeinen bisher unberührten Teil seines Wesens krank machte* [. . .]. (200, my emphases)

[*Oppressed and tormented* by [Heilner's] emotional scenes, Hans used the hours left to him to plunge himself, with a sort of frenzied zeal, into his work — work that nonetheless became more and more difficult for him. *That his old headaches returned came as no surprise to Hans,* but that he more and more frequently experienced hours of fatigue and idleness and had to goad himself just to get done what was necessary — that worried him deeply. [. . .]. *[He] sensed that his friendship with the oddball [Heilner] exhausted him and that it made some previously untouched part of himself ill* [. . .].]

Just after the Ephorus undertakes his "ungeschickten Rettungsversuch" (213–15; his inept attempt to save Hans), Hans tries valiantly to work his way back into his former life and formerly impressive academic success at Maulbronn. But as the Ephorus had seen and foreseen, and as Hans now *knows,* Heilner's "schlechter Einfluss" (negative influence) remains a major cause of Hans's profound difficulties, and a major obstacle:

Von da an plagte Hans sich aufs neue mit der Arbeit. Es war allerdings nicht mehr das frühere flotte Vorwärtskommen, sondern mehr ein müh-seliges Mitlaufen, um wenigstens nicht zu weit zurückzubleiben. *Auch er wußte, daß das zum Teil von seiner Freundschaft herrührte,* doch sah er in dieser nicht einen Verlust und ein Hemmnis, vielmehr einen Schatz, der alles Versäumte aufwog — ein erhöhtes, wärmeres Leben, mit dem das frühere nüchterne Pflichtdasein sich nicht vergleichen ließ. [. . .] Und so spannte er sich immer wieder mit verzweifeltem Seufzer ins Joch. Es zu machen wie Heilner, der obenhin arbeitete und das Nötigste sich rasch und fast gewaltsam hastig aneignete, verstand er nicht. *Da sein Freund ihm ziemlich jeden Abend in den Mußestunden in Anspruch nahm, zwang er sich, morgens eine Stunde früher aufzustehen,* und rang mit der he-bräischen Grammatik wie mit einem Feinde. (215–16, my emphases)

[From this moment on Hans began anew to slave away at his work. But it was no longer his formerly quick, easy progress; now it was more an arduous keeping-up, so that at least he wouldn't fall too far behind. *Even he knew that this [change for the worst] was partially due to his friendship [with Heilner],* and yet he saw this friendship not as a loss or a hindrance for himself, but rather as a treasure that made up for everything he was not doing — as an elevated, more radiant life that could not be compared to his earlier sober, dutiful existence. [. . .]. He therefore took up his yoke again and again with sighs of despair. He didn't know how to do what Heilner did: Heilner studied superficially and could learn what was most necessary to know quickly, in an almost frantic rush. *Since his friend laid claim to his free time practically every evening, Hans forced himself to get up an hour earlier every morning,* and he began fighting with the grammar of Hebrew as if with an enemy.]

In remarkable confirmation of Dr. Strohmayer's description of "the weaklings who tire quickly and have difficulty recovering," this is the exact moment at which the first clear signs emerge of Hans's mental dissolution:

> Freude hatte er eigentlich nur noch am Homer und an der Geschichtsstunde. Mit dunkel tastendem Gefühle näherte er sich dem Verständnis der homerischen Welt, und in der Geschichte hörten allmählich die Helden auf, Namen und Zahlen zu sein, und blickten aus nahen, glühenden Augen und hatten lebendige rote Lippen und jeder sein Gesicht und seine Hände — einer rote, dicke, rohe Hände, einer stille, kühle, steinerne, und ein anderer schmale, heiße, feingeäderte. (216)

> [Only Homer and his history class still gave him pleasure. He kept feeling his way, darkly, toward an understanding of the Homeric world, and in history the heroes gradually stopped being only names and dates, and they looked at him from close on with burning eyes and had vibrant red lips and each its own face and hands — one's hands were red, plump, and raw; one's calm and cool, like stone; and another's slender, warm, and finely veined.]

*

Once Hermann Heilner is seen clearly as opponent, antagonist, villain — and there is much more, mostly negative, to see — the novel opens for new readings. In his essay "Begegnung mit Vergangenem," Hesse himself points a way forward, describing *Unterm Rad* in the very same paragraph both as "Schulroman" and "Schülerroman" (a novel critical of schooling practices *and* a novel about schoolboys) — a neat confirmation of his final self-critical ambivalence toward the book (572). As a "Schülerroman" written by "a poet and not a prosecutor" (Steudel), *Unterm Rad* may be read again, beyond allegory and autobiography, as a drama of characters and character, a story of adolescent friendship and betrayal whose central scenes play out in a boarding school against a backdrop of illness, *Angst*, ambition, and loneliness.

Hans's need for friendship drives the plot. After Hans betrays Heilner for the sake of his ambition — by knowingly failing to stand up for his friend after Heilner's spectacular public punishment by the Ephorus (201–3) — Hans's feelings of shame and "das plötzlich erwachte Bewußtsein seiner

Schuld gegen Heilner" (210; his suddenly awakened consciousness of his guilt toward Heilner) — begin to transform and mature him: "Es war irgend etwas in [Hans] anders geworden, ein Jüngling aus einem Knaben [. . .]" (210; Something had changed in Hans, the little boy had become a young man). To make up for his betrayal, Hans shows himself willing — and in the face of his deathly fear of failure, heroically willing — to give up all he is and all he has dreamed of becoming for Heilner's forgiveness and for the hope of restoring their broken friendship: "Du mußt, Heilner! Ich will lieber *Letzter* werden, als noch länger so um dich herumlaufen" (211, my emphasis; You have to, Heilner. I would rather become *the worst student in the class* than keep avoiding you like this). Hans knows, or "feels darkly" (200), that this friendship is a Faustian bargain, that Heilner makes him ill, but still Hans welcomes and embraces "das neue Glücksgefühl" (212; the new feeling of happiness) and later the "erhöhtes, wärmeres Leben" (215; the elevated, more radiant life) that this friendship brings him. Hans apparently believes, at least at first, that he has the strength to survive Heilner's insidious influence. Even after his daily academic work has devolved into "ein mühseliges Mitlaufen" (215; an arduous keeping-up) and his own mental health has begun to crumble, Hans keeps faith with his friend. For such devotion, Hans earns continued torment ("peinigen") by Heilner and, at the moment of his greatest need, not reward or thanks, but the betrayal of unexplained and inexplicable abandonment. The effects on Hans of Heilner's "flight" from Maulbronn are seen in chapters 5 through 7, where his friend's desertion and silent absence haunt him.[51]

For readers attuned to Heilner's character and the narrator's ironic attitude toward him, his abandonment of Hans is more confirmation than surprise. From the beginning, Heilner sees his friendship with Hans as only a "Vergnügen und Luxus, eine Bequemlichkeit oder auch eine Laune" (198; a diversion and a luxury, a comfort or even a whim). Heilner stays attached to Hans only "weil er ihn brauchte" (199; because he needed him). Hans for Heilner is "lediglich eine angenehmes Spielzeug, sagen wir eine Art Hauskatze" (199; really just a nice toy, let's say a kind of pet).

Heilner's flight from Maulbronn has been read almost universally as an essential and symbolic part of Hesse's uncompromising "school novel" and, indeed, allegorically, of Hesse's own life: as an admirable victory of individual and artist against the allegedly repressive, authoritarian, unjust educational system of Wilhelmine Germany and as Heilner's — allegorically Hesse's — "healing." Heilner's abandonment of Hans, when mentioned at all, is usually explained away as an unfortunate result of the "principle of polarization" or as the "character assassination" that somehow sets Hermann Hesse free. But the novel tells a different story. In the text, Heilner flees for one reason: because the Ephorus bans him from accompanying Hans on the daily convalescent walks he must now take on physician's orders. As Heilner explains to the Ephorus in their climactic confrontation: "er sei Giebenraths Freund und niemand habe das Recht, ihnen den Verkehr miteinander zu verbieten" (225–26; he is Giebenrath's friend and no one has the right to forbid them to spend time together). But Heilner's "flight" the next day, supposedly untertaken to show the Ephorus "daß [Heilners] Wille stärker war als Befehle und Verbote" (227; that [Heilner's] will was stronger than any commands and prohibitions), is not therefore a heroic or symbolic blow against a repressive system and for individualism, freedom from "Fremdbestimmung" (control by others; Michels), or Hesse's favorite virtue, "Eigensinn" (self-will; see Stelzig 1988, 99). Heilner's flight is instead a trivial and self-defeating protest against a non-repressive "command." The Ephorus had banned Heilner from walking with Hans only "*in nächster Zeit*" (226, my emphasis; "*for the time being*"). This is a measured and reasonable prohibition, given Heilner's obvious negative influence on the ailing Hans.[52] But in fleeing Maulbronn, Heilner triumphantly makes the Ephorus's temporary prohibition *permanent*. To show the Ephorus that "no one has the right to keep [him] from spending time" with his friend, Heilner runs away, thereby guaranteeing that he will never be able to spend time with his friend again. Instead of showing the Ephorus that Heilner's "will was stronger," Heilner reveals only that he himself is badly confused and that Hans, despite Heilner's feisty defense of friendship, means little to him. Heilner in fact abandons Hans, without warning or explanation, to the sad fate that Heilner, more than any character or force in the novel, has worked hard to prepare Hans for: life "beneath the wheel." This is hardly a heroic or positive symbolic act, nor one that may be said to "call into question" or even "to provoke" "the educational system."[53] Heilner's flight is an empty gesture that hurts only Hans. It is an act of protest only in Heilner's troubled imagination.[54]

Notes

Thanks to Mary Finseth and her interlibrary loan staff at the University of Wisconsin-Eau Claire for their usual heroic work; to Andreas Solbach in Mainz, Michael H. Weber in Potsdam, Reinhard Laube of the Deutsches Literaturarchiv Marbach, and especially Hesse bibliographer Jürgen Below for references and materials; to Johannes Strohschänk and Audrey Fessler for helpful discussions; and to my students in Introduction to Reading German Literature (Fall 2007), who tackled *Unterm Rad* with tenacity, and read well.

[1] D. J. Enright, "Hesse vs. Hesse," *New York Review of Books* 11, 4 (12 September 1968), quoted as in http://www.nybooks.com/articles/11571 (accessed 1 July 2008).

[2] Hesse called the novel "the story of a Swabian schoolboy" in a letter to his publisher Samuel Fischer (28 December 1903; unpublished). Quoted as in Siegfried Unseld, *Hermann Hesse: Werk und Wirkungsgeschichte* (Frankfurt am Main: Suhrkamp, 1987), 38.

[3] Theodor Ziolkowski, *The Novels of Hermann Hesse: A Study of Theme and Structure* (Princeton, NJ: Princeton UP, 1965).

[4] Hugo Ball, *Hermann Hesse: Sein Leben und sein Werk* (Berlin: S. Fischer, 1927), 54–55. Please note: in the following, all translations into English from primary and secondary works in German are my own.

[5] Heinz Stolte, *Hermann Hesse: Weltscheu und Lebensliebe* (Hamburg: Hansa-Verlag, 1971), 44. Joachim Noob begins a critique of this "principle" in *Der Schülerselbstmord in der deutschen Literatur der Jahrhundertwende* (Heidelberg: Winter, 1998), 163–64.

[6] Joseph Mileck, *Hermann Hesse: Life and Art* (Berkeley: U of California P, 1978), 36.

[7] Volker Michels, "Unterm Rad der Fremdbestimmung. Zur Aktualität von Hesses Frühwerk," afterword to *Unterm Rad: Roman in der Urfassung* (Frankfurt am Main: Suhrkamp, 1982), 213–14.

[8] Karl-Heinz Hucke identifies this practice as the unacknowledged point of most Hesse criticism. See Hucke's *Der integrierte Außenseiter: Hesses frühe Helden* (Frankfurt am Main and Bern: Peter Lang, 1983), 13.

[9] Donald Heiney, "A Dream of Puppets in an Allegory," review of *Beneath the Wheel*, translated by Michael Roloff (Farrar, Straus & Giroux, 1968), *Christian Science Monitor*, 15 October 1968, 9; original emphasis.

[10] See Hermann Hesse, *Unterm Rad: Mit einem Kommentar von Heribert Kuhn* (Frankfurt am Main: Suhrkamp, 2002), 241.

[11] Klaus Johann, *Grenze und Halt: Der Einzelne im "Haus der Regeln." Zur deutschsprachigen Internatsliteratur* (Heidelberg: Winter, 2003), 100–101.

[12] Suhrkamp advertising blurb on the volume "*Unterm Rad*": *Entstehungsgeschichte in Selbstzeugnissen des Autors*, ed. Volker Michels (Frankfurt am Main: Suhrkamp: 2008): http://www.suhrkamp.de/titel/titel.cfm?bestellnr=45883 (accessed 6 August 2009); my emphasis.

[13] Ninon Hesse, ed., *Kindheit und Jugend vor Neunzehnhundert: Hermann Hesse in Briefen und Lebenszeugnissen, 1877–1895* (Frankfurt am Main: Suhrkamp Verlag, 1966).

[14] Richard C. Helt, ". . . *A Poet or Nothing at All*": *The Tübingen and Basel Years of Hermann Hesse* (Providence and Oxford: Berghahn Books, 1996), 25. On this point see also Eugene L. Stelzig, "A Child Possessed: *Eigensinn* as Hermann Hesse's Identity Theme," *Germanic Review* 56, 3 (Summer 1981): 116.

[15] Hucke insisted in 1983 that "the strict separation of author from work should be automatic ["selbstverständlich"] for scholars of literature" (12). In 2003 Johann made a similar point (101). And as Siegfried Unseld pointed out years ago: "The real conflicts among the pupils and the major crisis that Hermann Hesse experienced" at this time in his life are *not* depicted in *Beneath the Wheel* (1987, 39). Stelzig makes the same objection in more detail in *Hermann Hesse's Fictions of the Self: Autobiography and the Confessional Imagination* (Princeton, NJ: Princeton UP, 1988), 97.

[16] Hesse, letter to Karl Isenberg, 25 November 1904, *Gesammelte Briefe*, vol. 1, 1895–1921, ed. Ursula and Volker Michels and Heiner Hesse (Frankfurt am Main: Suhrkamp, 1973), 130–31. Further references to the *Gesammelte Briefe* will be cited as *GB* with volume and page number.

[17] For these details, see Ninon Hesse and Gerhard Kirchhoff, eds., *Kindheit und Jugend vor Neunzehnhundert: Hermann Hesse in Briefen und Lebenzeugnissen*, vol. 2: 1895–1900 (Frankfurt am Main: Suhrkamp, 1978), 549–50, and Siegfried Greiner, *Hermann Hesse: Jugend in Calw. Berichte, Bild- und Textdokumente und Kommentar zu Hesses Gerbersau-Erzählungen* (Sigmaringen: Jan Thorbecke, 1981), esp. 30–35. Isenberg probably also knew that Hesse's experiences in Calw, Göppingen, and Maulbronn had not been terrible enough to justify his narrator's vitriol. See Thomas Bertschinger, *Das Bild der Schule in der deutschen Literatur zwischen 1890 und 1914* (Zurich: Juris Druck + Verlag, 1969), 126–51, and Greiner, 30–35.

[18] Based on Hesse's essay "Erinnerungen an Hans" (Memories of Hans, 1936), which contains most of what we know about Hans's difficult school experiences in Calw, "fast umgebracht" (almost killed) is an exaggeration. See *Sämtliche Werke*, vol. 12: *Autobiographische Schriften II*, ed. Volker Michels (Frankfurt am Main: Suhrkamp, 2001). All references to this essay are to this edition.

[19] One can sense here how fruitful a reception study of *Unterm Rad* might be. Volker Michels has explained the novel's ferocious tone by suggesting that "the author had just recently escaped the circumstances that led to the ruin of his protagonist Hans Giebenrath. [. . .]. In 1903, Hesse was still too close in time [to these events] for a more tolerant assessment" (1982, 208–9). But G. W. Field has noted that "Hesse waited for more than a decade for these episodes in his life to simmer down before he effected an esthetic distillation." See Field, *Hermann Hesse* (New York: Twayne Publishers, 1970), 27.

[20] Hesse, "Begegnung mit Vergangenem," in *Sämtliche Werke*, vol. 12: *Autobiographische Schriften II*, ed. Volker Michels (Frankfurt am Main: Suhrkamp, 2001), 571–72.

[21] For the "original version" published in the *Neue Zürcher Zeitung*, I quote Volker Michels, ed., *Unterm Rad: Roman in der Urfassung*, 213–14. For the version in print from 1905 to 1951: *Unterm Rad* (Berlin: S. Fischer, 1927), 163–64. For the latest version: *Unterm Rad* in *Sämtliche Werke*, vol. 2, ed. Volker Michels (Frankfurt am Main: Suhrkamp Verlag, 2001, [2]2003), 183. Unless noted, all parenthetical references to *Unterm Rad* are to the 2001 edition.

[22] In Göppingen, Hesse himself had regular instruction from 7:30 AM to noon and from 1:30 to 4:00 PM, then a "Landexamenstunde" (a preparatory class for the state examination) from 5 to 7 PM. Lights went out by 9:00, but Hesse "reports lying awake until very late thinking of his Greek and Latin" (Bertschinger, *Das Bild der Schule*, 138). Hans J. Hahn has commented that "even a weekly workload of ten to sixteen lessons plus homework should not weaken a young person so much that his or her physical development is negatively effected." See Hahn, "Störfälle, oder Probleme des integrierten Außenseiters, in den pädagogischen Romanen Hermann Hesses und in Carsten Probsts *Träumer*," in *Hermann Hesse Today / Hermann Hesse heute*, ed. Ingo Cornils and Osman Durrani (Amsterdam, New York: Rodopi, 2005), 164.

[23] On his final trip home from Maulbronn, Hans's "Angst vor seinem enttäuschten Vater, dessen Hoffnungen er betrogen hatte, beschwerte ihm das Herz" (120; his fear of his disappointed father, whose hopes Hans had dashed, made his heart heavy). Hans's father later "[gab] sich alle Mühe, den Ärger seiner Enttäuschung über Hans zu verbergen" (123; tried very hard to conceal his annoyance and disappointment in

Hans). Neither of these reactions is evidence for "eine vergewaltigte Kindheit" (a violated [or raped] childhood).

[24] Fr. Steudel: "Ein neuer Schülerroman," *Blätter für die deutsche Erziehung. Monatsschrift für die Gebildeten aller Stände* 5.2 (Birkenwerder, February 1905), 19–21; original emphasis. Quoted here from a copy graciously provided to me by Jürgen Below.

[25] Although Waltraud Wende reads Hermann Heilner as a "fictionalized mouthpiece for pedagogical reform ideas," Heilner's native recalcitrance, petty misbehaviors, and sometimes witty attempts to combat Hans's diligence do not amount to a critique of the educational system of the day. See Wende, "'Die Schule ist die einzige moderne Kulturfrage, die ich ernst nehme.' Zur Relation zwischen literarischen Texten und soziokulturellen Erfahrungsräumen am Beispiel von Hermann Hesses Schulgeschichte *Unterm Rad*," in *Hermann Hesse und die literarische Moderne. Kulturwissenschaftliche Facetten einer literarischen Konstante im 20. Jahrhundert. Aufsätze und Materialien*, ed. Andreas Solbach (Frankfurt am Main: Suhrkamp, 2004), 219.

[26] Franz Servaes, "Hermann Hesses zweiter Roman," *Neue freie Presse*, no. 14794 (Vienna, 29 October 1905): n.p.

[27] Gabriele Wohmann, "Hermann Hesse, *Unterm Rad*," in Wohmann, *Ich lese. Ich schreibe. Autobiographische Essays* (Neuwied: Luchterhand, 1984), 82. Published originally as "Romane von Gestern — heute gelesen. Mord durch allmähliche Vergiftung. Hermann Hesses *Unterm Rad*," *Frankfurter Allgemeine Zeitung*, 16 April 1980, 25.

[28] Sikander Singh, *Hermann Hesse* (Stuttgart: Philipp Reclam jun., 2006), 87.

[29] *Duden Bedeutungswörterbuch*, vol. 10 of *Der Duden in 10 Bänden* (Mannheim: Bibliographisches Institut, 1970).

[30] *Duden, die Sinn- und sachverwandten Wörter: Wörterbuch der treffenden Ausdrücke*, vol. 8 of *Der Duden in 10 Bänden* (Mannheim: Bibliographisches Institut, 1972).

[31] *Wahrig Deutsches Wörterbuch*, 7. vollständig neu bearbeitete und aktualisierte Auflage (Gutersloh and Munich: Bertelsmann Lexikon Verlag, 2000).

[32] Michael Müller, *"Unterm Rad,"* Interpretationen. Hermann Hesse. Die Romane (Stuttgart: Philipp Reclam jun., 1994), 11.

[33] Fritz Böttger, *Hermann Hesse: Leben, Werk, Zeit*. Mit einem Essay von Hans-Joachim Bernhard (Berlin-GDR: Verlag der Nation, 1974), 129.

[34] Martin Pfeifer, *Hesse-Kommentar zu sämtlichen Werken*, revised and expanded edition (Frankfurt am Main: Suhrkamp, 1990), 107.

[35] Helga Esselborn-Krumbiegel, *Hermann Hesse: Literaturwissen für Schule und Studium* (Stuttgart: Philipp Reclam jun., 1996), 43. And Esselborn-Krumbiegel, *Hermann Hesse, Unterm Rad: Erläuterungen und Dokumente* (Stuttgart: Philipp Reclam jun., 1995), ²2003, 5.

[36] *Wahrig Deutsches Wörterbuch* (2000) defines "zermalmen" as "heftig zerdrücken, zerquetschen, in kleinste Teile drücken oder zerbrechen; (fig.) völlig vernichten" (to crush violently, squash utterly, press or shatter into the smallest pieces; [fig.] utterly destroy).

[37] *Deutsches Wörterbuch*, ed. Jacob Grimm and Wilhelm Grimm (Leipzig: S. Hirzel, 1864–1960), see "Rad" in http://germazope.uni-trier.de/Projects/DWB (accessed 28 Dec. 2007).

[38] In the same way, there is no biographical or textual justification for the surprisingly widespread notion that Hesse's title implies the (probably apocryphal) "juggernaut": Lewis W. Tusken claims that "beneath the wheel" "may well be taken from Hindu ceremonies, where devotees [. . .] would sometimes throw themselves beneath the wheel of the huge moving statues of Shiva [. . .]." See Tusken, *Understanding Hermann Hesse: The Man, His Myth, His Metaphor* (Columbia: U of South Carolina P, 1998), 59.

[39] This should give pause to those (like Müller himself) who assert that Giebenrath's story "ist [. . .] im Grunde [. . .] schon zu Ende" (is [. . .] basically [. . .] already over) at the start of Chapter 5 (Müller, *"Unterm Rad," Interpretationen*, 24, 27). Hesse clearly didn't think so. In this context, I note that Giebenrath's death did not anticipate, foreshadow, or prefigure Hans Hesse's 1935 suicide. Some critics, perhaps seeking to impute an extra-human prescience to Hermann Hesse, have suggested that it might have been so. See e.g. Christian Immo Schneider, *Hermann Hesse* (Munich: C. H. Beck, 1991), 42–43; or Helt, ". . . *A Poet or Nothing at All,"* 24, note 15.

[40] Paul Mog, "Opfertode. Hesses *Unterm Rad* und die literarische Schulkritik der Jahrhundertwende," in *Hermann Hesse 1877–1962–2002,* ed. Cornelia Blasberg (Tübingen: Attempto, 2003), 19.

[41] Andreas Solbach, "Dezisionistisches Mitleid: Dekadenz und Satire in Hermann Hesses *Unterm Rad,"* in *Hermann Hesse Today,* ed. Cornils and Durrani, 69 and 71. In this group Solbach names Mark Boulby, *Hermann Hesse: His Mind and Art* (Ithaca: Cornell UP, 1967); Hucke, *Der integrierte Außenseiter;* Stelzig, *Hermann Hesse's Fictions of the Self;* Esselborn-Krumbiegel, *Demian: Die Geschichte von Emil Sinclairs Jugend. Unterm Rad. Interpretationen* (Munich: Oldenbourg, 1989); Müller, *"Unterm Rad," Interpretationen;* and Esselborn-Krumbiegel, *Hermann Hesse: Literaturwissen für Schule und Studium.* I would add Bertschinger, *Das Bild der Schule;* Rainer Kolk, "Literatur, Wissenschaft, Erziehung. Austauschbeziehungen in Hermann Hesses *Unterm Rad* und Robert Walsers 'Jakob von Gunten,'" in *Nach der Sozialgeschichte: Konzepte für eine Literaturwissenschaft zwischer historischer Anthropologie, Kulturgeschichte und Medientheorie,* ed. Martin Huber und Gerhard Lauer (Tübingen: Niemeyer, 2000), 223–50; Carsten Gansel, "Von Angst, Unsicherheit und anthropologischen Konstanten — Modernisierung und Adoleszenzdarstellung bei Hermann Hesse," in *Hermann Hesse und die literarische Moderne,* ed. Solbach, 224–55; Wende, "'Die Schule ist die einzige moderne Kulturfrage"; and of course Solbach himself, especially "Dezisionistisches Mitleid."

[42] Hans Rudolf Schmid, *Hermann Hesse* (Frauenfeld and Leipzig: Verlag von Huber & Co., 1928), 74, 76.

[43] The quotation is from Gayle L. Davis's review of the very helpful *Cultures of Neurasthenia from Beard to the First World War,* ed. Marijke Gijswijt-Hofstra and Roy Porter (Amsterdam, NY: Rodopi, 2001), in *Social History of Medicine* 15 (2002): 525–27; see http://shm.oxfordjournals.org/cgi/reprint/15/3/525 (accessed 14 Jan. 2008). See also Dr. Andreas Steiner, *"Das nervöse Zeitalter": Der Begriff der Nervosität bei Laien und Ärzten in Deutschland und Österreich um 1900* (Zurich: Juris-Verlag, 1964); Joachim Radkau, *Das Zeitalter der Nervosität: Deutschland zwischen Bismarck und Hitler* (Munich and Vienna: Carl Hanser Verlag, 1998); and Volker Roelcke, *Krankheit und Kulturkritik: Psychiatrische Gesellschaftsdeutungen im bürgerlichen*

Zeitalter (1790–1914) (Frankfurt and New York: Campus Verlag, 1999). On over-burdening in schools (*Schulüberbürdung*), see Radkau, *Das Zeitalter der Nervosität*, 315ff.; Gijswijt-Hofstra and Porter, eds., *Cultures of Neurasthenia;* and Gerhard Haring, *Schulstress — Die Wiederkehr eines alten Problems: Die Überbürdungsdebatte im 19. Jahrhundert als Hintergrund zur Bewertung der Schulstreßdiskussion in den 70er Jahren des 20. Jahrhunderts* (Berlin: Technische Universität, 1980).

[44] Wilhelm Strohmayer, *Vorlesungen über die Psychopathologie des Kindesalters für Mediziner und Pädagogen* (Tübingen: Verlag der H. Laupp'schen Buchhandlung, 1910), 30.

[45] Rolf Meister, "Über die Darstellung von Psychosen in Dichtung und Literatur der Moderne. Eine psychiatrische Betrachtung." Dissertation, Psychiatrische und Nerven-klinik, University of Münster, Germany, 1968.

[46] Adolf Schweckendiek, *Könnt ich Magie von meinem Pfad entfernen: Neurosenkund-liche Studien an Gestalten der Dichtung* (Berlin: Hans Lungwitz-Stiftung, 1970).

[47] In "Dezisionistisches Mitleid," especially in his brilliant analysis of Hesse's ironical treatment of Hermann Heilner (74–76), Solbach has recognized Heilner as Gieben-rath's "antagonistischer Dämon" (74; antagonistic daemon) but not fully as his op-ponent or enemy.

[48] Anonymous, review of *Beneath the Wheel, Kirkus Reviews*, 1 August 1968, 841.

[49] Review of *Beneath the Wheel, Saturday Review*, 28 September 1968, 40.

[50] We can infer the length of this headache-free time. Bertschinger reports that Hesse started in Maulbronn on 15 September. Just before Giebenrath's headaches return, we read of "spätherbstliche Regenwolken" (late autumn rain clouds) and cold (200); the next page announces "stürmische, dunkle Novembertage" (201; stormy, dark No-vember days).

[51] Clearly, both Hans's profound emotional attachment to Hermann Heilner (see their tender kiss, for example, on 195–96) and all of chapters 5 through 7 need further detailed examination.

[52] Christian Immo Schneider makes this same point: "And as a pedagogue myself, I can't really criticize the Ephorus for trying to warn the ever impressionable Hans Giebenrath against spending time with his rebellious friend Hermann Heilner" (45).

[53] Volker Michels has written of Hans's "brilliant friend Hermann Heilner (H.H.), who, like Hesse himself, breaks out of the seminary and thereby provokes the edu-cational system and calls it into question." See Michels's "Nachwort des Herausgebers" in *Unterm Rad* (2001, [2]2003), 560.

[54] If anything transparently autobiographical is lurking here, then it must be self-critical, perhaps a late concession by Hesse to Ephorus Palm that his emotional state at Maul-bronn really was full of "immature, sentimental world-weariness"; or perhaps a late apology to Wilhelm Lang, Hesse's special friend at Maulbronn, whom he abandoned — and whose friendship he lost — when he "fled." For details, see Ninon Hesse, ed., *Kindheit und Jugend*, esp.194–95.

2: *Roßhalde* (1914): A Portrait of the Artist as a Husband and Father

Osman Durrani

W ORK ON *ROSSHALDE* KEPT HESSE BUSY during a critical period in his life, and it is convenient to locate this short but multi-layered text at an intersection between the realist and symbolist phases of his career.[1] It has been described as the culmination of his first creative phase, as his "most realistic novel,"[2] yet it is riddled with ambiguities and told in an ironic manner that anticipates the less direct, more consciously encrypted style of the author's later novels *Demian, Der Steppenwolf,* and *Das Glasperlenspiel.* The title itself is marked by an ironic distance from the human sphere, the term *Roßhalde* denoting a hillside where horses are kept, a place where they may disport themselves, but also an area in which they are restrained from free movement. It is an appropriate choice, directing attention away from individual people to a natural, shared environment. The designation of this text as a "novel" may also be questioned. It was originally published as an "Erzählung" and as such was serialized in a magazine.[3] Despite running to eighteen chapters and having several centers of interest, it does in some respects straddle the generic divide between the novel and the long short story or *Novelle.* Like a tragedy in the Grecian manner — another comparison occasionally made[4] — it observes the unities of time, place and action if not entirely, then surely more closely than most novels do.

The focus is on six characters, a husband and wife, two sons, a friend of long standing, and a manservant, all of whom are caught up in what at times seems like a hothouse experiment, interdependent on each other, emotionally and on other levels, who seek but rarely attain their individual freedom of self-expression and happiness.

There are good reasons for regarding Hesse's fourth novel as autobiographical, as most of his critics do. Writing as recently as 2002, Klaus Walther allocates just two paragraphs to it, concentrating entirely on parallels with Hesse's private circumstances: "Roßhalde reflects in many ways his life situation."[5] Not only does the artist at its center resemble the author, but the book possesses a prophetic quality, "eine merkwürdige Voraussage," in that Hesse's own son Martin was affected by a similar illness to Pierre's just a few months after its completion.

The prevailing autobiographical approach to the novel is undoubtedly encouraged by the initial focus on an artist figure who has several commonalities with the author. Yet the events are narrated in the third person with the assistance of many probings into characters' minds and frequent recourse to *erlebte Rede,* with attention shifting between Roßhalde's occupants, each of whom elicits periodic interest when he or she steps into the foreground, only to recede and be displaced by another. Individual scenes are described concisely, yet in remarkable depth, frequently with filmic precision: "Da klang von Pierres Zimmer schneidend ein lauter, gellender Schrei herüber, der riß Veraguths wehmütigen Traum mitten durch. Alle sprangen mit erbleichten Gesichtern empor, die Flasche fiel um, rollte über den Tisch und klirrte zu Boden" (*SW* 3:135; "And then his dream was shattered by a piercing scream from Pierre's room. All three jumped up with pale faces, the carafe was overturned, rolled over the table, and fell to the floor," *R* 202).[6] We shall need to consider whether the majority of critics are right to base their readings of this richly detailed work solely on the marital problems to which the artist is prone. It will also be important to assess whether Veraguth's eventual breakout does indeed promise a resolution and a new beginning, and why the novel's focus shifts away from the artist's role as a husband toward that of a father. The intriguingly ambiguous character of Otto Burkhardt also calls for close scrutiny, with a view to determining his motivation and the effect that he has on the central character.

Johann Veraguth is presented as an outwardly successful painter in the prime of life, a father of two sons, Pierre, aged seven, and Albert, some ten years older. Veraguth's wife, Adele, is introduced as a cultured but, in her husband's view at least, emotionally frigid wife with whom there have been tensions in the past. These have led to an almost total breakdown in their relationship, to the extent that they now occupy separate living quarters on their extensive estate. As the novel unfolds, a few areas of disagreement receive attention, mostly in the form of hints rather than elaborate descriptions, providing some of the qualities of a novel of marital breakdown in the manner of Flaubert's *Madame Bovary,* Tolstoy's *Anna Karenina,* and Fontane's *Effi Briest.* Yet in sharp contrast to the pattern established by these and other icons of the genre, there is no obvious incompatibility to drive a wedge between the couple, no act of adultery is reported beyond a few oblique hints; indeed, the erotic aspect of the failing couple's relationship merits no comment whatsoever. Hesse himself took pains to emphasize that this is not yet another novel about the consequences of wrong choices precipitously made through inexperience or ignorance. Something that no one could have predicted has gone wrong over the twenty years or so that the marriage has endured, and the consequences are now utterly beyond repair. There are no flashbacks to the days of courtship, because these are not relevant; "[die] unglückliche Ehe, von der der Roman handelt, beruht gar nicht auf einer falschen Wahl" (the unhappy marriage which is the subject of the novel is not the result of a wrong choice)[7] — an assertion that cannot be proved or disproved in a text that refuses insight into the couple's past.

It is perhaps for this reason that the couple's emotions for one another are rarely mentioned; it is presented as given that they should have cooled down and cannot be rekindled. This acceptance of the inevitable, this refusal to examine the causes or to explore remedial strategies, contributes to the novel's modernity; there is no need to delve into minutiae or to invite the reader to observe the moments of joy and intimacy that precede the breakdown. The tragedy could not have been avoided; it is deeply embedded in the nature of the two individuals who can no longer live together. Thus an air of melancholy rather like that of Goethe's *Die Wahlverwandtschaften* hangs over the country mansion that gives the novel its name, and whatever physical, temperamental, or intellectual dysfunctionalities may have kept the couple apart in the past, these command relatively little interest. The only explanation of how the marriage fell apart is given in chapter 5 over drinks with a friend, but, as will be shown, this, too, raises renewed questions as it seeks to provide answers.

Roßhalde is a country mansion surrounded by gardens of various descriptions — a lawn, a chestnut grove, a lime grove, and a wilder, more overgrown area with a lake, to which the painter has withdrawn. But it is not a remote country idyll: there are servants, motor-cars are available to ferry guests to and fro, electric lighting and telephones have been installed. It resembles the large house outside Bern that had belonged to the painter Albert Welti and which Hesse, his wife Maria and their children occupied in September 1912, and like that house it became, for its inhabitants, not just a refuge but also a prison. Its very layout is a blueprint for a divided existence, containing, as it does, an elegant, slightly run-down residence and a decrepit summer pavilion (the term "Lusthäuschen" was evidently chosen for its ironic properties) in the form of an ancient temple that has fallen on evil days: "das schöne, etwas verkommene Herrenhaus mit dem Stall und ein kleines tempelartiges Lusthäuschen im Park, dessen Portal schief in verbogenen Angeln hing und an dessen einst mit blauer Seide tapezierten Wänden Moos und Schimmel wuchs." (*SW* 3:7; "the fine, slightly run-down manor house with its stable, and in the park a small temple-like summer house, its door hanging askew on bent hinges and its walls, formerly hung with blue silk, covered with moss and mold," *R* 1). This may not tally completely with Welti's mansion, which was rented, not bought outright, but the similarities are there in the relative proximity to a nearby town no less than in the ostentatious opulence that somewhat exceeds what an artist — even a successful one — would normally be able to afford. There are spacious parks and gardens, as well as a lake, and when Albert decides to take his brother on an excursion, several carriages and a choice of horses appear to be at his disposal.[8]

Unlike *Unterm Rad* and *Peter Camenzind*, *Roßhalde* does not conform to the established pattern of the *Bildungsroman*. It spans a few weeks at most, and even the central character remains a shadowy figure who may be a great artist, but whose inner development is not traced chronologically. Art is Veraguth's vocation, but Hesse provides conflicting statements about its merits. At one point it is stated that he never produced a failure ("er, der keine mißglückte Tafel oder Leinwand aus den Händen gab," *SW* 3:71 / "and he, who never sent a bungled drawing or painting out into the world," *R* 100), elsewhere, that neither his adoring seven-year-old son nor his manservant actually enjoyed looking at his work (*SW* 3:21–22).

As a person, Veraguth is in some respects the antithesis to the seraphic aesthete. He is selfish, embittered, possessive, periodically obsessed by his art, hostile not only to his wife but also to his older son, blind to the blandishments of his friend Otto Burkhardt, and determined to win his younger son away from his estranged wife. He refuses to separate from her for fear of losing him. He is short-tempered and domineering, and even interferes in the marital plans of his servant, Robert, giving him precisely eight days to break off his engagement to a fiancée whom he himself has never met (*SW* 3:110). In his youth he had often been violent ("[Er], der früher gewohnt gewesen war, frohe Tage lärmend in die tiefe Nacht hineinzuziehen und im Ärger die Stühle zu zerschmettern," *SW* 3:76–77 / "he who had formerly prolonged happy days boisterously into the night and smashed chairs in anger," *R* 109). Now, when Albert visits him in his studio, he begins a long monologue and pays no attention to his son ("Der Maler hörte nicht," *SW* 3:69 / "The painter was not listening," *R* 97). He does not even try to deal with his failing marriage by attempting a reconciliation, never discusses his plans, but merely informs Adele of his decisions.

> "Ihr sollt einmal ungestört miteinander leben, du und Albert — und auch Pierre, sagen wir etwa für ein Jahr. Ich dachte mir, es würde dir bequem sein, und für die Kinder wäre es gewiss ganz gut. Sie leiden doch beide etwas darunter, daß — daß wir nicht so recht mit dem Leben fertig geworden sind. Auch uns selber wird bei einer längeren Trennung alles klarer werden, meinst du nicht?" (*SW* 3:96)

> ["You'll live together undisturbed, you and Albert — and Pierre, too — for about a year, let's say. I thought it would be convenient for you, and it would certainly be a good thing for the children. It weighs

on them a bit that . . . that we haven't managed our life so very well. And we ourselves ought to see things more clearly after a prolonged separation. Don't you think so?" (R 139)]

Adele is quick to observe that this is not a prelude to a discussion but an irreversible decision: "Dein Entschluss scheint ja festzustehen" ("Your mind seems to be made up," R 139). There is one rather remarkable scene that takes place between husband and wife in chapter 8, where a reconciliation seems almost possible, but the opportunity is missed, as Adele asks, in a slightly too probing manner, about the progress of his work. With masterly irony, Hesse depicts Veraguth's vulnerable points, his covert longing for happiness, and his refusal to find it in his wife. The choice of a symbolic banana at this point can hardly be fortuitous:

> Er schälte eine Banane und roch befriedigt an der reifen, nahrhaft und mehlig duftenden Frucht.
> "Wenn es dich nicht stört, möchte ich noch den Kaffee hier nehmen," sagte er schließlich.
> Sein Ton war von schonender Freundlichkeit und etwas müde, als behage es ihm, hier auszuruhen und es ein wenig gut zu haben.
> "Ich lasse ihn sofort bringen. — Du hast viel gearbeitet?" (SW 3:74)

> [He peeled a banana and took pleasure in the mealy, nutritious smell of the ripe fruit.
> "If it doesn't inconvenience you, I should like to take my coffee here," he said finally. His tone was friendly, considerate, and a trifle weary, as though it would soothe him to rest here and enjoy a little comfort.
> "I'll have it brought in. — Have you been working hard?" (R 104)]

Hereupon his mood suddenly changes, and it is this harmless, solicitous question that, improbably, sets the seal on their separation and shows that the artist's fastidious disposition can verge on the neurotic. These incidents make it difficult to read Veraguth as a self-portrait except as an ironic one with caricature-like properties. As Lewis Tusken comments, the impression we are given is "that of a particular artist who feels very sorry for himself,"[9] and the narrator actually confirms that he is a "damaged individual" in the course of a long list of his many sorrows in chapter 8 (SW 3:71–72).

Seen in the context of those nineteenth-century social novels in which marital breakdowns figure prominently, this represents a new departure. Where we might expect deceit, a paramour, a major or minor infidelity, there is nothing of the sort. Neither Veraguth nor his wife could be accused of overtly adulterous behavior. Instead, they appear to agree that each was to blame in his or her own way for what happened, in circumstances apparently beyond their control. Adele does show signs of bitterness, yet does nothing to influence her husband's decision:

"Das ist nun das Ende von Roßhalde," sagte sie mit einem Ton tiefer
Bitterkeit, und sie dachte dabei an die Zeit ihrer Anfänge, an Alberts
Babyjahre, an alle ihre damaligen Hoffnungen und Erwartungen. Das
war also das Ende davon. (*SW* 3:108)

["Then this is the end of Rosshalde," she said in a tone of deep bitterness, thinking of the early days, of Albert as a baby, and of all her old
hopes and expectations. So that was the end of it. (*R* 159, translation
amended)]

There are questions here that the novel never even attempts to answer,
unspoken mysteries that most readers might want the author to clarify,
but Hesse does not oblige. Adele, "die verschlossene Frau" — the reserved
woman — in the narrator's words (*SW* 3:29), remains passive, guilty only
of having forfeited her husband's affections in years gone by. Both parties
agree that they were to blame for some of their shared tragedy, and are
now inclined to be gentle and forgiving towards one another: "[Laß] uns
nicht von Schuld reden" (*SW* 3:96; "[. . .] let's not talk about blame," *R*
140). They take their meals apart when it suits them and together when it
suits them. Veraguth repeatedly uses the term "Kind," "child" (*SW* 3:108)
to address his wife, in a manner that is at once intimate and patronizing.

Yet there are many points in the novel when physical matters, holding
hands, embracing, and even the naked human body are foregrounded. It
is the function of Otto Burkhardt, Veraguth's long-absent friend, to re-
kindle interest in them. One of the first things they do together is to swim
in the nude (*SW* 3:30). Looking round the painter's studio, the visitor is
quick to observe its austerity; "er vermisste bekümmert alle Zeichen von
Behagen, kleinem Komfort und genießerischer Mußezeit" (*SW* 3: 27; "he
noted with concern the absence of any sign of well-being, creature comfort, or enjoyment of leisure," *R* 31). The painter has renounced all
worldly pleasures; his routine is composed of "Arbeit und Askese" (work
and asceticism); even his hair is characterized as "vorzeitig ergrauend"
(*SW* 3:26–27; prematurely graying, cf. *SW* 3:129) and there is something
stifling about the very ambience in which his art is nurtured:

Also so entstanden diese Bilder [. . .] in Räumen, die nur Arbeit und
Entsagung kannten, wo nichts Festliches, nichts Unnützes, kein lieber
Tand und Kleinkram, kein Duft von Wein und Blumen, keine Erin-
nerung an Frauen zu finden war. (*SW* 3:27)

[So this is how these pictures [. . .] were made; they were made in
rooms that knew only work and self-denial, where one could find
nothing festive, nothing useless, no cherished baubles or bric-a-brac,
no fragrance of wine or flowers, no memory of women. (*R* 31)]

The impasse is one that all of Hesse's truly creative figures must recognize and transcend, as Klingsor and Goldmund do. The artist's visitor is of a radically different temperament. When he walks across the estate, one can almost see his hips swing:

> Er schlenderte bequem unter den Bäumen hinweg, und Veraguth sah ihm nach, wie seine Gestalt und sein Gang und jede Falte seiner Kleidung Sicherheit und ruhige Lebensfreude verkündete. (*SW* 3:27)

> [He sauntered off slowly under the trees and Veraguth looked after him, observing how his stature and his gait and every fold of his clothing breathed self-assurance and serene enjoyment of life. (*R* 32)]

When the two men begin to relax and reminisce about their youth, it is Burkhardt who brings up the subject of their erstwhile sweetheart, Meta Heilmann. Through a series of hints and probings, both men tease out each other's secret longings for a girl whom neither has forgotten. Here again, Veraguth reveals himself to have been the unsuccessful outsider; Burkhardt's deviousness is revealed in the story about Meta's glove, which he had stolen from her long ago and about which even his best friend knows nothing (*SW* 3:32).

This is just one of many instances in which Otto Burkhardt is shown in a wavering, uncertain light. He is clearly something of a womanizer, and in the company of Adele, whom he flatters with cavalier-like attentions and gifts of carefully chosen oriental bric-à-brac, he plays the part of the wealthy colonial landowner: "'Ich [. . .] bin im Begriff, ein reicher Nabob zu werden'" (*SW* 3:29; "I'll soon be a wealthy nabob," *R* 34).[10] This contrasts sharply with what he says in his letter to Veraguth: "'ich habe in den letzten vier Jahren, ehrlich gesagt, keine zehn Taler verdient'" (*SW* 3:14; "to be perfectly frank, I have not earned ten talers in the last four years," *R* 11), for which reason he expects something of a drubbing from his family. The most telling detail is revealed when the traveler shows his friend a series of photographs that he claims to have taken in the East. Sensing how important visual images are for an artist like Veraguth, he has carefully planned to ensnare his friend by means of this most appropriate of devices: "Es war seit vielen Jahren sein Wunsch, Veraguth einmal mit sich nach Ostasien zu locken und ihn eine Weile drüben bei sich zu haben" (*SW* 3:35; "For years It had been his wish to lure Veraguth to East Asia and keep him there with him for a while," *R* 43). This in itself is a curious formulation, given that Veraguth has long felt the urge to leave the restrictive milieu of Roßhalde. Yet Hesse goes to great lengths to portray Burkhardt as a slyly operating seducer figure. As soon as the artist asks to see pictures of the Orient, Burkhardt senses that moment for which he had been waiting has finally arrived, and as he unpacks the photographs he tries to appear calm while awaiting his friend's reaction "mit der heftigsten Spannung" (*SW* 3:35; with the most burning suspense). His collection of scrupulously and artificially posed snapshots and their manufacture are described in great detail. Significantly, they are described as "bait": "Sie waren Burkhardts Köder" (*SW* 3:36; "They were Burkhardt's bait," *R* 44). Deviously, Burkhardt implies that he took many of the pictures himself; the narrator reveals that he employed a young Englishman in Singapore and a Japanese in Bangkok to comb through the countryside and capture subjects such as attractive rural locations, monuments, people, and activities, whose cumulative effect is to play on Veraguth's creative imagination.

> Er zeigte Bilder von Häusern, Straßen, Dörfern, Tempeln, Bilder von fabelhaften Batuhöhlen bei Kuala Lumpur und der wildschönen, brüchigen Kalk- und Marmorberge in der Gegend von Jpoh [. . .], Bilder von Malaien, Chinesen, Tamilen, Arabern, Javanern [. . .], nackte athletische Hafenkuli, dürre alte Fischer, Jäger, Bauern, Weber, Händler, schöne goldgeschmückte Weiber, dunkle nackte Kindergruppen, Fischer mit Netzen, Sakeys mit Ohrringen, welche die Nasenflöte spielten, und javanische Tänzerinnen in starrendem Silberschmuck. (*SW* 3:36)

> [He showed him pictures of houses, streets, villages, and temples, of fantastic Batu caves near Kuala Lumpur, and of the jagged, wildly beautiful limestone and marble mountains near Ipoth, [. . .], of Malays, Chinese, Tamils, Arabs, and Javanese, naked athletic harbor coolies, wizened old fishermen, hunters, peasants, weavers, merchants, beautiful women with gold ornaments, dark groups of naked children, fishermen with nets, earringed Sakai playing the nose flute, and Javanese dancing girls bristling with silver baubles. (*R* 44–45)]

Small wonder that the artist should succumb to the charm of such alluring subjects as dancers decked out in glistening silver, beautiful women with gold ornaments, muscular dockworkers, and groups of naked children. There is something unwholesome in all this, although, true to his calling, Veraguth responds as a painter should: "'Man könnte das alles malen'" (*SW* 3:36; "One might paint all that," *R* 45). There follows a discussion in which Veraguth expounds his theory that the artist must communicate a vision of things "so wie begabte Kinder sehen" (*SW* 3:38; as gifted children see them). The key significance of this excursus will become clearer in due course.

Many critics have ignored Burkhardt's underhand motives, and some have gone so far as to praise him for his selfless devotion to his friend. It would be wrong to dismiss Otto Burkhardt as a fraud, even though a roguish streak does appear in him, often ignored or misrepresented by reviewers.[11] As Veraguth elaborates his views on the importance of the naïve perspective in art and surveys scenes yet to be painted, the focus switches from the painter to his friend: "Burkhardt schwieg und hörte seinem Freunde zu, im Herzen voll Mitleid. Wie er mich anlügen will! dachte er mit heimlichem Lächeln" (*SW* 3:38–39; "Burkhardt said nothing. His heart was full of compassion as he listened to his friend. How hard he tries to lie to me, Burkhardt thought with a secret smile," *R* 49). If Burkhardt is to be believed, it is Veraguth who is now playing fast and loose with the truth, pretending to be involved in great projects that are unlikely ever to come to fruition. But some doubt remains as to who is right and who is wrong, and the ever-shifting perspective gives the narrative an instability that is part of its fascination and part of its modernity.[12]

Later, Burkhardt is again given the role of illuminating his friend's deteriorating mental state. After an uncomfortable meal, taken in the company of the older son, now returned from boarding school, the visitor begins to reflect on what he has just witnessed: "Erst in dieser Stunde fühlte Otto Burkhardt bis ins Innerste die Vereinsamung und hoffnungslose Kälte, in der seines Freundes Ehe und Leben erstarrt und verkümmert war" (*SW* 3:45; "It was only then that Otto Burkhardt became fully aware of the loneliness and hopeless coldness that had descended on his friend's marriage and life," *R* 58). The great art that Veraguth has produced and that earned him fame across the globe is nothing more than an escape from the sad reality of a failed marriage. There are no clues as to whether we should accept this thesis. The critics maintain that this marriage has failed because the artist cannot sustain it; the friend assumes, rightly or wrongly, that Veraguth's art has flourished precisely because his marriage has failed. Here, too, the reader faces a question deliberately left open to conflicting interpretations. Yet in one important respect Burkhardt is wrong to assume that a "the chill of hopelessness" has descended on his friend; the warmth of Veraguth's feelings for his young son continues to sustain him while he lives.

Burkhardt undergoes a remarkable series of permutations: introduced, by means of a letter, as a close and caring friend, he is then shown to behave like a deceiving tempter, before providing a sympathetic perspective on Veraguth's tragic loneliness. In the following chapter he reverts to his role as the confidant to whom the painter is able to reveal the story of his marriage. Here, in chapter 5, the sequence of events that led to the breakdown, hinted at elsewhere, is given its clearest, if still puzzling, expression. What is remarkable in the story of this broken-down marriage is that the causes are so trivial and nugatory, and yet sufficient to ruin a relationship between two cultured and well-intentioned people. Where one might have expected a confession of some clandestine passion, there is nothing more than a minor difference of temperament in Veraguth's criticism of his wife: "Schwung hat sie nie gehabt; sie war ernsthaft und schwerlebig;

ich hätte das vorher wissen können" (*SW* 3:48; "She was never very lively; she was solemn and heavy, I might have noticed it sooner," *R* 65).

Given Veraguth's introverted personality, it would seem that in this respect at least, the couple were not exactly incompatible. Yet he presents himself as a victim, and the most serious accusation he can level against Adele is that she is unable to share his moods and inflexible whenever he attempts to salvage the situation:

> "War ich ärgerlich und unzufrieden, so schwieg sie und litt, und kam ich bald darauf mit dem Willen zu einem besseren Verständnis, bat ich sie um Verzeihung oder suchte ich sie in einer Stunde froher Laune mitzureißen, so ging es nicht, sie schwieg auch da und beharrte immer verschlossener in ihrem treuen, schwerfälligen Wesen." (*SW* 3:49)

> ["When I was irritable and dissatisfied, she suffered in silence, and a little later when I tried to patch things up and come to an understanding, when I begged her to forgive me, or when, in an excess of good spirits, I tried to sweep her off her feet, it was no good; she kept silent and shut herself up tighter than ever in her heavy fidelity." (R 65)]

There is grudging acknowledgment of her better qualities even in this comment; the woman may not be outgoing, she may be *schwerfällig,* but she is also faithful and loyal to him, *treu.* She even shares his artistic temperament, at least insofar as she takes pleasure in playing four-handed pieces on the piano with her older son. In this increasingly uncomfortable predicament, his art becomes his refuge: "Ich fing an fleißig zu werden und habe so allmählich gelernt, mich in die Arbeit wie in eine Burg zu verschanzen" (*SW* 3:49; "I became more and more industrious and gradually learned to take refuge in my work," *R* 66). Here is another clear indication that it was not art that caused the marriage to fail, but marital failure that caused the art to flourish.

Although no affairs are mentioned, they cannot be ruled out. "Ich verliebte mich mit einem gewissen wehmütigen Leid in hübsche junge Mädchen, aber es ging nie tief genug" (*SW* 3:49; "I fell in love with pretty, young girls, but what I felt was a kind of melancholy envy; it never went deep enough," *R* 66) is as much as the painter is prepared to reveal, tantalizingly hinting at a confession, only to retract it in the same breath. It is at this point that Veraguth arrives at the heart of his confession. If he is to be believed, the marriage failed not because of his wife, still less because of the "pretty young girls" with whom he admits having fallen in love from time to time. The real cause was his eldest son, Albert, his and his wife's inordinate love for whom kept them together: "Wir hatten ihn beide sehr lieb, die Gespräche über ihn und die Sorgen um ihn hielten uns beisammen" (SW 3:50; "We both loved him very much and worrying over him kept us together," *R* 67). Thus their relationship survives until jealousy sets in and the father experiences the anguish of seeing his son — his only child, at that point in time — drift away from him: "ich habe mehrere Jahre mit beständiger Angst zugesehen, wie er ganz langsam kühler gegen mich wurde und mehr und mehr zur Mutter hielt" (*SW* 3:50; "[. . .] and then for several years I looked on in constant anguish as he grew cooler and cooler toward me and more and more attached to his mother," *R* 67).

Veraguth's flawed relationship with his eldest son is one of the mysteries that Hesse has, no doubt intentionally, embedded within this text. It seems unlikely that the boy is naturally spiteful, although the incident in which he threw a knife (or knives) at his father would certainly indicate a fiery temperament (*SW* 3:86–87). One might argue that his father, himself given to public displays of anger in his youth and still frequently irritable, at times "sonderbar nervös" (*SW* 3:61; "strangely nervous," *R* 84), has passed on a virulent temperament to the boy. More probably, and more insidiously, the boy has turned out to resemble his mother both physically and in other respects, and with the deterioration of the marriage is identified by his father as being of the other party. There is also the possibility of an incestuous component, at least in the form of a suspicion in Veraguth's restless and tormented mind, speculation along these lines being encouraged by the regular "four-handed piano-playing" sessions in which mother and son regularly indulge their shared passion for music. In the tenth chapter, where mother and son have their most intimate conversation, Albert does his best to persuade his mother that he has acquired her qualities while Pierre "hat mehr von Papa" (*SW* 3:79–81; has [inherited] more from Papa).[13]

Yet this is not the end of the painter's parental career. The couple has a second son, born after the initial estrangement, who was conceived during a period of renewed intimacy occasioned by the older son's illness. Things are now back where they started, with Veraguth having to fear that Pierre, too, will eventually follow his older brother and side with his estranged wife. The very child that brought them together is now the wedge that drives them apart.

After the painter has made his full confession, Burkhardt reverts to the role of the selfish observer motivated by a desire to control his friend under the guise of providing assistance:

> Nun sah er tief in den dunklen Brunnen, aus dem Johanns Seele sich mit Kräften und mit Leiden sättigte. Und zugleich empfand er einen tiefen, freudigen Trost darüber, dass er es war, der alte Freund, dem sich der Leidende eröffnet, den er angeklagt, dem er um Hilfe gebeten hatte. (*SW* 3:55)

> [Now he saw deep into the dark spring from which Johann's soul drew the strength and suffering in which it was steeped. And at the

same time he felt a deep, joyous consolation at the fact that it was he, the old friend, to whom the sufferer had bared himself, whom he had accused, and whom he had begged for help. (*R* 75)]

This is no unselfish observer, still less a disinterested helper; he is a man with a mission, the most innocent aspect of which is perhaps a desire to bask in the reflected glory of his outwardly more successful and renowned companion. Hesse returns to the underlying ambiguity at the close of chapter 5, where the artist, having recovered his composure, shares childhood memories while his companion listens "mit beinahe widerwilligem Vergnügen" (*SW* 3:56; "with almost reluctant pleasure," *R* 75); we sense the barest touch of disappointment that his friend has now regained his strength. He uses the following day to press home on Veraguth the need to tear himself away from his cloying domestic circumstances, taunting him with grandiose clichés calculated to wound his pride ("'[Du] hast den Anschluß ans Leben verloren'" / "you've lost your contact with life"), goading him with the thought that his son Pierre might be better off without him (*SW* 3:57 / *R* 78).

It is worth mentioning that his many promises of a better life include an erotic component: "Du kannst bei mir malen und reiten, du kannst auch Tiger schießen oder dich in Malaiinnen verlieben — es gibt hübsche [. . .]" (*SW* 3:58; "With me you'll be able to paint and ride horseback, you'll be able to hunt tigers too and fall in love with Malay women — some of them are pretty [. . .]," *R* 80). The first sign of the success of his scheme follows soon after these seductive overtures, when Veraguth asks for permission to keep the photographs that had been prepared for the purpose of ensnaring him: "Bitte, laß mir die Photographien da" (*SW* 3:59; "Please leave the photographs here," *R* 80). These, we recall, are the "bait" that his friend has had expressly made for this purpose; they contain scenes of seductive dancers and naked bodies. Like Faust, asking to look again into the witch's mirror, the painter now wants to keep hold of these images, whose magic, we feel, has begun to work on him. The visitor can thus depart with a foretaste of his mission's success.

At this point it is worth taking a closer look at Hesse's portrayal of Frau Adele Veraguth. Having been warned from the outset that Veraguth's marriage was plagued by "Zerwürfnisse" (quarrels, *SW* 3:7), the reader might expect her to come across as a something of a harridan. But there is more sorrow than anger or ill will in her demeanor. She engages in a variety of womanly activities, cutting flowers in the garden, receiving gifts from her visitor, presiding at table, and discussing her husband's plans for herself and her children. She rebukes her older son when he is rude and cares for her younger son when he falls ill. The first description marks her out as "serious" and "disappointed": "Die große Gestalt mit dem ernsthaften und enttäuschten Frauengesicht" (*SW* 3:16), but goes no further. The reader might expect an argument, or at least some pointer as to who is in the right and who is in the wrong, but nothing of the kind materializes. Instead, Veraguth is placed in a dubious light, when he eavesdrops on mother and child and secretly plans to alienate his young son from his estranged wife, tempting him away from her like a thief. This shows him at his most vulnerable: not as an artist, not as a husband or lover, but as a jealous and overpossessive father:

> Aber diesen Kleinen wollte er nicht verlieren, ihn nicht. Er wollte ihn als Dieb hinterm Zaun belauschen, er wollte ihn locken und an sich ziehen, und wenn auch dieser Knabe sich von ihm abwenden würde, dann wollte er nicht mehr leben. (*SW* 3:17)

> [But this child he would not lose, no no. Like a thief behind his hedge he would spy on him, he would lure him and win him, and if this boy should also turn away from him, he had no desire to live. (*R* 16)]

It is a telling sign of Adele's sensitivity to her husband's wishes that she sees through the subterfuge, and, recognizing how much Pierre means to him, magnanimously cedes the boy to his father at the end of the novel (*SW* 3:128).

Adele is thus characterized by personal sadness, but also by a clear-sighted and generous spirit that enables her to understand her husband's concerns without, however, being able to satisfy him on a personal level. There are times when the narrator allows the reader to glimpse her erstwhile hopes and aspirations (*SW* 3:108). There are others when she seems firm and purposeful, such as when she refuses to leave Pierre "alone" with his father (*SW* 3:19). If she has a failing, it is that she cannot fully grasp the underlying causes of the breakdown of her marriage: "sie hatte zwar aufgehört, ihren Mann zu lieben, sah aber noch heute den Verlust seiner Zärtlichkeit als ein traurig unbegreifliches, unverschuldetes Unglück an" (SW 3:18; "though she had ceased to love her husband, she still regarded the loss of his affection as a sadly incomprehensible and undeserved misfortune," R 18).

An important altercation takes place, not between Adele and Johann, but between Adele and her older son, Albert. Arriving back from the boarding school to which he has been banished, Albert makes a fuss about seeing his father, which culminates in a declaration of hate. Adele tries her best to mediate and, with no obvious trace of bitterness, advises her son to let the matter rest. She is not one to provoke an argument: "'Man muß die Dinge kennen, die man zu ertragen hat. Aber man muß das, was weh tut, nicht aufwühlen, mein Kind'" (*SW* 3:40; "It's good to be conscious of what we have to bear. But we mustn't churn up the things that hurt us, child," *R* 51). And with that, they return to their favorite occupation, playing duets on the piano.

In what has been said so far, there is very little to suggest that the problems raised in the novel are peculiar to artists. And yet this is the way in which *Roßhalde* is almost always read in literary criticism — when it is discussed at all.[14] Theodore Ziolkowski, for example, mentions it but once in his influential 361-page study, *The Novels of Hermann Hesse,* implying that, like other novels preceding the author's post–World War I break-through, it is little more than autobiographically tinged *Unterhaltungs-literatur:*

> The inner turmoil in the life of the painter Veraguth remains on a private level that reflects, to be sure, Hesse's own confused marital situation, but affords not the slightest hint of the almost archetypal self-seeking so characteristic of the later works.[15]

Lewis Tusken puts it bluntly: "*Roßhalde* is Hesse's attempt to analyze his marriage problem."[16] Recent German criticism has not progressed much beyond combining autobiographical parallels with reflections on the prob-lematic life of the artist. Sikander Singh, who reveals cursory familiarity with the text by consistently mis-spelling the name of Burkhardt as Burck-hardt, observes:

> The novel thematizes not only the psychological conflict of a married couple, but also the failure of the artist at bourgeois existence, for which the couple's relationship only serves as a cipher.[17]

Yet it is difficult to see any connection between Veraguth's failed marriage and his vocation as an artist. His problems, insofar as they are placed be-fore the reader, have more to do with common human emotions such as jealousy than with incompatible lifestyles. Adele, as we have observed, pos-sesses an artistic talent, albeit a musical one.

Yet there plainly is a biographical component in the figure of Otto Burkhardt. Although he bears some of the traits of the "alter ego" figures who appear in the author's earlier narratives, he is neither the inwardly liberated Hans Heilner of *Unterm Rad* nor the lovable friend that Richard was to Peter Camenzind. Nor is he rounded enough or sufficiently posi-tive to become the tutelary spirit that was to surface in *Demian*. His morals are as dubious as his finances. At times he seems inclined to rescue his friend from the emotional stalemate of his marriage, but we also read that he had planned to lure him to East Asia for selfish reasons long be-fore he heard about his deteriorating family circumstances. The carefully composed snapshots, accompanied by casual references to beautiful Malay women, are introduced as part of a strategy designed to play on Veraguth's most vulnerable points. There are good reasons why this should be so. Burkhardt represents temptation of a very specific type: the lure of the East. But he does this in the guise of a hedonistic entrepreneur, as refer-ences to his involvement in money-making ventures such as rubber-tree plantations make clear. This was the wrong approach to the Orient, as Hesse was to realize on his own personal journey undertaken during September to December 1911. Thus the autobiographical elements go far beyond exploring the status of the artist; the unreliable tempter reproduces its author's disillusionment about travel to the East in the guise of a tiger-shooting colonial "Nabob." Given the "disappointment" which Hesse himself experienced on his journey,[18] this could hardly be otherwise. Veraguth may be taken as representing Hesse on the eve of his departure to India, and the narrative anticipates its unsatisfactory outcome through the figure of the shady playboy-cum-entrepreneur.

The most controversial aspect of Burkhardt's argumentation concerns the boy Pierre, from whom Veraguth is unwilling to be separated. It is in this character that, in my view, Hesse's most distinctive achievement in this novel is to be found. Pierre is one of several figures whose thoughts and feelings the narrator reproduces; it is certainly not true to say that everything is seen through the painter's eyes. As we shall see, the world of the seven-year-old boy is explored with remarkable sensitivity.

Pierre is introduced, typically, in the garden, in a delicate situation that has a painterly quality. His father is lurking behind a hedge, eavesdropping on a conversation between the boy and his mother, and already at this point his jealousy can be sensed; the verbs *spähen* (to spy) and *lauschen* (to eavesdrop) are associated with him.

The conversation between mother and son is simple enough, revolving around the natural environment ("Wie heißen die Blumen da?," *SW* 3:16 / "What are those flowers called?," *R* 15). Yet it ends in disillusionment for the young boy, when his mother fails to provide answers that satisfy his curiosity. The bees cannot, he realizes, think of each flower as a "Honigblume," because if they did, all flowers would have the same name. And his response is to belittle his mother's answer and to reflect on the inadequacies of the older generation when it comes to explaining the things that interest him:

> "Honigblumen!" dachte er geringschätzig und schwieg. Er hatte es längst erfahren, daß man gerade die hübschesten und interessantesten Dinge nicht wissen und erklären kann. (*SW* 3:16)

> ["Honey flowers!" he said contemptuously, and fell silent. He had discovered long ago that the prettiest and most interesting things are the very ones that cannot be known or explained. (*R* 15)]

Pierre possesses not only an enquiring mind, but also a beautiful body. There is something slightly disturbing about the way in which Hesse lingers on the details of his physique:

> In seinen braunen Haaren spielte das Licht, die nackten Beine standen mager und sonnenbraun in der Helle, und wenn er sich bückte, sah

man im weiten Ausschnitt seiner Bluse unter dem braungebrannten Nacken die weiße Haut des Rückens hervorschimmern. (*SW* 3:16)

[The light played over his brown hair, and his bare legs stood thin and sunburnt in the bright glow, and when he bent down, his loose-fitting blouse revealed the white skin of his back below his deeply tanned neck. (*R* 15)]

The reader is invited, in this vivid depiction, to share Veraguth's emotional attachment to his young son, his admiration of the "precocious" boy's physical beauty: "Veraguth stand hinter der Hecke und hörte zu, er betrachtete das ruhige, ernsthafte Gesicht seiner Frau und das schöne, frühreif zarte seines Lieblings [. . .]" (*SW* 3:16–17; "Veraguth stood behind the hedge and listened; he observed the calm earnest face of his wife and the lovely, prematurely fragile face of his darling [. . .]," *R* 16).

Yet what is remarkable about the unfolding narrative is the extent to which Pierre himself becomes the center of interest in the ensuing text. He becomes an important character in his own right, and is seen in many situations that have no direct connection with the artist. In the next chapter, there is a long conversation between Pierre and Veraguth's manservant, Robert, in which the boy not only holds his own against the older man, but also displays a maturity far beyond his years. Again, the adult is accused of failing to understand him "'Du verstehst mich gar nicht!'" (*SW* 3:20; "You just don't understand [me]!" *R* 21); and when they start to talk about the paintings in the studio, the boy manages to express both admiration and skepticism about his father's work: "Darum habe ich die Bilder gern, ich spüre, daß Papa sie gemacht hat. Aber eigentlich gefallen sie mir nur halb" (*SW* 3:21; "That's why I like his pictures, because I feel that Papa made them. But, to tell you the truth, I only half like them," *R* 23). Here, at least, Robert would appear to agree with the boy's assessment: "Robert war in seinem Innern durchaus derselben Meinung" (*SW* 3:22; "At heart Robert agreed perfectly," *R* 23).

From the first chapter onwards, we never lose sight of the boy. In the third chapter he converses in an adult manner with Burkhardt, poring over a map as he attempts to trace the latter's journeys. His physical delicateness is mentioned more than once; for instance in the passage "Pierre wiegte voll Vergnügen seinen schlanken Oberkörper hin und her" (*SW* 3:33; "Pierre's slender torso rocked back and forth with pleasure," *R* 41). In the fourth chapter, there is another indication of his extreme sensitivity, when he listens to his brother playing the piano, only to realize that Albert is talking down to him as adults do to children. As this insight into his thought processes is delivered, it is accompanied by a level of detail far in excess of what a character study of Veraguth would require:

In Alberts Frage hatte er etwas von dem Ton gespürt, in welchem nach seinen Erfahrungen die meisten Erwachsenen zu Kindern redeten und dessen verlogene Freundlichkeit und unbeholfene Überheblichkeit er nicht leiden mochte. Der große Bruder war ihm willkommen, [auf] diesen Ton aber gedachte er nicht einzugehen. (*SW* 3:41)

[In Albert's question he had sensed a trace of the tone which in his experience most grownups assumed in speaking to children; he could not bear its sham friendliness and ponderous arrogance. He was glad his big brother had come [. . .]. But that tone, no, he wouldn't put up with it. (*R* 53)]

He walks away from his brother and seeks out his father, with whom he finds it easier to communicate. Here again, he displays a precocious disillusionment with the adult world: "Die meisten Menschen verstehen ja gar nicht recht, was man sagt und will, aber Onkel Burkhardt versteht mich gleich" (*SW* 3:43; "Most people don't really understand what I mean when I say something, but Uncle Berkhardt understands right away," *R* 56). Little does he realize, sitting on Burkhardt's knee and playing with the buckle of his belt, that this is the man who is trying to drive a wedge between him and his father!

In fact, Pierre becomes increasingly important in the narrative and there are times when he displaces the other characters. He is, as Veraguth confesses in chapter 5, the center of his life, and yet he is not seen so much through Veraguth as through his own experiences, which are communicated directly to the reader. Chapter 7 is significant in that it is here that the symbolic painting is described, in which Pierre occupies a central position between his estranged parents: "ein Kind, stillfroh und ohne Ahnung der über ihn lastenden Wolke" (*SW* 3:61; "a child, tranquilly happy and without suspicion of the cloud hanging over him," *R* 84). This is often picked up by critics as the central image of the novel,[19] and its function is certainly to communicate the parents' alienation and the vulnerable position of the child in a marriage that is breaking down. Equally important is Pierre's relationship to nature; Tusken goes so far as to speak of a "St. Francis-like relationship to life around him."[20] Yet in the same chapter in which this painting is briefly mentioned, more space is given to Pierre's attempts to rescue a mouse from a predatory cat, and while this, too, may have a symbolic function, the warmth of the boy's emotions quickly communicates itself to his father and the reader.

Even as this happens, there are portents that this will be Veraguth's last love, for instance, "Ach, nie mehr im Leben würde er eine solche Liebe fühlen können wie zu diesem Knaben" (*SW* 3:65; "Oh, never again in his life would he experience such love as he did for this child," *R* 90). And we are not allowed to forget that all the while Veraguth has been brooding over the "bait" his friend has left behind, "Stunde um Stunde allein, in den Anblick der indischen Photographien vertieft" (*SW* 3:61; "for hours alone [. . .] immersed in the Indian photographs," *R* 85).

The novel is divided into eighteen chapters, ten of which deal directly with the successive phases of Pierre's illness. It is a curious fact that few critics have noted this, and there has been little discussion of its significance. The novel can be more conveniently disposed of as a statement about the artist's marriage, and yet far more time is expended on the artist's son than on his wife. Thus we cannot agree with Singh's assertion that "although the other figures in the novel have paradigmatic functions, their individuality is staged only schematically."[21] There are several points at which Pierre's experience of his illness is conveyed directly and not observed through the eyes of his parents. He thereby loses his subordinate role as the artist's son in the same measure as the artist, in turn, is represented not as Adele's husband but as Pierre's father.

In chapter 9, Veraguth is agitated when his son does not return from a short excursion with Albert. Remembering the time when he used to spend his nights smashing chairs, his old bitterness returns, as he longs to be reunited with his son: "Aller Groll und alle Bitterkeit kam wieder in ihm auf, und zugleich ein sehnliches Verlangen nach seinem Knaben, dessen Blick und Stimme allein ihn froh machen konnten" (*SW* 3:77; "All the resentment and bitterness rose up in him, and at the same time an intense longing for his boy, whose voice and glance alone could give him joy," *R* 109). Yet curiously, as soon as the boy is found, he repairs to a Weinstube on his own, and then confirms to Burkhardt that he intends to accompany him to India.

From this point on, in chapters 10 through to 17, Pierre occupies center stage. The focus shifts directly onto him when he wakes up the next morning "später als sonst und ohne Lebensfreude" (*SW* 3:81; "later than usual and without zest," *R* 116). We follow his peregrinations through the house and garden, his thoughts about his family and about God ("Wahrscheinlich war es mit dem lieben Gott auch nichts," *SW* 3:81 / "Probably God-in-His-Heaven was a fake too," *R* 118), and his ultimately unsatisfactory visit to his father's studio. Although the latter appears pleased to see him and kisses him, Pierre must realize that his parent is not in the mood to be disturbed: "[Er] merkte genau, daß der Vater aufatmete und froh war, ihn gehen zu sehen" (*SW* 3:85; "and it did not escape him that his father was relieved to see him go," *R* 122). It is typical of Hesse that he should show how the intelligent child can read the mind of an adult and recognize the grown man's self-absorption behind an outward display of affection.

Nor are we spared any of the unpalatable and, in the end, heartwrenching details of Pierre's struggle against the illness as it gains a hold over him. There are passages that display a clinical knowledge of the progress of meningitis in a young boy. From the early vomiting to the final agonized screaming, nothing is spared: the headaches, the sensitivity to light, even the temporary relapses that give the parents hope that he has recovered and will pull through, all are meticulously recorded in natural-istic, scientifically observed detail. Yet side by side with the parents' agita-tion and the doctor's marvelously observed fatalism, we are never allowed to lose sight of the boy's own perception of what is happening to his body. His feverish nightmare is recorded with filmic precision over several pages (*SW* 3:90–93), culminating in a sense that his father, while not con-soling him, at least acknowledges that both are prone to a similar grief, before he, too, walks away from the distressed child (*SW* 3:92).

There follow many ups and downs: Pierre does not die quietly, and his agony extends over many pages, with rays of light (*SW* 3:98–100, 134) followed by sudden, cruel downturns, screams and hideous physical dis-tortions (*SW* 3:101, 136). A further sign of Veraguth's failure not only as a husband but also as Pierre's father is that he never abandons his plan to go abroad, but chats about tiger-shooting and tropical outfits as the disease takes hold of his son. Only in the final stages does he hold vigil beside the dying child's bed. Here, too, the focus is more often on the child than on the parents. His every contortion is registered, his mech-anical kicking, his screaming, the way he bangs his hand bloody against the metal bedpost. The narrator takes it in and sets it down, and in a final bold step accompanies the boy to the very bourne of life and crosses briefly into the beyond:

> Der war weit weg in einer anderen Welt, er wanderte dürstend durch ein Höllental von Pein und Todesnot, und vielleicht schrie er jetzt eben nach dem, der neben ihm auf seinen Knien lag und der gerne jede Qual gelitten hätte, um seinem Kinde zu helfen." (*SW* 3:136)

> [He was far away in another world, wandering thirst-parched through a hell of torment and death, and there perhaps, in the valley of hell, was crying out for the very man who was kneeling by his side, who would gladly have suffered every torment to help his child. (*R* 203)]

Deaths of young children were no rarity at the turn of the twentieth century, neither in reality, nor in literature. The novels of Dickens and Dostoevsky, the plays of Holz and Schlaf, Ibsen and Hauptmann, show sick and dying children in many countries and settings. It has been pointed out that Hesse's immediate inspiration may have been Hanno Budden-brook, and there are certainly affinities in the way Hesse and Thomas Mann treat small children in their novels, Mann's Nepomuk Schneidewein being the best known example of its type.[22] Both may use the child in similar fashion, the underlying objective being to show the loss that a great artist must suffer in the pursuit of his career, yet Hesse differs from

Mann in that his Pierre has been omnipresent throughout the novel and is thus a central rather than an episodic figure, as Hanno and Nepomuk are. It is also a matter for debate whether Veraguth ever was, or will be, the great artist who, like Leverkühn, must needs ride roughshod over his peers to achieve originality.

The ending, in the eighteenth chapter, signals a new beginning, with the artist bathed in bright sunlight, determined not to lose another precious hour of his life (SW 3:142), yet this new life will take him, in the company of a wily colonialist, to a world of rubber-tree plantations, tiger hunting,[23] and cute native dancers. Minutes earlier, as Tusken observes, the sky had been full of approaching rain clouds, and the upbeat declaration that follows may be little more than a faint hope.[24] The fact that the symbolic painting he executed at Roßhalde is described as "eines seiner größten und schönsten Werke" (SW 3:72; "one of his greatest and most beautiful works," R 102) does not suggest that India will be a turning point in the evolution of his art.

Those critics who maintain that the novel is primarily a character sketch of Veraguth, or that it traces a crisis in the life of an artist, tend to ignore the importance of Pierre for an understanding of what Hesse was trying to achieve. G. W. Field is one of relatively few readers who has looked more closely at this figure and related him to the author's interest in child psychology.[25] Yet his significance goes beyond a realistic investigation of how children feel and how their parents feel toward them, admittedly a topic of growing importance in a century that was becoming increasingly interested in the child's experience of the world. What Hesse does here is far more complex and far more rewarding: he uses the child's perspective to illustrate a theory of art that was propounded, earlier in the novel, by Veraguth himself:

> Nicht dieses wohlbekannte Stückchen Natur, gesehen von einem guten Beobachter und vereinfacht von einem guten, schneidigen Maler, aber auch nicht sentimental und holdselig wie von einem sogenannten Heimatkünstler. Es muß ganz naiv sein, so wie begabte Kinder sehen, unstilisiert und voller Einfachheit. (SW 3:38)

> [Not your famous excerpt of nature seen by a good observer and simplified by a skillful energetic painter, and not sweet and sentimental either, as a painter-of-the-native-scene would do it. This picture must be perfectly naïve, as seen through the eyes of a gifted child, unstylized and full of simplicity. (R 48)]

It is here, in this programmatic excursus, that Hesse reveals an ambition that could equally apply to himself. He, too, had begun to tire of the closely observed environment, no less than of the sentimental approach to which locally based artists ("Heimatkünstler") are prone. In these few brief words, we have the antidote: the child's perspective, unstylized, naïve. *Roßhalde* is the first novel in which this direct approach is converted into practice; it accounts for the privileged position given to Pierre's dream, to his thoughts, to his suffering. Only when this is recognized will it be possible to read the novel as something more complex than yet another novel of marital breakdown and to understand why the perspective has to shift from the adult to the child, who becomes the victim of the tragedy and thus shares the focus with his father.

It is evident that *Roßhalde* has, until now, remained one of Hermann Hesse's less well known works in the Anglo-Saxon world. It was the last of the major novels to be translated into English. When it appeared in 1970, the alleged "Hesse boom" had all but spent itself. Yet by then there had been no fewer than three separate translations into Japanese, while in Germany, it had sold an impressive total of 720,000 copies.[26] A reconsideration now seems overdue. *Roßhalde* has been hailed as Hesse's "most realistic novel," and as the one that should therefore appeal most directly to the English-speaking reader.[27] The case for re-visiting this text becomes yet more pressing when one recognises that Hesse has here succeeded in exploring the instabilities of an intensely private world with unrivalled intensity, as this chapter has attempted to demonstrate.

Notes

[1] Rudolf Koester, *Hermann Hesse* (Stuttgart: Metzler, 1975), 29.

[2] George W. Field, *Hermann Hesse* (New York: Macmillan, 1970), 112.

[3] First publication was in *Velhagen und Klasings Monatshefte,* 1913; the bound edition followed a year later.

[4] Field, *Hermann Hesse,* 37.

[5] Klaus Walther, *Hermann Hesse* (Munich: DTV, 2002), 57. See also notes 12–14, below.

[6] References to *Roßhalde* in this essay are to *Sämtliche Werke,* vol. 3: *Die Romane: Roßhalde. Knulp. Demian. Siddhartha,* ed. Volker Michels (Frankfurt am Main: Suhrkamp, 2001) and will be given using the abbreviation *SW* 3 and page number. Most English translations are from *Rosshalde,* trans. Ralph Manheim (New York: Farrar, Straus, and Giroux, 1970) and are given in parentheses and quotation marks using the abbreviation *R* and page number. When no quotation marks or page number is present, the translations are the author's or editors' own.

[7] Letter to Hesse's father, 16 March 1913, *Gesammelte Briefe,* vol. 1: *1895–1921,* ed. Ursula and Volker Michels (Frankfurt am Main: Suhrkamp, 1990), 242.

[8] For further discussion of the topography, see Mimi Jehle, "The 'Garden' in the Works of Hermann Hesse," *German Quarterly* 24 (1951): 42–50, and Sikander Singh, *Hermann Hesse* (Stuttgart: Metzler, 2006), 105–6.

[9] Lewis W. Tusken, *Understanding Hermann Hesse: The Man, His Myth, His Metaphor* (Columbia: U of South Carolina P, 1998), 71.

[10] Compare this with another statement Burkhardt makes: "'ich [. . .] entwickele mich allmählich zum Erbonkel'" (*SW* 3:23; "I'm gradually developing into an inheritance uncle," *R* 25).

[11] Kurt Tucholsky, for example, speaks admiringly of their relationship: "Da möchte man Hermann Hesse danken, dass ers uns wieder einmal geschrieben hat, wie fest dieses Band zwischen zwei Männern sein kann, gesponnen ohne hinterhältige Absichten, ohne Herrschsucht, geknüpft von Individualität zu Individualität, von Mensch zu Mensch" (At this point one would like to thank Hermann Hesse for once again documenting how strong this bond between two men can be, a bond created without ulterior motives or any desire for domination, simply linking one individual to another fellow human being). *Die Schaubühne,* Nr. 17, 23 April 1914, 485.

[12] Lüthi assumes that Burkhardt's views on art conflict with Veraguth's. If the friend does indeed view art as a means of "Betäubung," the artistically manufactured but ultimately fraudulent photographs he has had made would be an appropriate example of the misuse of art. See Hans Jürg Lüthi, *Hermann Hesse — Natur und Geist* (Stuttgart: Kohlhammer, 1970), 22.

[13] See also note 20, below.

[14] *Roßhalde* has long been neglected by mainstream Hesse scholarship. Ziolkowski devotes one, Freedman two paragraphs to it. There are few references in Harold Bloom's recent volume in the Modern Critical Views series, where the title is once given as *Robhalde.* Theodore Ziolkowski, *The Novels of Hermann Hesse: A Study in Theme and Structure* (Princeton: Princeton UP, 1967), 4–5; Ralph Freedman, *Hermann Hesse: Pilgrim of Crisis* (London: Jonathan Cape, 1979), 162–63; Harold Bloom, ed., *Hermann Hesse* (Broomhall, PA: Chelsea House, 2003), 180.

[15] Ziolkowski, *Novels of Hermann Hesse,* 5.

[16] Tusken, *Understanding Hermann Hesse,* 67.

[17] Singh, *Hermann Hesse,* 100.

[18] "[. . .] die Reise selbst war eigentlich eine Enttäuschung" (. . . the trip itself was a disappointment), he wrote in a letter to Romain Rolland, *Gesammelte Briefe,* vol. 2: *1922–1935,* ed. Ursula and Volker Michels (Frankfurt am Main: Suhrkamp, 1979), 56.

[19] Singh, *Hermann Hesse,* 100–101. A linocut image by Emil Rudolf Weiss, intended to reproduce this key work, appears on the cover of the original printed edition; see Singh, 99.

[20] Tusken, *Understanding Hermann Hesse,* 68. To this it should be added that neither of Veraguth's sons is presented in a consistently positive light. Pierre is repeatedly described as "verwöhnt" (*SW* 3:20, 79) and Albert shares a violent streak with his father, whom he apparently once attacked with knives (*SW* 3:86–87), displaying what Singh terms "unüberwindbarer ödipaler Hass" (95; unconquerable Oedipal hatred). Among the relatively few specific traits ascribed to Albert are an aversion to local wine and romantic music, failings in Veraguth's eyes and possible indicators of insensitivity (*SW* 3:44).

[21] Singh, *Hermann Hesse,* 101.

[22] See James White, "Echo's Prayers in Thomas Mann's *Doktor Faustus,*" *Monatshefte für den deutschen Unterricht* 42 (1950): 393–94, and Osman Durrani, "Echo's Reverberations. Notes on a Painful Incident in Thomas Mann's *Doktor Faustus,*" *German Life and Letters* 37 (1984): 125–34.

[23] Before his departure, Veraguth promises to bring back a tiger skin (*SW* 3:97). Shooting big cats may have been a fashionable sport at the time, but it does not accord well with the "St. Francis-like" view of nature that Pierre represents.

[24] Tusken, *Understanding Hermann Hesse,* 70.

[25] Field, *Hermann Hesse,* 37. See also Joseph P. Strelka, "Hermann Hesses *Roßhalde* psychoanalytisch gesehen," *Acta Germanica* 9 (1976): 77–186.

[26] Siegfried Unseld, *Hermann Hesse, eine Werkgeschichte* (Frankfurt am Main: Suhrkamp, 1973), 41; Martin Pfeifer, *Hermann Hesses weltweite Wirkung* (Frankfurt am Main: Suhrkamp, 1973), vol. 1, 288.

[27] Field, *Hermann Hesse,* see note 2, above.

3: The Aesthetics of Ritual: Pollution, Magic, and Sentimentality in Hesse's *Demian* (1919)

Andreas Solbach

HERMANN HESSE'S *DEMIAN*[1] reflects the crisis in the author's life that began in 1912 with the serious illness of his son Martin and the family's move from Gaienhofen to Bern. It continued as his wife's mental condition deteriorated, finally resulting in their permanent separation and eventual divorce. During the years before the novel's publication in 1919,[2] Hesse's deep emotional turmoil about the war, his father's death, and personal and professional repercussions of his journalism aggravated the crisis equally as much as his enormous workload. In 1916, while writing *Demian,* Hesse received psychotherapy from J. B. Lang,[3] who soon became his close friend.[4]

Most interpreters locate *Demian* within an ideological matrix of religion and psychology, centering on ideas of Jung, Bachofen, Nietzsche, and Hölderlin, as well as on Gnostic notions. Wackenroder, Novalis, and Keller are also seen as influences, a modest selection given Hesse's comprehensive knowledge of literature.[5] Efforts to establish the novel's unifying themes and an over-arching, coherent meaning have met with only limited success, owing precisely to how evident the sources and literary influences are. Most commentators emphasize a particular point of view to lend consistency to their arguments, which ultimately pits advocates of religious interpretations against those favoring psychological approaches. As neither C. G. Jung nor Nietzsche, named most frequently as influences, can readily be assigned to a particular discipline, readings differ less as to the materials cited than in the rigidity of the conclusions drawn from them. These analyses, often pedantic attempts to link each character to a Jungian concept, are the very opposite of readings that focus on dominant ethical and political ideas.[6] Though both sides present accurate, significant observations, neither approach represents convincingly the novel's total scope.

In contrast to *Peter Camenzind* and *Unterm Rad, Gertrud* (1910) and *Roßhalde* (1914) were artistically conventional and received little acclaim. Hesse knew that he had to act decisively as an artist to prove his mettle as an author to himself and to a literary marketplace transformed by the war.

There was a danger, however, that his political ideas, his ever stronger pacifism, would alienate the bourgeois public. He had to achieve four goals at once: first of all, he had to advance artistically beyond his own pre-war ideas and styles, so that he could influence the literary discourse under circumstances that the war had changed utterly. Hesse could not and would not present themes from his early works to please increasingly conservative audiences; he was too young and ambitious to guide his career into that kind of blind alley. Secondly, he did not wish to abandon his hard-won ideological stance, by no means yet his final position, as a liberal pacifist, but — his third imperative — he did not want to lose his middle-class readers. Hesse knew full well that he was a bourgeois author like the Mann brothers, with whom he shared many literary themes, as well as a part of the reading public, and so was not about to veer further to the left politically. In this respect, Hesse remained an unconventional liberal all his life, a characteristic attitude for southwest Germany.[7] Lastly, Hesse believed that reaching these goals would help him to overcome his personal crisis and release new energies.

Technically, making *Demian* achieve his second and third aims was Hesse's greatest problem. He solved it ingeniously by publishing it under a pseudonym, thereby improving the chances of fulfilling his fourth need. Success as a pseudonymous author clearly improved his self-confidence as an artist and a man, proving that he had something to say even under radically changed circumstances. *Demian*'s success also established a public of middle-class readers who emphatically approved of it, even if they presently had to realize that they had been fooled. By publishing under a pseudonym, finally, Hesse had realized his most important goal: to be widely recognized by critics and readers alike as the voice of a new generation shaped by the war. He had made possible a new beginning for his career by establishing his legitimacy as a highly regarded writer, worthy to participate in the most significant discourses of the time. But had he truly realized his purposes as an artist and political thinker? As far as possible. At best, *Demian* is politically ambivalent: on the one hand, the soldier achieves a mythic status, purified in spirit and intellect as all men yearn to be, his humanity renewed; on the other hand, one senses palpable regret that this *renovatio* and *reformatio* of the people of Europe is only possible with such destruction, to which Demian himself falls victim. With a sure instinct, Hesse avoids describing warfare itself, thus leaving its nature an open question and inviting approval both from pacifists and defenders of the war.

Some readers of the time, especially the youngest, who were often close to the German Youth Movement (Wandervogel), were fascinated by the way the story invited them to identify with its various characters. Lulu von Strauß und Torney summed it up: "Out of spiritual hunger, one person or another found *Demian*. He read, and he felt as though a blindfold had been lifted from his eyes. Read and found — himself."[8] And Gerhart Sieveking remarked: "Ever since reading *Demian,* we can behold the world only through his eyes."[9]

Because younger readers accepted the fiction that the pseudonymous author belonged to their own generation, they readily identified themselves with him. But this accounts only partially for the *sinceritas,* the honesty that affirmed for them the truth of the narrator's story. Readers and reviewers perceived the novel primarily as a stylization "that does not follow any literary theories or fads,"[10] as Rudolf Kayser noted, and indirectly follows the tradition of the *sermo humilis,* which speaks of the highest matters in the simplest words.[11]

There is a strong temptation to read *Demian*'s claim to true-to-life authenticity, eschewing artistic devices entirely, telling only plain facts, as enjoining emulation of its attitudes, a secular *imitatio Christi.* The text provides many such signals, most emphatically through Demian and his mother, who are depicted almost like figures in the Gospels.[12] This reading helps in understanding the text, suggesting as it does a secularized *politica christiana;* yet it is bound to those sources and ideas that influenced the author directly and linked him to his readers at the time through a web of shared facts and notions. And yet, the novel's great impact and enduring popularity[13] must stem from an interpretive model on a higher level of abstraction than Christian symbolism or Jungian psychoanalysis can offer. Both of these ideological systems are extraordinarily significant, but they are only surface phenomena whose deep structure remains to be analyzed.

Before turning to this task, however, a seemingly obvious observation has to be clearly stated, as it establishes a vital connection between *Demian* and Hesse's earlier works: ruminations on the necessary conditions for telling a convincing story are recurrent in Hesse's works, and he returns time and again to the rhetorical device of *sinceritas,* sincerity.[14] If the ultimate purpose of a text is to persuade, it must be believable, which also requires sincerity, so a strategy must be devised to convince the reader. In this sense, the "natural," "artless" style that Hesse's narrator in *Demian* cultivates is anything but artless. It is rhetoric at its most artificial. The art of rhetoric requires that simple, unadorned speech, the most humble kind of style, be used for ordinary topics. It is also used in religious instruction because of its accessibility and because it exemplifies humility, the attitude such teachings seek to elicit from readers. The rhetorical austerity and simplicity of Hesse's novel is just as calculated as the pseudonymous authorship, intended to confer a sense of authenticity to a story purporting to be fact, not fiction.[15]

Hesse's protagonists are always on their way to life, whether portrayed as adults desiring to escape their isolation or as children or adolescents in the throes of individuation, all wish intensely to take part in life's fullness, to transcend their own limited being. Their common starting point is a sense of being incapable of living, of facing an obstacle that the protagonist cannot (yet) overcome. A sharp distinction is drawn between uneventful everyday life and an authentic life of intensive experiences and truly meaningful being. An individual is challenged to enter upon the promised new life, not to be understood as the symbolic expression of a limited psychoanalytic theory, but as an initiation, whose ritual imposes a symbolism of its own, harkening back to anthropological origins more ancient and poetic than any modern theories. Thus, we are dealing, not only in *Demian,* but also, within their own specific situations, in *Siddhartha* and in *Steppenwolf,* with literary descriptions of "rites of passage" as Arnold van Gennep and Victor Turner understood the term.[16] It should be noted that van Gennep presented his groundbreaking studies almost ten years before Hesse published *Demian,* though it is unlikely that Hesse, though interested in ethnology, was aware of them.

Van Gennep observed that, in traditional societies, each stage in a person's life (birth, puberty, marriage, etc.) is accompanied by ceremonies. These transitions also have a spatial dimension, as each social group occupies a specific space or sector, separated from its neighbors by a "neutral zone" of variable dimensions.

Were one to compare societies to houses, all of the doors in modern civilizations would be wide open, and transitions easy compared with traditional societies, in which "sections are carefully isolated and passage from one to another must be made through formalities and ceremonies [. . .]"[17] In this respect, rooms, houses, and thresholds are especially significant in Hesse's novels, for they define the territories of the sacred and the profane.

Van Gennep distinguishes between "preliminal rites" that select and set the participant apart, transformative "liminal" or "threshold rites" that enable transcendence to the next stage, and "postliminal rites" that integrate the subject into the new sphere of being. The "preliminal rites" signify that the subject is temporarily giving up a previous social status, and the "postliminal rites" signify his reintegration with the social realm, following transformation by way of the "liminal rites."

Demian's basic design can be usefully described in terms of "rites of passage": first, gradual separation from the parental family as a preliminal rite and then the long threshold phase of the rites of transformation, which are also rituals of initiation. The liminal phase is of special concern, for it is here that the "novice," separated from parents and family, is made familiar with the precepts and practices of new and larger spheres of being. Van Gennep focuses mainly on initiation into totem societies and "magico-religious brotherhoods," which suits our purposes too, for Emil Sinclair's "mark of Cain" could be seen as analogous to a totemic sign, and the circle of Demian and Frau Eva as a magico-religious secret society. More interesting for the present inquiry, however, are Victor Turner's more comprehensive and complex analyses in *The Ritual Process: Structure and Anti-Structure* (1969) and *From Ritual to Theatre: The Human Seriousness of Play* (1982). Before turning to the threshold phase of the protagonist's initiation ritual, we must look more closely at the preliminal rites, as they play a larger part in our literary case study than merely separating the hero from his family home, and they reveal a rather complex structure.

Demian and Hesse's short story *Kinderseele* (1919) have significant features in common, and in at least one respect the story develops the central problem more clearly than does the novel, and merits consideration here.[18] In both texts, typically for Hesse, two essential structures are contrasted as diametrical opposites: "our world" and "the other world." "Our world" signifies "father's house,"[19] and, disturbing to modern readers, the dichotomy of "ours" and "theirs" becomes understood as the opposition between good and evil. This simple but heavy-handed argumentation has hypnotized many readers and interpreters, who have difficulty in seeing beyond its striking dualism. Actually, it is quite easy to understand this construction of opposites. The part that is "ours," of light, and the good is depicted vividly as the world of childhood and "father's house," the most important elements of which are protection, safety, and an all-embracing sense of security. This *securitas* also represents, in respect to hermeneutics, absolute confidence in one's interpretive judgment. From its point of view, all things have a definite meaning and purpose, because *sinceritas* is its guiding maxim in comprehending the world. It guarantees that moral and aesthetic judgments made in its name by priests, interpreters, and educators, the fathers, in short, are unassailable, and thus grounded in religion. The narrator describes compellingly the positive feelings that arise from the synergy of *sinceritas* and *securitas* in a powerful recollection of childhood's freedom from all cares. This joyous state can endow a child's experiences in the world with vivid immediacy; its loss, however, can arouse feelings of inconsolable craving for this "paradis artificiel."

The other pole of this dualism is constituted by the world of the alien, the other, which cannot be judged with certainty. This mysterious world is the opposite of "father's house": it is a realm of uncertainty, danger, and dishonesty. Its nature eludes stable, durable description; entropy and chaos reign there, not logical regularity and order. Its dominant characteristic, however, is a striking ambiguity, which is incompatible with Protestantism's system of hermeneutics, in which only a word's literal sense constitutes meaning. Whereas certainty arises from a fundamentalist reading of the world and language, which accepts, beyond literal meanings, only figurative language pertaining to Christ, the ambiguity of the world of the other is founded upon the rhetorical nature of language and a culture's indeterminate signs. Hesse's narrative worlds derive their peculiar energy from the fact that this dualism does not remain rigid, bringing the two worlds to a tragic collision; rather, both the world of safety and honesty and that of danger and uncertainty reveal inner contradictions. The sphere of order reveals a negative side, becoming rigid and immovable and culminating in an oppressively one-dimensional view of life, while the "negative" sphere of disorder offers varied, colorful attractions, expressing its powerful dynamism. While rigid, literal-minded order does confer security behind a shield of sincerity, it leads ultimately to death, because it cannot accommodate change. On the other hand, while the perilous domain of ambiguous signs is impelled by rhetorical deception, it expresses nothing less than life itself. It is no wonder that the world of the "other" and "alien" entices, seduces, and captivates Hesse's protagonists.

It is obvious that "father's house" corresponds to the situation that precedes the rites of the liminal phase, the way of life from which the novice must be freed if he is to find his place in the "other" world, which is still unfamiliar. But even in Hesse's dualistic design anthropological points of view come to light that deserve closer scrutiny. The world of the father is characterized by a sense of purity and hygienic order: "Zu dieser Welt gehörte milder Glanz, Klarheit und Sauberkeit, hier waren sanfte freundliche Reden, gewaschene Hände, reine Kleider, gute Sitten daheim" (D 237; "It was a realm of brilliance, clarity, and cleanliness, gentle conversations, washed hands, clean clothes, and good manners"; R/L 5) The world outside, on the other hand, is filthy, smelling of unwashed bodies, presenting amorphous, grotesque shapes and the danger of infection with deadly diseases:

> In dieser zweiten Welt gab es Dienstmägde und Handwerksburschen, Geistergeschichten und Skandalgerüchte, es gab da eine bunte Flut von ungeheuren, lockenden, furchtbaren, rätselhaften Dingen, Sachen wie Schlachthaus und Gefängnis, Betrunkene und keifende Weiber, gebärende Kühe, gestürzte Pferde, Erzählungen von Einbrüchen, Totschlägen, Selbstmorden. [. . .] Betrunkene schlugen ihre Weiber, Knäuel von jungen Mädchen quollen abends aus den Fabriken, alte Frauen konnten einen bezaubern und krank machen [. . .] überall quoll und duftete diese zweite, heftige Welt [. . .]. (D 238)

> [This second world contained servant girls and workmen, ghost stories, rumors of scandal. It was dominated by a loud mixture of horrendous, intriguing, frightful things, including slaughterhouses and prisons, drunkards and screeching fishwives, calving cows, horses sinking to their death, tales of robberies, murders, and suicides. [. . .] [D]runkards who beat their wives, droves of young girls pouring out of factories at night, old women who put the hex on you so that you fell ill, [. . .] — everywhere this second vigorous world erupted and gave off its scent. (R/L 6)]

In *Purity and Danger: An Analysis of Concepts of Pollution and Taboo* (1966),[20] which has also influenced literary criticism, the anthropologist Mary Douglas pointed out that concepts of purity and peril influence cultures in establishing their values. To her, uncleanness is "the by-product of a systematic ordering and classification of matter, in so far as ordering involves rejecting inappropriate elements."[21] Uncleanness is never an isolated phenomenon, but always an expression and part of structures of explication and regulation. Douglas proceeds from the central observation that for traditional societies the impure and the sacred are often not separated. Such societies believe further that "[h]oliness is the attribute of Godhead. Its root means *set apart*."[22] In her analysis of the book of Leviticus she continues:

> Granted that its root means separateness, the next idea that emerges is of the Holy as wholeness and completeness. [. . .] This much iterated idea of physical completeness is also worked out in the social sphere and particularly in the warriors' camp. [. . .] In short, the idea of holiness was given an external, physical expression in the wholeness of the body seen as a perfect container. Wholeness is also extended to signify completeness in a social context. An important enterprise, once begun, must not be left incomplete.[23]

Hesse's narrator, Emil Sinclair, strives to achieve just this wholeness and completeness by undergoing the initiatory rite that gives him the power to live with the dark side of the world, both within himself and outside. Thus, perfection is an attribute of holiness, which demands that individual elements of creation must be separated from one another. Further remarks by Douglas also appear relevant to Hesse's novel. "Developing the idea of holiness as order, not confusion, this list [i.e. Leviticus] upholds rectitude and straight-dealing as holy, and contradiction and double-dealing as against holiness."[24] The holy is to be seen as the principle of the antirhetorical, that principle associated most closely with "father's house." The notion of order, on the other hand, does not necessarily accommodate modern ideas of its nature, at least not at first glance, for the ritual accepts and affirms the power of disorder, as does Emil Sinclair.

> In the disorder of the mind, in dreams, faints and frenzies, ritual expects to find powers and truths which cannot be reached by conscious effort. Energy to command and special powers of healing come to those who can abandon rational control for a time.[25]

Such powers and truths, seemingly magical, permit the novice to share in the spell or to perform it himself as he undergoes the rituals of the liminal phase. However, this phase also subjects novices to an ordeal of uncleanness and defilement; they are separated from society and become a kind of filth themselves. Not infrequently, they are regarded as dead, and they often are permitted, indeed ordered, to behave like delinquents.[26]

It is no wonder that the initiate is under a taboo,[27] for he submits to rituals that, by means of defilement and by treating him as such, acquaint him with the secrets and practices of magic, enabling him later to take his place as a responsible member of the community. But the culture's rules about pollution and purity are not suspended by the contamination that individuals undergo; on the contrary, this liminal ritual can be seen as a preventive inoculation of the initiate's psyche. He is purposely infected with a relatively benign moral "pathogen," which his mind and body can contend with and overcome, thus enhancing his abilities and endowing him with greater power.

Sinclair's goals in life change in the course of the novel, whose greater part is dedicated to the workings of the liminal ritual. The narrator rarely speaks in the first person, for his dominant concerns are with Demian. Initially, in his preliminary state of mind, the narrator, reflecting solely his own experience, affirms that the fascinating world of darkness and the other possesses evil, devilish qualities. This intrusion of religious rhetoric suggests the ways of thinking that the "rites of passage" are meant to overcome. Characteristically, in the world of *Demian*, Emil's entry into the liminal phase is not clearly marked; at first, the world of the "other" is cautiously probed in an act of controlled transgression. From the start, the gateway of Emil's home is significant, separating the father's world from that of life. In *Kinderseele*, it is named at the very beginning: "Unser Vaterhaus, das groß und hell an einer hellen Straße lag, betrat man durch ein hohes Tor, [. . .] [E]s [war] immer ein Übergang in eine andere Welt, in 'unsere' Welt" (K 179; "Our father's house, large and bright on a bright street, was to be entered through a high gateway, [. . .] it [was] always a passage from another world into 'our' world").

At the very outset in *Demian*, Kromer attempts to extort money from Emil on the threshold of his own home, dashing Emil's hopes of limiting the risk of his controlled transgression, his boastfulness. The reassurance Emil seeks in imagining himself as a returning Prodigal Son is meaningless. He tries to gain acceptance in Kromer's gang or "clan" by doing his bidding and being humiliated by him. The older boy's attraction stems from his semi-adult posturing and from the sense of danger he projects,[28] as Sinclair soon finds out when Kromer tries to blackmail him with his tale of having stolen apples. Outwardly, he could possibly foil the attempt by admitting to the lie, but Emil's insistence that he had told the truth and thus must fear exposure shows that the situation is analogous to traditional magic. It is clearly based on the magical power of telling a story, as is done in liminal rituals. In a rite of initiation into one of a clan's groups, initiates tell stories of thefts they have committed, insisting they are real.

If an initiate admits it is a fiction, he forfeits all chance of ever joining the group, having divested himself of the magical power of storytelling. Neither *Demian*'s author nor the protagonist find this result acceptable, but Emil can find no way to free himself from his dilemma, and becomes depressed and ill. In fact, he did become infected in the world of the "others," which the text emphasizes through metaphors of contamination and disease, all associated with the taboo against physical contact:

> [I]ch war tief und schuldvoll in die fremde Flut versunken, in Aben-teuer und Sünde verstrickt [. . .]. Ich trug Schmutz an meinen Füßen [. . .]. Schicksal lief mir nach, Hände waren nach mit ausgestreckt [. . .]. Meine Sünde war [. . .], daß ich dem Teufel die Hand gegeben hatte. [. . .] Nun hielt der Teufel meine Hand, nun war der Feind hinter mir her. (*D* 245–46)

> [I, guilty and deeply engulfed in an alien world, was entangled in ad-ventures and sin, [. . .] My feet had become muddied [. . .] I was haunted by misfortune, it was reaching out toward me [. . .] My sin [. . .] consisted in having shaken hands with the devil [. . .] the enemy was behind me. (R/L 13–14)]

The Kromer episode, Emil's infection by the alien world, is only a pre-requisite to the many forms his liminal rituals are to take. Thus contami-nated, Sinclair loses his sense of security in the world of his father, even though, once rescued from Kromer by Demian, he seems briefly to regain it. The experience permanently destroys in him the boundary between dis-sembling and sincere expression; it destabilizes the bases of integrity and judgmental certainty, setting in their place skepticism and wariness toward appearances and ideas. Even before Demian reveals to him that critical judg-ments based on knowing the "true" and the "good" grow out of fears and resentments, Sinclair senses that he is not only chosen, but also superior:

> Dabei funkelte ein sonderbar neues Gefühl in mir auf, ein böses und schneidendes Gefühl voll Widerhaken: ich fühlte mich meinem Vater überlegen! Ich fühlte, einen Augenblick lang, eine gewisse Verachtung für seine Unwissenheit [. . .]. Es war ein erster Riß in die Heiligkeit des Vaters, es war ein erster Schnitt in die Pfeiler, auf denen mein Kin-derleben geruht hatte, und die jeder Mensch, ehe er er selbst werden kann, zerstört haben muß. (*D* 246–47)

> [A strange new feeling overcame me at this point, a feeling that stung pleasurably: I felt superior to my father! Momentarily I felt a certain loathing for his ignorance. [. . .] It was the first rent in the holy image of my father, it was the first fissure in the columns that had upheld my childhood, which every individual must destroy before he can become himself. (R/L 15)]

Emil's harmonious, literal-minded bond with his father's world has been destroyed. He no longer feels that he is an immediate part of it. The thought of dying makes him fearful, since henceforth, thanks to his alienation from his former life, his world will be dominated by ambiguity, the possibility that he will be deceived and even deceive himself, and because, through his new awareness, the horror of life's impermanence overshadows his being.[29] Sinclair reacts with symptoms of mental and physical illness; just as with initiates in actual rituals, his "madness" is fundamental to the development of the liminal phase.

Further developments are linked to the rites of detachment that centered on the fictional theft and blackmail, which Max Demian finally resolves. Made fatherless by fate, he possesses an aura of maturity, power, and knowledge, like someone who has completed his initiation and belongs to a special group, separate from the others: "Zwischen uns kindischen Jungen bewegte er sich fremd und fertig wie ein Mann, vielmehr wie ein Herr" (D 253; "In contrast to us, he seemed strange and mature, like a man, or rather like a gentleman": R/L 22). Demian assumes a magical function, accompanying the initiate through the liminal phase and guiding his rituals. In this role he is clearly apart from the everyday world of the fathers.[30] Demian's chief function, aside from the Kromer episode, is to explain Emil's status to him and to familiarize the novice with his magical practices.

First of all, Demian acquaints the younger novice with his special calling by pointing out to him the threshold, in both the literal and figurative senses. In the crest over the doorway's keystone, Demian perceives a sparrowhawk, whose image, inconsequential at that moment, is to become Sinclair's totemic sign: he is its bearer and it bears him. At once sign and signified, it dominates the way over the threshold; it expresses Sinclair's character figuratively, serving too as his talisman of protection, defense, and magical power. It is also the visible evidence and concrete metaphor of the initiate having been elected to the group; like Cain, he bears a mark. The images are composed identically. From the forehead, or from the gateway's apex, downward, the totemic sign is inscribed upon the bearer in such a way that people perceive immediately that he is different, but do not know why.

In the discussion that ensues, Demian, using the Old Testament example of Cain and Abel, develops the most important instrument of his magical training. In the liminal phase, according to Van Gennep, the novice is to learn "to manipulate the sacra according to precise rules without danger from the supernatural."[31] But he must first confront the "sacra," the magical objects and actions that frighten him, since, as Van Gennep writes, "the exposing of these bogeymen of their childhood is the central event of the ritual."[32] But while the initiate in traditional societies "learns" one or more ritual techniques whose magical power he does not doubt, Emil is subjected to a radical demolition of his illusions that overturns entirely his conception of the world, which is especially vulnerable because it depends upon questionable presumptions such as the polar opposition of honest speech and dissembling rhetoric. Demian begins by assailing the hermeneutics of literal meanings, upon which the postulate of honest expression is based. "Die meisten Sachen, die man uns lehrt, sind gewiß ganz wahr und richtig, aber man kann sie alle auch anders ansehen, als die Lehrer es tun, und meistens haben sie dann einen viel besseren Sinn" (D 255; "Most of the things we're taught I'm sure are quite right and true, but one can view all of them from quite a different angle than the teachers do — and most of the time they then make better sense"; R/L 24). Asserting that a text may have a meaning, allegorical or otherwise, beyond its literal wording means that all signs may be arbitrary and fosters skepticism in all matters. The Bible's exemplary story of fratricide — that of Cain and Abel — is not chosen by chance. What at first seems to be a casual mention of the story leads Demian to re-read it skeptically, undermining the premises of the story as they are traditionally conceived. From this re-reading emerges a theme of the greatest importance: Emil's realization that he, too, bears the mark.

There is a significant paradox inherent here, for the process of initiation is based upon the arbitrary nature of signs and, consequently, the possibility of differing interpretations. However, the mark of the chosen, the totemic animal or the mark of Cain, appears to be non-arbitrary or literal, so that the deeper, ultimately magical significance of the distinguishing sign contradicts the argument on which it is based. Hesse avoids this paradox only by affirming the mark as a *sacrum,* thus as a magical object.[33] In his interpretation, Demian cites a philosophical argument that suggests Nietzschean origins:

Es war da ein Mann, der hatte etwas im Gesicht, was den andern Angst machte. Sie wagten nicht ihn anzurühren, er imponierte ihnen, er und seine Kinder. [. . .] Dieser Mann hatte Macht, vor diesem Mann scheute man sich. Er hatte ein "Zeichen." Man konnte das erklären, wie man wollte. [. . .] Also erklärte man das Zeichen nicht als das, was es war, als eine Auszeichnung, sondern als das Gegenteil. [. . .] Daß da ein Geschlecht von Unheimlichen und Furchtlosen herumlief, war sehr unbequem, und nun hängte man diesem Geschlecht einen Übernamen und eine Fabel an, um sich für alle die ausgestandene Furcht ein bißchen schadlos zu halten. (D 255–56)

[Here was a man with something in his face that frightened the others. They didn't dare lay hands on him; he impressed them, he and his children. [. . .] This man was powerful: you would approach him only with awe. He had a "sign." You could explain this any way you

wished. [. . .] So they did not interpret the sign for what it was — a
mark of distinction — but as its opposite. [. . .] It was a scandal that a
breed of fearless and sinister people ran about freely, so they attached a
nickname and myth to these people to get even with them, to make
up for the many times they had felt afraid. (R/L 24–25)]

In Demian's reading, Cain becomes a strong man, whose charismatic power the weak try to tame with defamatory intrigues. According to Demian's
critique of traditional ideology, religion interprets Cain's extraordinary
powers as a sign of his evil character in order to conceal the weakness of
common humanity. The way the powerless multitude reads this sign gives
it the force of a law because, once defined, it also imposes a moral judgment. This problem preoccupied not only Nietzsche, but also the philosophy of the Greek Sophists, with whom Socrates and Plato contended.
The dispute has come down to us as the *nomos-physis* debate. Its basic problem, the question of the validity, applicability, and efficacy of laws that
humans have established — by definition subject to change — is very much
alive today.[34] Critics of the *nomoi* (laws) resort to various arguments, some
of them grossly contradictory. Nature is seen by some as Darwinistic, letting the strongest prevail through the "survival of the fittest," enabling
them to establish their own laws. Others assume the existence of humanistic laws of Nature, which apply to all nations.[35] Demian clearly does not
care about the philosophical consequences of his theory, which is intended entirely to reveal to Sinclair his role and his status, for he too bears
the mark as one of the chosen.[36]

Sinclair realizes this immediately upon remembering that he had felt
superior to his father: "Ja, da hatte ich selber, der ich Kain war und das
Zeichen trug, mir eingebildet, dies Zeichen sei keine Schande, es sei eine
Auszeichnung und ich stehe durch meine Bosheit und mein Unglück höher
als mein Vater, höher als die Guten und Frommen" (*D* 257; "Yes, at that
moment I, who was Cain and bore the mark, had imagined that this sign
was not a mark of shame and that because of my evil and misfortune I
stood higher than my father and the righteous, the pious"; R/L 26).

Demian liberates Sinclair from Kromer's blackmailing, and Sinclair's
newly found knowledge that he is one of the chosen disappears in his regression into the "radiant world" of his father's house. The narrator makes
a perceptive comment about the reason for his regression:

[I]n Wahrheit war es nichts als Angst. Denn Demian hätte mehr von
mir verlangt als die Eltern verlangten, viel mehr, er hätte mich mit
Antrieb und Ermahnung, mit Spott und Ironie selbständiger zu machen versucht. Ach, das weiß ich heute, nichts auf der Welt ist dem
Menschen mehr zuwider, als den Weg zu gehen, der ihn zu sich selber
führt! (*D* 269)

[[I]n reality it was entirely because of my fear. For Demian would have been far more exacting than my parents; he would have tried to make me more independent by using persuasion, exhortation, mockery, and sarcasm. I realize today that nothing is more distasteful to a man than to take the path that leads to himself. (R/L 38)]

It is only with the onset of puberty that Sinclair liberates himself, when he meets his spiritual mentor again in confirmation class. Demian appears to him once more as an exceptional being with a charismatic aura. He demonstrates his magical powers in feats of telepathy and continues to instruct Sinclair; proceeding from his theory of the mark of Cain to a re-evaluation of the thief on the cross. As in the earlier example, the sinner's stubbornness is seen not as a grave transgression, but rather as a mark of distinction that makes him a hero: "[D]er ist ein Kerl und hat Charakter. Er pfeift auf eine Bekehrung, die ja in seiner Lage bloß noch hübsches Gerede sein kann, er geht seinen Weg zu Ende und sagt sich nicht im letzten Augenblick feig vom Teufel los, der ihm bis dahin hat helfen müssen" (*D* 280; "No, the other [thief], he's a man of character. He doesn't give a hoot for 'conversion,' which to a man in his position can't be anything but a pretty speech. He follows his destiny to its appointed end and does not turn coward and forswear the devil who has aided and abetted him until then"; R/L 50–51). Demian criticizes the faintness of heart that brought about Sinclair's regression and has, temporarily at least, retarded the initiation process. His arguments are significant, as they all have a literary orientation. The regression may only be "talk," empty rhetoric without power to persuade, no more than a "Pfaffengeschichte, süßlich und unredlich, mit Schmalz der Rührung und höchst erbaulichem Hintergrund" (*D* 280; "a priest's fairy tale, saccharine and dishonest, touched up with sentimentality and given a highly edifying background"; R/L 50); yet he also compares himself implicitly with Mephisto and Sinclair with Faust. The allusion to Goethe is not as significant, however, as the emphasis on the rhetorical principle of ambiguity, which, surprisingly, is here set against the demand for *constantia,* constancy. In this way, Demian introduces a new phase in the initiation process, one that apparently contradicts its basic assumptions. For *constantia* is nothing less than the complement of *sinceritas,* which had previously been displaced, for the sake of better understanding the dissembling nature of language and the world, by the conviction that all things can be defined and interpreted in different ways. Accordingly, Demian then sets forth the idea that the world does not exist within the opposition of Good and Evil, but is rather to be understood as a fabric, often impenetrable, of myriad desires and motives:

Aber die Welt besteht auch aus anderem. Und das wird nun alles einfach dem Teufel zugeschrieben, und dieser ganze Teil der Welt, diese ganze Hälfte wird unterschlagen und totgeschwiegen. [. . .] Aber ich meine, wir sollen alles verehren und heilig halten, die ganze Welt, nicht bloß diese künstlich abgetrennte, offizielle Hälfte! (*D* 281)

[But the world consists of something else besides. And what is left over is ascribed to the devil. [. . .] But I mean we ought to consider everything sacred, the entire world, not merely this artificially separated half! (R/L 51)]

With the "something else besides" Demian has in mind "our entire sexual life," which teachers, given this rigid dichotomy, demonize and criminalize, assuming their opinions to be infallible. Demian argues, to the contrary, that human instincts, "die natürlichsten Dinge von der Welt" (*D* 281; "the most natural things in the world"; R/L 51), are not in themselves good or evil, but derive moral character only from the ways we use them. We may apply this notion to other elements of the novel, such as magical and ritual processes, and we might even regard it, as Hesse did, as a poetological principle for all literature.[37] Such a perspective may also help with the problem we have touched upon already, namely, resolving the link between *sinceritas* and the rhetorical nature of practical and artistic language.

In evoking this complex, Hesse reconfigures the essential hermeneutic problem of early Protestant leaders, who, while wishing to adhere to literal meanings of words in order to establish the stability of the canonical texts and therewith of the faith, nonetheless could not avoid perceiving ambiguities in the Biblical text. To resolve this problem, Luther developed a Christ-centered system of hermeneutics that regards possibly extra-literal, metaphoric meanings as applying exclusively to Christ, so that definite meanings can be conferred upon ambiguous passages.[38] Hesse insists that any philosophy of life must deal with the world's ambiguity and the rhetorical nature of language; yet, if a person is to be initiated into that world, there must be some assurance that he can assign reliable meanings to the phenomena he will encounter. To resolve this paradox, Hesse must, with different assumptions, find a solution similar to Luther's Christ-centered system. Hesse differs from the great Reformer in proceeding from the idea that a multitude of dimensions of meaning must be dealt with, but, like him, he establishes a stable basis for forming opinions and assigning valid meanings to phenomena. In the place of Christ and His death on the cross, Hesse sets a person's development of his own individuality as the means to salvation.

Naturally, this idea stands in stark contradiction to traditional Christian conceptions, and given its Nietzschean turn, it is not especially original. What is new and stimulating, however, is that it implicitly postulates that becoming an individual is a continuing process, whose immanent claim to mediate a kind of redemption, even if taken on purely secular terms, can easily be misunderstood as being anti-religious. A kind of "decisionism" is operative here, the necessity of having to decide, which, in Hesse's case as in that of the concept's chief proponent, Carl Schmitt, results from the impossibility of a final and indisputable decision. The uncertainties of the aesthetic, political, and ethical dimensions of meaning and judgment demand an abrupt, direct, and immediate decision. Hesse plays down the aspect of immediacy, while the category of exceptionality plays a special role, for according to Schmitt: "He who makes decisions under exceptional conditions is sovereign."[39] Crucial for Hesse in all of his works is the sovereignty of the individual, which becomes manifest when this individual declares that he is an exception from other men. The individual proclaims his distinction as a bearer of the sign (not Abel, but Cain, not the repentant thief, but the "stubborn" sinner), expressing the essence of that status in the "rites of passage," which symbolize the unity of his life's goal with the path leading to it. Skepticism and disillusionment make possible the novice's separation from his former life. Initiation derives its significance from being conferred only under exceptional circumstances. At this point, however, flaws in this construct are revealed. Because the hero sets himself apart as exceptional, as manifested in the performance of the initiation process, there is no motive for a transition from the liminal phase to that of reintegration. As we shall see shortly, *Demian* has precisely this problem in common with Hesse's other novels. Demian's admonition to "get serious," to establish and affirm one's own sovereignty as a unique individual, is merged with a lofty conception of a universal, holistic human nature that affects Sinclair profoundly:

> In mir aber trafen diese Worte das Rätsel meiner ganzen Knabenjahre, das ich jede Stunde in mir trug und von dem ich nie jemandem ein Wort gesagt hatte. [. . .] Die Einsicht, daß mein Problem ein Problem aller Menschen, ein Problem alles Lebens und Denkens sei, überflog mich plötzlich wie ein heiliger Schatten, und Angst und Ehrfurcht überkam mich, als ich sah und plötzlich fühlte, wie tief mein eigenstes, persönliches Leben und Meinen am ewigen Strom der großen Ideen teilhatte. Die Einsicht war nicht freudig, obwohl irgendwie bestätigend und beglückend. Sie war hart und schmeckte rauh, weil ein Klang von Verantwortlichkeit in ihr lag, von Nichtmehrkindseindürfen, von Alleinstehen. (*D* 282)

> [His words, however, touched directly on the whole secret of my adolescence, a secret I carried with me every hour of the day and of which I had not said a word to anyone, ever. The realization that my problem was one that concerned all men, a problem of living and thinking, suddenly swept over me and I was overwhelmed with fear and respect as I suddenly saw and felt how deeply my own personal life and opinions were immersed in the eternal stream of great ideas. Though it

offered some confirmation and gratification, the realization was not really a joyful one. It was hard and had a harsh taste because it implied responsibility and no longer being allowed to be a child; it meant standing on one's own feet. (R/L 51–52)]

This insight that the struggle he would undergo for his sovereignty as a person constitutes both the goal and the process of the initiation creates in Sinclair the space needed for the "rites of passage." Here, Demian functions not only as guide and helper, but also as the incarnation of a magical sovereignty, which is associated with a sense of utopian rapture, a mysterious trance, which lets him appear to have magical powers. Demian's withdrawal into himself both fascinates and frightens Sinclair:[40]

[E]twas ging von ihm aus, etwas umgab ihn, was ich nicht kannte. [. . .] Der Anblick machte mich zittern. [. . .] Ich hing mit gebanntem Blick an seinem Gesicht [. . .]. Der wirkliche Demian aber sah so aus, so wie dieser, so steinern, uralt, tierhaft, steinhaft, schön und kalt, tot und heimlich voll von unerhörtem Leben. [. . .] Nie war ich so vereinsamt gewesen. (*D* 285)

[[S]omething emanated from him, something surrounded him that was unknown to me. [. . .] I trembled at the sight. [. . .] My spellbound eyes were fixed on his face.[. . .] The real Demian, however, looked like this, as primeval, animal, marble, beautiful and cold, dead yet secretly filled with fabulous life. [. . .] Never had I been so alone. (R/L 55)]

In Demian, his companion and guide, Sinclair sees himself as the magus he is to become. "Es wurde nun alles anders. Die Kindheit fiel um mich her in Trümmer" (*D* 286; "Now everything changed. My childhood was breaking apart around me"; R/L 56). The preliminary rites have accomplished Emil's separation from his "father's house," the threshold has been passed. The true ritual can now begin.

Following these elaborate preparations, we are surprised at how little is gained in the liminal phase. The basic attitudes of the chief protagonists and their decision to change are more important than the actual rituals of transition, which nonetheless can easily be described. They include the events of chapters 4 through 7, which are concerned mainly with the ideal figure of Beatrice and the eccentric Pistorius. Significant for this section's ritualistic character are the magical images that Sinclair produces, which serve both as means of communication and as *sacra*.

By leaving his native city and his parents' household, the narrator concludes the ritual of separation. He finds it easy to depart, and he is preoccupied with his inner life:

Der Abschied von der Heimat gelang sonderbar leicht [. . .]. Jetzt war ich ganz verwandelt. Ich verhielt mich völlig gleichgültig gegen die äußere Welt und war tagelang nur damit beschäftigt, in mich hineinzuhorchen und die Ströme zu hören, die verbotenen und dunklen Ströme, die da in mir unterirdisch rauschten.

[My leave-taking form home was surprisingly easy. [. . .] Now I had completely changed. I behaved with utter indifference to the world outside and for days on end voices from within preoccupied me, inner streams, the forbidden, dark streams that roared beneath the surface. (R/L 57)]

In his quest for "life," however, he soon reaches the limits of normal social behavior and undergoes that painful phase of puberty known as "the awkward age" and characterized by confusion, rapid oscillations between feelings of inferiority and superiority, dark urges, and sexual desire. Remembering his idyllic childhood, he sees himself as a pariah, as *abiectus,* and yet there enters into his revulsion a feeling that his life has been enhanced, that he is on the path he must follow to his initiation:

Also so sah ich innerlich aus! Ich, der herumging und die Welt verachtete! [. . .] So sah ich aus, ein Auswurf und Schweinigel, betrunken und beschmutzt, ekelhaft und gemein, eine wüste Bestie, von scheußlichen Trieben überrumpelt. [. . .] Trotz allem aber war es beinah ein Genuß, diese Qualen zu leiden. [. . .] Es war doch Gefühl, es stiegen doch Flammen, es zuckte doch Herz darin! Verwirrt empfand ich mitten im Elend etwas wie Befreiung und Frühling. (*D* 291)

[So that's what I looked like inside! I who was going about contemptuous of the world! I who was proud in spirit and shared Demian's thoughts! That's what I looked like, a piece of excrement, a filthy swine, drunk and filthy, loathsome and callow, a vile beast brought low by hideous appetites. [. . .] In spite of everything, I almost reveled in my agonies. [. . .] At least it was feeling of some kind, at least there were some flames, the heart at least flickered. Confusedly I felt something like liberation amid my misery. (R/L 62)]

Despite having surrendered to contamination, Emil preserves within himself his sense of the sacred and its fundamental demand that he put his life in order by distinguishing himself from others. He is released from his misery by a sacred ritual object that will be extraordinarily significant for *Demian* and for Hesse's entire oeuvre: a picture, more precisely a portrait. Emil happens to encounter a young lady with a "kluge[n] Knabengesicht" (*D* 295; "an intelligent and boyish face"; R/L 66) whom he names Beatrice in honor of Dante's venerated ideal and to whom he will never speak; she is the incarnation of the sacred he has chosen.

> Plötzlich hatte ich wieder ein Bild vor mir stehen, ein hohes und ver-
> ehrtes Bild — ach, und kein Bedürfnis, kein Drang war so tief und
> heftig in mir wie der Wunsch nach Ehrfurcht und Anbetung. [. . .] Sie
> stellte ihr Bild vor mir auf, sie öffnete mir ein Heiligtum, sie machte
> mich zum Beter in einem Tempel. (*D* 295–96)

> [Suddenly a new image had risen up before me, a new and cherished
> image. And no need, no urge was as deep or as fervent within me as
> the craving to worship and admire. [. . .] She raised her image before
> me, she gave me access to a holy shrine, she transformed me into a
> worshiper in a temple. (R/L 66)]

Emil transforms the image he has conceived into a real object of ritual by
painting a picture that is directly antithetical to his made-up stories of thie-
very. The attempt to join Kromer's "clan of hunters and gatherers" was a
story told poorly and dominated by a simple, self-interested lie. The saintly
image he now produces, however, does not look like the model; rather, it
looks like Demian and serves as the projection of an ideal self, which is
the goal of ritual practices meant to cleanse the novice of magical contamination and achieve a new, higher level:

> Dieser Kult der Beatrice änderte mein Leben ganz und gar. Gestern
> noch ein frühreifer Zyniker, war ich jetzt ein Tempeldiener, mit dem
> Ziel, ein Heiliger zu werden. Ich tat nicht nur das üble Leben ab, an
> das ich mich gewöhnt hatte, ich suchte alles zu ändern, suchte Rein-
> heit, Adel und Würde in alles zu bringen, dachte hieran in Essen und
> Trinken, Sprache und Kleidung. Ich begann, den Morgen mit kalten
> Waschungen [. . .]. Ich benahm mich ernst und würdig, trug mich auf-
> recht und machte meinen Gang langsamer und würdiger. (*D* 296–97)

> [This cult of Beatrice completely changed my life. Yesterday a pre-
> cocious cynic, today I was an acolyte whose aim was to become a saint.
> I not only avoided the bad life to which I had become accustomed, I
> sought to transform myself by introducing purity and nobility into
> every aspect of my life. In this connection I thought of my eating and
> drinking habits, my language and dress. I began my mornings with
> cold baths [. . .] My behavior became serious and dignified; I carried
> myself stiffly and assumed a slow and dignified gait. (R/L 67–68)]

Quite evidently, we have before us here a novice in the midst of a liminal
ritual who has created a sacred object that he carefully conceals, worships
only in the evening, and treats like a crucifix. He realizes gradually that his
holy image evokes not only Beatrice and Demian, but himself as well, not
in the sense of a portrait, but as a sign of the individuality of his person, of
his predestined sovereignty as a goal and a path, which becomes clear when
he "magically" happens upon a masterful statement by Novalis, which he
immediately understands: "Schicksal und Gemüt sind Namen eines Be-

griffs" (D 299; "Fate and temperament are two words for one and the same concept"; R/L 70)

The central lesson that Sinclair must absorb during his liminal rites — that there is no such thing as coincidence — again appears to contradict the principle that life and language confront us with ambiguous signs. His encounter with the Beatrice-figure is just as non-coincidental as those later with Demian and Pistorius. The function of both experiences is only to discredit the principle of coincidence. Demian acquaints him with the conservative idea that most significantly counters coincidence: "Es ist so gut, das zu wissen, daß in uns drinnen einer ist, der alles weiß, alles will, alles besser macht als wir selber" (D 301; "It's good to realize that within us there is someone who knows everything, wills everything, does everything better than we ourselves"; R/L 72).

Once Emil has understood the purpose of the initiation, the magical image ceases to dominate and is replaced by another ritual icon that he creates, reproducing from memory his "clan's" original "totemic sign" that Demian had pointed out over the threshold of his home. This time he does not seek to portray an almost abstract, impersonal principle (character = destiny), but rather to grasp the image of his particular destiny. Finally, he sends the icon to Demian, who magically conveys to Emil his explicatory *subscriptio*: "Der Vogel kämpft sich aus dem Ei, das Ei ist die Welt. Wer geboren werden will, muß eine Welt zerstören. Der Vogel fliegt zu Gott. Der Gott heißt Abraxas" (D 305; "The bird fights its way out of the egg. The egg is the world. Who would be born must first destroy a world. The bird flies to God. That God's name is Abraxas"; R/L 76).[41]

This new stage presents the novice with a further task: clearly, the mythic godhead Abraxas symbolizes what it is that Sinclair must now comprehend. Through rather wooden mechanics of the plot, Emil is quickly introduced to Pistorius, his guide for this phase, who familiarizes him with this religious figure and the ideas associated with him. The quest for Abraxas is inspired by a cursory discussion of that divinity during a Greek lesson,[42] culminating in a brief description: "Wir können uns den Namen etwa denken als den einer Gottheit, welche die symbolische Aufgabe hatte, das Göttliche und das Teuflische zu vereinigen" (D 306; "We may conceive of the name as that of a godhead whose symbolic task is the uniting of godly and devilish elements"; R/L 78) Thus, Abraxas functions as a mythological and ritual symbol for ideas that Demian had expressed in the second chapter, and Pistorius contributes no further thoughts of his own, treating Abraxas simply and rather schematically as a totem or the insignia of a secret society.

The process of the rites of passage moves decisively forward when the Abraxas myth comes to be associated for Sinclair with the theme of sexuality and life through a dream[43] in which he encounters his mother, who, in his embrace, turns into a figure resembling Demian, arousing bliss mixed with deep feelings of guilt: "Diese Gestalt zog mich an sich und nahm mich in eine tiefe, schauernde Liebesumarmung auf. Wonne und Grausen waren vermischt, die Umarmung war Gottesdienst und war ebenso Verbrechen. [. . .] Ihre Umarmung verstieß gegen jede Ehrfurcht und war doch Seligkeit" (*D* 308; "This form drew me to itself and enveloped me in a deep tremulous embrace. I felt a mixture of ecstasy and horror — the embrace was at once an act of divine worship and a crime. [. . .] Its embrace violated all sense of reverence, yet it was bliss"; R/L 79). He comes to understand that he is summoning Abraxas in his dream fantasy, thus performing a ritual act.

The action that follows, until the parting with Pistorius, is accompanied by constant recurrences of the dream fantasy. Its ultimate function is merely to prepare for the concluding ritual of the liminal phase, upon which the rituals of re-integration must follow in order to complete the initiation. At this point we also encounter the novel's motto, which expresses the function of the initiatory rites, to guide the novice into life: "Ich wollte ja nichts, als das zu leben versuchen, was von selber aus mir herauswollte. Warum war das so sehr schwer?" (*D* 309; "I wanted only to try to live in accord with the promptings which came from my true self. Why was that so very difficult?"; R/L 80). Breaking through to life is naturally connected with the dream fantasy, and the appeal to Abraxas means accepting these dreams and the wishes from which they arise, not suppressing them: "Wenn man von Abraxas weiß, darf man es nicht mehr tun [d.h. die Liebesträume verdrängen]. Man darf nichts fürchten und nichts für verboten halten, was die Seele in uns wünscht" (*D* 322; "When you know something about Abraxas, you cannot do this [i.e. suppress your dreams of love] any longer. You aren't allowed to be afraid of anything, you can't consider prohibited anything that the soul desires"; R/L 95). At this point Sinclair reaches a remarkable convergence of arguments, which he is unable to resolve and which he cannot escape. The initiate learns to judge actions by whether they enhance the actor's personal sovereignty and are in keeping with his destiny. When the narrator protests, "[man dürfe] doch nicht alles tun, was einem einfällt" (*D* 322; "But you can't do everything that comes to your mind!"; R/L 95), Pistorius has no convincing rebuttal, for his position depends essentially on affirming relativism and ambivalence. As was previously the case, the only answer lies in adapting the identity of character and destiny to the particular case at hand:

> Wenn Ihnen wieder einmal etwas recht Tolles oder Sündhaftes einfällt, Sinclair, wenn Sie jemanden umbringen oder irgendeine gigantische Unflätigkeit begehen möchten, dann denken Sie einen Augenblick daran, daß es Abraxas ist, der so in Ihnen phantasiert! Der Mensch, den Sie töten möchten, ist ja nie der Herr Soundso, er ist sicher nur

eine Verkleidung. Wenn wir einen Menschen hassen, so hassen wir in seinem Bilde etwas, was in uns selber sitzt. (*D* 322)

[If you happen to think of something truly mad or sinful again, if you wanto to kill someone or want to commit some enormity, Sinclair, think at that moment that it is Abraxas fantasizing within you! The person whom you would like to do away with is of course never Mr. X but merely a disguise. If you hate a person, you hate something in him that is part of yourself. (R/L 95)]

Such a radical program, founded on moral relativism, cannot be controlled unless the concept of sovereign individuality can progress beyond its most basic imperatives. A person facing the moral dilemma of the permissibility of all actions, as long as they serve to realize the goals of personal sovereignty and the destiny of his character, can evade it only by turning radically inward and limiting himself to his own concerns. The world and life then become a screen upon which subjective ideas and fantasies are projected; hence, a murder occurs merely as an imagined act.[44] This "philosophic-moral" argument also exposes a poetological problem. If the ambiguity of the world and language, the ambivalent rhetoricity of life, is inescapable, if the only true measure of ideas and decisions lies in casting one's lot with one's own daimon and destiny through a decisive act of personal sovereignty, then turning radically inward has two results: it liberates the protagonist from reality and its laws, for the boundary between reality and illusion disappears, and, consequently, a poetic relativism establishes itself. It is no longer clear whether a "real" phenomenon possesses reality in itself or whether it only has significance as a product of a subject's imagination. This extends the principle that meanings in poetry and rhetoric are ambivalent beyond its original limits, permitting most of *Demian*'s interpreters to evaluate Frau Eva and much else merely as aspects of the narrator's subjectivity.[45]

Pistorius instructs the novice to transform the radical action desired by his daimon into ritual, and thus to sublimate reality through ritual: "Statt sich oder einen andern ans Kreuz zu schlagen, kann man aus einem Kelch mit feierlichen Gedanken Wein trinken und dabei das Mysterium des Opfers denken" (*D* 322; "Instead of crucifying yourself or someone else, you can drink wine from a chalice and contemplate the mystery of the sacrifice"; R/L 95). By undergoing his initiation not only aided by ritual but *as ritual,* the protagonist separates himself from the world, which now must no longer be fought for and won in real life, but is perpetually present as a projection of his inner being.

This turn has far-reaching consequences. First, in regard to ritual, there is a risk that valuing it so highly will make it the absolute plane of reality for the subject. If the hero can conquer life in performing the rituals of initiation, there is no longer any reason for him to progress beyond the liminal rites to those of re-integration. Second, in regard to the poetological constitution of the text, extending the notion of the ambiguity of language brings about an essential uncertainty in judging the text's fictional character. To what degree is the world of the narrative reality and to what degree is it a projection of the narrator's consciousness? There is no longer any criterion that prohibits regarding anything or everything about the text as symbolic of someone's state of mind — or any state of mind at all. On its surface, Hesse's novel remains "realistic" and full of concrete details, but it is uncertain whether the individual pieces are real. Does Frau Eva exist? If so, what is she "really" like? How much about her, and which elements, are projections of the narrator? What is their significance for him or the reader?

Clearly, the author has grasped this poetological problem precisely. In proposing a solution, he attempts to justify all of the elements of his poetics of ritual, albeit with some highly problematic results. First of all, he must overcome the tendency to extend the liminal phase any further within Emil's story. To this end, he creates a thematically dominant ritual that he names "Jacob Wrestling" in the title of chapter 6, alluding very consciously to the Old Testament. Here such motifs recur as the ecstatic worship of an image and the condemnation of a holy woman as a whore, of intentional contamination and degradation. The initiate falls into a trance, which is performed as a ritual struggle, for he hears the words of Jacob wrestling with the Angel: "Ich lasse dich nicht, du segnest mich denn" (D 237; "I will not let thee go except thou bless me"; R/L 100).

The blessing of the "Divinity" represented in the ritual icon, which, strictly speaking, represents only a part of Emil's own psyche, a figment of his imagination, evidently concludes the ritual process, and we may assume that he wholeheartedly affirms his autonomous decision to achieve personal sovereignty. A moment of intoxicating ecstasy completes the ritual process: he burns the portrait and eats its ashes.

Following successful completion of the ritual, the novice must leave the liminal phase and begin the rites of re-integration. To accomplish this, Hesse has Emil quarrel with Pistorius, whose purpose has been fulfilled. Sinclair confronts his mentor with this fact, precipitating the break.[46] He reproaches him with pursuing purely "antiquarian" interests[47] and thus with being out of touch with life and incapable of fulfilling his dream of founding a religion. Emil goes on to describe his goals for his own life:

> Es gab keine, keine, keine Pflicht für erwachte Menschen als die eine: sich selber zu suchen, in sich fest zu werden, den eigenen Weg vorwärts zu tasten, einerlei wohin er führte. [. . .] Wahrer Beruf für jeden war nur das eine: zu sich selbst zu kommen. [. . .] Seine Sache war es, das eigene Schicksal zu finden, nicht ein beliebiges, und es in sich auszuleben, ganz und ungebrochen. (D 334–35)

[An enlightened man had but one duty — to seek his way to himself, to reach inner certainty, to grope his way forward, no matter where it led. [. . .] Each man had only one genuine vocation — to find his way to himself. [. . .] His task was to discover his own destiny — not an arbitrary one — and live it out wholly and resolutely within himself. (R/L 107–8)]

These goals differ from Demian's ideas only in the range of their concerns and the terseness and power with which they are expressed. But Emil's concluding reflections introduce a new tone and style:

Viel Einsamkeit hatte ich schon gekostet. Nun ahnte ich, daß es tiefere gab, und daß sie unentrinnbar sei. [. . .] Dann blickte ich in mich und sah meinem Schicksalsbild in die offenen starren Augen. Sie konnten voll Weisheit sein, sie konnten voll Wahnsinn sein, sie konnten Liebe strahlen oder tiefe Bosheit, es war einerlei. Nichts davon durfte man wählen, nichts durfte man wollen. Man durfte nur sich wollen, nur sein Schicksal. (D 336)

[I had already felt much loneliness, now there was a deeper loneliness still which was inescapable. [. . .] Then I would gaze into myself and confront the image of my fate. Its eyes would be full of wisdom, full of madness, they would radiate love or deep malice, it was all the same. You are not allowed to choose or desire any one of them. You were only allowed to desire *yourself,* only your fate. (R/L 109)]

With the completion of the ritual, the style takes on kitschy overtones, and the novel lapses into hollow sentimentality in discussing, towards its close, two major themes that emerge inexorably from earlier developments. Let me recapitulate briefly: Breaking through to fully experiencing life is configured as the ritual initiation of a novice and is based on two prerequisites: first, the adoption of a relativistic worldview that is based on the conviction that possible meanings of phenomena, whether in life or in texts, are subject to a universal indeterminability. In order to overcome this relativism and begin the initiation in earnest, a decision must be made to limit the scope of rhetorical ambivalence. This decision lies in the self-affirmation of the subject, that is, in adopting as a maxim that all phenomena are to be examined and judged in reference to how they enhance the development of the subject's own character as destiny. However, establishing the subject's decision as absolute results in a moral dilemma of every individual having a different system of ethics: the classical "war of everyone against everyone." Resorting once more to individualization resolves this dilemma, for the subject's actions are taken to be metaphoric in character. To support this way of conceiving the world, it is necessary to assume that the essence of the world's being, from its primal beginnings to the future, has been magically implanted into each member of the human species, that is, that the world is an idea. Seen hermeneutically, this amplifies radically the principle of linguistic and moral indeterminacy, leading to a dual solipsism. The initiation into life now concentrates on the rituals themselves, which are no longer the means, but the ends of the initiation, for they have become life itself. Thus, the ritual no longer introduces the novice to life, rather, it itself is life, which is, after all, a projection of the individual's consciousness. The novice finds fulfillment in the repetition of of the ritual, which signifies only itself. A second, hermeneutic, solipsism results, for the principle of ambiguity becomes overextended, foreshortened, and, through abstraction, established as being absolute. Because the subject must necessarily assign ambiguous meanings to data (the traditional "hermeneutic circle"), which no longer refer to life in a real world, not only are meanings uncertain, but a radical randomness prevails, for no judgment regarding a particular consciousness can be communicated. Within the subject, ritual stages a non-referential interiority, whose laws and history can no longer be communicated by mutual consent.[48] In this climate of arbitrariness, sentimentality and ideological themes, which previously had been avoided, become possible.

Thus, Demian's mother, Frau Eva, is introduced with rude directness as the real-life incarnation of the great ritual dream. In a chiaroscuro somewhere between reality and the narrator's fantasy, she achieves an indecipherable double-existence as a widowed single mother with a rather eccentric son, a sorceress murmuring mysterious incantations, and, simultaneously, in a personal union, goddess of a mystical secret cult of which she is the chief priestess.

Discussions between Demian and Emil about "those who bear the mark," which begin soon after they "fatefully" meet again, are analogous to the mystical-mysterious figure of Frau Eva. Demian's critical diagnosis of the age rests upon ideas first stated by Ferdinand Tönnies in his influential study, *Gemeinschaft und Gesellschaft* (Community and Society, 1887):[49]

> Alles vertraute, heimliche, ausschließliche Zusammenleben [. . .] wird als Leben in Gemeinschaft verstanden. Gesellschaft ist die Öffentlichkeit, ist die Welt. [. . .] Gemeinschaft ist das dauernde und echte Zusammenleben, Gesellschaft nur ein vorübergehendes und scheinbares. Und dem ist es gemäß, daß Gemeinschaft selber als ein lebendiger Organismus, Gesellschaft als ein mechanisches Aggregat und Artefact verstanden werden soll.[50]

> [When people live together intimately, domestically, exclusively [. . .] that is life as a community. Society is the public sphere, the world. [. . .] Community is the enduring and authentic way of living together, society only temporary and illusory. Accordingly, we should regard community as a living organism and society as a mechanical assemblage and artifact.]

Demian speaks in a similar vein:

> Überall, sagte er [=Demian], herrsche Zusammenschluß und Herden-
> bildung,[51] aber nirgends Freiheit und Liebe. Alle diese Gemeinsamkeit
> [. . .] sei eine Zwangsbildung, es sei eine Gemeinschaft aus Angst, aus
> Furcht, aus Verlegenheit, und sie sei im Innern faul und alt und dem
> Zusammenbruch nahe. (*D* 340–41)

> [Everywhere, [Demian] said, we could observe the reign of the herd
> instinct, nowhere freedom and love. All the false communion [. . .]
> was an inevitable development, was a community born of fear and
> dread, out of embarrassment, but inwardly rotten, out worn, close to
> collapse (R/L 114–15)]

Demian expects "clashes" that will bring about the end of the world; upon
this background "those who bear the mark" are defined:[52] "Um das, was
von uns bleibt, oder um die von uns, die es überleben, wird der Wille der
Zukunft sich sammeln" (*D* 342; "Around what remains of us, those of us
who survive, the will of the future will gather"; R/L 116). Here, for the
first time, contemporary readers are addressed directly, as they will shape
the future. They too have undergone an initiation; the war, as Hesse sees
it, has transformed them.[53]

Two concealed motifs are significant here: on one hand, Hesse accepts
the experience of warfare as equivalent to individual "rites of passage,"
which, like the war, are essentially accessible to everyone. On the other
hand, he identifies those for whom the war was a true *metanoia* — a spiritual transformation and reorientation — as equivalent to the community
of the "bearers of the mark." This enables him to adopt dual perspectives
regarding the war that confound readers even today, but that are easily
explained in terms of my analysis. When Hesse, writing on politics, condemns war on the one hand, and on the other sees it as a "cleansing" and
the starting point for a radical rearrangement of European culture and morality, the hermeneutic ambivalence we have observed is once again revealed. As a historical phenomenon, war is despicable, but as a personal and
national ritual it can be understood as a concrete metaphor for the fates of
men, and questions of guilt and morality are not raised in this context. The
war ultimately becomes a self-referential ritual because it can convey any
meaning that is assigned to it. The only way out of this spiral of relative
values leads to the community of the "bearers of the mark" gathered
around Frau Eva and Demian:

> Uns Gezeichneten lag keine Sorge um die Gestaltung der Zukunft ob.
> Uns schien jedes Bekenntnis, jede Heilslehre schon im voraus tot und
> nutzlos. Und wir empfanden einzig das als Pflicht und Schicksal: daß
> jeder von uns so ganz er selbst werde, so ganz dem in ihm wirksamen
> Keim der Natur gerecht werde und zu Willen lebe, daß die ungewisse

Zukunft uns zu allem und jedem bereit finde, was sie bringen möchte. (D 349–50)

[We, who bore the mark, felt no anxiety about the shape the future was to take. All of those faiths and teachings seemed to us already dead and useless. The only duty and destiny we acknowledged was that each of us should become so completely himself, so utterly faithful to the active seed which Nature planted within him, that in living out its growth he could be surprised by nothing unknown to come. (R/L 123–24)]

Like the war, Frau Eva is a pure symbol, open to any meaning at all. She is a *sacrum*, a ritual icon, the prayer to which is its own fulfillment, an image in a dream that cannot be fulfilled and becomes transformed into countless further dream images. These transformations ultimately become Frau Eva's actual reality, because they are unique to her. This mystical-mythical figure's totality corresponds to that of the entire text: abstract potentiality. This potentiality remains abstract because it finds its goal and fulfillment in itself, never assuming concrete form: it is the decision for indeterminacy. "Unsere Aufgabe war, in der Welt eine Insel darzustellen, vielleicht ein Vorbild, jedenfalls aber die Ankündigung einer anderen Möglichkeit zu leben" (D 348; "Our task was to represent an island in the world, a prototype perhaps, or at least the prospect of a different way of life"; R/L 122) Yet this open, abstract potentiality yearns for a purpose, and it follows from what has been said that its only possible purpose is to be a part and function of a ritualistic realization of a person's own character as his fate. This is the function fulfilled by Frau Eva: to be a semiotically open *sacrum* for the community of "bearers of the mark," while the community itself fulfills this function for humanity's future development. In this connection, Hesse frequently speaks less of Germany[54] than of Europe:[55]

Die Seele Europas ist ein Tier, das unendlich lang gefesselt lag. Wenn es frei wird, werden seine ersten Regungen nicht die lieblichsten sein. [. . .] Dann wird unser Tag sein, dann wird man uns brauchen, nicht als Führer oder neue Gesetzgeber — die neuen Gesetze erleben wir nicht mehr -, eher als Willige, als solche, die bereit sind, mitzugehen und da zu stehen, wohin das Schicksal ruft. [. . .] Die wenigen, welche dann da sind und mitgehen, werden wir sein. Dazu sind wir gezeichnet [. . .]. Alle Menschen, die auf den Gang der Menschheit gewirkt haben, alle ohne Unterschied, waren nur darum fähig und wirksam, weil sie schicksalbereit waren. (D 350)

[The soul of Europe is a beast that has lain fettered for an infinitely long time. And when it's free, its first movements won't be the gentlest. [. . .] Then our day will come, then we will be needed. Not as leaders or lawgivers — we won't be there to see the new laws — but rather as those who are willing, as men who are ready to go forth and stand prepared wherever fate may need them. [. . .] The few who will be ready at that time and who will go forth — will be us. That is why we are marked [. . .] All men who have had an effect on the course of human history, all of them without exception, were capable and effective only because they were ready to accept the inevitable. (R/L 124)]

Not surprisingly, the reasoning behind this idea, which readers at the time could find plausible and convincing, relies on an analogy from evolutionary biology:

Man muß sich das immer biologisch und entwicklungsgeschichtlich denken! Als die Umwälzungen auf der Erdoberfläche die Wassertiere ans Land, Landtiere ins Wasser warfen, da waren es die schicksalbereiten Exemplare, die das Neue und Unerhörte vollziehen und ihre Art durch neue Anpassungen retten konnten. [. . .] Sie waren bereit, und darum konnten sie ihre Art in neue Entwicklungen hinüber retten. Das wissen wir. Darum wollen wir bereit sein. (D 350–51)

[Always, you must think of these things in evolutionary, in historical terms! When the upheavals of the earth's surface flung the creatures of the sea onto the land and the land creatures into the sea, the specimens of the various orders that were ready to follow their destiny were the ones that accomplished the new and unprecedented; by making new biological adjustments they were able to save their species from destruction. [. . .] [T]hey were ready, and could therefore lead their species into new phases of evolution. That is why we want to be ready. (R/L 124–25)]

The goal of the "rites of passage," then, appears to be to instill preparedness and openness for humanity's future development. As convincing as Demian's argument seems, it is also ambivalent, for his sentiments amount to readiness for his own sacrificial fate in the coming war, which he prophesies and in which he dies. Sinclair, on the other hand, explicitly discusses the situation following the catastrophe. Through this dual, ultimately antithetical, structure, Hesse evokes two significant complexes of themes and motifs. He desires to establish a meaning for the war's incredible human toll, and in this sense *Demian* is an unconventional message of condolence, a *consolatio*. We may regard this part of the argument as the dangerous complement to what is to follow. The sentimentalized discourse of accepting fate is, like rhetorical speech generally, accessible to every kind of perversion and any ideology at all. Reverence for the victims and his wish to console the survivors make the author suppress this danger, for the idea of the community of the "bearers of the mark" fulfills another function for Sinclair, which grows out of the first:

> Und je starrer die Welt auf Krieg und Heldentum, auf Ehre und an-
> dere alte Ideale eingestellt schien, je ferner und unwahrscheinlicher
> jede Stimme scheinbarer Menschlichkeit klang, dies war alles nur die
> Oberfläche, ebenso wie die Frage nach den äußeren und politischen
> Zielen des Krieges nur Oberfläche blieb. In der Tiefe war etwas im
> Werden. Etwas wie eine neue Menschlichkeit. [. . .] Die Urgefühle,
> auch die wildesten, galten nicht dem Feinde, ihr blutiges Werk war
> nur Ausstrahlung des Innern, der in sich zerspaltenen Seele, welche
> rasen und töten, vernichten und sterben wollte, um neu geboren wer-
> den zu können. (*D* 363)

> [The more singlemindedly the world concentrated on war and hero-
> ism, on honor and other old ideals, the more remote and improbable
> any whisper of genuine humanity sounded — that was all just surface,
> in the same way that the question of the war's external and political
> objectives was superficial. Deep down, underneath, something was
> taking shape, something akin to a new humanity. [. . .] The most
> primitive, even the wildest feelings were not directed at the enemy;
> their bloody task was merely an irradiation of the soul, of the soul
> divided within itself, which filled them with the lust to rage and kill,
> annihilate and die, so that they might be born anew. (R/L 138)]

Sinclair's true goal lies in his being prepared to accept his own destiny,
which finds its analogy in the war. He sees himself primarily as a member
of the ritual community of "those who bear the mark."

The narrator is unable and unwilling to leave the liminal phase; his
participation in the real world is unreal, for his true reality is the plane of
ritual within the ritual community, with whose *sanctissima* he would like
to merge as much as possible. Victor Turner describes Gennep's liminal
phase in that sense as *communitas,* his term for the state of "liminality,"
which we have characterized as hermeneutic ambivalence: "The attributes
of liminality or of liminal *personae* ('threshold people') are necessarily ambiguous [. . .]."[56] They elude the strictures of laws, morality, and customs.
Initiates and novices, persons at the border or the threshold, all appear
impoverished and weak; they are powerless and must obey their leaders.
At the same time, an intense communal loyalty and a remarkable solidarity
arise from this situation of weakness equally shared. Turner perceives two
models of communal life here, structure and anti-structure, which oppose
and complement each other and operate in alternation with each other.

From an anthropological and sociological perspective, the liminal phase
serves to reinforce the idea that high and low, power and powerlessness
are complementary constants in life and to inculcate in those members of
society who are later to wield power an understanding of its just and appropriate exercise by having them experience weakness. However, *com-*

munitas, as defined by Victor Turner, includes other marginalized social groups and individuals:[57]

> Communitas, or the "open society," differs in this from structure, or the "closed society," in that it is potentially or ideally extensible to the limits of humanity. In practice, of course, the impetus soon becomes exhausted, and the "movement" becomes itself an institution among other institutions — often one more fanatical and militant than the rest, for the reason that it feels itself to be the unique bearer of universal human truths.[58] [. . .] Exaggeration of communitas, in certain religious or political movements of the leveling type, may be speedily followed by despotism, overbureaucratization, or other models of structural rigidification. For [. . .] those living in community seem to require, sooner or later, an absolute authority, whether this be a religious commandment, a divinely inspired leader, or a dictator.[59]

The dangers we remarked upon in analyzing the text could not be named more clearly, yet, as suggested already, Sinclair avoids this form of the ideology of *communitas.* The narrator refuses simply to rejoin society. His sense of the indeterminacy of phenomena, that perceptions are mere phantasms of an individual consciousness, has degraded reality too much for him to be able to return to it. Yet the community of the "marked" cannot offer him a home,[60] for it is without guidance, producing, on one hand, a precarious fatalism that is prey to any ideology and, on the other, the danger that it will give rise to a totalitarian ideology of rigorous egalitarianism inspired by a radicalization of the "ritual powers of the weak."[61] Symbiosis, even uniting with the dominant figure of the ritual group, proves illusory, for such a fusion would replace the delicate ambivalence between reality and dream with a brutally singular meaning. The sheltering community can only represent an ideal ideological construct that has liberated itself from reality and been conducted into a "twilight zone." Sinclair's *communitas* can only be a haunted house, a dream vision that appears as the symbolic expression of his own inner state, as a moment of epiphany, of revelation, or as an accidental constellation of fragments of reality. Every reality has exactly the meaning that an individual assigns to it.

But what kind of fate awaits Sinclair, who has intimations of his death even within the tranquil life of the community?

> Und je und je ergriff mich über dies Glück eine tiefe Trauer, denn ich wußte wohl, es konnte nicht von Dauer sein. Mir war nicht beschieden, in Fülle und Behagen zu atmen, ich brauchte Qual und Hetze. Ich spürte: eines Tages würde ich aus diesen schönen Liebesbildern erwachen und wieder allein stehen, ganz allein, in der kalten Welt der anderen, wo für mich nur Einsamkeit oder Kampf war, kein Friede, kein Mitleben. (*D* 358)

[Yet at any moment this happiness would produce in me the deepest melancholy, for I knew very well that it could not last. It was not my lot to breathe fullness and comfort, I needed the spur of tormented haste. I felt that one day I would waken from these beloved images of beauty and stand, alone again, in the cold world where there was nothing for me but solitude and struggle — neither peace no relaxation, no easy living together. (R/L 133)]

What possibilities for living in reality are there for such a wanderer between the worlds? A life as a priest, an intellectual, an artist? These are the ideas that Hesse would test aesthetically in *Siddhartha, Steppenwolf,* and *Narziß und Goldmund;* novels whose protagonists present possible solutions to the riddle presented in *Demian.*

— *Translated by Michael M. Metzger*

Notes

[1] The letter *D* followed by a page number denotes quotations from *Demian,* which are taken from Hermann Hesse, *Roßhalde. Knulp. Demian. Siddhartha,* vol. 3 of *Sämtliche Werke,* ed. Volker Michels (Frankfurt am Main: Suhrkamp, 2001); R/L followed by a page number denotes quotations from Hermann Hesse, *Demian: The Story of Emil Sinclair's Youth,* trans. Michael Roloff and Michael Lebeck (New York: Bantam, 1968).

[2] For biographical particulars, see Ralph Freedman, *Hermann Hesse: Autor der Krisis. Eine Biographie* (Frankfurt am Main: Suhrkamp, 1991).

[3] See H. Hesse, *"Die dunkle und wilde Seite der Seele": Briefwechsel mit seinem Psychoanalytiker Josef Bernhard Lang 1916–1944,* ed. Thomas Feitknecht (Frankfurt am Main: Suhrkamp, 2006).

[4] During psychotherapy, it is entirely unthinkable for the therapist and the patient to have a private personal relationship. By current standards, a therapy cannot succeed under these circumstances. Hence it is no suprise that in this case the therapist himself becomes a kind of patient, as the editor of this correspondence reports. See Thomas Feitknecht's foreword to *"Die dunkle und wilde Seite der Seele,"* 14ff.

[5] A summary appears in Walter Jahnke's *Hermann Hesse: Demian. Ein er-lesener Roman* (Paderborn: Schöningh, 1984).

[6] See examples in *Hermann Hesse: Politische und wirkungsgeschichtliche Aspekte,* ed. Sigrid Bauschinger and Albert Reh (Bern: Francke, 1986), especially Robert Conrad, "Socio-political Aspects of Hesse's *Demian,*" 155–65.

[7] This is not contradicted by Hesse's statement in 1918 that he stands "very, very far to the left" politically (Michels, ed., *Materialien zu Hermann Hesses "Demian,"* 2 vols. [Frankfurt am Main: Suhrkamp, 1993, 1997], 1:128; subsequent references to this source will be given as Michels, *Materialien* and volume and page number). Hesse is speaking here of his consistent pacifism, which was an idea shared by no party of that time; today that would not be different. He made the remark before

the founding of the German Communist Party; the Social Democrats had voted in favor of the war.

[8] Lulu von Strauß und Torney, "Hermann Hesse" (1922), in Michels, *Materialien*, 2:63.

[9] Gerhart Sieveking, "Hermann Hesse und wir Jüngsten" (1921), in Michels, *Materialien*, 2:52. Also see Ernst Glaesers descriptive paean "Erinnerung an Demian" (1937), in Michels, *Materialien*, 2:73–75.

[10] Rudolf Kayser, "Emil Sinclais *Demian*" (1919), in Michels, *Materialien*, 2:11.

[11] See, inter alia, Erich Auerbach, "Sermo humilis," *Romanische Forschungen* 64 (1952): 304–64.

[12] Theodore Ziolkowski convincingly portrays the figurations of Christ in *The Novels of Hermann Hesse: A Study in Theme and Structure* (Princeton: Princeton UP, 1965), 87–145; significantly, the chapter on *Demian* is entitled "The Gospel of *Demian*."

[13] By far the greatest number of copies of the novel began to be — and are being — sold fifty years after its first printing.

[14] See Wolfgang Kayser, *Die Wahrheit der Dichter: Wandlung eines Begriffs in der deutschen Literatur* (Hamburg: Rowohlt, 1959) (Rowohlts deutsche Enzyklopädie, vol. 87); Lionel Trilling, *Sincerity and Authenticity*, 7th ed. (Cambridge, MA: Harvard UP, 1964); David Perkins, *Wordsworth and the Poetry of Sincerity* (Cambridge, MA: Belknap Press, 1964); Leon Guilhamet, *The Sincere Ideal: Studies on Sincerity in Eigteenth-Century English Literature* (Montreal: McGill-Queen's UP, 1974).

[15] Cf. Adolf Grolman, "Vom Advent der Seele" (1921), in Michels, *Materialien*, 2:57. Concerning literary confessions as a genre, see Ulrich Breuer, *Bekenntnisse: Diskurs — Gattung — Werk* (Frankfurt am Main: Lang, 2000) (Finnische Beiträge zur Germanistik, vol. 3).

[16] The discussion that follows is based on Arnold van Gennep, *The Rites of Passage* (London: Routledge, 1960 [first published 1908 in French]), Victor Turner, *The Ritual Process: Structure and Anti-Structure* (New York: Routledge, 1969), and Victor Turner, *From Ritual to Theatre: The Human Seriousness of Play* (New York: Performing Arts Journal Publications, 1982) using the abbreviations *Rites, Ritual,* and *Theatre* respectively.

[17] Van Gennep, *Rites*, 26.

[18] Hermann Hesse, "Kinderseele," in *Die Erzählungen 1911–1954*, ed. Volker Michels (Frankfurt am Main: Suhrkamp, 2001) (*Sämtliche Werke*, vol. 8). Hereafter cited as K.

[19] D 237; K 179.

[20] Mary Douglas, *Purity and Danger: An Analysis of Concepts of Pollution and Taboo* (London: Routledge, 1966).

[21] Douglas, *Purity*, 35.

[22] Douglas, *Purity*, 49.

[23] Douglas, *Purity*, 51–52.

[24] Douglas, *Purity*, 53.

[25] Douglas, *Purity*, 94.

[26] "During the marginal period which separates ritual dying and ritual rebirth, the novices in initiation are temporarily outcast. For the duration of the rite they have no place in society. [...] Then we find them behaving like dangerous criminal characters. They are licensed to waylay, steal, rape. This behaviour is even enjoined on them. To behave anti-socially is the proper expression of their marginal condition" (Douglas, *Purity*, 96–97).

[27] It is not possible to explore here the interesting arguments offered by the psychoanalytical perspective; see Sigmund Freud, *Totem und Tabu: Einige Übereinstimmungen im Seelenleben der Wilden und der Neurotiker* (Frankfurt am Main: Fischer, 1999) (*Gesammelte Werke*, vol. 9) and Franz Steiner, *Taboo* (New York: Philosophical Library, 1956). Julia Kristeva's fundamental study, *Powers of Horror: An Essay on Abjection* (New York: Columbia UP, 1982) must be mentioned here, as must her *Black Sun: Depression and Melancholia* (New York: Columbia UP, 1989). Hesse's *Demian* offers numerous starting points for any psychoanalytic interpretation seeking to look beyond the simple representation of Jungian archetypes with the help of Kristeva, Freud, and Lacan.

[28] Interestingly, Kromer appears as a kind of hunter-gatherer and projects a sense of the archaic.

[29] The shadow as metaphor plays an important part in *Demian* from the very beginning, as Jungians have been foremost in pointing out. I don't find it necessary to assign such specific significance to a literary motif that is so common. Shadows appear and function in many discursive contexts from antiquity onward, and they also play an important role in the ethnology of cultures.

[30] He shares other attributes with traditional sorcerers: he is rumored to belong to an unusual sect and to possess great wealth and extraordinary physical strength. (D 258; R/L 27) It is believed that he defeats opponents with "magical" acts and not through violence. The way Demian deals with Kromer reinforces this idea.

[31] Van Gennep, *Rites*, 79.

[32] Van Gennep, *Rites*, 79.

[33] Hesse's poetic conception here depends on the identity of the semiotic sign with the distinguishing sign (the mark of Cain), so that the sign becomes a stigma — and vice versa. The subversive element, then, lies in the inversion of the order, in making the stigma dominant: "The first element of the story, its actual beginning, was the mark" (D 255; R/L 24).

[34] This discussion cannot be pursued in detail here; I mention it only to give a sense of the intellectual scope of Hesse's text. Regarding the nomos-physis problem, see W. K. C. Guthrie, *The Sophists* (Cambridge: Cambridge UP, 1971) and G. B. Kerferd, *The Sophistic Movement* (Cambridge: Cambridge UP, 1981).

[35] This is not meant in regard to evolutionary biology, as it is not the strong who survive, but those who can best adapt to new circumstances; the idea that nature postulates laws of "humane" feelings such as filial love or gratitude is untenable from a biological point of view. In both cases, "nature" must be understood in a metaphoric sense.

[36] Nonetheless, these conclusions reveal a central problem of the text: Demian's philosophy of power does not overtly call for a kind of "super-man," an "Über-

mensch" in the sense of contemporary enthusiasm for Nietzsche, but it could easily be understood as doing so. The protagonist's ambivalent attitude toward war is in keeping with such a reading, as critics have frequently noted. See *Hermann Hesse: Politische und wirkungsgeschichtliche Aspekte,* ed. Sigrid Bauschinger and Albert Reh (Bern: Francke, 1986). Demian, however, whom we may imagine as a precocious high-school student and not as a mature thinker, seems to represent a mediating position that, proceeding from a more complex idea of nature, does not set forth the purely egoistic-utilitarian thesis of "might makes right." Contrary to the *nomos* vs. *physis* controversy, Demian's argument does not relate to society insofar as he assigns to the individual an absolute right to his own being; the individual reserves for himself a domain, *vita solitaria,* which he must defend against the totalitarian demands of society. It is not difficult to perceive here the model of "liminal rites," which prepares such a domain and serves as a community of initiates similarly chosen. A comment: The "marked" Harry Potter is not very different; he too undergoes a ritual initiation in a group of initiates of equal status, among whom he nevertheless plays a special role.

[37] Hesse is not alone in this belief; the idea that literature in itself is neither good nor evil, but depends for its effect on the uses to which it is put, has been familiar since antiquity.

[38] Regarding Luther, see Gerhard Ebeling, *Luther: Eine Einführung in sein Denken,* 4th revised ed. (Tübingen: Mohr, 1981).

[39] Carl Schmitt, *Politische Theologie: Vier Kapitel zur Lehre von der Souveränität* (1922; Berlin: Duncker & Humblot, 1985), 11. Also: Carl Schmitt, *Der Begriff des Politischen* (1932; Berlin: Duncker & Humblot, 1991).

[40] Here again, the allusion to the magical-religious is evident. Rudolf Otto mentions "fascinosum" and "tremendum" as characteristics of the sacred. See Otto, *Das Heilige: Über das Irrationale in der Idee des Göttlichen und sein Verhältnis zum Rationalen* (1979; reprint, Munich: Beck, 1987).

[41] If Emil still worships the holy image of Beatrice, that is also ritualistic behavior, if only in a dream and *in effigiem.* Before he creates the picture in the first place, he dreams of Demian pointing out the heraldic bird, which is constantly transformed in his hands: "Zuletzt aber nötigte er mich, das Wappen zu essen. Als ich es geschluckt hatte, spürte ich mit ungeheurem Erschrecken, daß der verschlungene Wappenvogel in mir lebendig sei, mich ausfülle und von innen zu verzehren beginne" (D 303; "In the end he obliged me to eat the coat of arms! When I had swallowed it, I felt to my horror that the heraldic bird was coming to life inside me, had begun to swell up and devour me from within"; R/L 73–74).

[42] Evidently, Hesse chooses this "scientific" introduction in order to convey to his readers the factuality of this godhead; otherwise they could have assumed that he had created a convenient fiction.

[43] The special significance of this dream is given great emphasis; it is "der wichtigste und nachhaltigste meines Lebens" (D 307; "the most important and enduringly significant of my life"; R/L 79).

[44] Here, the groundwork is being laid for the complex of problematic motifs in *Steppenwolf* that will culminate in the fantasized murder of Hermine.

[45] Such ideas are confirmed by Pistorius: "Die Dinge, die wir sehen [. . .] sind die-selben Dinge, die in uns sind. Es gibt keine Wirklichkeit als die, die wir in uns haben. Darum leben die meisten Menschen so unwirklich, weil sie die Bilder außerhalb für das Wirkliche halten und ihre eigene Welt in sich gar nicht zu Worte kommen lassen" (D 323; "The things we see [. . .] are the same things that are within us. There is no reality except the one contained within us. That is why so many people live such an unreal life. They take the images outside them for reality and never allow the world within to assert itself"; R/L 96). It is easy to connect such thinking with the psychedelic "revolution's" philosophy of drugs. Hesse's *Demian* does suggest such a scenario, but it is artistically valid because it is not represented as a solution, but as a problem that is solved neither here nor in *Steppenwolf.*

[46] The narrator treats this parting as a thematic part of the ritual; the ability to turn away at the right moment becomes a result of the successful initiation. See: D 330–31; R/L 104ff.

[47] In using the term "antiquarian" here (D 332–33; R/L 105) Hesse is drawing from the second of Nietzsche's "Unzeitgemäße Betrachtungen" (Thoughts Out of Season), *Vom Nutzen und Nachtheil der Historie für das Leben* (On the Uses and Misuses of History), in which Nietzsche differentiates three ways to regard history: the monumental, the antiquarian, and the critical. In part, Hesse does Pistorius an injustice in understating his eccentric unconventionality, which does not quite fit in with an "antiquarian" nature. The echo of Nietzsche is significant in light of the true approach to history, the "critical," which will characterize the final chapters.

[48] This is the reason for Hesse's often expressed aversion to engaging in explorative psychological conversations, as becomes evident in the idea that people talk too much and that nothing good comes from that.

[49] Ferdinand Tönnies, *Gemeinschaft und Gesellschaft: Grundbegriffe der reinen Sozio-logie,* revised ed. (Darmstadt: Wissenschaftliche Buchgesellschaft, 1970). In his study, Tönnies also deals with ethnological research, which he uses in formulating his theses.

[50] Tönnies, *Gemeinschaft,* 3, 5. Further points of agreement with Tönnies cannot be discussed here.

[51] The term "herd" and compounds derived from it suggest, in the first instance, Nietzsche's *Zarathustra;* but it can also be associated with early theorists of the psychology of the masses, e.g.: Gustave Le Bon, *Psychologie der Massen* (Stuttgart: Kröner 1911; first published in French, 1895) and Sigmund Freud, *Massen-psychologie und Ich-Analyse,* which, however appeared in 1921, after *Demian.* Direct influences are less a consideration than the fact that the author came to grips with ideas current at the time, doubtless, too, so that his book would enjoy the greatest possible popularity.

[52] Demian mentions the mark of Cain at the start of their conversation as an iden-tifying characteristic. (D 340; R/L 114).

[53] Demian comments almost cynically: "Es wird mir ja im Grunde kein Vergnügen machen, Gewehrfeuer auf lebende Menschen zu kommandieren, aber das wird ne-bensächlich sein" (D 360; "Of course, it's not going to be any fun to order men to fire on living beings, but that will be incidental"; R/L 136).

[54] Hesse expressly shared Nietzsche's reservations about nationalism, especially the narrow-minded nationalism of the Germans.

[55] Hesse is alluding here, as he often does, to Novalis, in this case to his great essay *Die Christenheit oder Europa* (Christendom or Europe).

[56] Victor Turner, *The Ritual Process,* 95.

[57] The obvious analogies with M. Bakhtin's concept of the carnivalesque cannot be discussed here.

[58] This assurance that they belong to the group of "those prepared for their fates," which will determine future events, characterizes both Sinclair and Demian. Turner associates these movements with situations of extreme historical and political change, such as the period of the First World War: "Mostly, such movements occur during phases of history that are in many respects 'homologous' to the liminal periods of important rituals in stable and repetitive societies, when major groups or social categories in those societies are passing from one cultural state to another. They are essentially phenomena of transition" (Turner, *Ritual Process,* 112).

[59] Turner, *Ritual Process,* 112, 129. Max Weber described the problem of the institutionalization of charismatic and communitarian movements vividly and in classical form in *Wirtschaft und Gesellschaft: Grundriss der verstehenden Soziologie* (1925) 5th rev. ed. (Tübingen: Mohr, 1990) and Karl Mannheim: *Ideologie und Utopie* (1929; Frankfurt: Klostermann, 1985.

[60] Frau Eva declares at the very beginning: "Heim kommt man nie [. . .]. Aber wo befreundete Wege zusammenlaufen, da sieht die ganze Welt für eine Stunde wie Heimat aus" (D 345; "One never reaches home. [. . .] But where paths that have affinity for each other intersect, the whole world looks like home, for a time"; R/L 119).

[61] Turner, *Ritual Process,* 102.

4: *Klein und Wagner*

Stefan Höppner

COMPOSED IN MAY AND JULY 1919, the middle text of Hesse's *Klingsor* volume has received little critical attention to date. This is all the more surprising since *Klein und Wagner* is not only the first major text the author composed in Montagnola, and is also proof that Hesse had begun to adapt psychoanalysis to his own needs, adding his own twist to the more orthodox understanding of C. G. Jung's theories that had dominated *Demian*. Moreover, the novella introduces key themes and motifs that dominate Hesse's writing during the following decade or so, including, in particular, some striking connections to *Steppenwolf*. Finally, the extreme concentration of this piece is particularly notable: among Hesse's major tales, this text has the smallest number of characters, the shortest time span, and arguably the most concentrated treatment of theme. According to Hesse's biographer Joseph Mileck, the five chapters of the text can be interpreted as equivalent to the five acts of a drama.[1] The combination of these elements makes *Klein und Wagner* one of the most fascinating texts of the author's middle years.

Klein und Wagner tells the story of Friedrich Klein, a middle-aged minor clerk who has embezzled from his employer and absconded to Northern Italy or Ticino, the Italian-speaking part of Switzerland — the text remains deliberately vague about this — with forged documents. However, Klein is not a common criminal, but rather a self-alienated, tormented bourgeois in search of peace and self-fulfillment. While pondering his fate, he recognizes that his primary motivation was a "Zwang und Drang,"[2] a compulsion and urge, to murder his wife and children, which he could only avoid by entirely abandoning his old life. This dark drive is associated with the name Wagner, which alludes to the famous composer and also an actual German schoolteacher who in September 1913 had killed his wife and children. In spite of his flight, Klein fails to transcend his pain: instead of feeling liberated, he regards himself as a victim of his own thoughts, his brain "ein Kaleidoskop, in dem der Wechsel der Bilder von einer fremden Hand geleitet wurde" (210; "a kaleidoscope in which the shifting images were directed by another's hand," *Klein* 46). Throughout the novella, Klein repeatedly ponders suicide — that he is serious about this is indicated by the fact that he carries a gun.

In this desperate situation he meets "die Gelbe" (229), a young blonde courtesan who mingles with the local art crowd. Initially appalled by her looks, he is increasingly drawn to her, although his stance remains ambivalent: "Etwas an ihr lockte, erzählte von Glück und Innigkeit, duftete nach Fleisch und Haar und gepflegter Schönheit, und etwas anderes stieß ab, schien unecht, ließ Enttäuschung fürchten" (237; "Something about her lured him, spoke of happiness and intimacy, was redolent of flesh and hair and groomed beauty, and something else repelled, seemed inauthentic, made him fear disappointment," *Klein* 82). To Klein, the color of her hair soon symbolizes her great vitality as well as her connection to the eternal feminine.[3] After he overhears her name, Teresina, and watches her dance, they finally meet.

During a long conversation in the park during the following morning, they recognize they have something in common, being tormented by the present, occupying a position in-between the underworld and an honorable, bourgeois society. At the same time, Teresina embodies a state that Klein desires for himself: "Wenn Sie tanzen [. . .] sind Sie wie ein Baum oder ein Berg oder Tier, oder ein Stern, ganz für sich, ganz allein, Sie wollen nichts anderes sein als was sie sind, einerlei ob gut oder böse" (246; "When you dance [. . .] you're like a tree or a mountain or an animal, or like a star, altogether alone, altogether by yourself. You don't want to be anything different from what you are, whether good or bad," *Klein* 94).[4] When Teresina asks him about his background, he refuses to give a straightforward answer: "Sie wollen mich ja nicht verstehen und auch sich selber nicht [. . .] Sie versuchen es mit dem Verbrecher und mit dem Geisteskranken, Sie wollen meinen Stand und Namen wissen. Das alles aber führt nur weg vom Verstehen, [. . .] ist vielmehr Flucht vor dem Verstehenwollen" (248; "You don't want to understand me, or yourself either. [. . .] You've tried it with the idea of a criminal and a madman. You want to know my name and status. But all that only leads away from understanding. [. . .] it's an escape from wanting to understand [. . .]," *Klein* 95–96). After this conversation, he feels reconciled with nature, and experiences the Southern landscape as an epiphany. In the evening he walks to a remote village and seeks to participate in the simple life of the Italian-speaking peasants. After a harmonious evening, his neglected hostess enters Klein's chamber to sleep with him, but during their love-making he feels shaken by the premonition that love is only bound to disappoint him, and flees the house.

Fighting the thought of suicide, Klein strays through the Southern night. For a brief moment, he even places his head on the railway tracks (261). Exhausted, he feels he has temporarily overcome his demons, falls asleep, and dreams of a theater with a sign over the entrance spelling either "Lohengrin" or "Wagner." Upon entering, he stabs a monstrous woman who resembles both his wife and the Italian peasant woman; simultaneously, another identical woman attempts to strangle him. Upon waking up, Klein recognizes the significance of his dream:

Das Theater mit der Aufschrift "Wagner," war das nicht er selbst, war es nicht die Aufforderung, in sich selbst einzutreten, in das fremde Land in seinem Innern? Denn Wagner war er selber — Wagner war der Mörder und Gejagte in ihm, aber Wagner war auch der Komponist, der Künstler, das Genie, der Verführer, die Neigung zu Lebenslust, Sinnenlust, Luxus — Wagner war der Sammelname für alles Unterdrückte, Untergesunkene, zu kurz Gekommene in dem ehemaligen Beamten Friedrich Klein. (262)

[The theater called "Wagner" — was that not himself, was it not an invitation to enter into his own interior being, into the foreign land of his true self? For Wagner was himself — Wagner was the murderer and the hunted man within him, but Wagner was also the composer, the artist, the genius, the seducer, lover of life and the sense, luxury — Wagner was the collective name for everything repressed, buried, scanted in the life of Friedrich Klein, the former civil servant. (*Klein* 116)]

The following morning, Klein finally returns to his hotel and invites Teresina to take a boat to nearby Castiglione with him to gamble at the local casino there — a wish of hers he had overheard in an earlier conversation. Klein is motivated by his infatuation for Teresina and their apparent similarities of character. But while gambling bores him quickly, his lover continues for many hours — not because she is addicted to gambling, but because she aims to win enough to give up her profession. Although Klein gradually becomes aware of their fundamental differences, and although his fear and desire blend into one, they are still attracted to each other, and end the night as lovers.

In the long run, however, their relationship leaves Klein unfulfilled, and he and Teresina ultimately remain strangers throughout the text. During one humid summer night, Klein awakes appalled and ponders murdering Teresina, who now temporarily reminds him of his wife. Once again he threatens to repeat Wagner's deeds — and his dream. Klein "war in das Theater Wagner eingetreten" (276; "had entered Wagner's theater," *Klein* 134). However, when he looks into Teresina's mirror, Klein recognizes that it is himself he wants to kill. He finally walks to the lake, steals a boat, rows out on the water and lets himself drop into the waves. Before he drowns, he recognizes that his suicide is ridiculous and unnecessary. Nonetheless, he undergoes an epiphany in which he finally lets go of his ego (as well as his alter ego, Wagner). In dying, he eventually finds the fulfillment he desires:

Jetzt vernahm Klein seine eigene Stimme. Er sang. Mit einer neuen, gewaltigen, hellen, hallenden Stimme sang er laut und hallend Gottes Lob, Gottes Preis. Er sang im rasenden Dahinschwimmen, inmitten der Millionen Geschöpfe, ein Prophet und Verkünder. Laut schallte sein Lied, hoch stieg das Gewölbe der Töne auf, strahlend saß Gott im Innern. Ungeheuer brausten die Ströme hin. (283)

[Now Klein heard his own voice. He was singing. With a new, mighty, high, reverberating voice he sang loudly, loudly and resoundingly sang God's praise. He sang as he floated along in the rushing stream in the midst of the millions of creatures. He had become a prophet and proclaimer. Loudly, his song resounded; the vault of music rose high; radiantly, God sat within it. The streams roared tremendously along. (*Klein* 144)]

In his death, Klein both fails and meets his goals, unable to transcend his earthly struggles, while at least achieving a "symbolic reunification with totality."[5]

Klein und Wagner was first published in October 1919, printed in *Vivos voco,* a short-lived periodical edited by Hesse and Richard Woltereck. The intellectual monthly's aim was "to bring together disaffected or unaligned members of the fragmented German youth movement into a coherent group which would work for the reconstruction of a new German society."[6] Woltereck (1877–1944) was a prominent German zoologist who had put his professorship on hold to work for the German embassy in Bern, where he and Hesse joined forces to distribute and publish books for the Deutsche Kriegsgefangenenfürsorge, or aid to prisoners of war.[7]

Later, *Klein und Wagner* was also included in the *Klingsor* volume (1920) alongside the tales *Kinderseele* (written while still residing in Bern) and *Klingsor's Letzter Sommer,* another product of the first flash of creativity Hesse experienced in Montagnola (see Ralph Freedman's article in this volume). In 1931, *Klein und Wagner* found its place in the collection *Weg nach innen,* alongside *Siddhartha* and — once again — the *Klingsor* novella. Beginning with Hugo Ball's Hesse biography,[8] many interpretations have thus focused on *Klein und Wagner* as part of the "journey inward" characteristic for the author's middle period rather than looking at the text as an autonomous whole.

At the time, Hesse himself considered *Klein und Wagner* "das Beste, was ich bisher gemacht habe, ein Bruch mit meiner früheren Art und der Beginn von etwas ganz Neuem. Schön und holdselig ist diese Dichtung nicht, mehr wie Cyankali, aber sie ist gut und war notwendig"[9] (the best that I have done so far, a break with my earlier style and the beginning of something completely new. Beautiful and lovely this work is not, more like cyanide, but it is good and was necessary). Stylistically, *Klein und Wagner* marks a new departure insofar as both the vocabulary and the metaphors are now strongly influenced by Expressionism.[10] As Rolf Georg Bogner points out, the text is remarkably rich in the parallelisms, repetitions, and synesthetic effects typical for the literature from this period[11] — a tendency that Hesse even radicalized in *Klingsors letzter Sommer*.[12]

Autobiography

Among the most obvious features of *Klein und Wagner* are the striking autobiographical parallels. Hesse closely identified with all protagonists from this period — "Ich [. . .] war Sinclair, war Klingsor, war Klein etc. und werde noch manches sein"[13] (I . . . was Sinclair, was Klingsor, was Klein, etc. and will be many other things too), as he wrote to his analyst, Joseph Bernhard Lang. In spite of this general tendency, *Klein und Wagner* is arguably, as Joseph Mileck has written, "the most ruthless of Hesse's many self-exposures."[14] The publication in 2006 of the correspondence between Hesse and Lang has demonstrated just how much of Hesse's thinly veiled autobiography went into the text: by 1919, Hesse's first wife Maria (Mia) Hesse-Bernoulli had been diagnosed as mentally ill. The author was still uncertain whether to seek a divorce. In addition, he feared the responsibility for raising their three sons, Bruno, Heiner, and Martin. Beneath Klein's identification with the murderer Wagner, Martin Stingelin argues, lurks a "barely dismissable impulse to snuff out one's own family — with the aim of getting rid of responsibility and clearing the way for the possibilities of artistic development."[15] At the same time, Hesse was still reeling from the death of his father and the inimical German responses to his opposition to the First World War. In the spring of 1919, Hesse finally succumbed to his urge to escape and left Bern for Ticino, where he would soon settle down in the mountain village of Montagnola.

Amidst this inner turmoil, Lang sheltered his patient from some of the immediate consequences of his escape: he was instrumental in finding a home for Hesse's children, paid visits to Mia Hesse, and contacted Mia's brother Fritz Bernoulli about a possible divorce.[16] Moreover, Lang shared his friend's general skepticism about marriage. While Hesse's protagonist Veraguth in *Roßhalde* only doubts that married life is incompatible with artistic creativity, Lang launched an attack on marriage in general:

> Your marriage and family conflict is a contemporary one; I encounter it with all human beings who are strongly progressively oriented. The marriage itself will have to be overcome after all. The bonds of the family must be undone. Isn't it strange that most founders of religions were against monogamous marriage: it exists, like all monopolies, as an academic arrangement for order and maintenance of the status quo, for the dear state, which hates and must hate all progressivism.[17]

In fact, shortly thereafter it was Lang who sought to solve the problems with his own wife and children in a similar fashion and even asked Hesse for advice on how to proceed.[18]

Whereas the character Klein remains trapped in his identification with Wagner, writing down his story proved instrumental for Hesse in overcoming his deep personal crisis, at least for the time being: "Klein ist ein Stück Hesse und wird es immer sein, und ohne ihn, ohne die Übertragung meines Leidens in diesen Spiegel, hätte ich dies Leiden nicht ertragen. Es ist meine Rettung gewesen, daß ich in die Einsamkeit ging und vollkommen Tag und Nacht in meiner Dichtung lebte"[19] (Klein is a part of Hesse and will always be; without him, without the transference of my suffering into this mirror, I would not have been able to bear this suffering. It was my salvation that I escaped into solitude and lived completely, day and night, in my writing). To Hesse, writing *Klein und Wagner* fulfilled a clear therapeutic purpose: "Je weniger wir uns vor unserer eigenen Phantasie scheuen, die im Wachen und im Traum uns zu Verbrechern und Tieren macht, desto kleiner ist die Gefahr, daß wir in der Tat und Wirklichkeit an diesem Bösen zugrund gehen"[20] (The less we shy away from our own imagination, which in waking and in dreams makes us into criminals and animals, the less danger there is that we in fact and reality meet our downfall due to this evil). Hesse thus eventually succeeded in regaining artistic freedom, even if only temporarily, by pushing his family aside. However, as the following essays in this book will demonstrate, this newly won freedom did not mark the end of his personal crisis.

Klein and Wagner, or: What's in a Name?

The names Hesse chose for his protagonist's double nature are highly significant. "Klein" of course points to the protagonist's "kleinbürgerlich" or petty bourgeois origin, but also to the small-mindedness that prevents him from finding a solution short of suicide for his inner conflicts. At the same time, the surname Klein hints at his insignificance and his status as a "braver Beamter" (211; obedient official). While Klein's exact job is never mentioned, his status as a *Beamter,* or petty official, suggests that he has previously been a low-ranking member of the bureaucratic machinery so often associated with modern society. In this context, one of Hesse's contemporaries, the philosopher and sociologist Alfred Weber (1868–1958), described a profound bureaucratization of society that threatened to progressively eliminate any freedom the individual still had.[21] Historically, the term *Beamter* refers to an employee of the state, whose duty, in exchange for lifelong employment, it is to carry out any order from his supervisors. In German-language cultures, the *Beamter* is thus often associated with elaborated bureaucratic procedures, sometimes inefficient, murderous, or bizarre — a criticism most prominent in the writings of Franz Kafka.[22] In this light, Klein not only breaks from the secure existence of the bourgeois family man; by identifying with Wagner, he also wrestles himself free from the powerful grip of a modern bureaucracy that had both employed and exerted control over him.

At the same time, Klein's first name Friedrich points to various figures in German literary history and philosophy that were of great importance to Hesse, such as Schiller, Hölderlin, and Hegel,[23] but also von Hardenberg (Novalis), and most of all, Nietzsche. The combination of "Friedrich" and "Klein" marks the juxtaposition of genius and criminal,[24] or at least of genius and everyday bourgeois — a symbol of the violent split tormenting Klein.[25]

The name Wagner points to a more complex relationship. As Klein himself notices, the name Wagner alludes to both the composer Richard Wagner and the mass murderer Ernst Wagner (224). While the latter is of greater significance to the story, some attention should be paid to the composer as well. When the name Wagner suddenly emerges in the text, it is the famous Richard Wagner who first comes to mind. As a young man, Klein had enthusiastically embraced Wagner's music, especially the opera *Lohengrin*. Later, he had become more critical. Now, Klein concludes, he has grown to hate Wagner because he reminds him of the mistakes of his youth, "weil Jugend und Schwärmerei und Wagner und all das ihn peinlich an Verlorenes erinnerten, weil er sich von einer Frau hatte heiraten lassen, die er nicht liebte, oder doch nicht genug" (224; "because youth and artistic enthusiasm and Wagner and all the rest reminded him painfully of things he had lost, because he had let himself be married by a woman he did not love, or at any rate not in the right way, not sufficiently," *Klein* 64). Initially, then, Wagner figures merely as a convenient symbol for Klein's self-hatred, since he is not yet fully aware of his destructive and auto-destructive impulses.

Klein's rejection of Richard Wagner can be read as an autobiographical reference as well. Very much like Klein, as a young man Hesse was fascinated by the composer,[26] and Wagner figures prominently in the early texts. In Hesse's breakthrough novel, *Peter Camenzind* (1904), it is a musician named Richard who introduces the protagonist to the contemporary arts, and it is a passage from Wagner's *Die Meistersinger von Nürnberg* that he first plays to Camenzind.[27] Later in life, Hesse became much more skeptical of Wagner — a tendency that peaks in *Steppenwolf,* where Harry Haller encounters an endless black-clad caravan in the Magic Theater, consisting of nothing but superfluous parts in the orchestrations of Wagner and Brahms.[28] In *Klein und Wagner* there are no signs of this mockery, and the only piece of music the text explicitly mentions is *Lohengrin,* formerly Klein's favorite piece (224). However, like Klein, the protagonist in Richard Wagner's opera is a man who needs to guard his true identity from others as well; uttering his true name would spell doom. Finally, when Klein dreams of the murder scene in the "Theater Wagner," he is uncertain whether the sign above the entrance says "Wagner" or "Lohengrin."

The frequent allusions to the composer Wagner in connection with Klein's first name lead to an alternative reading of the novella: on a second level, it is possible to read *Klein und Wagner* as homage to and a distancing from Nietzsche, whose reception arguably bore a great influence on Hesse's early works. Like Klein, Nietzsche started out as a Wagner enthusiast and greatly shaped the subsequent Wagner reception through his treatise *Die Geburt der Tragödie aus dem Geiste der Musik* (The Birth of Tragedy out of the Spirit of Music, 1872). Nietzsche's enthusiasm, however, later turned into ambivalence and even rejection, documented in the essay *Der Fall Wagner* (The Case of Wagner, 1888). Nietzsche's antipathy toward Wagner, based on his disappointment with the composer's aesthetic and political philosophies, is "der Haß des enttäuschten Liebhabers,"[29] as is Klein's. In this respect, Klein's struggle with Richard Wagner can be interpreted as a tribute to Nietzsche's conflict with the composer. Since Klein and Wagner are essentially the same person, and Klein's hatred is also a form of self-loathing, the novella can also be read as a poetical version of Hesse's distancing from Nietzsche. If Nietzsche is like Klein, his most significant shortcoming would then be that he remained trapped in his inner conflicts (such as his conflict with Wagner) and was unable to transcend to the higher spiritual planes he aspired to and which he described in his writings. That is to say that Hesse portrays the limitations of Nietzsche's philosophy in Klein and thus arrives at the insight that the philosopher can no longer serve as a guide to his own inner struggles.

On the whole, however, the novella deals much less with the composer than it does with the *other* Wagner. From this perspective, it is surprising that criticism has hitherto paid little attention to Hesse's choice. Few studies on this issue have been published,[30] and they leave some important questions unanswered.

In September 1913, Ernst August Wagner (1874–1938), a schoolteacher from the Stuttgart area, first murdered his wife and his four children, and then went on a killing spree in Mühlhausen, a nearby village, killing eight and wounding twelve more people.[31] He had even planned to continue his spree and end it with a dramatic climax in a palace in nearby Ludwigsburg.[32] Although Wagner had carefully planned his crime, he was not sentenced to death — the lawful punishment at the time — but instead transferred to a mental institution, where he died an old man. Throughout his lifetime, Wagner remained famous due to numerous writings published by his psychiatrist, Robert Gaupp. Although the first of them, *Zur*

Psychologie des Massenmords: Hauptlehrer Wagner von Degerloch, was published in 1914,[33] Hesse does not appear to have read it, nor did he apparently read any of Gaupp's clinical studies that continued to appear over the next few decades. It is more likely that he heard about Wagner from Otto Hartmann, a fellow pupil from his Maulbronn days,[34] and from the philosopher Christoph Schrempf (1860–1944), a friend and mentor of Hesse's, to whom Wagner had sent one of his farewell letters before he went on his killing spree.[35] In this letter, he had asked the "free thinker" and former theologian to provide for the publication of his writings[36] — a request Schrempf did not fulfill.

Klein readily identifies with Ernst Wagner because the schoolteacher does what he does not dare;[37] and although Klein remembers his disgust upon first hearing about the crime, he now re-interprets his initial reaction: "Schon damals [. . .] habe sein Innerstes dessen Tat verstanden, verstanden und gebilligt, und seine so heftige Entrüstung und Erregung sei nur daraus entstanden, daß der Philister und Heuchler in ihm die Stimme des Herzens nicht habe gelten lassen" (221; "Even then [. . .] you understood his act in your heart, understood and improved it, and your outrage and agitation sprang only from your own philistine, hypocritical refusal to admit what you really knew inwardly," *Klein* 60). Klein now realizes that the crime he would officially be persecuted for — embezzling — was only secondary to his urge to escape his family in order to avoid repeating Wagner's crimes (218–19). Klein realizes his double nature as a potential killer *and* a Philistine, unable to decide between these options.

Although Hesse — like his protagonist — hardly seems capable of actually committing such an atrocious crime, it is obvious that the case of Ernst Wagner provided him with a convenient image of his own struggles, which he then committed to writing. In this respect, it is instructive that *Klein und Wagner* deals only with part of the actual crimes. While Klein repeatedly refers to Wagner's murder of his family, the subsequent killing spree is never mentioned. Whether Hesse actually knew about this part of the story when he wrote *Klein und Wagner* is not known. In any case, it is important to note that Klein does not know, or does not remember, these facts. Most likely, he represses the other crimes from his memory because they do not fit his identification with his "teacher," Wagner. While Klein's aggressions are directed at his family, at Teresina, and at himself, he is not driven by revenge for any real or imagined injustice. For the real Wagner, in contrast, murdering his family seems to have been secondary to his grander schemes. In the first place, the schoolteacher was driven by his desire to take revenge on the people of Mühlhausen,[38] where he served as a teacher from 1901 to 1902, felt unfairly treated, and first met his wife, with whom he lived in an unhappy marriage.[39]

It is possible that Ernst Wagner may have served as a reference point for Hesse, since his name offered a neat link to Hesse's former favorite composer, which he then complemented with a main character bearing the first name of his former main philosophical influence. But there are further reasons to be taken into consideration: It is possible that Hesse also identified with Wagner because the killer was from Hesse's own home area, Swabia.

Last but not least, there is a biographical parallel that seems to have remained unexplored to this day: Like Hesse, Ernst August Wagner was a writer. Starting in 1894, he composed numerous dramas. Most of these plays dealt with biblical and historical figures, such as Nero, David, or Absalom. Moreover, Wagner composed two treatises related to his work (*Der Unteroffizier-Schulmeister* and *Die Deutsche Rechtschreibung*), as well as an autobiography, whose title *Auch Einer* was taken from Friedrich Theodor Vischer's then-popular novel of 1879, while its tone was modeled on Nietzsche's autobiographical writings. Except for some self-published dramas, Wagner's writings remained unpublished during his lifetime.[40] Wagner regarded himself as equal or superior to Schiller, his fellow Swabian:[41]

> [I]ch weiß nicht, wie Theaterkritiker und sogar Literaturgeschichtsschreiber dazu kommen können, von einer neuen Ära des deutschen Dramas zu schreiben. Denn mich kennen sie ja gar nicht. [. . .] [I]ch will es euch laut in die Ohren schreien, daß ich der größte Dramatiker der Gegenwart bin. Jeder Satz, den ich schreibe, legt Zeugnis davon ab.[42]

> [I don't know how theater critics and even literary historians could come to write of a new era of German drama. Because they don't know of me at all. . . . I want to shout it loudly in your ears that I am the greatest contemporary dramatist. Every sentence that I write bears witness to that.]

In Wagner, Hesse may have recognized his own darker sides as an author. Often plagued by self-doubts about his writings, he may have asked himself whether his art was in fact just as worthless as Wagner's plays. According to his own "Kurzgefaßter Lebenslauf" (Brief Curriculum Vitae, 1925), these self-doubts became especially prominent in the wake of the deep crisis during and after the First World War,[43] the very period during which Hesse composed *Klein and Wagner*. From a biographical point of view, the case of Wagner may have supported and enlarged these self-doubts, possibly rendering his own literary efforts as questionable as those of an obvious madman.

Moreover, the biographies of Hesse and Wagner intersected in at least one point. Like the schoolteacher, Hesse had turned to Christoph Schrempf before, attracted by the former theologians' fame as a free spirit (12:428).

In or around 1897, Hesse submitted a manuscript for publication in Schrempf's journal *Die Wahrheit,* which he referred to as perhaps the first piece he had attempted to publish (12:429). Both Hesse and Wagner thus shared the experience of having their writings rejected by Schrempf, whose defiance of religious and political authorities had obviously fascinated both writers — Schrempf had stepped down as a Protestant priest because he refused to give up his convictions. Although Schrempf did not publish Hesse's early manuscript, the young writer did not stop idolizing his prospective mentor, and remained in close contact with him until Schrempf's death in 1944. As previously mentioned, Schrempf was very likely one of two personal sources Hesse drew on in the composition of his text.

Psychoanalysis and Transformation

Like many works after *Demian, Klein und Wagner* is heavily informed by Hesse's reception of psychoanalysis (see the article by Volker Michels in this volume). However, while *Demian* capitalized on a linear process of individuation, according to which every new obstacle eventually serves to guide first-person narrator Emil Sinclair to a new level of consciousness, Wagner remains trapped in his inner divisions.

Hesse's initial interest in psychoanalysis grew out of his own crisis. After a nervous breakdown in the spring of 1916, Hesse began his therapy with Lang, who was a disciple of C. G. Jung. Inspired by a first personal meeting with Jung in 1917, Hesse also began with intensive studies of Jung's writings.[44] The intense discussions with Lang as well as Hesse's studies of Jung found their immediate expression in *Demian* (see the chapter by Andreas Solbach in this volume). Shortly thereafter, Hesse began to study the writings of Sigmund Freud.[45] Psychoanalytical theories continued to have a major impact on Hesse's writings at least until the early 1930s, although he added his own twists to the theories of both Freud and Jung. In his essay *Künstler und Psychoanalyse* (Artist and Psychoanalysis, 1918), Hesse describes psychoanalysis as a powerful tool in the artistic process: "keinen Zauberschlüssel, aber doch eine wertvolle neue Einstellung, ein neues vortreffliches Werkzeug"[46] (no magic key, but nevertheless a worthwhile new orientation, an excellent new tool). He names three reasons why writers should study Freud's and Jung's theories: first, they re-establish the power of imagination and its universal role in human interaction, thereby justifying the useful role of the writer in society; second, after undergoing analysis, the writer will continue to profit from his close connection with his own unconscious; and third, psychoanalysis demands honesty toward oneself, enabling the artist to confront bitter truths that nonetheless lead to improved, more powerful writings (14:353–56).[47]

It is no wonder then, that even the first reviewers of *Klein und Wagner* recognized how crucial Hesse's adaptation of psychoanalysis is to the interpretation of the novella. When the poet Klabund reviewed the text, he remarked that Hesse's novella was "fast wissenschaftlich exakt" (almost scientifically exact), that especially the dream sequences were in accordance "mit den jüngsten psychologischen Erkenntnissen" (with the most recent psychological discoveries).[48] Although Hesse is one of the first German-language writers who actually underwent psychoanalytical therapy,[49] he was by no means the only contemporary writer exploring the mind of the pathological criminal. Other examples include Georg Kaiser's play *Von morgens bis mitternachts* (From Morning to Midnight, 1916)[50] and Georg Heym's tale *Der Dieb* (The Thief, published 1913). It is remarkable that it is once again the expressionists whose interests Hesse shares.[51] Few of their texts, however, adhered as closely to actual psychoanalytical theory as Hesse's.

The way Wagner's dreams express his hidden inner conflicts is deeply indebted to Freud's and Jung's dream theories, in which the dreamer's unconscious conflicts are played out in a symbolical form, thus revealing his or her desires and anxieties. The dream sequences in *Klein und Wagner* are carefully constructed in this fashion. At the same time, Klein remains the sole interpreter of his own dreams, and thus takes on the role of his own therapist, alternating the symbolic world of the unconscious with careful and detailed interpretations,[52] finding the "real" significance of a dream through repeated readings of the same sequence.

This is exemplified by a dream Klein has while still riding on the train:

> Er saß, so träumte ihm, vorn auf einem Automobil, das fuhr rasch und ziemlich waghalsig durch die Stadt, bergauf und — ab. Neben ihm saß jemand, der den Wagen lenkte. Dem gab er einen Stoß in den Bauch, riß ihm das Steuerrad aus den Händen und steuerte selber, wild und beklemmend über Stock und Stein, knapp an Pferden und Schaufenstern vorbei, an Bäume streifend, daß ihm die Funken vor den Augen stoben. (213)

> [He was sitting, he had dreamed, in the front seat of an automobile that was moving rapidly and rather recklessly through a city, up and down hills. Beside him sat someone who was driving. In the dream he gave the driver a punch in the stomach, snatched the wheel from his hands, and now drove himself, drove wildly and terrifyingly over hill and dale, barely skirting horses and shop windows, grazing trees so closely that sparks flashed in his eyes. (*Klein* 49–50)]

Right away, Klein reads this sequence as a tale of self-empowerment: "Ja, es war besser, selber zu steuern und dabei in Scherben zu gehen, als immer von einem anderen gefahren und gelenkt zu werden" (213; "Yes, it was better to drive yourself even if it meant peril than always to be driven and directed by others," *Klein* 50). At the same time, Klein remains uncertain about the identity of the faceless chauffeur: "Er konnte sich an kein Gesicht, keine Figur erinnern — nur an ein Gefühl, eine vage Stimmung . . . Wer konnte es gewesen sein? Jemand, den er verehrte, dem er Macht über sein Leben einräumte[.] [. . .] Vielleicht sein Vater? Oder einer seiner Vorgesetzten? Oder — war es am Ende — ?" (213–14; "He could not remember any face or shape, merely the feeling of someone else, a vague, obscure mood. . .Who could it have been? Someone he respected, whom he allowed to have power over his life[.] [. . .] Perhaps his father? Or one of his superiors? Or — or was it after all . . .?," *Klein* 50).

The sentence remains unfinished, indicating both Klein's strained search and his unconscious attempt at veiling the truth. True, Klein finds an immediate answer: "Es war seiner Frau wegen geschehen, einzig seiner Frau wegen. Wie gut, daß er es endlich wußte" (214; "It had all been done because of his wife, solely because of his wife. How good that he knew that at last," *Klein* 50–51). However, the overemphasis on his wife already indicates that this is not the whole truth. Starting from this first dream, Klein gradually recognizes how he has become complicit in the suppression of his own personality, if only by internalizing the moral values of society. Klein eventually realizes that his only path to liberation lies, as Heinz W. Puppe puts it, in his absolute, unconditional self-realization, even at the expense of society, even if the ultimate result is self-destruction.[53]

In this struggle for self-realization, Teresina functions for Klein as what Jung called the "anima," the feminine side of the male individual. In a certain sense, she is not so much an independent character as a mirror of his own struggles.[54] Even before their first conversation, Klein regards her as "ein Mensch, der seinen eigenen Himmel und seine eigene Hölle hat, welche niemand mit ihm teilen kann" (239; "a person who has his own heaven and his own hell, which no one can share with him," *Klein* 84) — in other words, he projects his own struggles onto her and invites her to do the same (248).

According to Heinz W. Puppe, Klein's development can be described as a process consisting of three stages: in the first stage, before his escape, he was the passive object of bourgeois conventions. In the second stage, Klein gradually becomes aware of his needs and limitations, striving to achieve self-realization and overcome those elements and relations that had previously functioned as obstacles; Klein's violent inner struggles are the result of the contradictions between internalized conventions and true needs. It is this stage that makes up most of the text. It is only with the third stage, however, that Klein comes to the conclusion that, to overcome bourgeois conventions, he has to abandon himself to fate, let go of his personality and die.[55]

In order to achieve transcendence, however, Klein needs to leave Teresina behind as well. There are two main reasons for this: in spite of their apparent similarities, Teresina remains tied to bourgeois society. Not only does she depend on wealthy men to pay for her living, she also exposes her bourgeois nature when she and Klein go gambling in Castiglione. She does not play for excitement, but to gain financial independence (249). Klein realizes this as he observes her: "Er sah sie bei einem andern Tisch stehen und ihr Geld wechseln. [. . .] Sie sah nachdenklich, besorgt und sehr beschäftigt aus, wie eine Hausfrau. [. . .] Wie lang sie mit den tausend Franken ausreicht! dachte er gelangweilt, bei mir ging das schneller" (267–68; "He saw her standing at another table and changing her money. [. . .] She looked thoughtful, anxious, and very busy, like a housewife. [. . .] How long she makes a thousand franks last! he thought, bored. It was faster for me," *Klein* 122–23). Even at the most intimate of moments, when Klein and Teresina are about to consummate their affair, she disrupts the romantic atmosphere when she suddenly realizes that she has left her money on the boat and immediately returns there to reclaim it (272). For all her Bohemian attitude, Teresina eventually reveals herself to be not so different from the bourgeois society she seeks to overcome: it is financial, not psychological independence she strives for — a level that Klein leaves behind in the first chapter, when he realizes that the money he has embezzled is meaningless. In Hesse's terms, Teresina's struggle is thus necessarily doomed to fail.

Eventually, just when their love affair begins in earnest, their supposed common ground proves to be an illusion. When Teresina admonishes Klein for living "wie ein Selbstmörder" (273; like a suicide) she speaks the truth without realizing it. In turn, Klein stops regarding Teresina as a mirror image of himself; but instead of realizing that he had idolized his own projection, he feels betrayed and disillusioned (275). However, Klein not only stops regarding Teresina as a partner in crime; he even begins to view her as the enemy:

> So hatte er einst auch seine Frau zuweilen liegen sehen[.] [. . .] Nun sah er ihr Gesicht, im Schlaf so fremd, so ganz bei sich selbst, so ganz von ihm abgewandt. [. . .] Schwindel! Schwindel! [. . .] Mit diesem schönen Leib, mit dieser Brust und diesen weißen, gesunden, starken, gepflegten Armen und Beinen würde sie ihn noch oft verlocken und ihn umschlingen und Lust von ihm nehmen und dann ruhen und schlafen, [. . .] schön und stumpf und dumm wie ein gesundes schlafendes Tier. (274–75)[56]

> [In the past he had sometimes seen his wife lying that way beside him. [. . .] Now he saw her face, so alien in sleep, so utterly absorbed, so utterly turned away from him. [. . .] Fraud! Fraud! [. . .] With her

lovely body, with those breasts and those white, strong, healthy arms and legs, she would still tempt him often and embrace him and derive pleasure from him and then rest and sleep deeply, [. . .] beautiful and torpid and stupid as a healthy, sleeping animal. (*Klein* 132–33)

At this point, Klein is ready to do in reality what he had previously only done to the anonymous woman in his dream, that is, stab Teresina with a knife: "Nun stand er, Wagner, am Bett einer Schlafenden, und suchte das Messer! — Nein, er wollte nicht" (277; "Now he, Wagner, stood by the bed of a sleeping woman and was seeking the knife! No, he would not," *Klein* 136). This scene is of double significance: At the very moment Klein has come to fully identify with the killer, he realizes that identification with Wagner is not his true goal, that he needs to overcome his projection and eliminate himself; in Rudolf Koester's words, Klein's decision not to kill his lover but rather to commit suicide "marks the birth of a new man."[57]

Here, it becomes obvious that *Klein and Wagner* is more than just a literary case study in Jungian theory, and that Hesse is adapting psychoanalysis for his own ends. While both Freud and Jung aim to bring their patients' inner conflicts to light, they do so in order to enable them to deal with their struggles, to cope with life, and, ultimately, to find a place in society. *Klein und Wagner,* however, promotes self-realization through self-annihilation, dropping out of society instead of fitting in. In this context, Johannes Cremerius speaks of a "pietistisches Mißverständnis der Psychoanalyse" (Pietistic misunderstanding of psychoanalysis) in Hesse's writings, wherein analysis is not so much geared toward self-recognition, but rather aims at rooting out the patient's "evil side" altogether. Hesse's understanding of psychoanalysis is thus characterized by a universal feeling of guilt that has in roots in his deeply religious upbringings.[58] In this connection, Sikander Singh states:

> Friedrich Klein — and this is a further ironic paradox of the text — the prototype of a modern human being, of the despairing atheist, finds his way back to an old image . . . He quotes the one abandoned by all, the son of man, Jesus in the Garden of Gethsemane.[59]

If all human guilt has its roots in the original sin of Judeo-Christian religion, then it is impossible to overcome — for Hesse himself as much as for Klein. At the same time, the ending is hardly a pessimistic one: by "surrender[ing] willingly to the universal process of unending flux"[60] in a Dionysian *unio mystica*[61] modeled on the crucifixion of Christ, Klein attains an irrevocable salvation.

From the point of view of orthodox psychology, Hesse's version of psychoanalysis may rightfully be regarded as the result of a profound misreading. From an aesthetic point of view, however, this misunderstanding proves to be highly productive: from *Demian* on, it provided

Hesse with a viable model for displaying his character's inner struggles with a clarity and depth unachieved in his earlier texts.

Steppenwolf Anticipated?

Klein und Wagner can thus be read as a prelude to *Der Steppenwolf* (1927). While the later novel is much more complex in structure (see the essay by Martin Swales in this volume), *Klein und Wagner* already plays with some of its most important themes and motifs. Like Klein, Harry Haller is on the run from his marriage, feeling trapped in the deep inner split between bourgeois identity and its violent, destructive other; Klein and Haller both seriously consider solving their conflicts by committing suicide (though Haller stops short of actually carrying it out). Both protagonists seek to come to terms with their destructive tendencies through their relationship with prostitutes, whose grace and almost animalistic vitality are embodied by their love of dancing. Even their physical descriptions are highly similar.[62]

The tormented main character and his female other first seem to be complementary parts of a whole, united in their dropping out of the bourgeois mainstream. As Klein remarks: "Sehen Sie, das ist die Ähnlichkeit, die wir beide haben: wir beide tun hie und da, in seltenen Augenblicken, das, was in uns ist. Nichts ist seltener, die meisten Menschen kennen das überhaupt nicht" (247; "You see, there is the resemblance between us; both of us here and now, at rare moments, do what is in us. Nothing is rarer. Most people can't do that at all," *Klein* 94). The inner turmoil of both characters is not simply the result of an individual pathology, but also a sign of the times, the result of Europe's and especially Germany's moral and philosophical disorientation in the wake of the First World War.

However, while Klein and Haller deal with similar conflicts, the results are strikingly different. Harry goes through with murdering Hermine, even if she turns out to be only a projection, whereas Klein ends up killing himself. Moreover, Haller's passage through the Magic Theater lacks the religious epiphany Klein experiences while drowning. To a certain extent, then, Haller remains in control even during ecstasy. He learns that his struggle to transcend his everyday existence in favor of immortality is far from over; he will have to continue his struggle throughout his life, and in order to do so will have to embrace the multiple facets of his self, including its darker aspects. In contrast, Klein remains unable to overcome his inner split and thus succumbs to his suicidal urges, finding peace not in accepting the facts of life, but in giving up his personality altogether. Only in death does he become one with the universe. In many ways, then, *Der Steppenwolf* picks up where *Klein und Wagner* leaves off, carrying the conflicts at the novella's core to solutions that are, in comparison, more satisfying — both in terms of the protagonists' struggles and Hesse's aesthetic achievement.

Notes

[1] Joseph Mileck, *Hermann Hesse: Life and Art* (Berkeley: U of California P, 1978), 145.

[2] Unless otherwise stated, *Klein und Wagner* is quoted from Hermann Hesse, "Klein und Wagner," in *Sämtliche Werke*, ed. Volker Michels, vol. 8: *Die Erzählungen 3. 1911–1954* (Frankfurt am Main: Suhrkamp, 2002), 210–83; here, 211. Subsequent references to this work are cited in the text using the page numbers. References to other volumes in this edition are cited in text with volume and page number. English translations of *Klein und Wagner* are from Richard and Clara Winston's translation, "Klein and Wagner," published in *Klingsor's Last Summer* (New York: Farrar, Straus and Giroux, 1970), 45–144, and are given in parentheses or brackets and indicated by the designation *Klein* and page numbers.

[3] Reso Karalaschwili, "Die Taten des Lichts: Zur Farbgebung in *Klein und Wagner* und *Klingsors letzter Sommer*," in *Wege zu Hermann Hesse: Dichtung Musik Malerei Film — 5. Internationales Hermann-Hesse-Colloquium Calw 1988*, ed. Friedrich Bran and Martin Pfeifer (Bad Liebenzell: Gengenbach, 1989), 105. Through her blond hair, Teresina thus becomes associated with similar female characters in Hesse's works, such as Beatrice in *Demian*, Maria in *Steppenwolf*, as well as Goldmund's mother, Lydia, Julie, and Agnes in *Narziß und Goldmund* (see ibid.).

[4] For Sikander Singh, Klein's assessment of Teresina's dancing recalls Nietzsche's concept of the Dionysian; see Sikander Singh, *Hermann Hesse* (Stuttgart: Reclam, 2006), 135.

[5] Theodore Ziolkowski, *The Novels of Hermann Hesse: A Study in Theme and Structure* (Princeton, NJ: Princeton UP, 1965), 28.

[6] Jonathan Harwood, "Weimar Culture and Biological Theory: A Study of Richard Woltereck (1877–1944)," *History of Science* 34 (1996): 353.

[7] For an overview of Woltereck's life and work, Harwood, "Weimar Culture and Biological Theory," 347–77.

[8] Hugo Ball, *Hermann Hesse: Sein Leben und sein Werk* (Berlin: S. Fischer, 1927).

[9] Hermann Hesse, letter to Louis Moilliet, 24 July 1919, in Hermann Hesse, *Gesammelte Briefe*, vol. 1, ed. Ursula Michels and Volker Michels (Frankfurt am Main: Suhrkamp, 1973), 407. Subsequent references to this edition will be indicated by the abbreviation *GB* and volume and page numbers.

[10] Singh, *Hermann Hesse*, 130.

[11] Ralf Georg Bogner, "Hermann Hesse und der Expressionismus," in *Hermann Hesse und die literarische Moderne*, ed. Andreas Solbach (Frankfurt am Main: Suhrkamp, 2004), 112–13.

[12] See also Bogner, "Hermann Hesse und der Expressionismus," 116–17.

[13] Hermann Hesse, letter to Josef Bernhard Lang, 26 Jan. 1920, in Hermann Hesse, *"Die dunkle und wilde Seite der Seele": Briefwechsel mit seinem Psychoanalytiker Josef Bernhard Lang,* ed. Thomas Feitknecht (Frankfurt am Main: Suhrkamp, 2006), 159.

[14] Mileck, *Hermann Hesse: Life and Art,* 142. See also Hugo Ball's remark: "*Klein und Wagner* remains totally tied to the Bern experiences. The war, the breakup of the marriage are pursued and suffered through all the way to their consequences in dreams" (Ball, *Hermann Hesse,* 194–95).

[15] Martin Stingelin, "Freie Fahrt für freie Künstler: Wie Hermann Hesse vor seinen Kindern und dem bürgerlichen Leben floh und welche Rolle sein Psychoanalytiker dabei spielte," *Literaturen* 6 (2006): 37.

[16] Feitknecht, "Vorwort," in Hesse, *"Die dunkle und wilde Seite der Seele,"* 14.

[17] Josef Bernhard Lang, letter to Hermann Hesse, 23 Sept. 1919, in *"Die dunkle und wilde Seite der Seele,"* ed. Feitknecht, 102–3.

[18] See Josef Bernhard Lang, letter to Hermann Hesse, 15 June 1920, in *"Die dunkle und wilde Seite der Seele,"* ed. Feitknecht, 171. The connections between Hesse and Lang go even further: at the time of writing the letter quoted above, Lang was having a short yet passionate affair with Ruth Wenger, later to become Hesse's second wife.

[19] Hermann Hesse, letter to Ida Huck, Feb. 1920, cited in Siegfried Unseld, *Hermann Hesse: Werk und Wirkungsgeschichte,* 2nd ed. (Frankfurt am Main: Suhrkamp, 1985), 76.

[20] Hermann Hesse, letter to Carl Seelig, 1919, in *GB* 1:424.

[21] Alfred Weber, "Der Beamte" (1927), in *Haben wir Deutschen nach 1945 versagt?: Politische Schriften: Ein Lesebuch,* ed. Christa Dericum (Frankfurt am Main: S. Fischer, 1982), 29–52.

[22] In this context, it is interesting to note that Alfred Weber, who taught at the University of Prague from 1904 to 1907, was also Kafka's doctoral advisor. For an informed recent analysis of the role of bureaucracy in Kafka's writings, see: Barry Murnane, *"Verkehr mit Gespenstern": Gothic und Moderne bei Franz Kafka* (Würzburg: Ergon, 2008), 187–234.

[23] Kurt J. Fickert, "The Portrait of the Artist in Hesse's *Klein und Wagner,*" *Hartford Studies in Literature* 6 (1974): 180.

[24] Fickert, "The Portrait of the Artist in Hesse's *Klein und Wagner,*" 180.

[25] "Es waren immer zwei Friedrich Klein dagewesen, ein sichtbarer und ein heimlicher, ein Beamter und ein Verbrecher, ein Familienvater und ein Mörder" (225; There had always been two Friedrich Kleins there, a visible and a secret one, an official and a criminal, a family father and a murderer).

[26] Mileck, *Hermann Hesse: Life and Art,* 142.

[27] Hesse, *Peter Camenzind,* in *Sämtliche Werke,* ed. Volker Michels, vol. 2: *Die Romane: Peter Camenzind. Unterm Rad. Gertrud* (Frankfurt am Main: Suhrkamp, 2001), 38.

[28] Hesse, *Der Steppenwolf,* in *Sämtliche Werke,* ed. Volker Michels, vol. 4: *Die Romane: Der Steppenwolf. Narziß und Goldmund. Die Morgenlandfahrt* (Frankfurt am Main: Suhrkamp, 2001), 193.

[29] Karl Schlechta, "Anmerkungen," in Friedrich Nietzsche, *Werke in zwei Bänden,* ed. Schlechta, vol. 2 (Frankfurt am Main: Zweitausendeins, 1999), 713.

[30] Those that have been published include Johannes Cremerius, *Freud und die Dichter* (Freiburg: Kore, 1995), 91–129; Bernd Neuzner and Horst Brandstätter, *Wagner: Lehrer Dichter Massenmörder — Samt Hermann Hesses Novelle* Klein und Wagner (Frankfurt am Main: Eichborn, 1996); Bernd Neuzner, "Hermann Hesse und der Massenmörder Wagner," in *Hermann Hesse und die Psychoanalyse: "Kunst als Therapie" — 9. Internationales Hermann-Hesse-Colloquium in Calw vom 8.-10. Mai 1997,* ed. Michael Limberg (Bad Liebenzell: Gengenbach, 1997), 177–94.

[31] For a detailed description of Wagner's crimes, see Neuzner and Brandstätter, *Wagner: Lehrer Dichter Massenmörder,* 18–30.

[32] See Neuzner and Brandstätter, *Wagner: Lehrer Dichter Massenmörder,* 38–39.

[33] Robert Gaupp, *Zur Psychologie des Massenmords: Hauptlehrer Wagner von Degerloch: Eine kriminalpsychologische und psychiatrische Studie* (Berlin: Springer, 1914).

[34] Neuzner, "Hermann Hesse und der Massenmörder Wagner," 181.

[35] Printed in: Neuzner and Brandstätter, *Wagner: Lehrer Dichter Massenmörder,* 44–50.

[36] Neuzner and Brandstätter, *Wagner: Lehrer Dichter Massenmörder,* 49.

[37] On a related note, Eugene Stelzig reads Wagner's name as a wordplay on the German verb *wagen,* which means "to dare"; see Eugene Stelzig, "Ticino Legends of Saints and Sinners" [1988], in *Hermann Hesse,* ed. Harold Bloom (Broomall, PA: Chelsea House, 2003), 200.

[38] In a fragment of his autobiography, Ernst Wagner wrote: "[E]s ist notwendig, daß ich hingehe. Es ist auch notwendig, daß ich die Meinen mitnehme. Meine Frau könnte ja wohl leben, aber wie könnte ich dann die Kinder töten? Für sie selbst ist es übrigens auch gut, wenn sie das nicht überlebt. Ich töte alle 5 aus Mitleid" (cited in Neuzner and Brandstätter, 87; It is necessary that I die. It is also necessary that I take my family with me. My wife could certainly live, but how could I then kill my children? For her too it is also good if she doesn't live through it. I am going to kill all five out of sympathy). In Hesse's tale, these motives are subject to a complete reinterpretation. The pain of Klein's self-torment and his search for spirituality replace Wagner's actual paranoia and desire for revenge: "Da war Wagner eines Nachts aufgestanden und hatte gesehen, daß es keinen Sinn habe, noch mehr, noch viele solcher Nächte voll Qual aneinander zu reihen, daß man dadurch nicht zu Gott komme, und hatte das Messer geholt" (275; "And then one night Wagner had sprung up and had seen that there was no longer any sense to adding more, many more such nights of torture to one another, that they did not bring him any closer to God, and he had gone for the knife," *Klein* 133).

[39] See Neuzner and Brandstätter, *Wagner: Lehrer Dichter Massenmörder,* 57.

[40] For a list of Wagner's self-published texts, see Neuzner and Brandstätter, *Wagner: Lehrer Dichter Massenmörder,* 299–300.

[41] Neuzner and Brandstätter, *Wagner: Lehrer Dichter Massenmörder,* 124–26.

[42] Neuzner and Brandstätter, *Wagner: Lehrer Dichter Massenmörder,* 112. Wagner's self-aggrandizement only reached its peak after the publication of *Klein and Wagner.* In 1926, Wagner accused the popular Franz Werfel of plagiarizing his own dramas in the latter's play *Schweiger* (1923). Wagner eventually tried to take the issue to court in 1927, but although the case was investigated by the police, no legal proceedings were initiated. This defeat only fueled Wagner's rage, turning his hatred into pure anti-Semitism (Werfel was Jewish). Werfel in turn insisted that he had not read Wagner's writings (Neuzner and Brandstätter 206). See Neuzner and Brandstätter, 188–206.

[43] Hesse, "Kurgefaßter Lebenslauf," in *Sämtliche Werke,* ed. Volker Michels, vol. 12: *Autobiographische Schriften II. Selbstzeugnisse. Erinnerungen. Gedenkblätter und Rundbriefe* (Frankfurt am Main: Suhrkamp, 2003), 53–55. Subsequent references to this work will be indicated by volume and page number in parentheses.

[44] Günter Baumann, "'Es geht bis aufs Blut und tut weh. Aber es fördert. . .': Hermann Hesse und die Psychologie C. G. Jungs," in *Hermann Hesse und die Psychoanalyse,* ed. Limberg, 42. In 1921, Hesse briefly underwent therapy with Jung himself. Unsatisfied, however, Hesse later returned to his friend Lang, with whom he achieved more lasting results.

[45] Johannes Cremerius, "Hermann Hesse und Sigmund Freud: Hesses Freud-Rezeption und sein öffentliches Eintreten für die Psychoanalyse," in *Hermann Hesse und die Psychoanalyse,* ed. Limberg, 30.

[46] Hesse, *Künstler und Psychoanalyse,* in *Sämtliche Werke,* ed. Volker Michels, vol. 14: *Betrachtungen und Berichte II: 1927–1961* (Frankfurt am Main: Suhrkamp, 2003), 352. Subsequent references to this volume will be indicated by volume and page number in parentheses.

[47] See also Cremerius, "Hermann Hesse und Sigmund Freud," 36.

[48] Cited in Unseld, *Hermann Hesse: Werk und Wirkungsgeschichte,* 75. Similarly, Joseph Mileck argues that both *Demian* and *Klein und Wagner* "would almost prompt one to think of clinical reports." At the same time, it remains unclear whether Hesse really "became so engrossed in his psychological self that his work tended to suggest more the effort of the analytic talent than that of a creative artist," as Mileck claims in his *Hermann Hesse and His Critics* (Chapel Hill, NC: U of North Carolina P, 1958), 22.

[49] Cremerius, *Freud und die Dichter,* 93.

[50] For a detailed comparison of Kaiser's play with Hesse's novella, see Rudolf Koester, "Kaiser's *Von morgens bis mitternachts* and Hesse's *Klein und Wagner:* Two Explorations of Crime and Human Transcendence," *Orbis Litterarum* 24.4 (1969): 237–50. According to Koester, the crucial difference between both texts is that "*Klein und Wagner* is concerned with the dissection of a psyche," whereas "*Von morgens bis mitternachts* dissects a society, undermined by false values" (245).

[51] See also Bogner, "Hermann Hesse und der Expressionismus," 112–13.

[52] Heinz W. Puppe, "Psychologie und Mystik in *Klein und Wagner* von Hermann Hesse," *PMLA* 78 (1963): 128.

[53] Puppe, "Psychologie und Mystik in *Klein und Wagner,*" 130.

[54] Lou Reed expressed this beautifully in a song for The Velvet Underground: "I'll be your mirror, reflect what you are / In case you don't know [. . .] When you think the night has seen your mind / that inside you're twisted and unkind / Let me stand to show that you are blind [. . .] Cause I see you" (Lou Reed, "I'll Be Your Mirror," 1967, *Between Thought and Expression: The Selected Lyrics of Lou Reed* [New York: Hyperion, 1991], 3).

[55] Puppe, "Psychologie und Mystik in *Klein und Wagner,*" 131.

[56] Mark Boulby merely regards Klein's relationships with women as variations on the Don Juan motif, in the same vein as Goldmund's move "from lover to lover in search of that permanence which is never to be found" (Mark Boulby, "Narziß and Goldmund," 1967, *Hermann Hesse,* ed. Harold Bloom [Broomall, PA: Chelsea House, 2003] 94). This interpretation, however, completely overlooks Klein's murderous intentions and their function for his development.

[57] Koester, "Kaiser's *Von morgens bis mitternachts* and Hesse's *Klein und Wagner,*" 250.

[58] Cremerius, *Hermann Hesse und Sigmund Freud,* 37.

[59] Singh, *Hermann Hesse,* 136.

[60] Koester, "Kaiser's *Von morgens bis mitternachts* and Hesse's *Klein und Wagner,*" 249.

[61] Hans Jürg Lüthi, *Hermann Hesse: Natur und Geist* (Stuttgart: Kohlhammer, 1970), 71.

[62] Fickert, "The Portrait of the Artist in Hesse's *Klein und Wagner,*" 183.

5: *Klingsors letzter Sommer* and the Transformation of Crisis

Ralph Freedman

Hesse's Inner Path

*K*LINGSOR'S LETZTER SOMMER IS PART OF a new kind of fiction that occupied Hermann Hesse immediately after the First World War. Along with *Siddhartha* and the lesser known *Klein and Wagner,* this brilliant novella explores the inner life through a correspondingly subjective language. These three works form a sequence: they appeared individually in the aftermath of the war and were re-published in 1931, as a collection called *Weg nach Innen* (The Way Within or The Inward Way), a title that pinpoints Hesse's intention precisely. Hesse took this title from a fragment in Novalis's collection called *Blütenstaub: "Nach Innen geht der geheimnisvolle Weg"* (Inward leads the secret way).[1] *Siddhartha* projects a transformation of an individual life caught within a larger world of Buddhist and Taoist religions, while *Klein und Wagner* portrays an actual change in identity, a "Jekyll and Hyde" syndrome, as yet another aspect of a self transforming itself. In *Klingsors letzter Sommer* the famous painter Klingsor recreates himself in art as well as in death.

A lost war and a chaotic present provided an overriding theme: the need for a fresh beginning by turning within, "transforming" the inner life into a new kind of "outer" life in another, imagined environment — true to the model of German Romanticism to which the "new" Hesse still owed a considerable debt. It remained the task of this generation to explore not only ways of portraying the inner life but also of transforming this inner life into artistic and spiritual figures.

Among all of Hesse's writings at this time, *Klingsors letzter Sommer* stands out as his sharpest "critique" of individual and societal crisis. For what could be more like "crisis" than the naked threat of death?

In Klingsor, the painter facing the end of his life, Hesse created an overpowering figure, in part a product of his imagination, in part taken from people he knew in his self-imposed exile in southern Switzerland. Magic determines the painter's name: "Klingsor" alludes to the figure of the magician in Wolfram von Eschenbach's *Parzival,* who was able to see sounds and hear colors, as well as to "Klingsohr," the magical teacher of poetry in the Romantic novel *Heinrich von Ofterdingen* by Novalis.

If Klingsor's name calls up echoes from the past, the figure he represents is even more suggestive. Klingsor is not a poet like Novalis but a great painter. Although Hesse's poetic self is represented by a minor figure named "Hermann," a blond young man of little significance, the artist par excellence in this novella is Klingsor, who has distinguished forebears of his own. The obvious model is Vincent Van Gogh, whose fervor and intoxication Hesse admired and brought to life. In fact, Hesse first had a factual monograph in mind. In May 1919, a young law student and journalist, Carl Seelig, had asked Hesse to contribute such a monograph on Van Gogh. Seelig had supported Hesse's work on behalf of German war prisoners by purchasing some of his drawings and efforts as a painter, which reminded him of Van Gogh's work. When the monograph failed to materialize, Hesse replaced it with his fiction. Volker Michels, who revealed these striking parallels between Van Gogh's letters from Arles and Hesse's letters to Seelig from Ticino, suggested a corresponding parallel between Hesse's state of mind and Van Gogh's in his difficult relationship with Paul Gauguin.[2]

Hesse's invention of the figure of Klingsor went hand in hand with his own growing interest in a new form of expression — shapes and colors — to transform mental states into words, into paintings, and, ultimately, by a process of synesthesia, to combine the two. For this novella represents a turning point not only in Hesse's work as a writer — his use of language that assumed an expressionist style — but also as a painter in his own right, roaming through the countryside with easel and palette. Though the delicate watercolors of his newly chosen southern homeland were strikingly different from Klingsor's fierce explosions, Hesse's painting remains part of his own, and Klingsor's, artistic revolution.

Stefan Zweig referred to this transformation by pointing out Hesse's leap from the naturalistic and idealistic poet-painter of the Black Forest to a *Sprachkünstler* (an artist of language) freed from naturalism, who consciously recomposes Van Gogh's colors into a passionate dispute between darkness and light.[3]

Hesse's Work: A Mirror

Practically all of Hesse's books reflect themes and episodes in his life, but in this novella (as in some others, like *Die Morgenlandfahrt*), autobiographical references serve a specific function. We know that Hesse had freed himself from his Bern household soon after the end of the war. He had separated from his wife Mia and was able to place his three young sons with friends. So he felt free to wander in the Italian-speaking south of Switzerland, which became the stage and background of this novella. He was free now . . . except for the guilt that gnawed at his conscience.

Both the freedom and the guilt are represented in the story of Klingsor, facing his impending death from an unspecified but fatal illness. As we trace Hesse's own movements during this time, we discover that they reflect, item by item, Klingsor's wandering on his infernal itinerary from life to death. The autobiographical references within this journey are too clear to be ignored. From the first page on, step-by-step, we encounter a disguised Hermann Hesse. The novella becomes an allegory.

It is a paradoxical journey. As Klingsor wanders through the countryside, the shapes he portrays on his canvas are connected in time to each other by words that set the pace which carries us from one way station to another within the allegory. Klingsor's home is on one level the now-famous Casa Carmuzzi, where Hesse was to live for many years. But the Casa also serves as a "magical castle" in an atmosphere of guilt shared by the poet and his persona, Klingsor. Starting from this "castle," Hesse/Klingsor moves from one stage to another in his death-bound pilgrimage. If for the author the flight had been an escape from the guilt-laden past toward a weightless freedom, his character rises through the stages of his pilgrimage to the inevitable encounter with, first, the grandiose self-portrait, then the fact of death.

Where does this novella that culminates in death begin? Klingsor, the great artist, is "sick unto death," as the freedom his author has gained in his escape to the Ticino landscape is transformed into both grail and grave for his character. Klingsor — like Everyman — carries his death inside him, and yet for one last summer he lives to celebrate once more. His farewell to life will be a final orgy — with wine, friends, and women — but it will create yet another orgy, a grand vision of world and death — a reflection of crisis.

This crisis included orgiastic elements that compose both the inner and outer forms of an astonishingly rich novella. Hesse's robust, self-consciously expressionistic language helps create this effect. Both his perception of life and his awareness of its passing are portrayed through shapes and colors that mark the progress of the allegory: for example, at the end of the day, foreseeing the end of Klingsor's life, Hesse writes:

> Erloschen war die Welt, die er gemalt hatte, erloschen der gelb und grüne Himmel, ertrunken die blaue helle Fahne, ermordet und verwelkt das schöne Gelb.[4]

> [Extinguished was the world he had painted, extinguished the green and yellow sky, the bright blue flag; slain and withered was the lovely yellow.[5]]

What was Hesse's design in choosing such colorful language, other than creating a new atmosphere to mark his chosen Ticino exile? The poet, the speaker, the interlocutor sought to echo his own self, reflecting himself in his protagonist, the "new" artist. An alternation of references marks the allegory, where distinct way stations in Klingsor's rise to his culminating vision morph into his descent into death.

The novella is carefully constructed. It begins with Hesse's sense of the place, as he saw it during his creative summer of 1919, portrayed through Klingsor's eyes. From the four-room apartment in the Casa Camuzzi, Klingsor, like Hesse, looked down from his balcony to view the symphony of the senses below:

> Klingsor stand nach Mitternacht, von einem Nachtgang heimgekehrt, auf dem schmalen Steinbalkon seines Arbeitszimmers. Hinter ihm sank tief und schwindelnd der alte Terrassengarten hinab, ein tief durchschattendes Gewühl dichter Baumwipfel, Palmen, Zedern, Kastanien, Judasbaum, Blutbuche, Eukalyptus, durchklettert von Schlingpflanzen, Lianen, Glyzinien. Über der Baumschwärze schimmerten blaßspiegelnd die großen blechernden Blätter der Sommermagnolien, riesigen schneeweiße Blüten dazwischen halbgeschlossen, groß wie Menschenköpfe, bleich wie Mond und Elfenbein, von denen durchdringend und beschwingt ein inniger Zitronengeruch herüberkam. Aus unbestimmter Ferne her mit müden Schwingen kam die Musik geflogen, vielleicht eine Gitarre, vielleicht ein Klavier, nicht zu unterscheiden. . . . Sternlicht floss durch das Waldtal, hoch und verlassen blickte eine weiße Kapelle aus den endlosen Wäldern, verzaubert und alt. See, Berge und Himmel flossen in der Ferne ineinander. (285)

> [Just back home after a night walk, Klingsor stood on the narrow stone balcony of his studio. Below him, dizzyingly precipitate, the old terrace gardens dropped away, a densely shadowed tangle of treetops, palms, cedars, chestnuts, judas trees, red beech and eucalyptus, intertwined with climbing plants, lianas, wisterias. Above the blackness of the trees the large glossy leaves of the summer magnolias gleamed pallidly, the huge, snow-white blossoms half shut among them, large as human heads, pale as moon and ivory. From the massed leafage, penetrating and rousing, a tartly sweet smell of lemons drifted toward him. From some indefinite distance languorous music winged its way toward him, perhaps a guitar, perhaps a piano; there was no saying . . . Starlight flowed through the wooded valley. High and deserted, a white chapel, enchanted and old, peered out of the endless forest. In the distance, lake, mountains, and sky flowed together. (146)]

This scene epitomizes many others Hesse describes both in his métier of words and in his paintings. Indeed, Hesse saw this time of visual creation as a supplement to and replacement of his powers as a writer, as he found himself in the midst of a new phase of creativity — the greatest since the time of writing *Demian* two years before. For all its deathlike overtones, this introductory passage shows that *Klingsors letzter Sommer* dramatized Hesse's *arrival,* the beginning of his new life. It was, as he once called it, a painting of his dreams.

The novella gently but steadily develops in several phases. Among Klingsor's most intimate friends we meet the man he calls "Louis der Grausame" (Louis the Cruel). Why "cruel"? Isn't this name just a cover for Hesse's good friend from Geneva, the painter Louis Moillet?

Whatever this relationship may have been in life, for Klingsor, the persona, the artist *par excellence,* it presents the point where art at its liveliest becomes deadly for the man. Louis becomes considerably more than an intimate friend. He is "cruel" because his flightiness provides no support. His figure consists only of constantly flowing feelings. His fluidity, refusing to stay anywhere, is connected to Hesse's idea of the artistic spirit: the eternal vagabond who drinks, sunbathes, and enjoys women, but who, in spite of his sensual abandon, raises serious questions about art as a worthwhile enterprise.

> "Ob diese ganze Malerei eigentlich einen Wert hat?" sagte Louis auf dem Ölberg und in Cartago, nackt im Grase liegend, den Rücken rot von der Sonne. Man malt doch bloss faute de mieux, mein Lieber. Hättest du immer das Mädchen auf dem Schoss, das dir gerade gefällt, und die Suppe im Teller, nach der heute der Sinn steht, du würdest dich nicht mit dem wahnsinnigen Kinderspiel plagen. Die Natur hat zehntausend Farben, und wir haben uns in den Kopf gesetzt, die Skala auf zwanzig zu reduzieren. (291)

> ["I wonder whether all this painting business has any real value," Louis said on the Mount of Olives lying naked in the grass, his back red from the sun. "You know we only paint for lack of anything better to do, my friend. If you had only the girl you fancy on your lap at the moment and your favorite soup in your plate, you wouldn't bother with this senseless, childish game. Nature has ten thousand colors and we've taken it into our heads to reduce the spectrum to twenty." (158)]

Following the section entitled "*Louis*" we encounter a variety of similar episodes, such as "*Der Kareno-Tag,*" which introduces Hesse's second wife Ruth Wenger as Rebekka, the Queen of the Mountains.[6] An interpolated letter by Klingsor to someone named Edith alludes to Hesse's friend Elizabeth Rupp. "*Die Musik des Untergangs*" featuring a character described as an Armenian astrologer provides a mask for the architect, Josef Englert. Another mythified passage is called "*Abend im August,*" which laces the wonders of nature and wine with abandoned lovemaking. Following a return to the beginning, with a letter written to "*Louis den Grausamen*" (Louis the Cruel), the work reaches its predestined climax: "*Das Selbstbildnis,*" the Self-Portrait.

Heights of Sublimation

According to Freud, a work of art is developed by re-channeling drives ("Umleitung der Triebe"), a process he called "sublimation," a form of "transformation." Hesse reworked his identity by giving himself the names of two Chinese poets of the eighth century, which were left purposely undisguised: "Li Tai Pe" and "Thu Fu." These were both poets who represented aspects of Klingsor/Hesse's vision of the artist-creator: Li Tai Pe as hard-drinking popular icon; Thu Fu as sufferer, ironically aware of spiritual and social decay at court and elsewhere in society.[7]

For Hesse, the idea of sublimation or transformation is the key not only to art but also to a vision of life and death that points the way to art. As psycho-aesthetic theory, this question had occupied him for some time, beginning with the essay "Künstler und Psychoanalyse," which he had written earlier in Bern. At the time of "Klingsor" he continued this debate, weighing the pros and cons of Freud's original concept and Jung's further exploration. What *is* new in this novella is the vision of death — the "ultimate" crisis vision as an aspect of art. When Louis leaves, the light goes out.

Thus, several figures wearing the masks of men as well as women of Hesse's circle accompany Hesse and therefore Klingsor at this time of a new beginning with precisely the urge toward art that determines his protagonist. They do so by representing the chiaroscuro of a high feeling for life as well as a melancholy consciousness of death.

In the section entitled *Die Musik des Untergangs* — the "music of doom," we hear another voice, one that accepts the transformation — Louis's "sublimation" — of crisis, but is oriented specifically towards the dark side. The figure representing Josef Englert is the "Armenian magician," the voice of an artist who, along with his creation, senses his own demise. Louis speaks of the freedom of the senses, of the relation of art to the unconscious, whereas the magician speaks of these things too, but under the sign of death.

> Sieh da meine Hand. . . . diese braune Hand. Sie hat mit vielen Pinseln gemalt; sie hat neue Stücke der Welt aus dem Finstern gerissen und vor die Augen der Menschen gestellt. Die braune Hand hat viele Frauen unter dem Kinn gestreichelt, und viele Mädchen verführt. Diese liebe Hand, Freunde, wird bald voll Erde und voll Maden sein; keiner von euch würde sie mehr anrühren. Wohl, eben darum liebe ich sie. Ich liebe meine Hand, ich liebe meine Augen. Ich liebe meinen weissen, zärtlichen Bauch, ich liebe sie mit Bedauern und mit Spott und mit grosser Zärtlichkeit, weil sie alle bald verwelken und verfaulen müssen. (319)

> [See my hand, . . . this brown hand. It has painted with many brushes; wrested fresh segments of the world and placed them before men's eyes. This brown hand has fondled many women under the chin and has seduced many girls . . . This dear hand, my friends, will soon be full

of earth and maggots; none of you would want to touch it any longer. Very well, that's the reason why I love it. I love my hand, I love my eyes, I love my soft white belly; I love them with regret and with scorn and with great tenderness, because they must all wither and decay so soon. (196)]

Hesse prefaces this passage with powerful thoughts, "We who are dying know more of death . . . we are humans, not stars."[8] These sentences are part of the music of doom, testifying to the bitter substance of this allegory. They designate not only the inferno of the depressed spirit but also a further cosmic panorama: the *underside* of sublimation. The "Armenian astrologer" has confirmed his magic power.

A special class of such figures is formed by the various women — representing erotic encounters — who become the passports to Hesse's new life in Ticino. Most of these women, usually actual persons endowed with fictional names, come from the exciting time when Hesse gave himself to his recent discovery of liberty — of freedom in art and life — as in the novella Klingsor gives himself over to ultimate freedom — his death. One of these figures is Hesse's not-so-romantic second wife, Ruth Wenger, who was prosaic by contrast to her fictional mask. For in the novella she is enveloped in regal romance:

Plötzlich stand die Königin der Gebirge da. Schlanke elastische Blüte, straff und federnd ganz in Rot, brennende Flamme, Bildnis der Jugend. (303)

[Suddenly the Queen of the Mountains stood there, a slender lissome flower, body straight and pliant, all in red, burning flames, image of youth. (174–75)]

These passages also include patently wishful physical encounters. For example, a love scene with a peasant woman reflects a wish dream, which often recurs in Hesse's books, rather than a believable episode. A sturdy farm wife allows the great painter to work in her yard; he asks for a drink of water; they fix each other with a hard look; later she follows him into the mountains; her approaching footsteps are heavy with sensuous meaning. Their language is only of the body as he beds her under the pine trees. This scene, by no means unusual in Hesse, not only portrays an expressionistic cliché of the time, but also the romantic ambience surrounding the sexual myths by which his admirers of the youth movements of his time lived.[9]

Yet the novella concludes with an image of final significance for Klingsor's creation: an anonymous woman who, in a way, becomes the godmother of his final creation.

The Ultimate Self-Portrait

The book ends with Klingsor's vision of his achievement and his death: the creation of this great artist's self-portrait. The scenes leading up to it are memorable. I will now embroider on this scene in order to dramatize the mood of imagination and death that engulfs Klingsor at this critical moment. A woman lying on the couch with him observes him with growing alarm as she sees him scrutinizing his own image in the mirror again and again with great excitement, staring at his own distorted face. Does the woman already discern her own face in the imagined painting? Has she already become part of the great magician who painted the world along with himself? We recognize the scene as an allegory of life, of art, of the fear of death — of the painter as well as the woman.

> Und nicht sein Gesicht allein, oder seine tausend Gesichter, Malte er auf das Bild, nicht bloss seine Augen und Lippen, die leidvolle Talschlucht des Mundes, den gespalteten Felsen der Stirn, die wurzelhaften Hände, die zuckenden Finger, den Hohn des Verstandes, den Tod im Auge. Er malte in seiner eigenwilligen, gedrängten und zuckenden Pinselschrift sein Leben dazu, seine Liebe, seinen Glauben, seine Verzweiflung. (331)

> [And it was not only his face, or his thousand faces, that he painted into this picture, not only his eyes and lips, the pained ravine of his mouth, the cleft cliffs of his forehead, his rootlike hands, his twitching fingers, the mockery of reason, the death in his eyes. In his idiosyncratic, over-crowded, concise, and jagged brush script he painted his life along with it, his love, his faith, his despair. (212–13)]

One has the feeling — and here I fantasize again — of looking into the eyes of this anonymous woman who is filled with dread. She does not want to be dragged into the death that lives in Klingsor's eyes. We visualize the bronzed arms and the suntanned shoulders quietly, respectfully covered with the sheet before she stealthily disappears with frightened steps. She never comes back, says the text. Naturally, she never comes back. Yet she remains in the picture; she lives in the canvas. But she is nonetheless dead, for she is part of the painting of death.[10]

The multiplicity of mirrors in this novella strikes the reader forcefully at this point. Each place, each person, is reflected in a distorted fashion, which gives a clue to Hesse's use of pseudonyms throughout the novella. Klingsor, painter and mask for Hesse, is named for literary figures of the past: a poet, a dark sorcerer. Klingsor sees himself mirrored, a series of reflected glimpses, increasingly distorted. His self-portrait is in itself a reflection, a distorting mirror, which exalts and immortalizes the hero. Through his creation of this mirrored labyrinth, Hesse has transformed his own fear of dying, recomposing death through art.

In this way, this stunning novella, prospecting for the treasure of the subconscious, renders a compelling picture of human greatness against a background of the human condition.

Notes

[1] See Theodore Ziolkowski, *The Novels of Hermann Hesse* (Princeton: Princeton UP, 1965), 13. Hesse's collection actually contains extended works of prose, *Klingsor, Siddhartha,* and *Klein und Wagner* as well as *Kinderseele.*

[2] See Volker Michels in *Hermann Hesse: Sämtliche Werke,* vol. 8 (Frankfurt am Main: Suhrkamp Verlag, 2001), 523.

[3] Zweig reference is from Volker Michels, ed., Hesse, *Sämtliche Werke,* vol. 8, 524.

[4] *Klingsors letzter Sommer,* in Hesse, *Sämtliche Werke,* vol. 8, ed. Volker Michels. All references to the German original text will be to this edition by page number.

[5] Hermann Hesse, *Klingsor's Last Summer,* trans. Richard and Clara Winston (New York: Farrar, Straus and Giroux, 1970), 188. Subsequent references to this translation are by page number.

[6] *Klingsors letzter Sommer, SW* 8:303; *Klingsor's Last Summer,* 174–75. See quotation below regarding the "Queen of the Mountains."

[7] See also Joseph Mileck, *Hermann Hesse, Life and Art* (U of California P, 1978), 149.

[8] *Klingsors letzter Sommer, SW* 8:319; *Klingsor's Last Summer,* 196.

[9] *Klingsors letzter Sommer, SW* 8:322–23; Freedman, *Hermann Hesse, Pilgrim of Crisis,* 206–7.

[10] Freedman, "Im Gedenken zum Todestag Hermann Hesses, des Dichters der Krisis," *Krisen als Wege zur Einheit,* ed. Uli Rothfuss (Calw: Sparkasse Pforzheim Calw, 2003), 56–58.

6: *Siddhartha*

Adrian Hsia

T HE ESSAY HAS THREE PARTS. The first part deals with the interpretation of the novel in accordance with international Hesse scholarship,
while the second part discusses the English translations and their accompanying introductions of *Siddhartha*. The third part examines the similarities between Hesse's message as expressed in the novel and some tenets of
Zen Buddhism.

An East-Western Interpretation of *Siddhartha*

As early as 1923, one year after the publication of *Siddhartha,* Hesse emphasized that he had found the deepest truth in the Upanishads, the
thoughts of Buddha, Confucius, Lao Zi (Hesse's transcription: Lao Tse),
and the New Testament. He reiterated the same thought in 1958 with
specific reference to *Siddhartha:* that the novel is the confession of a man
of Christian origin who left the Church early in his life in order to learn to
understand other religions, especially the Indian and Chinese forms of belief.[1] This perspective on the novel, not only carrying the authoritative
stamp of the author, but subscribed to by most critics of today, will be the
foundation of our analysis of *Siddhartha*.

Hesse had begun writing the novel in December 1919 and completed
the first part by August 1920. He then had to put it aside because he had
exhausted his own experience of searching for knowledge and his personal
reaction to the teaching of Buddha. He was at a loss how to depict the
further development of Siddhartha, which culminates in his enlightenment.
It seems that C. G. Jung was instrumental in the work's completion. Hesse
had several sessions of psychotherapy with him in Küsnacht, a suburb of
Zurich, in May and June 1921. The therapy helped him "to create a space
within us in which God's voice can be heard,"[2] as he wrote in a letter during this period. Having a new focus, Hesse was able to look beyond Buddhism for inspiration. At this point, Lao Zi seemed to have come to his
aid: Hesse confessed in a letter of February 1922 (a few weeks before he
took up writing *Siddhartha* again) that the novel departed from Brahman
and Buddha, but would end in Tao.[3] He took up writing again in March
1922 and completed the novel in May. The novel was then published in

October of the same year. A few weeks after the publication of the novel, Hesse again wrote in a letter to Stephan Zweig dated 27 November 1922 that Siddhartha's wisdom or enlightenment was closer to Lao Zi's teaching than the Buddha's. Having said this, we should not lose sight of other vital statements of Hesse's to the effect that the novel is a very European book because of its emphasis on individualism.[4]

Siddhartha is divided into two parts: the first part has four chapters; the second has eight. The critic Leroy Shaw suggested that the first four chapters correspond to the "Four Noble Truths,"[5] and that the following eight correspond to the "Eightfold Path" of Buddhism.[6] It is possible that Hesse was thinking of these tenets in a general way when he began to write, but it is highly unlikely that he intended each chapter to correspond to one specific tenet. For example, although the first noble truth is that life is suffering, the reader encounters Siddhartha as an adolescent who has yet to encounter suffering. The young Siddhartha's father ignores the Atman (personal soul or true self) in him, which results in the boy's infinite, unstillable longing for it. This is more Hesse than Buddhism, a religion that sees desire as the cause for suffering, and suffering as a fact of all existence: "Birth is suffering; aging is suffering; death is suffering; grief, lamentation, bodily pain, mental pain and despair are suffering; not getting what one desires, that too is suffering: In brief the five aggregates subject to grasping are suffering."[7] The first chapter does not depict any of these sufferings. Indeed, the young Siddhartha longs to leave home to begin his search for knowledge to attain Atman. In the second chapter, as a disciple of the Samanas, he is, however, taught the opposite; he learns how to escape Atman and assume another identity temporarily. Dissatisfied that Atman remains unreachable, he goes in search of Buddha for a solution. In the third chapter he learns of and rejects Buddha's teaching without hesitation (while accepting him as a role model), and in the fourth his awakening is described. He is now conscious of the absolute necessity of finding his own path to enlightenment. His desire is stronger than ever and he is not suffering because of it. For the next four chapters he goes into the world to do everything proscribed by the eightfold path. Only in the eighth chapter does he realize that all his activism has only brought him unnecessary suffering. The last four chapters could be construed as corresponding to the prescribed eightfold path: "right occupation" (in the case of the ferryman), right effort (in that of the son), right contemplation (in the case of Om), and right meditation (as exemplified by Govinda). However, it is exactly in these last four chapters that Lao Zi comes to the aid of Hesse's Siddhartha, because the ferryman in the ninth chapter is the embodiment of Tao, as I have indicated elsewhere.[8] Thus, the "Four Noble Truths" and the "Eightfold Path" cannot be the structural foundation of the novel, even though the numbers correspond neatly.

Theodore Ziolkowski advances the theory that the structure is triadic, each part having four chapters, with the river being the dividing line.[9] Hesse would have agreed to this, because the threefold development corresponds to his mode of thinking. Moreover, the life of the protagonist is actually divided into three stages. Hesse himself set the first four chapters apart: after his encounter with the Buddha and his decision to find his own individual way to enlightenment, Siddhartha leaves the realm of the spirit in order to immerse himself in the world of sensual pleasures. He becomes a lover, a merchant, and finally a gambler. His spiritual quest is all but forgotten. I believe, as I have written elsewhere, that this total reversal was inspired by another Taoist philosopher, Lie Zi, whose book Hesse read in a German translation. According to the Chinese sage, every act has to be carried to the very end before a real change can take place.[10] Thus Siddhartha goes from one extreme (the quest for Atman) to total immersion in the material and sensual world that Hesse called "die Kinderwelt," the world of the child people. Only now is Siddhartha ripe for the third and final stage, the way to enlightenment, depicted in the last four chapters.

At the end of the eighth chapter, Siddhartha escapes from the world of the child people and enters the world of the ferryman, the embodiment of Tao. Siddhartha lives with him on the river bank in tranquillity until his former lover, the courtesan Kamala, suddenly arrives at the river on her way to the Buddha. She has with her a boy. Siddhartha did not know that his lover was pregnant when he escaped from the world of the child people. Now he sees his son for the first time, but just as the three are united, Kamala dies of a snake bite. Now Siddhartha has to take care of his son, who resents having to call a stranger his father. In the course of time, Siddhartha develops into a caring and possessive father, an image of his own father when he was young. Buddhist and Taoist tenets teach that all desires and attachments lead to unnecessary suffering and constitute obstacles to enlightenment. Siddhartha has to learn, as his own father before him, that he cannot live for his son and has to let him pursue his own individual path. This is the last obstacle Siddhartha has to overcome before he can find his Atman, his true self, which is in tune with Brahman, the universal entity. Or to put it in Christian terms, before he can find God.

Another interesting interpretation has been presented by Reso Karalaschwili, who examines numerical symbolism as a compositional principle of *Siddhartha*.[11] However, Karalaschwili's primary concerns are the symbolic meanings of the numbers two, three, and four in the Indian culture; he also shows, as an afterthought, their meanings in the Western world. He almost entirely leaves out the numerology that is prominent in Chinese culture. Any reader of Dao De Jing would point out the significance of the passage that from one emerges two, two then produces three, three yields four, and four gives birth to the whole world. In all three cultures, we find

unity, duality, triad (or trinity), and tetrad. We could call the unity or oneness God, Tao, or Brahman; the duality is still best represented by the two
terms *yin* and *yang;* the triad signifies totality of the upper realm; while
the tetrad represents totality of the lower realm and is also a symbol of
our earth (the four corners of the world, the four seasons). Thus Siddhartha goes through three stages, each described in four chapters. He experiences and overcomes the duality of the world and reaches unity.

We are reminded that the novel has twelve chapters, that is, three times
four. Apart from the symbolic meaning of three and four mentioned above,
twelve, being the product of three times four, signifies totality and can be
arranged in a perfect circle, as Ziolkowski, Karalaschwili, and and I have
shown.[12] Very early, from the Samanas, Siddhartha learns the meaningless
repetitiveness of moving in circles. He also learns from them how to project oneself, through meditation, into all kinds of objects, such as a bird,
an animal, or even a carcass, however, one has to return to oneself after
meditation. On another occasion, Siddhartha poses the question whether
those who hope to escape the cycle of reincarnation are not in fact walking in circles as well. Govinda denies this, and expresses his belief that the
path is actually a spiral and that he and Siddhartha have climbed many
steps. Siddhartha disagrees, pointing out that the oldest Samana has been
going in circles for sixty years without reaching his goal. In this short exchange, the difference in perception between Siddhartha and Govinda is
shown very clearly. Obviously, one day, Govinda will not be able to keep
pace with his friend. However, they leave the Samanas together to go to
the Buddha, who has, through the teaching of Nirvana, brought the wheel
of rebirth to a halt. When they reach him, Siddhartha realizes that the
Buddha's achievement is a personal one; only the Buddha alone is beyond
suffering and rebirth. Even though Siddhartha feels that the Buddha's
teaching is the wisest, he is certain that there is no doctrine, no prescribed
path to enlightenment as if mounting a spiral-shaped path, climbing higher with every step. And yet, enlightenment remains an intellectual exercise
of walking in circles. At this point, Siddhartha has reached his first awakening; he will no longer follow the teachings of others, be it the Samanas
or the Buddha. He and Govinda part ways.

Now the law of duality comes into force. Siddhartha goes in a direction opposite to that of spirituality and loses himself gradually in sensuality and material life until he is transformed into just another member of
the "Kindermenschen," the child people. It is ironic that while Govinda
believes he is walking upwards, Siddhartha knows he is, like water, flowing downwards. This downward movement of water is a phenomenon
characteristic of Tao, as described in Dao De Jing.[13] Eventually Siddhartha
reaches the bottom and is ready for another awakening, this time from
the world of Sansara. Every time he experiences an awakening, he finds

himself near the river, and eventually crosses it. The ferryman Vasudeva[14] is there to ferry him across, as if to give the finishing touch to the process of transformation. When Siddhartha experiences his second awakening, it is the ferryman's job to lead him onto the path to enlightenment by showing him natural contemplation, which is listening to and learning from the river: acquiring the quality of water. It flows downward, moves upward as vapor, comes down again as rain, and joins the streams and rivers. It is deep and shallow; it swallows and absorbs everything (while possessing nothing). It reflects everything and it is not burdened with knowledge or craving for anything, not even Atman or Brahman. It is present everywhere in one form or another, and time has no meaning for it. It just is. Vasudeva is the demonstrator of this natural phenomenon. Elsewhere I have called him the personal embodiment of Tao, while Karalaschwili has preferred to use the term Brahman. But these are just different names for the same phenomenon.

Vasudeva practices *wuwai* or non-action. He has no theory, he prescribes no regulations or rules, he establishes no church, and has no disciples. He ferries people across the river, he cooks, he eats, he sleeps, and he hardly ever talks. He has no teaching and no theories, he only shows Siddhartha by his own example to listen to the river, learn from the river, and acquire the quality of the river. However, Siddhartha has yet to overcome the final hurdle, the possessive love of a father, his invisible link to their world, which he has long since physically left. Now the past has caught up with him. He has learned the art of love from Kamala, without, it seems, becoming involved emotionally. The same does not seem to be true for her. When it becomes known that Buddha is dying and will enter nirvana soon, people from all over the land go to pay him their last respects. Kamala and her son are among them. They approach the river, and now it is Kamala's turn to cross it. However, it is not her destiny to survive crossing this river so full of symbolic meaning for Siddhartha. She dies of a snake bite a short distance from the ferry. The last scene is described thus:

> Kamala blickte ihm unverwandt in die Augen. Sie dachte daran, daß sie zu Gotama hatte pilgern wollen, um das Gesicht eines Vollendeten zu sehen, um seinen Frieden zu atmen, und daß sie statt seiner nun ihn gefunden, daß es gut war, ebenso gut, als wenn sie jenen gesehen hatte.

> [Kamala gazed intently into his [Siddhartha's] eyes. She thought about how she had wanted to make a pilgrimage to see Gautama in order to behold the face of a Perfect One, to breathe in his peace, and now she had found not Gautama but this man, this was good, just as good as if she had seen the other one.[15]]

Kamala no longer sees a difference between Gautama and Siddhartha, but the latter has yet to experience total enlightenment. And the peace he has found as the ferryman's assistant will soon be shattered by his son.

The next chapter, simply entitled "The Son," brings the reader back to the first scene of the novel, when Siddhartha was a child. Now, as father, he tastes the same agony he had caused his own father — or rather an agony even more intense. The situation is more complicated now because father and son are strangers. In addition, Siddhartha's son is utterly spoiled, while the young Siddhartha was, at least on the outside, obedient to his father. Everything he has learned from the river is not sufficient to win over his son, who finally runs away. Siddhartha suffers long and hard. He has to learn to accept this suffering and to learn that his son is now going his own way, as he did when he was young. When he accepts this as a natural process, he passes the last stage of development. Vasudeva has fulfilled his duty, and passes on his role to Siddhartha, who has now reached the realm of Om. Perhaps someday he too will introduce someone to the river. In this final stage of enlightenment, when the unity is felt as omnipresent, the river, an apt symbol for Tao, becomes insignificant. Now Siddhartha is really like the Buddha, or Vasudeva for that matter. A stone is as good a symbol as the river to serve as example of the eternity of the moment. Time and differences become irrelevant. However, Hesse does posit a prerequisite: love. One has to love animate and inanimate things, even a common stone. One has to affirm the necessary existence of everything. Everything is a reality and must therefore be affirmed.

Above we have sketched the circuitous development of Hesse's Siddhartha to enlightenment. He is, however, although foregrounded, only one of the three characters in the novel who have reached this stage. The other two are the Buddha and the ferryman. Of these two, the former appears in the novel as the apparent enlightened one. Although Hesse does not describe his path to enlightenment, the reader knows that the historical Buddha was born a prince and lived a life of sensual pleasure and luxury until he discovered that living is suffering because of death, old age, sickness, and so on. He therefore left the comfort of his kingdom and became an ascetic, living — not unlike the protagonist of Hesse's novel — in the forest, until, after years of intense meditation, he attained enlightenment. The paths of the Buddha and Siddhartha are comparable, only they developed in reverse directions. The Buddha developed from sensual and luxurious life to asceticism and spirituality, while Siddhartha's path is from asceticism and spirituality to sensuality. It is remarkable that Siddhartha rejects the doctrine formulated by the enlightened one while accepting his state of enlightenment.

The historical Buddha determines the time and space of the novel. However, the reader is aware that all three are fictional; we are not discussing a historical (time) novel about India (place) or the Buddha (person). We are dealing with a creation or re-creation of Hesse's mind. That the personal name of the Buddha is Siddhartha, the same as Hesse's protagonist and the title of the novel suggests that Hesse is creating a fictional rival of the Buddha. That Hesse characterized his Siddhartha as incorporating European individualism, the most pronounced trait of the author, is an indication that the protagonist represents Hesse in many ways. Hesse's Siddhartha admits that the world described by the Buddha is a perfect, eternal chain linking cause and effect, but this "unity of the world" is interrupted and destroyed by opening a gap (the doctrine of the Nirvana) in the construct. This Siddhartha, as the mouthpiece of Hesse, rejects, because it has become an intellectual game. However, Hesse's protagonist does not deny that the Buddha has attained enlightenment, but he insists that the latter did not reach the enlightened state by following someone else's teaching and that no one can copy another individual's way to enlightenment.

Subsequently, Siddhartha has to turn to the other enlightened character in the novel, the ferryman Vasudeva, who is not a teacher and has no disciples. He seems to have no past; the reader knows practically nothing about him except that he once had a wife. It is not known when and under what circumstances he attained enlightenment. He is always there to ferry people, and particularly Siddhartha, across the river. He is a man of little or no words, a simple man without a doctrine. He is an ideal prototype of a Taoist sage on the model of Lao Zi, entirely different from the Buddha and Siddhartha. He is neither a determined seeker, nor does he try to solve the problem of life by slipping through a gap in an intellectually constructed world. All his senses are alive, not being buried or burdened by accumulated intellectual debris. He lives by his instincts, and his Atman is in tune with Brahman, that is, he is in uninterrupted communion with Tao. His symbol is the river in all its phases of transformation. He leads Siddhartha to the river and remains on the scene until his ward has become one with the river. The river and Vasudeva are both in their own ways manifestations of Tao, which is, as we shall see later, literally present in all objects.

In chapter 5 of book XXII of Chuang Zi's *True Classic of the South Flower Country,* a book Hesse admired, there is a parable with the title "Where is Tao."[16] The first answer is: it is omnipresent. The second answer is: it is in the ant. The third answer is: it is in the weed. The next answer is: it is in the sounding tile, a kind of music instrument. The last answer is: it is in the dung. This seemingly illogical order of objects of decreasing importance, from the abstract to animate and later inanimate things until the unspeakable, excrement, is reached, makes the point that Tao is indeed everywhere. Nothing is too low or dirty to be a part of Tao. Hesse's Siddhartha demonstrates the omnipresence of Tao by using a stone, which by itself is a less transparent symbol than the river. When Govinda fails to understand, Siddhartha asks his friend to kiss his forehead. With the touch of the kiss, Siddhartha is transformed into the river of life with the whole universe in flux. Time, place, and individual objects have no significance and are united in Tao. There is no doubt that Siddhartha has attained enlightenment. Govinda recognizes this, but he does not understand Siddhartha's explanation using the example of the stone, nor does he comprehend the significance of the demonstration of the universal unity in flux. He will remain a seeker who does not reach his goal.

English Translations of *Siddhartha* and Their Introductions

Literary works need readers, both casual and professional. The latter voice their interpretations as critiques. More than eight decades after the publication of *Siddhartha,* there are, of course, many different opinions on the work. Playing a prominent role here is the linguistic divide between those who do and those who do not read German. Hesse of course wrote in German, but the novel is also very popular in English. Even though there is no reliable statistical information, given the fact that English speakers are many times more numerable than German speakers, it is likely that *Siddhartha* has more Anglophone than German readers. What do these readers encounter when they read *Siddhartha* in one of its many English translations?

The first one, by Hilda Rosner, was published in 1951[17] and was brought out in paperback in 1957. Even though it has neither an introduction, nor a translator's preface, nor even a simple table of vital dates in the author's life and career, it was this translation along with that of Hesse's other popular novel *Steppenwolf* (first published in German in 1927 and translated into English in 1929) that inspired the beatnik and the hippie generation and made Hesse a cult author in the United States. Moreover, Rosner's translation was the only one available for roughly half a century, having been reprinted many times. So that for that time period, most Anglophone readers, unless they did research on their own, read the novel without any background information. This fact makes the enormous success of the novel and the popularity of its author even more remarkable.

The situation began to change only around the turn of the millenium. In 1999, Penguin Classics brought out a new translation by Joachim Neugroschel with a detailed introduction by Ralph Freedmann. Both are quite celebrated in their respective domains. Neugroschel was born in Vienna, Austria, and moved to New York at a young age. He has a degree in English and Comparative Literature from Columbia University and calls

German his native tongue. He began his career by translating two books from English into German. Later in life, he rendered into English from German, Yiddish, French, Italian, and Russian. In 1994, he was awarded the French-American Translation Prize. He also won three PEN Translation Awards. He is credited with having translated 200 titles so far. Besides Hesse, he has also translated Thomas Mann's and Franz Kafka's works into English. He compares the task of a translator with that of an actor: both can play many and different roles. He professes that he does not translate literally, but rather the style, the rhythm, and the music.[18] This method is most essential for translating *Siddhartha,* which the author of the introduction to Neugroschel's translation, Ralph Freedman, has deemed a lyrical novel.[19] Freedman was born in Hamburg and emigrated to the U.S. before Nazi Germany forbade Jews to leave the country. After his study on the lyrical novel, which includes *Siddhartha,* Freedman published *Hermann Hesse: Pilgrim of Crisis.*[20] With its expanded German edition, Freedmann became the author of the most definitive biography of Hesse. His introduction to *Siddhartha* is an important complement to Neugroschel's translation. To put it in perspective, the translated text has about 130 pages, while the introduction counts 26 pages, including "Suggestions for Further Reading."

Freedman establishes that the First World War and the death of his father caused Hesse to change fundamentally, leaving the neo-Romantic phase behind. He names four factors that facilitated the transformation. First, the personal crisis caused by the death of his father and the increasing mental instability of his first wife, Maria Bernoulli, the mother of his three sons. Second, Hesse's increasing involvement with the spiritual world of the East, especially China and India, focusing on the unity of all things and beings of the universe. Third, his involvement with psychoanalysis: he was first treated by a disciple of C. G. Jung, and later by Jung himself, so that a personal friendship evolved. This impact of this relationship would have even a stronger impact on the subsequent novel, *Steppenwolf.* Fourth, he began his inward journey, looking for answers within himself instead of in the outside world. This was a result of his preoccupation with psychoanalysis as well as with the Eastern notion of the unity of the universe.

Regarding *Siddhartha* in particular, Freedman emphasizes three factors: first, that the novel links Western sensibility with Eastern ideas; second, that there is an "unmistakable Western persona in the wings of the Eastern stage" (xviii); and third, that the novel is an intellectual biography of the "search of the source of the self within the self" (xix). With this special brand of Western sensibility and Eastern thought, Siddhartha rejects Buddha's doctrine of nirvana, because it undermines the universal unity. Even though Freedman pays tribute to the Eastern presence in

Hesse's worldview, we feel that his analysis of the East is only skin deep. It is hoped that the present essay will make up for this shortfall in an otherwise excellent interpretation. Freedman himself regrets that the Anglophone world has not been able to profit from the German-language scholarship on Chinese and Indian elements in Hesse's thinking.[21]

Without comparing Neugroschel's translation with Hilda Rosner's, Freedman praises Neugroschel's very highly. He considers the rendition not only elegant, but also imaginative. For a lyrical novel such as *Siddhartha*, as Freedman puts it, Hesse "uses words as expressions of sensed thought rather than as verbalized thought in promoting the idea of unity above the inner divisions of people and the fissures of societies in crisis" (xxviii–xxix). He believes that Neugroschel's translation reflects Hesse's style with fine sensibility, a view that we tend to agree with.

One year after Neugroschel's translation, in 2000, the Buddhist New Age publisher Shambhala published a new translation by Sherab Chödzin Kohn. In Tibetan tradition, Shambhala is the mythical kingdom in the Himalayas that later inspired the story of Shangri-la. The publishing house was an offshoot of the counterculture movement of the sixties and was founded in 1969 in San Francisco. Its success can be measured by the fact that in 1974, Random House became the official distributor of Shambhala books. This was an indication that the counterculture was beginning to join the mainstream. The publishing house moved in 1976 to Boulder, Colorado, in order to be close to its major author, the Tibetan Buddhist teacher Chögyam Trungpa, who founded Naropa University there in 1974. Shambhala Publications started its business with the title *Meditation in Action* by the same Tibetan guru. Altogether, Shambhala has published twenty-one titles by the guru, not including his *Collected Works* in eight volumes which appeared in 2004. This same Chögyam Trungpa is also the teacher of the translator of the Shambala edition of Hesse's *Siddhartha*, Sherab Chödzin Kohn.

Shambhala Publications is one of the rare publishing houses that supplies its own readers, because Shambhala is also a community of 165 meditation centers spread across North America and Europe, and even in some Asian countries such as Korea and Thailand. This perhaps explains that besides a hardcover edition of *Siddhartha*, there is also a paperback, a small-format paperback (which fits in a shirt pocket) and an audio edition of Kohn's translation. According to the meager information supplied by Shambhala, Sherab Chödzin Kohn has been a teacher of Buddhism and meditation for over thirty years. Moreover, he is the author of *A Life of the Buddha* (1994; paperback 2009). With Samuel Bercholz, one of the two original co-founders of the publishing house, he also edited *Entering the Stream: An Introduction to Buddha and his Teachings* (1993). Another edition followed in 1997 with the title *An Introduction to Buddha and his*

Teachings, which was in turn followed by a 2002 edition simply titled *Buddha and his Teachings.* In 1998, Kohn also co-authored a volume titled *The Wisdom of the Crows and other Buddhist Tales.* With this background, Kohn can be called *Siddhartha's* Buddhist translator. As a matter of fact, his "Translator's Preface" is the most informative of all introductions to English translations of *Siddhartha.*[22] He writes that even though Hesse's *Siddhartha* represents the author's journey to the East, in the present Anglophone world, it was the East that traveled to the West, since, for example, his own teacher was a Tibetan.

Kohn echoes Ralph Freedman's opinion that Hesse was a pilgrim of crisis and would attract readers any time society finds itself in crisis. He believes that we presently are also in a crisis, which he calls the "fertility dance with the microchip . . ." which, he says, must ". . . surely provoke a further acute outbreak of spirituality" (viii). This analysis sheds light on the phenomenon that within the eight years from 1999 through 2006 three new English translations of *Siddhartha* were published (including the next one to be discussed). Kohn even goes further with the prediction that with the perennial human yearning for spirituality, Hesse's work "cannot really go out of style." In addition, he is also the only translator to point out that "Hesse's grasp of Buddhist thinking was imprecise. He did not escape touches of theism and thoughts of sin . . ." (ix). He also thinks that *Siddhartha's* doctrine "is not sharp, but sweetly and naively eclectic" (ix). Kohn's Buddhist perspective has probably prevented him from realizing that with his novel Hesse was presenting a parallel path or message to that of the Buddha. He therefore intended it to be eclectic, not doctrinaire. Hesse was presenting a syncretic belief, not the fundamental view of any rigid doctrine. Nevertheless, Kohn's knowledge of Buddhism enabled him to recognize a certain resemblance between Hesse's eclectic doctrine and Zen Buddhism. This phenomenon we shall take up again when we discuss the next translation. In the meantime, we shall give a brief analysis of the introduction to Kohn's Buddhist translation.

The introduction is written by Paul W. Morris; it was previously published as "*Siddhartha:* Hermann Hesse's Journey to the East" in *Tricycle: The Buddhist Review.*[23] Unlike Freedman, who fully documents the sources of his views, the present introduction has no footnotes, although Morris does offer a bibliography of half a dozen titles in English. From this fact and the opinions Morris expresses in the introduction, it can be assumed that German scholarship on Hesse and China and India was not accessible to him. When he writes about generalities, he is quite correct. He informs the readers correctly that Hesse "created his own exotic blend of Eastern spirituality that was a synthesis of Hinduism, Buddhism, and Taoism, combined with his burgeoning knowledge of Western psychoanalysis" (xii). However, Morris's assertion that no other religion besides Christianity "permeated [Hesse's] life and work more than Buddhism" (xii) is more the fervent wish of a Buddhist rather than an objective fact, for, as we have established in the first part of this essay, Hesse treated Hinduism, Buddhism, Taoism, and Christianity — in both its Catholic and Protestant manifestations — as equals, although, to suit his argument of the moment, he sometimes did not emphasize all elements. Morris also errs when he tries to be specific. He writes, for example, that "Hesse's portrayal of India is based less on his own travels to the subcontinent and more on an imagined notion of 'the Orient' . . ."(xii). But in his lifetime, Hesse only left Europe once, in 1911. Furthermore, he never set foot on the Indian subcontinent. The closest he got to India was Colombo (a topic we shall pick up again later).

In his effort to make Hesse appear more Buddhist than he really was, Morris tends to misrepresent Hesse. Even though he knows of Hesse's interest in psychoanalysis, he does not seem to know that Hesse was treated by C. G. Jung himself in the summer of 1921. It was this treatment plus his renewed interest in Lao Zi that pulled Hesse out of his acute depression and consequently enabled him to complete the second part of the novel in two months, But Morris tries to convince us that Hesse snapped out of the depression and was able to finish the novel because "he grew more familiar with Buddhist doctrine" (xvi). Quite the contrary: in a diary entry of January 1921, Hesse insisted that his Siddhartha would not want Nirvana when he dies, but to be reborn again.[24] A few weeks later, he again stated his disagreement with Buddhist doctrine, calling it too rational.[25] A few years later, in a letter to a PhD candidate, he made the categorical statement that *Siddhartha* was the expression of his liberation from Buddhism.[26] Morris quotes Hesse saying that "we allow Buddha to speak to us as vision, as image, as the awakened one, the perfect one, we find in him, almost independently of the philosophic content and dogmatic kernel of his teaching, a great prototype of mankind" (xvi), and this is very similar to what Siddhartha said to the Buddha: "I have never doubted you for a moment . . . that you are Buddha, that you have attained the goal, the highest . . . You have found the deliverance from death. It came to you from your own seeking . . . It did not come through a teaching! And — this is my thought, O Sublime one — no one is granted deliverance through teaching . . . That is why I . . . leave all teachings and teachers and to reach my goal alone or die."[27] This is Siddhartha's categorical statement. It is also Hesse's conclusion, up to a point. He had been attracted by Buddhism in his younger years, about the time he was also attracted to Schopenhauer, but his enthusiasm eventually waned, as his critical remarks written during his visit to the Buddhist temples in Kandy, in today's Sri Lanka, in 1911 bear witness,[28] but he retained his respect for the Buddha his entire life. We need a balanced approach to Hesse's view of Buddhism in order to do justice to the novel.

Morris also errs in other details. He writes that Hesse resumed working on *Siddhartha* in early 1922 and "quickly completed the eight chapters that comprise Part Two" (xvi). The problem is that, after the publication of Part I (first 4 chapters) in July 1921, the first three chapters of Part II were published under the title "Siddharthas Weltleben. Drei Kapitel aus einer unvollendeten indischen Dichtung" (Siddhartha's Profane Life: Three Chapters from an Incomplete Indian Poetic Work) in the same year's September issue of the journal *Genius*.[29]

In 2006 a new English translation by Susan Bernofsky was published.[30] Of the four translations, only Neugroschel and Bernofsky translate the original subtitle, "Eine indische Dichtung." Neugroschel renders it as "An Indian Tale." Freedman thinks this translation misleading, because the German word can either mean any imaginative work in general or a poetic work in particular. For Hesse, who always wanted to be a poet, "Dichtung" can only imply a poetic work. Does Bernofsky's rendition, "An Indian Poem," do more justice to the German original? Perhaps it does. Or perhaps one should revert to Freedman's phrasing and call it "An Indian Lyrical Novel."[31] The new translation is accompanied by a "biographical note," an introduction by Tom Robbins (who describes himself as an "author of eight offbeat but popular novels"), and a "translator's preface," plus a glossary of Indian terms. The biographical note is precise and informative. It outlines the major publications by Hesse, the date of the first English translation of the novel, and recounts reactions to the novel from informed readers such as Thomas Mann. It provides the reader with good background information.

The introduction by the American novelist Robbins is a different matter. He has some valid insights, but errs in many factual matters. It is obvious that he is not conversant with Hesse scholarship, not even with the many books and essays available in English or even Freedman's introduction to Neugroschel's rendition. He characterizes Hesse as "steeped in German mysticism and Asian philosophy" (xiii), which according to him represent two of many components of Hesse's mind; he also adds in parenthesis that Hesse was twice in the Far East. If he had taken the trouble to read the biographical note included in Bernosky's translation, he would have learned that Hesse took "a formative trip to the East Indies in 1911" (vi). It is never mentioned that he visited anywhere in Asia again. As a matter of fact, Hesse never visited the Far East, but instead only what the Germans called *Inselindien* (literally "island India," today's Sri Lanka), *Hinterindien* (literally "behind India," the Malay Peninsula, including Singapore), and Sumatra, a part of the former Dutch East Indies. Today we would say Southeast Asia. It is also of interest to note that Robbins thinks

Siddhartha is equivalent to "a road movie," even though Hesse's hero walks barefoot. He further claims "a superficial resemblance" (xv) between *Siddhartha* and Kerouac's *On the Road,* and contrasts Hesse's novel with W. Somerset Maugham's *The Razor's Edge,* commenting that though "parallels definitely exist, the differences between the two books are nearly as pronounced as those between a Chicago hotdog and a Bombay curry." These are curious, even frivolous remarks. However, they do show how *Siddhartha* has become a part of the Anglo-American cultural fabric. But how is this indigenized Siddhartha originally created by Hesse interpreted? Robbins suggests that Hesse reduced Hinduism and Buddhism "to their essence, and what remains of this double boiler is a systemless system that perhaps most closely resembles Zen" (xvii). He believes that Hesse did not mention Zen in the novel because of historical accuracy, since it was founded in China over a millennium after the book's action, and it was many centuries later (somewhere in the 11th or 12th century) before it was accepted in Japan. For this reason Siddhartha could not be a Zen master. Robbins does not explain the resemblances between the philosophy espoused by the novel and Zen Buddhism.

Siddhartha and Zen

But was Hesse aware of Zen Buddhism at the time when he was writing the novel?[32] We remember that the Buddhist translator Kohn also recognized a close resemblance between the worldview espoused in the novel and Zen. When Hesse was writing *Siddhartha,* Zen was still practically unknown in the West. But late in his life he did become interested in this form of Mahayana Buddhism practiced in China and Japan. Let us trace the development. Before the novel was published as such, the first part was first published in 1921 in a journal. When the last five chapters of the second part were completed, Hesse also published all eight chapters together and dedicated it to his cousin, the Japanologist Wilhelm Gundert, who was on home leave from being a missionary in Japan.[33]

The Japanese philosopher Daisetz Teitaro Suzuki (1870–1966) was the first to introduce Zen Buddhism to the West. In 1934, he published *An Introduction to Zen Buddhism,* the first work on Zen Buddhism in a Western language. A German translation was published in 1939, with a preface by Carl Gustav Jung.[34] A copy of this book is in Hesse's personal library, which is preserved in Marbach, Germany. In this copy, we can see that several quotes in Jung's preface had been underlined by Hesse. The following two are the most instructive: "Buddha is nothing other than the mind or rather that of the perceiver of this mind"; and "gaining insight in one's own nature with attainment of Buddhahood."[35] These tenets, especially the second one, correspond perfectly to Hesse's anti-doctrinaire convictions as expressed in *Siddhartha*. Until his cousin Wilhelm Gundert took up the translation of *Bi Yan Lu,* a compendium of Zen Buddhism teachings, and shared it with Hesse, there is no evidence that Hesse made any efforts to study Zen. In a letter to his cousin dated 19 May 1956, he wrote about these sessions. When the first volume of Gundert's translation of the original Chinese work was published in 1960 (the second volume followed seven years later), Hesse was so enthusiastic that he compared his cousin's achievement to that of Richard Wilhelm, to whom Hesse owed his knowledge of Chinese classics. Although Gundert, despite what one might conclude from Hesse's dedication of the second part of the novel to him, did not play a role in the composition of *Siddhartha,*[36] his name is nevertheless listed in the "Glossary of Sanskrit Terms, Deities, Persons, Places, and Things" in Bernofsky's English translation of *Siddhartha*. It is curious that Gundert's name is otherwise not to be found in the book. One gets the impression that his name stands as an alibi for Tom Robbins's interpretation. It is also interesting that even though Robbins erred in historical details — given that Siddhartha was published in 1922, or before Zen was known in the West, so that Hesse could not have known of it when he wrote the novel — it is, in my view, legitimate to compare Hesse's worldview with Zen, because it is the result of a marriage of Tao and Dharma.

Tom Robbins can be considered a prototypical Anglophone reader with little or no German background who appreciates *Siddhartha* as a general work of art. He mentions Dostoyevsky, Maugham, Kerouac, and the "New Age," among others, to construct an ahistorical, fictionalized kind of post-Hesse. The person of the author and the scholarly research on his works are of little interest to Robbins. His introduction may be an interesting, even illuminating exercise, but can easily distort both author and work.

The translator Susan Bernofsky seems to share Robbins's view that historical details are of less significance. If she had read the "biographical note" more carefully, she would not have written in the preface that Hesse "fled to neutral Switzerland" (xx) before the First World War was over. It is documented, of course, that Hesse moved with his family in September 1912 — nearly two years before the First World War *began* — to Oster-mundgen, not far from Bern.[37] Bernofsky's characterization of the novel is also peculiar. She writes: "Siddhartha is a child of his [Hesse's] time, a fin de siècle youth who has put on a loincloth and monk's robe for a fancy-dress ball" (xx). To the students of Hesse's works, this statement falsifies the personality and the time of the author and puts both in a trifling light, because Hesse's works reflect, as a rule, a crisis situation, both on the personal and general level. The following comment is, to use an understatement, offbeat as well: "One might notice, for one thing — as Tom Robbins did when he read this new translation — that Hesse has populated his novel with improbable fauna: chimpanzees and jaguars, creatures to be found in India only in zoos" (xx). These animals cannot be found in the novel. Bernofsky concludes that *Siddhartha* is "a powerful metaphor whose very distance from the European reality of the time just goes to show how unbearable that reality was" (xx). This is certainly partially true and contradicts the earlier assertion of a "fancy-dress ball"; yet to postulate this as the ultimate aim of the novel seriously limits its scope. Tom Robbins comes closer to the mark when he says "that Hesse has *his* traveller remind us emphatically that 'Wisdom cannot be passed on.' And that reminder may be the hardest, most valuable jewel in this literary lotus" (xviii). But instead of grappling with a creature of our own creation, we should focus on the author and his work, even though — or perhaps especially when — we are reading a translation.

Neither Hilda Rosner nor Sherab Chödzin Kohn translate the subtitle of *Siddhartha* — "Eine indische Dichtung" — while Neugroschel translates it as "An Indian Tale" and Bernofsky renders it as "An Indian Poem," as we have seen above. This subtitle is quite problematic, because in the novel Hesse's hero rejects the tenets of both Hinduism and Buddhism. Or to be more precise, in the case of Hinduism, he retains the notion of unity in the sense of all-inclusiveness and the correspondence of Atman to Brahman, but rejects Hindu doctrine and rites. With Buddhism, the situation is even more complicated: Siddhartha looks upon the historical Buddha as his role model while refusing to believe that the teachings and the structural system of Buddhism have any general validity. Because of this ambiguous position of Hesse and his alter ego Siddhartha, two groups of interpreters have evolved, each emphasizing a different aspect. Scholars close to the Indian culture tend to overlook Hesse's objection to certain tenets of Indian spirituality, while those of Christian background stress the rejection and believe that Hesse was subtly re-affirming Christianity by emphasizing Christian love. The latest representative of the first group is Kamakshi P. Murti, whose doctoral dissertation, containing a chapter on *Siddhartha,* was published in 1990 as *Die Reinkarnation des Lesers als Autor.*[38] Murti is very critical of her predecessors, especially Vridhagiri Ganeshan,[39] and criticizes him for presenting the novel as expressing Hesse's conviction that Indian spirituality, especially as manifested in Hinduism, represents the ultimate wisdom (101). She herself seems to believe that Hesse was swaying between Christian and Indian religions, as the heading of the section "Siddhartha. Christian history of salvation or Buddhist path to redemption?"[40] suggests. Consequently, she finds a way to evade the issue by going into stylistic analysis in order to demonstrate how the language of the novel is indebted to Sanskrit, a language Hesse did not know (he acquired his knowledge of India through translations). A link between the rhythmic and repetitive prose of the novel and the translation of any

Indian classic has not been established. Nevertheless, it is obvious that contemporary interpreters with an Indian background do not insist that Hesse's novel was exclusively indebted to Hinduism as Ganeshan once did.

A similar tendency can also be observed in critics belonging to the Christian group, with the theologian Christoph Gellner as the latest representative. His book, entitled *Hermann Hesse und die Spiritualität des Ostens,* sums up this development. Eastern or Asian spirituality has become increasingly acceptable and is respected by many Christians. Gellner believes that Hesse's intense suffering under the rigid Christian orthodoxy practiced by his parents alienated him from the religion to such an extent that he turned to Asia for spiritual relief. From his first encounters, around 1900, with adherents of philosophies and lifestyles beyond European conventions — "vegetarians, nudists, and theosophists on Monte Verità" — he advanced to Hinduism and Buddhism, and around 1907, at the age of thirty, proclaimed himself Buddhist.[41] Soon afterwards, he changed this exclusive position and included Chinese spirituality in his worldview. Now, when Hesse discussed his beliefs, he often mentioned China and India in one breath.[42] The title of Gellner's chapter on *Siddhartha* is an eye-opener: "The Indian Element is Not of Chief Importance"; and one of the subheadings reads: "Liberation from Indian Thoughts."[43] Gellner does not claim, however, that Hesse had discarded Hinduism and Buddhism altogether, just that they were no longer dominant for him. We are reminded that Hesse never ceased to be a Christian (although he often swayed between Protestantism and Catholicism). Especially in *Siddhartha,* the so-called Indian lyrical novel, he insisted on the presence of Christian love. As we have seen, his Christianity had been modified by Asian spirituality, or as Gellner formulates it, the new Asian perception of Christianity.

To conclude, we shall take a final look at Sherab Chödzin Kohn's and Tom Robbins's contention that Siddhartha's message mostly resembles Zen. Only Kohn gives us an indication why this is so. He remarks that in the final chapter of *Siddhartha,* "Hesse does not quite give us the 'return to the market place' found in the last of the ten Zen ox-herding pictures, but the utter excoriation of ego . . . is vivid enough" (ix). In an elaborate footnote, Kohn describes these pictures:

> A series of ten pictures, well-known in the Zen tradition, depicts the stages of the path to enlightenment. The process begins with a man searching for an ox, symbolizing the practitioner trying to get a handle on his awareness. After a long time the man finds that ox's footprints, next he glimpses the animal, finally catches it, tames it, and is able to ride it home. Since the practitioner has now at last become one with his awareness, in the seventh picture the ox disappears; in the eighth the man disappears (ego is gone), and the picture is empty. In the ninth, emptiness disappears — again there are phenomena, ap-

pearing brilliant and clear without the projections of ego. In the tenth picture, the man re-appears, a nondescript old fellow heading for the market place on foot; he drinks at the sake shop, he bargains, he gossips, and whomever [sic] encounters him experiences awakening. (x)

Hesse, who died shortly after the publication of the first volume of his cousin's translation of *Bi Lan Yu,* did not know this series of pictures. Admittedly, the ninth picture does bear some resemblance to Siddhartha's progress. Yet Hesse would never have agreed to the tenth picture, which would imply that whoever reads the novel would be enlightened. It would also mean that whoever sees the Buddha would be enlightened, including Govinda. Hesse would never have entertained such a thought, because it is too mechanical and denies the unity of self and the universe, the ultimate state of enlightenment important to Hesse.

We have already characterized Zen Buddhism as a marriage of Tao and dharma. Even though Hesse learned about Zen decades later, when he was in his seventies, many symbols in the novel we analyzed such as the river are derived from Taoist teachings. However, these can easily be related to Zen symbolism. We shall take a closer look in this regard. We know that Hesse was familiar with *Bi Yan Lu.* This book belonged to the "Yünmen" school of Zen Buddhism in China. Literally, "Yünmen" means cloud gate. Hesse was very happy that he had finally found a form of Buddhism he could accept.[44] This joy he expressed through two of his fictional characters: Josef Knecht and Carlo Ferromonte in *Das Glasperlenspiel* (The Glass Bead Game), Hesse's last novel, first published in Zurich in 1943. In 1960 he wrote in the fictive letter entitled "Josef Knecht an Carlo Ferromonte," published a year later, that with Zen the essence of Buddha acquired a Chinese face.[45] This school of Buddhism echoes Hesse preference for doctrine without words and his emphasis on Christ or Tao or Buddha or Atman within us perfectly.

We shall take Hesse's story "Innen und Aussen" (Inside and Outside), written in 1919 and published a year later, as an example. At that time, Hesse had yet to hear of Zen Buddhism. In the story, the character Erwin is the mouthpiece of Hesse. He pronounces the maxim: nothing is external; nothing is internal; because what is external is internal. We shall compare this passage with the teaching of master Hui Neng (638–713), the sixth patriarch of Zen Buddhism in China, who established the southern branch, from which the Yünmen school is derived. Hui Neng said: ". . . to those whose hearts and words are good and for whom the internal and external are one, meditation and wisdom are identified. Self-enlightenment and practice do not consist in argument."[46] In other words, if one practices meditation, words and arguments become unnecessary and inside and outside are one and the same.

If we juxtapose Hesse's *Siddhartha* and Hui Neng's teaching, we gain the impression that they are paraphrasing each other. Since we are already familiar with Hesse's novel, I shall quote Hui Neng:

> . . . in my system . . . absence of thought has been instituted as the main doctrine, absence of phenomena as the substance, and non-attachment as the foundation.[47]

We remember that from the samanas, Siddhartha learned meditation by thinking, that is, by projecting his Atman into another being or thing, which he then has to unlearn. In the world of the child people he becomes attached to possessions, which he has to dispose of, and in his final stage he has to overcome the attachment to his son. Only then can he reach the stage he calls awakening. What is this awakening other than self-enlightenment?

Hui Neng even explains indirectly why Siddhartha has to learn from the river instead of following the way of Buddha:

> [In its ordinary process], thought moves forward without a halt; past, present, and future thoughts continue as an unbroken stream. But if we can cut off this stream by an instant of thought, the Dharma-Body will be separated from the physical body, and at no time will a single thought be attached to any dharma. If one single instant of thought is attached to anything, then every thought will be attached. That will be bondage. But if in regard to all dharmas, no thought attached to anything, that means freedom.[48]

Is this not the same lesson that Siddhartha learns from the river in order to gain the realm of unity?

One year before he died, Hesse wrote the poem entitled "Junger Novize im Zen-Kloster" (Young Novice in a Zen Monastery), in which the novice is struggling to grasp the world of Maya. The last stanza of the poem gives advice:

> Sammle dich und kehre ein
> Lerne schauen, lerne lesen!
> Sammle dich — und Welt wird Schein.
> Sammle dich — und Schein wird Wesen.[49]
>
> [Gather yourself and turn inward
> Learn to observe, learn to read!
> Gather yourself — and the world becomes appearances.
> Gather yourself — and appearances become essences.]

Here, the real world and the world of Maya, or appearances, are the same, only the mindset is different. With proper meditation, one recognizes the world of Maya, and, again with meditation, the world of appearance (Maya) becomes essential again. In a way, the poem's advice reflects the development of Siddhartha. He has to learn to perceive in order to penetrate the world of appearance, and then he has to learn further to use his natural or instinctive qualities to lift the veil of Maya to see the real world. Hesse and his alter ego made a similar journey through the world of appearances or the "Kinderwelt" (the world of the child people) in the novel to themselves, where they find Atman, Tao, Brahman, or God.

Notes

[1] See Hermann Hesse, *Sämtliche Werke,* ed. Volker Michels, vol. 12: *Autobiographische Schriften II. Selbstzeugnisse. Erinnerungen. Gedenkblätter und Rundbriefe* (Frankfurt: Suhrkamp, 2003), 213. Subsequent references will be given as *SW* 12 and page number.

[2] Ralph Freedman, *Hermann Hesse: Pilgrim of Crisis.* (New York: Pantheon Books, 1978), 225.

[3] Adrian Hsia, *Hermann Hesse und China* (Frankfurt am Main: Suhrkamp taschenbuch, 2003), 237.

[4] See Volker Michels, ed., *Materialien zu Hermann Hesses "Siddhartha"* (Frankfurt am Main: Suhrkamp, 1974), 2:21.

[5] Leroy R. Shaw, "Time and the Structure of Hermann Hesse's Siddhartha," in Symposium, 11.1 (Fall 1957): 204–24. The four noble truths are: 1. Life is equivalent to suffering; 2. The cause of suffering is craving for pleasure and fulfillment; 3. Suffering can be eliminated by extinguishing craving and desire; 4. Follow the eightfold path to end desire and suffering.

[6] The eightfold path consists of: 1. Right views; 2. Right resolve; 3. Right speech; 4. Right behavior; 5. Right occupation; 6. Right effort; 7. Right contemplation; 8. Right meditation.

[7] http://www.buddhanet.net/e-learning/buddhism/bp_sut23.htm [6 March 2009]

[8] Adrian Hsia, "Siddhartha und China," in Michels, ed., *Materialien zu Hermann Hesses "Siddhartha,"* 2:195–205.

[9] Ziolkowski, "Siddhartha — die Landschaft der Seele," in Michels, ed., *Materialen zu Hermann Hesses "Siddhartha,"* 2:133–61.

[10] Hsia, *Hermann Hesse und China,* 102.

[11] Reso Karalaschwili, "Die Zahlensymbolik als Kompositonsgrundlage in H. Hesses 'Siddhartha,'" in Michels, ed., *Materialien,* 2:255–71.

[12] Michels, ed., *Materialien,* 2: 266.

[13] Cf. Adrian Hsia, "Siddhartha und China," in Michels, ed., *Materialien zu Hermann Hesses "Siddhartha,"* 2: 195–205.

[14] In Hindu mythology, Vasudeva is the father of Krishna, but he bears no resemblance to the ferryman.

[15] Hermann Hesse, *Siddhartha: An Indian Poem,* translated by Susan Bernofsky (New York: Modern Library, 2006), 96.

[16] Hesse read this in Richard Wilhelm's translation, namely: *Das wahre Buch vom südlichen Blütenland*, 1912.

[17] New York: New Directions Publishing Corporation, 1951.

[18] See "An Interview with Joachim Neugroschel, Translator and Editor of *The Shadows of Berlin*," http://www.eclectica.org/v10n1/glixman.html (accessed 24 July 2009).

[19] See Ralph Freedman, *The Lyrical Novel: Studies in Hermann Hesse, André Gide, and Virginia Woolf* (Princeton: Princeton UP, 1963).

[20] (New York: Pantheon Books, 1978). An expanded German translation was published as *Hermann Hesse: Autor der Krisis. Eine Biographie* (Frankfurt: Suhrkamp 1982).

[21] In footnote 15 of his introduction Freedman cites two studies and regrets that they have not been translated into English: Vridheri Ganeshan's *Das Indienerlebnis Hermann Hesses* (Bonn: Bouvier 1974), and Adrian Hsia's *Hermann Hesse und China* (Frankfurt: Suhrkamp, 1974). It is also of interest to note that in Freedman's "Suggestions for Further Reading" there is one item he considers "highly recommended": "Hermann Hesse and the East" by Adrian Hsia. Freedman regrets its "relative inaccessibility."

[22] We are reminded that Hilda Rosner did not provide her readers with a preface, while Neugroschel only wrote that his translation was based on the original version of 1922. Susan Bernofsky's preface will be discussed later.

[23] Fall 1999, vol. IX, no. 1.

[24] Hermann Hesse, *Sämtliche Werke*, ed. Volker Michels, vol. 11: *Autobiographische Schriften I. Wanderung. Kurgast. Die Nürnberger Reise. Tagebücher* (Frankfurt: Surkamp, 2003), 631. Subsequent references will be given as *SW* 11 and page number.

[25] Hesse, *SW* 11:640.

[26] Hermann Hesse, *Gesammelte Briefe*, 4 vols., ed. Ursula and Volker Michels (Franfurt am Main: Suhrkamp, 1973–1986), here 2:96.

[27] Quoted from Neugroschel's translation, 32–33.

[28] "Der Buddhismus von Ceylon ist hübsch, um ihn zu photographieren und Feuilletons darüber zu schreiben; darüber hinaus ist er nichts als eine von den vielen rührenden, qualvoll grotesken Formen, in denen hilfloses Menschenleid seine Not und seinen Mangel an Geist und Stärke ausdrückt." *SW* 13:272–75. (The Buddhism on Ceylon is pretty, so you can take pictures and write magazine articles about it. Beyond that it is nothing more than one of the many sentimental, painfully grotesque forms in which helpless human suffering expresses its need and its lack of spirit and strength.)

[29] Cf. Chrisph Gellner, *Hermann Hesse und die Spiritualität des Ostens* (Düsseldorf: Patmos, 2005), 125.

[30] Hermann Hesse, *Siddhartha: An Indian Poem*, translated by Susan Bernofsky (New York: Modern Library, 2006).

[31] We are reminded of the title of another study by Freedman: *The Lyrical Novel: Studies in Hermann Hesse, André Gide, and Virginia Woolf*, 1963.

[32] A word of clarification is perhaps in order here. The word "Zen," as it is known in the West, is the Japanese pronunciation of the Chinese ideogram "Chan," meaning meditation. The Chinese character is, in turn, derived from Sanskrit "dhyāna" (or "Jhāna" in Pali). Bodhidharma, the founder of the Shao Lin (Japanese pronunciation: Shorin) Temple, famous for its martial arts, was also the founder of Chan Buddhism. In the course of Tang Dynasty, it was introduced to Japan.

[33] Gundert, when he finally returned to Germany in 1936, occupied the chair of Japanology at the University of Hamburg. In the 1950s, he began to translate a part of the Zen Buddhist canon *Bi Yan Lu* into German, often discussing the translation with Hesse.

[34] It was translated by Hans Zimmer and published by Curt Weller & Co. in 1939. Cf. my *Hermann Hesse and China* for a chapter on Hesse and Zen, pages 115–38.

[35] See Hsia, *Hermann Hesse and China*, 132.

[36] Hesse's dedication of the second part of the book to his cousin was probably meant as congratulation, since Gundert received his doctorate from the University of Hamburg at that time.

[37] Cf. Martin Pfeifer, *Hesse Kommentar zu sämtlichen Werken* (Munich: Winkler, 1980), 42.

[38] Kamakshi P. Murti, *Die Reinkarnation des Lesers als Autor: Ein Rezeptionsgeschichtlicher Versuch über den Einfluß altindischer Literatur auf deutsche Schriftsteller um 1900* (Berlin: Walter de Gruyter, 1990).

[39] Vridhagiri Ganeshan, *Das Indienbild deutscher Dichter um 1900* (Bonn: Bouvier, 1975).

[40] The German original: "Christliche Heilsgeschichte oder buddhistischer Erlösungsweg?," 105.

[41] Gellner, *Hermann Hesse und die Spiritualität des Ostens*, 51.

[42] Gellner, *Hermann Hesse und die Spiritualität des Ostens*, 89–90.

[43] The German original versions: "Das Indische ist nicht die Hauptsache: 'Siddhartha'" and "Befreiung vom indischen Denken."

[44] Cf. Hsia, *Hermann Hesse and China*, 123.

[45] Cf. "Das Buddhawesen bekam ein neues, ein chinesisches Gesicht," Michels, ed., *Materialien*, 449.

[46] Quoted from Wm. Theodore de Bary, Wing-Tsit Chan, and Burton Watson, eds., *Sources of Chinese Tradition* (New York: Columbia UP, 1964), 1:352–53.

[47] De Bary, et al., eds., *Sources of Chinese Tradition*, 353.

[48] De Bary, et al., eds., *Sources of Chinese Tradition*, 353.

[49] This poem was first published in *Akzente* (1961): 185–86. Quoted from Hsia, *Hesse and China*, 135.

7: *Der Steppenwolf*

Martin Swales

Hermann Hesse's *Der Steppenwolf* (1927) belongs to a group of some six novels, all written and/or published within the period 1920 to 1933, which, by common consent, represent the canonical contribution of the German novel to High Modernism. The others are Kafka's *Das Schloss,* Thomas Mann's *Der Zauberberg,* Döblin's *Berlin Alexanderplatz,* Broch's *Die Schlafwandler,* and Musil's *Der Mann ohne Eigenschaften.* All of these works have at least three features in common. One is that they register an urgent sense of cultural transition, a crisis that expresses itself as a virulent collision of old and new values. Another is their need to find — or at least to gesture towards — a conclusion that holds out the promise of some kind of consoling, perhaps even redemptive, solution. The third feature they share is an acute form of novelistic self-consciousness: that is to say, they are novels that thematize their own narrative performance as part of the cultural analysis that they are concerned to offer. All of them are, by any standards, challenging works. Part of the challenge they pose is that they work simultaneously on a number of interpretative levels.

The event sequence of *Der Steppenwolf* is as follows. The novel consists of three different, but overlapping, narrative texts. It opens with a brief statement by an unnamed and unspecified bourgeois narrator. He lives in a large house belonging to his aunt. A new tenant arrives: one Harry Haller, the "Steppenwolf" of the novel's title, a man who feels himself to be a radically fractured self, part decent, respectable human being, part violent, instinctual wolf. The bourgeois narrator registers the strangeness and reclusiveness of Haller, and is both alienated by and attracted to him. While he finds it difficult to form a clear picture of the strange lodger's way of life, he feels with great urgency that this enigmatic figure is symptomatic of contemporary Europe's troubles. When Haller disappears as mysteriously as he has arrived, he leaves behind a mass of papers. And the bourgeois narrator decides to pass those papers on to us, the readers, by publishing them. They consist for the most part of Harry's own account of his recent experiences — and, by this token, they have a certain confessional force. We learn that he has private means; while he disapproves of capitalism, he lives off the interest from certain funds and investments. He is a critical intellectual, but he despises most other intellectuals; he is a pacifist who is troubled by the rising tide of bellicosity in the world around him. He loves the domestic solidity of the bourgeois world, yet feels that his own divided personality precludes him from identifying with it. One evening, in an alleyway of the old town, he sees, or thinks that he sees, a doorway above which an inscription makes propaganda for a "Magic Theater." His attempt to enter is thwarted, but he subsequently acquires from a peddler a brief tract entitled "Tractat vom Steppenwolf."

Harry's own narrative is interrupted at this point, and we are given the treatise to read. It is a psychological-cum-philosophical analysis of none other than Harry himself. It suggests that he must learn to get beyond the crude dualism of understanding himself as part man, part wolf; rather, he consists of multiple selves. And in the closing lines of the "Tractat" there is the intimation that, if only Harry could attain the serenity of the so-called Immortals, who are, we presume, the authors of the "Tractat," he will be able to smile at and come to terms with his own multiplicity of being. Harry is little comforted by the "Tractat." He accepts a dinner invitation from a professor with whom he is acquainted, but, appalled by his host's philistinism and nationalism, he leaves in fury. In a pub he is accosted by a young woman, Hermine, a prostitute, who decides to take him in hand. She helps him to enjoy pleasures that hitherto he has hardly known. She reconciles him to jazz by teaching him to dance; she arranges for him to be introduced to the pleasures of sex by Maria. He also meets, through Hermine, Pablo, a saxophonist. In the closing phase of the novel Harry attends a masked ball and then, his inhibitions much lifted by the drugs Pablo supplies, he enters a Magic Theater, where he discovers facets of his personality that have long been hidden. At the climax of the Magic Theater sequence Harry kills Hermine; for this he is condemned by Pablo, who seems to speak with the authority of the Immortals, condemned for having introduced real emotions (presumably jealousy) into the high fictionality of the Magic Theater. Harry's account ends on the note of failure — but with the promise that Pablo and Mozart, and with them the wisdom of the Immortals, are waiting for him.

Part of the difficulty posed by an attempt to do what I have just done — to summarize the events of the novel — is that one finds oneself uncertain about the status of the events as events. Not only does relatively little happen; one cannot be entirely sure about the definition of the little that happens. Are the events portrayed as genuinely occurring in a recognizable outer world? Or are they part of an elaborate dream sequence? Either way, the events are, as one might put it, very discursive, very much talked about, explained and interpreted. We are left in no doubt that they mean a great deal; but their particularity is left shrouded. To this quality, a kind of over-determined narrativity, I shall return later in this chapter.

I have already suggested, in my attempt to link *Der Steppenwolf* with other novels of German High Modernism, that Hesse's narrative can be viewed on a number of levels: historical, philosophical, and psychological. These levels are, of course, not water-tight; rather, they constantly interact with each other. But for purposes of interpretative clarity it makes sense initially to treat them separately. Moreover, it is helpful to identify each strand of meaning with a particular section of the novel. That is to say: the historical theme is particularly in evidence in the introductory account provided by the bourgeois narrator; the philosophical theme dominates the "Tractat"; the psychological concern comes to the fore in Harry's own "Aufzeichnungen."

As I have already indicated, the bourgeois narrator, who is present in the opening few pages of the text, is not linked to Harry by any close ties of friendship or intimacy. But occasionally, often as the result of a brief meeting, Harry allows the bourgeois narrator insight into another realm, a domain that is somehow foreign yet utterly germane to him. At one point the narrator writes: "Ueberhaupt machte der ganze Mann den Eindruck, als komme er aus einer fremden Welt, etwa aus überseeischen Ländern, zu uns und finde hier alles zwar hübsch, aber ein wenig komisch"[1] (8; "Altogether he gave the impression of having come out of an alien world, from another continent perhaps. He found it all very charming and a little odd": 5) It is worth registering at this point that virtually all the relationships in the novel are of this kind; they are not fueled by interpersonal urgency, rather they represent the coming together of different experiential worlds. What matters in Harry's relationships to Hermine, Maria, and Pablo is less the particular experiential interaction that occurs than the interpretive chemistry that results. The bourgeois narrator registers, and is partly offended by, Haller's strangeness, his melancholy, his irony. Yet he also is at pains, at the end of his account, to stress that he is publishing Harry's papers because they have a vital degree of interpretative purchase on the disarray of contemporary life:

> Durch meine Bekanntschaft mit Haller ist es mir möglich geworden, sie (die Aufzeichnungen, M.S.) teilweise zu verstehen, ja zu billigen. Ich würde Bedenken tragen, sie anderen mitzuteilen, wenn ich in ihnen bloss die pathologischen Phantasien eines einzelnen, eines armen Gemütskranken sehen würde. Ich sehe in ihnen aber etwas mehr, ein Dokument der Zeit, denn Hallers Seelenkrankheit ist — das weiss ich heute — nicht die Schrulle eines einzelnen, sondern die Krankheit der Zeit selbst, die Neurose jener Generation, welcher Haller angehört, und von welcher keineswegs nur die schwachen und minderwertigen Individuen befallen scheinen, sondern gerade die starken, geistigsten, begabtesten. (23)

[But owing to my acquaintance with Haller I have been able, to some extent, to understand them, and even to appreciate them. I should hesitate to share them with others if I saw in them nothing but the pathological fancies of a single and isolated case of a diseased temperament. But I see something more in them. I see them as a document of the times, for Haller's sickness of the soul, as I now know, is not the eccentricity of a single individual, but the sickness of the times themselves, the neurosis of that generation to which Haller belongs, a sickness, it seems, that by no means attacks the weak and worthless only but, rather, precisely those who are strongest in spirit and richest in gifts. (24)]

This, then, is the historical emphasis that the bourgeois narrator gives to Harry's confession. That affirmation of Harry's importance does, of course, also extend to Harry's psychological crises; and the narrator also knows that that personal disarray interlocks with philosophical questions as regards human being in the world:

Haller gehört zu denen, die zwischen zwei Zeiten hineingeraten, die aus aller Geborgenheit und Unschuld herausgefallen sind, zu denen, deren Schicksal es ist, alle Fragwürdigkeit des Menschenlebens gesteigert als persönliche Qual und Hölle zu erleben. (24)

[Haller belongs to those who have been caught between two ages, who are outside of all security and simple acquiescence. He belongs to those whose fate it is to live the whole riddle of human destiny heightened to the pitch of a personal torture, a personal hell. (25)]

In this remark from the narrator, the notion of Harry's expulsion from sheltered innocence raises the psychological issue; the reference to all the questionableness of human life points us towards philosophical concerns. But, even so, the thrust of the bourgeois narrator's diagnosis of Harry is primarily historical, and it illuminates the fate of those who are "zwischen zwei Zeiten geraten": caught between two times.

Just as the bourgeois narrator's account of Harry's behavior tallies in certain particulars with Harry's own account — his sitting on the stairs savoring the smell of the bourgeois household — so, too, the narrator's diagnosis of the historical parameters of Harry's experience is taken up elsewhere in the text. In other words, the corroborative interplay between the various narrative sections of Hesse's novel is extensive. The historical issue is raised in Harry's own account — in, for example, his allergic reaction to many facets of the world around him. He speaks to Hermine about the climate of aggression and war-mongering that is to be registered on all sides:

Keiner will den nächsten Krieg vermeiden, keiner will sich und seinen Kindern die nächste Millionenschlächterei ersparen, wenn er es nicht

billiger haben kann. Eine Stunde nachdenken, eine Weile in sich gehen und sich fragen, wieweit man selber an der Unordnung und Bosheit in der Welt teilhat und mitschuldig ist — sieh, das will niemand!
Und so wird es also weitergehen, und der nächste Krieg wird von
vielen tausend Menschen Tag für Tag mit Eifer vorbereitet. (114)

[Nobody wants to avoid the next war, nobody wants to spare himself
and his children the next holocaust if this be the cost. To reflect for
one moment, to examine himself for a while and ask what share he
has in the world's confusion and wickedness — look you, nobody
wants to do that. And so there's no stopping it, and the next war is
being pushed on with enthusiasm by thousands upon thousands day
by day. (134)]

Above all else, Harry is appalled by the travestying of the achievements of
high bourgeois culture in the modern world. In discussion with his land-
lady he reflects on the inroads of technology into culture:

Man werde, vielleicht schon sehr bald, entdecken, dass nicht nur ge-
genwärtige, augenblickliche Bilder und Geschehnisse uns beständig
umfluten, so, wie die Musik aus Paris und Berlin jetzt in Frankfurt
oder Zürich hörbar gemacht wird, sondern dass alles je Geschehene
ganz ebenso registriert und vorhanden sei und dass wir wohl eines
Tages, mit oder ohne Draht, mit oder ohne störende Nebenge-
räusche, den König Salamo und den Walther von der Vogelweide
werden sprechen hören. Und dass dies alles, ebenso wie heute die
Anfänge des Radios, den Menschen nur dazu dienen werde, von sich
und ihrem Ziele weg zu fliehen und sich mit einem immer dichteren
Netz von Zerstreuung und nutzlosem Beschäftigtsein zu umgeben.
(102)

[The discovery will be made — and perhaps very soon — that there
were floating round us not only the pictures and events of the trans-
ient present in the same way that music from Paris or Berlin was now
heard in Frankfurt or Zurich, but that all that had ever happened in
the past could be registered and brought back likewise. We might well
look for the day when, with wires or without, with or without the
disturbance of other sounds, we should hear King Solomon speaking,
or Walter von der Vogelweide. And all this, I said, just as today was
the case with the beginnings of wireless, would be of no more service
to man than as an escape from himself and his true aims, and a means
of surrounding himself with an ever closer mesh of distractions and
useless activities. (118)]

It is worth remembering that some nine years after the publication of
Hesse's *Der Steppenwolf* Walter Benjamin published a justly famous essay
entitled *Das Kunstwerk im Zeitalter seiner technischen Reproduzierbarkeit*

(The Work of Art in the Age of Its Technological Reproducibility). Like Haller, Benjamin perceives that the impact of technology on the dissemination of works of art has profoundly to do with a broader historico-cultural disturbance that he sees as generating on the one hand fascism's will to aestheticize politics and on the other communism's commitment to the politicization of art. I am not seeking to claim any direct influence or overlap here; rather, I merely want to suggest that for both Benjamin and Hesse the inroads of technology into the aesthetic domain is the engine for far-reaching social change, and the impact of that change can be little short of devastating. There are, of course, many further implications to the historical import of *Der Steppenwolf* that could be explored; but what has been argued so far may suffice to indicate the broad outlines of the historical symptomatology that is at work in the novel.

Now we turn to the philosophical theme of Hesse's text. The "Tractat," which, it seems, has been written by the Immortals who watch over Harry's adventures, tells us at one point:

> Der Mensch ist ja keine feste und dauernde Gestaltung (dies war, trotz entgegengesetzter Ahnungen ihrer Weisen, das Ideal der Antike), er ist vielmehr ein Versuch und Übergang, er ist nichts andres als die schmale, gefährliche Brücke zwischen Natur und Geist. (63)

> [Man is not by any means of fixed and enduring form (this, in spite of suspicions to the contrary on the part of their wise men, was the ideal of the ancients). He is much more an experiment and a transition. He is nothing else than the narrow and perilous bridge between nature and spirit. (70)]

The remark echoes the contention of Nietzsche's Zarathustra:

> Der Mensch ist ein Seil geknüpft zwischen Tier und Uebermensch — ein Seil über einem Abgrunde.
> Was gross ist am Menschen, das ist, dass er eine Brücke und kein Zweck ist. (*Also sprach Zarathustra*, Section 4)

> [The human being is a rope strung between animal and superman — a rope above an abyss.
> What is great about the human being is that he is a bridge and not a purpose.]

Harry registers the instability of human selfhood in terms of a dualism, one that pits two selves (man and wolf) against each other. But, according to the Immortals, he has to learn that processes of separation and fracturing are endemic to human life:

> Jede Geburt bedeutet Trennung vom All, bedeutet Umgrenzung, Absonderung von Gott, leidvolle Neuwerdung. Rückkehr ins All, Auf-

hebung der leidvollen Individuation, Gottwerden bedeutet: seine Seele so erweitert haben, dass sie das All wieder zu erfassen vermag. (66)

[All births mean separation from the All, the confinement within limitation, the separation from God, the pangs of being born ever anew. The return into the All, the dissolution of painful individuation, the reunion with God means the expansion of the soul until it is able once more to embrace the All. (73)]

That primal and ever-repeated fracturing trauma sets up longings for wholeness that are as intense and revelatory as they are unrealizable in earthly existence. Yet, even within earthly limitations, certain advances can be made. According to the Immortals, Harry must learn that what calls itself selfhood is, in the last and most truthful analysis, a multiplicity of potential and actual personae, and that bourgeois culture may have a way of being philosophically equal to the task of sustaining equilibrium in the midst of dizzying plurality:

Das "Bürgerliche" nun, als ein stets vorhandener Zustand des Menschlichen, ist nichts anderes als der Versuch eines Ausgleiches, als das Streben nach einer ausgeglichenen Mitte zwischen den zahllosen Extremen und Gegensatzpaaren menschlichen Verhaltens. (54)

[Now what we call "bourgeois," when regarded as an element always to be found in human life, is nothing else than the search for a balance. It is the striving after a mean between the countless extremes and opposites that arise in human conduct. (59)]

And the "bourgeois" (understood by the Immortals less as a sociohistorical than as an ontological category), if only they can capitalize cognitively on it, may have within reach that epistemological made known as humor which can acknowledge and indwell in multiple allegiances:

Der Humor bleibt stets bürgerlich, obwohl der echte Bürger unfähig ist, ihn zu verstehen. (. . .) Einzig der Humor, die herrliche Erfindung der in ihrer Berufung zum Grössten Gehemmten, der beinahe Tragischen, der höchstbegabten Unglücklichen, einzig der Humor (vielleicht die eigenste und genialste Leistung des Menschentums) vollbringt das Unmögliche, überzieht und vereinigt alle Bezirke des Menschenwesens mit den Strahlungen seiner Prismen. (57–58)

[Humor has always something bourgeois in it, although the true bourgeois is incapable of understanding it. [. . .] Humor alone, that magnificent discovery of those who are cut short in their calling to highest endeavor, those who falling short of tragedy are yet as rich in gifts as in affliction, human alone (perhaps the most inborn and brilliant achievement of the spirit) attains to the impossible and brings every aspect of human existence within the rays of its prism. (62–63)]

The notion — and theme — of laughter runs throughout the novel and comes to a head in the Magic Theater extravaganza that provides its climax. There Harry learns to discover the many possibilities that slumber unacknowledged within him: the austere pacifist can take delight in technological warfare, the ascetic intellectual discovers that he can desire many women. The theater itself owes its magic to the fact that it is a place of irony, of knowing detachment, of experiencing not authentically but in the "as if" of fiction. And this, it seems, is the lesson the Immortals (who embrace not only Mozart and Goethe but also Pablo the saxophonist) have to teach Harry — although he is not yet ready to accept it.

It is now time to turn to the psychological implications of *Der Steppenwolf*. As we know from the poems in the collection "Krisis: ein Stück Tagebuch," a number of which Hesse published in 1927, with the complete collection appearing in 1928, Hesse himself was in a state of profound psychological turmoil at the time of writing *Der Steppenwolf*. The poems are, in many ways, less challenging than the novel; they are somewhat unreflective, perhaps even self-pitying. But even so, the anguish is hurtfully present. And that disarray can be felt in the novel. From his own account we learn that Harry is subject to violent mood swings; and the negative swing of the pendulum brings him frequently close to suicide. He is bemused by his own dualism, by the fact that he, the wolf, should take lodgings in a highly respectable bourgeois household. Yet that household reeks of his childhood home. And it seems that home, the site of his early years, has not only produced the fractured personality but also harbors the possibility of healing. When he meets Hermine, he guesses her name because she is the re-incarnation of his boyhood friend Herrmann. In the Magic Theater she appears dressed like a boy; her appeal is hermaphroditic:

> Ohne sie nur berührt zu haben, unterlag ich ihrem Zauber, und dieser Zauber blieb selbst in ihrer Rolle, war ein hermaphroditischer. Denn sie unterhielt sich mit mir über die Kindheit, über meine und ihre, über jene Jahre vor der Geschlechtsreife, in denen das jugendliche Liebesvermögen nicht nur beide Geschlechter, sondern alles und jedes umfasst, Sinnliches und Geistiges, und alles mit dem Liebeszauber und der märchenhaften Verwandlungsfähigkeit begabt, die nur Auserwählten und Dichtern auch noch in späteren Lebensaltern zuzeiten wiederkehrt. (158)

> [Without so much as having touched her I surrendered to her spell, and this spell itself kept within the part she played. It was the spell of a hermaphrodite. For she talked to me about Herman and about childhood, mine and her own, and about those years of childhood when the capacity for love, in its first youth, embraces not only both sexes, but all and everything, sensuous and spiritual, and endows all things

with a spell of love and a fairylike ease of transformation such as in
later years comes again only to a chosen few and to poets, and to them
rarely. (190)]

As in Freudian psychoanalysis, the possibility of some kind of comfort and
healing reaches back into early experience. Yet here, in Hesse's world, we
also hear Jungian aspirations towards wholeness, towards a re-integration
of the multi-faceted personality. The (in part drug-induced) hallucinations of the Magic Theater provide intimations of both the presence and
the negotiability of the multiple selfhood — even if Harry is not yet able
psychologically to grasp the possibility and make it work for him.

It is now time to take stock of what emerges from the triple narrative
modality (bourgeois narrator, "Tractat," Harry's papers) and the triple
thematic force (historical, philosophical, psychological) of the text. At one
level, the novel achieves considerable richness of statement. But there are
two limiting factors: one has to do with an unclarity in the text; the other
has to do with its discursivity. Let me begin with the unclarity — and it
concerns the killing of Hermine. It seems that, in the closing phase of the
novel, Harry fails to enter into the fictionality, into that play of possibility
(as opposed to the incarnation of actuality) that is the governing signature
of the Magic Theater. Certainly it is for that offense that he is condemned
at the end of the novel:

> Meine Herren, vor Ihnen steht Harry Haller, angeklagt und schuldig
> befunden des mutwilligen Missbrauchs unseres magischen Theaters.
> Haller hat nicht nur die hohe Kunst beleidigt, indem er unsern
> schönen Bildersaal mit der sogenannten Wirklichkeit verwechselte und
> ein gespiegeltes Mädchen mit einem gespiegelten Messer totgestochen
> hat, er hat sich ausserdem unseres Theaters humorloserweise als einer
> Selbstmordmechanik zu bedienen die Absicht gezeigt. (201)

> [Gentlemen, there stands before you Harry Haller, accused and found
> guilty of the willful misuse of our Magic Theater. Haller has not alone
> insulted the majesty of art in that he confounded our beautiful picture
> gallery with so-called reality and stabbed to death the reflection of a
> girl with the reflection of a knife; he has in addition displayed the
> intention of using our theater as a mechanism of suicide and shown
> himself devoid of humor. (245)]

The verdict is forthright. "Sie sollen lachen lernen, das wird von Ihnen
verlangt. Sie sollen den Humor des Lebens, den Galgenhumor dieses
Lebens erfassen" (202; "You have got to learn to laugh. That will be required of you. You must apprehend the humor of life, its gallows-hu-
mor": 246). The force of this is clear within the logic of Hesse's novel.
Yet curiously the actual text does not corroborate the accusation. Harry
enters the Magic Theater in a spirit of experimentation. One of the fictive

realms he enters is labeled "Wie man durch Liebe tötet" (190; How one kills through love). This, then, like everything else in the Magic Theater, is fiction, not fact. At an earlier juncture of the novel Hermine tells Harry that one day he will kill her. When he does kill her in the Magic Theater, he does so in quotation marks as it were. He is carrying out her command, and his actions seem to be muffled by a kind of detached aestheticism:

> Ich öffnete. Was ich hinter der Türe fand, war ein einfaches und schönes Bild. Auf Teppichen am Boden fand ich zwei nackte Menschen liegen, die schöne Hermine und den schönen Pablo, Seite an Seite, tief schlafend, tief erschöpft vom Liebesspiel, das so unersättlich scheint und doch so schnell satt macht. Schöne, schöne Menschen, herrliche Bilder, wundervolle Körper. Unter Herminens linker Brust war ein frisches rundes Mal, dunkel unterlaufen, ein Liebesbiss von Pablos schönen schimmernden Zähnen. Dort, wo das Mal sass, stiess ich mein Messer hinein, so lang die Klinge war. Blut lief über Herminens weisse zarte Haut. (195–96)

> [I opened it. What I saw was a simple and beautiful picture. On a rug on the floor lay two naked figures, the beautiful Hermine and the beautiful Pablo, side by side in a sleep of deep exhaustion after love's play. Beautiful, beautiful figures, lovely pictures, wonderful bodies. Beneath Hermine's left breast was a fresh round mark, darkly bruised — a love bit of Pablo's beautiful, gleaming teeth. There, where the mark was, I plunged in my knife to the hilt. The blood welled out over her white and delicate skin. (238)]

We are given no hint of a resurgence of "real," that is to say unregenerate, emotion. There is no intimation of jealousy or rage. This is a fictive moment, a moment of aesthetic semblance (the recurrence of the adjective "schön" is particularly noteworthy). Yet Harry is condemned for having brought reality to bear in a place of make-believe. But in my view the text does not support that accusation.

To register this inconsistency may seem to be unnecessarily carping. But two matters need to be noted. One is that this is a crucial moment in the novel. The stylistic failure at this all-important juncture, is, then, no mere peccadillo; it does matter profoundly. And the other is that this flaw is symptomatic of a larger weakness in the novel — which has to do with the discursivity to which I have already drawn attention. *Der Steppenwolf* is a text that keeps on commenting on itself, talking about itself, about its own significance. The bourgeois narrator at one point comments:

> Es war mir nicht möglich, die Erlebnisse, von denen Hallers Manuskript erzählt, auf ihren Gehalt von Realität nachzuprüfen. Ich zweifle nicht daran, dass sie zum grössten Teil Dichtung sind, nicht aber im Sinn willkürlicher Erfindung, sondern im Sinne eines Ausdrucksver-

suches der tief erlebte seelische Vorgänge im Kleide sichtbarer Ereignisse darstellt. (22)

[It was not in my power to verify the truth of the experiences related in Haller's manuscript. I have no doubt that they are for the most part fictitious, not, however, in the sense of arbitrary invention. They are rather the deeply lived spiritual events which he has attempted to express by giving them the form of tangible experiences. (22)]

Yet this threatens to de-substantialize the novel, to make it much more an exercise in talking-about rather than in telling. There is, then, a kind of discursive overkill at work; the novel keeps on interpreting itself on every page — and this imparts a degree of sameness to the text — despite the triple narrative perspective that is, on the face of it, so important in a novel that is all about multi-perspectivity. One could, in other words, wish that the bourgeois narrator might sound more resolutely bourgeois, that the Immortals might sound notes of transcendental otherness, that Harry's own account could have greater experiential urgency and sting.

Yet to raise these questions is only to remind ourselves that we need another — perhaps more differentiated — way of expressing the importance of *Der Steppenwolf,* because it is and remains a profoundly important novel. And here one aspect of the novel can help us to a more just appreciation of its worth. That aspect involves the whole issue of literary reception — of the ways in which and the extent to which Hesse's *Der Steppenwolf* engages with earlier literature, and its susceptibility to a particular kind of hugely volatile reception in the twentieth century.

To begin with the presence of earlier literature as part of the statement made by *Der Steppenwolf,* it is important to recall Hesse's upbringing within the tradition of Swabian piety. From this he derived an intense reverence for the life of the mind, for the interrelationship of things physical and things spiritual. Precisely that cast of mind made him especially receptive to a number of genres and key works within the German literary tradition. One thinks initially of that form of novel that has often been claimed to be the major German contribution to the European novel — the Bildungsroman. The genre emerges to prominence in the eighteenth century with Wieland's *Agathon* and Goethe's *Wilhelm Meisters Lehrjahre.* (That the eighteenth century is important in this context needs hardly surprise us; it is worth noting that one of Harry Haller's favorite books is *Sophiens Reise von Memel nach Sachsen,* an epistolary novel that was enormously popular in eighteenth-century Germany). What Wieland and Goethe achieve is a novel form in which the governing event sequence is devoted to the quest of a young person (usually a male rather than female) for a full and differentiated understanding of the unfolding human self in all its complexity and richness. Both Wieland and Goethe (and those who succeed them as practitioners of the Bildungsroman) are less concerned with practicalities, with (as one might put it) where the next meal is coming from, than with inward matters, above all with the complex coexistence within the self of multiple possibilities of being. To put the matter most simply: Harry Haller's quest is part of a long literary tradition. What follows from this preoccupation is a spiritualization of the novel's event sequence: when the protagonist meets other characters, they open up for him new domains of experience — and those domains are as much within him as they are properties of the outer world. Hesse's *Der Steppenwolf* is manifestly indebted to this novel tradition, and the indebtedness extends even to particular details of the event sequence. Goethe's *Wilhelm Meisters Lehrjahre* (Wilhelm Meister's Apprenticeship, 1795–96) has a secret society or "Geheimbund," the "Turmgesellschaft," that keeps watch over Wilhelm's doings. Its equivalent in Hesse's novel is the Immortals. Wilhelm's initial ambition is to join the theater, because he senses there a realm in which both the bohemian way of life and the experience of watching and creating fictions extends and transforms his selfhood. The links with Harry Haller's Magic Theater are manifest. Above all, the Bildungsroman is an inherently ironic narrative constellation, one in which human richness is pitted against human limitation, and some of that ironic trajectory can be heard in the notion of humor in *Der Steppenwolf.*

To link Hesse's work with the tradition of the Bildungsroman is, however, to explore only one facet of the novel's complex intertextuality. Two other instances deserve mention, and they both derive from Goethe's work (and he, we recall, is one of the most frequently mentioned of the Immortals). One is his early novel *Die Leiden des jungen Werthers* (The Sufferings of Young Werther, 1774). It is very different from *Wilhelm Meister's Lehrjahre* and the Bildungsroman in that it explores, with ferocious intensity, not the unfolding of the human self but rather its capacity for self-destruction. The novel ends with Werther's suicide. Many passages of Harry's despair echo Werther. Moreover, his discovery of the beauty of physical movement through dance is almost exactly paralleled by Werther's delight in seeing his beloved Lotte dancing. There is also an important structural link between Goethe's and Hesse's novels. Werther's life is told for the most part in his own words — through his letters. These letters are published by an editor figure who prefaces them with a brief introduction, and then, as Werther's state of mind degenerates, steps into the narrative to recount its catastrophic closure. The narrative situation of *Der Steppenwolf,* with the bourgeois narrator who publishes Harry's papers, is not dissimilar. What is different is that we have no closure to Hesse's novel: we do not know what happens to Harry after the Magic Theater adventure; and there is no structural framing — the bourgeois narrator does not return at the end.

A final instance of relationship between Hesse and Goethe needs to be mentioned, and it concerns Goethe's *Faust*. In one respect Harry Haller is no "Bildungsroman" hero; he is old (nearly fifty), whereas the protagonists of the Bildungsroman are typically adolescents. Harry's discontent with the sterile life of the intellectual, his craving for powerful, immediate experience is very close to Goethe's Faust. The following two statements from Harry Haller would not be out of place in the mouth of Goethe's hero:

> Es brennt alsdann in mir eine wilde Begierde nach starken Gefühlen, nach Sensationen, eine Wut auf dies abgetönte, flache, normierte und sterilisierte Leben. (28)

> [A wild longing for strong emotions and sensations seethes in me, a rage against this toneless, flat, normal and sterile life. (31)]

> Aber nicht Wissen und Verstehen war es, was not tat, wonach ich mich so verzweifelt sehnte, sondern Erleben, Entscheidung, Stoss und Sprung. (SW4, 104)

> [But what I needed was not knowledge and understanding. What I longed for in my despair was life and resolution, action and reaction, impulse and impetus. (120)]

Moreover, Hesse's text is full of references to the two souls that are at war within Faust's selfhood. These two souls relate in many respects to the man/wolf dualism that haunts Harry. In Faust the essential friction is that between mind and matter, between the reflective, observing, questioning self and the physical, raw, instinctual self. That friction generates the disquiet, the sheer restlessness and energy that is both Faust's tragedy and his glory. Moreover, like Haller, Faust is constantly aware of the multiple collisions between old and new cultures; he registers the abrasiveness and destructiveness of the new world — but also its sheer transformative drive. In a whole number of ways, then, Goethe's great drama is omnipresent in *Der Steppenwolf.*

One could go on illustrating the intertextual echoes that pass between *Der Steppenwolf* and earlier works from the German literary tradition. And I do not wish to belabor the point. What needs, however, to be stressed is that these intertextual moments endow Hesse's novel with an impressive richness and intensity that is not immediately apparent from straightforward scrutiny of the words on the page. *Der Steppenwolf* is almost a kind of echo-chamber filled with earlier voices. That condition links with the thematic purpose of the novel. It is crucially about the interplay of old and new forms of culture, about the self and its world as multiple and pluralist rather than unitary. What may seem on first reading to be a somewhat narrow, self-obsessed text in fact constantly obliges us to hear other texts, other voices as part of the statement that it makes.

In a different — but not unrelated — way the history of the reception of *Der Steppenwolf* in the twentieth century also provides us with a wealth of voices that echo and amplify the text. The early responses to the novel in the late 1920s and early 1930s are, not surprisingly perhaps, divided. Hostile critics saw the novel as scandalous in its frankness about sexuality, drugs, and popular culture, and regarded it as a symptom rather than a diagnosis of contemporary decadence. Other critics saw it as a tired last flickering of high bourgeois culture (Mozart, Goethe) that sought to answer modern trashiness by invoking outworn values. Positive responses welcomed the novel's debate with the vulgarity of modern culture and approved of its concern to find higher spiritual values behind and beyond the triviality of the modern world.

Postwar responses to *Der Steppenwolf* are similarly varied. Hesse was awarded the Nobel Prize for Literature in 1946 — it was, to put it mildly, remarkable that a German writer should be so honored in the immediate aftermath of the Nazi horrors. This award produced an upsurge of interest in his work. Yet some ten years later Hesse fell into disfavor. For many years he had lived a reclusive life in Montagnola, in the Ticino, the Italian part of Switzerland; and in the 1950s he was dismissed as a questionably self-stylizing guru. Academic critics in Germany found his work too schematic, simplificatory, perilously close to earnest kitsch. Yet strangely, at precisely this time (the late 1950s) English-speaking commentators discovered Hesse. For Colin Wilson, *Der Steppenwolf* was a key work in the context of modern exploration of the outsider figure. In the United States Joseph Mileck, Theodore Ziolkowski, and Ralph Freedman all upheld Hesse's importance. Ziolkowski showed the structural sophistication of *Der Steppenwolf,* and Freedman invoked Hesse's writing as belonging within the tradition of the lyrical novel, of the kind of narrative that concerns itself with inwardness rather than with outwardness. And then, in the wake of the scholarly enthusiasm for Hesse, but totally unconnected to it, there was the response of the hippie generation. For Timothy Leary, the guru of that generation, *Der Steppenwolf* was crucially about the psychedelic fracturing of the narrow self, about the discovery, through drugs, of the filmic, kaleidoscopic richness of which the human psyche, once liberated from societal constraints, is capable. In 1970 Berkeley had a Steppenwolf Bar and a Magic Theater. Chicago had a Magic Theater Company, Philadelphia had a Magic Theater Coffee House. And the rock group Steppenwolf performed with great success across America — and beyond.

This intense response from outside Germany to a German novel is quite without equal in the twentieth century. The fervor, the extent to which *Der Steppenwolf* became a cult book, a Bible for a youthful generation is, intriguingly, echoed by the intense response, across late eighteenth-century Europe, to Goethe's *Werther,* a novel which, as we have noted, is intertextually related to *Der Steppenwolf.* Clearly, the reception accorded to a novel is not the necessary proof of its quality. Goethe's *Werther* has remained a classic of German literature; this is less true of *Der Steppenwolf.* Yet it is impossible not to hear the reception as responding to, partaking of, and amplifying certain energies within the text.

What, then, are we to make of *Der Steppenwolf?* Two points need to be made by way of conclusion. One is that Hesse's novel, as we have registered, is about the virulent collision of old and new values. And the explosive and volatile story of its reception, from violent repudiation to euphoric worship, seems to enact that very theme. When the hippie generation makes a cult book of the novel, they enact in some way the cultishness of the novel. As the epigraph to both Harry Haller's narration and to the "Tractat," "Nur für Verrückte" (For Madmen Only), suggests, the world to which these papers offer access is one situated at the margins of the established social consensus. The novel ends with Mozart and Pablo waiting. The hippies felt that they were answering that call. "Eintritt nicht für jedermann" — "Entry not for everyone" — is one of the slogans of the Magic Theater that shimmers on the shiny surface of the wet pavement. Timothy Leary's followers felt that entry was for them; *Der Steppenwolf* is about the quest for a new kind of faith, and they felt that that faith was within their grasp.

My second concluding observation concerns what I have called the over-determined nature of the text. *Der Steppenwolf* explores the quest for multiperspectivity; and on first reading one has the impression that that multiperspectivity is embodied in the three different narrative strands of the novel. (The shifting of narrative ground is conveyed particularly urgently in German editions of the novel, which print the whole of the "Tractat" in italics. Regrettably English-language editions often ignore this typological marker of difference.) Yet on closer reading, the three narrative strands tend to merge into one; they circle about the same value scheme. (Admittedly there are occasions when we do sense a perspectival pluralism. Hermine is a case in point. As a figure, she oscillates between being on the one hand the experienced prostitute who knows how to deal with a client who is a frustrated, aging intellectual and on the other a voice from the spiritual universe of the Immortals.) But for the great part Hesse's novel is worryingly uni-vocal. Except that, when we hear the process of its reception as an attendant sounding board, then the text becomes pluri-vocal in its force. We read, as it were, with those other voices in our ears. We find ourselves responding to *Der Steppenwolf* not just as one novel in its own right but also as a phenomenon of textual multiplicity. That is to say: we register it as a debate with older forms of literature and with twentieth-century literature, and as a debate with our own culture — with, for example, novels of so-called magical realism (Salman Rushdie, Günter Grass, Gabriel Garcia Marquez, Mario Varges Llosa) and with postmodernity's love affair with virtual reality and cybertext. In the process, the novel itself and the experience of reading it becomes exciting, maddening, frustrating, intriguing — and above all, enriching. And for that, we should be grateful.

Notes

[1] References to the novel in this essay are to Hesse, *Der Steppenwolf,* in *Sämtliche Werke,* vol. 4, *Die Romane: Der Steppenwolf. Narziß und Goldmund. Die Morgenlandfahrt,* ed. Volker Michels (Frankfurt am Main: Suhrkamp Verlag, 2001) and will be given by page number in parentheses. English translations, which follow the German and are also indicated by page number, are from *Steppenwolf,* trans. Basil Creighton (New York, Toronto, London: Bantam Books, 1969).

8: Hermann Hesse's *Narziss und Goldmund:* Medieval Imaginaries of (Post-)Modern Realities

Frederick A. Lubich

H ERMANN HESSE'S NOVEL *Narziss und Goldmund* was published in 1930 and became the most successful book during his lifetime.[1] The novel is set in the Middle Ages and depicts the story of a friendship between two men, whose personalities are veritable case studies in character opposites. Whereas Narziss finds an intellectual home and spiritual sense of belonging in the cloister of Mariabronn, Goldmund seeks fulfillment in his perennial vagabonding through the world. At the end of his adventurous life he returns to the cloister in order to settle down as a sculptor, striving to transform his worldly experiences into works of exquisite art. During Goldmund's extended absence, Narziss has risen to the lofty position of abbot, in which capacity he represents and reflects the powers and the teachings of his Catholic Church.[2] Why would this medieval story of two very different friends, leading lives of, respectively, the *vita contemplativa* and the *vita activa* be such a success with modern readers? One of the answers probably lies in Hesse's thematic structure of the novel. The Romantics of the nineteenth century had already cultivated a deep affinity with the Middle Ages, and their relationship to that earlier time period became a congenial mode of reflection for Hesse, the neo-Romantic author of the twentieth century. Like a distant mirror, its medieval imaginaries project across the centuries central aspects of our modern and postmodern realities. Focusing on the development of intellectual history, this narrative mirror reflects specifically Adorno and Horkheimer's "dialectics of enlightenment," Nietzsche's "transvaluation of values," and last but not least, the eclipse of all reason, which characterized the genius and the insanity of Germany's cultural history. This essay will trace this trajectory and illustrate the various reflections of the novel's medieval modernity.

Essential for the understanding of the exemplary differences in the character formation of Narziss and Goldmund is the recognition that they are modeled after cultural archetypes. Narziss represents the patriarchal world order of an androcentric culture, whose societal hierarchy is based on male authority, maintained by social and sexual repression, and focused on spiritual values that find their quintessential apotheosis in God the Father, residing in heaven. Goldmund, by contrast is associated with the matriarchal myth of a gynocentric utopia, whose ideal state is characterized by female authority, based on social equality and sexual permissiveness, and centered in the material world, which finds its symbolic representation in the pagan Mother Goddess, living on earth. Whereas the patriarchal paradigm represents Christianity's historical reality, the matriarchal counter model did not emerge until Johann Jakob Bachofen's encyclopedic study *Das Mutterrecht* (1861).[3] Its explorations of matriarchal myths in pre-historic cultures were soon complemented by Carl Gustav Jung's teachings of psychological archetypes.[4] Together, this psychomythic model of the *magna mater* or Great Mother was to influence a wide variety of modern discourses ranging from Marxism and psychoanalysis to contemporary feminism.[5]

On a psychological level, Goldmund figures as an illustrative case study for the object relations theory of Melanie Klein, a former student of Sigmund Freud. According to her model, human relations are characterized by the experience and memory of a pre-oedipal symbiosis between mother and child. In her seminal essay "A Study of Envy and Gratitude" (1956), she delineates the splitting of the *mater imago* into a "good" and "bad" mother, depending on the amount of nurturing she grants her child.[6] Goldmund's early years at the cloister are marked by memories that cast his mother into a dark and dubious light:

> Die Mutter war etwas, wovon man nicht sprechen durfte, man schämte sich ihrer. Eine Tänzerin war sie gewesen, ein schönes, wildes Weib von vornehmer, aber unguter und heidnischer Herkunft. [. . .] nach einigen Jahren der Zahmheit und des geordneten Lebens hatte [sie] sich ihrer alten Künste und Übungen wieder erinnert, hatte Ärgernis erregt und Männer verführt [. . .] war in den Ruf einer Hexe gekommen und schließlich für immer verschwunden. (62)

> [His mother was something one must not speak about, someone to be ashamed of. She had been a dancer, a beautiful, wild creature of cultivated but unworthy and heathen origin. [. . .] But after a few years of tame and orderly life, she had resorted to her old skills and habits, had created scandals and seduced men [. . .] She had acquired the reputation of being a witch and had finally [. . .] disappeared forever. (49)]

These early memories of his mother are obviously passed down to Goldmund by his father, and they are tainted by paternal resentment and patriarchal prejudice. From time immemorial, men have desired women's youthful beauty and associated them with the divine, yet on the other hand have demonized them as wicked sorceresses in league with the devil. The pervasive witch hunts throughout the Middle Ages are tragic testimony to the cruel realities of such male fantasies.[7]

Narziss encourages Goldmund to reconnect with his own true and undistorted memories of his early years: "Du hast deine Kindheit vergessen, aus den Tiefen deiner Seele wirbt sie um dich" (50; "You have forgotten your childhood. It is crying out to you from the depths of your soul," 40). It is in the world of his dreams that Goldmund begins to recover his forgotten childhood:

> Tief sank der Jüngling in diese Träume [. . .] In ihnen stand nicht nur geliebte Vergangenheit wieder bezaubernd auf: Kindheit und Mutterliebe, strahlend goldener Lebensmorgen; es schwang in ihnen auch drohende, versprechende, lockende und gefährliche Zukunft. Zuweilen erschienen diese Träume, in denen Mutter, Madonna und Geliebte eins waren, ihm nachher wie entsetzliche Verbrechen und Gotteslästerungen, wie niemals mehr zu sühnende Todsünden; zu anderen Malen fand er in ihnen alle Erlösung, alle Harmonie [. . .] es waren Geheimnisse der Mutter, sie kamen von ihr, sie führten zu ihr. (66)

> [The youth sank deep into these dreams. [. . .] In those dreams it was not only the beloved past that magically re-emerged: childhood and mother love, the radiant, golden morning o life; in them there also reverberated a menacing, promising, enticing and perilous future. At times these dreams, in which mother, Madonna and lover were one, would later appear to him as terrible crimes and blasphemies, mortal sins beyond all atonement; at other times he found in them all salvation, all harmony [. . .] but they were secrets of his mother, they came from her, they led to her [. . .]. (52)]

In these dreams, oedipal fantasies of maternal love merge with Christian pangs of conscience about deadly sin and eternal damnation, only to reconfigure themselves again, crystallizing in the image of the mythic Mother Goddess, reaching out to her son and embracing him as her lover. (This mother-son embrace is the matriarchal pre-configuration of the Christian *pieta*, in which the living son of the Mother Goddess returning to her womb/earth is transformed into the dead son of God the Father returning to his spirit/heaven).

In order to further explore Goldmund's complex bond with his mother and her symbolic world, we need to look at Hesse's own psychological struggle, which to varying degrees informed the creation of his literary figures. In a personal crisis during the time of the First World War, Hesse underwent psychotherapy with one of the first analysts trained in Jungian depth psychology. His novel *Demian* is a direct reflection of this experience.[8] Just as Hesse had benefited from such treatment, he now has Narziss fulfill the role of a therapeutic guide who encourages his friend to trust and follow his deepest dreams. Thus, this medieval monk, steeped in the scholastic thinking of his time, makes a strong case for the modern movement of psychoanalysis, which began to gain momentum around

1900 with the publication of Sigmund Freud's *Traumdeutung* and reached a culmination point of sorts toward the end of the twentieth century. Especially the last third of the twentieth century saw a great popularization of a wide variety of psychoanalytical theories and therapies. Since the 1990s these therapeutic self-explorations resulted in a syndrome which became known as "recovered memories," in which growing numbers of people "re-experienced" traumatic events from their early childhood. Public awareness of this phenomenon was enhanced by the testimony of several celebrities. However, as it turned out, these "recovered memories" were largely not shameful memories of a "bad mother" but rather of a "bad father." Freud's seduction theory, which he later reformulated to protect, as some argued, the patriarchal family, proved to be true after all. Not only did the father figure in these "recovered memories" all too often emerge as a sexual abuser of his children; in Europe his authority and moral integrity was also often severely compromised by his involvement with the politics and atrocities of fascist and communist dictatorships.

Narziss might not sanction all of Goldmund's daring dreams, but with his encouragement to explore the world of his subconscience, the psychic realm of mythic archetypes, he opens a new door to the self-understanding of modern man. As Goldmund leaves the monastery of Mariabronn, he begins to follow the "Ruf der Mutter" (195; "his mother's call," 150). Virtually enacting Klein's theory, Goldmund's early lovers all embrace him as their child, calling him "Goldmündchen" (81; "my sweet Goldmund," 64), "Goldmündlein, mein Kind" (82; "Goldmund, my little one," 64), and "mein armer kleiner Junge" (125; "my poor boy," 98). In addition to this playful repetition of the primal scene, Goldmund's (pre-) oedipal yearnings imbue his sexual experiences with the innocence of a perennial child. Throughout his life and his many erotic escapades, he will retain this child-like nature and remain "stürmisch und unersättlich," "ein großes Kind" (314; "impetuous and insatiable"; "a big child," 240).

Every era in history has had such *Wunderkinder* of love who break culture's sexual codes and moral conventions. However, as a social and cultural prototype they did not emerge until the end of the 1960s when they became known as "flower children." They came together as "kids" in Woodstock, celebrating their "summer of love" as an exuberant "Paradise Now." Ideally speaking, this is the collective fulfillment of all of Goldmund's solitary dreams. As the girl who will be his first love discovers him sleeping in a meadow full of summer flowers, we read: "Blumen hatte er gepflückt, sah sie mit Lächeln" (80; "He had picked some flowers, she saw with a smile," 63). The scene could not be more symbolic for young Goldmund, the flower child, waiting to be awakened by the girl's kiss. And when he later recalls her, he compares her to a flower: "Sie lächelte mich an wie eine Blume" (84; "and [she] smiled at me like a flower," 66). This flower imagery culminates in the description of Goldmund's most important lover many years later, whom he calls a "Zauberblume," a magic flower (263). The poetic convention of identifying female sexuality with floral imagery is part of a centuries-old tradition that equates virginity, defloration, and maternal fertility with the natural cycle of flowering and fruition. With the German Romantics, man's longing for life and love eventually found a poetic expression in the symbolic Blue Flower with its multifaceted mystic meanings. When generations later Woodstock's "children of paradise" identified themselves with "flower power," they tapped into the same sexual and mystical imaginary.

Closely related to the flower children and their favorite theme of free love is the erotic nature of Goldmund's dreams:

> Viel vergessene Kindheit kam in diesen Mutterträumen herauf, aus unendlichen Tiefen und Verlorenheiten blühten viele kleine Erinnerungsblumen [. . .] von Fischen träumte er zuweilen, die schwammen schwarz und silbern auf ihn zu, kühl und glatt, schwammen in ihn hinein, durch ihn hindurch, kamen wie Boten mit holden Glücksnachrichten aus einer schöneren Wirklichkeit, schwanden schwänzelnd und schattenhaft [. . .] Von einem Garten träumte er oft, einem Zaubergarten mit märchenhaften Bäumen [. . . und . . .] tiefen blaudunklen Höhlen; zwischen den Gräsern blickten funkelnde Augen unbekannter Tiere, an den Ästen glitten glatte sehnige Schlangen, an Reben und Gesträuchen hingen groß und feuchtglänzend riesige Beeren, die schwollen beim Pflücken in seiner Hand und vergossen warmen Saft wie Blut oder hatten Augen und bewegten sich schmachtend und listig. (66)

> [Much forgotten childhood surfaced in these mother-dreams. Out of lost, bottomless depths blossomed many small flowers of memory [. . .]. Sometimes he would dream of fish that swam towards him, black and silvery, cool and smooth: swam into him, through him, like messengers with good tidings from a more beautiful reality, then vanished, weaving and shadowy [. . .]. And there was a garden he often dreamed of, a magic garden with fabulous trees [. . . and . . .] deep, dark-blue caverns; from out of the grass flashed the eyes of unknown beasts, and along the branches slithered smooth, sinuous snakes. From vines and shrubs hung huge, moistly glistening berries which, when picked, swelled in his hand and spilled warm juice like blood, or had eyes [that] moved, salacious and sly. (52)]

Clearly, what all these organic images of flowers, fish, snakes, the swelling of fruits and the spilling of fluids add up to is the orgasmic imaginary of sexual intercourse. On a psychosexual level, Goldmund is regressing into the maternal cavity, floating blissfully in the amniotic fluids of the nurturing womb. Thus, the Romantic blue flower has permutated into the "dark blue" cave, turning his mother, the whole of mother earth into one wet dream. On a mythological level, these dream scenes of procreation are interwoven with sceneries of paradise, thereby intertwining the physical origin of man with the biblical account of the genesis of mankind.[9] Like God, Goldmund becomes the creator of life on earth:

> Oft träumte er schwimmende Fische und fliegende Vögel und jeder Fisch oder Vogel war sein Geschöpf, war von ihm abhängig und lenkbar wie sein Atemzug, strahlte wie ein Blick, wie ein Gedanke von ihm aus, kehrte in ihn zurück. (66)

> [He often dreamed of fish swimming and birds flying, and each fish or bird was his creature, was dependent on him and controllable like his breathing, radiated from him like a glance or a thought, and re-entered him. (52)][10]

Goldmund's psychomythic experiences reflect a modern psychedelic consciousness that Timothy Leary, the acid guru of the '68 generation, propagated with the slogan "Turn on, tune in, drop out." The three aspects of this frame of mind can be traced in Hesse's novel. First, the "turning on" and opening up of a vivid imagination: Goldmund's mellifluous dream imagery, which combines the world of flora and fauna into erotic configurations, surfaced for the first time as a generic style in the prints, paintings, and book illustration of the Art Nouveau movement of the turn of the nineteenth to the twentieth century.[11] The revival of this style in the late 1960s and its transformation into the colorful arabesques of posters and record covers became an expression of the psychedelic spirit of these days of hallucinogenic trips. Passages like those in which Goldmund's blue flower dreams are described in a stream-of-consciousness style were congenial textual guides for mellow mushroom trips into a blossoming lotus land of cosmic consciousness.[12]

Second, Leary's second motto of "tuning in" also resonates very much with the sensibilities of the times as well as those of Hesse's hero, and they manifest themselves in a cultivated love for music. This was another artistic medium through which the free-floating sexual energies of the times could be channeled and amplified. From silly love songs to the Dionysian dithyrambs of bands like The Doors and Led Zeppelin, or Pink Floyd and Deep Purple, with their suggestive color associations, the popular music of the 1960s and 1970s like no other musical genre before literally rocked the sexual energies of youth all over the world with their raving melodies. Historically, this growing eroticization of music dates back to the time of the French trouvères and troubadours in the eleventh and twelfth centuries. Their musical celebration of female beauty became the model for the German *minnesang* tradition of the High Middle Ages. Goldmund too wanders in the footsteps of these itinerant minstrels. Although he primarily works as a draftsman and sculptor, he also plays the lute. However, his favorite musical instrument is the body of a beautiful woman. After many years of wandering, he does find the perfect embodiment of his musical dreams in Agnes, the mistress of a powerful count and governor. It is the classical situation, in which according to all the rules of courtly love, the traveling gleeman would serenade such a mistress as *hôhe frouwe,* praising her many virtues. *Frauenlob* of that nature usually served the purpose of currying favor with the spouse of the serenaded beauty, who could grant the wandering minstrel a secure ministerial position. In Goldmund's case, forget the position. He is much more interested in the "hohe Gestalt" (254; "tall figure," 194) of the mistress herself — and high strung as she is, she soon grants him his desire to display all his minstrel's skills: "Noch nie hatte der Spielmann auf einer solchen Laute gespielt, noch nie hatte die Laute unter so starken und kundigen Fingern geklungen" (256; "Never had the minstrel played on such a lute; never had the lute responded to such strong, expert fingers," 195).[13]

Leary's last suggestion of "dropping out" also finds in Goldmund a willing follower. His childlike nature, his lifelong resistance to settling down, are obvious indications of his refusal to give up his carefree youth. This becomes most evident in his repeated lamentations about the passage of time: "Schön war das Leben [. . . und . . .] rasch verwelkt die Jugend" (220, see also 311 et passim; "How beautiful was life, how [. . .] swiftly withering was youth!," 169). Goldmund's aversion toward growing old is not in tune with a medieval worldview. To age with dignity was the time-honored goal of man throughout Christian history. The image of an ancient God the Father with infinite wisdom and eternal authority was the highest role model for graceful aging and dignified longevity. It was not until the twentieth century that youth became the new cultural ideal. From the aesthetics of Art Nouveau — which is aptly called *Jugendstil,* the style of youth, in German — to the evolution of pop culture and the tumultuous student politics in the 1960s and 1970s, rebels with and without a cause radically de-valorized adulthood, the social establishment, and its cultural institutions. "Unter den Talaren der Muff von tausend Jahren," under the gowns the musty smell of a thousand years, became one of the most popular slogans of the German student movement, which in turn found its American variation in the rebel cry "Don't trust anybody over thirty." This distrust of the older generation was also the other side of the desire to stay, in the words of Bob Dylan, "Forever Young." Thus, "dropping out" of time, refusing to age, never staying long in any place, and always following the flow of dreams, fantasies, and erotic opportunities makes Goldmund an exemplary "drop-out" long before it became a global youth movement.

Linked with the cult of youth is the cultivation of the body, the body young and beautiful, made and ready for love. Or as Goldmund sees it: "das Spiel der Geschlechter, das stand ihm obenan [. . .] dies schien ihm den Kern alles Erlebens zu enthalten" (178–79; "the play of the sexes — this had priority for him [. . .] this seemed to him to comprise the core of all experience," 138–39, translation modified). Not surprising for a minstrel, who always has *minne* on his medieval mind, but this statement also captures the quintessence of the sexual revolution of the twentieth century. The revalorization of human sexuality since the Victorian Age reached its symbolic culmination in the late 1960s with the rebellious cry of international youth calling on each other to "make love not war." Hailing the dawn of the Age of Aquarius, this most famous counterculture slogan suggested nothing short of replacing the belligerent history of the fathers, full of war and male aggression, with a utopian future dedicated to peace, love, and human compassion.[14] Such sweeping politics demanded change of the highest order: Ultimately, the biblical God of Wrath was to capitulate to the mythical Goddess of Love. Her commandments culminated in *The Joy of Sex*, teaching all her lovers the multiple ways to please each other. Not surprisingly, the book became a runaway bestseller throughout the 1970s.

Looking back on his life of many loves, Goldmund comes to the conclusion: "das Spiel, die Liebe, das Behagen ohne Gedanken — das gedieh unter Männern nicht, dazu brauchte es Frauen und Wandern und Schweifen und immer neue Bilder" (311; "playfulness, love, contentment unmarred by thought — did not flourish among men; for that there had to be women and new places and constantly new impressions," 238). As diffuse as this retrospective summary may appear, it does telescope central aspects of western societies in the twentieth century, bringing their various aspects into sharper focus, as the following explorations show:

First, the notion of "Spiel": all things playful appeal to Goldmund as a "großes Kind" and even more to the child in all of us, middle-aged "baby boomers," and their children. As never before, we want games and entertainment, thereby converting our parks into amusement parks, our time into leisure time, and our culture as a whole into a virtual multi-functional PlayStation.[15] Into this turbulent *Spassgesellschaft*, the medieval *Spielmann* returns rejuvenated as modern playboy determined to be fit for fun. Given this new game of survival of the fittest, playboys and playmates like Goldmund and his youthful lovers are the clear winners. In this light, the religious passion plays of the Middle Ages have become modernity's secular plays of passion.

A second and central aspect in Goldmund's worldview is the importance of "Frauen," the role of women in society. Under the law and order of patriarchy, women had been the perennial losers in the battle of the sexes. This did not change until the 1920s, when German women were granted the right to vote and the so-called "New Woman" began to gain equal footing with men in their play for power and pleasure.[16] In America, part of the image of the "New Woman" would gradually transfigure into the icon of the "Wonder Woman," a formidable reflection of the popular imagination, half archetype, half comic strip. The stage to which she would ascend were the dream factories and projection screens of Hollywood, from where she soon would rule over mankind, ravishingly revamped as dark gorgon and gorgeous goddess of the silver screen. Not surprisingly, Goldmund's erotic conquest of the governor's mistress bears a striking resemblance to these cinematic stagings of female power and pleasure: "Es war eine Frau zu Pferde, ein großes hellblondes Weib mit neugierigen, etwas kühlen Blauaugen, mit festen Gliedern und einem blühenden Gesicht voll Lust zu Genuss und Macht" (251; "It was a woman on horseback, tall, fair-haired, with probing, somewhat aloof eyes, firm taut limbs and a face alive with the desire for pleasure and power," 192). Whereas Goldmund believes to recognize in her "blonde lachende Lebensfülle" once again "das Bild seiner Mutter [. . .] wie er es damals, als Knabe in Mariabronn im Herzen getragen" (254; "fair-haired, laughing vitality . . . the image of his mother as he had carried it in his heart when a boy at Mariabronn," 194), the first readers of the novel in the 1930s would more likely have imagined her as a blond, buxom bombshell à la Jean Harlow, Mae West, and Jayne Mansfield.[17]

The stunning rise of the dazzling diva in the Hollywood cinema of the 1920s and 1930s coincided with the systematic decline of patriarchal powers and authorities in the Old World, ranging from the fall of the czar of Russia and the emperors of Germany and Austria-Hungary to the twilight of God himself in his much-challenged kingdom of heaven. Klaus Theweleit has written about this pivotal time period: "An die Stelle der gestorbenen Transzendenz Gottes [wird] die neue Transzendenz des weiblichen Geschlechts, das den Mangel aufhebt, gesetzt"[18] (In place of the dead transcendence of God was set the new transcendence of the female sex, which filled the void). What imaginary woman could better deliver modern man from need, from all kinds of depressions and deprivations, than the nurturing Mother Goddess, the archetypal *alma mater*? In antiquity, she was identified with the cornucopia, providing milk and honey in abundance and a plethora of other earthly delights and material luxuries. In Hesse's imagined Middle Ages, she nursed and nurtured Goldmund's insatiable thirst for women: "Trink mich aus, Geliebter" (256; "Drink up all of me, beloved," 195) coos Agnes, and it seems that she in turn fulfills most generously all of his wildest childhood dreams: "Ihnen blühte das Paradies" (256; "For them, paradise blossomed," 195)[19]

In 1975, the French feminist theorists Hélène Cixous and Catherine Clément published *La Jeune Née* (The Newly Born Woman), which became a founding text of the French *écriture féminine*, redefining female writing as writing the body unbound. In her preface to the English edition of the book, Sandra Gilbert summarized the stream-of-consciousness style of this collaborative text as the voice of a woman "newborn and yet archaic, a voice of milk and blood, a voice silenced but savage."[20] As a Freudian expression of the "return of the repressed," of female potential repressed throughout patriarchal history, it is a raging rhapsody in "which silenced women must finally find ways to cry, shriek, scream, and dance in impassioned dances of desire" (xi). Excess is the mode and style with which this repressed returns: "excess desire, excess rage, excess creative energy" (xii). Gilbert concludes her synopsis of the *Newly Born Woman*: "Think of her [. . .] flying [. . . a . . .] utopian body [. . . in . . .] orgasmic freedom" (x–xi). This is the soaring "voice of the uterus" (Cixous), finally liberated, ready to take on wings of desire and exalt in erotic pleasures, in boundless *jouissance*.[21] *La Jeune Née* is a new Marseillaise for women, a beacon to guide them in liberating themselves from men — and ultimately emancipate them too. Liberté, humanité, sensualité are their ancient ideals, reborn in the here and now. Seen in the larger context of its cultural continuum, *La Jeune Née* is the magic transformation of psychedelic "flower power" into psychosexual "Frauen-Power," Goethe's *Ewig Weibliche* up to date — and Goldmund's final rendezvous with Agnes, "seine schöne, königliche Geliebte" (262; "his beautiful, regal mistress," 202). Her "Spielmann" is fully aware of his royal challenges:

> Um das Glück dieser Nacht zu erleben, um diese wunderbare Frau so beglücken zu können, dazu hatte es seines ganzen Lebens bedurft, all der Schulung durch Frauen, all der Wanderung und Not, all der durchwanderten Schneenächte und all der Freundschaft und Vertrautheit mit Tieren, Blumen, Bäumen, Wassern, Fischen, Schmetterlingen. Es bedurfte dazu der in Wollust und in Gefahr geschärften Sinne. (262–63)

> [To know the happiness of that night, to be able to make that wonderful woman so happy; this had required his entire life, all that women had taught him, all his journeyings and sufferings, all that tramping through snowy nights and all the friendship and familiarity with animals, flowers, trees, waters, fish, butterflies. It required senses sharpened in sensuality and danger [. . .] (202)]

It is in this lifelong *education sentimentale et sensuelle* that Goldmund develops an emotional sensibility and erotic sophistication that transcends by far the conventional boundaries of masculine sexuality. His intimate knowledge of creation and his passionate admiration of all its wonders make him a perfect match for his mistress and her erotic expectations, as they resonate with Cixous' characterizations of *La Jeune Née* ("Her libido is cos-

mic [. . .] spacious singing Flesh." [Cixous, 88, capitalization by Cixous]).
To highlight this exorbitant sensuality, the novel's central scene may be
cited one more time: "Noch nie hatte die Laute unter so starken und
kundigen Fingern geklungen." The author concludes: "Alles nur irgend
dem Menschen erlebbare Glück schien ihm in diesem Augenblick zusammengeronnen" (256; "All the happiness a human being could experience
seemed to come together in this moment," 244).

The third aspect in Goldmund's looking back is the motif of "Wandern und Schweifen": Only life on the road with all its trials and tribula-
tions will teach Goldmund the art and magic of perfect love, step by step,
woman by woman. He is a medieval pilgrim in pursuit of modern happiness, searching for the "Madonna and Geliebte" (66) in every good
woman. Whether they are comely or homely, innocent or experienced, he
can learn from all of them. His erotic education begins in the flowery
meadows close to Narziss's monastery, where Lise, his first lover, initiates
him into the mysteries of sex: "Die holde kurze Seligkeit der Liebe wölbte
sich über ihn, glühte golden und brennend auf, neigte sich und erlosch"
(80; "The sweet, brief bliss of love arched over him, flared up in golden
flames, subsided and died away," 64). This romantic description of his first
love already adumbrates the sparkling horizon of his last love, but it also
foreshadows another future experience, the modern one-night stand. Goldmund's lifelong wanderlust from village to village in search of erotic adventures became in the sixties and seventies the lifestyle of countless so
called "swinging singles." Many of them had sworn off the bourgeois limitations of a conventional marriage and its traditional family values in order
to embrace the much more bohemian lifestyle of hopping from bar to bar
and bed to bed in search of partners full of fun and spontaneous frivolities
— and full of fear of commitment.[22] In the 1970s, Goldmund's restless
"Wandern und Schweifen" would have found an ideal female companion
in Erica Jong and her novel *Fear of Flying*, which glamorizes casual sex
with perfect strangers from a modern woman's point of view.[23] Can the
heroine of *Fear of Flying* reach in her erotic raptures the heights of the
"flying utopian body" of the Newly Born Woman? God(dess) only knows.
In its own way, Jong's narrative became a defining novel for the 1970s
and, together with Cixous and Clément's manifesto, is a pathbreaking —
and at times breathtaking — document of the continuing social self-lib-
eration and sexual self-realization of the New Woman, the Newly Born
Woman, born to be sexy and single.

Goldmund's adventurous bachelorhood is linked with his need for personal independence. Time and again we read "Ich muss in die Freiheit"
(201; "I must have my freedom," 153) and hear him jubilate "im . . .
Taumel der wiedergewonnenen Freiheit" (204; "in the first rapture of freedom regained," 157). The idea of personal freedom did not gain philo-

sophical momentum until the Age of Enlightenment. However, since then the notion of civil and political liberties has emerged as one of modern history's most powerful forces, which has been pushing for the liberation and emancipation of modern man and modern woman as well as sexual, ethnic, and religious minorities.[24]

Closely related to the notion of freedom and independence is the concept of social mobility. Certainly a very common modern analog of Goldmund's medieval vagabonding is today's global tourism. During the Middle Ages, only a very small fraction of the population traveled, including craftsmen, pilgrims, scholars, soldiers and merchants, and of course minstrels and vagabonds. The vast majority of the population was tied to the land for life, tilling the soil as farmers in bondage to their feudal overlords. Nowadays, cheap last-minute flights take millions of tourists around the globe. Complementing the short-term traveling routines of today's accidental tourists in search of fun and recreation are the growing patterns of long-term migration, which to varying degrees are forced upon whole segments of populations. The trends established by the persecution and expulsion of millions of ethnic and religious minorities in the first half of the twentieth century and the economic migration of guest workers and refugees fleeing utter poverty in its second half promise to continue in the twenty-first century.[25]

Similarly, the world's countless resident aliens share with Goldmund many degrees of alienation, arising from their sense of personal uprootedness and cultural homelessness. Goldmund's romantic wanderlust often alternates with a rueful *weltschmerz* that has its sources in a complex sense of "Heimatlosigkeit" (123, 127, 141, 144 et passim). Part of his dejection is probably a combination of "envy and guilt," to reformulate Klein's object relations theory. Goldmund feels envious of those who have homes and guilty about the possibility of having wrecked them by seducing good wives into careless adultery. But Goldmund's mood swings, his feelings of being down and out, have even deeper roots. "Ihn durchdrang stärker als jemals das Gefühl des Heimatlosen, der kein Haus oder Schloss oder Klostermauern zwischen sich und der großen Angst gebaut hat." (144; "More strongly than ever he was pierced by a sense of homelessness, of having failed to build house or monastery walls between himself and the great fear [. . .]," 111). This great anxiety already foreshadows the "transcendental homelessness" social and cultural critics have repeatedly diagnosed as the major malaise of modern man.[26]

A positive aspect of Goldmund's sense of alienation, and intricately linked with it, is his awakening concern for the welfare of all creatures. This becomes most pronounced in his observations at village markets, where he is struck by the suffering of dying animals: ". . . wie die Fische mit schmerzlich geöffneten Mäulern und angstvoll starren Goldaugen sich still dem Tod ergaben oder sich wütend und verzweifelt gegen ihn wehrten. Wie schon manches Mal ergriff ihn ein Mitleid mit diesen Tieren und ein trauriger Unmut gegen die Menschen." (187, see also 247; ". . . the fish, with agonized, gaping jaws and frightened, staring gold eyes, quietly resigned themselves to death, or fiercely and desperately fought it off. As on many other occasions, he was seized by pity for these creatures and by a sorrowful resentment of human beings," 145). This empathy with the suffering of animals is no longer part of the medieval mind, which was quite comfortable torturing humans, as Goldmund himself witnesses and as numerous artifacts, chronicles of witch hunts, and the arsenals of torture chambers from medieval Europe amply document. Goldmund's heartfelt commiseration with the suffering and dying creatures is very much characteristic of the modern mind, whose ecological concerns have spawned a wide variety of organizations oriented toward concern for non-human beings, ranging from the prevention of cruelty to animals to the preservation of endangered species. While the peace movement of the 1960s protested against the war of their fathers, the Greenpeace movement of the following decades organized worldwide strategies to protect Planet Earth.

Goldmund's compassion for the well-being of all creatures as well as his vivid imagination about the interrelatedness of all forms of life have much in common with the nascent Gaia consciousness, whose evolving New Age Spirituality includes a rediscovery of the pagan cults by Wiccans, the reconstruction of matriarchal myths by contemporary scholars, and an "Earth Day" for all of us, reminding everyone of the precious and precarious nature of Mother Earth. Deeply in touch with her seasons, and in tune with her natural rhythms, Goldmund sees the world as a unique gift from his mother, and as he awaits death, he returns this gift to her: "ihr gab er den Wald, die Sonne [. . .] in die mütterlichen Hände zurück" (270; "to her he [. . .] gave back the forest, the sun, [. . .] into those maternal hands," 207), so that the wealth of the earth can be regenerated and shared with generations to come. ("Re-cycling" is the magic word).[27]

The fourth and last aspect of Goldmund's retrospective, which gains a major importance in modern culture, is his fascination with images ("und immer neue Bilder," 311). Throughout the novel, Goldmund's wanderlust is driven by an intense *Augenlust*. In his fixation on images, he is the exemplary counterpart to Narziss, who tells him at the end of his journey through life: "für dich bestand die Welt aus Bildern, für mich aus Begriffen" (294; "For you the world consisted of images, for me of concepts," 225). This characterization further reinforces the exemplary difference between their patriarchal and matriarchal worldviews, as the following delineation further illuminates. According to Narziss, *Genesis* means: in the beginning was the Word (Logos) and the Word was in God. As Goldmund begins to refocus his view of the world, he finally arrives at the opposite end of such cosmogonic mythology: in the beginning was Eros, and Eros was one with the Goddess whose boundless love for life created the universe.[28] In this reversal of perspective, Narziss's blind faith in God the Father in heaven turns into Goldmund's blind love for the Mother Goddess on Earth, who after all reveals herself visually in all of her material abundance — and seeing is believing.[29] This cosmic change in perspectives from Narziss's fervent belief in an eternal afterlife in heaven to Goldmund's acute awareness of the ephemerality of life on earth has lasting consequences. In a universe where the material world has become the center of cultural consciousness, caring for the earth and its well-being becomes increasingly important. In addition, the shift from Narziss's culture of "Begriffe" to Goldmund's world of "Bilder" anticipates the epochal turn from the verbal to the visual, from the (written) word to the image, in short, from the sacred to the secular, and eventually to the spectacular world of our present-day show-business culture and its omnipresent stargazing and idol worshipping.

In the novel, this systematic inversion from the spiritual to the secular finds its most symbolic representation in the Madonna statue of Meister Niklaus, Goldmund's admired mentor and master: "Es war eine Mutter Gottes aus Holz [. . .] so lebendig, so schön [. . .] wie er sie nie gesehen zu haben meinte" (156; "It was a wooden statue of the Madonna [. . .] more alive, more tender and soulful, than anything he remembered ever having seen before," 122). His father confessor cautions him that some think "das sei keine rechte Mutter Gottes, sie sei viel zu neumodisch und weltlich" (156–57; "she is not a fitting Madonna, that she is much too modern and worldly," 122). Matriarchal scholarship has long argued that the Christian Madonna is an iconic split-off from the stock imagery of the ancient Great Mother, and that the Catholic invocation of her as *stella maris* represents a last worldly reflection of the *Urmutter*, the *prima materia* as *anima mundi*, the orgasmic freedom of the world to be born. In Meister Niklaus's statue this sublimated representation of the virginal divine is brought back down to earth again and re-invested with all the sensuous beauty of human flesh and blood.[30]

Meister Niklaus's recreation of the divine in explicitly human form is a medieval anticipation of the Renaissance. In the history of the visual arts, this systematic shift from the sacred to the secular began around 1500, but not until the late nineteenth century did artists such as Félicien Rops (1833–98) thematize it in pictures of blasphemous crucifixions. However, no artist rendered the metamorphosis of the Madonna from medieval to modern more expressively than Edward Munch (1863–1944) around the turn of the century. His various representations of this figure endow her with all the attributes of a sensuous woman, if not decadent *femme fatale*. Her languid, naked torso projects concupiscent carnality, which in one version is further highlighted by a frame containing shapes that clearly suggest sperm, thereby connecting male sexuality with female fertility. With the arrival of Art Nouveau around 1900, this process of secularization moved into its final iconographic stage, panerotic diffusion. The contemporary Viennese architect Adolf Loos (1870–1933) famously declared "All art is erotic." And Hesse's Goldmund, with all his "Schulung durch Frauen" could not agree more. As he finally returns home to the monastery at the end of his life to settle down as a sculptor, he creates an elaborate bas-relief depicting the Garden of Eden. Repeatedly he calls his recreation of paradise not only a labor of love but also a work of "Wollust" (303, 307; "lust," 139). Goldmund fails however to give final shape to the dream of his life. "Das Bild der Menschenmutter" (170; "the image of the secular Eve-mother," 135) in which female sensuality and female spirituality would form a beatific unity, remains a vision beyond dreams. Although throughout his life Goldmund experienced moments of ecstatic paradise, his artistic failure to give it permanent shape is also telling testimony to the unreachable ideals of modern man and his doomed hopes to find lasting sexual and spiritual happiness through his imagined modern other, his larger-than-life madonna as passionate lover and perfect mother.[31] "Paradise Now," the "restorative utopia" of Bachofen's Great Mother, will always remain out there, "back in the future," where in the past decades the theorists of postmodern worldviews have been imagining the last frontier. There, the images of our visions might be picture perfect but still not real.

Complementing the powerful sexual current which runs through Goldmund's life story is a homoerotic undercurrent that characterizes Narziss's monastic world. As Michel Foucault has demonstrated in his *History of Sexuality*, the discourse formation on human sexuality did not begin until the Age of Enlightenment. Sex in the Dark Ages was primarily sin, associated with death and damnation. And homosexuality did not even dare to speak its name or articulate its desire — maybe with one clandestine exception: the numerous depictions of the martyred body of Saint Sebastian have been recognized — though not until the twentieth century — as secret icons of the gay community.[32] Hesse's novel also contributes to the cautious coming-out of such a homoerotic subculture in ecclesiastical institutions. As we are introduced at the beginning of the novel to the cloistered world of Mariabronn, we find several references in this direction. About young Narziss we read for example: "dass er wunderbar Griechisch konnte, liebten die Gelehrten an ihm. Dass er so edel und fein war, liebten beinahe alle an ihm, viele waren in ihn verliebt" (11; "The scholars loved him for his wonderful Greek. Almost everyone loved him for his nobility and refinement; many fell in love with him," 9). During his long tenure at the monastery, the abbot, Daniel, has witnessed his share of such

romantic entanglements: "Viele Jünglingsfreundschaften hatte er in mehr
als vierzig Jahren Klosterleben mit angesehen, sie gehörten ins Bild des
Klosters, sie waren hübsche Zugabe, waren zuweilen ein Spass, waren
zuweilen eine Gefahr" (41; "In more than forty years of monastic life he
had observed many friendships between youths. They were part of the monastery scene, a pleasant bonus, sometimes amusing, sometimes dangerous," 32). Abbot Daniel's remarkable openness about such male bonding
in his monastery is only surpassed by young Narziss's own explicit confession to Goldmund: "Du schläfst an der Brust der Mutter, ich wache in
der Wüste [. . .] Deine Träume sind von Mädchen, meine von Knaben
. . ." (51; "You sleep on your mother's breast, I keep vigil in the desert.
[. . .] Your dreams are of girls, mine of boys [. . .]," 41). The last three
periods are as fraught with hidden significance as the famous hyphen in
Kleist's novella *Die Marquise von O. . . .*[33]

The church's history of demonizing sexuality and female sexuality in
particular is complemented by an even more insidious defamation, that is,
the age-old prejudice against the Jews as the murderers of Christ. During
the Middle Ages, this accusation was further compounded by the charge
of the blood libel, in which Jews were accused of slaughtering Christian
children for ritual purposes. In times of crisis such slandering invariably
led to catastrophic consequences for the Jews. As the Great Plague
ravishes the world around him, Goldmund watches with horror: "In einer
Stadt sah Goldmund mit grimmigem Herzen zu, wie die ganze Juden-
gasse brannte, Haus an Haus, rundum stand das johlende Volk, und die
schreienden Flüchtlinge wurden mit Waffengewalt ins Feuer zurück-
gejagt. Im Irrsinn der Angst und Erbitterung wurden überall Unschuldige
totgeschlagen, verbrannt, gefoltert" (232; "In one town Goldmund
watched in suppressed rage as an entire Jewish sector burned, house after
house, while the howling mob stood round and the screaming victims were
driven back by force of arms into the flames. In the madness of fear and
frustration, innocent people everywhere were being beaten to death,
burned to death or tortured," 177). When Goldmund meets the Jewess
Rebekka, he learns about the cruel fate of her people first hand. "Ihr
Vater, der war samt vierzehn anderen Juden auf Befehl der Obrigkeit zur
Asche verbrannt worden" (235; ". . . her father who, with fourteen other
Jews, had been burned to ashes by order of the authorities," 179). What
he sees and hears about the horrors of such pogroms will leave an in-
delible impression on Goldmund. Years later, after he has returned to Mariabronn and Narziss, he interrupts one of their lofty conversations with
a question out of the blue: "Eine Frage, Narziss: habt ihr auch einmal
Juden verbrannt?" (282; "One question, Narcissus: Did the monastery
ever burn Jews?," 216). Narziss's answer is evasive: "Juden verbrannt? Wie
sollten wir? Es gibt ja bei uns keine Juden" (282, "Burn Jews? How could

we? There are no Jews where we are," 216). Yet Goldmund does not let his friend off the hook that easily: "Versteh mich. Narziss! Ich meine: Kannst du dir denken, dass du in irgend einem Fall den Befehl zum Um-bringen von Juden geben würdest oder doch deine Einwilligung dazu? Es haben ja so viel Herzöge, Bürgermeister, Bischöfe und andere Obrig-keiten solche Befehle gegeben" (282; "Don't misunderstand me, Narcissus! What I mean is, can you imagine a case in which you would give the or-der to kill Jews, or at least your consent? After all, so many dukes, mayors, bishops and other authorities have given such orders," 216). At the latest here at this telling passage, associations with the Holocaust can no longer be ignored. After the increasingly rabid antisemitism of the growing Nazi movement during the Weimar Republic, accompanied by the assassination of several prominent Jewish politicians and public figures (Landauer, Luxemburg, Liebknecht, Rathenau), fears that the madness of medieval pogroms might repeat itself were not unfounded. As it turned out, the Third Reich and its systematic mass murder of Jews, organized by the high-est power of state and condoned if not sanctioned by its various churches, would surpass the wildest imagination of any pre-Holocaust novelist. In hindsight, the medieval horror scenes Goldmund witnesses crystallize into a magnifying glass under which the future large-scale preparations for the "Final Solution" become already visible like a rising specter.[34] Goldmund watches with horror, "wie die Knechte mit Stangen und Bootshaken die Toten von den Wagen rissen und sie zu Haufen in das große Loch stießen [. . .] übereinander geschmissen, viele nackt" (215; "as the men dragged the bodies from the carts with poles and boat-hooks and shoved them in piles into the big pit [. . .] thrown on top of each other, many of them naked," 165). Such graphic snapshots conjure up the stacks of naked corp-ses in the extermination camps, piled up like logs ready to be burned in ovens. The novel's ominous foreshadowing of the Holocaust is further underscored by a psychological syndrome that in recent years has become known as survivor's guilt. There is no doubt that the orphaned Rebekka suffers from it: "Sie [. . .] hatte fliehen können, war nun aber verzweifelt zurückgekehrt und klagt sich an, dass sie sich nicht habe mitverbrennen lassen" (235; "After managing to escape she had now returned in despair, overcome with remorse at not having let herself be burned with them," 179).[35] In this world of cruel persecution and deadly destruction, perpe-trated mainly by masculine aggression and sanctioned by predominantly pa-triarchal authorities, Rebekka, the distraught survivor, stands as a solitary and desperate reminder of the other possible world, the realm of nurtur-ing life and cherishing love, associated with the archetype of the feminine divine. It would take centuries until such an alternative model would gain major momentum and be able to substantially transform social realities and cultural ideals.

Just as in the final years of the Second World War and the Holocaust, the world around Goldmund turns into a wasteland of moral depravity and human desperation: "Das ganze weite Land stand unter einer Wolke von Tod, unter einem Schleier von Grauen [. . .] Massengräber [. . .] die Pestknechte und Spitalbüttel herrschten wie Henker" (231; "the whole wide country was under a cloud of death, under a veil of horror, [. . .] mass graves [. . .] the men paid to remove the corpses held sway like hangmen," 177). Here, Mother Nature unveils herself as a devouring monster, and mankind colludes with her transmogrification, turning hospital helpers into brutal henchmen. In the universe of the concentration camps, the medieval torturers would return as modern doctors, engaging in cruel medical experiments in which death was always the final diagnosis.

Goldmund's intense visual perception and graphic depiction of the horrors around him find a stunning correspondence in the German Jewish painter Felix Nußbaum and the strangely medieval features of his rendition of Holocaust scenes. Paintings like "The Damned" (1944) depict the persecuted as crazed somnambulists and walking dead in the manner of Bosch's and Brueghel's late medieval tableaux. Nußbaum's paintings are visual narratives in which the rampages of the Brown Pest of National Socialism appear like a *déjà vu* of the Black Death during the Middle Ages. Watching the dammed of his own time, Goldmund too gets seized by the panic of death, fleeing its pandemic by taking refuge with the living, the hysterical survivors: "Oft floh er zu den heftigen Festen der Lebenslustigen, überall klang die Fiedel des Todes, er lernte ihren Klang bald kennen, oft nahm er teil an den verzweifelten Gelagen, oft spielte er dabei die Laute oder tanzte beim Pechfackelschein durch fiebernde Nächte mit" (232; "Often he would join some frenzied celebrants of the lust to live — Death's fiddle was to be heard everywhere and he soon learned to recognize its sound — or he would participate in those desperate feasts, perhaps play the lute or join in the dancing by the light of pitch flares throughout the feverish night," 177). Such delirious descriptions are evocative transliterations of the stock imagery of the medieval *Totentanz*. Its morbid choreography appears directly telescoped into paintings like Nußbaum's "Organ Grinder" (1943) and "The Skeletons Play for a Dance" (1944). In Theresienstadt, Hitler's showcase concentration camp, Weimar's Jewish artists would finally be forced to perform their own dance of death. Germany, the land of music, had morphed into a dancing morgue, whose grotesque world Paul Celan would capture in his famous poem "Todesfuge." "Der Tod ist ein Meister aus Deutschland," this often quoted line from Celan's poem describes most emblematically the production of death "made in Germany," that is, its perfection of mass murder, which the Nazis industrialized on a monstrous scale and efficiently and systematically exported all over Europe.

This mastery of death is — vice versa — complemented by a master narrative of love. Like no other country in the world, the culture of German-speaking countries has produced and propagated the seminal theories of the sexual revolution, from Bachofen's *Mother Right* to Marcuse's *Eros and Civilization* (1955). As we have seen, the themes of love and death and their baroque tropes of *carpe diem* and *memento mori* are intricately woven into the text of Hesse's novel. Given Germany's antithetical proclivities, its modern madness and ingenuities, it even managed to raise love and death to the sublime synthesis of a romantic *Liebestod*. In Wagner's operas of death and desire, this theme becomes a central leitmotif whose chthonic crescendos and celestial climaxes have transported generations of opera lovers around the world. Goldmund knows all about its melodramatic rises and final collapses of opposites. He hears it in the moaning of his enraptured mistress: "töte mich" (256; "kill me," 195) and he recognizes it again in the grand and grim finale, hovering over a landscape devastated by the plague, "das wilde Lied des Todes [. . .] süß und verführend, heimwärts lockend, mütterlich" (234; "Death's wild song [. . .] sweet and seductive, beckoning homewards, maternal," 178). But the maternal dance of love has become a macabre dance of death, and the voice from the womb (Cixous) is turning into the call from the tomb (Bachofen), revealing the Freudian "Unheimliche" in all its uncanniness.[36] Excess of love and excess of death, of ecstasies and agonies, the sheer shedding and spilling of blood, sweat, semen, and tears, it is Goldmund's life story and it is also the history of Western civilization in the twentieth century. Narziss, with his scholarly erudition, might call it a "historia passionis," a history of passion in which the double meaning of the Latin word "passio" connotes and intertwines the ecstasy of lovers with the agony of those tortured and murdered. (The outbreak of AIDS at the end of the twentieth century would twist this *Liebestod*-motif, this double bind of "Leiden" and "Leidenschaft" one more time into a reality of epidemic proportions, making especially members of the gay community martyrs of their own sexual liberation.) Till the end of his life, Goldmund will cherish the memories of his lovers and the happiness of their love, and he will be haunted even more by the memory of the dead and the horrors of their death: "Ich denke an Rebekka, an die verbrannten Juden, an die Massengräber, an das große Sterben" (283; "But I'm thinking of Rebekka, of the Jews who were burned, of the mass graves, of the countless deaths," 217). Since then, for Goldmund the cries of love, its *petit mort*, reverberate more and more with the cries of the dying, "das große Sterben."

Long before commemorating the Holocaust became a kind of negative identity for his country, Goldmund stands *betroffen* and *heimgesucht* by the medieval prelude of its modern insanity. Since the 1990s Germany's official labor of mourning has evolved into a veritable memory culture, a collective exercise of "recovered memory." In Freudian terms, the Holocaust has become the narcissistic wound in Germany's painful recovery of national pride and identity. And this narcissistic injury is also a festering thorn in the side of the Catholic Church and its institutional memory. Narziss illustrates this — *nomen est omen* — with striking clarity. His failure to see and avert evil, that is, the age-old curse of antisemitism, has over the centuries become the blind spot of the Catholic Church. The rationale of not seeing, or not being able to see, was after all an essential part of the church's theodicy. Furthermore, Narcissus, according to myth, was only interested in seeing himself, the reflection of his own beauty, "so edel und fein" he was, just like Narciss. The cloisters of the church served a similar purpose of self-reflection, thereby blocking out the ugly world and the misery of those outside. In this institutional double blindness of faith and self-absorption, Narziss figures as a kind of fictional *doppelgänger* of Nuntius Pacelli, the Vatican's emissary to the Third Reich, who as the later Pope Pius XII would stand accused of having ignored the persecution of the Jewish people under National Socialism.[37] With his doctrinal belief that Jews are responsible for the murder of Christ, with his allegiance to a powerful institution that is deeply tainted by the history of antisemitism and with his wishful or unwitting thinking ("Es gibt ja bei uns keine Juden"), Narziss becomes a potential precursor of Hitler's willing executioners and their radical determination to make Germany "judenfrei." Like Pacelli, the pontifex of Rome, Narziss, the abbot of Mariabronn, stands compromised by his personal and institutional failure to help all those who are oppressed and persecuted.

For Goldmund, the experience of the plague and its deadly toll on humanity left him not only psychologically traumatized, it also affected him spiritually with lasting consequences. Having survived its physical devastation and moral corruption, he tries to come to terms with it, to confess his sins, and, even more important, to understand God's purpose with all of this: "Lieber Gott, warum hast du uns so geschaffen, warum führst du uns solche Wege? Sind wir nicht deine Kinder? Ist nicht dein Sohn für uns gestorben? Gibt es nicht Heilige und Engel, um uns zu leiten?" (240; "Dear Lord, why hast Thou created us like this, why dost Thou lead us along such paths? Are we not Thy children? Did not Thy Son die for us? Are there not saints and angels to guide us?," 183). One more time, Goldmund plays the naïve child, asking his father in heaven for divine guidance and reassurance. But not even a father confessor is present to respond: "Wohl gab es Beichtstühle in der Kirche, doch in keinem einen Priester; sie waren gestorben, lagen im Hospital, waren geflohen" (240; "But although there were confessionals in the church, in none of them was there a priest. They had died, were in hospital, had fled," 183). Goldmund's doubts, which have been mounting for years, finally topple over into disbelief and defiance. "Oder sind das alles hübsche erfundene Geschichten, die man den Kindern erzählt und über die die Pfaffen selber lachen? Ich bin irr an dir geworden, Gottvater, du hast die Welt übel geschaffen, schlecht hälst du sie in Ordnung" (240; "Or are these all charming stories invented for children and laughed at by the priests themselves? I have lost faith in Thee, O Lord. Thou hast created an evil world, and Thou dost not look after it well," 183). After a long enumeration of injustices, inequities and above all endless human miseries, Goldmund cries out: "Hast du uns denn ganz vergessen und verlassen, ist dir die Schöpfung ganz entleidet, willst du uns alle zugrunde gehen lassen?" (240, "Hast Thou then quite forgotten and deserted us? Canst Thou no longer tolerate Thy creation? Dost Thou want us all to perish?," 183). Echoing Christ's own agony on the cross ("my father, why hast thou forsaken me"), Goldmund leaves the confessional distraught and disillusioned.[38]

Years later, close to the end of his journey through life, Goldmund finally accepts the loss of his Christian faith. After his heavenly night with his royal paramour, Goldmund gets caught by the governor's guards and thrown into a dungeon where he awaits his execution. Quickly his high spirits give way to the darkness of sullen soul searching: "Er wusste nicht, ob es einen Himmel gebe, und einen Gottvater, und ein Gericht und eine Ewigkeit. Er hatte in diesen Dingen seit langem jede Gewissheit verloren" (270; "He didn't know if there was a heaven and a heavenly Father, and a Judgment and an eternity. He had long lost all certainty in such things," 207). At the last minute, Goldmund is saved from death by a mysterious priest who turns out to be Narziss. Although very thankful, Golmund remains rather unimpressed by this fabulous, if not miraculous intervention. After many more disputations with Narziss about God and his world, the man of the church finally comes to the conclusion: "Du scheinst ein Heide geworden zu sein" (288, "You have evidently become a heathen!," 220). At that time in history, this was a serious charge. During the Middle Ages, even avowed Christians fighting to preserve the purity of the faith were executed and burned at the stake, as the fates of Jan Hus, Savonarola, Giordano Bruno, and others show. In Goldmund's case, his uncompromising probing and questioning has made a deep impression on Narziss: "Die Welt, in der er lebte und Heimat hatte, seine Welt, sein Klosterleben, sein Amt, seine Gelehrsamkeit, sein schön gegliedertes Gedankengebäude waren ihm durch den Freund oft stark erschüttert und zweifelhaft geworden" (315; "The world in which he lived and had his home, his world, his monastic life, his office, his scholarship, his nicely organized thought structure, had often been violently shaken and cast into doubt by his friend," 241). Narziss's religious doubts are the beginning of cracks in the theological constructs of his church, and they would soon widen in historical reality, leading inexorably to the schismatic movement of the

Protestant Reformation. This critical process of Christian self-reflection gained new momentum during the Age of Enlightenment and culminated at the end of the nineteenth century in Nietzsche's epochal pronouncement "God is dead."[39] Since then, the specter of nihilism has haunted Europe, and the Death of God became Christianity's worst nightmare.[40]

This modern sense of transcendental abandonment is clearly articulated and anticipated in Goldmund's medieval endeavors to communicate with God. With his desperate question "Hast du uns denn ganz. . . . verlassen?" Goldmund's lifelong quest for a higher truth traces this centuries-old trajectory of losing faith in God to its very end in modernity. The burning ghettos of medieval Jews are — eternal recurrence of the same — the fiery furnaces of modern extermination camps. The fears of the Middle Ages that the world would soon come to an end — with Dürer's horsemen as its harbingers — have finally come true: Apocalypse Now — that is, Auschwitz, the crucible, in which the Judeo-Christian belief in God is most severely tested. As the earth becomes hell and heaven does not fall, Good must have either made a pact with Evil or disappeared altogether. "God left in 1941," this sentence attributed to the Jewish philosopher Emanuel Levinas might be apocryphal after all, but it does encipher most poignantly the spiritual disillusionment of many Holocaust survivors and countless post-Holocaust thinkers. Their disbelief probably reached its most astounding articulation when Pope Benedict XVI visited Auschwitz in the fall of 2006 and was overheard wondering: "Where was God?" (Nietzsche forbid).

"Credo, quia absurdum": I believe because it does not make sense. This was the syllogistic reasoning of medieval theologians, professing their faith despite and because of the world's many adversities and atrocities. After all the dialectics of enlightenment and the eclipse of all reason, after all the unbelievable and unimaginable realities of the twentieth century — after Auschwitz — "*Non* credo, quia absurdum" has become the only logical response for millions of former believers. "Die Kirche war leer," Goldmund realizes on his last visit to church, "hohl klangen [seine] Schritte im Steingewölbe wider" (240; "The church was empty, [. . .] and [his] footsteps echoed hollowly from the vaulted stone ceiling," 183). Those hollow halls reverberate even more loudly throughout modern Europe, where church attendance has dropped dramatically in recent decades. In their homilies and encyclicals church authorities have been deploring this trend with growing frequency as a rapid "re-paganization" of Christian Europe. Poor Narziss: he saw this one coming. His "Credo, quia absurdum" finds its distant but powerful echoes in the Absurd Theater of the 1950s, in which Samuel Beckett's play "Waiting for Godot" (1953) restaged the world as a theatrical *reductio ad absurdum*.

Since God the Father in heaven had remained painfully silent, Goldmund follows the "call of the mother," the joyful seductions of Mother Earth. Whereas God the Father remains the *deus absconditus*, the proverbially hidden God, she keeps revealing herself in a multitude of erotic epiphanies, in the beauty of women, the wonders of life, and the ecstatic experience of love. Abundance, peace, freedom and happiness in the here and now, in other words, the archetypal aspects of the female divine, are her paradisical promises. Following her with eyes wide open, Goldmund pursues a most alluring dream into the future despite and even because of all the disillusionments he has experienced in reality.

In his own lifetime, Goldmund witnesses much goodness and much evil, including the apparent disappearance of the ultimate good, which was supposed to be God. Looking beyond good and evil, following Nietzsche's notion of a radical transvaluation of all traditional values, one has to ask how this moral and spiritual transformation might play itself out and coalesce into a new, postmodern worldview. After all that has been written, said, and done, mankind still invokes God's holy name. According to Scriptures, he will return at the end of time to redeem the world. Perhaps God's second coming is revealed in the return of the ancient Goddess? Perhaps, the silent, ascetic God of the New Testament is aching like the God of the Old Testament, is yearning like thunderous, irascible Yahwe — who, according to the gnostic revelations of the medieval Kabala, is still searching for his mystical Shekina, his lost divine female other? Perhaps their holy reunion would heal mankind, make it whole again, a newborn wo-man-kind, dancing and soaring together, turning the Day of Judgment into a Day of Jouissance? — Monotheists will protest such flights of fancy, atheists will scoff at such New Age Spirituality. But most of us should be able to agree with Hesse on this: For the changes and challenges of the future, "dazu braucht es Frauen." Or as a graffiti of the 1970s put it: "Die Zukunft wird weiblich sein oder gar nicht." The writing is still on the wall.

Notes

[1] See Heribert Kuhn, commentary to Hermann Hesse, *Narziss und Goldmund* (Frankfurt: Suhrkamp, 2003), 368. All subsequent quotes from the novel are from this edition also and are cited parenthetically by page number. The English translation of the novel by Ursule Molinaro, which has been on the American market since 1968, is commendable, as it catches the medieval melody and imagery of the novel altogether quite well: *Narcissus and Goldmund* (New York: Farrar, Strauss and Giroux, 1968; reprint New York: Macmillan, 2003). English translations of quotations from the novel are from Molinaro, cited by page number.

[2] For a succinct analysis of Narziss as a reflection of the teaching of Thomas of Aquinas and other theologians of the High Middle Ages, see Ralf R. Nicolai, *Hesses*

Narziss und Goldmund: Kommentar und Deutung (Würzburg: Königshausen und Neumann, 1997).

[3] Johann Jakob Bachofen, *Das Mutterrecht,* in Bachofen, *Gesammelte Werke,* vols. 2 and 3 (Basel: Schwabe, 1948).

[4] Carl Gustav Jung, "Die psychologischen Aspekte des Mutterarchetyps," in C. G. Jung, *Gesammelte Werke,* vol. 9 (Olten & Freiburg: Walter, 1976), 89–124.

[5] For a summation of the psychomythic aspects of the *magna mater* see Erich Neumann, *Die Große Mutter: Der Archetyp des Großen Weiblichen* (Zurich: Rhein, 1956). For further details on the reception history of matriarchal mythography in the first third of the twentieth century, see Frederick A. Lubich, "La loi du père versus le désir de la mère. Zur Männerphantasie der Weimarer Republik," in *Wann ist der Mann ein Mann — Zur Geschichte der Männlichkeit,* ed. Walter Erhart and Britta Herrmann (Stuttgart, Weimar: Metzler, 1997), 249–70.

[6] Melanie Klein, "A Study of Envy and Gratitude," in *The Selected Melanie Klein,* ed. Juliet Mitchell (New York: The Free Press, 1987), 211–99.

[7] For an exemplary analysis of the construction of various female stereotypes in literary and cultural history see Sylvia Bovenschen, *Die imaginierte Weiblichkeit: Exemplarische Untersuchungen zu kulturgeschichtlichen und literarischen Präsentationsformen des Weiblichen* (Frankfurt: Suhrkamp, 1979). For an illustrative study of the return of negative female stereotypes and evil archetypes in modern art of the nineteenth and twentieth century, see Bram Dijkstra, *Idols of Perversity: Fantasies of Feminine Evil in Fin-de-Siècle Culture* (New York, Oxford: Oxford UP, 1986).

[8] See Frederick A. Lubich, "Bachofens Mutterrecht, Hesses *Demian* und der Verfall der Vatermacht." *Germanic Review* 65.4 (1990): 150–58.

[9] Goldmund is not alone with such visions of paradise. He finds a soul mate in Thomas Mann's novel *Der Zauberberg,* where Hans Castorp, "Sorgenkind" (!) par excellence, experiences at the height of a life-threatening snowstorm very similar epiphanies of Elysian ecstasies. For a close reading of this text and its larger context see Frederick A. Lubich, "Thomas Manns *Der Zauberberg* — Spukschloß der Großen Mutter oder die Männerdämmerung des Abendlandes," in *Deutsche Vierteljahrsschrift für Literaturwissenschaft und Geistesgeschichte* 67. 4 (1993): 729–63. To a degree, Narziss and Goldmund are even literary reflections of Thomas Mann and Hermann Hesse. Goldmund is a poetic projection of Hesse, the bohemian wanderer and principal representative of Germany's neo-Romantic modernity, Narziss an intellectual reflection of Mann, the well-established representative of German classical modernity, and an earlier incarnation of Thomas von der Trave in *Das Glasperlenspiel,* Hesse's last and most explicit homage to his friend.

[10] Such mental permutations and interpenetrations are reminiscent of the "participation mystique" that is characteristic of the psychomythic world of the ancient Eleusinian mother mysteries (see Neumann, *Die Große Mutter,* passim). On a modern level, Hesse's narrative rhythm and his tendency toward repetition of themes and imagery are reminiscent of D. H. Lawrence's impassioned prosody.

[11] In Gustav Klimt's numerous paintings of sensuous females flourishing amid flowers and floating in deep waters, this erotic stream-of-consciousness style found its most gifted exponent.

[12] For a recent account of those high times see Barry Miles, *Hippie* (New York: Sterling, 2004), whose lavish illustrations make it an informative sourcebook on the lifestyles and art forms of that period.

[13] Goldmund must have struck all the chords of Nietzsche's true musicians "die [. . . in . . .] der Musik gleichsam ihren Mutterschoß haben und mit den Dingen fast nur durch unbewusste Musikrelationen in Verbindung stehen" (who find their womb in the world of music and who connect with the material world almost only through unconscious musical relations) (*Geburt der Tragödie* in *Werke in Sechs Bänden*, vol 1, ed. Karl Schlechta [Munich: Hanser, 1980], 116).

[14] The German word "Befriedigung" clearly reflects this deeper connection between social peace and sexual satisfaction, a connection that was central to both the utopian ideals of matriarchal cultures and the movement for peace and free love of the '68 generation.

[15] This play principle has also become a defining feature of postmodern aesthetics in a variety of art forms ranging from literature to painting and architecture. See Charles Jencks, *Post-Modernism: The New Classicism in Art and Architecture* (New York: Rizzoli, 1987).

[16] In Germany, the emerging popular culture of cabaret, cinema, and music halls, with its mix of sassy showgirls and serious female artists, propagated this multifaceted liberation to such a degree that Weimar's mass culture became identified with woman. Already Hitler had raged against the growing femininization of Weimar Germany. For an exemplary analysis of its central features see Andreas Huyssen, "Mass Culture as Woman: Modernism's Other," in Andreas Huyssen, *After the Great Divide: Modernism, Mass Culture, and Postmodernism* (Bloomington: Indiana UP, 1986), 44–62.

[17] For a popular account of the rise of the silver screen goddess see Kenneth Anger, *Hollywood Babylon* (San Francisco: Simon and Schuster, Straight Arrow Books, 1975).

[18] Klaus Theweleit, *Männerphantasien*, vol. 1, *Frauen, Fluten, Körper, Geschichte* (Reinbek bei Hamburg: Rowohlt, 1980), 395.

[19] The encouragement "Trink mich aus, Geliebter" further enforces Goldmund's link with Melanie Klein's concept of the "good mother," whom she defines as the source of all post-oedipal joys: "The capacity to fully enjoy gratification at the breast forms the foundation for all later happiness" ("A Study of Envy and Gratitude," 215). Thus, Goldmund's namesake, his "golden mouth," becomes another signifier for his blissful relationship with the maternal body.

[20] Gilbert, preface to Hélène Cixous and Catherine Clément, *The Newly Born Woman* (Minneapolis: U of Minnesota P, 1988), ix. All subsequent quotes are taken from this edition.

[21] Gilbert explains the term as used by Cixous and Clément: "Jouissance implies a virtually metaphysical fulfillment of desire that goes far beyond any satisfaction that could be imagined by Hugh Hefner and his minions" (xvii).

[22] For a study of this lifestyle of hippies as reconstructed yuppies see David Brooks, *Bobos (Bourgeois Bohemians) in Paradise: The New Upper Class and How it Got There* (New York: Simon and Schuster, 2000).

[23] Jong's semi-autobiographical novel reprises the Jungian archetype of the Bachofenian, bacchanalian Aphrodite: "Mit stets neuen Männern paart sich die gleiche Urmutter" (Bachofen, 157; with ever-new men the same Ur-Mother pairs herself).

[24] In historical hindsight, Bachofen's definition of Dionysian matriarchy and his predictions of the return of its "restorative utopia" has become a self-fulfilling prophecy, as one of his most succinct definitions of its cultural ideals shows: "Es hat das Gesetz des leiblichen Lebens, Freiheit und Gleichheit unter den Menschen, an die Spitze gestellt, alle Unterschiede, welche aus politischen Gesichtspunkten stammen, aufgehoben, Fesseln gelöst [. . .] Glanz und Pracht des Lebens befördert und dem Fleische Emanzipation gebracht" (592–93; "It had given the law of life, freedom and equality amongst all human beings its highest priority, it had eliminated all differences which had been the result of socio-political conditions, it had done away with restrictions [. . .] propagated the splendor and magnificence of life and it had emancipated the flesh").

[25] In a cover story on this new "Völkerwanderung," the German magazine *Der Spiegel* characterized our present-day world as a "Welt der Wandernden" and quoted the *Weltkommission für internationale Emigration,* which concluded "dass Migration das wesentliche Thema des 21. Jahrhunderts werden könnte" (*Der Spiegel*, July 2, 2006, 68; that migration could become the primary issue of the twenty-first century).

[26] The spectrum ranges from books like *Der unbehauste Mensch* (1951) by the conservative cultural critic Hans Egon Holthusen to studies such as *Die Theorie des Romans* (1920) by the socialist critic Georg Lukács, in which he coined the term "transzendentale Obdachlosigkeit" (transcendental homelessness). In Freud's essay "Das Unheimliche" (1919) the psychological aspects of home and loss of home, of belonging and abandonment, find their analytical explication in the child's early relationship with its mother. ("Das Unheimliche," *Studienausgabe in zwölf Bänden,* ed. Alexander Mitscherlich, Angela Richards, and James Strachey [Frankfurt: Fischer, 1992], 4, 241–74).

[27] During the past two decades several books on this ecological consciousness, rooted in matriarchal earth religions, have appeared. Some of them are serious academic studies, others are in a more popular vein. To name but a few: Manfred Kurt Ehmer, *Göttin Erde, Kult und Mythos der Mutter Erde: Ein Beitrag zur Ökosophie der Zukunft* (Berlin: Clemens Zerling, 1994); Monica Sjöö and Barbara Mor, *The Great Cosmic Mother: Rediscovering the Religion of the Earth* (San Francisco, Harper and Row, 1987); Adele Getty, *Goddess, Mother of Living Nature* (London: Thames and Hudson, 1990); Gloria Feman Orenstein, *The Reflowering of the Goddess* (New York: Pergamon Press, 1990); and Elinor W. Gadon, *The Once and Future Goddess: A Sweeping Visual Chronicle of the Sacred Female and her Reemergence in the Cultural Mythology of Our Time* (New York: Harper and Row, 1987).

[28] Logos and Eros: the synthesis of both creative principles is "Eros im Wort," which crystallizes in Thomas Mann's novella *Der Tod in Venedig* into the sparkling sentences of "anderthalb Seiten erlesener Prosa" (in H. T. Lowe-Porter's translation, "that page and a half of choicest prose"; *Death in Venice and Seven Other Stories* [New York: Vintage, 1936]) and disseminates into the rich and colorful prose of Mann's complete oeuvre, culminating in his late novel *Der Erwählte* in a polyse-

mantic text that could be characterized by what Roland Barthes has called a "Babel Heureuse," a happy Babel. (Thomas Mann, *Der Tod in Venedig* in *Gesammelte Werke in 13 Bänden*, vol. 8 [Frankfurt: Fischer, 1990], 492). For a detailed analysis of this interplay between language and sexuality in Mann's work, see Frederick A. Lubich, *Die Dialektik von Logos und Eros im Werk von Thomas Mann* (Heidelberg: Carl Winter, 1986).

[29] In his quest to understand "was die Welt im Innersten zusammenhält" ("what secret force hides in the world and rules its course"; *Faust I*, 382–83, trans. Walter Kaufmann), Goethe's Faust too comes to the realization that it was Eros who created the world, and he calls upon him to return and rule again: "So herrsche denn Eros, der alles begonnen" ("Now let Eros, first cause of all, reign and be crowned"; *Faust II*, 8479, trans. David Luke). See Goethe's *Faust*, trans. by Walter Kaufmann (Garden City, New York: Anchor Books, Doubleday Company, Inc, 1963), 95; and Johann Wolfgang von Goethe, *Faust, Part Two* trans. by David Luke (Oxford, New York: Oxford UP, 1994), 122.

[30] Since Goldmund is a *minnesänger*, well experienced in the theory and practice of "hohe Minne" and "niedere Minne," Meister Niklaus's masterpiece might remind Goldmund also of the Marian poetry of Walther von der Vogelweide, in which the religious trope of the gate of paradise, the *porta paradisi*, as it was referred to in medieval texts, figures as a symbol of the virginal sex of the mother of Christ, through which "der künec hêrlîche wart ûz und in gelân" (through which the Lord in his magnificence had passed [literally: had been let in and out]), (Walther von der Vogelweide, *Gedichte: Mittelhochdeutscher Text und Übertragung*. Selected, translated and commented by Peter Wapnewski [Frankfurt: Fischer, 1973], 214). This Christian poem completes the mystical circle of exit and return, which defines the sexual-existential relationship of the mythical Mother Goddess and her Lover Son.

[31] Where Goldmund, the sculptor, failed, Madonna Ciccone will try again. Her ever-changing sexual persona is the next stage in the evolution of reconfiguring the sensuality and spirituality of the contemporary iconic female. For a more elaborate account see Frederick A. Lubich, "Hermann Hesses *Narziss und Goldmund* oder 'Der Weg zur Mutter'. Von der Anima Mundi zur Magna Mater und Madonna (Ciccone)," in *Hermann Hesse Today — Hermann Hesse Heute*, ed. Ingo Cornils and Osman Durrani (Amsterdam: Rodopi, 2005).

[32] Thomas Mann's reference to the figure of Saint Sebastian in *Der Tod in Venedig* (1912) is one of the first ones in a canonical piece of modern German literature. If one compares the baroque representations of the martyrdom of Saint Sebastian with the camp aesthetics of such contemporary visual artists as Pierre et Gilles, whose airbrushed photographs blend the iconography of saints with imagery of sado-masochistic sexuality, then the iconic status of Saint Sebastian and his importance for the gay imagination becomes quite transparent.

[33] Have such cloistered dreams about handsome boys always remained dreams? The many sex-abuse scandals which have been rocking the Catholic Church since the late 1990s provide quite a clear — and stunning — answer. Whatever the complete truth may be, for the benefit of the church, one needs to carefully differentiate between healthy homosexuality and pedophiliac pathology.

[34] In 1932, *Narziss und Goldmund* became the first of Hesse's novels to be translated into Hebrew (Heribert Kuhn, commentary to *Narziss und Goldmund*, 368). By the same token, Nazi authorities banned the book in 1941, "weil darin die Erzählung eines Pogroms vorkommt," as Hesse wrote in a letter of 1944, "und weil ich es ablehnte, diese Erzählung beim Neudruck wegzulassen" (because in it I describe a progrom . . . and because I refused to leave out this description when it was reprinted; quoted in Kuhn, commentary, 367) Hesse's refusal further indicates that the account of the pogrom in the novel was not just another historical incident, but a central part of his narrative design; and in 1941, its medieval fictionality was gaining dramatically in contemporary reality.

[35] In Ruth Klüger's memoirs *Weiter leben*, the guilt of the concentration camp survivor becomes a veritable leitmotif, but also an additional incentive to succeed. For a closer reading of the psychological complex see Frederick A. Lubich, "Surviving to Excel: The Last German Jewish Autobiographies of Holocaust Survivors Ruth Klüger, Marcel Reich-Ranicki, and Paul Spiegel," in *Modern Judaism* 25.2 (2005): 189–210.

[36] The deeper, archetypal identity of *Mutterreich* and *Totenreich* is an underlying theme in Bachofen's matriarchal archeology. For a larger correlation of the theme of music and its relation to magic and madness in the works of both Hermann Hesse and Thomas Mann, see G. W. Field, "Music and Morality in Thomas Mann and Hermann Hesse," in *Hesse: A Collection of Critical Essays*, ed. Theodore Ziolkowski (Englewood Cliffs, NJ: Prentice Hall, 1973), 94–111.

[37] Since Rolf Hochhuth's publication of his drama *Der Stellvertreter* (The Deputy) in 1963, in which he fictionalized Pacelli's controversial role, the debate about the Vatican's failure in the Holocaust has not abated.

[38] The Mexican expressionist painter José Orozco transformed this profound disillusionment of Christ and his Christian followers into the startling image of an angry Son of God, who with the blow of an axe hacks his cross into splintering pieces. This iconoclastic destruction of the principal symbol of Christianity completes and complements the sacrilegious representation of Munch's Madonna. Thus, the Mother of God and the Son of God stand united in their revolt against God the Father.

[39] For an elaboration of this historical continuum, see for example Thomas Mann's 1947 essay "Nietzsches Philosophie im Lichte unserer Erfahrung" (Thomas Mann, *Gesammelte Werke, Reden und Aufsätze*, vol. 9, 675–712) and his novel, published in the same year, *Doktor Faustus: Das Leben des deutschen Tonsetzers Adrian Leverkühn erzählt von einem Freunde* (*Gesammelte Werke*, vol. 6).

[40] Considering the death of God, Nietzsche made the philosophical exhortation "Bleib der Erde treu": "Stay true to the earth." In his treatise "Probleme der Lyrik," the poet Gottfried Benn rephrased this metaphysical inversion, this turning of God and his world upside down, as modernity's "Transzendenz nach unten" (Downward transcendence).

9: Beads of Glass, Shards of Culture, and the Art of Life: Hesse's *Das Glasperlenspiel*

Paul Bishop

"GLASS BEADS, AS THE SAYING GOES, are thought equal to pearls," we read in one of the epistles of St. Jerome.[1] Jerome makes frequent use of this image (which in fact derives from Tertullian) to convey the idea of *value* — not least the value of one's life, and of the choices made during it. In turn, the notion of value is one of the central ideas in Hesse's novel about glass beads, and about a strange game one can play using them — the Glass Bead Game.

Hesse began work on *Das Glasperlenspiel* in February 1932, shortly before he left Zurich and moved to Montagnola.[2] Although fragments of the novel, particularly some of the poems, were published in literary journals in the intervening years, it did not appear in its entirety until 1943, when it was published in two volumes by Fretz & Wasmuth in Zurich, after the National Socialist government had forbidden Hesse's previous publisher, S. Fischer Verlag, from publishing it in Germany. The novel is thus a product of over ten years' work and reflection, representing the culmination of his literary career: it is widely regarded as his greatest novel. Its long genesis is reflected in the complexities of structure and its narrative perspectives, not to mention its distinctive narrative style.

The book has a peculiar tone, due not least to this narrative style,[3] which is characterized by a mixture of narrative voices, all of which display a remarkable, even uncanny similarity. The novel purports to be the work of an anonymous narrator who has assembled various manuscripts (10) concerning Josef Knecht, who becomes the Master of the Glass Bead Game, and whose life is narrated in the novel (from his childhood in Berolfingen and his training in the Game at Waldzell to his appointment as Ludi Magister).[4] From certain comments it seems that the narrator is himself a former pupil of Knecht and a player of the Glass Bead Game (262–63). *Das Glasperlenspiel* bears the subtitle "Versuch einer Lebensbeschreibung des Magister Ludi Josef Knecht samt Knechts hinterlassenen Schriften" (A Tentative Sketch of the Life of Magister Ludi Joseph Knecht Together with Knecht's Posthumous Writings), and in addition to the twelve chapters that constitute the "Lebensbeschreibung" (one of which contains "Das Schreiben des Magister Ludi an die Erziehungsbehörde"

[Magister Ludi's Letter to the Educational Authorities] and their reply), it consists of the introductory section, "Das Glasperlenspiel: Versuch einer allgemeinverständlichen Einführung in seine Geschichte" (The Glass Bead Game: A General Introduction to Its History for the Layman) and the posthumous writings of Knecht — that is, the poems of his student years and the three autobiographical exercises (or "Lebensläufe") he wrote.

In some ways it is an odd biography, for anything psychological or biological is omitted, as Oskar Seidlin noted as early as 1948, and there are virtually no female figures.[5] (In Kastalien itself, we learn, "die Gefahr, sich an Frauen oder an sportliche Exzesse zu verschwenden, ist nicht eben groß" [98; "the danger of wasting himself on women or on losing himself in sports is also minimal," 97].) In other ways, too, it does not claim to be a complete account, for the editor reports he has not had access to the secret archives of the "Erziehungsbehörde." From the assembled documents, however, emerges the path of Josef Knecht's life, a path described as going "im Kreise [. . .], oder in einer Ellipse oder Spirale, oder wie immer, nur nicht geradeaus, denn das Geradlinige gehörte offenbar nur der Geometrie, nicht der Natur und dem Leben an" (349; "a circle, or an ellipse or spiral or whatever, but certainly not a straight line; straight lines evidently belonged only to geometry, not to nature and life," 350).

Such a "documentary" approach had, of course, been used by Hesse before: in *Der Steppenwolf* (1927), which consists of the "Vorwort des Herausgebers"; the "Aufzeichnungen" of the central character, Harry Haller; and the "Traktat vom Steppenwolf" (Foreword from the Editor; Writings; Tractate of the Steppenwolf). Yet these two works are linked by more than just narrative technique. We learn that a forerunner of the Glass Bead Game was known as "magisches Theater," which features towards the end of the *Steppenwolf* novel (32).[6] And the motif of dualism underlies both novels, as it does *Demian* and Hesse's other works, not least *Narziß und Goldmund* (1930) and *Die Morgenlandfahrt* (Journey to the East, 1932), which, like *Das Glasperlenspiel*, foreground the theme of hierarchical or religious orders.[7] On occasion the narrator cites his sources or mentions the identity of those who have apparently transcribed their conversation with Knecht (for example, 41, 59, 83, 96, 129, 169, 182, 215, 238, 231 and 252, 255, 266), but the narrator and his sources alike tend to cultivate a somewhat affected and equivocal style, which conforms to "der gangbare, unpersönliche Behördenstil" ("the conventional, impersonal officialese," 340) in which the high-ranking officials of Kastalien themselves write (339). For one critic, Hesse's mature style is "closely related to the art of Glass Bead Playing itself."[8] Not least in the sense of languor (or to put it uncharitably: *longueur*) to which it sometimes gives rise, the sheer placidity of style is sometimes reminiscent of Kafka, although in its utter strangeness it recalls Goethe's *Wilhelm Meister*.[9] Through the introduction of magical realist elements, moreover, "die Geschichte vom Ende unseres verehrten Meisters" loses its status as history and becomes instead "eine Legende [. . .], einen Bericht, gemischt aus echten Nachrichten und dunkeln Quellen zusammengeronnen" (262–63; "the history of our venerated Master's last days" . . . "a legend, an account compounded of authentic information and mere rumors"; 265).

Following hints made by Hesse, some critics, such as Willy and Edith Michel, have placed *Das Glasperlenspiel* in the tradition of the Utopian novel.[10] Other critics, however, including Oskar Seidlin and Barbara Belhalfaoui, have argued that the republic of Kastalien — named after the spring, sacred to Apollo and the Muses, on Mount Parnassus — is not so much a utopia as a myth.[11] Only its chronological setting in the future — according to a note by Hesse, in the twenty-fifth century[12] — can it be said to resemble a work of science fiction, although it has evident dystopian elements; it is, as Hesse told G. B. Fischer, "die Fiktion einer datierten Zukunft" (the fiction of a dated future).[13] So in this new era technology does not seem to have advanced very far, as the references to radio and to automobile travel suggest, but the *mental attitude* of the future is very different. Occasional reference is made in the text to "die Erschütterungen und Krisen der letzten großen Kriegsepoche," to "das 'kriegerische' Jahrhundert" or to "die 'feuilletonistische Epoche'" (164, 322; cf. 14–15; "the shocks of the last great epoch of wars," "Century of Wars [. . .] the Age of Feuilleton," 165, 324), out of the ruins of which the Order of the Glass Bead Game and Kastalien have arisen. And there are indirect references to the contemporary politics of Hesse's time, when, in his letter to the Order, Knecht envisages the possibility that, once again, the generals will dominate parliament, a belligerent ideology will arise, and education and scholarship will be made to serve the ends of war (327).[14]

Thus the reader of the novel is placed simultaneously in two different positions vis-à-vis the timeline of the novel, and the status of the Glass Bead Game, indeed of Kastalien itself, is correspondingly ambiguous. Depending on the chronological perspective — looking back in time to their origins and to their state during Knecht's childhood, or looking ahead in time to their decay during the lifetime of Josef Knecht, or looking even further ahead in time to their renewal following his death — the Glass Bead Game, the Order, and Kastalien are valued positively, negatively, and finally positively again, as Ziolkowski has pointed out.[15] Or as Otto F. Bollnow puts it, "der Dichter selbst [hat] die Welt Kastaliens ja nur als eine Seite dargestellt, die im Verlauf der Darstellung relativiert wird" (62; the poet himself represented the world of Kastalien only as a page that is relativized in the course of the presentation).[16] The following diagram seeks to make clear these different time-lines and the corresponding valuations of Kastalien and, mutatis mutandis, the Game:

	FUTURE 3	Narrator prepares account of Josef Knecht's life: time of narration	Kastalien #3 (valued as +)
x [present of novel]			
	FUTURE 2	Josef Knecht's later life as Ludi Magister	Kastalien #2 (valued as −)
	FUTURE 1	Josef Knecht's childhood	Kastalien #1 (valued as +)
xx [our age]	PAST 1	Age of the Feuilleton	
	PAST 2	History of culture and humankind	

x = location of the reader in narrative time
xx = actual location of the reader in historical time

In his "Einführung" to the Glass Bead Game, the narrator speaks of the ancient ideal of wisdom and of the reformation of intellectual life that began in the twentieth century and led to the establishment of Kastalien and to the Glass Bead Game (9). But what *is* the Glass Bead Game? The problem here is well stated in one of Hesse's sketches for the novel, where he notes that the Game is "nicht leicht anschaulich zu beschreiben, da so kompliziert und außerdem ja noch gar nicht erfunden"[17] (not easy to describe clearly, because so complicated and besides not even invented yet). For to be fully utopian, the Glass Bead Game must be unimaginable to us, readers in a pre-utopian state, and so it turns out to be. The Game is described variously as "das ideale Ziel einer Universitas Litterarum" (12; "the ideal goal of a *universitas litterarum*," 7); as an understanding of "die ästhetische Seite" of life (an aesthetic side that, seen in its entirety, i.e., both physical and mental, is "ein dynamisches Phänomen," a dynamic phenomenon), comprehended "im Bild rhythmischer Vorgänge" (96; "an image of rhythmic processes," 94); as a game in which everything becomes all-meaningful, leading "ins Zentrum, ins Geheimnis und Innerste der Welt, in das Urwissen" (105; "into the center, the mystery and innermost heart of the world, into primal knowledge," 105); as "das Spiele der Spiele" (34, 103; "the Game of games," 28); as (so Knecht tells his friend and assistant Tegularius) "unser königliches Spiel" ("our royal game"), as a *lingua sacra*, "eine heilige und göttliche Sprache" (106; "a sacred and divine language," 105); as neither religion, nor philosophy, nor even the traditional conceptions of art (to which it is, however, the closest), but as "eine Kunst *sui generis*" and superior to all three (126; 126); as something almost sacramental, although ultimately "das Spiel bleibt Spiel" (169; "the game remains a game," 169); as "das edle Spiel" (211; "the noble game," 213) in which the idea of universality finds its highest and most perfect expression; and as the union of the three principles of scholarship, veneration of the beautiful, and meditation (291). In the idyll *Stunden im Garten* (1936) Hesse described the Game as "eine hübsche Erfindung, / Deren Gerüst die Musik und deren Grund Meditation ist" (a pretty invention, / Whose framework is music and whose basis is meditation).[18]

The intellectual antecedents of the Game are said to be numerous. The narrator mentions Pythagorean thought and Hellenistic Gnosticism; ancient Chinese and Arabic-Moorish culture; scholasticism, humanism, and Romanticism. Among the specific names mentioned in the text are Nicholas of Cusa (1401–1464), from whose works a lengthy quotation is taken (10; cf. 35);[19] Peter Abelard (1079–1142), G. W. Leibniz (1646–1716), and G. W. F. Hegel (1770–1831) (12); the fictitious figure of Albertus Secundus (a portmanteau created from the names of the scholastic theologian Albertus Magnus [ca. 1206–80] and the Dutch Renaissance poet Johannes Secundus [1511–36]); and, again with quotation, Novalis (1772–1801) (13–14).[20] We also learn that Knecht's favorite reading as a student in Waldzell included Leibniz, Kant (1724–1804), and the Romantics, especially Hegel (79). The Game itself is said to consist in part of "Analogien and Assoziationen," some legitimate (in the sense of universally comprehensible), some private (that is, subjective) (59). Knecht offers the example from his schooldays of the associations between the fragrance of some elder bushes and Franz Schubert's setting (D 686) of Ludwig Uhland's poem "Frühlingsglaube" (Spring Belief) which begins "Die linden Lüfte sind erwacht" (The gentle breezes are awakened). In the description of Knecht's submission to the annual competition in Waldzell, we learn of the difference between formal and psychological (or pedagogical) methods of construction of the Game (177). According to Knecht's own conception of the Game,

> "das Spiel [. . .] umschließt nach absolvierter Meditation den Spieler so, wie die Oberfläche einer Kugel ihren Mittelpunkt umschließt, und entläßt ihn mit dem Gefühl, eine restlos symmetrische und harmonische Welt aus der zufälligen und wirren gelöst und in sich aufgenommen zu haben." (178)

> [The game [. . .] encompasses the player after the completion of meditation as the surface of a sphere encompasses its center, and leaves him with the feeling that he has extracted from the universe of accident and confusion a totally symmetrical and harmonious cosmos, and absorbed it into himself. (178)]

In an early sketch for the novel dating back to 1932, Hesse conceived of the Game as "höchste Kultur," as embracing "Musik, Geschichte, Weltraum, *Mathematik*" (music, history, space, *mathematics*).[21] Some eight years later, in a letter of 22 February 1944 to Rolf von Hoerschelmann,

Hesse wrote that "das Glasperlenspiel ist eine Sprache, ein komplettes System; es kann daher auf jede denkbare Weise gespielt werden, von einem und improvisierend, von mehreren und nach Plan, wetteifernd oder auch hieratisch"[22] (the Glass Bead Game is a language, a complete system; it can therefore be played in every conceivable way, by one person and by improvising, by several and according to plan, competitively or in a hieratic way). One of the major literary intertexts for the Game, however, is surely Friedrich Schiller (1759–1805) and his conception of aesthetic play, according to which "der Mensch spielt nur, wo er in voller Bedeutung des Worts Mensch ist, und er ist da ganz Mensch, wo er spielt" (the human being only plays when he or she is in the fullest sense of the word a human being, and *a human being is only fully one when he or she plays*). In *Über die ästhetische Erziehung des Menschen in einer Reihe von Briefen* (On the Aesthetic Education of Mankind in a Series of Letters, 1795), Schiller enunciated an ideal according to which "der frivolste Gegenstand muß so behandelt werden, daß wir aufgelegt bleiben, unmittelbar von demselben zu dem strengsten Ernste überzugehen" (the most frivolous theme must be so treated that it leaves us ready to proceed directly from it to some matter of the utmost import), and "der ernsteste Stoff muß so behandelt werden, daß wir die Fähigkeit behalten, ihn unmittelbar mit dem leichtesten Spiele zu vertauschen" (the most serious material must be so treated that we remain capable of exchanging it forthwith for the lightest play).[23]

More specifically still, the narrator hints that the Glass Bead Game is the game of literature itself. An example of an outstanding exponent of the Game is the former Magister, Thomas von der Trave — a concealed reference to the German novelist, Thomas Mann (1875–1955), born on the river Trave in Lübeck[24] — whom the narrator praises for "seine glänzend aufgebauten, formal unübertrefflichen Spiele" that are also said to reveal "eine nahe Vertrautheit mit den hintergründigen Problemen der Spielwelt" (123; "the brilliant construction and unequalled form of his games . . . his total grasp of the subtlest problems of the Game's world," 123). In this sense, the narration of *Das Glasperlenspiel* (and especially the description of the Glass Bead Game) is itself an example of a glass bead game.

Yet to return to the novel: how, within its fictional economy, is the Game actually meant to be played? In his early drafts, before the character of Knecht had been conceived, the invention of the Game is attributed to a well-to-do bourgeois called Reinhold Klaiber, and takes the form of a rather complicated and highly intellectualized game of cards.[25] In the "Einleitung" of the final version, we learn that the Glass Bead Game is a mode of playing with the totality of contents and values of a culture, and that all the insights of art and scholarship become an immense body of intellectual values, on which the single Game-player plays like an organist on an organ (11–12). In his poem "Orgelspiel," dating back to early 1937, we find another development of this idea of cultural organist (10:342–47). Essential to the Game is the problem of knowledge, and the Game can be understood as a tool designed to facilitate the organization of cultural knowledge in an age of information overload.[26] Over time, the narrator tells us, the Games became a public ceremonial, lasting for days or weeks, during which the players lived as ascetically as the penitent participants in the spiritual exercises of St. Ignatius (34). Each Game states, elaborates, varies, and develops one, two, or three themes, much like a piece of music — an important idea in the novel (34). Its interdisciplinary nature is exemplified by its exploration of the parallels between, say, a piece of classical music and the formulation of a natural law (34).

The novel includes the description of an annual Game over which Knecht presides in front of thousands of onlookers (238–40). Beyond the need for such accessories as an abacus on which are strung glass beads of various sizes, shapes, and colors (26), or a luminous golden stylus and a small tablet, together with time and space to meditate (238), however, it is beyond our comprehension to understand how the Game operates, and indeed this must be so. For we are still members of "das 'feuilletonistische' Zeitalter" (14; "Age of feuilleton," 24) which, beginning with Nietzsche's discovery that the creative period of our culture is over, is characterized by "die öde Mechanisierung des Lebens, das tiefe Sinken der Moral, die Glaubenslosigkeit der Völker, die Unechtheit der Kunst" (19; "the dreary mechanization of life, the profound debasement of morality, the decline of faith among nations, the inauthenticity of art," 15). To us, the members of the Order and the players of the Glass Bead Game must seem as they do to Knecht's friend and counterpart, Plinio Designori. We must look up to them, as he does, "zu ewig heiteren, ewig spielenden und ihr ewiges Dasein genießenden, keinem Leide erreichbaren Göttern oder Übermenschen" (284; "God or Supermen, forever serene, forever playing, forever enjoying your own existences, forever immune to suffering," 286).

That said, there is, as Designori also points out, another way of looking at these players. For it turns out that the Glass Bead Game is not the ultimate game, and there is a transcendence beyond the transcendence that the Game represents. Magister Thomas warns of the danger of the Game becoming mere theological philosophizing or, in the words of Kant, "eine Zauberlaterne von Hirngespinsten" (126; "a magic lantern of chimeras," 126).[27] And after his promotion to the status of Magister Ludi, Knecht comes to realize the Game has its own hidden *diabolus*, and that it can lead to empty virtuosity, to the egotistic satisfaction of artistic vanity, to sheer ambitiousness, and to the acquisition (and misuse) of power over others (214). The symbol of this danger, and of the propensity to selfishness, vice, and absurdity, is the twice-mentioned figure of Faust (214; cf. 97). Even in his close friend, Fritz Tegularius — interpreted variously as representing Nietzsche, or an aspect of Hesse's own self[28] — Knecht sees not only a "wunderlicher Einzelner," but also "der Repräsentant eines entartenden und niedergehenden Kastaliens" (247; "eccentric individual" . . . "the prototype of a deteriorating Castalia," 249). Thus Tegularius represents a warning of the future ahead for Kastalien: he is "den Typus des Kastaliers nämlich, wie er einmal werden könnte, wenn nicht durch neue Begegnungen und Impulse das Lebens Kastaliens sollte verjüngt und gekräftigt werden können" (247; "a portent of the Castalian as he might some day become unless the life of Castalia were rejuvenated and revitalized by new encounters, new forces," 249).

As Knecht comes to realize, and as he points out in the circular letter in which he tenders his resignation as Magister, all is far from well in Kastalien. Indeed, there is evidence that Designori's critique of the Glass Bead Game — that it is regressive, sterile, a game for eunuchs — is valid (84). Early on we learn that the elitism of the Game, and its being reserved for the cream of an exclusively aristocratic intelligentsia, are not universally admired (118–19); Knecht begins to wonder how long the interest of the citizens of Kastalien in the institutions of the "pädagogische Provinz" and in the practice of the Glass Bead Game will last (251). The dangers, he writes in his letter to the "Erziehungsbehörde," are both internal — the Game itself is imperiled, the whole of Kastalien (the Order, the "Behörde," the colleges, the archives) infected by hubris, conceit, arrogance, an air of superiority, and ungrateful exploitativeness — and external — he outlines the worrying political developments and historical trends. Ahead lies only calamity; a crisis, to which Knecht has no solution to offer. In Hegelian terms, the spirit of Kastalien is that of "der zu sich selbst gekommene Geist" (Hegel 389), which means, as Otto Seidlin has written: there is no way forward and no chance of anything new.[29] In its turn, this crisis affects Knecht. It turns out that he, too, faces calamity, albeit one to which there is a solution, embodied in the complementary figure of Plinio Designori, the representative of the other pole of Knecht's personality (250; cf. 240). The "servant" (*Knecht*) needs the "master" (*De-signori*)[30] — thus Hesse embodies in his onomastic philological symbolism[31] the theme, running through his work, of the reconciliation of opposites: sense and intellect, dark and light, mother and father, sensuality and ascesis, and — ultimately — *Seele* and *Geist*.[32] While, during their student days, Knecht goes walking or swimming, practices playing fugues by Froberger, and reads Hegel, Designori visits his family, courts girls, and stays in elegant clubs (87). And while, in their careers, Knecht is appointed Magister Ludi, Designori goes into law, becomes a government official, and marries the daughter of a party leader. What the narrator emphasizes, however, is the mutual dependency of these two paths, of these two tendencies or antipodes of life. In Hegelian terms, Knecht and Designori must recognize each other in a mutual, reciprocal way — "sie anerkennen sich als gegenseitig sich anerkennend."[33] Morever, this dualism is something immanent to Knecht: the narrator speaks of "die Zweiheit oder Polarität" within Knecht himself, "diese Spaltung oder besser diese unaufhörlich pulsierende Polarität in Knechts Seele" (240; "the duality or [. . .] polarity"; "this dichotomy in Knecht's soul, or rather this ever-alternating polarity" 242), just as he speaks of "das Gleichgewicht in Designoris Seele" (294; "Designori's psychic equilibrium," 296).

Likewise, Kastalien represents one way of looking at the world, but it is not the only one. As Seidlin observes, Kastalien represents, so to speak, the realm of the Father, which has repressed the maternal realm without which, however, it cannot survive,[34] an interpretation that opens the way for a matriarchal reading in terms of Bachofen.[35] In the words of the narrator, "die Tendenz zum Bewahren, zur Treue, zum selbstlosen Dienst an der Hierarchie" and "die Tendenz zum 'Erwachen', zum Vordringen, zum Greifen und Begreifen der Wirklichkeit" ("the tendency toward loyalty, toward unstinting service of the hierarchy"; "the tendency toward 'awakening,' toward advancing, toward apprehending reality," 250) are related to each other like Yin and Yang (250). Such statements represent Hesse's response to those critics who accused him of retreat into ultra-aesthetic exclusivity, into escapist mysticism, and into hapless hand-wringing in the face of political events. Indeed, the conflict between aesthetics and ethics is one of the great themes of the novel, and "der alte Wettstreit zwischen Ästhetisch und Ethisch" ("the old conflict between aesthetics and ethics," 121) is said to be the central problem in Knecht's life (121).

The solution to the dangers facing the Glass Bead Game lies in a coming-to-terms with (what for Knecht is) "ein brennendes Verlangen nach Welt, nach Menschen, nach naivem Leben" (252; "a wild craving the world, for people, for unreflective life," 253). It lies in leaving the world of Kastalien, while retaining its supreme sense of cheerful serenity or "Heiterkeit," a key term in German classical aesthetics (289). "Ein rechter Glasperlenspieler," Knecht tells Designori (in one of the most important conversations in the novel), "[sollte] von Heiterkeit durchtränkt sein wie eine reife Frucht von ihrem süßen Saft" ("A proper Glass Bead Game player ought to be drenched in cheerfulness as a ripe fruit is drenched in its sweet juice," 292); such cheerfulness or serenity is — anticipating Tito's dance and his own early-morning death in the icy waters of the mountain-lake? — "ein heiteres, lächelndes Schreiten und Tanzen mitten durch die Schrecken und Flammen der Welt, festliches Darbringen eines Opfers" (291; "a serene, smiling, striding forward and dancing through the terrors and flames of the world, the festive offering of a sacrifice," 292). Look up at the night sky, says Knecht, and you will know this deepest insight and love, this affirmation of all reality — "das Geheimnis des Schönen und die eigentliche Substanz jeder Kunst" (290; "the secret of beauty and the real substance of all art," 291). The solution, as Ignacio Götz has noted, lies in accepting the truth taught by the old Music Master that "die Wahrheit wird gelebt, nicht doziert" (72; "Truth is lived, not taught," 69).[36]

But if such a solution exists in theory, it is ultimately, in practice, a mysterious one. When Knecht resigns his post as Magister Ludi, he leaves for the capital, where he has undertaken to act as personal tutor to Tito, Designori's wayward son. But, as Curt von Faber du Faur argues, it is Tito who — assuming (much like Tadzio in Thomas Mann's *Der Tod in Venedig* [1912]) the function of the Hermes psychopompos (or, more accurately, his youthful, diminutive form, Telesphorus) — has much to teach Knecht.[37] After he has been driven out to a cottage in the mountains, the next morning Knecht finds a dressing-gown laid by his bed, and he walks down to the lake. As the world comes alight in the radiance of the dawn, Tito performs a mystic dance to the rising sun: a celebration of the breaking day, and an expression of his oneness with the elements. "Dieser Fest- und Opfertanz des panisch Begeisterten" ("This celebratory and sacrificial dance of one inspired by Pan") is both pagan and uncultured, yet Knecht watches Tito's ecstatic performance in wonderment. In contrast to what Ziolkowski has called the "stiff and hyperintellectual" style of the rest of the novel (1961, 207), the language of these final paragraphs is rich and powerful in its evocation of the landscape and the dance; its imagery and symbolism have been compared with the conclusion of the Klassische Walpurgisnacht in *Faust II*.[38] Tito's dance is the last sight Knecht witnesses, for, challenged to a swimming race in the icy waters of the lake, he drowns.

Thus the final chapter, "Die Legende," brings the "Lebensbeschreibung des Magister Ludi Josef Knecht" to a close, but not the novel itself. There follow the thirteen poems from Knecht's student years,[39] and the three "Lebensläufe" attributed to Knecht. According to Hesse's letter of January 1955 to Rudolf Pannwitz, the original impulse behind the novel had been the idea of reincarnation — a symbol, that is, for what is stable among the flux and for the continuity of tradition and intellectual life.[40] Evidence of this idea is most clearly seen in the three "Lebensläufe" and, in fact, the narrator observes that "es lebte ein Rest des alten asiatischen Wiedergeburts- und Seelenwanderungsglaubens in dieser freien und spielerischen Form hier fort" (100; "here there survived a remnant of the ancient Asiatic belief in reincarnation and transmigration of souls in this free and playful form"). The function of such an autobiography, the narrator tells us, was to exercise the imagination, to encourage its writers to regard the personality as no more than a mask, and in certain cases — but not, surely, in these texts — as an attempt to write in the style of previous centuries.

In the words of the narrator, the three "Lebensläufe" might well be regarded as "den vielleicht wertvollsten Teil unseres Buches" (101; "possibly the most valuable part of our book," 101), and their function has been the subject of much critical discussion.[41] Taken together, two critics have suggested, the "Lebensläufe" show Knecht to be a "historically conscious" hero, who is "constantly evolving and widening his horizons."[42]

The first "Lebenslauf," "Der Regenmacher," is set far in the past, in an ancient, matriarchal society. It tells of a boy in the village, named Knecht, who becomes the apprentice of Turu, the Rainmaker. Like the disciples in Novalis's *Die Lehrlinge zu Sais,* Turu is able to "read" nature, and to discover hidden meanings in the objects of the natural world (430–31). Turu falls out with his disciple, Maro, who is unable to act, as a pupil, in the service of culture, as Turu does in his role as teacher (435). (Here Knecht inserts an excursus on the consequences for those periods of history when the wrong people come to acquire leading positions in communities, schools, academies, and governments.) When a meteor shower sends the villagers into panic, Turu's decision to channel their terror into something manageable by means of ritualistic prayer, rather than an appeal to reason, prevents the community descending into madness. (Even Richard Dawkins, the evolutionary biologist and campaigning atheist, might find in this scene a plausible argument for the social function of religion.) But Turu knows the phenomenon bodes ill; the demons are against him and nothing he does succeeds. Soon he must summon the courage to save the village from starvation and illness by sacrificing himself. When Knecht assumes the office of Rainmaker and dons the ceremonial robes and the tall fox-fur headdress, his first official act is to place Turu's freshly sacrificed body on the ritual fire. By foregrounding the theme of self-sacrifice, this "Lebenslauf" offers a comment on Knecht's death in "Die Legende," but it also highlights the role in cultural life of ritual in general and music in particular — early prototypes, as it were, of the hyper-sophisticated Glass Bead Game.

The second "Life," "Der Beichtvater" (The Father Confessor) is set in the early centuries of Christianity, during the age of the Desert Fathers — to be precise, in the time of St. Hilarion (ca. 291–371). Josephus Famulus leaves the city of Gaza to live as a hermit in the desert, where his gift of listening brings many people to visit him. Over time he becomes assailed by a complete absence of joy (454), and is tempted to contemplate killing himself (accompanied by a horror of the idea of pagan human sacrifice, a link to the previous life) (455–56; cf. 457) — a pathological form of the acedia of which so many solitaries and saints of the desert complain. Having abandoned his cave, Josephus overhears two camel drivers discussing one Father Dion, also known as Pugil, famed for the stringency of the penances he demands. Under the tree of an oasis, Josephus discovers this holy man, but he does not recognize him until the next day. Josephus becomes Dion's disciple, but is amazed that his master does not correct the astrological mythology espoused by a pagan scholar who is passing by. Dion's distinction between mythology and true faith, which accords a value, albeit superficial, to the former, is another powerful argument for tolerance in matters of belief. Before his master dies, Joseph learns from Dion that, when they met, Dion had been making a pilgrimage to seek him; when Joseph finds Dion in his last sleep, the saint's face is illumined, like that of the Music Master, with a radiant smile.

The third "Life," called the "Indischer Lebenslauf," is set in the ancient India of the Vedic period and the golden age of Hinduism. In many respects it echoes the style of Hesse's earlier novel set in India, *Siddhartha* (1922),[43] but thematically it addresses more directly than any other part of *Das Glasperlenspiel* the role of war, which remains on the margins of the "Lebensbeschreibung des Magister Ludi."[44] Little Prince Dasa (whose name means "servant") is the son of the warrior Ravana, an incarnation of Vishnu in his avatar as Rama, but he is displaced in the affections of his stepmother by her own son, Nala. One day Dasa discovers in the forest a holy man, or yogi, in the midst of his meditations (again, a link to the previous "Life"); over time he gets used to bringing him gifts. Later, living in the capital amid its spectacular festivals, he forgets this experience, and marries the beautiful Pravati. When she deserts him for his half-brother, the young Rajah, Dasa kills his rival, and becomes a vagabond in the forest — where he again comes across the yogi. Dasa builds his own hut, and learns from the silent yogi the art of meditation. Tormented by anguished dreams, Dasa asks the master how he can attain peace and tranquility, to which the yogi only laughs and responds — alluding to the Hindu doctrine of the illusoriness of the world — "Maya! Maya!"[45] While seeking to know more from the yogi, Dasa suddenly hears his wife's voice, and returns with her to become prince. Prince Dasa becomes a pupil of the Brahmans, cherishes his wife and their son, and defends the kingdom against a hostile neighbor in a series of battles that he eventually loses. His son dead, his wife shocked to silence, he is taken to a dungeon — but when he awakes, he is back in the forest. It is as if Dasa has been taken by the yogi into the "magisches Theater" of *Der Steppenwolf*.[46] Has his life been a dream? How is one to tell, when all reality is a dream, when it is "Spiel und Schein [. . .], Schaum und Traum" ("a game and an appearance, all foam and dream," 518) — when it is, in a word, "Maya" (514)? Having gained insight into the illusoriness of the-All-that-is-Maya, Dasa becomes the disciple of the yogi, never to leave the forest again. Once again, the "Lebenslauf" offers a comment on Knecht's life through its debate on the nature of reality, its focus on the nature of vocation, and the insights apparently gained through meditation (another integral part of the Glass Bead Game).

In fact, a fourth "Lebenslauf," mentioned by the narrator, was planned by Knecht — and, indeed, by Hesse — involving the life of a Swabian pastor who had abandoned the service of the Church for his interest in music (602–703). Remnants of this project can be found in the references to such prominent representatives of the mystical tradition as F. C. Oetinger (1702–82), for whom Hesse had a special affection (101), and the Lutheran scholar J. A. Bengel (1687–1752), whose work on the New Testament is held to mark the beginning of modern textual criticism (101; cf. 147–48, 156).[47] Both theologians came from Swabia, the part of Germany where Hesse himself was born. Although some critics, such as Ziolkowski and Boulby, have suggested that the fourth "Lebenslauf" constitutes nothing less than a key to the novel,[48] Ann and John White have suggested rather that the conclusion of the work with the "Indischer Lebenslauf" strengthens it.[49]

Clearly, *Das Glasperlenspiel* is a novel of ideas: in fact, it is saturated with cultural references, and the major drama of the work lies in the intellectual (rather than emotional or, certainly, sexual) development of its central figure, the Magister Ludi Josef Knecht. This intellectual-historical aspect represents part of Hesse's ambition, as expressed in his letter of May 1934 to Ernst Morgenthaler, "gegenüber den heute herrschenden Tendenzen nicht bloß eine Utopie nach vorn, in die Zukunft zu bauen, sondern sie auch nach hinten, in die Jahrhunderte zurück, einigermaßen zu verankern" (in contrast to the current tendency not only to build a utopia in the future, but as it were to anchor it in the past, back into the centuries).[50] Hence the various echoes and resonances of major writers and thinkers — for instance, of Goethe.[51] Instead of Wilhelm *Meister* we have Josef *Knecht;*[52] and "Knecht" is the name applied to Faust, both by the Lord in the "Prolog im Himmel" in *Faust I* and by Mephistopheles in the "Finstere Galerie" when Faust descends to the realm of the Mothers in *Faust II*.[53] The "Turmgesellschaft" of the *Wilhelm Meister* novels reappears in Kastalien in the form of the Order, and explicit mention is made of the notion of the "pädagogische Provinz" (53).[54] A more covert tribute to Goethe has been detected in the figure of the Music Master.[55]

The extent to which Hesse is not just drawing on cultural material, but also transforming it, is debatable. Oskar Seidlin suggests that "das Bild des goetheschen Menschen" is reaffirmed in Josef Knecht (272; the image of the Goethean human being), while Inge Halpert argues that *Das Glasperlenspiel*'s conception of the "pedagogic province" is very different from Goethe's, and that while the terms *vita activa* and *vita contemplativa* occupy a prominent place in the novel, they do not signal that Hesse has adopted "a Goethean attitude toward men and the world."[56] The real debt to Goethe resides, rather, in the adoption of the underlying structural idea of "Stufen" (cf. 407; stages, phases), of a "Stufengang" or "Spirale," a progression of stages, or a spiral, as found in the *Wanderjahre*.[57]

Then again, the presence of Thomas Mann in the novel can be felt in various ways: not simply in the figure of Thomas von der Trave, but (at a deeper level) in the proximity between Mann's playful conception of *Ironie* and Hesse's notion of *Heiterkeit,* described by Knecht as "höchste Erkenntnis und Liebe," as "Bejahen aller Wirklichkeit, Wachsein am Rand aller Tiefen und Abgründe" (290; "supreme insight and love, affirmation of all reality, alertness on the brink of all depths and abysses," 291). In terms of literary technique, both Mann and Hesse use a technique called montage: the integration of extensive passages of (disguised) quotation into the fabric of their novels, as Ziolkowski has pointed out.[58]

Mann most clearly deployed the montage technique in his late novel *Doktor Faustus* (1947), which displays several similarities with *Das Glasperlenspiel*. In fact, Mann adopted a posture of amazement when he read *Das Glasperlenspiel,* telling Agnes E. Meyer on 8 March 1944 that it had been "etwas wie ein heilsamer Choc" when the book arrived, and describing the work as, among other things, "unübersetzbar" and "enorm deutsch" (something of a positive shock; untranslatable; enormously German).[59] Hesse shrewdly remarked that the passages of musical analysis in Mann's novel of works by the novel's central artist figure, the composer Adrian Leverkühn, reminded him of Tegularius.[60] These similarities include: first, the pseudo-documentary style; second, a complex time-horizon; third, a coming-to-terms with cultural history; fourth, the thematic concern with the relation between ethics and aesthetics; and fifth, the importance attached to music and its mathematical structure.[61]

Corresponding to such passages in Mann's novel as Wendell Kretzschmar's lectures on musicology (chapter 8), Zeitblom's and Leverkühn's discussion of polyphony (chapter 22), and the descriptions of Leverkühn's compositions, *Apocalipsis cum figuris* and *Doctor Fausti Weheklag* (chapters 34 and 46), are passages in Hesse's novel that are more understated and more abstract, but no less evocative and intriguing, such as the narrator's remarks on the function of music (25), Knecht's comments on music in his lectures (37–38 and 77–78), the poem "Stufen" as (so Tegularius tells us) a text about the nature of music (344), and Knecht's statement of his aspiration to lead his life in accordance with the structure of music, "Thema um Thema, Tempo um Tempo [. . .], nie müde, nie schlafend, stets wach, stets vollkommen gegenwärtig" (367; "from theme to theme, from tempo to tempo, [. . .] never tiring, never sleeping, forever wakeful, forever in the present," 368). In addition, there are many moments when the plot turns on a musical performance: Knecht and the old music-master playing music together (44–46), the music-master performing for Knecht in his room in the former monastery of Monteport

(68), the music-master's preoccupation with a sonata by Gabrieli (88–92), Pater Jakobus playing a sonata by Purcell in his room after vespers (145), and Knecht's performance of the same piece at the end of his conversation with Designori (291–92).

The importance for the Glass Bead Game of music and mathematics alike, and the appreciation of the former in terms of the formal structures of the latter, hints, as several critics have noted, at an even deeper intellectual engagement on Hesse's part: his response to Plato.[62] After all, Hesse entertained a longstanding interest in Plato: in 1908 he included in a list of essential reading the *Phaidon,* the *Gorgias,* and the *Symposium;* in the 1930s he read some of the translations of and commentaries on Plato produced by Kurt Hildebrandt, a member of the circle around Stefan George; and in 1946 he named Plato — along with Spinoza, Schopenhauer, Nietzsche, and Jacob Burckhardt — as among the influences on his own thought.[63] In his history of the Glass Bead Game the narrator refers to the Platonic academy (12), and in his "Rundschreiben" (encyclical) to the "Erziehungsbehörde," Knecht engages explicitly with Plato's chief political thesis — that the philosopher should rule the state (328). Indeed, one critic has argued that the conception of the novel in general, and its fictitious Latin motto in particular, are modeled on Socrates' comment in *The Republic* (473 a) on the possibility of the ideal state.[64] Another speaks of the "uncanny similarity" of the parallels between Knecht's schooling and the stages of Plato's educational scheme, and between Knecht's own life and example and Plato's conception of "the guardian."[65] Even more specifically, attention has focused on the common importance attached to the roles of mathematics and music,[66] and to the interrelation of *vita contemplativa* and *vita activa.*[67] In a letter of February 1944, Hesse spoke of Kastalien, the Order, and its meditative scholarliness as "eine ewige, platonische in diversen Graden der Verwirklichung schon oft auf Erden sichbar gewordene Idee."[68]

From Plato, too, is derived the idea of the nobility ("Adel"), and its peculiar status with regard to the Glass Bead Game. In the "Rundschreiben" Knecht speaks of social history in terms of the creation of nobility, be it (politically) by birth or (culturally) by education. Yet all forms of nobility face the same characteristic disease (319). In Knecht himself Tito recognizes the qualities of "Adel," "Vornehmheit," "Herrentum," which appeal in turn to "die edlen, guten, ritterlichen, die höheren Strebungen und Kräfte" of his interlocutor (387; "nobility," "innate aristocratic quality," and "masterly nature"; "good, chivalric, higher aspirations and forces," 387). But this idea is given a Nietzschean twist: in line with Zarathustra's pronouncement that a new nobility should arise, Knecht's resignation suggests that its basis will be not biological, but spiritual (*geistig*) — after all, Tito reflects, Knecht is "vornehm," despite the fact his father could have been anyone, even a cobbler (387). And Pater Jakobus describes the Benedictine Order as an organization whose task is to take men and to transform them — "sie durch Erziehung, nicht durch Eugenik, durch den Geist, nicht durchs Blut zu einem Adel zu machen" (152; "to make a nobility of them, not by eugenics, not by blood, but by education and the spirit," 152).

And there is a further Nietzschean, anti-Platonic twist: the insistence in the novel on the importance of history. As Pater Jakobus tells Knecht, there can be no nobility — "kein adliges und erhöhtes Leben" — without the knowledge of devils and demons, and the struggle against these — "das Wissen um die Teufel und Dämonen und [. . .] den beständigen Kampf gegen sie" (259). The theological terminology is appropriate, given that the speaker is the learned monk-historian of Mariafels, the great Benedictine monastery where the music-master had once studied and to which Knecht is sent on a mission in an ambassadorial role.[69]

At the very beginning of his account of Knecht's life, the narrator comments that to write history *is* literature, for the third dimension of history is fiction (39). Pater Jakobus describes the study of history as "eine sehr ernste Aufgabe [. . .] und vielleicht eine tragische," for to write history means "sich dem Chaos überlassen und dennoch den Glauben an die Ordnung und den Sinn bewahren" (151; "it is a very serious task [. . .] and possibly a tragic one"; "submitting to chaos and nevertheless retaining faith in order and meaning," 151). After his first year in office as Magister Ludi, Knecht resumes his historical studies (250–51, 252). By contrast, Tegularius dismisses the philosophy of history (and, in particular, Marxism!) as a waste of time (253), to which Knecht responds that all art — all "objektivierten Geist" — is the outcome of a struggle for liberation (254). Although Tegularius represents the decline of Kastalien, even he becomes absorbed in history when asked to research "die düstere Vorzeit des Ordens" for Knecht's petition to the "Erziehungsbehörde" (309–10; "the dark prehistory of the Order"). In the resulting "Rundschreiben," Knecht refers to Hegel as the "geistvollste Blüte und zugleich gefährlichste Wirkung" of "d[ie] sogenannte Geschichtsphilosophie" ("most spiritual blossoming and at the same time the most dangerous effect of the so-called philosophy of history") and champions the cause of history. "Wir selbst sind Geschichte," he tells his senior colleagues, "und sind an der Weltgeschichte und unserer Stellung in ihr mitverantwortlich" (323; "We are ourselves history and share the responsibility for world history and our position in it," 325), before going on to give an historical overview of the development of Kastalien that forms a counterpart to the history of the Glass Bead Game provided in the narrator's introduction. In reply, the head of the "Erziehungsbehörde" congratulates Knecht on his (implicitly Nietzschean) view of history, not as a scholarly end in itself, but as directly applicable to contemporary needs, and attributes it to Knecht's being a disciple of Pater Jakobus, a figure Hesse identified as based on the Swiss historian Jacob Burkhardt (1818–97).[70] In fact, as Ziolkowski has shown, the postscript to Knecht's "Rundschreiben" is a direct, almost word-for-word quotation from Burckhardt's essay "Das Revolutionszeitalter."[71] For the critic G. W. Field, there is "an odd combination of Hegel and Burckhardt" in the novel's "Hegelian drive to a higher unity in which the individual plays his sacrificial role in the pattern of Burckhardt's declaration [about the greatness of individuals]."[72]

The oddness, if such it is, about Knecht's innate sense of "die Vergänglichkeit alles Gewordenen" and "die Problematik alles vom Menschengeist Geschaffenen" (241; "the transitoriness of all that has evolved" and "the problematical nature of everything created by the human mind," 243) is its transmutation into his keen sense of reality. Through his friendship with Designori, through his conversations with Pater Jakobus, and through his historical studies, Knecht acquires "eine wache Ahnung von der Wirklichkeit" (244; "a lively sense of its reality," 246). History, he tells Tegularius, deals precisely with reality: "Abstraktionen sind entzückend, aber ich bin dafür, daß man auch Luft atmen und Brot essen muß" (254; "Abstractions are fine, but I think people also have to breathe air and eat bread," 256). In turn, what Knecht means by reality is what he also calls Life (252), and what is so frequently referred to in the novel as his awakening ("Erwachen") is concerned not with "die Wahrheit und die Erkenntnis," but rather with "die Wirklichkeit und deren Erleben und Bestehen" (350; "truth and cognition"; "experiencing and proving oneself in the real world," 351). Thanks to Pater Jakobus, Knecht encounters history, and discovers what it means to be "nicht nur ein Kastalier, sondern auch ein Mensch" (369; "not only a Castalian, but also a man," 370), which involves a coming-to-terms with and an entering-into "die Welt und ihr Leben" (369; "the world and its life," 370). To borrow Bollnow's words from his commentary on Knecht's poem "Doch heimlich dürsten wir . . ." (But secretly we thirst), such a coming-to-terms involves understanding the tension between "geistiges Leben" and "[der] Untergrund der Wirklichkeit" (spiritual life and the background of reality); naming and even affirming "Nacht und Blut und sogar Barbarei, diese schreckliche Welt, aus der die Ordnung des 'Glasperlenspiels' uns grade befreien sollte" (night and blood and even barbarism, this terrible world, from which the order of the Glass Bead Game is supposed to free us); and accepting "diese chaotische und böse Welt" as "die einzig ursprüngliche Wirklichkeit" (this chaotic and evil world; the only original reality).[73]

If such is the importance of writing history, how much greater is the importance of *making* history! Knecht's "Erwachen" follows precisely the threefold developmental schema of Hesse's 1932 essay "Ein Stückchen Theologie,"[74] a schema that consists of: (1) a move from innocence to guilt; (2) a move from guilt to despair; (3) finally, a move from despair to decline — *or* to redemption, to a "drittes Reich" of the spirit, to the experience of a condition beyond morality and the law — to faith (12:152–64). Speaking to Meister Alexander before he finally leaves Hirsland, Knecht reflects on the roles of life and death in the process of awakening, on the various "Stufen and Räume" ("stages and rooms"), on the presence during "die letzte Zeit eines Lebensabschnittes" of "eine Tönung von Welke und Sterbenwollen, welche dann zum Hinüberwechseln in einen neuen Raum, zum Erwachen, zu neuem Anfang führt" (367; "each successive period in one's life bears within itself, as it is approaching its end, a note of fading and eagerness for death. That in turn leads to a shifting to a new area, to awakening and new beginnings," 368). At the end of the "Lebensbeschreibung" it is left open what Knecht's fate signifies: is it the sudden decline of an individual unfit for life in the real world? Or a final transcendence? Or is it (in an Hegelian manner) both?

As critics such as Bollnow have recognized, the novel's ending presents us with "eine ernstliche Schwierigkeit," inasmuch as "das letzte Wort bleibt ein Rätselswort" (a serious difficulty; the last word remains a word-riddle).[75] Seidlin interprets Knecht's death, and its effect on his pupil, as a final act of transcendence (in the Hegelian sense of annulment, preservation, and elevation).[76] For Hilde Cohn, the ending symbolizes the idea of "death and rebirth," especially given the (Jungian?) significance of water in Hesse's work as "those powers of nature" that "absorb and recreate."[77] Others, including Kenneth Negus,[78] have ascribed a sacrificial significance to Knecht's death, in this respect following Hesse's own suggestion in a letter of January 1944 to his son, Bruno, that "dieser Tod ist kein Zufall, sondern er ist ein Opfertod, und der junge Tito wird dadurch tiefer angefaßt und fürs ganze Leben verpflichtet, als es auf irgendeine andre Art hätte geschehen können."[79] When Tito picks up Knecht's dressing-gown and rubs himself dry with it, we see him preparing, so to speak, to assume Knecht's mantle.[80] And Ziolkowski argues that one of the beneficiaries of Knecht's sacrifice — if that is what it is — is the narrator.[81]

The mysterious significance of Knecht's death perhaps provides the best perspective from which to appreciate an element of the novel hitherto unaddressed (and on which, for reasons of space, we can only briefly touch): namely, the influence of the East on Hesse's thinking. As well as being dedicated to "den Morgenlandfahrern" (travelers to the East, a reference to Hesse's story of 1932),[82] the novel embodies the theme of the East in the figure of the Älterer Bruder and his hermitage in the bamboo grove (111–13). During his time at the bamboo grove (113–18), Knecht perfects his knowledge of the Chinese oracle-book, the *Book of Changes* or *I Ching*, and it is here that his "awakening" begins (117).[83] Just as Knecht realizes that the Glass Bead Game itself has an interior, esoteric aspect that

points to "die Tiefen, wo nur noch der ewige Atem im ewigen Ein und
Aus sich selbst genügend waltet" (107; "into those depths where the eternal Atman eternally breathes in and out, sufficient unto itself," 107), so
he delights in the subtleties of the ancient oracular texts. Much of Hesse's
knowledge of the *I Ching* was mediated by the German sinologist Richard Wilhelm (1873–1930), also a friend of C. G. Jung (1875–1961), with
whom Hesse underwent analysis. So Hesse would have understood entirely the appropriateness of the sign of Mong ("Youthful Folly"), whose
accompanying verdict Hesse cites in the text in Wilhelm's translation (116),
to Knecht's situation in chapter 3, as well as that of the hexagram Lü ("The
Wanderer"), which results from Knecht's consultation prior to setting off
for Mariafels (134). J. C. Middleton has argued that, read in the ideo-
grammatic context of the *I Ching*, the final scene of the "Legende" embodies imagistically the union of the complementary opposites, *yin* and
yang, to which the novel often refers (105, 250, 268), and which constitutes the central feature of his meditative vision prior to his election as
Magister Ludi (199).[84] More important, in the bamboo grove Knecht
comes to understand that the Älterer Bruder has sought to escape all that
is problematic about the Glass Bead Game by means of "ein Verzicht auf
das Heute und Morgen zugunsten eines Vollkommenen, aber Vergan-
genen" ("renunciation of the present and the future in favor of something
perfect enough, but past," 119); and he also realizes that this way is not
his way. "Aber welches war sein Weg?" (119–20; "But what then was the
way for him?," 119). This becomes the central question in Knecht's life
— and in the reader's engagement with it.

Das Glasperlenspiel has been rightly compared to Mann's even more
monumental *Joseph und seine Brüder*, to his *Doktor Faustus*, and to Hermann Broch's *Die Schlafwandler* (The Sleepwalkers, 1932), especially its
philosophical essay on the "Zerfall der Werte" (disintegration of values).[85]
Written against the historical backdrop of the collapse of European culture and its descent into global war, *Das Glasperlenspiel* opposes to Alfred
Rosenberg's *Der Mythus des zwanzigsten Jahrhunderts* a different and older
myth — the myth of Castalia, the sacred fountain where the Pythia used
to bathe.[86] Yet, like Thomas Mann, Hesse's goal was "den Mythos den
fascistischen Dunkelmännern aus den Händen zu nehmen und ihn ins Humane 'umzufunktionieren'" (to take myth out of the hands of the fascist
shadow men and transform it into the humane).[87] Where Thomas Mann
succeeded in rescuing myth by means of the formula "Mythos plus Psychologie," Hesse's fictional world in *Das Glasperlenspiel* might well be described as "Mythos plus Bürokratie" — a parody of bureaucracy, that is,
in the form of the republic of Kastalien, its orders and its hierarchy. Faced,
as we are today, with the collapse of the *Bildungsideal* in the West and
across the globe, with the debate on the role of "elites" in education, and

with all the other characteristics of a post-Nietzschean age and the "Zeiten des Schreckens und tiefsten Elends" (334; "Times of terror and deepest misery," 335), there is arguably no better time than now to read and engage with *Das Glasperlenspiel*. As Pater Jakobus, in the words cited by Knecht in the postscript to his "Rundschreiben" puts it, "wenn aber beim Elend noch ein Glück sein soll, so kann es nur ein geistiges sein, rückwärts gewandt zur Rettung der Bildung früherer Zeit, vorwärts gewandt zur heitern und unverdrossenen Vertretung des Geistes in einer Zeit, die sonst gänzlich dem Stoff anheimfallen könnte" (334; "But if any happiness at all is to be extracted from that misery, it can be only a spiritual happiness, looking backward toward the conservation of the culture of earlier times, looking forward toward serene and stalwart defense of the things of the spirit in an age which otherwise might succumb wholly to material things," 335). By presenting us in the novel with lengthy passages of encomium of the Glass Bead Game as well as a critique of its ideals, and by hinting at a restitution of those ideals on a higher, vitalist level, Hesse allows his readers to indulge their hyperaesthetic imagination at the same time as he reminds them of the responsibilities of Art to Life. Thus the Glass Bead Game — the Game, and the novel itself — remains, as Hesse intended it to be, a source of consolation and inspiration:

> Aber er [= der Tag] komme nun früh oder spät
>   oder komme auch niemals,
> Immer wird mich, so oft ich des Trostes bedarf,
>   Josef Knechtens
> Freundlich sinnvolles Spiel,
>   den alten Morgenlandfahrer,
> Aus den Zeiten und Zahlen entrücken
>   zu göttlichen Brüdern,
> Deren harmonischer Chor
>   auch meine Stimme mit aufnimmt.   (9:614)

> Whether it [the day] comes soon or later
>   or even if it never comes at all,
> Then, whenever I am in need of comfort,
>   Josef Knecht's
> Friendly and meaningful game
>   will pluck me, old traveler to the east,
> From the times and the figures
>   to the divine brethren,
> Whose harmonic chorus
>   takes my voice up into its own.

Notes

[1] Jerome, Letter CXXX §9; cf. Letter LXXIX §9 and CVII §8. Jerome's source is Tertullian, *Ad martyras,* §4.

[2] See G. W. Field, "On the Genesis of the Glasperlenspiel," *German Quarterly* 41 (1968): 673–88; and Joseph Mileck, "*Das Glasperlenspiel:* Genesis, Manuscripts, and History of Publication," in *Hesse Companion,* ed. Anna Otten, 189–221 (Frankfurt am Main: Suhrkamp Verlag, 1970).

[3] In a letter to G. B. Fischer of 28 January 1933, Hesse spoke of "die Schaffung einer gereinigten Atmosphäre" (the creation of a purified atmosphere). Quoted from Volker Michels, ed., *Materialien zu Hermann Hesses "Das Glasperlenspiel,"* 2 vols. (Frankfurt am Main: Suhrkamp, 1973–1974), 1:60. Michels's work will be cited henceforth as Michels, ed. *Materialien zu H. H.s "Das Glasperlenspiel"* and volume and page number.

[4] All references to the text of *Das Glasperlenspiel* in this essay are to the edition of *Die Romane: Das Glasperlenspiel,* volume 5 of the *Sämtliche Werke,* ed. Volker Michels (Frankfurt am Main: Suhrkamp, 2001), indicated by page numbers in parentheses. The translations used here are from *Magister Ludi: The Glass Bead Game,* trans. Richard and Clara Winston (New York: Bantam, 1970); parenthetical page references following the translations refer to this edition.

[5] Oskar Seidlin, "Hermann Hesses *Glasperlenspiel,*" *Germanic Review* 23 (1948): 263–73; here 266. Hesse himself addresses this fact in his "Warum kommen im 'Glasperlenspiel' keine Frauen vor?" in *Autobiographische Schriften II: Selbstzeugnisse. Erinnerungen. Gedenkblätter und Rundbriefe,* vol. 12 of *Sämtliche Werke,* ed. Volker Michels (Frankfurt am Main: Suhrkamp, 2003), 231–34. Subsequently cited by volume and page number.

[6] Cf. *Die Romane: Der Steppenwolf. Narziß und Goldmund. Die Morgenlandfahrt,* vol. 4 of *Sämtliche Werke,* ed. Volker Michels (Frankfurt am Main: Suhrkamp, 2001), 33, 156–203.

[7] Seidlin, "Hermann Hesses *Glasperlenspiel,*" 270. As Walter Kaufmann has pointed out, Hesse shared with Nietzsche the ideal of a "Bildungs-Sekte," of "Kreise [. . .], wie die Mönchsorden waren, nur mit einem weiteren Inhalt" (Sect of education; circles . . . like the monk's orders were, only with a broader content). Friedrich Nietzsche, *Sämtliche Werke.* 14 vols. (Munich/Berlin and New York: Deutscher Taschenbuch Verlag/de Gruyter, 1988), 7:32 [62]-[63], 776; Walter Kaufmann, *Nietzsche: Philosopher, Psychologist, Antichrist* (Princeton, NJ: Princeton UP, 1974), 418.

[8] Christian J. Schneider, "Hermann Hesse's 'Glasperlenspiel': Genesis, Structure, Interpretation," in *Hesse Companion,* ed. Anna Otten, 222–59.

[9] Curt von Faber du Faur, "Zu Hermann Hesses 'Glasperlenspiel,'" *Monatshefte* 40/4 (April 1948): 177–94.

[10] Willy Michel and Edith Michel, "Das Glasperlenspiel: Pädagogische Utopie, dialektische Entwicklung und hermeneutische Erinnerung," in *Hermann Hesse Romane,* Stuttgart: Reclam, 1994, 132–68; here 134–35.

[11] Seidlin, "Hermann Hesses *Glasperlenspiel*," 264; Barbara Belhalfaoui, "Utopie und Geschichte in Hesses Glasperlenspiel: Nachgewiesen anhand der Lebensläufe," *Recherches germaniques* 10 (1980): 182–204.

[12] See Hesse's note accompanying the publication of the "Einleitung" in *Die neue Rundschau* in 1934. Theodore Ziolkowski, "*The Glass Bead Game:* Beyond Castalia," in *The Novels of Hermann Hesse: A Study in Theme and Structure* (Princeton, NJ: Princeton UP, 1965), 283–338; here 303.

[13] Michels, ed. *Materialien zu H. H.s "Das Glasperlenspiel,"* 1:60.

[14] See Ronald Gray, "Hermann Hesse: The Prose and the Politics," in *Weimar Germany: Writers and Politics,* ed. Alan Bance, 14–25 (Edinburgh: Scottish Academic Press, 1982), 24.

[15] Ziolkowski, "*The Glass Bead Game:* Beyond Castalia," 303.

[16] Otto F. Bollnow, *Unruhe und Geborgenheit im Weltbild neuerer Dichter* (Stuttgart, Berlin, Cologne, Mainz: W. Kohlhammer, 1953), 62.

[17] Cited from Michels, ed., *Materialien zu H. H.s "Das Glasperlenspiel,"* 1:314. Cf. *Das Glasperlenspiel,* 571.

[18] *Die Märchen. Legenden. Übertragungen. Dramatisches. Idyllen,* vol. 9 of *Sämtliche Werke,* ed. Volker Michels (Frankfurt am Main: Suhrkamp, 2002), 614. Subsequent references to this volume will be by volume and page number.

[19] See von Cusa's *Idiota de Mente* (The Layman on the Spirit), chapter 9, 125: 4–10 Nikolaus von Kues, *Philosophische-Theologische Werke,* 4 vols (Hamburg: Felix Meiner, 2002), vol. 2, pp. 83–85.

[20] "Zueignung," *Heinrich von Ofterdingen,* in Novalis, *Werke,* ed. Gerhard Schulz (Munich: C. H. Beck, 1969), 129.

[21] Cited from Michels, ed., *Materialien zu H.H.s "Das Glasperlenspiel,"* 1:314.

[22] Cited from Michels, ed., *Materialien zu H.H.s "Das Glasperlenspiel,"* 1:241.

[23] Schiller, letter 15, §9; letter 22, §5 (Schiller 106 and 156). For further discussion, see G. W. Field, "On the Genesis of the Glasperlenspiel," *German Quarterly* 41 (1968): 673–88; here 686; and Curt von Faber du Faur, "Zu Hermann Hesses 'Glasperlenspiel,'" 177–94; here 193.

[24] See Warren R. Maurer, "Trends in Literary Scholarship: German Literary Onomastics: An Overview," *German Quarterly* 56/1 (January 1983): 89–105; here 98; and Joseph Mileck, "Names and the Creative Process: A Study of the Names in Hermann Hesse's 'Lauscher,' 'Demian,' 'Steppenwolf,' and 'Glasperlenspiel,'" *Monatshefte* 53 (1961): 167–80; here 176.

[25] See the "Erste, handschriftliche Fassung" (May/June 1932), "Zweite Fassung" (August 1932), and "Dritte Fassung" (1933) of the "Einleitung" (Included in *SW,* vol. 5, 519–69).

[26] On the various solutions to the longstanding problem of "information overload," see the following three articles in the *Journal of the History of Ideas* 64/1 (2003): Daniel Rosenberg, "Early Modern Information Overload," *Journal of the History of Ideas,* 1–9; Ann Blair, "Reading Strategies for Coping With Information Overload ca. 1550–1700," 11–28; and Brian W. Ogilvie, "The Many Books of Nature: Renaissance Naturalists and Information Overload," 29–40.

[27] Kant, *Kritik der praktischen Vernunft* (Stuttgart: Reclam, 1961), part 1, book 2, section 2, chapter 7, page 223.

[28] These alternatives are raised and discussed, respectively, by Joseph Mileck in his "Names and the Creative Process: A Study of the Names in Hermann Hesse's 'Lauscher,' 'Demian,' 'Steppenwolf,' and 'Glasperlenspiel,'" *Monatshefte* 53 (1961): 167–80; here 175, and Hilde D. Cohn in her "The Symbolic End of Hermann Hesse's 'Glasperlenspiel,'" *Modern Language Quarterly* 11/3 (September 1950): 347–57; here 352.

[29] The quote is from G. W. F. Hegel, *Phänomenologie des Geistes* (1807; Frankfurt am Main: Suhrkamp, 1986), 389. Seidlin's point is from his "Hermann Hesses *Glasperlenspiel*," 265. As G. W. Field has noted, interest in Hegel's philosophy may have been mediated to Hesse by Otto Engel's commemorative article on Hegel, published — in the feuilleton section! — in Stuttgart's *Neues Tageblatt* of 14 November 1931. (Field, "On the Genesis of the Glasperlenspiel," *German Quarterly* 41 [1968]: 673–88; here 678–79).

[30] Joseph Mileck, "Names and the Creative Process," 175.

[31] Onomastics is concerned with the study of the forms and origins of words, especially proper names.

[32] Ralph Freedman, "Romantic Imagination: Hermann Hesse as a Modern Novelist." *PMLA* 73/3 (June 1958): 275–84; here 278. The master categories of *Geist* and *Seele* are probably derived from Ludwig Klages (1872–1956), as has been discussed extensively by Max Schmid, in his *Hermann Hesse: Weg und Wandlung* (Zurich: Fretz & Wasmuth, 1947), 12–14, 94–96, 100–102, 210–12. See also Faber du Faur, "Zu Hermann Hesses 'Glasperlenspiel,'" 193.

[33] The quotation is from Hegel, *Phänomenologie des Geistes,* 147; see also Willy Michel and Edith Michel, "Das Glasperlenspiel: Pädagogische Utopie," 162–63.

[34] Oskar Seidlin, "Hermann Hesses *Glasperlenspiel*," 268.

[35] See Edmund Remys, *Hermann Hesse's "Das Glasperlenspiel": A Concealed Defense of the Mother World* (Bern: Peter Lang, 1983).

[36] Ignacio Götz, "Platonic Parallels in Hesse's *Das Glasperlenspiel*," *German Quarterly* 51/4 (November 1978): 511–19; here 516.

[37] Faber du Faur, "Zu Hermann Hesses 'Glasperlenspiel,'" 193.

[38] G. W. Field, "Goethe and *Das Glasperlenspiel:* Reflections on 'Alterswerke,'" *German Life and Letters* 23 (1969): 93–101; here 90–100.

[39] See Hesse's comments "Über die Gedichte 'Besinnung' und 'Stufen,'" in Hesse, *Gesammelte Werke in zwölf Bänden,* vol. 11 (Frankfurt am Main: Suhrkamp, 1987), 99–100; see also Mileck, "The Poetry of Hermann Hesse," in *Hesse Companion,* ed. Anna Otten (Frankfurt: Suhrkamp, 1970), 267–68; Ziolkowski, *"The Glass Bead Game:* Beyond Castalia," in *The Novels of Hermann Hesse,* 307–10.

[40] Letter to Rudolf Pannwitz of January 1955, Michels, ed., *Materialien zu H. H.s "Das Glasperlenspiel,"* 1: 294.

[41] See Sidney M. Johnson, "The Autobiographies in Hermann Hesse's *Glasperlenspiel*," *German Quarterly* 29/3 (May 1956): 160–71, and I. A. White and J. J.

White, "The Place of Josef Knecht's 'Lebensläufe' within Hermann Hesse's *Das Glasperlenspiel*," *Modern Language Review* 81 (1986): 930–43.

[42] White and White, "The Place of Josef Knecht's 'Lebensläufe,'" 943.

[43] Hesse himself drew another link between *Das Glasperlenspiel* and *Siddhartha* (Hesse, 95). *Gesammelte Werke in zwölf Bänden*, vol. 11, 90–98; here 95.

[44] White and White, "The Place of Josef Knecht's 'Lebensläufe,'" 936–37.

[45] In June 1936 Hesse had read a book by the German Indologist, Heinrich Zimmer (1890–1943): *Maya: Der indische Mythos* (Stuttgart and Berlin: Deutsche Verlags-Anstalt, 1936). Michels, ed., *Materialien zu H. H.s "Das Glasperlenspiel,"* 1: 41.

[46] White and White, "The Place of Josef Knecht's 'Lebensläufe,'" 937.

[47] Gerhard Wehr, *Die deutsche Mystik: Mystische Erfahrung und theosophische Weltsicht — Eine Einführung in Leben und Werk der großen deutschen Sucher nach Gott* (Bern, Munich, Vienna: Otto Wilhelm Barth Verlag, 1988), 287–303; and Wehr, *Philosophie: Auf dem Suche nach Sinn* (Augsburg: Pattoch Verlag, 1990), 119–33.

[48] Ziolkowski, "Hermann Hesse: *Der vierte Lebenslauf*," *Germanic Review* 42/2 (March 1967): 124–43; Mark Boulby, "'Der vierte Lebenslauf' as a Key to 'Das Glasperlenspiel,'" *Modern Language Review* 61 (1966): 635–46.

[49] White and White, "The Place of Josef Knecht's 'Lebensläufe,'" 936.

[50] Michels, ed., *Materialien zu H. H.s "Das Glasperlenspiel,"* 1:88–89.

[51] G. W. Field, "Goethe and *Das Glasperlenspiel*," 93–101.

[52] Joseph Mileck, "Names and the Creative Process," 175; Inge D. Halpert, "Wilhelm Meister and Josef Knecht," *German Quarterly* 34/1 (January 1961): 11–20; here 11.

[53] Hilde D. Cohn, "The Symbolic End of Hermann Hesse's 'Glasperlenspiel,'" *Modern Language Quarterly* 11/3 (September 1950): 347–57; here 355. The original passage in *Faust* reads: "Kennst du den Faust?" "Den Doktor?" "Meinen Knecht!" (*Faust I*, l.299; Do you know Faust? The doctor? My servant!); "Er schließt sich an, er folgt als treuer Knecht" (*Faust II*, l.6294; He joins, he follows as a true servant).

[54] See *Wilhelm Meisters Wanderjahre*, book 2, chapter 8, cited, as are all references to works by Goethe in this essay, from the Hamburger Ausgabe of Goethe's *Werke* (Hamburg: Christian Wegner, 1948–1960), here, vol. 8, 244–59.

[55] Inge D. Halpert, "The Alt-Musikmeister and Goethe," *Monatshefte* 52 (1960): 19–24; Rudolf Koester, "Hesse's Music Master: In Search of a Prototype," *Forum for Modern Language Studies* 3 (1967): 135–41; see also Field, "Goethe and *Das Glasperlenspiel*," 96.

[56] Inge D. Halpert, "Vita activa and vita contemplativa," *Monatshefte* 53 (1961): 159–66; here 160, 165.

[57] See the explanation of "die Bedeutung des Stufengangs" by "der Aufseher" in *Wilhelm Meisters Wanderjahre*, book 2, chapter 1 (*Werke* 8:150–51); the meaning of the progression of steps; the supervisor; and the description of Makarie as "in einer Spirale, sich immer mehr vom Mittelpunkt entfernend und nach den äußeren Regionen hinkreisend" (449; orbiting in a spiral, always distancing itself from the midpoint and toward the outer regions). For further discussion, see Willy Michel,

"Krise und dialektischer Werdegang des *Magister Ludi* Josef Knecht," in *Crisis and Commitment: Studies in German and Russian Literature in Honor of J. W. Dyck,* ed. John Whiton and Harry Loewen, 168–90 (Waterloo, Ontario: U of Waterloo P, 1983), 168; Michel and Michel, "Das Glasperlenspiel: Pädagogische Utopie," 163.

[58] Ziolkowski, "*The Glass Bead Game:* Beyond Castalia," 284 and 312.

[59] Thomas Mann, *Selbstkommentare: "Doktor Faustus" und "Die Entstehung des Doktor Faustus"* (Frankfurt am Main: Fischer Taschenbuch Verlag, 1992), 22.

[60] See Hesse's letter to Thomas Mann of 12 December 1947, Michels, ed., *Materialien zu H.H.s "Das Glasperlenspiel,"* 1:280.

[61] For discussion of the novel in relation to Mann's *Doktor Faustus,* see Helmut Koopmann, "Brüderlichkeit auf große Distanz: Zu Thomas Manns 'Doktor Faustus' und Hermann Hesses 'Glasperlenspiel,'" in *Ein Leben für Dichtung und Freiheit: Festschrift zum 70. Geburtstag von Joseph P. Strelka,* ed. Karlheinz F. Auckenthaler, Hans H. Rudnick, and Klaus Weissenberger (Tübingen: Stauffenberg, 1997), 351–69.

[62] The critics include Götz, "Platonic Parallels in Hesse's *Das Glasperlenspiel*"; Charles Senn Taylor, "The Platonism of Hesse's *Das Glasperlenspiel,*" *Monatshefte für den deutschen Unterricht* 74/2 (1982): 156–66; Ziolkowski, "Modes of Hesse's Political Allegory: A Platonic View," in *Hermann Hesse: Politische und wirkungsgeschichtliche Aspekte,* ed. Sigrid Bauschinger and Albert Reh, 187–203 (Bern: Francke Verlag, 1986).

[63] Ziolkowski, "Modes of Hesse's Political Allegory: A Platonic View," 196–97; Andrew L. Yarrow, "Humanism and Deutschtum: The Origins, Development, and Consequences of the Politics of Poetry in the George-Kreis," *Germanic Review* 58/1 (Winter 1983): 1–11.

[64] Ziolkowski, "Modes of Hesse's Political Allegory," 194. Socrates' comment runs: "Don't compel me necessarily to present [the good city] as coming into being in every way in deed as we described it in speech [but] if we are able to find that a city could be governed in a way most closely approximating what has been said, say that we've found the possibility of these things coming into being on which you insist." Cited from Alan Bloom (ed. and trans.), *The Republic of Plato* (New York: Basic Books, 1991), 153.

[65] Götz, "Platonic Parallels in Hesse's *Das Glasperlenspiel,*" 513, 517.

[66] Taylor, "The Platonism of Hesse's *Das Glasperlenspiel.*"

[67] Halpert, "Vita activa and vita contemplativa."

[68] Michels, ed., *Materialien zu H. H.s "Das Glasperlenspiel,"* 1:241.

[69] This monastery, like Mariabronn in *Narziß und Goldmund,* is based on the monastery of Maulbronn, whose seminary Hesse attended (Mileck, "Names and the Creative Process," 177).

[70] See Hesse's letter to Robert Faesi of 1 November 1943, in Michels, ed., *Materialien zu H H.s "Das Glasperlenspiel,"* 1:232; for discussion, see also Mileck, "Names and the Creative Process," 175.

[71] Ziolkowski, "*The Glass Bead Game:* Beyond Castalia," 314.

[72] Field, "On the Genesis of the Glasperlenspiel," 679. Ziolkowski has pointed out that the classic statement of Burckhardt's view of the great world-historical individuals can be found in his *Weltgeschichtliche Betrachtungen* (Ziolkowski "*The Glass Bead Game:* Beyond Castalia," 315–16); see Jacob Burckhardt, "Das Individuum und das Allgemeine (Die historische Größe)," in *Weltgeschichtliche Betrachtungen,* ed. Rudolf Marx (Stuttgart: Alfred Kröner, 1978), 207–48 (especially 229).

[73] The poem is found on page 398. The quotation is from Bollnow, *Unruhe und Geborgenheit im Weltbild neuerer Dichter,* 68–69.

[74] Belhalfaoui, "Utopie und Geschichte in Hesses Glasperlenspiel," 185–86; White and White, "The Place of Josef Knecht's 'Lebensläufe,'" 939.

[75] Bollnow, *Unruhe und Geborgenheit im Weltbild neuerer Dichter,* 58.

[76] Seidlin, "Hermann Hesses *Glasperlenspiel,*" 269.

[77] Cohn, "The Symbolic End of Hermann Hesse's 'Glasperlenspiel,' 356.

[78] Kenneth Negus, "On the Death of Joseph Knecht in Hermann Hesse's *Glasperlenspiel,*" *Monatshefte* 53 (1961): 181–89.

[79] Michels, ed., *Materialien zu H. H.s "Das Glasperlenspiel,"*1:235.

[80] J. C. Middleton, "An Enigma Transfigured in Hermann Hesse's *Glasperlenspiel,*" *German Life and Letters* 10 (1956): 298–303; here 301.

[81] Ziolkowski, "*The Glass Bead Game:* Beyond Castalia," 302 and 328–29.

[82] Murray Peppard, "Hermann Hesse: From Eastern Journey to Castalia," *Monatshefte* 50 (1958): 247–56.

[83] Adrian Hsia, *Hermann Hesse und China: Darstellung, Materialien und Interpretation* (Frankfurt am Main: Suhrkamp Verlag, 1974), 272–300.

[84] Middleton, "An Enigma Transfigured in Hermann Hesse's *Glasperlenspiel,*" 300.

[85] For *Joseph and His Brothers,* Seidlin, "Hermann Hesses *Glasperlenspiel,*" 263; for *Doktor Faustus* and for Broch, Ziolkowski, "*The Glass Bead Game:* Beyond Castalia," 283 and 292 respectively.

[86] David L. Miller, "*Ad maiorem gloriam Castaliae:* Hermann Hesse and the Greek Gods and Goddesses," *Spring* 1975: 152–62.

[87] See Thomas Mann's letter to Karl Kerényi of 18 February 1941 in Mann and Karl Kerényi, *Gespräch in Briefen* (Munich: Deutscher Taschenbuch Verlag, 1967), 105.

10: Hesse's Poetry

Olaf Berwald

THE PRECISION AND SUSTAINED MUSICALITY of Hesse's prose abundantly indicate that the author is a poet whose work cannot be contained in one literary genre. Surprisingly, his robust body of lyrical texts, whose impact on a worldwide readership equals that of his prose works, has widely been ignored by literary scholars. From the 1890s until the day of his death in 1962, Hesse, who downplayed the importance of his novels and defined himself primarily as a poet, wrote around 1,400 poems.[1] Beginning in 1896, his lyrical works circulated in journals, and throughout his writing life, Hesse frequently included poems in his voluminous correspondence, often accompanied by his own drawings and watercolors.[2] Hesse's epistolary corpus constitutes an integral part of his literary work, and future studies have yet to approach the multigeneric, hybrid structure of his letters and their incorporation of poems in the nexus of his dialogic social praxis spanning over seven decades.

Hesse's first book of poetry, *Romantische Lieder* (Romantic Songs), was published in 1898, followed by *Gedichte* (Poems, 1902), *Unterwegs* (On the Way, 1911), and *Musik des Einsamen* (Music of the Lonely, 1914). Between the end of the First World War and the beginning of the German Nazi regime, Hesse published the poetry volumes *Gedichte des Malers* (Poems of the Painter, 1920), *Italien* (Italy, 1923), *Ausgewählte Gedichte* (Selected Poems, 1921), *Krisis* (Crisis, 1928), *Trost der Nacht* (Comfort of the Night, 1929), and *Jahreszeiten* (Seasons, 1931). Five more books of poems followed: *Vom Baum des Lebens* (From the Tree of Life, 1934), *Neue Gedichte* (New Poems, 1937), *Zehn Gedichte* (Ten Poems, 1940), *Der Blütenzweig* (The Blossoming Twig, 1945), and *Stufen* (Steps/Stages/Phases, 1961).[3] Since 1942, numerous partial and comprehensive editions of Hesse's lyrical works have appeared and continue to be produced. More than one million copies of Hesse's poetry books have been sold in Germany alone, and several thousand musical compositions are based on Hesse's poems.[4]

Scholars, however, with very few exceptions, such as helpful recent contributions by Görner and Huber, still have not even begun to approach Hesse's lyrical output with the thoroughness and perceptive openness that these multilayered yet accessible texts invite. Apart from reiterated divisions of Hesse's lyrical output into distinct phases based upon a narrow understanding of the author's biography, and redundant recyclings of evocative but unnuanced labels such as "confessional poetry in the spirit of Goethe," patient reflections on Hesse's lyrical works remain an exception.[5]

The most succinct characterizations of Hesse's poems have been offered by fellow writers. For example, Thomas Mann, in a book review from 1929, combines what could be considered an ironical left-handed compliment with an astute observation that puts a finger on a precarious aesthetic tension that permeates Hesse's lyrical texts:

> Hesses bezaubernde Lyrik weiss eine sensitive Modernität in Laute von volkstümlicher Romantik zu kleiden.[6]

> [Hesse's enchanting poetry successfully clothes a sensitive modernity in sounds that resemble popular Romanticism.]

Hesse's poems, Mann suggests, perform a paradoxical dress rehearsal. Twentieth-century sensitivities and crises are clothed or covered in, and, one might add, obscured by nineteenth-century art forms established by late German Romanticism. Mann's dictum is still a useful point of departure for discussing aesthetic tensions in Hesse's poems between high-modernist self-awareness and a deceptively conservative reliance on traditional forms.

Hesse's lyrical works make ample use of but also subtly subvert traditional rhyme schemes and metrical structures. The unconventional individual voices and personae that emerge from Hesse's poems refuse to simply break away from traditional poetological patterns.[7] The poet rather embarks on the more ambitious project of crafting experimental breathing space within established forms. Adhering to lyrical conventions without becoming predictable, Hesse's poems avoid the false dichotomy between reader-friendliness and complexity. The poems are accessible without rendering reality harmless. The reader is challenged to question conventional assumptions about normalcy and ethical boundaries.

The following reflections present Hesse's poetry from three different but closely related perspectives, discussing its inherent and explicit poetics, examining the degree to which Hesse can be considered a political poet, and outlining the ways in which Hesse's poems examine the process of dying.

I. On Language and Poetics

In his essay "Über Gedichte" (On Poems), first published in 1918 and revised in 1954, Hesse writes:

Ein Gedicht ist [. . .] eine Entladung, ein Ruf, ein Schrei, ein Seufzer, eine Gebärde, eine Reaktion der erlebenden Seele, mit der sie sich einer Wallung, eines Erlebnisses zu erwehren oder ihrer bewusst zu werden sucht. [. . .] Es spricht ja zunächst lediglich zum Dichter selbst, ist sein Aufatmen, sein Schrei, sein Traum, sein Lächeln, sein Umsichschlagen.[8]

[A poem is [. . .] a discharge, a call, a scream, a sigh, a gesture, the soul's response to an experience, its way of resisting or understanding emotional intensity.[. . .] First and foremost, it addresses the poet himself and is his way of breathing again, his scream, his dream, his smile, his lashing about.]

Hesse's insistence on the intense somatic presence of poetry ("discharge," "scream," "kicking and fighting") is echoed by contemporary poets, including American poet laureate Robert Pinsky, who emphasizes that poetry in general "is the most physical of all art forms."[9]

In his numerous book reviews of poetry publications, a genre that Hesse used to develop his own poetics, he does not pledge allegiance to one specific poetological dogma. For example, while praising Oskar Loerke and what he conceives as a singular "balance of stylistic vigor and experiential strength" in Wilhelm Lehmann's poems, Hesse also supports new experimental lyrical voices, including Arno Holz and Paul Celan.[10] In 1925, Hesse welcomed Holz's monumental lyrical work-in-progress.[11] Hesse was also one of the first vocal supporters of Celan's poetry, a fact that has not yet entered scholarly awareness. In his review of Celan's volume *Mohn und Gedächtnis* (1952), Hesse highlights that he was "very fond of the way in which this poet dares to try something new without losing sight of, or cutting ties with, living literary tradition."[12]

An emphasis on the fruitful dialectic of lyrical innovation and humanistic literary tradition is also at the center of Hesse's immediate response to Brecht's death. Writing to his friend and publisher Peter Suhrkamp in August 1956, Hesse identifies Brecht as "the only German communist poet" whose poems were still nurtured by "the generous, broad foundation of a comprehensive literary education," and expresses his unrestricted "love and respect" for Brecht's lyrical works, "from the beginnings until today."[13] In his 1938 preface to his friend Emmy Ball-Hennings's poetry volume, *Blume und Flamme,* Hesse reiterates his programmatic call for a creative equilibrium between poetry's complementary and mutually enriching appetites for language as joyful play and as a path toward a "struggle for truth,"

oft wieder wie aus Spiel und reiner Künstlerfreude am Schönen entstanden, aus Freude am Bild, aus Freude an der Sprache, aus zartestem Gehör für ihre Unterströmungen und Melodien. Aber dann sind diese Bücher doch wieder nicht "reine," nicht vom Leben und seinen

Kämpfen gelöste Dichtungen und sind das Gegenteil von "l'art pour
l'art," sie sind ein Kampf um Wahrheit [. . .] (*SW* 20:266)

[often reemerged as if out of playfulness and pure artistic joy, out of a
fascination with an image, a fascination with language, the finest ear
for its undercurrents and melodies. But then again, these books are
not "pure" poetic works, not isolated from life and its battles, and they
are the opposite of "l'art pour l'art," they fight for truth]

Many of Hesse's poems simultaneously thematize and perform their
own poetics. Hesse's "Ode an Hölderlin" (Ode to Hölderlin, 1913), far
from merely being symptomatic of the renewed interest in Hölderlin in the
context of the rediscovery of his late fragments, constitutes an unusually
close stylistic symbiosis with Hölderlin's (1770–1843) work. Hesse's apos-
trophic poem directly (re-)turns to his Swabian predecessor as having had
the most incisive impact on him. Addressing Hölderlin as "friend of my
youth," the lyrical persona laments hyperreflexive modernity and its ob-
session with violent dichotomies, and the loss of intellectual and social
balance associated with an idealized image of Greek antiquity, a loss that
is mourned in Hölderlin's work. A mellifluous, seamless intertextual palimpsest, Hesse's poem is not only a lyrical evocation of solidarity with
Hölderlin's search for lost Greek tradition and postreflexive relief. Inviting the reader to concentrated receptiveness, Hesse's "Ode" is also a
solitary artistic achievement. Its lucid beauty is nourished by, but moves
beyond a stylistic symbiosis with Hölderlin's odes. Embodying a dialogic
gesture that transforms "Gespräch" into "Gesang" (conversation into
song), Hesse's poem also pursues Hölderlin's symphilosophical project of
non-violent thinking in the face of spiritual disintegration:

Keiner kennt dich, o Freund; weit hat die neuere Zeit
Sich von Griechenlands stillen Zaubern entfernt,
Ohne Gebet und entgöttert
Wandelt nüchtern das Volk im Staub. (*SW* 10:193)

[Nobody knows you, oh friend. The more recent era
Has abandoned Greece's silent magic,
Void of prayer and of gods
The people walk sober in the dust.]

In his poem "Sprache" (Language, 1928), Hesse articulates an unusually high degree of epistemic optimism regarding the cosmic function
of language:

Nach Sprache sehnt sich alles Leben
[. . .]
Und jedes Lied und jedes Buch

Und jedes Bild ist ein Enthüllen,
Ein neuer, tastender Versuch,
Des Lebens Einheit zu erfüllen.
In diese Einheit einzugehn,
Lockt euch die Dichtung, die Musik,
[. . .]
Was uns Verworrenes begegnet,
Wird klar und einfach im Gedicht:
[. . .]
Die Welt hat Sinn, das Stumme spricht. (*SW* 10:309–10)

[Everything living longs for language
[. . .]
And every song and every book
And every painting is a discovery,
A fresh attempt at feeling one's way into
fulfilling life's oneness.
Poetry, music lures you
To step into this oneness,
[. . .]
All the obtuseness we encounter,
Becomes lucid and simple in poetry.
[. . .]
The world has meaning, that which is mute speaks.]

The central role of music for Hesse's poetics is made explicit in his poems "Konzert" (1919), "Zu einer Toccata von Bach" (On a Bach Toccata, 1935), and "Orgelspiel" (Play of the Organ, 1937).[14]

Hesse's lyrical work exhibits palinodic oscillations between a pronounced trust in language's potential to shelter and transmit dialogic truth on the one hand, and satirical skepticism on the other, for example in his poem "Belehrung" (Instruction, 1927), whose opening lines postulate that words are "a scam":

Mehr oder weniger, mein lieber Knabe,
Sind schliesslich alle Menschenworte Schwindel. (*SW* 10: 291)

[More or less, my dear boy,
all words that humans utter are a scam.]

In his poem "Buchstaben" (Letters), written in 1935, Hesse presents a thought experiment that involves a "primitive," or an alien, who encounters the elements of language for the first time. Faced with the demonic artificiality of language, this visitor suffers a mental breakdown and only recovers after he has destroyed the threatening "non-world" of indecipherable letters:

Und endlich würde dieser Wilde schreien
Vor unerträglicher Angst, und Feuer schüren
[. . .]
Dann würde er vielleicht einschlummernd spüren,
Wie diese Un-Welt, dieser Zaubertand,
Dies Unerträgliche zurück ins Niegewesen
Gesogen würde und ins Nirgendland,
Und würde seufzen, lächeln und genesen. (*SW* 10:330–31)

[And finally this primitive would scream
Out of unbearable fear, and would fan a fire
[. . .]
Then perhaps, falling asleep, he would sense
How this non-world, this magic bauble,
This unbearable is sucked back
Into Neverbeen and Nowhereland,
And he would sigh, smile and recover.]

One of Hesse's few rhymeless poems, "Louis Soutter," composed in 1961, is written in the voice of the eponymous Swiss painter and violinist (1871–1942), who was institutionalized for the last two decades of his life.[15] This long poem is presented as a soliloquy of an artist who recapitulates how his paintings and sonatas, artworks that at the beginning of his career turned out "beautiful" and in line with harmonizing rules ("Schöne korrekte Bilder"), changed since he began to feel the piercingly mocking stare of death, a haunting presence that can only temporarily be bracketed:

Aber einmal sah mir durchs Fenster
Lachend mit kahlen Kiefern
Der Tod herein, und das Herz
Fror mir im Leibe, fror mir,
Friert mir noch heut. Ich floh,
Irrte hin, irrte her.
Aber sie fingen mich, sperrten mich ein,
Jahr um Jahr. Durch mein Fenster
Hinter dem Gitter glotzt er,
Glotzt und lacht. Er kennt mich. Er weiss.
[. . .]
Nicht korrekt, nicht schön, sondern richtig
Mal ich mit Tinte und Blut, male wahr. Wahrheit ist schrecklich.
Aber ich decke mein Blatt mit Strich an Strich,
Loser, dichter, grau, silbern, schwarz,
Lasse die Züge der Hieroglyphen
Wollig wuchern wie Moos,

[. . .]
Manchmal vergess ich,
Manchmal bann ich die Angst,
[. . .]
Weiß ich, in meinem Rückern,
Jenen stehen und lachen.
Er kennt mich. Er weiß. (*SW* 10:395–96)

[But once Death was looking into my window
Laughing with bleak jaws, and my heart
Froze in my body, froze
It still freezes today. I escaped,
Ran back and forth.
But they caught me, imprisoned me,
year after year. Through my window
Behind the bars he stares,
Stares and laughs. He knows me. He knows.

[. . .]
I paint
Not correctly, not beautifully, but the way things are
I paint with ink and blood, I paint in truth. Truth is terrifying.
But I cover my sheet stroke by stroke,
More loosely, more dense, grey, silver, black.
I allow the hieroglyphs' features
To grow untrimmed like wool, like moss,
[. . .]
Sometimes I forget, sometimes I bracket fear,
[. . .]
I know, behind my back,
That one standing and laughing.
He knows me. He knows.]

Here Hesse continues a tradition of rendering realities without cosmetic enhancement, a tradition that has one of its modern sources in Georg Büchner's novella *Lenz* (1831): the protagonist in this prosopopoeic poem, who feels constantly observed and mocked by Death, both uses and alters a famous passage from Rilke's *Duino Elegies* ("Ein jeder Engel ist schrecklich") to "Wahrheit ist schrecklich." Changing artistic style, this text suggests and exemplifies, can be an attempt to counter one's fear of death.

In his 1953 poem "Regen im Herbst" (Rain in Autumn, 1953), Hesse presents artists as keepers of an all-encompassing "Alles" who "help preserve and transform" it in "pious remembrance" into "word, painting, and song."[16] This auxiliary function of artists has pantheistic implications. Hesse's late poem "Kleiner Gesang" (Little Song), written in May 1962, addresses poetry as a "Schleier von Schönheit und Trauer": a "veil" that is not only made of but also used by "beauty and mourning," a veil that revealingly covers not a face but "the abyss of the world."[17]

II. Polis, Poetry, and Non-Violence

In Hesse's oeuvre, crises in and between polis and psyche cannot be neatly disentangled. Reading Hesse as a political poet is both a reduction and one of several indispensable ways to approach his work. While most of his lyrical texts implicitly contain political layers, the poems that will be discussed in this section unmistakeably target political issues. For example, "Im Frühling 1915," written during the First World War in March 1915, presents radically contrasting cuts from dream scenarios. Images of "human bodies filled with rage," of "pain staring out of hollow eyes," and even of "the poor god of love" being lost and running "across the field of bloodshed afraid and shivering" are followed by an ironically utopian stanza that emphasizes nature as a realm of soothing quiet, culminating in "the world having become a child" that is capable of an untarnished new beginning because it has no conceptual categories for "fear and pain and death":

> Manchmal seh ich nichts als schwarzen Haß,
> Menschenleiber wutverbissen,
> Schwache Seelen ohne Maß
> In Verbrechen hingerissen,
> Leid aus hohlen Augen stierend,
> Und der arme Gott der Liebe irrt,
> Ehe alles dunkel wird,
> Übers Blutfeld bang und frierend.
>
> Aber neue Blumen bringt
> Unsre Wiese jeden Tag,
> Amselschlag
> Aus der Ulme süß und dunkel schwingt,
> Und die Welt weiss nichts von Morden,
> Und die Welt ist Kind geworden,
> Daß wir mit beklommenem Atem stehen
> Und im duftend lauhen Wehen
> Angst und Leid und Tod nicht mehr verstehen. (*SW* 10:230)[18]

> [Sometimes I see nothing but dark hatred,
> human bodies deeply absorbed in rage,
> Weak souls lacking moderation
> Torn into crimes,
> Suffering staring out of hollow eyes,
> And the poor god of love disoriented,
> Before everything darkens,
> Runs across the bloodfield, fearful and shivering.

But our meadow brings
new flowers every day,
the blackbird's song
vibrates out of the elmtree sweet and dark,
And the world does not know anything about murdering,
And the world has become a child,
So that we stand here with our breath restrained
And amidst the fragrant mild breeze
Do not comprehend fear and suffering and death anymore.]

In his 1931 poem "Absage. Als Antwort auf einige Anfragen, warum ich mich nicht auf die Seite der Kommunisten stelle" (Refusal: A Response to Some Inquiries about Why I Don't Side with the Communists), Hesse, who took Marxist analyses seriously and worried about what he called the "Americanization" of Asia, vehemently rejects Stalinism and refuses to be co-opted by any party by pointing out structural affinities between the Soviet regime and Nazi Germany, even before the temporary alliance between Stalin and Hitler became public. The salient point that Hesse's poem reiterates is that all regimes that proliferate violence and are based on the abuse of power have to be overcome, and that their propaganda and their methods are practically interchangeable:

Lieber von den Faschisten erschlagen werden
Als selber Faschist sein!
Lieber von den Kommunisten erschlagen werden
Als selbst Kommunist sein!

Wir haben den Krieg nicht vergessen. Wir wissen,
Wie das berauscht, wenn man Trommel und Pauke rührt.
Wir sind taub, wir werden nicht mitgerissen,
Wenn ihr das Volk mit dem alten Rauschgift verführt.
[. . .]
Wir glauben alle die hübschen Phrasen nicht mehr,
Mit denen man uns in den Krieg gepeitscht und geritten —
Auch die Euren, rote Brüder, sind Zauber und führen zu Krieg und Gas!
Auch Eure Führer sind Generäle,
Kommandieren, schreien und organisieren.
Wir aber, wir hassen das,
Wir trinken den Fusel nicht mehr,
Wir wollen Herz und Vernunft nicht verlieren,
Nicht unter roten noch weißen Fahnen marschieren.
[. . .]
Und im Namen der Menschheit auf unsre Brüder schießen!
(*SW* 10:568–69)[19]

[Better to be beaten to death by the fascists
Than to be a fascist oneself!

Better to be beaten to death by the communists
Than to be a communist oneself!

We have not forgotten the war. We know
How intoxicating it is to play the kettledrum
We are deaf, we are unmoved,
When you seduce the people with the old drug.
[. . .]
We do not believe all those nice phrases anymore,
With whom they whipped and rode us to the war
Yours as well, red brothers, are fabricated and lead to war and gas!
Your leaders are generals, too,
Commanding, screaming, organizing.
But we, we hate all that,
We do not drink the rotgut anymore,
We do not want to abandon heart and reason,
We neither want to march under red nor under white banners.
[. . .]
And shoot at our brothers in the name of humanity!]

In "Für Max Hermann," a poem written for and addressed to his exiled fellow poet Max Hermann Neisse in 1933, the year in which the Nazis took power in Germany, Hesse presents any act of artistic creation as an act of resistance against state-sponsored murder: Despite the rise of extreme nationalism, Hesse maintains, the free individual will endure and an all-the-more-intimate nexus of solidarity will emerge between those "who resist the raw temptation" to become complicit with any brutal regime:

Fester sind die Wenigen verbunden,
die der rohen Lockung widerstehn
und in friedlich schöpferischen Stunden
durch den Garten ihrer Liebe gehn,
guten Willens ihre Werke bauen,
ob die Welt auch rings in Hass erkaltet:
denn der Zukunft kann getrost vertrauen,
wer die reine Flamme wohl verwaltet. (*SW* 10:569–70)

[The few form an alliance all the stronger,
Those who resist brutal temptation
And who in peacefully creative hours
walk through the garden of their love,
Build their works in good will,
Even if the world around them cools in hatred:
Because those who are loyal keepers of the pure flame
Can serenely trust the future.]

Written three weeks after the state-sponsored "Reichskristallnacht" pogroms in Nazi Germany in November 1938, Hesse's poem "Nachtgedanken" (Nocturnal Thoughts) contrasts the mutual butchering of humans, fear-driven installments of leaders, and supine obedience with the maternal peacefulness of nature:

> Wir Menschen schlagen einer den andern tot,
> [. . .]
> Kriechen vor Herrschern, die unsre Angst uns gab,
> [. . .]
>
> Aber unter uns treulich hält stand die Erde,
> Waltet mütterlich-stumm die Natur (*SW* 10:357)

> [We humans beat one another to death,
> [. . .]
> Crawl in front of rulers that our fear gave us,
> [. . .]
>
> But faithfully beneath us the earth holds remains resilient,
> nature sustains the order like a mother without words]

This sharp contrast culminates in a programmatic and poignant job description for future poets, including the lyrical persona and the author himself. Both a dialogic appeal and a reflective soliloquy, "Nachtgedanken" outlines indispensable political and existential aspects of becoming a precise and useful poet and, along the same lines, a person who maintains, or regains, his or her sanity and awareness even in times of mass destruction:

> Lass durchs Wort, durch Blick und Gebärde
> Liebe herein, und die alte, wartende Erde
> Wird dir, und es wird dir der Vater Geist
> Seinen Sinn und die ewigen Kräfte erschließen,
> Du wirst Heimat im Chaos entdecken,
> Und es werden die sinnlosen Schrecken
> Schaubar, tragbar, deutbar: mitten im Rachen
> Deiner Hölle wirst du zum Leben erwachen. (*SW* 10:357–58)

> [Make the word, glance, and gesture
> Permeable for love, and the ancient, anticipating earth
> Will, and father spirit will
> Unlock its meaning and the eternal powers,
> You will discover home within the chaos,
> And you will be capable of seeing the meaningless terrors,
> of carrying their weight, of interpreting them: locked inside the throat
> Of your hell, you will awake to life.]

At the end of August 1939, Hesse composed the long scenic poem "Kriegerisches Zeitalter" (War-Driven Era), a text in several voices whose speakers include an old man who is saddened and angered by the beginning of a new war, a "patriot" who parrots Horace's propaganda verse of organized slaughter being "dulce et decorum," a "warrior" who clings to "order" as an antidote to the disintegration of values, a passionately utopian young soldier who, while serving on the frontlines, insists on the necessity of overcoming irrational nationalism, and a narrator who describes the cruel deaths of young men on the battlefield and goes on to sketch the ways in which new generations grow up on stories that glorify the latest war. A kaleidoscope in multiple voices, the text does not take sides, and indicates that all the speakers are partially blind to the reality that they either embrace or deny. The poem leaves it to the reader to define the degree to which children might outgrow the forced fascination with pseudoheroic family stories. Alternating between different speakers whose stances toward state-sanctioned violence only differ by degree, this poem sketches a phenomenology of cross-generational psychological preparation for, and ultimately compliant continuation of, warfare. The final word in the poem is given to the children and to the young man who imagines human beings outgrowing party affiliations and national labels ("nicht mehr den Parteien / Noch Nationen angehörend"), and a global return to sanity and love:

> Aus den Trümmern, die wir lassen,
> Aus den Wunden, die wir schlagen,
> Aus dem Töten, Brennen, Hassen
> Wird das Neue dennoch tagen:
> [. . .]
> Dass am Ende unsre Erde
> Eins und Geist und Liebe werde. (*SW* 10:359–62)

> [Out of the ruins that we leave,
> Out of the wounds that we inflict,
> Out of the killing, burning, hatred
> Nevertheless the new will dawn:
> [. . .]
> That in the end our earth
> Will become one and spirit and love.]

In February 1945, Hesse contributed a transnationally therapeutic poem to a Swiss radio transmission, "Dem Frieden entgegen" (Approaching Peace):

> Aber wir hoffen. Und in der Brust
> Lebt uns glühende Ahnung

Von den Wundern der Liebe.
Brüder! Uns steht zum Geiste,
Steht zur Liebe die Heimkehr
Und zu allen verlornen
Paradiesen die Pforte offen.

Wollet! Hoffet! Liebet!
Und die Erde gehört euch wieder. (SW 10:377–78)

[But we hope. And in our heart
A glowing premonition is alive
Of the wonders of love.
Brothers! The return to the spirit,
To love
And the gate to all paradises
Lost is open to us.

Have the will! Hope! Love!
And the earth belongs to you again.]

Hesse was, however, not given to conventional gestures of reconciliation. Instead, a provocative legacy of Hesse's poems results from a fruitful tension between psyche and polis that might best be described as resilient ironic anger or stubbornly hopeful "defiance" ("Trotz"), the keyword of his poem "Späte Prüfung" (Late Challenge), composed in November 1944:

Scherbenberg und Trümmerstätte
Ward die Welt und ward mein Leben.
Weinend möcht ich mich ergeben,
Wenn ich diesen Trotz nicht hätte,

Diesen Trotz um Grund der Seele,
Mich zu stemmen, mich zu wehren,
Diesen Glauben: was mich quäle,
Müsse sich ins Helle kehren,

Diesen unvernünftig zähen
Kinderglauben mancher Dichter
An unlöschbar ewige Lichter,
Die hoch über allen Höllen stehen. (SW 10:374–75)

[Mountain of shards and place of ruins
The world became and my life became.
Weeping I would give up,
If I did not embody this defiance,

This defiance for the sake of the soul's foundation,
To push and fight back,

If I did not have this faith: Whatever torments me,
Will have to turn into brightness,

This irrational stubborn
childlike faith of some poets
In inextinguisable eternal lights
That stand high above all infernos.]

Elaborating on the closing argument encapsulated in "Späte Prüfung," one might affirm that, independent of affiliations with any political organization, the decision to work as a poet in itself constitutes an act of continued resistance against global destructiveness.

III. Self-Observation and Perceptive Release

Self-alienation is a thematic core that is approached head-on, and without providing any antidotes, in several Hesse poems that are written in the first person. For example, the lyrical voice in his poem "Vereinsamung" (Isolation, 1911–12), realizes "mit Grauen / Wie mir das eigne Herz zur Fremde wird" (*SW* 10:186).

Composed in 1925 and 1926 and integrated into his *Steppenwolf* novel, although first published in Berlin's *Die neue Rundschau* (1926) and in the *Neue Schweizer Rundschau* (1927), Hesse's poetry collection *Krisis: Ein Stück Tagebuch* (Crisis: A Piece from a Diary), which came out as a book edition with Samuel Fischer in Berlin in 1928, continues to puzzle academic readers because of its uncompromising refusal to comply with aesthetic or moral norms. In his 1927 monograph on Hesse, Hugo Ball, one of the founders of the Dada movement who later wrote works on religion and philosophy and also worked as a political publicist, a writer whom Hesse respected as his closest intellectual friend and the only one who fully comprehended his work ("der einzige meiner Freunde, der [. . .] die Notwendigkeit meiner Denkart und meiner gesamten Tätigkeit im Innersten begriffen hat"),[20] offers a succinct, if emotive, outline of the aesthetic tension and radical ethical labor that underlies Hesse's *Krisis* texts:

> Bitterkeit und Schwermut sind in diesen Gedichten bis zum Zerspringen des Instrumentes gediehen. [. . .] Verse [. . .] von einer unvergleichlichen Intensität und Trauer [. . .] Die alte verbergende Form ist nach allen Seiten zersprengt, ein neuer Rhythmus schwingt. Was er den Dichter gekostet hat, das werden nur diejenigen beurteilen können, die Hesses Diskretion, die seine Leidenskraft und seine Zähigkeit im Verbergen kennen.[21]

> [In these poems, bitterness and melancholy have increased to such a degree that the instrument is about to crack. [. . .] Verses [. . .] of incomparable intensity and mourning [. . .] The old sheltering form is

shattered everywhere, a new rhythm vibrates. Only those who know about Hesse's discretion, his capability to endure suffering, and his resilient insistance on hiding, will be able to assess what it [this new style] has cost him.]

Approaching an anonymous plurality of female bodies, the lyrical persona in Hesse's *Krisis* poem "Paradies-Traum" rehearses the process of dying by undergoing drug-induced immersions into erotic self-abandonment and self-extinction. Far from celebrating a spiritualized form of erotic ecstasy, this text retraces a psychological conflict between feelings of guilt, a pronounced lack of free will, and an unfulfilled desire to break free from the suffocating vocabulary of moral condemnation:

Erlösch ich mir und bin der Welt vereint.
Und weiss: auf diesen ruhmlos sündigen Pfad
Weht Gottes Atem mich, ich muss es dulden,
Muss weiter treiben, tiefer mich verschulden
Im Rausch der Lust, im Bann der bösen Tat.[22]

[I sense myself being extinguished, becoming one with the world.
And I know: God's breath is blowing me
on this fameless sinful path, I have to endure it,
Have to drift further, run up more debts and guilt
Intoxicated by desire, under the spell of the evil deed.]

In a matter-of-fact manner, the final poem of Hesse's *Krisis* cycle, "Am Ende," presents the fear of dying without any resort to hopes for reconciliation, let alone spiritual redemption:

Weiss ich warten das gewohnte Grauen.
Langsam geh dem Feinde ich entgegen,
Eng und enger schnürt mich ein die Not.
Das erschrockne Herz mit harten Schlägen
Wartet, wartet, wartet auf den Tod. (*SW* 4:245)

[I sense the usual terror waiting.
Slowly I walk toward the enemy,
tight and tighter misery is strangling me.
The terrified heart with hard beats
Is waiting, waiting, waiting for Death.]

Not so much in contrast with, but adding a complementary perspective to the project of facing internal "terrors" without subjecting them to complacent visual hygiene, Hesse's 1937 poem, "Durchblick ins Seetal" (View into Lake Valley), alludes to, and indeed continues, the problematization and satirical subversion of idyllicism in Hölderlin's late series of poems, his "Turmgedichte," composed from the 1810s until his death in 1843.[23] The lyrical "we" in Hesse's text consciously clings to momentary anesthetic resignation and emphatically blinds itself against anything that could disturb its idyllic forgetfulness, while subverting its own construction of harmony by reiterating the ambiguous and destabilizing verb "scheinen," a key term in Hölderlin's late poems:

> Festlich ordnen Dörfer, Haine, Matten
> Sich ins Bild, es scheint um Wohlgefallen,
> Scheint um Schönheit einzig hier zu gehen,
> · Um den Reigen bunt getönter Lichter:
> Spielzeug einem Maler oder Dichter,
> Scheint die Welt aus Licht nur zu bestehen,
> Das sich selbst erlebt, sich selbst gestaltet.
> Uns bezaubern Bühne und Kulissen,
> Und wir weigern uns vom Leid zu wissen,
> Das auch diese holde Welt durchwaltet. (*SW* 10:352–53)

> [Solemnly villages, groves, meadows arrange themselves
> Into the picture, it appears to be exclusively about agreeable delight,
> appears to be about beauty here,
> And to the round dance of colorful tinted lights:
> A painter's or a poet's toy,
> The World seems to consist of nothing but light,
> Experiencing itself, giving shape to itself.
> We are entranced by stage and sceneries,
> And we refuse to know of suffering,
> That permeates even this gentle, graceful world.]

By making a desire to ignore pain explicit, this poem, far from indulging in escapism, exercises an implicit form of media criticism, providing a subtle metacritical stance from which idyllicizing tendencies can be examined.[24]

Many of Hesse's aesthetically most accomplished, deceptively accessible yet subtly multilayered poems can also be read as providing practical introductions to conscious and serene dying.[25] For example, "Stufen" ("Steps," "Stages," or "Phases"), written in 1941 and arguably Hesse's most influential poem, rearticulates in the spirit of Goethe's late poems a serene acceptance of living and dying as a seamlessly rejuvenating process of metamorphotic maturation:

> [. . .]
> Und jedem Anfang wohnt ein Zauber inne,
> Der uns beschützt und der uns hilft, zu leben.

> Wir sollen heiter Raum um Raum durchschreiten,
> An keinem wie an einer Heimat hängen,
> Der Weltgeist will nicht fesseln uns und engen,

Er will uns Stuf um Stufe heben, weiten.
[. . .]

Es wird vielleicht auch noch die Todesstunde
Uns neuen Räumen jung entgegen senden,
[. . .] (*SW* 10:366)

[And magic inhabits every beginning,
Protecting us and helping us to live.

Our task is to perambulate range after range,
Without clinging as if to a home,
The world spirit does not want to constrain and contract us,
It wants to lift, expand us gradually.
[. . .]

Perhaps even the hour of our death will
Emit us afresh into new realms,
[. . .]]

In Hesse's 1946 poem "Skizzenblatt" (Sheet from a Sketch Pad), the renunciation of rhyme does not, as in the "Louis Sutter" prosopopoeia mentioned above, accentuate the lyrical persona's restlessness and emotional upheaval. Instead, its steadily gentle rhythm makes the process of dying palpable as a slow and serene walk "inland":

Einsam steht und rastet am Strande ein alter Mann,
Spürt den Wind im Haar, die Nacht und nahenden Schnee,
Blickt vom Schattenufer ins Lichte hinüber,
Wo zwischen Wolke und See ein Streifen
Fernsten Strandes noch warm im Lichte leuchtet:
Goldenes Jenseits, selig wie Traum und Dichtung.

Fest im Auge hält er das leuchtende Bild,
Denkt der Heimat, denkt seiner guten Jahre,
Sieht das Gold erbleichen, sieht es erlöschen,
Wendet sich ab und wandert
Langsam vom Weidenbaume landeinwärts. (*SW* 10:378–79)

[Lonely an old man stands on a beach and rests,
Senses the wind in his hair, the night and snow approaching,
Looks from the shadow bank into the light,
Where, between cloud and ocean a strip
Of the most distant beach still warmly shines in the light:
Golden beyond, blessed like dream and poetry.

He holds the shining image firmly in his eye,
Thinking of home, remembering his good years,
He sees the gold turning pale, sees it disappearing,

He turns away and wanders
Slowly away from the willow tree, inbound.]

Another poem that belongs in this group is the sonnet "Uralte Buddha-Figur in einer japanischen Waldschlucht verwitternd" (Buddha-Statue, Weathering in a Japanese Forest Gorge), composed in 1958, a text that not only offers a productive reception of Rilke's Buddha poems, but cultivates fresh ground for the sonnet, this seemingly most restraining of all lyrical genres:

Gesänftigt und gemagert, vieler Regen
Und vieler Fröste Opfer, grün von Moosen
Gehn deine milden Wangen, deine grossen
Gesenkten Lider still dem Ziel entgegen,
Dem willigen Zerfalle, dem Entwerden
Im All, im ungestaltet Grenzenlosen.
Noch kündet die zerrinnende Gebärde
Vom Adel deiner königlichen Sendung
Und sucht doch schon in Feuchte, Schlamm und Erde,
Der Formen ledig, ihres Sinns Vollendung,
Wird morgen Wurzel sein und Laubes Säuseln,
Wird Wasser sein, zu spiegeln Himmels Reinheit,
Wird sich zu Efeu, Algen, Farnen kräuseln, —
Bild allen Wandels in der ewigen Einheit. (*SW* 10:390)

[Pacified and gaunt, exposed to many rains
And many frosts, moss green
Your gentle cheeks, your large
Downcast eyelashes approach the end in silence,
Voluntary disintegration, freedom from becoming
In the universe, unshaped infinity.
Still the dissolving gesture announces
Your regal mission's nobleness,
And yet already seeks in moistness, mire, and soil,
Void of forms, the completion of their meaning,
Will be root tomorrow and foliage rustling,
Will be water, to mirror the sky's pureness,
Will ripple into ivy, algae, fern, —
Image of all change in timeless oneness.]

An inexhaustible source for reflections on poetics in the twenty-first century, Hesse's lyrical oeuvre invites thorough exploration, and demands multilayered forms of creative, dialogic reception. We have yet to discover the poet Hermann Hesse, and to face the aesthetic and ethical challenges his poems present and work through.

Notes

[1] See Michael Limberg, *Hermann Hesse* (Frankfurt am Main: Suhrkamp, 2005), 76: "[Hesse] sah er sich in erster Linie als Lyriker, der offen zugab, dass ihm jedes gute Gedicht lieber sei als drei Romane." ("Hesse first and foremost defined himself as a poet and openly admitted to prefer each good poem to three novels."). Ibid., 120: "Als Lyriker begann er, und noch am letzten Tag seines Lebens war er damit beschäftigt, dem Gedicht *Knarren eines geknickten Astes* seine endgültige Form zu geben." ("He started out as a poet, and even on the last day of his life he was busy bringing the poem 'Creaking of a Bent Branch' into its final shape."). All English translations in this essay are my own, O.B.

[2] I would like to thank the friendly and competent staff at Deutsches Literaturarchiv Marbach, where I studied Hesse's handwritten poetry manuscripts and correspondence in July and August 2007.

[3] For the most part, Hesse's poems are now available in the critical edition Hermann Hesse, *Sämtliche Werke,* vol. 10: *Die Gedichte,* ed. Volker Michels and Peter Huber (Frankfurt am Main: Suhrkamp, 2002). I will refer to this edition as *SW* 10 followed by page number. The earliest poems are included in *Sämtliche Werke,* vol. 1: *Jugendschriften,* ed. Volker Michels (Frankfurt am Main: Suhrkamp, 2001), 9–154.

[4] More than 2,100 musical compositions by 500 composers are listed in Georg Günter, *Hesse-Vertonungen: Verzeichnis der Drucke und Handschriften* (Marbach: Deutsche Schillergesellschaft, 2004). In his postface to the new critical edition of Hesse's poetry, Peter Huber estimates that Hesse's poems form the basis of around 5,000 musical pieces, see Peter Huber, "Nachwort des Bearbeiters," in *SW* 10:609–23; here 623. On the same page, Huber documents the sales figures for Hesse's poetry volumes.

[5] Two recent examples of recycling general notions about Hesse's poetry without providing careful analyses are Bernhard Spies, "Hermann Hesses Lyrik. Psychologisierung als Modernisierung," in *Hermann Hesse und die literarische Moderne. Kulturwissenschaftliche Facetten einer literarischen Konstante im 20. Jahrhundert: Aufsätze,* ed. Andreas Solbach (Frankfurt am Main: Suhrkamp, 2004), 118–33, and in Sikander Singh, *Hermann Hesse* (Stuttgart: Reclam, 2006), 247: "[. . .] im Sinne Goethes Bekenntnisdichtung" (confessional poetry as defined by Goethe).

[6] Mann's review is reprinted in Siegfried Unseld, ed., *Hermann Hesse: Werk- und Wirkungsgeschichte* (Frankfurt am Main: Suhrkamp, 1985), 169.

[7] See Peter Huber, "Nachwort des Bearbeiters," *SW* 10:622: "So scheut er sich nicht vor dem Gebrauch verschlissener Reimpaare, läßt häufig den Rhythmus aus dem metrischen Schema gleiten [. . .] Im Vergleich mit der Lyrik seiner Zeit ist Hesse seinen eigenen Weg gegangen." (He does not shy away from using overused rhyme pairs. Often he allows a disjunction of rhythm and metrical scheme [. . .] Compared with the lyric poetry of his time, Hesse pursued his own path.). Ibid., 620: "[. . .] die vordergründige Simplizität der Gedichte [ist] das Ergebnis eines oft langwierigen Arbeitsprozesses [. . .]" (the seeming simplicity of the poems is the result of an often long and painstaking work process).

[8] Hermann Hesse, *Sämtliche Werke,* vol. 14, ed. Volker Michels (Frankfurt am Main: Suhrkamp, 2002), 359–60. This key passage is also quoted in Singh, *Hermann Hesse,* 248.

[9] Robert Pinsky, private letter to the author, 1991.

[10] On Lehmann and Loerke, see Hesse's review "Über Wilhelm Lehmann" (1962), in *Sämtliche Werke,* vol. 20: *Die Welt im Buch V: Rezensionen und Aufsätze aus den Jahren 1935–1962,* ed. Volker Michels (Frankfurt am Main: Suhrkamp, 2005), 364–65; here 364: "Seit dem Tode Oskar Loerkes rechne ich ihn zu den wenigen, die ich ganz Ernst nehme. Er hat, was so selten ist, das Gleichgewicht von sprachlicher Potenz und Kraft des Erlebens." (Since Oskar Loerke's death, I count him among the few whom I take completely seriously. He possesses what is so rare, balance between poetic vigor and the power of experience.). Hesse's admiration for Oskar Loerke is also articulated in his review of Loerke's epistolary work, see ibid., 329–32.

[11] See Hesse, *Sämtliche Werke,* vol. 18: *Die Welt im Buch III: Rezensionen und Aufsätze aus den Jahren 1917–1925,* ed. Volker Michels (Frankfurt am Main: Suhrkamp, 2002), 476.

[12] See Hesse, *SW* 20:302: "Die Art, wie dieser Dichter Neues wagt, ohne den Zusammenhang mit der guten Überlieferung zu verlieren oder gar bewusst abzubrechen, ist mir sehr sympathisch." (The way in which this poet risks something new without losing or consciously breaking away from the nexus with good tradition is very much to my liking.).

[13] See Hesse, *Sämtliche Werke,* vol. 15: *Die politischen Schriften. Eine Dokumentation* (Frankfurt am Main: Suhrkamp, 2004), 789: "[. . .] seine Gedichte und Erzählungen liebe und schätze ich von den Anfängen bis heute, sein Tod ist auch mir ein Schmerz und Verlust. Er war der einzig wirkliche Dichter unter den deutschen Kommunisten, und der einzige, der noch auf der ganzen breiten Basis einer umfassenden literarischen Bildung stand." (I love his poems and stories and hold him in high esteem from his beginnings until today. His death is also my pain and loss. He really was the only real poet among the German communists, and the only one who still stood firmly on the whole broad foundation of a comprehensive literary erudition.).

[14] See Hesse, *SW* 10:245, 331, and 342–47.

[15] See Hesse's note in *SW* 10:396: "Louis Soutter, Maler und Musiker, lebte von 1871 bis 1942; als Maler und Violinist akademisch ausgebildet, Lieblingsschüler von Ysaye, übte wechselnd beide Berufe aus. Nach einem schweren Typhus erholte er sich nie wieder, die beiden letzten Jahrzehnte lebte er in einer Anstalt interniert. Dort zeichnete er die wilden genialen Blätter, die der Lausanner Verlag Mermod lang nach seinem Tode herausgab." (Louis Soutter, painter and musician, lived from 1871 to 1942; academically trained as a painter and violinist, Ysaye's favorite student, he alternated between both professions. He never recovered from a severe case of typhus, and he spent his last two decades in an institution. There he produced the wild drawings that display the mark of a genius, published by Mermod in Lausanne long after this death.).

[16] Hesse, *SW* 10:385: "Alles dauert in frommer Erinnerung, / Bleibt im Wort, im Bild, im Liede bewahrt, / Ewig bereit zur Feier der Rückkehr / Im erneuten, im

edlern Gewand. / Hilf bewahren du, hilf verwandeln [. . .]" (Everything lasts in pious remembrance, / Remains in the word, in the image, in love, / Eternally prepared for the celebration of return / In renewed, in nobler garment. / Help to preserve, help to transform).

[17] Hesse, *SW* 10:398: "Regenbogengedicht, / [. . .] / Schleier von Schönheit und Trauer / Über dem Abgrund der Welt." (Rainbow poem, / [. . .] / Veil of beauty and mourning / Above the world's abyss.).

[18] Görner's observation that Hesse's lyrical work offers a compelling blend of political and nature poetry ("eine politische Naturlyrik von unbestreitbarer Aussagekraft"), while remaining a general remark in his important essay, is a very useful description of this specific Hesse poem. See Rüdiger Görner, "Letzte Lieder. Zur Sprache des Späten in der Lyrik Hermann Hesses," in *Hermann Hesse Today / Hermann Hesse Heute*, ed. Ingo Cornils and Osman Durrani (Amsterdam/New York, Rodopi, 2005), 205–20; here 209.

[19] In an open letter written in the same year, Hesse reiterated his refusal to be affiliated with any party that promotes violence.

[20] Letter to Carla Fassbind, October 1927, shortly after Ball's death in the same year, in Hermann Hesse, Emmy Ball-Hennings, Hugo Ball. *Briefwechsel 1921 bis 1927*, ed. Bärbel Reetz (Frankfurt am Main: Suhrkamp, 2003), 543: "Ball war der einzige, den ich ganz ernst nahm, der einzige, mit dem ich sprechen konnte und mit dem volles gegenseitiges Verstehen mich verband [. . .]" (Ball was the only one whom I completely took seriously, the only one with whom I could talk and with whom I shared complete mutual understanding). See also Hesse's letter to Volkmar Andreae, September 21, 1927, ibid., 532: "Ich habe mit Ball den einzigen Menschen verloren, der mir geistig nahestand, der meine Sprache ganz und gar verstand, mit dem ich über geistige Dinge bis in die Tiefe sprechen konnte. Man findet so etwas nicht wieder. Er war der einzige meiner Freunde, der [. . .] mich verstand und die Notwendigkeit meiner Denkart und meiner gesamten Tätigkeit im Innern begriffen hat." (With Ball, I have lost the only one who was intellectually and spiritually close to me, who understood my language completely, with whom I could discuss intellectual and spiritural matters in depth. This is impossible to find again. He was the only among my friends who [. . .] understood me and who comprehended the necessity of my way of thinking and my whole work from the inside.).

[21] See Ball's monograph on Hesse's life and work, first published already in 1927 and now available in the edition of Ball's collected works, Hugo Ball, *Sämtliche Werke und Briefe. Band 8: Hermann Hesse. Sein Leben und sein Werk*, ed. Volker Michels (Göttingen, Wallstein, 2006), 169. Huber offers a less evocative but equally concise characterization of Hesse's *Krisis* project; see Peter Huber, "Nachwort des Bearbeiters," in *SW* 10:609–23; here 619–20: "[Hesse] verzichtet [. . .] weitgehend auf seine ästhetischen Prinzipien und reduziert den lyrischen Schmuck auf einen Rest, der angesichts der ungeschminkten Realitätsdarstellung schon fast verfremdend wirkt. Diese Texte, die trotz Reims kaum mehr lyrisch zu nennen sind [. . .]" (For the most part, Hesse leaves his aesthetic principles behind and reduces lyrical ornamentation to remnants that, juxtaposed with the naked rendering of reality, almost have a defamiliarizing effect. These texts that, despite the rhyme, can hardly be called lyrical anymore.).

[22] Since they are part of the novel *Der Steppenwolf,* these poems are not published in the critical Hesse edition's poetry volume, see Hesse, *SW* 4: *Die Romane. Der Steppenwolf. Narziß und Goldmund. Die Morgenlandfahrt* (Frankfurt am Main: Suhrkamp, 2001), 241–42.

[23] The relevance of Hölderlin's "Turmgedichte" for a reassessment of contemporary poetics and literary theory is discussed in my essay "Mythos und Methode. Notizen zur posthumanen Idylle," in *Derrida und danach? Tendenzen und Entwicklungen in literaturtheoretischen Diskursen der Gegenwart,* ed. Gregor Thuswaldner (Wiesbaden, VS Verlag für Sozialwissenschaften, 2008), 101–10.

[24] Görner's generalizing remark that Hesse's poems have "the tendency to defuse and oversimplify the complexity of modern life" ("Tendenz in seiner Lyrik, komplexe Daseinsprobleme zu verharmlosen") is the only moment in his otherwise insightful essay that runs the risk of adding to what he rightly criticizes in other critical works on Hesse's poetry: oversimplifications and unnuanced value judgments: "Es fällt nämlich auf, dass man beständig versucht hat, diese Lyrik pauschal zu werten." (It is striking that scholars have always tried to judge this poetry in unnuanced terms.). See Rüdiger Görner, "Letzte Lieder. Zur Sprache des Späten in der Lyrik Hermann Hesses," in *Hermann Hesse Today / Hermann Hesse heute,* ed. Cornils and Durrani, 220 and 218.

[25] According to Görner, Hesse embraced the art of poetry as a lifelong preparation for dying, see Görner, "Letzte Lieder. Zur Sprache des Späten in der Lyrik Hermann Hesses," in *Hermann Hesse Today / Hermann Hesse heute,* ed. Cornils and Durrani, 215: "Dichten wurde Hesse jedoch auch zu einer langen Einübung ins Sterben." (But for Hesse, writing poetry also became a long preparation for dying.).

11: "Ob die Weiber Menschen seyn?" Hesse, Women, and Homoeroticism

Kamakshi P. Murti

> *. . . in the masculine tradition the text is a woman, the pen a penis, and writing understood as coitus.*
> — Jane Gallop, *Thinking through the Body*, 1988

HERMANN HESSE CREPT INTO my consciousness in late 1950s India, not so surprisingly via *Siddhartha*.[1] At the time I was struggling with my own faith, attempting to distance myself from the Catholic nuns who were my teachers at school. The discussions I had with them about the truth value of religion, and what I perceived as their attempts to discredit Hinduism were very disquieting. I was simultaneously moved and resentful that a Western writer such as Hesse would deign to approach the complexities of a religion that I saw as my spiritual heritage. My carrying around a well-thumbed paperback edition of *Siddhartha* in my shoulder bag recalled an earlier generation of young readers — some two centuries before — who had carried Goethe's *Werther* in their pockets, and were sometimes driven to suicide because of it.[2] But the male protagonist, Siddhartha, did not interest me as much as Kamala, the courtesan turned *Bhikkhuni* (female Buddhist monastic). She exemplified the ideal of *Pativrata* (*pati* = husband; *vrat* = vow) prescribed by the Hindu *Shastras* (sacred treatises), of a woman who vows to remain staunchly loyal to her husband and who preserves her purity — physically, mentally, and spiritually. Feminist thought had not yet "threatened" the bastions of Hindu patriarchal institutions in my hometown.

"Saint Hesse among the Hippies"

It was the 1960s; I was studying in Germany. Crises of faith in institutionalized religion, in the establishment, and in the educational system in Europe, and a mounting awareness of illiteracy and poverty in my own country shocked me out of a complacency born of a privileged middle-class existence in India, and catapulted me into the arms of the "Achtundsechziger."[3] For many of us, German and non-German, Hesse seemed to offer an escape from this multifaceted crisis. The many utopian possibilities he offered in his works appeared seductively within reach, especially in the context of the 1960s counterculture movement. In fact, his appeal, like that of the young Goethe of *Werther* fame, went far beyond the confines of Germany. And then, quite as suddenly as it had begun, the "Hesse Boom" ended. In Germany the "Golf" generation had come of age.[4] At the same time the United States produced a generation of "Me! Me! Me!" status seekers.

Hesse the Rishi, or Seer

In India, the enthusiasm for Hesse never really waned; in fact, he, the twentieth-century writer, along with another German "guru," the nineteenth-century Indologist and philologist Friedrich Max Müller,[5] became even more sought after by young and old alike, and acquired more or less divine (or should I say "*nirvanic*"?) status.[6] German language institutes in India were named after Müller;[7] Hesse's *Siddhartha* was filmed in 1972 by Conrad Rooks with Indian actors.[8] Indian readers and viewers were flattered by this sudden interest in India, seeing it as a vindication of their newly-gained subject status. A postcolonial euphoria led us Indians to believe that there was a seamless thread between Vedic times (1500–500 B.C.E.) and twentieth-century India. The Mogul empire, the British Raj, every "foreign" thread in the fabric of Indian history that was seen as inauthentic, that is, "un-Indian," had been meticulously pulled out. The result was an outwardly pristine, albeit mendacious packaging of Hindu spirituality, infinitely accessible both to the Western seeker for the ultimate truth and to the scores of "maharishis" (great sages) who were willing to masticate and regurgitate this "absolute" truth for their fledgling pupils.

In April 2003, the well-known Hesse scholar Theodore Ziolkowski wrote:

> The year 2002, when the 125th anniversary of his birth coincided with the 40th of his death, was the Hermann Hesse Year par excellence in Germany and Switzerland. The jubilee reminds an American observer of nothing so much as the Hesse cult among U.S. youth in the 1960s, for which I coined the phrase "Saint Hesse among the Hippies" [. . .] The agency Stuttgart-Marketing offers "A Weekend with Hermann" (at 242 euros per head), featuring an excursion to Hesse's birthplace in nearby Calw, a three-course meal in the Hirsau monastery depicted in some of his stories . . .[9]

Hesse had once more become "marketable." But what had brought about his reincarnation? Jörg Drews bluntly states: "As a matter of fact . . . Hesse's work as an object of research and prominence within Germanistik is not held in very high esteem; this work is perhaps judged more skeptically precisely also within the context of its success with the youth of the world . . ."[10] Ingo Cornils and Osman Durrani, the editors of the 2005 volume *Hermann Hesse Today / Hermann Hesse Heute,* in which Drews's statement appears, counter it as follows:

> The uncertain and shadowy audience whose appetite for Hesse's novels brought him into the limelight may also explain why he slipped out of the public arena as quickly as he had entered it. As the sensational aspects of his "discovery" recede in the collective memory, it is timely to stand back and survey an important author's past, present and future place in the canon. He has not disappeared, but has remained a distinctive feature of the literary landscape on those continents he once took by storm. (8)

It is precisely those readers — pubescent or not — with their "uncertain and shadowy" existence, whose own homoerotic tendencies remained subservient to an unforgiving patriarchy, but who have now perhaps returned to read Hesse outside the closet, making the question in the title of this essay, "Ob Weiber Menschen seyn?" (Whether Women are Human Beings?),[11] central to an understanding of Hesse in a homoerotic frame. The "Weiber" could never be "Menschen" in an all-male discursive model. They were allowed to be muses, allegories, love- and sex-objects of inspiration. They were ahistorical beings in many ways, beyond or incapable of development — that was the extent of their "visibility." The homoeroticism pervading many of Hesse's writings may indeed be responsible for returning him to the literary canon as a writer who can be read differently in the relatively open and uninhibited sexual climate of the twenty-first century.

Cornils and Durrani rightly stress Hesse's utopian vision, his thoughts on youth and education, his work as a journalist and artist as being of significance in the twenty-first century. Another contributor to their volume, Frederick A. Lubich, discusses how Hesse also propagates a necessary paradigmatic shift from patriarchal reality to a "muttermythischen Utopie" (mothermythical utopia) in which the matriarchal premises of equality, freedom, and sensuality can be a future model for culture. This "muttermythische Unterwanderung der mittelalterlichen Patriarchatskultur" (mothermythical infiltration of the medieval patriarchal culture) according to Lubich, was the main reason for the rediscovery of Hesse in the 1960s and is the reason for the lasting worldwide effect of his works.[12] I am not comfortable with Lubich's assumption that Hesse imagined and instrumentalized a paradigmatic change from an oppressive patriarchy to a matriarchy full of utopian possibilities. What Lubich views as the subversive return of the "Große Mutter" is, as I will argue later, an attempt on Hesse's part to keep feminist agency at bay by freezing it into an archetypal mother figure and immobilizing it at the source of all *man*kind. Such a strategy removed women from the possibility of historical change, as I mentioned above.

Ultimately, I believe it is Hesse's language that continues to lure readers to his texts. According to Wolfgang Iser and Hans Robert Jauss of the Constance school of reception aesthetics, readers realize the potential of a text by filling in gaps or indeterminacies.[13] According to Iser, as summarized here by David Albertson, the reader does not search for a single objective meaning hidden within the text.

> Rather, literature generates effects of meaning for the reader in a virtual space created between reader and text. Although reader and text assume similar conventions from reality, texts leave great portions unexplained to the reader, whether as *gaps in the narrative* or as *structural limits of the text's representation of the world*. This basic indeterminacy "implies" the reader and begs her *participation in synthesizing, and indeed living, events of meaning throughout the process of reading*. Such a theory of aesthetic response *denies the simple dichotomy of fiction and reality*. According to Iser, fiction proposes alternate worlds created within the virtual reality of the text's meaning. In other words, in literature the actual and the possible can exist simultaneously. Literature thus takes on a greater human function of imagining beyond the given constraints of experience.[14]

In earlier readings of Hesse, I thought I had recognized Iser's notion of indeterminacies. Hesse appeared to urge a constant re-examination of social and individual conventions by deforming and defamiliarizing accepted perspectives.[15] Agnès Cardinal adapts Jauss's concept of the "Erwartungshorizont," "the series of expectations against which the reader tests or evaluates the text," to an analysis of Hesse's *Der Steppenwolf*.[16] Cardinal mentions how Jauss uses as an exploratory paradigm for his theory the example of *Don Quixote*,

> a novel which raised in the contemporary readership expectations of a certain kind — its title promised a tale of medieval chivalry and valour. When these expectations were frustrated, or only partially met, a tension arose, which resulted in a fruitful, dialectical exchange, in terms of the production and consumption of the text.[17]

However, Hesse's language was at once luminous and numinous. In other words, I soon discovered an underlying authoritarian tone in Hesse's texts, as if they were sacred and their exegesis was only to be carried out based on divine principles. This authoritarian tone intimidated the reader and discouraged her or him from entertaining any expectations or engaging in a "fruitful, dialectical exchange." It appeared at first to encourage the reader to participate in "synthesizing, and indeed living, events of meaning throughout the process of reading," to push the reader to a level of frustration that would lead to an altered consciousness. But then there were entire passages that ruled out this possibility. For example, Hesse describes a moment of epiphany in "Ein indischer Lebenslauf" (Indian Autobiography) in the volume *Aus Indien* (From India):

> Einige Male aber hatte er auch anderes empfunden, [. . .] wie da der eigene Leib und die eigene Seele ihre Schwere ablegen und im Atem eines größeren, reineren, sonnenhaften Lebens mitschwingen müßten, erhoben und aufgesogen von einem Jenseits, einem Zeitlosen und Unwandelbaren. Doch waren es Augenblicke und Ahnungen geblieben. Und er dachte, [. . .] er müßte es dahin bringen, daß der Meister sein Lehrer würde, daß ihn in seine Übungen und geheimen Künste einführte und auch ihn zu einem Yogin machte.[18]

> [A few times he had felt other sensations, . . . how there one's own body and one's own soul had to lay down their heaviness and rise up triumphantly in the breath of a greater, more pure, more sun-filled life, raised up and soaked in a hereafter, a timeless and unwavering. Still there were moments and premonitions. And he thought . . . that he must get the master to be his teacher, so that he would initiate him in his exercises and secret arts, and also make him into a yogi.]

Dreams here occupy the same level of reality as premonitions (*Ahnungen*). The search for a master, a "Yogin" who would help him attain the ultimate truth, is an irresistible part of the Western hero's quest, especially to a youthful reader. For the educated adult reader, there seems to be an intellectually challenging palimpsestic layering of German Romanticism,[19] Jungian philosophy, Bachofen's theory of matriarchy,[20] and Indian Advaita Vedantic philosophy,[21] with a pastiche of Confucianism, Schopenhauer, and Nietzsche). As the above quote shows, Hesse's seductively lyrical language, especially language that frees the body from all earthly constraints and allows it to fly (one cannot but help compare Hesse's protagonist to Harry Potter!) is irresistible. This combination of high priest and magician (a reminder of an earlier Romantic, Novalis, whose protagonists Heinrich and Klingsor resonate with similar *yogic* emanations[22]) raises Hesse's youthful reader's expectations of some kind of revelatory truth: Hesse ingeniously moves between the ambivalence of a novitiate who is himself seeking truth, and the self-assurance of a master who has already attained a Buddha-like stature.[23]

> Als ihm Kamaswami einstmals vorhielt, er habe alles, was er verstehe, von ihm gelernt, gab er zur Antwort: "Wolle mich doch nicht mit solchen Späßen zum besten haben! Von dir habe ich gelernt, wieviel ein Korb voll Fische kostet, und wieviel Zins man für geliehenes Geld fordern kann. Das sind deine Wissenschaften. Denken habe ich nicht bei dir gelernt, teurer Kamaswami, suche lieber du, es von mir zu lernen."[24]

[When Kamaswami once reminded him that he had learned everything from him, he replied: "Do not make such jokes. I have learned from you how much a basket of fish costs and how much interest one can claim for lending money. That is your knowledge. But I did not learn how to think from you, my dear Kamaswami. It would be better if you learned that from me."[25]]

Roles are clearly reversed here. In *Siddhartha* Hesse never states outright his belief in Europe's superiority over the Orient and the latter's need of enlightenment, as I have argued elsewhere.[26] The very name Siddhartha, Buddha's given name, seems to belie such a claim. But whereas the historical Buddha resisted the caste system introduced by the Northern Aryans, Hesse places his protagonist squarely within the Brahmin, that is, the priestly caste, thus privileging him with the ability to possess absolute knowledge within the Indian framework (Gautama Buddha was born in the *Kshartriya*, i.e. warrior caste, inferior to the Brahmin!). It becomes apparent very quickly, however, that Hesse's Siddhartha belongs to an even more rarified type of "Brahmin," namely the German Orientalist. Through this single stroke, as the historian Gyan Prakash has pointed out, Hesse affixes caste "as the one essence of India."[27] Prakash goes on to comment on the caste system as being complicit in the Orientalist project of constituting India as the Other in order to reestablish the Orientalist's belief in a stable, autonomous, and sovereign self.[28] Hesse ostensibly distances himself from the blatant overtones of colonialism by endowing his Siddhartha (and himself) authoritatively with the prestige of the Indian Rishi or seer. Just as the British used Lieutenant Colonel T. E. Lawrence as a "liaison" to the Arabs in the early twentieth century, the Orientalist Hesse makes use of Siddhartha to epitomize the perfect Brahmin youth to probe the Indian consciousness. The white Arab garb that Lawrence donned gives him the ability to slip in and out of his role as an "Arab." Such a role as a go-between allowed him to probe the Arab consciousness without relinquishing his identity as colonizer. Similarly, Siddhartha's Brahmin robes allow him to simultaneously be part of and above the colonized. As someone who is superior to the Indians by virtue of his Occidental vitality and life force, he proceeds to imagine them as a naïve race of "Kindermenschen" needing to be enlightened by one such as him. Like the Indologist Friedrich Max Müller, Hesse's use of the active Aryan against the lazy, lascivious Brahmin emerges very clearly in *Siddhartha*.[29]

Siddhartha hatte gelernt, Handel zu treiben, Macht über Menschen auszuüben, sich mit dem Weibe zu vergnügen, er hatte gelernt, schöne Kleider zu tragen, Dienern zu befehlen, sich in wohlriechenden Wassern zu baden. Er hatte gelernt, zart und sorgfältig bereitete Speisen zu essen, auch den Fisch, auch Fleisch und Vogel, Gewürze und Süßigkeiten, und den Wein zu trinken, der träge und vergessen *macht. . . . Aber immer noch hatte er sich von den andern verschieden und ihnen überlegen gefühlt, immer hatte er ihnen mit ein wenig Spott zugesehen, mit ein wenig spöttischer Verachtung* . . . (3:422; emphasis added)

[Siddhartha had learned how to transact business affairs, to exercise power over people, to amuse himself with women; he had learned to wear fine clothes, to command servants, to bathe in sweet-smelling waters. He had learned to eat sweet and carefully prepared foods, also fish and meat and fowl, spices and dainties, and to drink wine which made him lazy and forgetful. . . . *But he had always felt different from and superior to the others; he had always watched them a little scornfully, with a slightly mocking disdain* . . . (61)]

Siddhartha was the active Aryan who scorned the lazy Brahmin. For Hesse, evidently, the days of Western Europeans seeking the wisdom of the East were past. It was now the turn of the wise man from the *West* to offer the knowledge that once had its source in the East — a vindication of the belief that the West will ultimately triumph in all areas of knowledge.

As mentioned above, Frederick Lubich maintains that Hesse is truly interested in elevating the matriarchal premises of equality, freedom, and sensuality to the status of a cultural model for the future. However, his thesis — based on Bachofen's theory of matriarchy, that is, that motherhood is the *source* of human society, religion, morality, and decorum — is similar to the Orientalist's belief that the East is the *source* of knowledge. Both these sources — matriarchal and oriental — remain by definition at the beginning, immutable, and infinitely available to the needs of Western man.

In their program for the 2002 conference Herman Hesse Heute/ Hermann Hesse Today, from which the volume of the same name arose, the organizers Ingo Cornils and Osman Durrani cite "Hesse's continuing presence as a modern icon."[30] This becomes especially problematic in view of his inscription of women. There have been many analyses about how Hesse treats women as mere appendages to his own spiritual growth. The possibility of a homoerotic dimension, has, however, not been prominent in discussions, although it would explain to a great extent why the women in Hesse's works have no subject-position.

Socrates and Alcibiades?

Plato's *Symposium* (ca. 380 C.E.) is perhaps the earliest literary account of male friendship in the West, where the most beautiful youth in Athens, Alcibiades, offers himself as the lover of the philosopher Socrates. The ambiguity surrounding the concept of Platonic love, whether as masculine eros, or as a sublimated form of desire, forms an appropriate context for understanding Hesse's writings. In the following, I discuss the construction of the male protagonists and the women who frame them in four of Hesse's works — *Demian, Narziß und Goldmund, Der Steppenwolf,* and *Siddhartha,* paying special attention to the slippages that occur between homo- and heterosexual, colonial and post-colonial economies of desire. I will show that the female characters in these works are either reduced to an object or allegorical status (Frau Eva or universal mother in *Demian,* and the myriad women who go into the creation of the Madonna in *Narziß und Goldmund*) or become increasingly hermaphroditic to reflect and enable the consummation of the protagonist's homoerotic desires (Beatrice in *Demian,* Hermine in *Steppenwolf,* Kamala in *Siddhartha*), both processes resulting in the annihilation of the woman as subject. As Evi Petropoulou so eloquently states:

> . . . *the female character [almost] never occupies the organizing center of the narrative — even when Hesse emphasizes the individual woman* [. . .] In Hesse's work, the significance of woman is based on her "*mirror function*" [. . .] on her importance for the unfolding of the individuality of the subject. She represents *the Other* as the Foreign and Unfamiliar, perceived not as a threat to man's existence but as his missing part. *She seems to be in conscious possession of the other side of man that remains to be reached so that man may acquire the internal coherence and unity of his existence.*[31] (Emphasis added)

I agree with Petropoulou if she means by "missing part" that woman is a pre-defined static "Other" who waits passively for man to absorb her so that he "may acquire the internal coherence and unity of his existence." However, the word "conscious" in the last sentence of the above quote is debatable, as I will show later.

As mentioned earlier, there has been very little discussion in the scholarship about the homoerotic nature of the highly conflicted, yet enduring male friendships that Hesse's protagonists forge in the majority of his works.[32] I would go so far as to suggest that for Hesse homoerotic bonding is an escape from heterosexual responsibility. For the most part, critics have ignored the possibility of the homoerotic by using the concept of androgyny, implying a Jungian anima/animus, that is, a synthesis of the female and male archetypes. Miguel Serrano talks about "the Germanico-alchemical dream of the *Androgyne*" which, he asserts,

> is the *opposite of homosexuality* — whose aspiration is totality and the fusion of the opposites, the unity of Nietzsche's 'Self,' the inner *homo,* of *coelo, Demian,* beloved and admired by Sinclair; that is to say, by Hesse. His most intimate ego. *Narcissus and Goldmund.* In the original German version of *Steppenwolf,* the female protagonist is called Hermina, which is the feminine of Hermann. And this is the same

alchemical-tantrio game as in Mozart's *Magic Flute:* Pamino and Pamina. (Emphasis added.)[33]

Many critics have shown that Hesse's works are intensely autobiographical.[34] They have revealed how the other characters are extensions of the protagonist, representing various stages in his development toward self-realization in the Jungian sense. The following lengthy text by the prominent critic Joseph Mileck makes this element very clear:

> At the extremes of storytelling there are those writers who spin their yarns and those who document their lives. Hesse belongs to the latter. He had to write and he had to write about himself and there is little of the much he wrote that is not confessional in form and therapeutic in function. With rare exception, each of Hesse's major tales begins where the immediately preceding tale breaks off, scrutinizes and finds wanting its predecessor's concluding promise of better possibility, and then itself terminates abruptly on its own upbeat of new hope. [. . .] But autobiography is not just confined to narrative substance, it permeates the very narrative fabric of Hesse's art, no less in his minor than in his major works. Hesse's protagonists are self-projections not only in their concerns, thoughts, and feelings, but even in their persons and experiences and, with rare exception, in the worlds in which they live and the circles in which they move.[35]

In a male-defined and male-structured image of the self, women either slowly relinquish their femaleness, disappearing into the male persona, or they remain, as mentioned earlier, on an idealized or allegorical plane of being. By the time Hesse published his magnum opus *Magister Ludi* (The Glass Bead Game, 1943), women had become totally irrelevant (or redundant).

In her article "The Melancholic Structure of the Mind: The Absence of Object Relations in the Work of Hermann Hesse," Angelika Rauch-Rapaport aims to get away from a biographical focus, that is, a focus on women in Hesse's life as models for his female characters.[36] Pointing to the constant thematization of the "return to the mother at the end of the self's journey," Rauch-Rapaport suggests looking at Hesse's women characters in terms of the protagonists' inability to have meaningful and lasting relationships with them. Her premise is that Hesse did not have "a good internal mother-object," and his fictional characters therefore do not either. Consequently, Hesse went through life attempting to find himself, and his characters go through their lives trying to find themselves. Their "voyage to the self," says Rauch-Rapaport, "is a process of mourning, without however being able to give up the 'negative attachment' to the maternal-object."[37]

I agree with Rauch-Rapaport that Hesse's protagonists are unable to have meaningful and lasting relationships with women. However, I see the reason for such inadequacy not so much in their lack of a mother in infancy as in their ambivalence toward heterosexuality.

In her thoughtful paper "Darstellung und Bedeutung der weiblichen Figuren in Hermann Hesses Romanen der zwanziger Jahre," Petra Fricke attempts to recognize the important, albeit limited role that the female characters in Hesse's works play in helping the male protagonists to their goal of self-realization.[38] The sooner one realizes, however, that Hesse's women are more incidental to the plot than hitherto supposed, assuming importance only when they cast off the specificity of their gender or assume allegorical proportions (earth mother, Frau Eva, the Madonna), the easier it is to understand the male protagonists' problems.

In both Rauch-Rapaport's and Fricke's analyses, the emphasis is still on the protagonist's relationships with women within a heterosexual context. Craig Bernard Palmer is one of the few scholars who suggest that Jungian psychology and Eastern philosophy might not be the only approaches to understanding Hesse's texts: "[T]hose interpretations that take Jungian theories as their basis are not as productive to the understanding of *Steppenwolf* as they might be because they overlook the homosexual aspects of the text."[39] In regard to *Steppenwolf* and *Demian,* Palmer states that "the intersection of heterosexual and homosocial desires in this novel [*Steppenwolf*] is homosexual." I understand Palmer to say that an imposition of heteronormativity in society forces homosocial desires into a state of alienation that can be fulfilled only in a fictionalized realm. *Steppenwolf,* in fact, "radicalizes the convergence of homosocial and heterosexual relationships that the author had previously portrayed in *Demian* (1917)."[40] It is this convergence that I wish to examine more closely.

The narrative structure underlying the four works belongs to the genre of the Bildungsroman (novel of personal development), which usually traces the spiritual, moral, psychological, or social development and growth of the main character, usually male, typically from childhood to maturity. Hesse frames this growth in Jungian terms, giving the hero a shadow, a mentor, and a hinderer or tempter.

Demian (1919)

The words daemon and daimon, sometimes dæmon, are Latinized spellings of Greek διαμων, used purposely today to distinguish the daemons of Greek mythology, good or malevolent supernatural beings between mortals and gods, such as inferior divinities and ghosts of dead heroes, from the Judeo-Christian usage of demon, a malignant spirit that can seduce, afflict, or possess humans. Franz Kromer, the village bully, has the role of hinderer/tempter of the ten-year-old Emil Sinclair. Kromer fills Sinclair with fear, not only because he is socially unacceptable to Sinclair's family,

but also because Sinclair feels irresistibly drawn to this darker world that
Kromer represents: the world of Cain. Describing this world, Sinclair uses
words that recur in most of Hesse's works: chaos, madness, and dreams —
the realm of Dionysus. In stark contrast to the vigor and sensuality, or
Wollust (to use a Nietzschean term) that Cain's world promises is the Apol-
lonian world of brilliance and clarity, Protestant cleanliness and biblical
values associated with Sinclair's parents.

Demian senses Sinclair's inner conflict and advises him to find out "was
erlaubt und was verboten — ihm verboten ist" (3:283; "the actual meaning of 'permitted' and 'forbidden'"; 64) because "das Verbotene" is determined by men and hence not absolute.[41] Cain's is also the unfathom-
able, dark world of Frau Eva, who is an all-consuming, godlike figure: "In
sie hinein *verschwanden die Züge der Menschen, wie in eine riesige Höhle,*
und waren weg. Die Göttin kauerte sich am Boden nieder, hell schim-
merte das Mal auf ihrer Stirn" (3:363, emphasis added; "The ranks of the
people were *swallowed up into her as into a giant cave* and vanished from
sight. The goddess cowered on the ground, the mark luminous on her
forehead"; 169). As Edward Said has written, the eternal mother shares
many traits with the Oriental woman: "not only fecundity but sexual promise (and threat), untiring sensuality, unlimited desire, deep generative energies."[42] Hesse/Sinclair faces the threat of losing his individuality to Frau
Eva ("Sie war ein Meer, in das ich strömend mündete." [3:353; "She was
an ocean into which I streamed," 156]). However, his attempt to concentrate his whole consciousness and to think of Eva ("Ich wollte die Kräfte
meiner Seele zusammennehmen, um sie meine Liebe fühlen zu lassen, um
sie zu mir her zu ziehen" (3:359; "summoning all the strength in my soul
to let her feel my love and draw her to me," 163–64) is in reality a sum-
mons to Demian, for it is he who answers Sinclair's call, adding: "Es hat
noch niemand zu meiner Mutter Frau Eva gesagt, ohne sie zu lieben.
Übrigens, wie war das? *Du hast sie oder mich heute gerufen, nicht?*" (3:361,
emphasis added; "No one has called my mother Frau Eva who hasn't been
in love with her. You either called me or her today"; 166). As Palmer suggests, Frau Eva mediates Sinclair's homosocial desire for Demian. The
uncanny similarity between Frau Eva and Demian makes her more than a
mediator — she becomes and finally *is* Demian. Palmer suggests:

> Sinclair, Demian, and Demian's mother represent a triangulation of
> homosocial and heterosexual desires: the troubled male protagonist
> meets his ideal, wiser self in another man, and is brought closer to him
> through a female who shares many traits with the ideal man.[43]

I believe that Sinclair hides his desire for Demian under the disguise of a
heterosexual relationship with Frau Eva, but only because homoerotic de-

sire is a social taboo. Examples of Sinclair's desire for Demian abound in the work:

> Doch mußte ich ihn immerfort ansehen, er mochte mir lieb oder leid sein; kaum aber blickte er einmal auf mich, *so zog ich meinen Blick erschrocken zurück.* (3:253; emphasis added)

> [Yet I couldn't help looking at him, no matter whether I liked or detested him, but if he happened to glance my way I averted my eyes in panic. (27)]

> . . . aber statt Kromer war es diesmal Demian, der auf mir kniete. Und — das war ganz neu und machte mir tiefen Eindruck — alles, was ich von Kromer unter Qual und Widerstreben erlitten hatte, *das erlitt ich von Demian gerne und mit einem Gefühl, das ebensoviel Wonne wie Angst enthielt.* (3:259; emphasis added)

> [Yet this time it was Demian who knelt on me. And — this was totally new and left a deep impression on me — everything I had resisted and that had been agony to me when Kromer was my tormentor I suffered gladly at Demian's hands, with a feeling compounded as much of ecstasy as of fear. (34)]

> Und ich stand an einem Fenster, *hinterm Vorhang verborgen,* und schaute ihm zu. (3:272; emphasis added)

> [As I stood at the window behind the curtain and watched him [. . .]. (51)]

James Giles holds such voyeuristic behavior to be typical of someone "who is mentally replaying or fantasizing" about physically caressing the other person's body.[44]

In *Revolution in Poetic Language* (1974), Julia Kristeva distinguishes the semiotic (distinct from semiotics as the study of signs) from the symbolic.[45] The semiotic, according to Kristeva, is associated with the mother-infant dyad or union and the state of symbiosis and dependence before the infant acquires language. The semiotic is the pre-verbal signifying realm, a realm of exchange between mother and baby that functions through sound — the rhythmic pattern and tone of the voice — and through gesture, smell, touch. Important for my analysis of *Demian* is Kristeva's argument that in order to enter the symbolic (that is, formal language and social relations), this "other" of language — the semiotic — must be repressed. The mother's body mediates between the symbolic order and the semiotic *chora*.[46] Sinclair's dilemma lies in the fact that he cannot accept the symbolic, that is, heterosexual social relations as defined in a patriarchy. He is caught in a distressing, indeterminate state of being between the semiotic and the symbolic.

Beatrice belongs to those women in Hesse's works who increasingly transform themselves to reflect the protagonist's homoerotic desires, at the same time enabling the consummation of this desire with the male love-object. Through Sinclair's act of naming her Beatrice, she is allegorized. He calls her Beatrice, although he has not read Dante and knows about his Beatrice only from the *reproduction* of an English painting that he owns (3:295). Sinclair never addresses a single word to Beatrice, and places her in a holy shrine (3:298). Even in this holy shrine, woman is not the object of worship, but rather someone who gives Sinclair access to the actual love-object housed in this shrine: Demian. Beatrice is described as having "ein kluges *Knabengesicht.* [. . .] schon fast Dame, aber mit einem Anflug von Übermut und *Jungenhaftigkeit* im Gesicht, *den ich überaus gern hatte.*" (3:295; emphasis added; "[A]n intelligent and *boyish* face [. . .] A full-grown woman, but with a touch of exuberance, and *boyishness* in her face, and *this was what I liked above all*"; 80). He places himself within a heterosexual discourse (Dante and Beatrice), but admires that slender and *boyish* figure. That is to say, no attributes of female sexuality are allowed to spoil the possibility of homoeroticism. When Sinclair begins to paint Beatrice, it looks increasingly like a boy's face. It does not take too long for him to recognize that it is Demian's face (3:298–99). The girl he calls Beatrice does not arouse any emotion in him, only "ein sanftes Übereinstimmen, ein gefühlhaftes Ahnen: du bist mir verknüpft, aber nicht du, nur dein Bild; du bist ein Stück von meinem Schicksal." (3:300; "only a gentle harmony, a presentiment: you and I are linked, but not you, only your picture; you are a part of my fate," 86) a fate leading to his one passionate love, Demian.

In the end, characters and desires collapse into one: the mother, the object of Sinclair's heterosexual desire, disappears from the narrative, but not before she sends Sinclair a kiss via Demian, the object of his homosocial desire. While the kiss is symbolically heterosexual, it is homosexual in terms of the gendered bodies performing it.[47] As Palmer correctly points out, Sinclair's homosocial desire for Demian is mediated by the latter's *manly* mother. However, the kiss that Demian gives Sinclair at the end is quite explicit: "Ich schloß gehorsam meine Augen zu, ich spürte einen leichten Kuß auf meinen Lippen, auf denen ich immer ein wenig Blut stehen hatte, das nie weniger werden wollte"[48] (3:365; "I closed my eyes in obedience. I felt a light kiss on my lips where there was always a little fresh blood which never would go away"; 171).

Siddhartha (1922)

Siddhartha differs from the other works discussed in this text in two important ways. The first is Hesse's choice of South Asia as a backdrop for the story. The second is the way in which he feminizes a whole country, India. Characters, landscape, history — everything is effeminate, passive. By naming them "Kindermenschen," Siddhartha portrays the people of this vast country as if they have regressed to a primordial time.[49]

Why did Hesse choose this character, this country? Hermann Gundert, Hesse's maternal grandfather, the first missionary of the Basel Mission to Malabar, was invited in 1835 by Anthony Norris Groves, a private English missionary, to accompany him and his sons to Calcutta as house tutor. Gundert's influence on his grandson and indirectly on an entire generation of "India lovers" at the turn of the twentieth century cannot be denied.

Grandfather Hermann Gundert and grandson Hermann Hesse both feminized the colonial object. Gundert gradually shifted from missionary to colonial activities. As I have explained elsewhere, Gundert added to his initial missionary zeal the expression of an acute sense of European superiority and consequently the inferiority of the "Eingeborenen" (indigenous people) to whom he referred in his writings as "Sklaven," slaves.[50] Moreover, he saw the natives as caught in an eternally recurring pattern of sinful living, very much reminiscent of the biblical Sodom and Gomorrah. Such notions about the essentially effeminate nature of the natives can be found in the texts of many others who shared in the colonialist enterprise. For example, in 1872, the missionary William Butler described the natives of India as follows: "The Hindoos have long ceased to be a warlike people. The rich land which they conquered, its fertility, the abundance and cheapness of the means of life, and their inclination to indolence, which a warm climate fosters, have all been promotive of the effeminacy into which they have so generally sunk."[51] Such feminization was fundamental to colonial practices, as the anthropologist and historian Ann Laura Stoler points out,"Discursive management of the sexual practices of colonizer and colonized was fundamental to the colonial order of things."[52] The missionary was the perfect choice to play the role of policeman in matters of sexuality and promiscuity among the colonized. The "racially erotic counterpoint," the ultimate object of desire and moral decline, is the native woman with her burning sexuality.[53]

Werner Bieder's 1991 book on the Basler Mission describes grandfather Gundert's activities in India. One incident that he narrates throws an interesting light on the latter's perception of himself within the Indian context. In Melur, Southern India, soon after his arrival in the country, Gundert spots a Banyan tree:

> Ich sass vor dem schönsten und grössten Banyan, den ich in Indien gesehen, mit unzähligen durcheinandergewachsenen Stämmen: die Stille der Nacht, die milde Luft, die hellen Sterne — alles half mir ein-

mal auch recht dankbar zu seyn, dass Gott mich auf diesen Wegen geführt hat.[54]

[I sat before the most beautiful and biggest banyan tree that I had seen in India, with countless intertwined trunks: the stillness of the night, the mild air, the bright stars — everything helped me to be quite thankful that God had led me on this path.]

The image of Gundert sitting under a Banyan tree strikes a chord that is too familiar to ignore — that of the Buddha (and later Gundert's grandson in the guise of the Siddhartha) sitting under a similar tree and attaining nirvana.[55] The historian Gyan Prakash differentiates between the "old Orientalist, buried in texts and devoted to learning Sanskrit and Persian" and "the official, the scholar, and the modernizer," the representative of the British Raj. He sees the pendulum swinging from the "genuine respect and love for the Orient of William Jones . . . to the cold utilitarian scrutiny of James Mill, and then to missionary contempt."[56] As I have attempted to show elsewhere, the same ideological structure nevertheless constructed both discourses, however different they may seem on the surface. The pragmatic concern of empire was sometimes further away from the surface, sometimes closer, but it never completely vanished. There was no contradiction between an initial interest in the older India of Sanskrit, texts, and Brahmins, and the later on-the-spot official reports with "details on peasants, revenue, rent, caste, customs, tribes, popular religious practices, linguistic diversity, agro-economic regimes, male and female populations, and other such topics."[57] One merely separated the ancient Indian civilization with its magnificent monuments and literatures, as something that could not be remembered, from the current colonized space that was India, with its need for a civilizing mission from the West (the white man's burden). Thus William Jones's Orient could be constructed alongside of James Mill's and Hermann Gundert's, and each one profited from the others.

Siddhartha can be seen as a caesura in Hesse's writings, a break from the many demands on him that included his first wife's mental instability, his son's illness, and financial problems. In the face of a nervous breakdown, the Orient provided the perfect escape for him. Transcending the tradition of his grandfather Gundert and other Orientalists, he reinvented himself as a romanticized, almost mystical Indian Rishi or seer whose healthy, vigorous occidental body however had to be alert at all times to the danger of pollution from the diseased and infectious (especially female) oriental body. One could speculate that Kamala in Siddhartha possesses this all-consuming sexuality that threatens to emasculate Siddhartha unless the latter separates himself from her by virtue of his occidental power and virility. Unlike the pattern of relationships in Demian (and later in

Steppenwolf and *Narziß und Goldmund*), however, I would suggest that Siddhartha is not primarily interested in feigning a kind of male dominance within a heterosexual relationship. Like that of her counterparts in Hesse's other works, Kamala's agency is non-existent. She is merely another aspect of the life of these "Kindermenschen" that needs to be discovered, exposed, and finally penetrated. Since Kamala is a courtesan, the possibility of a consensual relationship is ruled out from the very start. She is after all a slice out of the *Kama Sutra,* a harem-like creature that was two-dimensional from the start, part of the exotic/erotic, mysterious Orient so titillating to the Western reader.[58]

Within the framework of colonialism and imperialism, such discursive measures seem inevitable. But the case of Hesse is of particular interest because readers both in the West and the East insist that Hesse did much to brighten the "tarnished" image of colonial India. Such a reading of Hesse strikes me as highly problematic. The fact that many important Indian nationalist historians, with their educational background anchored in the West, were themselves part of the continuing Orientalist discourse, does not make this dilemma any easier to resolve.

A closer look at Hesse's *Siddhartha* shows a rather curious return to the ways of the "old orientalists" that Prakash refers to as having had an apparently genuine respect and love for the Orient. Hesse puts on the garb of an Oriental seer here. Not surprisingly, central to his work is the distinction made by the indologist Max Müller between Aryans and ancient Hindus. The German Romantic dream of a nation does not admit to any spiritual or racial kinship with a historical India, but rather with an ancient India that, according to Müller, revealed the active side of the northern, European Aryans. This could be found in India only in the writings of the Vedic Rishis. Müller claims that this energy disappeared towards the end of the Vedic period (150 B.C.E.), turning inwards and becoming abstract and passive. Such passivity explained the lack in India of the expansionist ambition that was an integral part of European history. Müller concludes, therefore, that the heroic epics *Ramayana* (between 750 and 500 B.C.E.) and *Mahabharata* (between the 8th and the 4th century B.C.E.) signaled the end of India's vitality. He characterizes this transition by no longer calling the Indians of the post-epic period "Aryans" but instead "ancient Hindus."[59] The text's rhetoric feeds upon the intellectual and imaginative territory delineated by nineteenth-century German Orientalism.

Hesse goes a step further than Müller, removing himself from the sphere of mere scholarship (the Orientalist as scholar) and identifying himself with the ancient Aryan seer or Rishi. His is also not the covert colonialism that his grandfather, Gundert, practices. What makes this kind of Orientalist discourse so difficult to identify is the seductive power of Hesse's language, which maintains the Orientalist's emphasis on essentialized differences between East and West under the pretense of mediating between them.[60]

> Govinda wußte: dieser [Siddhartha] wird kein gemeiner Brahmane werden, kein fauler Opferbeamter, kein habgieriger Händler mit Zaubersprüchen, kein eitler, leerer Redner, kein böser, hinterlistiger Priester, und auch kein gutes, dummes Schaf in der Herde der Vielen. (3:373)

> [Govinda knew that he would not become an ordinary Brahmin, a lazy sacrificial official, an avaricious dealer in magic sayings, a conceited worthless orator, a wicked sly priest, or just a good stupid sheep amongst a large herd; 2]

The above quote perpetuates many of the stereotypical images that are associated with the Oriental: laziness, avarice, conceit, wickedness, stupidity. Hesse gives his reader the impression that he is genuinely concerned with providing new insights into the mind of the hitherto belittled Oriental. His narrative continues, however, to either appropriate the consciousness of the feminized, that is, emasculated Oriental subject, or to portray him as the stereotypical decadent Oriental despot. The following quote shows how Siddhartha remains a distant, superior observer of the decadence that surrounds him, not allowing himself to "go native,"

> Siddhartha hatte gelernt, Handel zu treiben, Macht über Menschen auszuüben, sich mit dem Weibe zu vergnügen, er hatte gelernt, schöne Kleider zu tragen, Diener zu befehlen, sich in wohlriechenden Wassern zu baden, Er hatte gelernt, zart und sorgfältig bereitete Speisen zu essen, auch den Fisch, auch Fleisch und Vogel, Gewürze und Süßigkeiten, und den Wein zu trinken, der träge und vergessen macht. Er hatte gelernt, mit Würfeln und auf dem Schachbrette zu spielen, Tänzerinnen zuzusehen, sich in der Sänfte tragen zu lassen, auf einem weichen Bett zu schlafen. Aber immer noch hatte er sich von den andern verschieden und ihnen überlegen gefühlt, immer hatte er ihnen mit ein wenig Spott zugesehen, ein wenig spöttischer Verachtung, mit eben jeder Verachtung, wie sie ein Samana stets für Weltleute fühlte. (3:422)

> [Siddhartha had learned how to transact business affairs, to exercise power over people, to amuse himself with women; he had learned to wear fine clothes, to command servants, to bathe in sweet-smelling waters. He had learned to eat sweet and carefully prepared foods, also fish and meat and fowl, spices and dainties, and to drink wine which made him lazy and forgetful. He had learned to play dice and chess, to watch dancers, to be carried in sedan chairs to sleep on a soft bed. But he had always felt different from and superior to the others; he had always watched them a little scornfully, with a slightly mocking dis-

dain, with that disdain which a Samana always feels towards the people
of the world. (61)]

On the surface, Hesse seems to want to distance himself from the
Orientalist/colonialist agenda, but I would argue that Hesse was not really interested in refuting it. Like other contemporary writers and travelers
from Europe, Hesse sought in the "East" an alternative spirituality to an
institutionalized Christianity that was stifling his own creativity. It was an
East, however, that lay in a distant, monumental, ahistorical past. Consequently, the Westerner could access such an East without being beset by
pangs of conscience about the brutal realities of colonialism. It was crucial
to keep early-twentieth-century India as a separate entity, an India that
was presented as degenerate and sorely in need of the West's "civilizing
mission" — a mission constructed to assuage those pangs of conscience.

> "Wie Govinda ist er," dachte er lächelnd, "alle, die ich auf meinem
> Wege antreffe, sind wie Govinda. Alle sind dankbar, obwohl sie selbst
> anspruch auf Dank hätten. Alle sind unterwürfig, alle mögen gern
> Freund sein, gern gehorchen, wenig denken. Kinder sind die Men-
> schen." (3:406)

> [He is like Govinda, he thought, smiling. All whom I meet on the way
> are like Govinda. All are grateful, although they themselves deserve
> thanks. All are subservient, all wish to be my friend, to obey and to
> think little. People are children. (41)]

If people are children, unable to think for themselves, they need lifelong discipline and guidance. The subtext of the white man's burden surfaces clearly here.

Hesse's own search for an alternate spirituality was similar in some ways
to the Charismatic and Pentecostal movements. As Manuel Vásquez per-
ceptively points out, "religion is one of the best vehicles to deal with both
the local and personal and also the global and the universal. . . . [These
movements] have universal messages of salvation and very personal strategies for coping with chaos."[61] Complicating Hesse's personal quest was his
perennial need for money as well as the various crises that befell him (his
son Martin's illness, his wife's schizophrenia, and the aftermath of the First
World War), which led to a need for the kind of cathartic writing that he
hoped *Siddhartha* would offer him. However, there is no shortcut to enlightenment, as he soon realized when faced with an unproductive gap of
almost one and a half years between the drafts of the first and second
parts of *Siddhartha*. Between 1919 and 1920 he managed to write the
first three chapters of the work, then abruptly stopped writing. Whereas the
first part led him on a quest for the ultimate truth and was therefore well
within the bounds of human endeavor, the second part promised the

reader the *attainment* of a nirvanic state of being — a challenge that Hesse knew he could not meet. The ensuing disappointment led to what I consider to be his most honest work, *Steppenwolf.* However, *Siddhartha's* immense popularity — despite Hesse's own misgivings about the success of the work — lies in the fact that on the one hand, Hesse saw himself as a sensitive *interpreter* of the Orient, thus appealing to the Western reader; on the other hand, by identifying himself with a Brahmin (Siddhartha), he offered the Eastern reader a possibility of identification.

But not only that. Hesse's recognition of his inability to offer in *Siddhartha* an ultimate form of redemption led to what I call a Felix Krullian way of organizing the world. Thomas Mann's Felix Krull, in the book of the same name, has the ability to win the favor of others by performing the roles they desire of him. Similarly, Siddhartha acquires the masterful ability to play any part he desires. Since the reader, according to the classic model of the confidence trickster story, colludes with the trickster, she or he is quite happy to be seduced into playing along with this performance. Siddhartha's appeal parallels Krull's in that he is able to not only experience "die große Freude" (the great joy) over sensual experience, but to allow the reader — whether male or female — to vicariously and intensely feel this joy, which is the reason for the otherwise inexplicably continuing popularity of *Siddhartha* in India. When Kamala accuses Siddhartha of being incapable of love, he says: "Ich bin wie du. Auch du liebst nicht — wie könntest du sonst die Liebe als eine Kunst betreiben. Die Menschen von unserer Art können vielleicht nicht lieben. . . ." (3:421; "I am like you. You cannot love either, otherwise how could you practice love as an art? Perhaps people like us cannot love," 59).[62]

Hesse the Orientalist

Siddhartha confirms the androcentric structures that are essential to Orientalism's growth. In this work, Hesse not only uses the prostitute, but also feminizes the Indian male (for instance, in a dream, Govinda turns into a voluptuous woman who accuses Siddhartha of abandoning him). In fact the root of the names Kamaswami and Kamala is *kamam* or sexual desire, symbolizing the excessive and infinitely available sexuality of the native, both male and female. In the figure of Kamaswami, whose energies are sapped by his greed and lust, Hesse constructs the effeminate Indian male along the lines expressed by the British historian Robert Orme (1728–1801): "Breathing in the softest climates, having so few wants and receiving even the luxuries of other nations with little labour from their own soil, the Indian must have become the most effeminate inhabitant of the globe."[63] The colonizer represented by Siddhartha finds such slothful behavior not only contemptible, but is compelled to defeat the corrupt, lying businessman at his own game, once more establishing his authority.

Unlike in the other works discussed in this essay, the relationship between Siddhartha and Kamaswami, or between Siddhartha and Govinda is no longer based on a desire for consensual sex, but on sexual aggression, a kind of possession of violence. Whereas Kamaswami exemplifies the corruptibility of the Oriental, Govinda typifies the passive, mentally deficient, effeminate Indian male.[64] Incapable of striking out on his own, he shows absolute deference to authority and shifts his allegiance from the Samana leader to Siddhartha to Buddha. The relationship between the Orientalist and the Oriental is clearly enunciated in the following lines: "Er sah die Menschen auf eine kindliche oder tierhafte Art dahinleben, welche er zugleich liebte und auch verachtete" (3:419; "He saw people living in a childish or animal-like way, which he both loved and despised," 57).[65]

Kamala, as the Oriental female, is, to apply the words of Edward Said, "less a woman than a display of impressive but verbally inexpressive femininity" (187). The association of an excessive sexuality with the Orient is a common Orientalist discursive element, not sex as contained and containable within the structure of Western morals, but an excess of sex, just as excess of any kind is synonymous with the Oriental. Hence it is the duty of the courtesan Kamala to initiate Siddhartha in the arts of the *Kama Sutra*.[66] After having been consumed to satisfy Siddhartha's sexual needs, this hypersexualized woman's disturbingly excessive (disturbing, because difficult to control) desire is then finally and completely contained: in her death. The parallel between the colonizing of India and Siddhartha's own absolute claim over Kamala's as yet unbounded sexuality is too striking to be ignored, especially in the context of postcolonial theory, which very often uses rape as a metaphor to describe the act of colonization. At the precise moment of total power over her, when he overcomes his initial fear of loss of self in her sexuality, he impregnates her with his seed. She releases her bird from its cage, that is, she gives up her soul to him, makes sure that her procreative energies are directed toward preserving his patrilineal identity by giving him a son, and then dies after recognizing him as the colonial master so to speak.

Interestingly, her death is due to a snakebite. In Hinduism, the snake has a divine status (it is one of the most sacred animals, second only to the cow), unlike the snake in Christianity, which has a less envious role! Within the Christian symbolism of what Hesse calls an Indian tale ("Eine indische Dichtung"), the snake ends Kamala's life just before she receives "enlightenment" from Siddhartha (3:446). Kamala, the former courtesan, is happy to die in Siddhartha's arms because in her eyes he has become the Buddha: "Sie dachte daran, daß sie zu Gotama hatte pilgern wollen, um das Gesicht eines Vollendeten zu sehen, um seinen Frieden zu atmen, und daß sie statt seiner nun ihn gefunden, und daß es gut war, ebenso gut, als wenn sie jenen gesehen hätte." (3:448; "It had been her intention to make a pilgrimage to Gotama, to see the face of the Illustrious One, to obtain some of his peace, and instead she had only found him, and it was good, *just as good as if she had seen the other*" [emphasis added]). India is thus triply colonized as a subservient or sublimated female or feminized body in this work:

1. As oriental man, feminized and passive.

2. As prostitute/courtesan — of the three women in the book, two are prostitutes.

3. As the Earth Mother (an Indian Frau Eva) for redemption — it is only through her that Siddhartha gains nirvana.

In *Siddhartha* Hesse finds a space that is "unpopulated" (as most colonized spaces are). In the interests of territorial expansion, it is incumbent on colonizers to perceive the lands that they colonize as blank spaces, unpopulated. Understandably, it is not expedient for the colonizer to attempt to fraternize with the native. As the colonized, the Indians are hardly material for such consensual relationships. Consequently, Siddhartha removes himself from the world of physical desire and suffering in a rather arrogant imitation of the Gautama, and dons the latter's "robes," proving that knowledge and wisdom are not necessarily the prerogative of the East!

As in almost all of Hesse's works, the feminine — here the whole country of India is weakened because of an assumed passivity — is sacrificed in the end to recuperate the Western colonizer and to re-establish an indisputably heterosexual patriarchal order. Interestingly enough, in all the other works discussed in this essay, Hesse consistently combats this patriarchal order that tries to impose heterosexual norms on him. However, *Siddhartha* has an added dimension, that of race. The intimate relationship between Orientalism and gender always contains this third, less visible aspect. It is instructive to read what Laura Stoler has to say in this context:

> Discourses of sexuality [. . .] could redraw the "interior frontiers" of national communities, frontiers that were secured through — and sometimes in collision with — the boundaries of race. These nationalist discourses were predicated on *exclusionary* cultural principles that did more than divide the middle class from the poor. They marked out those whose claims to property rights, citizenship, and public relief were worthy of recognition and whose were not. [Emphasis added.][67]

Hesse is also defined by these "exclusionary cultural principles."

Der Steppenwolf (1927)

There is no dissimulation in this most complex of Hesse's works. *Demian* and *Narcissus and Goldmund* possess an almost Harlequin-romance quality where plot, characters, style, and erotic scenes are formulaic and hence eminently accessible, especially to young readers. After all, as Rabine points out, the force of Harlequin "comes from its ability to combine, often in the same image, the [hero's] fantasy escape from these restraints and her idealized, romanticized, and eroticized compliance with them."[68] Although Harlequin romances are mostly concerned with women attempting to "balance the competing demands of work and love,"[69] Hesse's male protagonists also attempt to "imagine a different world, one in which the emotions matter more than workplace rules."[70]

Hesse's protagonist Harry Haller enters the text as a middle-aged man. We know very little about his childhood and adolescence. There is no love object to complete him. His alter ego is a wolf. But this is not a romanticized tale of a hero's quest for a unitary self. For the first time, Hesse breaks out of the mold of omniscient sage. Haller has no inhibitions about flaunting his "outsiderness" to society. The middle-class, heterosexual identity that has been imposed on him has begun to stifle him. Craig Bernhard Palmer expresses Harry's dilemma as "the fusion and confusion of homosocial and heterosexual desires."[71] The only way to resolve this desire on multiple levels, according to Palmer, is to enable Haller to make love to a man and a woman simultaneously. Haller falls in love, after all, with Hermine when she is dressed as a man. "In other words, homosociality becomes 'heterosociality,' and heterosexuality becomes homosexuality. Similarly, while Harry attempts to connect with Pablo intellectually and thus court him according to normal homosocial practice, Pablo responds to him sensually and suggests a sexual threesome in which Harry can make love to a man and a woman simultaneously."[72] Palmer rightly concludes that at the end both Hermine and the manly mother "can and must disappear so that the protagonist can realize the unified desire that he could previously only imagine by dividing it and attributing it to two genders."[73]

Hermine is like an androgynous flapper,[74] with distinct phallic attributes. According to Liz Conor, the flapper "stood for modernity's quest for truth, but on the other hand she represented sexual agency," an agency that might subvert traditional heterosexual norms.[75] Hermine is not averse to the gender mobility of "mannish" fashions. As Conor points out, "The boyishness of the Flapper was seen to be symptomatic of a rejection of the sexual responsibilities of maternity and womanhood proper,"[76] that is, of heterosexually normed behavioral constraints. But, as Conor adds, the Flapper ultimately remains heterosexual, since her "androgyny seemed

only to heterosexualize her, because it was effected, like modern heterosexuality, at the level of the eye."[77]

Unlike in *Demian* and *Narziß und Goldmund,* Hesse does not have
Hermine metamorphose into a Hermann, but instead attempts, in portraying her, to transcend the Jungian anima and animus and their integration to a point where an undivided self has no physical or metaphysical
equivalent (much like Nietzsche's attempt to go beyond a mere synthesis
of opposites). There is yet another difference between Harry Haller and
the others: the sense of shame he feels that prevents homosexuals from
reclaiming "disowned parts of the self and thereby [transforming their]
sense of self."[78] René Kaufman and Lev Raphael find this kind of shame expressed in sentences such as "Harry Haller [sei] ein Schädling und vater-
landsloser Geselle . . . und daß es natürlich mit dem Vaterland nicht
anders als übel stehen könne, solange solche Menschen und solche Gedanken geduldet würden und die Jugend zu sentimentalen Menschheits-
gedanken statt zur kriegerischen Rache am Erbfeind erzogen werde"
("Harry Haller was a noxious insect and a man who disowned his native
land, and that it stood to reason that no good could come to the country
so long as such persons and such ideas were tolerated and the minds of
the young turned to sentimental ideas of humanity instead of to revenge
by arms upon the hereditary foe") or "Es gibt für mich kein 'Vaterland'
und keine Ideale mehr" ("I have no country or ideals left").[79] They rec-
ommend the following procedure for escaping it:

> We must have new self-affirming words to say to ourselves to *replace*
> *the old shaming words, thereby engaging language.* Then we must ac-
> tually experience new feelings of love and respect for our essential self.
> That step engages affect. Finally we must actually create a new scene
> by actively visualizing someone else speaking the new words inside of
> us. It should be someone with whom we currently have a mutually
> respecting relationship or someone in the past like that.[80] [Emphasis
> added.]

Haller enters the Magic Theater in this very effort to engage language and
to "replace the old shaming words." He finds new languages at the Masked
Ball. Here is a Bakhtinian carnivalesque world where the themes of the car-
nival twist, mutate, and invert standard themes of societal makeup.[81] The
Masked Ball allows Haller to mock those in authority and satirize official
ideas about the unalterable nature of social identity, history, destiny, and
fate. This festive pleasure turns the world topsy-turvy, into a place where
destruction and creation are one.[82]

The women in *Demian, Siddhartha,* and *Narziß und Goldmund* are
erased. But in *Steppenwolf* it is the woman Hermine who orders Harry to
kill her as part of this cycle of destruction and creation. Pablo explains to
Harry that the latter's longing "nichts Andres bedeuten als den Wunsch,

Ihrer sogenannten Persönlichkeit ledig zu werden." (4:166; "means simply the wish to be relieved of your so-called personality," 196). His
individuality has to be shattered before he realizes that the belief in an
enduring unity "hat manche unangenehme Folgen" (4:180; "has many
unpleasant consequences"; 213). Pablo continues: "Wir zeigen dem-
jenigen, der das Auseinanderfallen seines Ichs erlebt hat, daß er die Stücke
jederzeit in beliebiger Ordnung neu zusammenstellen und daß er damit
eine unendliche Mannigfaltigkeit des Lebensspieles erzielen kann" (4:181;
"We demonstrate to anyone whose soul has fallen to pieces that he can
rearrange these pieces of a previous self in what order he pleases, and so
attain to an endless multiplicity of moves in the game of life," 214). In fact,
the invitation to Haller to enter the Magic Theater is meant "nur für Verrückte" (4:156; "for madmen only," 182). The German word "verrückt"
— to be mad or crazy — is much closer to what Haller experiences if one
separates the prefix "ver-" from "rücken," that is, dis-place, or re-move
from reality, for example move into an alternate reality. Since the world is
turned upside down in the carnevalesque Magic Theater, multiple sexualities are possible: "*Hermann* . . . erzählte mir nachher, *sie* habe diese
Frau nicht als Mann erobert, sondern als Frau, mit dem Zauber von Lesbos" (4:158–59; "Herman [. . .] told me afterwards that she had made a
conquest of her not as a man but as a woman, with the spell of Lesbos,"
186 [emphasis added]). (The use of the feminine pronoun "sie" in place
of the male noun "Hermann" reveals slippages in gender identity!). When
Harry stabs the reflection of Hermine with the reflection of a knife, it is
his final attempt to retain a cohesive and coherent identity. Hesse still uses
the woman, Hermine, to "heal" Haller; it is she who helps him laugh at
the game of life. At the end of the text, the many "Hallers" come to
recognize the healing promise of laughter, which has the potential to
destroy Harry Haller's singular ego. The symbolic death that Hermine
undergoes returns to her an identity that she can choose to combine with
Haller's — or not! This fleeting moment of agency for a woman is unusual in Hesse's works, but it underscores much more clearly his ongoing
struggle with his own sexuality. The fact that Hermine adopts the role of
aggressor and commands Haller to eradicate her from his consciousness
seems to indicate that when he re-emerges from the closet-like Magic
Theater, Haller (and Hesse?) is finally ready and willing to openly accept
and celebrate the ambiguities inherent in eroticism.

Narziß und Goldmund (1930)

The progression in Hesse's lifelong struggle to find a stable gender identity reveals itself in the titles of his works. In *Demian* the love object lives
in the Jungian collective unconscious of the protagonist, Emil Sinclair.

Siddhartha is the expression of an increasingly desperate search for alternate modes of existence, whether sensual or spiritual. *Steppenwolf* allows Haller for the first time to experience the creative fragmentation of what he had considered to be a singular ego. He discovers within himself various seemingly conflicting economies of desire.

Three years later, Hesse wrote a text the title of which seems to indicate a retreat into a pre-*Steppenwolf* state characterized by a unitary identity. It is clear from the title *Narziß und Goldmund* that the story is about two male protagonists and their relationship with each other. The title refashions the myth of Narcissus and changes it in interesting ways, making it possible for the protagonists to combat a heteronormative society on various fronts. Interestingly, the English translation recuperates the heterosexual. Geoffrey Dunlop's English translation of *Narziß und Goldmund*, entitled *Death and the Lover* removes whatever insights Haller had gained. Dunlop's English title is especially devastating because it implies the impossibility of a living and breathing relationship of consensual homosexuality.

Book Three of the homoerotic stories of Ovid's *Metamorphosis* tells of how Narcissus is loved by both girls and boys. He is cursed by a boy whom he has scorned and falls mortally in love with another "lovely boy" in the reflection of a pool. Echo, the nymph who falls in love with Narcissus but cannot speak because of Juno's curse, exhibits great similarities to Hesse's own construction of women. They are bereft of language, almost deprived of consciousness, and can only echo what men say — they are "Mimic Women," so to speak.[83] It is not coincidental that Hesse chooses to pair Narcissus with Goldmund and the latter's power of golden speech — something that is denied to Echo.

The first few pages of *Narziß und Goldmund* suffice to show what Palmer calls "the romance plot of monastic male homoeroticism":[84]

> [Sie] waren desto mehr von Narziß bezaubert, dem Wunderknaben, dem schönen Jüngling mit dem eleganten Griechisch, mit dem ritterlich tadellosen Benehmen, mit dem stillen, eindringlichen Denkerblick und den schmalen, schön und streng gezeichneten Lippen.[85]

> [[They] were all the more enamored of Narcissus, the handsome prodigy who possessed elegant Greek, impeccable manners, quietly penetrating thinker's eyes, and beautiful, sharply outlined lips. (5)]

Clara Tuite's description of the relationship between the Abbott and the Novice in Matthew Lewis's *The Monk* (1796)[86] could apply equally well to the homoerotic relationship between Narcissus and Goldmund in its specifically pedagogical and pederastic qualities, the kind of relationship, as Tuite explains, "which Foucault has defined in *The Use of Pleasure* as a characteristic homoerotic relationship between a younger and older man, based on an erotics of restraint, or "self-denial."[87] The monastic setting is most visible in *Narziß und Goldmund,* but the architectonics of monastic life are present in Hesse's other works as well, whether it is the cloistered, hallowed gaming halls in the Castalia of *Magister Ludi,* the forested yogic seclusion in *Siddhartha,* or the transgressively cloistered world of Cain in *Demian.* The Magic Theater in *Steppenwolf* frees Harry Haller from the restraints of the heterosocial world, but it inducts him into a circumscribed realm, ironically called immortal, where the players are pocket sized and Hermine can be killed because "sie hat es selbst so gewollt, ich habe nur ihren eigenen Wunsch erfüllt" (4:200; ". . .it was her own desire. I have only fulfilled her own wish," 238). As Foucault suggests, "repression is not the elimination of sexuality but a mechanism for the production or elaboration of a specific form of sexuality."[88] In each of these enclosed spaces, the protagonist has his sexual object safely transformed, repressed and/or eliminated.

> Narziß hatte recht wohl bemerkt, welch ein holder Goldvogel ihm da zugeflogen war. Er, der in seiner Vornehmheit Vereinsamte, hatte alsbald in Goldmund den Verwandten gewittert, obwohl er in allem sein Gegenspiel zu sein schien. . . . Aber die Gegensätze überspannte ein Gemeinsames. . . . *beide hatten sie vom Schicksal eine besondere Mahnung mitbekommen.*[89] (4:282; emphasis added)

> Narcissus knew only too well what a *charming golden bird had flown to him.* This hermit soon sensed a kindred soul in Goldmund, in spite of their contrasts. . . . But something they had in common bridged these contrasts: . . . *both bore the special mark of fate.* (17)

The "special mark of fate" had surfaced in *Demian* as the mark of Cain. Interestingly, the mark of Cain has been associated not just with the first murder in Judeo-Christian history, but also with racism,[90] and any "aberrant" sexual behavior, including homosexuality.

Goldmund spends a lifetime channeling his desires into sculpted figures. Two figures emerge from his artistic efforts: the universal mother in the form of the Madonna, and his love object, Narcissus, whom he sculpts to represent St. John, the beloved of Christ. Not coincidentally, Narcissus is given the name John after taking his vows (4:486). Even more striking is the fact that the early Christian church's greatest preacher, John, the bishop of Constantinople (349–407 C.E.), was known as Chrysostomos — "golden mouth" or "Goldmund" — because of his powers of oratory.[91] Toward the end of *Narziß und Goldmund,* the two protagonists are joined by the common name John.

When confronted by Narcissus, Goldmund is overwhelmed by desire and tries to restrain himself. It is not a denial of his passion, but rather an affirmation of his love, in which sexual tension is heightened.

Er hielt sich. Er bändigte sein Herz, er zwang seinen Magen, er jagte den Schwindel aus seinem Kopf. Er durfte jetzt keine Schwäche zeigen. (4:487; emphasis added)

[He controlled himself. He subdued his heart, forced his stomach to be calm, willed the dizziness out of his head. He could not show any weakness now. (262)]

Goldmund's adoration of the face symbolically hidden beneath the cowl — what Foucault calls "the covered face that solicits desire and the pleasure of deferral" — is marked by the restraint of the pederastic erotic economy, which involved, as Foucault points out, the necessity of "transforming ephemeral love into a mutual, egalitarian, and lasting relationship — that is, the sublimation of erotic interest into friendship."[92] The mechanism for the production or elaboration of the specific form of sexuality that Foucault talks about becomes obvious a few pages later in the novel. Narcissus sees in his friend's face "etwas blühen, das ihm seit den Knabenjahren nicht mehr geblüht hatte" (4:511; "something [flower] that had not flowered there since his boyhood years," 290). It is a smile of love and surrender.

Goldmund's use of the Madonna figure is part of his effort to contain his art within heterosexual norms. Hers is a syncretic role, providing a palimpsest for the actual source of inspiration — Narcissus/St. John. At the same time, her presence is essential for transforming his unrequited physical love into art.

In *Demian,* the semiotic seeps through the symbolic. Sinclair tries, at least outwardly, to maintain heterosocial and -sexual relations. According to Julia Kristeva, the semiotic is unnameable, whereas the symbolic asserts the power to name (just as Sinclair in *Demian* names the woman Beatrice). The heterosexual symbolic world denies Goldmund the power to name his male love-object. However, unlike in Demian, the universal mother is an image of Goldmund's own mother. There is, to paraphrase Kristeva, an even stronger semiotic relationship between this mother and Goldmund, *beyond* the constraints of the symbolic world structured by patriarchy.

The women Goldmund encounters within the parameters of accepted social and sexual behavior have no individuality. His vagabond life takes him from village to village, from woman to woman. Whether it is Lise, the gypsy, or the knight's daughter Lydia, he seeks to extract an essence from all these women, an essence that will allow him to sculpt his ultimate woman. She is the "original mother," the earth mother, Frau Eva. Narcissus tells him: "Du schläfst an der Brust der Mutter, ich wache in der Wüste. Mir scheint die Sonne, [. . .] deine Träume sind von Mädchen, meine von Knaben . . . (4:306; "You sleep at the mother's breast; I wake in the desert. For me the sun shines; for you the moon and the stars. Your dreams are of girls; mine of boys . . .," 45). The phrase "Brust der Mutter" takes on new meaning in the context of homosexuality when one thinks of Siddhartha's dream in which he is suckling at Govinda's breast. Or when Sinclair says: "Auch hatte ich Träume, in denen meine Vereinigung mit ihr sich auf neue gleichnishafte Arten vollzog." (3:353; "I had dreams, too, in which my union with [Frau Eva] was consummated in new symbolic acts," 156). The return to the semiotic, that is, the womb, gives the male protagonist the means to avoid a heterosexual patriarchal reality and remain in a "muttermythischen"[93] utopia that may or may not offer absolute equality, freedom and sensuality, but most certainly provides a sanctuary from pressure to conform to heterosexual norms.

Concluding Remarks

It is instructive to look at the chronology of Hesse's works in terms of his own developing homoeroticism. In 1917, *Demian* offered a first clear glimpse of Hesse's recognition of alternative sexualities. In 1922 he escaped to the East in his writing (interestingly, he did not set foot on Indian soil because of anxiety about dirt and poverty[94]). As mentioned earlier, I see his *Siddhartha* as a respite from multiple crises in his life, as well as anxiety about his own sexuality. Resorting to what I previously referred to as a luminous and numinous style of writing, Hesse finished the work, appealing to entire generations of grateful readers who were searching for an instant formula for nirvana. Had *Siddhartha* contained the ultimate truth about existence and the afterlife, Hesse would have put away pen and paper and sat under yet another Bodhi tree awaiting nirvana. However, his dissatisfaction with life continued and found expression in the year 1927 in *Der Steppenwolf,* perhaps the most honest of all Hesse's works and hence the one in which he was at his most vulnerable. It describes the schizophrenia that tortured him until the Immortals help him defy the old order. Finally, in 1930 the consensual homosexual relationship for which he had been searching found artistic expression in a return to the sanctuary of the semiotic chora, where Narcissus and Goldmund become one in what could be perceived as a state of death.[95]

There is no incontrovertible evidence to prove that Hesse was anything other than heterosexual. However, I have attempted to unravel the homoeroticism that his texts conceal. And the consensual homosexual relationship that one finds in each of the works I have discussed seems to take on a different form. His 1943 magnum opus, *Das Glasperlenspiel* (The Glass Bead Game), which earned him the Nobel Prize for Literature, infinitely defers the potential homoerotic tension between Knecht and Designori, placing it in an increasingly mathematical, cerebral realm of the "game," which sucks the lifeblood out of a potential relationship and ends in the death of the "servant" Knecht during his attempt to save his friend's son, Tito. In creating a male domain, Castalia, in the distant future (the year 2025), Hesse encounters difficulties similar to those in *Siddhartha* — such idyllic and utopian structures do not resolve the problems confronting him in his own century, in his own life.

Notes

[1] I would call Hesse's *Siddhartha* a popular study guide to Eastern mysticism.

[2] Goethe's epistolary and loosely autobiographical novel, *Die Leiden des jungen Werther* (The Sorrows of Young Werther, 1774), written when he was twenty-five years old, had a tremendous impact in Europe. Napoleon carried the book throughout most of his campaigns. It also started the phenomenon known as the "Werther-Fieber" and even led to copycat suicides (the protagonist Werther commits suicide at the end of the novel): supposedly more than 2,000 readers took their lives!

[3] The German student movement (commonly referred to as the "Achtundsechziger-Bewegung," or "movement of 1968") was largely a reaction against the perceived authoritarianism and hypocrisy of the German government and other Western governments. A wave of protests — some violent — swept Germany, fueled by overreaction by the police and encouraged by contemporary protest movements across the world (against the Vietnam war, against racial discrimination in the US, against the conditions in the so-called Third World). Following more than a century of conservatism among German students, the movement also marked a major shift to the left and radicalization of student politics.

[4] Named after Florian Illies's *Generation Golf: Eine Inspektion* (Berlin: Argon, 2000). Illies criticizes those born between 1965 and 1975 as being the most apathetic, self-indulgent generation of the last century.

[5] Müller (1823–1900) was best known for the critical edition of the *Rg-Veda* that he undertook in 1849 and completed in 1874.

[6] Rishis were sages who lived as dedicated vedic yogins in Indian spiritual history prior to yoga during the time in which the Vedas were written. Vedas are the first spiritual scriptures that have existed in written form.

[7] The Goethe Institutes in India are named Max Müller *Bhavan* in Friedrich Max Müller's honor.

[8] In 2002 the film was made available on VHS and DVD, mastered from the newly restored 35mm negative.

[9] Theodore Ziolkowski, "A Celebration of Hermann Hesse," April 2003, in *World Literature Today*. http://findarticles.com/p/articles/mi_go2101/is_200304/ai _n9280263 (accessed March 2, 2007).

[10] Jörg Drews, "'. . .bewundert viel und viel gescholten. . .': Hermann Hesses Werk zwischen Erfolg und Mißachtung bei Publikum und Literaturkritik," in *Hermann Hesse Today / Hermann Hesse Heute*, ed. Ingo Cornils and Osman Durrani. Amsterdamer Beiträge zur neueren Germanistik 58 (New York: Rodopi 2005), 27.

[11] In the year 1595 an anonymous Latin tract entitled "Ob die Weiber Menschen seyn?" (Are Women Human Beings?) was published. Translated into German in 1618, the tract was typical for the contentious debates that took place in the sixteenth century about woman as a human entity. This misogynistic attitude defined the spirit of that time period. The tract says among other things: "Wann ein Weib eine Tochter gebiert, so hat sie ihres gleichen, ein Monstrum nemblich geborn ... Es ist kein Thier so gifftig, das Weib ist noch gifftiger, ja teufflischer und boßhafftiger als der Teufel selbst ... Und gleich wie der Fuchs, der ausgezogen wird, erst nutz ist, also sind auch etliche Weiber erst etwas nutz, wenn sie sterben." (When a woman gives birth to a daughter, she has borne something equal to herself, namely a monster ... There is no animal so poisonous; woman is more poisonous, yes more devilish and evil than the devil himself ... And the same as the fox is only useful when it is skinned, so women are only worth something when they die.) "Die Standard" (unknown author) 14 November 2002.

[12] Frederick A. Lubich, "Hermann Hesses *Narziß und Goldmund* oder 'Der Weg zur Mutter': Von der Anima Mundi zur Magna Mater und Madonna (Ciccone)," in *Hermann Hesse Today / Hermann Hesse Heute,* ed. Cornils and Durrani, 55.

[13] David Albertson, "Wolfgang Iser," *Stanford Presidential Lectures in the Humanities and Arts* (2000), 2. http://prelectur.stanford.edu/lecturers/iser/.

[14] http://prelectur.stanford.edu/lecturers/iser/.

[15] http://prelectur.stanford.edu/lecturers/iser/.

[16] Agnès Cardinal, "Teaching Hermann Hesse's *Der Steppenwolf:* Some Reflections on Readers' Response," in *Hermann Hesse Today Today / Hermann Hesse Heute,* ed. Cornils and Durrani, 43.

[17] Cardinal, "Teaching Hermann Hesse's *Der Steppenwolf,"* 43.

[18] Hermann Hesse, *Aus Indien: Aufzeichnungen, Tagebücher, Gedichte, Betrachtungen und Erzählungen,* Suhrkamp Taschenbuch 562 (Frankfurt am Main: Suhrkamp, 1980), 336.

[19] Like Friedrich Wilhelm Schlegel, the German Romantic poet (1772–1829), Hesse criticizes modern culture for its analytic, reflective form of rationality, which encourages a disenchanting view of nature.

[20] The Swiss anthropologist and sociologist Johann Jakob Bachofen is most often connected with his theory of matriarchy, or *Mutterrecht,* first published in his 1861 book of the same name. This presented a radically new view of the role of women in a broad range of ancient societies. Bachofen assembled documentation meant to demonstrate that motherhood is the source of human society, religion, morality, and decorum. He concluded by connecting archaic mother right with the Christian worship of the Virgin Mary. Bachofen's conclusions about archaic matriarchy resonate to this day.

[21] *Advaita* = non-dual; *Veda* = knowledge; *Anta* = end or goal. Nondualism. The doctrine was consolidated by the Indian philosopher Adi Shankara (788 C.E.–820 C.E.).

[22] Novalis, pseudonym for Georg Philipp Friedrich Freiherr von Hardenberg (1772–1801). A leader of the so-called Jena Romantics, he is best known for his unfinished novels *Heinrich von Ofterdingen* and *Die Lehrlinge zu Sais.*

[23] Buddha: one who has achieved a state of perfect enlightenment. In the Pali Canon (the collection of primary Pali language texts which form the doctrinal foundation of Theravada Buddhism), the term "buddha" refers to anyone who has become enlightened (i.e., awakened to the truth, or *Dharma*) on her or his own, without a teacher to point out the Dharma.

[24] Hermann Hesse, *Siddhartha*, in *Sämtliche Werke*, vol. 3: *Die Romane: Roßhalde. Knulp. Demian. Siddhartha*, ed. Volker Michels (Frankfurt am Main: Suhrkamp, 2001), 406. All quotations from the novel in this essay are from this edition and will be referenced by the volume and page numbers.

[25] Hermann Hesse, *Siddhartha*, trans. Hilda Rosner (New York: New Directions, 1951), 56. All translations from *Siddhartha* in this essay are taken from this translation and will be referenced by page number.

[26] Kamakshi P. Murti, *India: The Seductive and Seduced 'Other' of German Orientalism* (Westport, CT: Greenwood Press, 2001), 111–12.

[27] Gyan Prakash, "Writing Post-Orientalist Histories of the Third World: Perspectives from Indian Historiography," *Comparative Studies in Society and History* 32.2 (April 1990), 393.

[28] Prakash, "Writing Post-Orientalist Histories," 393.

[29] Müller grants to the Aryans of northwest Europe a natural right to rule over the world: "The Teutonic race, the most vigorous and enterprising of all the members of the Aryan family . . . planted new states in the West and regenerated the *effete* kingdoms of the East . . . they preached Christianity and at last practiced it by abolishing slavery of body and mind among the slaves of West Indian landholders, and the slaves of Brahmanical soulholders, and they greeted at last the very homes from which the Aryan family had started." (Emphasis added.) Friedrich Max Müller, *Lectures on the Science of Language, Delivered at the Royal Institution of Great Britain in April, May & June 1861* (Delhi: Munshi Ram Manohar Lal, 1965), 236.

[30] Quoted from Cornils and Durrani, organizers, Hermann Hesse Heute/Hermann Hesse Today, Programme and Abstracts of Papers, http://www.german.leeds.ac.uk/utopie/hesseheute.htm (accessed 27 April 2009).

[31] Evi Petropoulou, "Gender and Modernity in the Work of Hesse and Kazantzakis." *CLCWeb: Comparative Literature and Culture* 2.1 (2000): http://docs.lib.purdue.edu/clcweb/vol2/iss1/5.

[32] In the following is a brief account of my understanding of the terms "homosexual," "homosocial," and "homoerotic": By "homosexual," I mean the state of being sexually attracted primarily to persons of the same sex, having sexual activity with a person of the same sex. My understanding of "homosocial" comes from the feminist and queer theorist Eve Kosofsky Sedgwick, who defined the term as "social bonds between persons of the same sex." Sedgwick saw homosocial desire as "the affective or social force, the glue . . . that shapes an important relationship" (1–2). She went on to explain that homosocial bonds can take many forms, and that there is a "continuum between homosocial and homosexual" (1). She also pointed out that the "glue" of desire can affect "an important relationship" in positive or negative ways (2). (Eve Kosofsky Sedgwick, *Between Men: English Literature and Male Homosocial Desire* [New York: Columbia UP, 1985]). The "homoerotic" concerns

homosexual love and desire and their arousal. All three terms are on a continuum, hence the difficulty in trying to define them as discrete terms. This ambiguity is crucial to my reading of Hesse's works.

[33] Miguel Serrano commenting on his book, *C. G. Jung and Hermann Hesse: A Record of Two Friendships* (Einsiedeln, Switzerland: Daimon Publishers, 1997). http://www.feastofhateandfear.com/archives/serrano1.html (accessed 27 April 2009).

[34] For instance, Martin Pfeifer, ed., *Hermann Hesses weltweite Wirkung: Internationale Rezeptionsgeschichte* (Frankfurt am Main: Suhrkamp Taschenbuch, 1977); Volker Michels, ed., *Materialien zu Hermann Hesses 'Der Steppenwolf'* (Frankfurt am Main: Suhrkamp Taschenbuch, 1973); Volker Michels, ed., *Materialien zu Hermann Hesses 'Das Glasperlenspiel,'* 2 vols. (Frankfurt am Main: Suhrkamp Taschenbuch, 1973); Christian Immo Schneider, *Hermann Hesse* (Munich: C. H. Beck, 1991).

[35] Joseph Mileck, *Hermann Hesse* (Berkeley: U of California P, 1981, xi.

[36] Angelika Rauch-Rapaport, "The Melancholic Structure of the Mind: The Absence of Object Relations in the Work of Hermann Hesse," in *Hermann Hesse Today Today / Hermann Hesse Heute,* ed. Cornils and Durrani, 83.

[37] Rauch-Rapaport, "The Melancholic Structure of the Mind," 84.

[38] Petra Fricke, "Darstellung und Bedeutung der weiblichen Figuren in Hermann Hesses Romanen der zwanziger Jahre" paper submitted to the Westfälische Wilhelms-Universität, 1996. http://www.gss.ucsb.edu/projects/hesse/papers/fricke.html (accessed April 2009).

[39] Craig Bernard Palmer, "The Significance of Homosexual Desire in Modern German Literature," http://www.gss.ucsb.edu/projects/hesse/papers/palmer-chap5.pdf (accessed April 2009).

[40] Palmer, "The Significance of Homosexual Desire," 2.

[41] Hermann Hesse,. *Demian,* in *Sämtliche Werke,* vol. 3, ed. Volker Michels (Frankfurt am Main: Suhrkamp, 2001), 283. Further quotations from this novel are from this edition and are indicated by the volume and page number. English translations are from Hermann Hesse, *Demian: The Story of Emil Sinclair's Youth,* translated by Michael Roloff and Michael Lebeck (New York: Harper & Row, 1965) and are indicated by page number.

[42] Edward Said, *Orientalism* (New York: Random House, 1978; Vintage House Edition, 1979), 188.

[43] Palmer, "The Significance of Homosexual Desire," 2.

[44] James Giles, *The Nature of Sexual Desire* (Westport, CT: Praeger/Greenwood, 2004), 87.

[45] For Kristeva, the symbolic is the sphere of representation, images, and all forms of fully articulated language.

[46] Kristeva uses the term *chora* to mean "a modality of significance in which the linguistic sign is not yet articulated as the absence of the object and as the distinction between the real and the symbolic." Julia Kristeva, *Revolution in Poetic Language,* 26.

[47] Palmer, "The Significance of Homosexual Desire," 2.

[48] Günter Baumann explains a similar kiss in *Siddhartha* as follows: "Wisdom cannot be taught, truth can only be experienced and this cannot be brought about intentionally. That is why Siddhartha asks his friend to kiss him. And obviously this kiss is more successful than words: Govinda is puzzled but because he loves his friend and he has some strange intuition, he kisses Siddhartha on his forehead. This kiss is the symbol of unintentional self-abandon, dedication and devotion of the ego to completeness, to the union of the universe, to the divine and this kiss suddenly brings about the unexpected experience of enlightenment the old man has looked for in vain." I see a situation analogous to that in *Demian* — Govinda's "strange intuition" is that of his desire for Siddhartha, a desire that he has tried to sublimate by following the Buddha. http://www.gss.ucsb.edu/projects/hesse/papers/baumann-hesse-and-india.pdf (accessed 3 February 2007). The fresh blood on Sinclair's lips reminds me of the blood a woman sheds in losing her virginity.

[49] When I came to the United States in the 1980s, I was not surprised to be greeted as *the* interpreter of Hesse and *Siddhartha* on every university and college campus where I taught. Hence, if someone had to teach a course on Hesse, it seemed to colleagues and students alike that I was the logical choice. Student enrollments also showed that Hesse, and especially his *Siddhartha*, was a particular favorite. Now more than ever I felt it incumbent on me to deconstruct some of Hesse's works and make his portrayal of women more transparent, especially since I myself was experiencing a mounting sense of being eroticized and exoticized. It was as if I had become a character in *Siddhartha*! At first, I could not comprehend this insistence in co-opting me into a colonial discourse that I was trying to battle at every turn. But then it occurred to me that this was the way the West perceived the East: through a two-way mirror of its own making. I was part of a discourse about a uniquely religion-obsessed India (and a uniquely transcendental Indian wisdom) — interpretable however only by the West — that had successfully penetrated our ostensibly postcolonial world. It is a discourse that permeates Hesse's writings.

[50] Murti, *India: The Seductive and Seduced 'Other' of German Orientalism*, 97.

[51] Rev. William Butler, D.D., *The Land of the Veda: Being Personal Reminiscences of India; Its People, Castes, Thugs, and Fakirs; Its Religions, Mythology, Principal Monuments, Palaces, and Mausoleums: Together with the Incidents of the Great Sepoy Rebellion, and its Results to Christianity and Civilization. With a Map of India, and 42 Illustrations. Also, Statistical Tables of Christian Missions, and a Glossary of Indian Terms Used in this Work and in Missionary Correspondence* (New York: Carlton & Lanahan; San Francisco: E. Thomas; Cincinnati: Hitchcock & Walden; 1872), 16.

[52] Ann Laura Stoler, *Race and the Education of Desire: Foucault's 'The History of Sexuality' and the Colonial Order of Things* (Durham, NC and London: Duke UP, 1995), 4.

[53] Stoler, *Race and the Education of Desire*, 6.

[54] Werner Bieder, *Erfahrungen mit der Basler Mission und ihrer Geschichte* (Basel: Helbing & Lichtenhahn, 1991), 79.

[55] Siddhartha sits beneath the Bodhi Tree in the ancient sacred forests of Uruvela (modern Gaya in Bihar, Northern India) and enters into a state of deep meditation.

Three days and nights pass, and his goal of enlightenment is realized. He becomes the Buddha, meaning the "Enlightened One."

[56] Prakash, "Writing Post-Orientalist Histories," 386. Sir William Jones (1746–94) was an English philologist and student of ancient India, particularly known for his proposition of the existence of a relationship among Indo-European languages. He served as a Supreme Court justice in India and founded the Asiatic Society, which stimulated worldwide interest in India and the Orient. James Mill (1773–1836) was a Scottish historian, economist, political theorist, and ·philosopher, and father of John Stuart Mill. In 1806 he began his *History of India,* which he took twelve years to complete. Although the work itself effected a complete change in the way the British governed India, it should be noted that Mill never visited the Indian colony, relying solely on documentary material and archival records in compiling his work. This fact has been understandably severely criticized, especially by the notable economist Amartya Sen, who won the Nobel Prize for economics in 1998.

[57] Prakash, "Writing Post-Orientalist Histories," 386–87.

[58] Kama = desire; Sutra = thread, which means a discourse threaded on a series of aphorisms. The *Kama Sutra* is an ancient Indian text, a *compendium* that was collected into its present form in the second century C.E. It is widely considered to be the standard work on love in Sanskrit literature. A small portion of the work deals with human sexual behavior.

[59] Murti, *India: The Seductive and Seduced "Other" of German Orientalism,* 36.

[60] Carol A. Breckenridge and Peter van der Veer, eds., *Orientalism and the Postcolonial Predicament — Perspectives on South Asia* (Philadelphia: U of Pennsylvania P, 1993), 23.

[61] From transcript of American Public Media program "Speaking of Faith," an interview by host Krista Tippett with Manuel Vásquez, co-author of *Globalizing the Sacred: Religion across the Americas"* (New Brunswck, NJ: Rutgers UP, 2003) broadcast on 29 July 2007.

[62] Hesse. *Sämtliche Werke.* Herausgegeben von Volker Michels. Frankfurt am Main: Suhrkamp Verlag, Band 3, 421.

[63] Quoted in Sara Suleri, *The Rhetoric of English India* (Chicago: U of Chicago P, 1992), 16.

[64] Murti, *India: The Seductive and Seduced 'Other' of German Orientalism,* 113.

[65] Murti, *India: The Seductive and Seduced 'Other' of German Orientalism,* 113.

[66] "The cultured person, and in particular the courtesan of Sanskrit literature, was expected to be educated in sixty-four *kalas* (arts and sciences), a term often equated with *silpa* 'art' or *vidya* 'science.'" (Ainslie Thomas Embree, Stephen N. Hay, William De Bary, *Sources of Indian Tradition: From the Beginning to 1800.* [New York: Columbia UP, 1988), 256.

[67] Stoler, *Race and the Education of Desire,* 7–8.

[68] Leslie Rabine, "Romance in the Age of Electronics: Harlequin Enterprises" (1985), in *Feminisms: An Anthology of Literary Theory and Criticism,* ed. Robyn R. Warhol and Diane Price Herndl (New Jersey: Rutgers UP, 1997), 978–79.

[69] Vicinus, Martha, and Deborah Rosenfelt, "Preface," in *Feminist Studies*, No. 1 (1985), 4.

[70] Vicinus, Martha, and Deborah Rosenfelt, "Preface," in *Feminist Studies*, No. 1 (1985), 4.

[71] Palmer, "The Significance of Homosexual Desire," 2.

[72] Palmer, "The Significance of Homosexual Desire," 2.

[73] Palmer, "The Significance of Homosexual Desire," 2.

[74] The term "flapper" is a British coinage that arose as early as 1912 from the comparison of these women with fledgling birds leaving the nest.

[75] Liz Conor, "The Flapper in the Heterosexual Scene." This online article is the final chapter of Conor's book *The Spectacular Modern Woman: Feminine Visibility in the 1920s* (Bloomington: Indiana UP, 2004). Online: *The Australian Common Reader Project,* http://www.api-network.com/main/index.php?apply=scholars&webpage=default&flexedit=&flex_password=&menu_label=&menuID=homely&menubox=&scholar=139 (accessed 3 May 2009).

[76] Conor, "The Flapper in the Heterosexual Scene."

[77] Conor, "The Flapper in the Heterosexual Scene."

[78] Palmer, "The Significance of Homosexual Desire," 6.

[79] Hesse, *Der Steppenwolf,* in *Sämtliche Werke,* vol. 4, *Die Romane: Der Steppenwolf. Narziß und Goldmund. Die Morgenlandfahrt,* ed. Volker Michels (Frankfurt am Main: Suhrkamp Verlag, 2001), 113 and 114. Further references to *Der Steppenwolf* are to this edition and will be given by volume and page number. English translations from this work are taken from Hesse, *Steppenwolf,* trans. Basil Creighton (New York, Toronto, London: Bantam Books, 1969), here 126 and 134; subsequent references will be indicated by page number following translation.

[80] René Kaufman and Lev Raphael, *Coming Out of Shame: Transforming Gay and Lesbian Lives* (New York: Doubleday, 1996) quoted in Palmer, "The Significance of Homosexual Desire," 7.

[81] The Russian philosopher, literary critic, and semiotician Mikhail Bakhtin saw carnivals and the carnivalesque as opportunities to dissolve class differences. Through costume and mask, a person could exchange bodies and be renewed, simultaneously providing a heightened awareness of one's sensual, material, and bodily unity and of one's community.

With the recent rise of information technology and the internet, creations of alternate worlds similar to Hesse's Magic Theater have become available online in the form of games in which an avatar becomes one's digital self. These virtual worlds are laboratories for the construction of identity, according to Sherry Turkle, a sociologist at MIT. Turkle and other sociologists have discovered that such an opportunity to try out different personalities leads in many cases to positive changes in the way the player is perceived in the real world.

[82] There are similarities here with Nataraja (The King of Dance), the dancing posture of the Hindu god Shiva, who performs his dance as a part of his divine duties of creation and destruction.

[83] In analogy to V. S. Naipaul's *The Mimic Men* (New York; Vintage Books, 1985).

[84] Palmer "The Significance of Homosexual Desire," 2.

[85] Hesse, *Narziß und Goldmund,* in *Sämtliche Werke,* vol. 4, ed. Volker Michels (Frankfurt am Main: Suhrkamp, 2001), 273. Further references to this work are to this edition and will be indicated by the volume and page number. English translations are from Hermann Hesse, *Narcissus and Goldmund,* trans. Ursule Molinaro (New York, Toronto, London, Sydney, Auckland: Bantam Books, 1971), references to which will also be indicated by page number.

[86] Clara Tuite, "Cloistered Closets: Enlightenment Pornography, The Confessional State, Homosexual Persecution and 'The Monk,'" in *Romanticism on the Net* 8 (November 1997), http://users.ox.ac.uk/~scat0385/closet.html (accessed 3 March 2007).

[87] Tuite. "Cloistered Closets."

[88] Foucault quoted in Tuite, "Cloistered Closets," http://www.erudit.org/revue /ron/1997/v/n8/005766ar.html (accessed 3 March 2007).

[89] Hermann Hesse, *Narcissus and Goldmund.* Trans. Ursule Molinaro (New York, Toronto, London, Sydney, Auckland: Bantam Books, 1971) 15.

[90] In eighteenth-century America and Europe, it was commonly assumed that Cain's "mark" was black skin and that Cain's descendants were black and still under Cain's curse. Accepting the theory that God had cursed black people, racists have used the curse as a Biblical justification for racism. These racial and ethnic interpretations of the curse and the mark have been largely abandoned even by the most conservative theologians since the mid-twentieth century, although the theory still has some following among white supremacists and an older generation of whites.

[91] There were countless legends about Chrysostomos in the Middle Ages. The Madonna is said to have asked him for a kiss. With that kiss, a golden glow surrounded his rather unskilled mouth, and he went on to become a famous preacher. http://www.heiligenlexikon.de/BiographienJ/Johannes_Chrysostomus.html (accessed 3 March 2007).

[92] Michel Foucault, *Use of Pleasure,* 233.

[93] Lubich, "Hermann Hesses *Narziß und Goldmund* oder 'Der Weg zur Mutter,'" in *Hermann Hesse Today / Hermann Hesse Heute,* ed. Cornils and Durrani, 55.

[94] A biographical note published by Suhrkamp states the following: "On September 6, 1911, Hermann Hesse boards the "Prinz Eitel Friedrich" in Genoa in the company of his friend, the painter Hans Sturzenegger, to travel to India, the country in which his grandparents, his father and his mother worked as missionaries. In actual fact, however, it turns out to be a trip not to India but to Indonesia: Penang, Singapore, Sumatra, Borneo, and Burma. The three-month itinerary touches the Indian subcontinent only peripherally. The ship does dock in Ceylon, where Hesse goes ashore, visits the sacred Buddhist shrines at Kandy, and climbs the highest mountain, yet the original plan to see the Malabar Coast comes to nothing. The educational trip to the Far East takes place at a time of reorientation. At home in Gaienhofen, where his third son, Martin, had just been born, Hesse feels increasingly estranged and ill at ease, and is gripped by wanderlust and a sense that a new phase in his life is about to begin. He dreams of a bachelor life. Yet the journey to India is a disappointment. The idealized image of India. as shaped by the stories

told by grandfather Hermann Gundert, proves to be elusive. He is, in fact, even disgusted by the reality of what he sees — the heat, the dirt, the colonialism, the social conditions, the obsequious nature of the Malays." http://www.hermann-hesse.de/eng/biographie/indienreise/indienreise.htm (accessed 24 June 2009).

[95] In all the other works discussed here, *Death and the Maiden* would have been an appropriate subtext. The theme is rooted in ancient mythological traditions: among the ancient Greeks, the abduction of Persephone (Proserpine among the Romans) by Hades (Pluto), god of Hell, is a clear prefiguration of the clash between Eros and Thanatos (= death). The young goddess gathers flowers in company of carefree nymphs when she sees a pretty narcissus and plucks it. At that moment, the ground opens; Hades comes out of the underworld and abducts Persephone. In Hesse's *Narziß und Goldmund,* it is Narcissus who plucks Goldmund out of a crowd and exerts a tremendous seductive force on him. He prefigures Thanatos in his black cowl at the end of the book, ready to abduct Goldmund and carry him away to the Elysian Fields in Hades, where, at least according to Roman mythology, souls were neither good nor evil.

Hesse discusses both of these intense events — sexual climax and the act of dying, and observes the conflation of the two in the women to whom his protagonists make love. But in *Narziß und Goldmund,* his *male* protagonist experiences orgiastic death — the sign of requited love?

12:   Hermann Hesse's Politics

Marco Schickling

I. Prelude: Hesse in the Age of Wilhelm II

DURING THE TIME IN WHICH Hermann Hesse was coming of age, the mass print media were just emerging as a force in German life. This had far-reaching consequences for the monarchy. According to Martin Kohl-rausch, ideological tensions between the imperial state of Wilhelm II and sectors of the press peaked in 1906, when 4,000 daily newspapers in Germany were publishing 25.5 million copies for a population of over 60 million, shaping opinions and the national mood.[1]

The history of Germany's Second Empire was characterized by mass phenomena. The new state's founding in 1871 was followed by the rise of political parties and their organizations, of labor unions, industrial trusts, religious associations, sports clubs, youth leagues, and the like. This in turn created a substantial market for publications catering to interest groups and political movements. Mandatory education and increased cultural awareness created large numbers of readers, a public of unprecedented size. Young Hesse was keenly interested in German periodicals of all kinds. He was reading important literary journals before 1900 and later contributed to them as an author and reviewer. From the beginning he studied — for instance as a bookseller in Basel around 1900 — how the print media functioned, the interests controlling them, and how they were manipulated. Later, he intended that his book reviews should educate his readers.

Hesse's experiences with journals dedicated to culture and politics began in 1907, when he joined *März*, a biweekly that he and Ludwig Thoma founded together with Conrad Haußmann, an attorney and member of the Reichstag for the German Democratic Party. It was backed by Albert Langen, who also published *Simplicissimus*, a Munich satirical journal that, like *März*, commented with extreme criticism and ridicule on events in Berlin surrounding Kaiser Wilhelm II from a south German perspective. The editors avoided appearing provincial by inviting French, Austrian, and Swiss authors to contribute, an international approach unusual in that nationalistic epoch. Hesse's commitment to *März* must also be read as a gesture of resistance to the power of Berlin's newspapers, whose ability to shape the public's opinions and tastes he never underestimated. How highly Hesse valued exchanging ideas and working with writers elsewhere in Europe, especially in France, can be seen in his turning away from *März* following the death of Langen, its cosmopolitan publisher, which caused the journal to become increasingly "German."[2] This change in *März*'s cultural attitudes reflects the political tensions then afoot in Europe, a result of imperialist rivalries.

These developments challenged for the first time Hesse's own international heritage and intellectual outlook. His mother, whose own mother was from Francophone Switzerland and whose father was Swabian, had been born in western India. His father had been born a Russian citizen in the Baltic town of Weißenstein.[3] One of Hesse's older stepbrothers was a British subject, having been born in colonial India, the other a citizen of Württemberg. Hesse later said of his origins: "Diese gemischte Herkunft verhinderte mich, je viel Respekt vor Nationalismus und Landesgrenzen zu haben" (*SW* 12:17; This mixed heritage prevented me from ever respecting nationalism and national borders very much). His parents spoke German, English, and occasionally French. Working for an international missionary society, his parents received guests from many countries, bringing great cultural variety to their homes in Calw and Basel.

Hesse's political attitude before the First World War reflects his liberal and democratic values. As a south German, he viewed political events in Prussia with severe but coolly critical disapproval. After the troubled and critical years of his childhood and youth, it was time for him to enter calmer — read "bourgeois" — waters. This he was able to do with the critical and financial success of his debut novel, *Peter Camenzind* and his marriage with the Swiss photographer Maria Bernoulli in 1904. He imagined the safe harbor of marriage and family as a lasting stabilizing force for his personality, which for the first few years proved to be the case. His editorial work for *März* helped to form his political ideas. Conrad Haußmann's articles for the journal criticized the autocratic "personal" rule of Wilhelm II, which was then coming under unremitting scrutiny and attack by most German newspapers, thanks to the Caligula Affair (1894), the Eulenburg Scandal (1906–7) and the charges of Byzantinism and the Camarilla Trials that followed, as well as the *Daily Telegraph* Affair. Haußmann and Thoma demanded parliamentarism for Germany as a consequence of these crises and in order to limit the power of the monarch. This was a position that Hesse surely shared and that had a major effect on his views.[4]

The new life that Hesse and his family began in an old farmstead close to the Swiss border in Gaienhofen on Lake Constance in 1904 is positively typical for the generation of those born around 1880. For what later become known as *Lebensreform,* a movement for the "reformation of life," an alternative to the customs and "advances" of Western European civilization, was the invention and development of specific groups of well-educated younger people. The art, architecture, fashions, and new ideas about nutrition and the human body inspired by *Lebensreform* all reflect the desire to abandon existing cultural norms, traditions, and the inhibitions that civilization imposed. Proclaiming the emancipation of the body through explicitly sexual themes, it seemed to embody the psychoanalytic process to which Freud had subjected the age. This also holds true for its rejection of bourgeois moral hypocrisy, expressed as strongly in Frank Wedekind's drama *Frühlings Erwachen* (Spring's Awakening, 1891) and Ludwig von Hofmann's erotically liberating painting *Frühlingssturm* (Spring Storm, 1894–95)[5] as in Henry van de Velde's "reform" dress for women of 1906, which was designed to be worn without a corset.

Nothing about these avant-garde ideas and stylistic trends, which as yet had not caught the attention of the masses and mass media, was "unpolitical." On the contrary, they represent, together with the rise of the public sphere and the media, modern processes of democratization from below. With his depictions of life close to nature and far from the cities (as he portrayed it in *Peter Camenzind*) and his later visits to the Monte Verità natural-healing spa near Ascona, Switzerland, Hesse clearly sympathized with these tendencies of the age.

Hesse was able to study the consequences of imperialism on the other side of the world on his voyage to the East Indies in 1911. He quickly realized how Dutch colonial rule and increasingly influential Chinese entrepreneurs were looting the island paradise of Indonesia and changing its society's structure. The first remarks on social conditions in Hesse's writings are found in his travel diary from this trip: "Immer wieder wundert und verletzt mich die Selbstverständlichkeit, mit der auch nette und redliche Weiße die Natives als Unterworfene und weit niedrigere Wesen ansehen" (I am often surprised and appalled by the casual way that even polite and decent white people regard the natives as their subjects and as a far lower order of being).[6] In this statement Hesse is describing an outgrowth of the Social Darwinist ideology that shaped the practices of the colonial powers and often too of missionaries. These new insights about economic, political, and religious connections in the Far East were then reflected in Hesse's book reviews, as when he discusses the books of the Dutch author and critic of colonialism Multatuli (Eduard Douwes Dekker).

Scholars have paid too little attention to the impact that Hesse's voyage to Asia had on his political ideas and on how he responded to the First World War. His experiences in the Netherlands East Indies conclude the first phase of his political education. Hesse was coming into his own as an active observer of the world's affairs.

II. The First World War
and Its Aftermath

The outbreak of the First World War found Hesse living in Bern, where he had moved in 1912 for the sake of his Swiss wife and the schooling of their three sons. The press would later mercilessly criticize Hesse for this change of residence, though it was for these purely domestic reasons.[7]

Hesse reacted to the start of hostilities in August 1914 with a sense of panic that his "religion," namely art, had lost its meaning. He feared that the struggle between a cultivated social order and the forces of capitalism would destroy the cultural life of Europe and especially of Germany. In his letters Hesse warned equally against the influence of Great Britain's global economic power and against Czarist Russia, which he saw as culturally backward. Drawing upon his experiences in Asia and relating them to the current events, Hesse hoped that the oppressed colonies of Indonesia might now rebel against their imperial overlords.[8] He worried that Europe might suffer the fate of the East, where Western powers corrupted ancient cultures and traditions, finally oppressing whole nations through territorial annexations and social transformations.

For Hesse as a cosmopolitan European, it must have been particularly painful to witness the "War of the Minds"[9] that was being waged even as the soldiers fought. This form of warfare, completely new to Hesse, involved open hostility against fellow artists and thinkers in "enemy" nations and was conducted primarily in the press. It threatened his very sense of being as a writer and intellectual. He reacted to the new situation with feeling, stating, on the one hand, that he believed in the German culture's historical mission, superiority, and predominance over other national cultures, but, on the other hand, that he found fault with the corruption of that culture by the relentless, opportunistic co-opting of German artists to serve hysterical nationalism. This politicization of the arts forced Hesse to take a cultural-political stand. On 3 November 1914, the internationally recognized *Neue Zürcher Zeitung* published Hesse's article, "O Freunde, nicht diese Töne!" It warned against misusing poets and thinkers for political purposes, insisting that their calling requires artists to remain neutral and distant from such matters. Hesse was trying desperately to keep politics out of the arts, appealing too to the innate humanity and cosmopolitanism of all of the arts. In rallying his fellow artists everywhere, Hesse anticipated a time after the war in which, he believed, capitalism's influence on daily life would be substantially weakened. It is one of the ironies of history that the war, as an accelerator of industrial development and modernization, led to just the opposite result.

Under these new circumstances, western civilization could no longer return to noble personal ideals, to the virtues of living simply and naturally, or an all-embracing humanism, all of which Hesse had believed in as a member of the *Lebensreform* generation. Until 1916, he tried persistently to see the war's positive aspects; he suggested, for example, that the possibility of sudden death enhanced a person's humanity, that extreme peril would imbue Germans with a more spiritual attitude towards living. Hesse had never before yielded to such illusions, and he was never to do so again. His writings early in the war risk being construed in a nationalist vein, such as when, in his preface to a poetry anthology for soldiers in 1915, he defined their mission as fighting for the universal sovereignty of the German spirit and culture against the interests of "finance and commerce."[10] Though he was here contradicting ideas in "O Freunde, nicht diese Töne!" Hesse hoped that cultural "imperialism" as he conceived it would foster an increase in humanity. Hesse's convictions had been deeply shaken.

His tone changed abruptly, however, when he repeatedly volunteered for the German Army but was rejected each time as too near-sighted. In the summer of 1915, as an alternative to military service, Hesse joined the Office of War Prisoner Welfare at the German Embassy in Bern. His closest colleague was Richard Woltereck, a professor of zoology and expert in marine biology from Leipzig, who as late as 1914 had been working with Bernhard von Bülow, the German Emperor's close friend and special envoy to Rome. Together they organized the Bücherzentrale für Kriegsgefangenenvorsorge (Central Book Depot of the Office of War Prisoner Welfare).[11] Its mission was to supply German soldiers held in foreign countries, especially France, with suitable reading matter. It aimed to relieve the stresses of camp life by helping the men to educate themselves, but also to meet the more advanced needs of interned workers, teachers, and students who were trying to conduct classes and seminars in the camps. In late 1918, the British held an estimated 328,000 prisoners of war, the French 350,000, and the Russians 2.25 million. As of October 1918, Germany was holding 2.4 million enemy soldiers.[12] This aspect of the Great War is nearly forgotten today.

Hesse asked German publishers to contribute books; in open letters and in private he begged for financial donations to pay for needed supplies. He had patriotic feelings for his fatherland and was happy to serve.[13] Finally, he established his own little textbook publishing house. As his duties involved cooperating with the Red Cross, a neutral organization, Hesse became more familiar with international law. All international welfare organizations based their activities on behalf of war prisoners on the articles of the Geneva Convention (1874/1906).

Hesse's homeland, at least its newspapers, in the editorial lockstep required by the political *Burgfrieden* or truce between Kaiser and Reichstag, did not thank him for his selfless dedication. Inured to the nasty ways of the press, Hesse was now assaulted by slanders reprinted time and again alleging that he "cravenly" left Germany in wartime and was now avoiding military service. For years, "traitor" and "coward" were the favored terms in this diatribe. Hesse's writings were condemned for lacking enthusiasm for Germany's cause and not showing unconditional solidarity with the fatherland. Although he defended himself in the press with Conrad Haußmann's support, Hesse lost many friends, and his reputation was gravely damaged. Having to acknowledge how many Germans had fallen prey to fanaticism, as painful as it was, was also an important step in Hesse's political maturation.[14]

During the war and in its immediate aftermath, Bern was a hotbed of activity for diplomats of the several belligerent nations, for political agitators, and for numerous newspapers and organizations. Many socialist conferences took place there, sometimes attended too by Trotsky and Lenin, a resident from 1914 to 1916.[15] This decidedly left-wing political climate influenced Hesse's thinking, as would soon become apparent after the war.

Pacifist groups were also active in Bern, issuing pamphlets and sponsoring lectures. Hesse felt challenged by their idealistic plans for a world at peace, but declared that their propaganda helped no one, least of all the war's victims, who concerned him most. Hesse's articles in the *Neue Zürcher Zeitung* and the *Frankfurter Zeitung* from this period are among his best political writings. In them, Hesse demanded that the German press stops attacking him, end sensationalist reporting of enemy war atrocities, and, last but not least, that the war itself be ended. He urged Germans on the "home front" at long last to express their widespread disgust with the war and to exert relentless pressure on their politicians. In his open letter, "An einen Staatsminister" (To a Minister of State, 12 August 1917), he accuses the minister of being so absorbed by the business of warfare that he has lost any sense of its catastrophic consequences for humanity. Hesse's insistence that the German government change its foreign policy became so vociferous that the Ministry of War demanded that he stop discussing current affairs. He responded by redoubling his newspaper writing, using the pseudonym "Emil Sinclair."

When the Armistice was declared in fall 1918, Hesse knew that he could not abandon the German people, humiliated by defeat and filled with resentment as they were. The most important task was to learn the right lessons from the disaster, so that a new war of vengeance would not ensue. Hesse felt he had to "immunize" returning German soldiers and prisoners of war, the "lost generation," against fanatical demagogues and revanchists, whether of the extreme right or radical left wings. It was clear to him that his efforts would be made tremendously more difficult by what he termed the "Gewaltfrieden" (extorted peace) of Versailles. His chief points were: (1) Germany must never become a world power; (2) the Treaty of Versailles must be revised to soften its harshest conditions and decrease the hostility many Germans felt for other nations, especially France; (3) the idea of the League of Nations must be supported; (4) socialism, while not a perfect solution, was at that time the most appropriate political alternative to the present state; (5) returning German soldiers must be re-integrated immediately into society; (6) society as a whole must be re-structured to achieve more social justice. During the turbulent postwar period, Hesse's proposals appealed to agitators for new political alternatives.

Johann Wilhelm Muehlon (1878–1944) lived in Gümlingen, near Hesse's home in Bern. On his estate, diplomats of the Entente discussed Europe's future with republicans, democrats, pacifists, and exiled writers. Among them were Ernst Bloch, Hugo Ball, Alfred H. Fried, René Schickele, and Annette Kolb. Fried edited the *Friedens-Warte* (Sentinel for Peace), the leading journal of middle-class pacifists, in which Hesse too published for a time. Starting in 1908, Muehlon had directed the war materiel department for Krupp in Essen, but resigned in 1914, believing that Germany was guilty of starting the war. Until 1917, he was Germany's ambassador to Switzerland. As Muehlon's guest, Hesse gained practical insights about the undercover diplomacy typical of the time.

In March 1919, as the designated prime minister of Bavaria's soviet government following the murder of Kurt Eisner, Muehlon asked Hesse to work with him in creating a new government in Munich. Hesse answered: "Mein Dienst und göttlicher Beruf ist der der Menschlichkeit. Aber Menschlichkeit und Politik schließen sich im Grunde immer aus. Beide sind nötig, aber beiden zugleich zu dienen, ist kaum möglich. Politik fordert Partei, Menschlichkeit verbietet Partei." (To foster Humanity is my duty and divine calling. But Humanity and politics are always mutually exclusive by their very natures. Both are necessary, but to serve both at once is hardly possible. Politics demands partisanship. Humanity forbids partisanship.).[16]

Hesse did, however, remain interested in political events. The Spartacist uprising in Berlin and the murders of the Socialists Rosa Luxemburg and Karl Liebknecht, whom Hesse esteemed, made clear to him that his most urgent task was to persuade German soldiers, returned from the front, without leadership, and all too ready to join the Freikorps, that they must not wage a civil war in their own homeland. He resorted to a favorite device of the time, an anonymous pamphlet.[17] *Zarathustras Wiederkehr: Ein Wort an die deutsche Jugend* (Zarathustra's Return: A Word to Germany's Youth) stated Hesse's program for re-educating the young people of Germany. He hoped they would take the collapse of Wilhelmine Germany as a chance for a new beginning, never again to follow blindly a political leader, a nationalistic program, or any other ideology. In a later edition, Hesse declared that decades of errors and miscalculations in social, cultural, and political developments had started Germany on the road to war:

> Erst wenige haben eine Ahnung von dem Verfall des deutschen Geistes, in dem wir lang vor dem Kriege schon lebten. Wir müssen nicht hinten beginnen, bei den Regierungsformen und politischen Methoden, son-

dern wir müssen vorn anfangen, beim Bau der Persönlichkeit, wenn wir wieder Geister und Männer haben wollen, die uns Zukunft verbürgen. (*SW* 15:221)

[Only a few people even now have any idea of the decay of the German spirit which we all endured long before the war. We must not begin with the final step, with politics and forms of government; rather, we must begin at the beginning by building a new structure for our personalities, so that we can hope for minds and men that promise a better future.]

In condemning prewar Germany, Hesse had in mind the German Reich that Bismarck established with "blood and iron" after the Franco-Prussian War, its misguided educational policies and practices, and, in particular, Prussian authoritarianism and militarism. In its style and content, the pamphlet seems too emotional and preachy, insufficiently specific and often repetitive. In perhaps its finest passage, Hesse speculates whether "Deutsches Wesen," "the German character" can bring about "Weltverbesserung," making the world better by elevating it morally and improving civilized life:

Freunde, wir sollten uns des Urteils darüber enthalten lernen, ob die Welt gut oder schlecht sei, und wir sollten auf diesen seltsamen Anspruch, sie zu verbessern, verzichten. Oft ist die Welt schlecht gescholten worden, weil der, der sie schalt, schlecht geschlafen oder zuviel gegessen hatte. Oft ist die Welt selig gepriesen worden, weil der, der sie pries, eben ein Mädchen geküßt hatte. Die Welt ist nicht da, um verbessert zu werden. Auch ihr seid nicht da, um verbessert zu werden. Ihr seid aber da, um ihr selbst zu sein. Ihr seid da, damit die Welt um diesen Klang, um diesen Ton, um diesen Schatten reicher sei. Sei du selbst, so ist die Welt reich und schön! Sei nicht du selbst, sei Lügner und Feigling, so ist die Welt arm und scheint dir der Verbesserung bedürftig. (*SW* 15:239–40)

[Friends, we must learn to withhold our judgment on whether the world is good or bad, and we should give up the strange wish to make it better. Often enough, those who condemn the world as bad have only slept badly or overeaten. Often too, someone blesses the world because he has just kissed a girl. The world is not here to be made better. And you too are not here to be made better. You are here to be the selves you are. Each of you is here to enrich the world with your own sound, your own tone, your own shadow. Be yourself, and the world is rich and beautiful. If you are not, you are a liar and coward, and the world will seem poor and deficient to you.]

Hesse skillfully contrasted a cultivated, dynamic individualism with the uniformity that war imposed on life, defining all of its aspects by the lowest common denominator. In this context, his essay "Eigensinn" (A Mind of One's Own, 1917)[18] is also a political statement, but more thoughtfully analytical and clearly formulated. Understandably, Hesse took the precaution of publishing it under the pseudonym "Emil Sinclair," since he argues in it that to be guided by one's "Sinn des Eigenen," a conviction about one's own essential being, is the highest personal virtue, drastically contradicting the dominant "Prussian-German" wartime imperatives of obedience, patriotism, and heroic sacrifice that rationalized the senseless slaughter at the front. Savagely, Hesse revealed how language is manipulated in the public sphere, as when distinguishing between "Heimatliebe" (love of the homeland) and the then more popular "Patriotismus":

> Der Patriotismus ist so eine [Tugend]. Ich habe nichts gegen ihn. Er setzt an Stelle des Einzelnen einen größeren Komplex. Aber so richtig als Tugend geschätzt wird er doch erst, wenn das Schießen losgeht — dieses naive und so lächerlich unzulängliche Mittel, "die Politik fortzusetzen." Den Soldat, der Feinde totschießt, hält man doch eigentlich immer für den größeren Patrioten als den Bauern, der sein Land möglichst gut anbaut. Denn letzterer hat davon selbst Vorteil. Und komischerweise gilt in unserer verzwickten Moral stets diejenige Tugend für zweifelhaft, die ihrem Inhaber selber wohltut und nützt! (*SW* 15:105)

> [I have nothing against patriotism, which is a proverbial virtue. It replaces a person's own love of home with something larger. But people especially appreciate it as a virtue when a shooting war starts, that naive and ludicrously insufficient "continuation of politics by other means." The soldier who kills our enemies is always considered to be a greater patriot than the farmer who cultivates his land as well as possible, since the farmer benefits from that himself. It is amusing to see how our perverse morality questions any virtue if it benefits or pleases the person practicing it.]

III. The Skepticism of the 1920s

Although there were a few sympathetic reactions to his articles, Hesse recognized that strong currents of antidemocratic ideology existed in German society, especially among the young, in addition to chauvinism, antisemitism and the glorification of violence. In the summer of 1922, hoping to counter the National Socialist movement that was already emerging, Hesse recommended a book on current affairs:

> Eine kleine Schrift *Verrat am Deutschtum* von Wilhelm Michel gibt Anlaß, auch einmal ein Wort über eine der hässlichsten und törichsten Formen jungdeutschen Nationalismus zu sagen, über die blödsinnige, pathologische Judenfresserei der Hakenkreuzbarden und ihrer zahlreichen, namentlich studentischen Anhänger. Es gab früher einen Antisemitismus, er war bieder und dumm, wie solche "Anti"bewegungen eben zu sein pflegen, und schadete nicht viel. Heute gibt es eine Art von

Judenfresserei unter der deutschen, übel mißleiteten Jugend, welche sehr viel schadet, weil sie diese Jugend hindert, die Welt zu sehen wie sie ist, und weil sie den Hang, für alle Mißstände einen Teufel zu finden, der dran schuld sein muß, verhängnisvoll unterstützt. Man mag die Juden lieben oder nicht, sie sind Menschen, häufig unendlich viel klügere, tatkräftigere und bessere Menschen als ihre fanatischen Gegner. Man mag sie, wo man sie als schädlich empfindet, auch bekämpfen, wie man gelegentlich gegen Übel kämpft, die man als notwendig kennt, die aber dennoch je und je zu erneutem Anlauf reizen. Daß man aber eine Menschenklasse schlechthin für das Übel in der Welt und für die tausend schlimmen Sünden und Bequemlichkeiten des eigenen, deutschen Volkes als Sündenbock aufstellt, ist eine Entartung so schlimmer Art, daß ihr Schaden allen Schaden, der je durch Juden geschehen sein mag, zehnfach aufwiegt. Die kleine Schrift *Verrat am Deutschtum* von Wilhelm Michel spricht darüber endlich ein deutliches Wort. Es möge Beachtung und Wirkung finden, namentlich unter den Studenten! (*SW* 15:345)

[Wilhelm Michel's pamphlet *Verrat am Deutschtum* (Germanness Betrayed) provides an occasion to speak out about one of the ugliest, most foolish forms of the latest version of German nationalism, namely the idiotic, diseased Jew-baiting of the bards of the swastika and their many supporters, especially among students. Antisemitism was formerly tame and stupid, as such "anti-" movements usually are, and was pretty harmless. Today's virulent Jew-baiting by misguided young Germans does a lot of harm, because it prevents these young people from seeing the world as it really is, and because it reinforces fatefully the tendency to find, for everything that is wrong, a devil who must be at fault. Whether one likes Jews or not, they are human beings, frequently infinitely more intelligent, energetic, and better human beings than their fanatical adversaries. If one considers them harmful, one may oppose them, as one opposes necessary evils that nonetheless have always spurred us on to further progress. But to make of a single group of people a scapegoat for all the evil in the world and for the thousand awful sins and the sloth of the German people itself is an act of degeneracy so terrible that it outweighs tenfold the very worst of the worst deeds that may have been done by Jews. Finally now, Michel's pamphlet addresses this clearly and honestly. May it find readers and inspire them to take action, especially among the students!]

Hesse published this challenge in *Vivos voco,* a journal of current cultural affairs that he founded in 1919 with Richard Woltereck, whose title, which means "I summon the living," they borrowed from the motto of Schiller's poem "Die Glocke" (The Bell). As a platform for new social and political ideas and designs, the journal called attention to the plight of those who were still enduring the effects of the war: returning veterans and mothers and children still suffering from illnesses caused by the food shortages of

1916–17. In addition to numerous book reviews, essays by Hesse appeared here, such as "Du sollst nicht töten" (Thou shalt not kill), offering ethical and moral guidance to young Germans at risk of falling into extremism. Hesse avoided making political propaganda for or against the Weimar Republic because he had confidence neither in the new parliamentary democracy nor in the popular platforms of the socialist or communist parties. Books from Germany and letters from readers, moreover, showed him that Germany's voters, some only recently enfranchised, were irascible, shaky in their convictions, or perhaps simply overwhelmed. The republic's many turbulent crises — assassinations, attempted putsches, inflation, strikes, and rebellions — well into the 1920s made Hesse more certain that his reserved attitude was correct, even though his close friend Conrad Haußmann was vice president of the National Assembly that had established the new state. Even positive developments did not change Hesse's attitude, such as Germany's joining the League of Nations in 1925, which he had been observing in action ever since attending a 1919 meeting of the League in Bern. He regarded Hindenburg's election in 1925 to the presidency of the republic as a setback, at once a sentimental embrace of the Wilhelmine past and the nation's "call for a strongman."

Hesse's political position regarding Germany is reflected in his encounters with Berlin's Prussian Academy of the Arts. In November 1926, after repeated invitations and appeals, he had reluctantly accepted the honor of an appointment to the academy, which promoted the significance of artists and the arts for the nation. Hesse was skeptical because the institution was an organ of the state, and he was concerned that artists might become financially dependent on it and in danger of losing their freedom of expression. Before six months had passed, Hesse was planning to resign. His fellow members Wilhelm Schäfer, Oskar Loerke, and Thomas Mann managed to dissuade him for a time. When he finally did leave the academy in 1930, Hesse described his motives to Schäfer, prophesying with striking clarity: "Beim nächsten Kieg wird diese Akademie viel zur Schar jener 90 oder 100 Prominenten beitragen, welche das Volk wieder wie 1914 im Staatsauftrag über alle lebenswichtigen Fragen belügen werden" (SW 15:339; In the next war, many members of this Academy will be among the 90 or 100 prominent figures who, as in 1914, are commissioned by the state to lie to the people about everything that matters in their lives). Hesse remembered all too well the start of the First World War, when, of all people, intellectuals and artists had pledged to support the kaiser's war policies and official propaganda. In the following years, the academy turned increasingly right-wing under the growing influence of chauvinist, nationalist writers, culminating in March 1933 with the declaration of fealty to the Nazi regime drafted by Gottfried Benn.[19] When, a year later, Thomas Mann tried to persuade him to re-join the academy, Hesse sent him his analysis of the political situation in

Germany based on his own ample experiences. It can also be seen as intending to open the eyes of the 1929 Nobel laureate:[20]

> Der letzte Grund meines Unvermögens zur Einordnung in eine offizielle deutsche Korporation ist mein tiefes Mißtrauen gegen die deutsche Republik. Dieser haltlose und geistlose Staat ist entstanden aus dem Vakuum, aus der Erschöpfung nach dem Kriege. Die paar guten Geister der "Revolution," welche keine war, sind totgeschlagen, unter Billigung von 99 Prozent des Volkes. Die Gerichte sind ungerecht, die Beamten gleichgültig, das Volk vollkommen infantil. Ich habe anno 1918 die Revolution mit aller Sympathie begrüßt, meine Hoffnungen auf eine ernst zu nehmende deutsche Republik sind seither längst zerstört. Deutschland hat es versäumt, seine eigene Revolution zu machen und seine eigene Form zu finden. Seine Zukunft ist die Bolschewisierung, mir an sich gar nicht widerwärtig, aber sie bedeutet eben doch einen großen Verlust an einmaligen nationalen Möglichkeiten. Und leider wird ihr ohne Zweifel eine blutige Welle weißen Terrors vorangehen. So sehe ich die Dinge seit langem, und so sympathisch mir die kleine Minderheit der gutgewillten Republikaner ist, ich halte sie für vollkommen machtlos und zukunftslos, für ebenso zukunftslos, wie es einst die sympathische Gesinnung Uhlands und seiner Freunde in der Frankfurter Paulskirche war. Von 1000 Deutschen sind es auch heute noch 999, welche nichts von einer Kriegsschuld wissen, welche den Krieg weder gemacht noch verloren noch den Vertrag von Versailles unterzeichnet haben, den sie wie einen perfiden Blitz aus heiterem Himmel empfinden. (*SW* 15:348–49)

> [The ultimate reason why I cannot be included in an official German body is my profound lack of confidence in the German Republic. This state, void of discipline and spiritual inspiration, emerged from the vacuum, the exhaustion that followed the war. The few good leaders of the "Revolution" that never took place were slaughtered with the approval of 99% of the people. The law courts are unjust, the officials indifferent, and the people totally infantile. In 1918, I welcomed the revolution with the greatest sympathy, but my hopes for a credible German Republic have long since been destroyed. Germany missed the chance to make its own revolution and find its own form. Its future lies in Bolshevization, which I don't find repellent in itself, but it does signify that unique possibilities have been lost to the nation. Unfortunately, too, it will doubtless be preceded by a bloody wave of white terror. That is how I have seen matters for some time now, and as much as I care for the Republic's few well-intentioned advocates, I think they are powerless and have no future, just as little future as the congenial ideals of Uhland and his friends had in the Paulskirche in 1848. 999 out of 1,000 Germans even today claim innocence of any guilt for the war, having neither waged it nor lost it, nor having signed the Treaty of Versailles, which they regard as a treacherous thunderbolt out of a clear blue sky.]

Hesse was using "white terror," a term current during the French Revolution and later used to describe the brutal suppression of the Russian and Bavarian revolutions, in reference to the methods then being used by the Nazi SA and SS against their opponents.

Hesse's growing faith in Communism during the 1920s had come about gradually, resulting from his journey to Asia, where he had observed capitalist exploitation in its most concentrated form, from Germany's failed revolution of 1918/1919, and from the Weimar Republic's politics.[21] He had read Marx and biographies of Lenin, Trotsky, and, later, Stalin. He finally declared his commitment to Communism in an open letter, "Brief an einen Kommunisten" (Letter to a Communist). Hesse states that he agrees with Communism's aims since his sense of history suggests that the time has come to organize society in this way. Hesse was motivated by his lifelong compassion for the poor and oppressed, those whom Marx had defined as the proletariat. (He demanded, among other things, equal educational opportunities for all.) He explained that he could not, however, subject himself to the discipline of any party, as political activism was not among the duties of a poet. The venality and opportunism of many fellow writers during the First World War had brought him to this conclusion. Hesse saw himself through and through as a supporter of communism, both through his work as a reviewer and essayist and through the material support he provided first to the prisoners of war and then to German colleagues threatened with exile during the 1930s, efforts through which he contributed to the lessening of hardship by sharing his private possessions with others. But he rejected any attempt to change the social order by force of arms.

IV. National Socialism and the Second World War

The 1930s brought dramatic political changes. In Germany, the global economic crisis caused unprecedented unemployment that, together with other economic and financial burdens, overwhelmed the government. Due to the weakness of the parliament and the quasi-dictatorial powers of the president, democracy was rapidly losing ground. In September 1930, widespread disillusion with the republic's politics brought the National Socialists a landslide victory in the Reichstag elections, accompanied by a strengthening of the radical left, the Communists. The failed "grand coalition" government was followed by a series of inept "president's cabinets," which, using emergency powers, increasingly curtailed civil rights. In the presidential election of March 1932, Hindenburg only narrowly defeated Hitler, who was gaining popularity with the aid of Alfred Hugenberg, the influential nationalist politician and newspaper czar. Hesse commented: "Der Ausfall der Wahl ist für den Moment beruhigend, aber im ganzen doch schlimm. Hitler weiß jetzt, daß er der zweite Mann im Reich ist und über 12 Millionen hinter sich hat" (*SW* 15:382; The election results are a relief for the moment, but very bad on the whole. Now Hitler knows that he is the second most important man in the Reich and that over 12 million are behind him).

On 26 November 1931, newspapers had obtained and published the so-called "Boxheimer Dokument," causing widespread anxiety. Werner Best, a National Socialist attorney and politician, had drafted the document in summer 1931 and party officials from the state of Hesse had given it their blessing while meeting at the Boxheimer Hof hotel near Bürstadt on the Bergstraße. Best believed that German Communists were planning to overthrow the government by force of arms, and that the Nazis should strike back by violently taking over the government. To that end, Best had drafted dictatorial directives and emergency regulations to suppress agitation, punish Communist putschists, possibly by death, and to put economic life entirely under state control. The document can be seen as a scenario for what occurred beginning in 1933, as it revealed the totalitarian design of a possible Nazi state. Hesse was well-informed about the Boxheimer Document and other events in Germany through the Swiss press and private letters, and his awareness would later play a major role in his rejection, after the war, of the claims of many Germans that they did not know of the plans or crimes of the Nazis, as will be seen below.

When President Hindenburg appointed Hitler chancellor of Germany on 30 January 1933, Hesse saw clearly that the next war, which he had been prophesying since the end of the First World War, in *Steppenwolf*, for example, was imminent. The fanatical enthusiasm of the Germans and their faith in a new order reminded him of the war frenzy of the summer of 1914. Hesse saw the demagogic corruption of his beloved German language by the Third Reich's grotesque jargon as a sign of a "Herrschaft des vollkommen Ungeistigen und Brutalen" (*SW* 15:400–401; a reign of totally mindless brutes). This debasement of German culture inspired him to create his magnum opus, *Das Glasperlenspiel* (The Glass Bead Game), which he had begun in 1932.

Presently, emigrants from Nazi Germany began to stream to Switzerland. The first refugees that Hesse harbored starting in March 1933 were Heinrich Wiegand, a Socialist journalist from Leipzig, the writers Thomas Mann, Bertolt Brecht, Bernhard von Brentano, and Kurt Kläber (alias Kurt Held), as well as the painter Gunter Böhmer. Later, Joachim Maass and Peter Weiss and others arrived. Brecht planned to settle in the Ticino region with Kläber, Anna Seghers, and Brentano, and sought Hesse's advice. These eyewitnesses informed Hesse thoroughly about events in Germany, for instance, that "große Gefangenen-Konzentrationslager" (*SW* 15:413; large prisoner-concentration camps) were being constructed there and that thousands of journalists were being dismissed or persecuted or their newspapers prohibited as part of "Gleichschaltung" (synchronization), the forcing of all aspects of culture and politics to conform to the Nazis' dictates. Despite having been warned by numerous German newspaper readers, Hesse continued even after 1933 to attempt to publish reviews of books by Jews, professing Christians, and foreigners in German papers.[22] By 1934, he was the only critic who dared to review favorably books by Jewish authors. German restrictions increasingly forced Hesse to publish these acts of intellectual resistance in Swiss newspapers, and only rarely in Germany. This provided an opportunity to influence Swiss readers, who, as letters informed him, did not all disapprove of Germany's new regime. Hesse understood very well why the Nazis had outlawed the Weimar Republic's rich production of outstanding literature, theater, music, and the visual arts, and the critical discourses associated with them, only to replace them with "synchronized" institutions that served the totalitarian state.

When from the mid 1930s on the German publishing industry was put under strict political regulation and the most renowned authors and publishers could work only in exile, Hesse found it even more difficult to make his criticism of the Nazis known. His final major effort, lengthy, detailed book reviews that were published in the Swedish journal *Bonniers Litterära Magasin* in 1935 and 1936, and in which he often praised emphatically books by exiled Jewish writers, brought forth a furious campaign against him in German newspapers and also, ironically, severe reproaches from the émigré press. Hesse's vantage point in neutral Switzerland made him the target of attacks from both left and right. Only then, when circumstances had made an objective discussion of literature impossible and dangerous, did Hesse stop writing literary reviews, though he continued to take an interest in émigré writers.

In Hesse's political writings and in his letters we find the answer to the question that was put to him again and again after 1933: why, living abroad, he had not taken part in the journalistic struggle of the émigrés against Nazi rule? In September 1939 he wrote:

> Wozu die Proteste? Wozu die witzigen Aufsätze über Hitler oder über die deutsche Unteroffiziersbegabung? Was geht sie mich an? Ich kann sie nicht ändern. Ich kann aber allen denen ein wenig helfen, die gleich mir die ganze säuische Machtstreberei und Politik in ihrem ganzen Tun und Denken sabotieren und Inseln des Menschentums und der Liebe bilden inmitten von Teufeltum und Totschlag. (*SW* 15:422)

> [Why these protests? Why these witty essays about Hitler and the talents of German noncoms? What business is that of mine? I cannot change these things. But I can give a little help to those who, like me, are bending all their thoughts and actions to sabotaging swinish power-grabbing and its politics and to create islands of humanity and love in the midst of devilry and slaughter.]

Hesse was skeptical about the émigrés' political activities because they were continually embroiled in internal disputes and thus unable to agree on actions in common against Nazi Germany. He also had to take care not to endanger his relatives in Germany, who could be held liable for his words, as well as Peter Suhrkamp, a courageous publisher and skilled tactician, who had been administering the house of S. Fischer, which published Hesse's works, ever since it had been formally transferred to "Aryan" ownership in 1936. Hesse's third wife, Ninon, was Jewish and still had relatives in Czernowitz (Chernovtsy), whose populace, as a result of the Hitler-Stalin pact, fell prey to forced resettlement, expropriation, and acts of terror by German and Rumanian troops as well as Russian forces.

Hesse responded to the protracted crisis by acting in positive, helpful ways, especially as many colleagues in the emigrant community were harming their own cause through persistent infighting. Hesse did, however, participate in acts of resistance. For years he argued bitterly with the aliens branch of the Swiss police, which gradually restricted the issuance of visas and residence authorizations to the point where it became nearly impossible to get them. Thanks to Hesse's interceding on their behalf, numerous intellectuals could make Switzerland the first stage of their exile.[23] He also made it possible for many to reside there for a time because he vouched for their financial and moral stability. This was often difficult, as Switzerland, fearing to be overrun by foreigners, out of latent antisemitism[24] and concerns about rising unemployment, resisted the entry of aliens and refugees, especially if they had no means of support.[25] After S. Fischer Publishers had been "aryanized" and split into a German part and a concern in exile, the Jewish publisher Gottfried Bermann Fischer was prevented from establishing the firm in Switzerland. As a result of Switzerland's laws of asylum, it had to establish refugee reception centers and internment camps, as the Alpine nation wished to be seen as nothing more than a way-station for refugees.

Hesse was certain that only a war could overthrow the dictatorship. Thus, he could not share the general relief that greeted the Munich Agreement of 1938 that the British Prime Minister Neville Chamberlain had negotiated. In late 1940, he wrote in a letter: "Diktatoren und Generäle müssen erschlagen, nicht belehrt werden" (*SW* 15:570; Dictators and generals must be killed, not lectured to). It was clear to Hesse that Germany would also lose the coming contest of arms.

Practically all of Hesse's journalistic writing and letters after 1933 aimed at helping that minority of Germans who maintained their human decency and intellectual integrity survive the Nazi era, so that when it was over, after the Second World War, it would be possible to build a better, more democratic Germany. For him, history had repeated itself, except that he was now concerned with the welfare of refugees instead of prisoners of war. Nonetheless, Hesse sent books to prison camps and internment centers in France, this time out of his own library.

V. Between East and West: The Postwar Period and Reconstruction

After the Second World War, in contexts ranging from the Nuremberg War Tribunals of 1945–46 to the ubiquitous denazification questionnaires, the Allies sought to assess to what degree ordinary Germans bore the guilt for Hitler's dictatorship. German readers now discovered Hesse, formerly slandered and disavowed, anew. Their letters to him, proclaiming innocence and ignorance of the totalitarian atrocities, represent a unique moment in the history of the German psyche. Hesse's horrified reaction is typified in his letter of 1 March 1946 to the popular Swabian writer Wilhelm Schussen, one of many such responses:

> Ihr habt also von allem und allem nichts gewußt! Nicht, daß Hitler durch seinen Münchner Putsch in seiner Gefährlichkeit bloßgestellt war, nicht, daß er von Euren "republikanischen" Behörden statt bestraft verhätschelt wurde, etc. etc., bis zum scheußlichen Boxheimer Dokument, das noch lange vor Hitlers Machtergreifung in allen deutschen Zeitungen stand, und das jedem nicht völlig Blindseinwollenden vollends die Augen öffnen mußte. Und dann, von 1935 an, konnte man in Eurem Land an keinem Kurort vorbeifahren, ohne große Tafeln zu lesen "Juden unerwünscht," von dem überall angebrachten "Juda verrecke" zu schweigen, aus dem jeder nicht Blinde die nahenden Pogrome deutlich ablesen konnte. [. . .] Die Mehrzahl meiner Freunde in Deutschland wußte Bescheid, und manche sind gleich 1933 emigriert, andre in den Folterkammern der Gestapo verschwunden, so wie die Angehörigen und Freunde meiner Frau fast ohne Ausnahme in Himmlers Gasöfen in Auschwitz etc. verschwanden! Man glaubt es Euch natürlich nicht, denn in diese Kunst des Nichtwissens und Unschuldigseins, während man gleichzeitig bis an die Knie im Blut watet, kann kein andres Volk sich je hineindenken. (*SW* 15:623–24)

> [So none of you had any idea of what was going on! Not that Hitler had been exposed as dangerous by his [1923] putsch attempt in Munich, not that he had been more spoiled than punished for that by the Republic's "loyal" officials, etc. etc., down to the disgusting Boxheimer Document, which German newspapers had published long before Hitler came to power, so that everyone not willfully blind had to have his eyes opened. And then, after 1935, it was impossible to drive past a resort in your country without reading "Jews Unwelcome" on large signs, not to mention "Down with the Jews!" that was scrawled everywhere, anticipating the pogroms that everyone not blinded had to see coming. [. . .] The

majority of my friends in Germany knew exactly what was going on; some emigrated in 1933, others disappeared into the Gestapo's torture chambers, just as my wife's friends and relatives almost without exception disappeared into Himmler's crematoriums at Auschwitz! It's only natural that no one believes you, as no other nation can imagine itself ignorant and innocent while wading knee-deep in blood.]

The lack of any change in his readers' ideas and attitudes makes it abundantly clear that there was no "Zero Hour" in Germany, when everything was to start afresh. That was brought home to Hesse by the fact that former Nazis continued to hold or had been named to important government positions. His relief efforts for Germany continued, however. Over two years, Hesse sent some 1,500 letters, sometimes also books, to German soldiers still interned in Egypt, Syria, France, Italy, England, and the United States. Hesse financed aiding his friends and colleagues in Germany by selling watercolors he had painted and handwritten copies of his poems. He also wrote articles challenging the German people finally to renounce nationalism and to acknowledge their guilt for the rise of Hitler and the war. The results were the same as after the First World War, for, as the writer Luise Rinser wrote to Hesse in May 1946: "Heute ist alles Politik, denn was wir tun, jedes Wort, das wir sprechen, hat politische Wirkung!" (*SW* 15:641; Everything is political today; anything we do, every word we speak has political repercussions). Once more, Hesse's ideas about Germany came under attack because he was convinced that Germans bore a collective guilt for the deeds of the defeated criminal regime. In countless resentful letters, Hesse had to confront once more the same persistent antisemitism that Max Frisch had observed in his postwar travels in Germany and Switzerland and that inspired him to write his drama *Andorra*.

Hesse was also critical of the churches for meddling in party politics. He criticized their failure to assess their errors during the Nazi period, especially the results of the Reichsconcordat of 1933 that regulated relations between the Catholic Church and the German state and lent Hitler greater legitimacy and international credibility. For Hesse, both the Catholic and Protestant churches had lost their moral authority entirely. Hesse's siblings in Germany belonged to Martin Niemöller's "Confessing Church," itself an act of opposition, and were in constant danger between 1933 and 1945 because their famous brother challenged the Nazis incessantly.

In 1946, Hesse published *Krieg und Frieden* (War and Peace) in Switzerland, a collection of his most important political articles since 1914.[26] Suhrkamp published an enlarged edition in Germany in 1949, a critical accompaniment to that year's founding of two new German states. The Soviet Union's aggressive foreign policy and Stalin's terror campaigns destroyed Hesse's faith in Communism and its promise of a more just distribution of power and wealth. He resisted gently but firmly all attempts by Communist officials of the German Democratic Republic to win him to their cause, seeing that they planned to use him only as a figurehead in their propaganda against the Federal Republic. In order not to aggravate further the coming struggle of East and West and West Germany's fear of "Bolshevism," Hesse implored his readers not to "throw Fascism and Communism into the same pot" ("Faschismus und Kommunismus nicht in einen Topf zu werfen"; *SW* 15:697). Needless to say, sectors of the German press reacted angrily to this attempt to see more in politics than black and white opposites.

Hesse reproached the Federal Republic with being "fast ein Anhängsel" (*SW* 15:728; practically an appendage) of the United States, and the Democratic Republic with being run by Moscow and with keeping its people in lockstep control. In 1950, as the Cold War worsened and fears of a nuclear World War III grew, discussions began about rearming West Germany and reintroducing compulsory military service. Hesse addressed an open letter to his German readers opposing such measures. His prediction of 1917 that alternative civilian duties would sooner or later have to be provided for conscientious objectors to military service slowly but surely proved true in the 1950s and '60s.[27]

Hesse admired greatly the "stubborn resistance" of the Hungarian people during the uprising of 1956 (*SW* 15:793). He was troubled, however, by events in Asia: the rearming of Japan, the Korean War, China's occupation of Tibet in 1950 and the dramatic rebellion against the occupation in 1959, which ended with the flight of the Dalai Lama into exile. Hesse respected China's ancient culture and had been impressed with the energy and enterprise of Chinese he had encountered in Asia in 1911. Forty years later, however, the assertive foreign policy of Mao's China caused him grave concern:

> Die Chinesen, einst das friedlichste und an kriegs- und militärfeindlichen Bekundungen reichste Volk der Erde, sind heute die gefürchtetste und rücksichtsloseste Nation geworden. Sie haben das heilige Tibet, neben Indien das frömmste aller Völker, barbarisch überfallen und erobert, und sie bedrohen dauernd Indien und andere Nachbarländer.[28]

> [The Chinese, once the most peaceful people on earth, hostile to war and militarism, today have become the most feared and ruthless nation. Like barbarians, they have attacked and conquered sacred Tibet, the most pious nation after India, and they constantly threaten India and other neighbors.]

All of these struggles, which made a million people refugees, confirmed for Hesse "that dreadful saying, supposedly uttered by Hegel, that the only thing we can learn from world history is that nothing has ever been learned from world history" ("jenen fatalen, angeblich Hegelschen Spruch: das einzige, was man aus der Weltgeschichte lernen könne, sei, daß noch nie aus der Weltgeschichte etwas gelernt worden sei"; *SW* 15:722).

Hermann Hesse's path to political enlightenment and maturation was a difficult one, yet typical for the war-torn and ideologically turbulent twentieth century. What stands out in his political writings is that Hesse, more than any other contemporary author, experienced events with visionary empathy and tried to help shape their impact. Even in his secluded home in Montagnola, he sensed changes in the world's political climate. From the First World War onward, he responded to wars and other political disasters by actively aiding hundreds of victims, an inestimable achievement in itself. Finally, in addition to his renown as a novelist and poet, Hesse deserves to be recognized as a great and constructive educator by virtue of his prodigious output of significant writings on politics and literature.

— *Translated by Michael M. Metzger*

Notes

[1] Martin Kohlrausch, *Der Monarch im Skandal: Die Logik der Massenmedien und die Transformation der wilhelminischen Monarchie* (Berlin: Akademie Verlag, 2005), 49.

[2] Helga Abret, *Albert Langen: Ein europäischer Verleger* (Munich: Verlag Langen-Müller, 1993), 203.

[3] Therefore Hesse assumed that he was technically Russian by birth. See Hermann Hesse, *Biographische Notizen (1923)*, in Hermann Hesse, *Autobiographische Schriften II: Selbstzeugnisse. Erinnerungen. Gedenkblätter und Rundbriefe*, vol. 12 of *Sämtliche Werke*, ed. Volker Michels (Frankfurt am Main: Suhrkamp Verlag, 2003), 17. Hereafter cited as *SW* 12 and page number.

[4] Kohlrausch demonstrates conclusively how the emerging functional relationship between the media and their public contributed to democratization or at least to the public's political education. Kohlrausch, *Der Monarch im Skandal*, 251–81.

[5] The motif of spring's awakening — which was also prominently connected to the *Lebensreform* movement — as well as the political situation prior to March 1848 (the *Vormärz*), when Germany's ill-fated liberal revolution began, were both alluded to in the title of Hesse's journal, *März*.

[6] Hermann Hesse, *Tagebuch der Indonesienreise* (1911), in Hermann Hesse, *Autobiographische Schriften I: Wanderung. Kurgast. Die Nürnberger Reise. Tagebücher*, vol. 11 of *Sämtliche Werke*, ed. Volker Michels (Frankfurt am Main: Suhrkamp Verlag, 2003), 354. Hereafter cited as *SW* 11 and page number.

[7] On 9 September 1911, during his Asian journey, Hesse had ended his poem "Gegenüber von Afrika" (Facing Africa) with this insight into his restless wandering: "Denn auch im Glücke kann ich auf Erden / Doch nur ein Gast und niemals ein Bürger werden." (Even with luck on earth I must roam / Always a guest and never at home.). Hermann Hesse, *Die Gedichte*, vol. 10 of *Sämtliche Werke*, ed. Volker Michels (Frankfurt am Main: Suhrkamp Verlag, 2002), 174.

[8] See his letter to his father of 9 September 1914 in Hermann Hesse, *Die politischen Schriften*, vol. 15 of *Sämtliche Werke*, ed. Volker Michels (Frankfurt am Main: Suhrkamp, 2004), 7–9. Hereafter cited as *SW* 15 and page number.

[9] *Krieg der Geister — Erster Weltkrieg und literarische Moderne,* ed. Uwe Schneider et al. (Würzburg: Königshausen und Neumann, 2000). Of interest in this context are also Trudi Tate, *Women, Men and the Great War* (Manchester: Manchester UP, 1995), and *Modernism, History and the First World War* (Manchester: Manchester UP, 1998).

[10] "Einführung" to the pamphlet *Zum Sieg: Brevier für den Feldzug,* in Hesse, *Die politischen Schriften, SW* 15:26–29.

[11] The large book depository of the War Prisoner Welfare Bureau was in central Bern at Gerechtigkeitsgasse 64. The Salvation Army had once occupied that space, which today houses the welfare office of the canton.

[12] *Enzyklopädie Erster Weltkrieg,* ed. Gerhard Hirschfeld et al. (Paderborn: Ferdinand Schöningh, 2003). On the situation in the camps: "The everyday life of interned ordinary soldiers and noncoms differed considerably from that of officers. Most prisoners were housed in large barracks sparsely furnished with wooden bunks, straw mattresses, and chairs; their food was provided by the camp's kitchen. Officers and enlisted men alike suffered from the endless monotony of prison life, which could lead to severe depression. 'Stacheldrahtkrankheit,' 'barbed wire disease,' or, in French, 'cafard,' were common to camps of all nations. Withdrawal, apathy, and endemic homesickness were common topics, for example, in the many camp newspapers that prisoners produced. In every larger camp, soldiers imprisoned and isolated for years, with packages and letters as their only bond with home, developed a unique prison camp culture" (641).

[13] Especially just after the war, Hesse complained about Switzerland's "cool neutrality," though he was a German citizen — or perhaps for that very reason. See his diary entry of 4 October 1914 in *SW* 11:422.

[14] Cf. Theodore Ziolkowski, "Spiegel der gestörten Psyche. Hermann Hesse und der Erste Weltkrieg," in *Krieg der Geister: Erster Weltkrieg und literarische Moderne,* ed. Uwe Schneider and Andreas Schumann (Würzburg: Königshausen & Neumann, 2000), 209–27.

[15] See *"Der sanfte Trug des Berner Milieus": Künstler und Emigranten 1910–1920,* ed. Josef Helfenstein and Hans Christoph von Tavel (Bern: Kunstmuseum Bern, 1988).

[16] Letter to Emil Molt of 18 November 1918, in Hesse, *Die politischen Schriften, SW* 15:206.

[17] Kohlrausch calls attention to political pamphlets as neglected historical source materials, emphasizing their significance to the political discourse of imperial Germany. Prohibited by the censors during and after the First World War, most of them appeared in neutral Switzerland. See Kohlrausch, *Der Monarch im Skandal,* 56–61.

[18] Originally, this text was part of the two-volume collection of Hesse's political writings that Volker Michels edited in 1977. It is now available in *Autobiographische Schriften II, SW* 12:101–6.

[19] See Inge Jens, *Dichter zwischen rechts und links: Die Geschichte der Sektion für Dichtkunst an der Preußischen Akademie der Künste* (Leipzig: Büchergilde Gutenberg, 1994), 207.

[20] As late as March 1933, Hesse complained in a letter to Rudolf Jakob Humm, a Swiss writer: "Thomas Mann ist mit mir befreundet, und die wenigen Male, wo er mit mir auf Soziales zu sprachen kam, stand er, bei aller intellektuellen Billigung des Sozialismus, mit dem Herzen so unendliche weiter rechts asl ich, war in seinem gepflegten

feinen Wesen so unangegriffen vom klaffenden Riß in der Welt, daß es mich schauderte, denn ich habe ihn aus anderen Gründen sehr gern." (*SW* 15:402; Thomas Mann is my friend; yet, on the few occasions when we have spoken about social problems, his heart, although he agreed with socialism intellectually, was so much more to the political right than mine, his refined nature was so oblivious to the world's yawning social abyss that I shuddered, as I like him very much for other reasons.).

[21] See Joseph Mileck, "'Ließe er sich ohne Flinten und Kanonen verwirklichen, wäre ich gerne dabei!' — Hermann Hesse und der Kommunismus," in *Hermann Hesse und die Politik*, ed. Martin Pfeifer (Bad Liebenzell/Calw: Verlag Bernhard Gengenbach, 1992), 59–86.

[22] Concerning Hesse's activities as a literary critic during the National Socialist period, see Marco Schickling, *Hermann Hesse als Literaturkritiker* (Heidelberg: Universitätsverlag Winter, 2005), 124–75.

[23] See Adolf Muschg, "Hermann Hesse und das Engagement," in *Hermann Hesse und die Politik*, 11–24.

[24] At the request of Switzerland, beginning in 1938, the passports of German Jews were stamped with the letter "J" for reasons of better surveillance and control.

[25] See *Deutschsprachige Schriftsteller im Schweizer Exil 1933–1950*, exhibition catalogue (Wiesbaden: Harrassowitz, 2002).

[26] The American edition appeared in 1970: Hermann Hesse, *If the War Goes On . . . Reflections on War and Politics*, translated by Ralph Manheim (New York: Farrar, Straus and Giroux).

[27] See his letter of 3 January 1917 to Hans Sturzenegger in *SW* 15:158–59.

[28] *Die Weltwoche* (Zurich), 30 October 1959, *SW* 15:807–8.

13:   Hermann Hesse and Psychoanalysis

Volker Michels

POETS HAVE BEEN FASCINATED BY their dreams ever since poetry itself
began. No one is more familiar with the impulses of the unconscious
than artists, who could not endure being deluged by such impressions without transposing them to their conscious minds and giving them expressive
forms and names. To align these sensations with their own drives, harmonize
their inner and outer being, integrate what suits them and fend off what
does not, artists use their creativity and invent weapons, as Hesse expressed
it, "gegen die Infamitäten des Lebens"[1] (against the infamies of life). In their
waking states, therefore, they achieve something very similar to the way
dreams function during sleep. While writing, they continue the dream's process of elucidation, and, with the aid of fantasy, the dream's more disciplined
sister, they form alternative worlds that are superior in their compelling
verisimilitude to the turbulent imagery of dreams. And, paradoxically, the
more subtly, unsparingly, and precisely they succeed in depicting what is apparently most private and subjective for them, the more objective, universal,
and transcendent it becomes, so that others too recognize themselves in
these representations and perceive their lives in the world more clearly.

Only few writers of the twentieth century were as prototypical in their
ability to depict their own being in this way as Hermann Hesse, who thereby
overcame the boundaries separating generations and cultures. Congratula-
ting Hesse on his seventy-fifth birthday, Thomas Mann wrote: "Auf Wieder-
sehen, lieber alter Weggenosse, durchs Tal der Tränen, worin uns beiden der
Trost der Träume gegeben war, des Spieles und der Form"[2] (Farewell, my
dear old companion through this vale of tears, where we both were granted
the solace of dreams, of play, and of form).

The solace of dreams? Like Thomas Mann, Hesse was dependent on
dreaming his way out of a daily existence that he found hard to bear. Both
struggled to meet the expectations of their parents and their schools. Their
inability to fulfill them was the decisive trauma that Thomas Mann and
Hesse had in common. The reason they both failed at the Gymnasium was
the very opposite of what their school reports stated. They were not lacking
in talent and good will, but rather had too much of both, which prevented
them from fitting into their parents' plans for their futures and from submitting readily to the educational methods then current. Whoever could not

endure the drudgery of storing, entirely without thinking, a maximum of the most diverse information within a minimum of time, ready to repeat it robotically on demand, was considered lazy or a dreamer. But if what he learned preoccupied a student and excited him, as Homer's *Odyssey* did Hans Giebenrath in *Unterm Rad* (Beneath the Wheel) or as Schiller's *Don Carlos* did Thomas Mann's Tonio Kröger, he lagged behind his class and was not promoted. If students are overwhelmed constantly with new information, they lose the desire to comprehend it meaningfully. And this dislike for unreflecting mental agility, an inability to conform and adopt smoothly the manner of others, forced Thomas Mann, like Hermann Hesse, to break off their secondary education, a stigma with momentous consequences for both. For the feelings of inferiority that it produced made them strive to disprove the accusations of dreaminess and sloth and to justify their being with the works of their lifetimes, which exceed in intelligence, painstaking skill, and cultural achievement everything that institutions of secondary and higher education can hope to realize. How ineradicable this early trauma must have been can be seen, for example, in Thomas Mann's taking up once more, at seventy-six in *Felix Krull,* his final novel, the motif of the confidence man that he had first sketched out in 1909. Similarly, Hermann Hesse, past seventy, still felt he needed to finish his schooling and pass the "Abitur" in order, perhaps, "doch noch etwas Rechtes zu werden"[3] (to become a respectable person after all).

In his fairy tale, "Kindheit des Zauberers" (The Sorcerer's Childhood, 1923), which looks back on his early youth, Hermann Hesse explores his earliest motives for dreaming. They are expeditions into the limitless. For children, whose sense for possibility is still more strongly developed than that for reality, find it difficult to grasp that something is impossible. Thus, from his earliest youth, Hesse felt

> eine gewisse Unzufriedenheit mit dem, was man Wirklichkeit nannte, und was mir zu Zeiten wie eine alberne Vereinbarung der Erwachsenen erschien. Eine gewisse bald ängstliche, bald spöttische Ablehnung dieser Wirklichkeit war mir früh geläufig und der brennende Wunsch, sie zu verzaubern, zu verwandeln, zu steigern [. . .] Reich und vielstimmig klang das Leben [. . .] aber schöner noch war die Welt meiner Wunschgedanken. Reicher noch spielten meine Wachträume. Wirklichkeit war niemals genug, Zauber tat not.[4]

> [a certain discontent with what people called reality, which at times seemed to me to be nothing more than something silly that grownups had agreed to acknowledge. Quite early, I tended, sometimes fearful, sometimes mocking, to reject this reality and to cherish the burning desire to make it magical, to transform it and make it more intense [. . .]. Life spoke with many voices and rich tones [. . .] but the world of my

wishful reveries was more beautiful still. My waking fantasies were richer still. Reality never sufficed. Magic was vitally necessary.]

But waking fantasies and wishful reveries are suspect, as they could render the adolescent unfit for the so-called serious business of living, which often requires a person to surrender everything about himself that deviates from a given norm.

The more Hesse, as he grew older, had to see the jungle of his fantasies and dreams, the enticing world of the possible, "begrenzt und in Felder geteilt und von Zäunen durchschnitten"[5] (set within borders, parceled into fields, and crisscrossed by fences), the more he wanted to become a sorcerer in order to preserve it for himself. But the necessary magical powers evidently existed only in fairy tales like those his mother read to him, and which he soon learned to imitate. His very first manuscript, "Die beiden Brüder" (The Two Brothers) is such a fairy tale. He wrote it at the age of ten to resolve qualms of conscience he felt towards his younger brother, a poetic reparation made in a conscious state, a potential dream pre-empted by his fairy tale.

Two impulses were to determine from then on the contents of Hesse's dreams: firstly, the need to break out of the cage of convention and so-called reality and expand his own potential to do justice to his own soul's far greater and more vital reality; secondly, the urge to define the resulting conflicts as legitimate questions.

The poetic energy of his dreams fascinated Hesse more than did their possible significance. Around the age of twenty at the latest, already while he was an apprentice bookseller in Tübingen, Hesse began recording his dreams in diaries, which unfortunately have not been preserved, except for the fragments "Aus meinem Traumbuch" (From My Book of Dreams), which have come down to us in a manuscript entitled "Zum 14. Juni 1898" (For June 14, 1898) that contained other sketches, poems, and impressions, and that he presented to his father for his fifty-first birthday.

These dream fragments appear again in Hesse's first book of prose, *Eine Stunde hinter Mitternacht* (One Hour Past Midnight, 1899), under the title "Der Inseltraum" (The Island Dream). Here, for the first time, he attempted to impose order on the poetic confusion of his dream contents and make them function meaningfully within the autobiographical narrative.

Just as Hesse developed into entire poems images and moods that spontaneously came to mind as first lines, motifs from his dreams could inspire him to shape them into literary works. He considered them a present from the soul — he gave an essay the title "Traumgeschenk" (Dream Gift) — a signal from the unconscious, the trace of the *Traumfährte* (Path of Dreams), — the title of a volume of his fairy tales — to be followed wherever it might lead, the journey to be recorded. In doing that, it is important to assimilate the dream's particular secret language to ordinary language, so that readers are sufficiently attuned to the writer. For as Hesse wrote in a letter to Hans

Reinhart in 1934, "in der Dichtung muß jenes Wunder zustande kommen, daß einer zwar seine ganz persönliche Sprache spricht und seine ganz eigenen Bilder sieht, daß aber seine Sprache und seine Bilder, sei es auch nur assoziativ, dem Anderen verständlich sind. Das unterscheidet ja eben den Traum von der Dichtung" (in poetry, that miracle must come to pass that someone speaks his own entirely personal language and sees his own unique images, but that his speech and his images are comprehensible to someone else, even if only by association. That is what distinguishes dreams from poetry). He continues: "Es wäre ja wunderbar, wenn man beim Dichten einfach die Traumbilder nachsprechen könnte, aber nur in ganz seltenen Fällen, und auch dann nur als Zufall, entstehen auf diese Weise wirkliche Gedichte: z. B. gibt es einige Verse von Hölderlin aus der Zeit des Wahnsinns, in denen das Hingegebensein an die eigene Innenwelt und die Kunst dichterischer Sprache für Momente wunderbar zusammentreffen"[6] (It would be wonderful to be able, while writing, simply to imitate the dream images directly, but it's very rare, at best a coincidence, for real poems to result. For instance, there are a few verses by Hölderlin from the time of his madness in which his total surrender to his inner world coincides wonderfully for moments at a time with the diction of poetic art). But that is the exception. For, as his novel *Gertrud* states, it is quite another thing "seinen Träumen nachzugehen und berauschte Stunden auszukosten, als unerbittlich und klar mit den Geheimnissen der Form wie mit Feinden zu ringen"[7] (to pursue one's dreams and savor hours of ecstasy than to wrestle, as though with enemies, relentlessly and coolly with the mysteries of form). The early manuscript "Inseltraum" is prototypical for this labor-intensive transformation of "dream gifts" into poetry, of the raw material into a shapely form, the process by which Hesse also transformed the many dream elements in his fiction.

Hesse selected individual motifs from each of the four dream fragments he had written down in 1898 and rearranged them in diverse ways to produce "Der Inseltraum." The dreams had been aroused by a reproduction of Arnold Böcklin's painting, "Villa am Meer" (Seaside Villa, 1864), which Hesse, at twenty, had hung in his room in the Herrenbergstraße in Tübingen. And "Der Inseltraum" became an ideal mythological creation indeed, in a classicist style, with a cypress grove, temples, and virgins at play, shot through with remembered autobiographical episodes that enliven Böcklin's motif and appropriate it in an entirely personal way.

"Inseltraum" is reminiscent not only of Böcklin's "Villa am Meer," but also of his "Frühlingslandschaft" (Spring Landscape, 1870), "Der Heilige Hain" (The Sacred Grove, 1882), "Die Lebensinsel" (The Isle of Life, 1888), "Der Gang zum Bacchustempel" (Procession to the Temple of Bacchus, 1890), and the famous "Toteninsel" (The Isle of the Dead, 1880/1883). In the same way, after the dreamer has had a healing sleep, all of the young women reappear who played the idealized role of Dante's Beatrice during

Hesse's boyhood and youth: Elise, the queen of the flowers, "Maria and Frau Gertrud," to whom Hesse had dedicated *Romantische Lieder* (Romantic Songs, 1899), his first book of poems; they are merged, however, into a single figure, the queen among the young women. Passing through the scenic backdrop of Böcklin's painting, when "plötzlich die ganze bemalte Wand hinweggerückt wird"[8] (suddenly the entire painted wall is moved away), she leads the dreamer through the real garden that the artist had painted back to where his boat is moored and invites him to come again, whenever he wishes to "draw on her light" — "Licht schöpfen," and, finally, when he "keines Ruders mehr bedarf"[9] (no longer needs an oar) to reach her.

After the turn of the century, Hesse abandoned this mythological-symbolistic style of storytelling, which had served to express his indistinct fears and desires through cryptic dream narratives, a manner that had been cultivated by the popular Flemish author Maurice Maeterlinck. In 1941, prefacing a new edition of *Eine Stunde hinter Mitternacht*, Hesse wrote that, as an apprentice bookseller at twenty, he had created for himself "ein Künstler-Traumreich, eine Schönheitsinsel [. . . als] Rückzug aus den Stürmen und Niederungen der Tageswelt in die Nacht, den Traum und die schöne Einsamkeit"[10] (an artist's dream kingdom, an island of beauty as a retreat from the storms and shallows of the daytime world into night, dreams, and lovely solitude). In *Hermann Lauscher,* his next prose work, however, he had undertaken "ein Stück Welt und Wirklichkeit zu erobern und den Gefahren einer teils weltscheuen, teils hochmütigen Einsamkeit zu entkommen. Der nächste Schritt auf diesem Weg, ein das Gesunde, Natürliche und Naive schon beinah übertreibender Schritt war dann der *Peter Camenzind,* in dem ich tatsächlich eine Art Befreiung fand"[11] (to capture something of the world and its reality and to escape the perils of a solitude at once timid and arrogant. My next step along this road, which nearly exaggerated a sense of the healthy, natural, and naive, was *Peter Camenzind,* in which I found a kind of liberation).

This did not mean that Hesse from then on no longer sought to eavesdrop on the hidden voices of his unconscious, to observe the impulses of his dreams, to follow their paths, and to note them down. Several of Hesse's writings during the first half of his life are visions, sometimes in the form of fairy tales, in which "Geister und Verstorbene, Gestalten der Wirklichkeit und des Glaubens, [. . .] Mögliches und Gewünschtes, Süßes und Grausiges Hand in Hand im stillen Dämmerlicht [vorkommt, sich teils] umrißlos ins Dunkle verliert oder sich im Ausdruck zum Symbol steigert," as he wrote in a review in 1912.[12] Here, Hesse wrote in another review from 1914, "ist die Schwelle, wo das Heute sich mit dem vor Jahrhunderten Gewesenen berührt. In unseren Träumen finden wir jene von der Logik entbundene Welt der Assoziationen und der Symbole wieder, aus welcher einst Sagen und Märchen aller Völker entstanden sind"[13] (ghosts and the dead, figures real or fancied, [. . .] the possible or the desired, the sweet and the horrible go hand in hand in the gloom, some drifting into the dark, some rising to be expressed as symbols. [. . .] This is the threshold on which the present and a centuries-old past touch. In our dreams, we encounter once more a world of alogical associations that gave rise to the legends and tales of all nations). Such tendencies are revealed, for instance, in Hesse's "Traum von den Göttern" (Dream of the Gods), written in February 1914 and presaging the First World War, "Singapur-Traum" (Singapore Dream, 1911), which touches upon his conflict with his father, a motif expressed more precisely in "Traum des Missionars" (The Missionary's Dream) in the story "Robert Aghion" of 1912, also written on the trip to Indonesia, in "Der schöne Traum" (The Beautiful Dream, 1912), and in "Flötentraum" (Flute Dream, 1913).

Just as had the souls of youthful and naive nations, Hesse at that time drank "harmlos aus dem Traumbrunnen, in welchem Fremdestes beisammen liegt und Übergänge von jeder Stufe des Daseins zu einer anderen möglich sind"[14] (in all innocence from the spring of dreams in which the strangest forms are commingled and transitions are possible from any level of being into any other), seemingly magical moods, in which he escaped for hours "der Kontrolle des Verstandes" (from reason's control) and grants fulfillment to "seinen Trieben in Wunschbildern"[15] (his desires in reveries). Here, Hesse was describing how he communed with his own poetic dreams in the course of discussing books by Martin Buber for the *Neue Zürcher Zeitung* in 1914. After 1916, this innocent attitude disappears: Hesse becomes increasingly interested in how dreams function as imaginary resolutions of real situations of failure and unfulfilled needs, and for the next decade he uses them as keys to understanding himself, dealing with reality, and progressing in his development.

We do not yet know exactly when Hesse first concerned himself with Sigmund Freud's classic work *Die Traumdeutung* (On the Interpretation of Dreams), which had appeared in 1900. His library contained the edition of 1914, the year in which Hesse first mentioned Freud in print in a favorable notice about Richard Löwenstein's monograph, *Nervöse Leute* (Nervous People) in the *Münchner Zeitung* of 18 December 1914. He wrote: "Freud und seine 'Psychoanalyse' haben erbitterte Gegner, und gewiß ist Freuds Methode noch mit subjektiven Vorurteilen behaftet, aber der Weg zur Erkennung und Heilung der 'Nervosität' ist von ihm gezeigt [. . .] Daß es dieselben psychischen Leiden waren, die Beethovens Symphonien und van Goghs Bilder geschaffen haben, ist eine andere Seite der Sache, und diese Seite verschweigt Löwenstein zu Unrecht"[16] (Freud and his "psychoanalysis" have bitter opponents, and Freud's method is certainly beset by subjective prejudices, but he has shown the way to the diagnosis and healing of nervous conditions [. . .] Löwenstein is wrong, however, in not mentioning that those very psychic sufferings created Beethoven's symphonies and Van Gogh's pictures).

In "Künstler und Psychoanalyse" (Artists and Psychoanalysis), an article in the *Frankfurter Zeitung* of 16 July 1918, his next published statement regarding Freud, Hesse warmly defended analytical psychology, declaring that in it he found confirmed "fast alle meine aus Dichtern und eigenen Beobachtungen gewonnenen Ahnungen bestätigt" (nearly all of the tentative insights he had ever gained from poets and his own observations). For Hesse, Freud affirms the value of fantasy and fiction for every artist. For psychoanalysis relies everywhere on the evidence of literature of the pre-psychoanalytic past. Hesse believed that artists too could find analysis fruitful, as it demands "eine Wahrhaftigkeit gegen sich selbst, an die wir nicht gewöhnt sind"[17] (an honesty towards oneself to which we are not accustomed).

> Wer den Weg der Analyse, das Suchen seelischer Urgründe, aus Erinnerungen, Träumen und Assoziationen, ernsthaft eine Strecke weit gegangen ist, dem bleibt als bleibender Gewinn das, was man etwa das "innigere Verhältnis zum eigenen Unbewußten" nennen kann. Er erlebt ein wärmeres, fruchtbareres, leidenschaftlicheres Hin und Her zwischen Bewußtem und Unbewußtem; er nimmt von dem, was sonst "unterschwellig" bleibt und sich nur in unbeachteten Träumen abspielt, vieles mit ans Licht herüber.[17]

> [Whoever has gone any distance in earnest on the path of analysis, of seeking primal psychic depths in memories, dreams, and associations, has won enduringly what might be called a more intimate relationship to his own unconscious. He moves between conscious and unconscious in ways that are warmer, more fruitful, more passionate. He brings to light notions that otherwise remain "below the threshold" or occur only in unnoticed dreams.]

Hesse considered examining dreams to be an extraordinarily productive method, for, as he wrote elsewhere, "der Traum ist das Loch, durch das du den Inhalt deiner Seele siehst, und dieser Inhalt ist die Welt. Die ganze Welt, von deiner Geburt bis heute, von Homer bis Heinrich Mann, von Japan bis Gibraltar, vom Sirius bis zur Erde, vom Rotkäppchen bis zu Bergson"[18] (the dream is the hole through which you see the content of your soul, and this content is the world. The whole world, from your birth until today, from Homer to Heinrich Mann, from Japan to Gibraltar, from Sirius to the Earth, from Little Red Riding Hood to Bergson). Thus, analysis, with its powers to educate, challenge, and inspire, is productive for no one more than for the artist, "denn ihm ist es ja nicht um die möglichst bequeme Anpassung an die Welt und ihre Sitten zu tun, sondern um das Einmalige, was er selbst bedeutet"[19] (for he is concerned with the unique phenomenon that his own being signifies, not with adapting to the world and its customs with optimal comfort).

Such assertions, but also Hesse's reservations, were anything but the fruits of his reading alone. For Hesse himself, two years previously, following his severe personal and ideological crisis of the early war years, had undergone psychoanalysis, the first German writer to do so, and thus spoke from experience.

In early April 1916, plagued by unbearable headaches, dizzy spells, and episodes of severe anxiety, Hesse entered Sonnmatt Sanatorium near Lucerne for seven weeks. In this private clinic, under the direction of the hydrotherapist Heinrich Ferdinand Hotz, a team of physicians of various specialties attended to the patients. Hesse wrote to Walter Schädelin on 3 May 1916 that he now had three doctors,

> welche zwar gemeinsam arbeiten, aber in vielem doch sehr divergieren, so daß meinem behandelten Ich je und je die Rolle einer letzten Instanz übrigbleibt. Der eine Arzt hier im Haus ist mein Sanatoriumsonkel, er berät mich in Diät etc., verschreibt mir Bäder, Güsse, Massagen und schwebt über dem Ganzen. Der zweite Arzt ist [der Internist] Hans Brun. Er hat mir gestern den Magen ausgepumpt [. . .] Der dritte ist ein Psychiater, die Kur bei ihm ist für mich nicht bloß die wichtigste, sondern auch die interessanteste"[20]

> [who do indeed work together, but disagree in many ways, so that my self, under treatment, is left to decide who is right. One doctor is my "sanatorium uncle," he advises me about my diet, etc., prescribes baths, showers, massages, and hovers over everything. The second is [the internist] Hans Brun. Yesterday, he pumped out my stomach. [. . .] The third is a psychiatrist, his treatments are the most important for me, and the most interesting.]

When Hesse found no relief in treatments with diathermy, a then-novel method that warmed body tissues by irradiating them with high-frequency waves of alternating current, only the possibility of psychotherapy remained, a method equally new. "Wir doktern zwar auch am Körper emsig herum," Hesse wrote on 20 May 1916 to his friend, the painter Ernst Kreidolf, "ich werde jetzt täglich von innen her elektrisch geheizt und mit Chlorophyll gefüttert. Aber wenn ich dabei auch ein Herkules werde, so bin ich damit vor Rückfällen in die schlimmsten nervösen Zustände gar nicht gesichert. Das muß im Gemüt und Willen vor sich gehen, und da ist zwischen Erkennen des Wahren und Tun immer ein Zwiespalt. Es geht mir diesmal ans Leben, und ich kann mich nimmer um eine entscheidende innere Krisis drücken"[21] (We are still diligently doctoring around on my body; [. . .] every day they warm me up electrically and feed me chlorophyll. But even if they make a Hercules of me, I still won't be at all safe from relapsing into the worst kinds of nervous states. [Healing] must occur in my mind and my will, and there is always a gap between understanding a truth and acting upon it. This time, it's a matter of life and death, and I can no longer avoid facing a decisive inner crisis).

Hesse's therapist, the Swiss psychoanalyst Josef Bernhard Lang (1881–1945) was, in the opinion of his teacher and colleague, C. G. Jung, who was six years his senior, a "very odd, but extraordinarily learned man." After completing his dissertation, "Word Association Experiments with Schizophrenics and Members of their Families," the graduate of the cathedral school at Einsiedeln had worked in several institutions, beginning as an intern at the Waldau mental hospital in Bern, the St. Urban psychiatric clinic in the canton of Lucerne, and later as medical director of the private mental hospital of Meiringen. While in Lucerne, he maintained a private practice on Schwanenplatz and also treated patients of the Sonnmatt Sanatorium. What Hesse had become aware of in theory by reading Freud's writings on humor, the interpretation of dreams, and human sexuality, he now found applied in practice to his own situation in twelve analytical conversations with J. B. Lang that lasted about three hours each. Thereafter, however, Hesse had to interrupt his stay at Sonnmatt, due to his work for the War Prisoners Welfare Bureau, which he also carried on in the sanatorium, and financial and family problems.

As his conflicts had by no means been resolved after such a brief treatment, Hesse agreed to see Lang as an outpatient. Between June 1916 and November 1917, for nearly a year and a half, Hesse traveled, every week at first, then more sporadically, from his home in Bern to Lucerne to consult Dr. Lang, a round trip of six hours. Never before in his life and never again did Hesse consult a physician that regularly and at such a requirement of time. Dream analysis was a major part of the therapy. The patient was required not only to recapitulate remembered dream fragments, but also to discover how they were linked to his past and current experiences. Only then was it the analyst's turn to translate the "manifest" dream content into psychological terms. If this procedure worked, it brought about a sense of liberation, a burden being lifted by the realization that one had attributed to subjective experiences and situations an excessively objective character.[22] Only then did it become possible for Hesse to play with "[den als unveränderlich vermuteten] Objekten zu spielen, auch mit den scheinbar starren Begriffen Krank und Gesund, Schmerz und Freude"[23] (those objects earlier seen as immutable and with the seemingly rigid notions of illness and health, pain and joy). In this way, despair could become mercy, whereby our life, by shedding a skin, opens itself up to renewed transformations. "Diese Erlebnisse des Erlöstwerdens sichern natürlich nicht gegen neue Verzweiflungen, aber sie fördern den Glauben daran, daß jede Verzweiflung von innen heraus überwindbar sei. Man wird nicht 'gesund', man verliert nicht den Schmerz, aber man beginnt wieder neugierig auf das zu werden, was uns noch bevorsteht, und findet den amor fati"[24] (Naturally, these moments of liberation do not immunize you against new fits of despair, but they promote the confidence that any despair can be overcome from within yourself. You don't become "healthy," you don't lose the pain, but you start to be curious about what is yet to come, and you find your *amor fati* [loving assent to your fate]). What Hesse, answering a reader's letter in April 1931, said regarding his psychoanalysis relates closely to a leitmotif in *Demian:* "Man muß seinen Traum finden, dann wird der Weg leicht. Aber es gibt keinen immerwährenden Traum, jeden löst ein neuer ab, und keinen darf man festhalten wollen." . . . "Ich lebe in meinen Träumen [. . .] Die anderen Leute leben auch in Träumen, aber nicht in ihren eigenen. Das ist der Unterschied"[25] (You must find your own dream, then the path becomes easy. But no dream lasts forever, each is succeeded by a new one, and you must not want to hold fast to any of them. . . . I live in my dreams [. . .] Other people also live in dreams, but they are not their own. That is the difference).

We are now able to trace the details of the difficult path that led to these results thanks to the dream diary that Hesse kept during the closing phase of his first psychoanalysis, and which his wife Ninon withheld from public view until thirty years after his death; scholars have had access to it only since 1995.

This diary, a typescript written on the old Smith-Premier machine with an italic typeface that Hesse had acquired in 1908 while living near Lake Constance, contains 111 single-spaced DIN A4 pages, with up to fifty-five lines per page. Like the printer's copy of *Demian,* they are typed for the most part on the reverse of stationery of the Welfare Organization for German War Prisoners in Bern. With the title *Möglichst vorurteilslos die Erlebnisse der Seele notieren*[26] (As free of prejudice as possible, write down the soul's experiences), this diary was first published in 1996. The original is untitled, but Hesse numbered the pages and dated his entries, beginning with 9 July 1917. That was about fourteen months after his analysis began, a time when his trips to Dr. Lang in Lucerne were becoming more irregular. No such dream diaries exist for the critical first phase of Hesse's analysis, from May 1916 to June 1917, when therapist and patient were meeting regularly. Only "Der schwere Weg" (The Hard Road) of May 1916, a loose allegory on the first twelve sessions, and "Eine Traumfolge" (A Succession of Dreams), written in October 1916, both later appearing in Hesse's *Märchen* (Fairy Tales), help to understand the obstacles to be overcome at the start of the therapy.

The dream diary begins at the time when Hesse was obliged to start a company of his own to publish books for the War Prisoner Relief Organization, an activity that made him even more indispensable in Bern than before. This circumstance most likely caused Hesse to continue the dream analysis in writing in order not to interrupt it, and also, if it became necessary, to be able to continue the therapeutic conversation by mail. Hesse's condition had been stabilized so much by then that he could agree with

C. G. Jung's maxim that "the unconscious functions well only when the conscious is fulfilling its tasks to the highest possible degree." This must have been the case at the time, for never before had Hesse been as strenuously challenged as by his welfare work during the war and his critical journalism during the period 1917–19.

The dream diary that Hesse kept between July 1917 and August 1918 is an important autobiographical document and indispensable to an understanding of the genesis of his works, especially regarding *Demian,* which appeared under a pseudonym in 1919. For Hesse himself, it was, as we have said, a means to continue his analytic dialogue with Dr. Lang,[27] as is revealed by several passages that read like letters to his doctor, for instance, "[. . .] I have nothing new to say about that, we have spoken about it often," on 24 July 1917, or "we have mentioned my attitude towards fame and the public," on 7 September 1917. To a large extent, however, especially toward their close, the entries become less of a dialogue with the therapist than a conversation Hesse is having with himself, which sometimes seems directed at readers or a public that does not know him, especially in such remarks as "Mia is my wife," on 22 July 1917, which his doctor would have known, or "In Zurich Dr. Lang and I agreed that I should start drawing or painting," on 5 August 1917. These passages suggest that the diary was not written exclusively for the therapeutic dialogue.

At the start of the entries, Hesse declares that he wishes to keep such a diary because he realizes that "bei mir der Trieb zu rascher Gestaltung und Ausmünzung [meiner Wahrnehmungen] das Erleben schädigt"[28] (my desire to give form [to my perceptions] and market them keeps me from fully experiencing them). Consequently, he hoped that the process of noting down his dream experiences would intensify their effect, which would be reinforced by their being analyzed rationally, either through his own interpretations or with professional help. The associations that Hesse himself found between his dreams and other aspects of his life are of special interest.

But Hesse did not try to rationalize every dream fragment in the diary as stemming from his own experiences and ideas, perhaps because, in the case of certain dreams, he wished to withhold clues from Dr. Lang, in order not to influence his interpretation, or simply because he was pressed for time or did not feel like doing more. Then too, Ninon Hesse removed some of his comments after his death. She had reviewed the diary for possible publication, as evidenced by the fact that pages were cut and re-joined with cellophane tape, and some are numbered in her writing. Seventeen passages, totaling a bit more than seven pages of the typescript, were sacrificed to her need for discretion and could not be found.

Even as he began the diary, Hesse found the task of representing dreams highly questionable. He realized that what could be remembered of a dream was not representative for the whole of the sleep process. For no one can remember psychic experiences during the initial phase of deep sleep. We can grasp, and just barely, only those dream residues we can reconstruct shortly before awakening. Hesse noted on 30 August 1917: "Ich habe oft Träume, wo Bilder gleichsam übereinander photographiert sind, was die Erinnerung erschwert"[29] (I often have dreams that are like double-exposed photographs, which makes remembering them difficult). Some dreams come to him as nearly indissoluble "clots of confusion," others as "bounteous series of fleeting images" that he compared with images painted on layered panes of glass, impossible to see through. He is determined, however, to see these difficulties positively, and finds solace in comparing his work on the diary with his efforts generally to express ideas in words. Just as the attempt to depict a dream is related to the world that the dream contains, the work of any artist relates to anything he attempts to represent. Even at best, only a fraction of what one really wants to say is expressed. Nonetheless, what is in order is not resignation, but the impulse to undertake constantly new attempts at expression. Hesse would certainly have shared Martin Walser's skepticism when he wrote in 1995: "Wenn es mir gelingt, einen Traum zu einem nicht ausrechenbaren Teil in Sprache wiederzugeben, ihn also festzuhalten, dann ist das schon eine zerstörerische Aktion. Aber wenn ich ihn dann auch noch, um ihn sozusagen zu verstehen, einer ihn deuten wollenden Sekundärsprache aussetze, dann ist er hin"[30] (If I succeed in reproducing in words even an infinitesimal part of a dream, to hold it in place, then that is a harmful action in itself. But if I then, in order to, as it were, understand it, were to expose it to a secondary language that purports to interpret it, the dream is utterly destroyed). Hesse, too, found that the jargon of psychoanalysis and its interpretive tools were not very helpful. Eight years after the dream diary, in the *Nürnberger Reise* (Journey to Nuremberg), he speaks of the "Panzer von allzuenger, allzu dogmatischer, allzu eitler Akademik" (the armor of an academicism that is all too narrow, dogmatic, and vain) surrounding psychoanalytic vocabulary that is as powerless "wie jeder Versuch, das Phänomen des Lebens zu vereinfachen, es auf eine wissenschaftliche, scheinbar exakte Formel zu bringen"[31] (as every attempt to simplify the phenomenon that is life, to reduce it to a scientific, seemingly exact formula).

Seen in this light, it is not surprising that Hesse rarely used psychoanalytic terms, not only in the dream diary, but also in later remarks on the subject. For example, he never mentions the Oedipus complex, the stereotyping phrase that academic psychology would most readily apply to him, given his problematic fixation on his mother and his conflict-laden relationship with his father. Only once does he use a term of C. G. Jung's: "Was mich an individuelles und kollektives Unbewußtes mahnt [. . .]"[32] (9 September 1917; What brings to mind the individual and collective unconscious [. . .]). Otherwise, Hesse is generally immune to academic jargon and, as a writer, is far more interested in the artistic aspect of the "nächtliche Spiele" (games of the night), such as "die Gleichzeitigkeit mehrerer Traumschichten, die ineinander übergehen können" (the simultaneity of several strata of dreams that can stream into one another), reminding him of the simultaneity of the real and the visionary, which he considers desirable as "ein Zustand, in dem wir gewissermaßen durch die Wirklichkeit hindurch wie durch Glas eine bedeutsamere, andere, höhere Welt sehen [können]"[33] (19 December 1917; a condition, in which we can, so to speak, see through reality as through glass into another, more meaningful, higher world). Fourteen years later, in *Die Morgenlandfahrt* (The Journey to the East), he wrote that "Das Glück der Träume [. . .] bestand aus der Freiheit, alles Erdenkliche gleichzeitig zu erleben, Außen und Innen spielend zu vertauschen, Zeit und Raum wie Kulissen zu verschieben"[34] (The pleasure of dreams lay in the freedom to experience all kinds of things at once, to interchange with playful ease internal with external states, to manipulate times and places like scenery on a stage). He believed that in the life of the unconscious, as expressed in the poetry of dreams, visions, and hallucinations, it is possible to transcend the complexities of one's individual existence to reach a timeless plane of universal being, of elemental situations of life, a state of mind congruent with the ideas of certain ancient mythologies, systems of belief, and religious cults.

Undoubtedly, the psychoanalytic treatments of 1916–18, which he resumed in 1920–21 during the difficulties he encountered in writing *Siddhartha,* were helpful to Hesse, in part too because he saw no alternative and accepted them as necessary. In 1918, in his retrospective article "Künstler und Psychoanalyse," he identifies his reasons. Psychoanalysis, he said, had compelled him to see, to perceive, to examine, and to take seriously those things about himself that he had most successfully repressed. Only in the intensive self-scrutiny of analysis, he continued, can one truly experience and penetrate to the essence of even part of one's own life story: "Über Vater und Mutter, über Bauer und Nomade, über Affe und Fisch zurück wird Herkunft, Gebundenheit und Hoffnung des Menschen nirgends [. . .] so erschütternd erlebt wie in einer ernsthaften Psychoanalyse"[35] (Nowhere else than in a serious psychoanalysis that makes us look backwards beyond father and mother, peasant and nomad, ape and fish, can we truly experience the origins, contingencies, and hopes of humanity).

In his dream diary, Hesse comes to terms unsparingly with the weaknesses and dubious sides of his personality. In contrast to *Demian,* the idealized psychic portrayal that it inspired, the diary has an entirely personal stamp; in depicting Hesse's personal problems, it reveals yet again what he expected of himself and others like him, as set forth in "Bekenntnis des Dichters" (The Poet's Confession) in 1927:

> Wir suchen unsere Zeit nicht zu erklären, nicht zu bessern, nicht zu belehren, sondern wir suchen ihr, indem wir unser eigenes Leid und unsere Träume enthüllen, die Welt der Bilder, die Welt der Seele immer wieder

zu öffnen. Diese Träume sind zum Teil arge Angstträume, diese Bilder sind zum Teil grausige Schreckbilder — wir dürfen sie nicht verschönern, wir dürfen nichts weglügen.[36]

[We do not seek to explain our time, to improve or instruct it, but rather, by exposing to it our own sufferings and dreams, to open up for it again and again the world of images, the world of the soul. In part, our dreams are terrible nightmares, the images horrific visions of doom — we must not embellish them, we must not cover them up with lies.]

Responding, decades later, to inquiries from his readers, Hesse always affirmed that his psychoanalysis had been good for him, especially because of the attention paid to dreams, whose self-regulating treatment of our problems let him marvel at "das Wunder der Seele [. . .] einerlei welche schönen oder anderen Seiten sie uns zeigen möge"[37] (the miracle that is our psyche, no matter whether it reveals to us our good sides or other ones). But he emphasized that the person being analyzed must do most of the work. He had found that reading several books by Freud and Jung had helped him more than the practical analytical techniques. As he wrote in a letter of November 1958 to Dr. Seidmann, "Später wurde mein Verhältnis zur Psychoanalyse kühler, teils weil ich viele Fälle erfolgloser, ja schädlich wirkender Analysen mit anzusehen bekam, teils aber auch, weil ich nie einem Analytiker begegnet bin, der ein echtes Verhältnis zur Kunst gehabt hätte"[38] (Later on, I became cooler towards psychoanalysis, in part because I had heard of cases where it had failed or even done harm, but also because I never met an analyst who had an authentic relationship to the arts). In April 1950, he wrote to Herbert Schulz that none of the many therapists he had known "sah in der Kunst etwas anderes als eine Ausdrucksform des Unbewußten; der neurotische Traum eines beliebigen Patienten war ihnen ebenso wertvoll und weit interessanter als der ganze Goethe. Mit dieser Erkenntnis war ich erst endgültig und völlig von der analytischen Atmosphäre frei. Die Kur ist mir aber im Ganzen gut bekommen"[39] (saw anything else in art but an expression of the unconscious; they found the neurotic dream of any patient at all just as valuable and far more interesting than all of Goethe. Knowing that, I was finally and completely free of the atmosphere of analysis. But, all in all, I found the treatments beneficial).

Hesse's acute sense that psychiatrists lacked understanding for artists, for what inspired them, and for the works themselves is intimately connected with his ideas about dreams. For, as he wrote to Christoph Schrempf in 1932, "Die Künste dienen [. . .] dem Leben, sie sind Funktionen wie Schlaf und Traum"[40] (The arts are there to serve [. . .] life, they are functions, like dreams and sleep); that is, they help to satisfy biological needs. But Hesse considered therapists who found the neurotic dreams of any patient just as valuable and even more interesting than all of Goethe to be nothing but learned philistines who could not conceive of the psychic antitoxins that he had developed from just these neuroses — as self-therapy at first, and then in aid of countless readers in surviving similar crises of their own. For, as Goethe remarked, "alles Gute was geschieht wirkt nicht einzeln. Seiner Natur nach setzt es sogleich das nächste in Bewegung"[41] (Nothing good that happens is an isolated event. In keeping with its nature, it immediately sets in motion the next thing). While the physician must concentrate on deviations from a norm and on pathological phenomena, nothing is as suspect to a creative person, who envisions and prepares for what is to come, as the so-called "normal." It is not the dreams that reveal to us our inmost desires that he mistrusts, but rather the outside world, which insists on conformity, placing between a person and his psyche "einen Wächter, eine Moral, eine Sicherheitsbehörde," and fails to acknowledge anything "was direkt aus dem Seelenabgrund kommt, ohne erst von jener Behörde abgestempelt zu sein" (a guard, a morality, a bureau of security . . . that rises from the soul's abyss unless it bear the bureau's stamp of approval). The quotation is from Hesse's article, "Sprache" (Language) from 1917, and he continues: "Der Künstler aber richtet sein ständiges Mißtrauen nicht gegen das Land der Seele, sondern eben gegen jene Grenzbehörde, und geht heimlich aus und ein zwischen Hier und Dort, zwischen Bewußt und Unbewußt, als wäre er in beiden zu Hause"[42] (But the artist constantly mistrusts not the land of the psyche but precisely that authority guarding the border, and he enters and leaves secretly, moving between here and there, between conscious and unconscious, as though he were at home in both). Only our dreams transcend these boundaries. For Hesse, they are at once a voice of the conscience and a driving force for progress and evolution, which makes use of the individual dreamer to advance its development, not caring in the least for what the current notions of normal or mad, sick or healthy might be. Hesse often spoke of how relative the terms "normal" and "mad" are: "Wir Künstler und Intellektuellen," he wrote on 29 November 1929 to Arthur Stoll, "sind ja heute alle Neurastheniker — vielmehr wir haben eigentlich keineswegs 'schwache' Nerven, sondern normale"[43] (We artists and intellectuals nowadays are all neurasthenics; actually, we have normal nerves, not weak ones). Or five years previously, in *Kurgast* (A Guest at the Spa):

> Die Psychiater erklären einen Menschen für gemütskrank, der auf kleine Störungen, kleine Reizungen, kleine Beleidigungen seines Selbstgefühls empfindlich und heftig reagiert, während derselbe Mensch vielleicht Leiden und Erschütterungen gefaßt erträgt, welche der Majorität sehr schlimm erscheinen. Und ein Mensch gilt für gesund und normal, dem man lange auf die Zehen treten kann, ohne daß er es merkt, der die elendeste Musik, die kläglichste Architektur, die verdorbenste Luft klaglos und beschwerdelos erträgt."[44]

[The psychiatrists call a person emotionally disturbed if he reacts strongly to little disturbances, little irritations, little insults to his self-esteem; yet that same person may be calmly suffering degrees of pain and distress, which most people find intolerable. And someone may be considered healthy and normal who never notices that he is being mocked and insulted, who tolerates uncritically the worst music, the most pathetic architecture, the stalest, dirtiest air without complaining.]

Thus, he wrote in a letter to Fritz Marti in 1929,

diese Neurosen am Ende auch eine Gesundheit sein, nämlich das einzig mögliche Reagieren beseelter Naturen auf eine Zeit, die nur Geld und Zahl und keine Seele mehr kennt.[45]

[Thus, these "neuroses" might actually be a kind of health, the only means that people with feeling souls have of reacting to an age that no longer knows about the soul, but only about cash and numbers.]

On the other hand, people who do not have such thick skins, who are beset by obstacles and unmet needs, tend to suffer from feelings of inadequacy and complexes that — if the function of dreams as a safety valve no longer suffices for them — must be resolved in their waking lives in different ways. During the day, Hesse notes in a letter of June 1929, the protective magic of the dream often fails because even the best dreamer when awake must take the outside world more seriously than he should. "Die Verrückten können das besser; sie erklären sich für Kaiser, und die Zelle für ihr Schloß, und alles stimmt wunderbar" (Madmen do it better. They declare themselves emperors and their cells their castles, and everything is just fine). It is his goal as an artist, Hesse says, to be able to transform the outside world magically without going mad. That is not easy to do, "dafür aber ist wenig Konkurrenz da. 99 Menschen von 100 haben ganz andere Ziele"[46] (but there is not much competition, as 99 people of 100 have completely different goals). And because things are that way, because most contemporaries, who provide physicians with the standard for "normality," cannot perceive and assess creative forms of psychic compensation, most psychiatrists too are insensitive to the possibility that it is valuable and significant when a writer "aus den Nöten und Beklemmungen seiner persönlichen Gebundenheit heraus [den Antrieb nehme], die Unvollkommenheit seines Lebens durch die Vollkommenheit seines Werkes zu erlösen"[47] (out of the needs and constraints of his personal life, is motivated to redeem the imperfections of his life by perfecting his art).

According to the criteria of psychoanalysis, Hesse noted in 1931 in his "Gedanken über Gottfried Keller" (Thoughts on Gottfried Keller), a writer who "den langen und mühseligen Umweg zur Sublimierung seiner Spannungen im Werk verschmäht, und der statt dessen eine Anpassungskur durchführt und 'normal' wird, wertvoller sein als jeder andere"[48] (disdains to follow the long and difficult detour to the sublimation of his tensions in his work, choosing rather to undergo the regimens of conformity and become "normal," must be of greater value than any other). That is why psychiatrists considered people such as Novalis, Hölderlin, Lenau, Beethoven, and Nietzsche nothing but severely pathological cases if they read their works without knowing who they were or of their stature. For the artist has only this advantage over the mentally disturbed: that he is not confined for being mad, but rather is respected for the work he creates. As Hesse wrote in a letter to the psychologist Theodor Schnittkin in 1928

> Daß diese Männer aus ihren Komplexen eine Welt geschaffen haben [und] daß *jede* kulturelle Leistung aus Komplexen kommt, daß Kultur überhaupt nichts andres ist als ein Einschalten von Widerständen und Reibungsgelegenheiten zwischen Trieb und Geist, und daß Leistungen nicht dort entstehen, wo Komplexe "geheilt" werden, sondern wo ihre Hochspannungen sich schöpferisch erfüllen, von alledem weiß die Analyse so wenig wie die moderne Wissenschaft überhaupt. Wie sollte sie auch. Der Zweck der Medizin, inklusive Analyse, ist ja nicht die Erkenntnis des Genies und der Tragik des Geistes, sondern ihr Zweck ist, zu bewirken, daß die Patientin Meyer womöglich ihr Asthma oder ihre nervösen Magengeschichten verliert. Der Geist läuft wahrlich auf anderen Pfaden, nicht auf diesen.[49]

> [That these men have created a world out of their complexes, [and] that *every* cultural achievement is born out of complexes, that culture itself is nothing but the result of resistances and frictions between the instinctive and the spiritual, and that creativity is not accomplished when complexes are "cured," but only when their intense powers can find productive fulfillment: psychoanalysis understands as little about such matters as modern science in general. How could it know any better? The purpose of medical science, including psychoanalysis, is not to acknowledge genius or the tragic aspects of the spirit; its purpose is, rather, to see to it that Mrs. Meyer, the patient, gets rid of her asthma or her nervous stomach. The human spirit truly chooses other paths, not these.]

In 1930, Hesse also devoted an entire chapter, well worth reading, of his "Notizen zum Thema Dichtung und Kritik" (Notes on Writing and Criticism) to the anti-intellectual influence of psychoanalysis on literary criticism, entitled "Psychologie der Halbgebildeten" (Psychology of the Half-Educated).

Even C. G. Jung considered art, the creative form of dreams and their sublimation, to be a mechanism of repression. Hesse did not dispute the point, but countered in September 1934 in reply to a letter from Jung that he himself applied that "noble" term, sublimation, only

> wo es mir erlaubt scheint, von "geglückter" Verdrängung zu reden, also von Auswirkung eines Triebs auf einem zwar uneigentlichen, aber kul-

turell hochrangigen Gebiet, zum Beispiel dem der Kunst [. . .] Und wo
ein begabter Mensch mit einem Teil seiner Triebkräfte solche Dinge
fördert, finde ich seine Existenz und sein Tun von höchstem Wert, auch
wenn er vielleicht als Individuum pathologisch ist. Was mir also während
einer Psychoanalyse unerlaubt scheint: das Ausbiegen in ein Scheinsub-
limieren, das scheint mir erlaubt, ja höchst wertvoll und erwünscht, wo es
gelingt, wo das Opfer Frucht trägt. Eben darum ist ja die Psychoanalyse
für Künstler so sehr schwierig und gefährlich, weil sie dem, der es ernst
nimmt, gleich das ganze Künstlertum zeitlebens verbieten kann. Geschieht das bei einem Dilettanten, dann ist es gut — geschähe es bei
einem Händel oder Bach, so wäre es mir lieber, es gäbe keine Analyse,
und wir behielten dafür den Bach.[50]

[where I deem it proper to speak of a successful repression, of the realization of an impulse within a figurative but culturally significant area,
e.g., in art. [. . .] And where a gifted person brings forth such works with
a part of his psychic energy, I find his existence and achievements to be of
the highest value, even if he personally is a psychopath. What I consider
unacceptable in psychoanalysis, to divert the patient into a pseudo-subli-
mation, seems permissible to me, indeed valuable and desirable, when it
is successful, when that sacrifice bears fruit. Psychoanalysis is so difficult
and dangerous for artists because it can forever forbid someone who takes
his art seriously from living for the sake of his artistry. If that happens to a
dilettante, fine, but if it happens to a Händel or a Bach, I would rather
there were no psychoanalysis, and we could hold on to Bach instead.]

Here, Hesse was speaking of the ancient practical truth of the purifying
influence of art, which resolves the visual riddles of the night into day-
dreams, gives them longer life, sublimates them as playful metaphors, thereby resolving conflicts with remarkable effects on society. That psychiatrists
have come to understand this is demonstrated wherever music, painting, and
literature are used for therapeutic purposes.

For more than a decade, between 1916 and 1927, Hesse used psychoanalysis and the interpretation of dreams to explore his inner self. This experience added greatly to the complexity and depth of his works without
diminishing their figurative immediacy. Fully conscious of the problem, he
avoided excessive involvement in the analytical process, which would have
put his powers of creative synthesis at risk. In this his reaction to psychoanalysis had much in common with the reaction of Rilke, who refused to
have his "angels" exorcised along with his "devils."

As he grew older, Hesse came to think less of the interpretation of
dreams as a medium of self-knowledge. In this, he was not quite as abrupt as
Goethe, who wrote to Herder in December 1788: "Die verwünschte Aufmerksamkeit auf Träume! Es ist doch immer das Traumreich ein falscher
Lostopf, wo unzählige Nieten und höchstens kleine Gewinnstchen unte-

reinander gemischt sind. Man wird selbst zum Traum, wenn man sich ernstlich mit diesen Phantomen beschäftigt"[51] (This damnable attention we pay to our dreams! The land of dreams is always a box of chances in a lottery containing countless losing tickets all mixed up with some bringing only tiny winnings. Anyone who takes these phantoms seriously will become a dream himself). Hesse was in no such danger; his dream-poem "Verzückung" (Rapture) declares:

Nichts ist außen, nichts ist innen,
Nichts ist unten, nichts ist oben,
Alles Feste will zerrinnen,
Alle Grenzen sind zerstoben[52]

[Nothing outside, nothing inside
Nothing below, nothing above,
All that's solid seeks to flow,
Every limit disappears]

He often quoted the Chinese thinker Chuang-tzu (ca. 350 BCE): "I dreamt I was a butterfly, and now I don't know whether I am a man dreaming he's a butterfly or perhaps a butterfly dreaming he's a man." As an artist, the surrealism of dreams drew his interest, the "Unerschöpflichkeit ihrer Spielphantasie, ihre geistreiche Kombinatorik und ihr oft hinreißender Humor"[53] (the inexhaustible inventions of their playful fantasies, their witty associations, and their often hilarious humor). Even in old age, Hesse felt so close to the world of dreams, fairy tales, and magic that his own life could seem like a fairy tale to him. In his "Kurzgefasster Lebenslauf" (Life Story Briefly Told), he wrote:

Oft sehe und fühle ich die Außenwelt mit meinem Innern in einem Zusammenhang und Einklang, den ich magisch nennen muß [. . .] Weil nun die sogenannte Wirklichkeit für mich keine sehr große Rolle spielt, weil Vergangenes mich oft wie Gegenwart erfüllt und Gegenwärtiges mir unendlich fern erscheint, darum kann ich auch die Zukunft nicht so scharf von der Vergangenheit trennen, wie man es meistens tut. Ich lebe sehr viel in der Zukunft.[54]

[I often see and feel that the world outside and my inward being are in a state of harmonious connectedness that I must call magical. [. . .] Because so-called reality is not very important to me now, because I am absorbed by things past as though they were present, and the present seems infinitely remote, I cannot separate the future from the past as sharply as most people do. I live in the future a great deal.]

The way that Hesse's books are read and appreciated today confirms the accuracy of that feeling. When his works encounter criticism and resistance, it is often because their provocative insistence that our species must evolve faster causes some readers discomfort. That was no less true during Hesse's lifetime; in 1926, for example, a young woman told him that she had dreamed that she was a monkey and that Hesse was trying to persuade her to become human. Commenting on this episode, Hesse wrote to his friend Hugo Ball on 23 November 1926: "In Träumen habe ich scheints keinen guten Ruf, doch sehe ich, daß die Träumer wenigstens nicht ihre schwächsten Antriebe mit meiner Maske bekleiden"[55] (It seems I don't have a good name in other peoples' dreams, but at least the dreamers don't dress up just their weakest impulses with a mask of my face).

— *Translated by Michael M. Metzger*

Notes

An earlier German-language version of this article appeared in Hermann Hesse, *Traumgeschenk,* ed. Volker Michels, 333–59 (Frankfurt am Main: Suhrkamp, 1996).

[1] From a letter of 23 July 1950, in Hermann Hesse, *Ausgewählte Briefe* (Frankfurt am Main: Suhrkamp, 1974), 346.

[2] Hermann Hesse/Thomas Mann, *Briefwechsel,* ed. Anni Carlsson and Volker Michels (Frankfurt am Main: Suhrkamp, 1999), 296.

[3] Hermann Hesse, "Traumtheater" (1948), in Hermann Hesse, *Sämtliche Werke,* vol. 14, *Betrachtungen und Berichte II. 1927–1961,* ed. Volker Michels (Frankfurt am Main: Suhrkamp, 2001), 248. Volumes of the *Sämtliche Werke,* once given a full citation in the notes to this chapter, will be cited by the abbreviation *SW* and volume and page number.

[4] Hermann Hesse, "Kindheit des Zauberers," in Hermann Hesse, *Sämtliche Werke,* vol. 9, *Die Märchen. Legenden. Übertragungen. Dramatisches. Idyllen* (Frankfurt am Main: Suhrkamp, 2002), 172.

[5] Hesse, "Kindheit des Zauberers," *SW* 9:186.

[6] Both quotations are from Hermann Hesse, *Gesammelte Briefe,* vol. 2, *1922–1935,* ed. Ursula and Volker Michels (Frankfurt am Main: Suhrkamp, 1979), 428–29.

[7] Hermann Hesse, *Gertrud,* in *Sämtliche Werke,* vol. 2, *Die Romane: Peter Camenzind. Unterm Rad. Gertrud* (Frankfurt am Main: Suhrkamp, 2001), 287.

[8] Hermann Hesse, *Eine Stunde hinter Mitternacht,* in *Sämtliche Werke,* vol. 1: *Jugendschriften,* ed. Volker Michels (Frankfurt am Main: Suhrkamp, 2001), 187.

[9] Hesse, *Eine Stunde hinter Mitternacht, SW* 1:187.

[10] Hesse, *Eine Stunde hinter Mitternacht, SW* 1:170.

[11] Hesse, *Eine Stunde hinter Mitternacht, SW* 1:171.

[12] From Hesse's review "Chinesische Geister- und Liebesgeschichten" (February 1912), in *Sämtliche Werke,* vol. 17: *Die Welt im Buch II. Rezensionen und Aufsätze aus den Jahren 1911–1916,* ed. Volker Michels with Heiner Hesse (Frankfurt am Main: Suhrkamp, 2002), 75.

[13] From Hesse's review "Die vier Zweige des Mabinogi" (December 1914), *SW* 17:396.

[14] From Hesse's review "Die vier Zweige des Mabinogi" (December 1914), *SW* 17:396.

[15] From Hesse's review "Die vier Zweige des Mabinogi" (December 1914), *SW* 17:396.

[16] From Hesse's review "Für Bücherliebhaber [IX]" (December 1914), *SW* 17:390.

[17] Hesse, "Künstler und Psychoanalyse" (1918), *SW* 14:352 and 354.

[18] Hesse, "Vom Bücherlesen" (1920), *SW* 14:371.

[19] Hesse, "Künstler und Psychoanalyse," *SW* 14:355.

[20] Hesse to Walter Schädelin, 3 May 1916 (unpublished).

[21] Hesse to Ernst Kreidolf, 20 May 1916 (unpublished).

[22] Hesse to Herrn P. Sch., mid April 1931. In Hesse, *Ausgewählte Briefe*, 51–52.

[23] Hesse to Herrn P. Sch., mid April 1931. In Hesse, *Ausgewählte Briefe*, 51–52.

[24] Hesse to Herrn P. Sch., mid April 1931. In Hesse, *Ausgewählte Briefe*, 51–52.

[25] Hesse, *Demian*, in *Sämtliche Werke*, vol. 3: *Die Romane: Roßhalde. Knulp. Demian. Siddhartha*, ed. Volkre Michels (Frankfurt am Main: Suhrkamp, 2001), 346 and 324.

[26] Hesse, "Traumtagebuch der Psychoanalyse 1917/1918," in *Sämtliche Werke*, vol. 11: *Autobiographische Schriften I. Wanderung. Kurgast. Die Nürnberger Reise. Tagebücher* (Frankfurt am Main: Suhrkamp, 2003), 444–617; here 446.

[27] The correspondence between Hermann Hesse and Josef Bernhard Lang has been made available as *Die dunkle und wilde Seite der Seele*, ed. Thomas Feitknecht (Frankfurt am Main: Suhrkamp, 2006).

[28] Hesse, "Traumtagebuch der Psychoanalyse 1917/1918," *SW* 11:446.

[29] Hesse, "Traumtagebuch der Psychoanalyse 1917/1918," *SW* 11:457.

[30] Martin Walser, "Die Stimmung, das Wissen, die Sprache," in Walser, *Über freie und unfreie Rede* (Eggingen: Isele, 1995), 40.

[31] Hesse, *Die Nürnberger Reise*, *SW* 11:162.

[32] Hesse, "Traumtagebuch der Psychoanalyse 1917/1918," *SW* 11:490–91.

[33] Hesse, "Traumtagebuch der Psychoanalyse 1917/1918," *SW* 11:534.

[34] Hesse, *Die Morgenlandfahrt*, *Sämtliche Werke*, vol. 4: *Die Romane: Der Steppenwolf. Narziß und Goldmund. Die Morgenlandfahrt*, ed. Volker Michels (Frankfurt am Main: Suhrkamp, 2001), 547.

[35] Hesse, "Künstler und Psychoanalyse" (1918), *SW* 14:355.

[36] Hesse, "Bekenntnis des Dichters" (1927), *SW* 14:395.

[37] Hesse to Carl Seelig, early 1919 (unpublished).

[38] Hesse to Peter Seidmann, November 1958. In Hesse, *Gesammelte Briefe*, 4:320–21.

[39] Hesse to Herbart Schulz, April 1950. In Hesse, *Gesammelte Briefe*, 4:54.

[40] Hesse to Christoph Schrempf, February 1932. In Hesse, *Gesammelte Briefe*, 2:319.

[41] J. W. Goethe, *Über die verschiednen Zweige der hiesigen Tätigkeit* (1795), in *Sämtliche Werke* (Munich edition; Munich: Hanser, 1986), 4:2:872–83; here 872, or Johann Wolfgang Goethe, *Über die verschiedenen Zweige der hiesigen Thätigkeit. Ein Vortrag*, in *Goethes Werke* (Weimar edition; Weimar: Böhlau, 1914), 53:175–92.

[42] Hesse, "Sprache" (1917), *SW* 14:345.

[43] Hesse to Arthur Stoll, 29 November 1929. In Hesse, *Gesammelte Briefe*, 2:232.

[44] Hesse, *Kurgast, SW* 11:123–24.

[45] Hesse to Fritz Marti, 17 August 1929. In Hesse, *Gesammelte Briefe*, 2:223.

[46] Hesse to Olga Diener, June 1929. In Hesse, *Gesammelte Briefe*, 2:216.

[47] Hesse, "Gedanken über Gottfried Keller" (July 1931), in *Sämtliche Werke*, vol. 19: *Die Welt im Buch IV. Rezensionen und Aufsätze aus den Jahren 1926–1934*, ed. Volker Michels with Heiner Hesse and Marco Schickling (Frankfurt am Main: Suhrkamp, 2003), 232.

[48] Hesse, "Gedanken über Gottfried Keller," *SW* 19:232.

[49] Hesse to Theodor Schnittkin, 3 June 1928. In Hesse, *Gesammelte Briefe*, 2:196.

[50] Hesse to C. G. Jung, September 1934. In Hesse, *Ausgewählte Briefe*, 127.

[51] J. W. Goethe to J. G. Herder, 27 December 1788. In J. W. Goethe, *Briefe der Jahre 1786–1814* (Zurich: Artemis, 1949), 131.

[52] From the poem "Verzückung," *Sämtliche Werke*, vol. 10: *Die Gedichte*, ed. Peter Huber (Frankfurt am Main: Suhrkamp, 2002), 258.

[53] Hesse, "Traumtheater," *SW* 14:246.

[54] Hesse, "Kurzgefaßter Lebenslauf" (1921/24), in *Sämtliche Werke*, vol. 12: *Autobiographische Schriften II. Selbstzeugnisse. Erinnerungen. Gedenkblätter und Rundbriefe* (Frankfurt am Main: Suhrkamp, 2003), 58.

[55] Hesse to Hugo Ball, 23 November 1926. In Hesse, *Briefwechsel 1921–1927 mit Hugo Ball und Emmy Ball-Hennings*, ed. Bärbel Reetz (Frankfurt am Main: Suhrkamp, 2003), 422.

14: On the Relationship between Hesse's Painting and Writing: *Wanderung, Klingsors letzter Sommer, Gedichte des Malers* and *Piktors Verwandlungen*

Godela Weiss-Sussex

INTERMEDIAL COMPARISON IS AN AREA of study that, though not new, has received fresh impetus in recent years, as we have come to recognize more and more clearly the extent to which the narrow confines of individual disciplines limit our search for a comprehensive understanding of creative works. But postulations of vague similarities are not enough. Like all generalizations, they obscure the precise detail of the relationship rather than elucidating it. On the other hand, as Erwin Panofsky established already in 1932, a one-to-one set of correspondences between texts and paintings cannot be established, as a direct "translation" from one medium to another is impossible. Any description of a picture in words cannot but distort — or even suppress — the original "voice" of the picture, even if only by adding an emphasis or evaluation in its description.[1] There are, however, clearly definable structural and thematic correspondences between paintings and literary texts; and intermedial comparison can and should explore these as scrupulously as possible.[2]

Where, as in Hesse's case, texts and paintings are produced by the same artist, this adds an extra interest to the inquiry. In such analyses of the work of "multiple talents," the starting point is the hypothesis that the artist's creative aims are the same in both media.[3] The investigation can thus focus on the relationship between the different realizations of this creative motivation. That Hesse pursued the same aims in his painting and writing is evident from comments such as one he wrote in a letter to the *National-Zeitung* in Basel in 1920: "Sie werden sehen, daß zwischen meiner Malerei und Dichtung keine Diskrepanz herrscht, daß ich auch hier nicht der naturalistischen, sondern der poetischen Wahrheit nachgehe"[4] (You will see that there is no discrepancy between my painting and my poetic work, that here also I pursue not naturalistic, but instead poetic truth). Representation of this poetic truth is not possible by mimetic efforts alone; it is the expression of a perceived connection and unison between the physical world and the subjective world of the artist — a capturing of external phenomena and an expression of innermost emotions at the same time.

This chapter will explore how Hesse developed the concept of art as the expression of poetic truth in his painting as well as in his writing in the first years of his working in both media, 1918 to 1922. It will analyze the interrelationship between word and picture in his works of these years, an interrelationship that, owing to his discovery and growing mastery of the new medium, had the most profound impact on his further development as a writer.[5]

Wanderung

Hesse started to paint at the age of forty, as a result of an acute personal crisis. He experienced the First World War and the hostility of the press because of his pacifist convictions as a conflict between himself and the world.[6] Furthermore, a severe illness of his youngest son in 1914, his wife's mental decline, and the death of his father in 1916 all deepened the crisis and caused, in Hesse's words, the loss of his home and his family (*SW* 12:54). With the foundations of his life eroded, he went through a period of severe doubt about himself, his abilities as a writer, and the value of literary writing at all.[7]

After undergoing psychoanalytical treatment in Lucerne in 1916 and on the suggestion of his analyst, Hesse took up painting; and during the following years, this activity was to take more and more room and importance in his life. In many of his letters from this period, he gives clear insights into the significance that painting took on for him as a refuge and support.[8] The richness and beauty of the Tessin landscape, which he first encountered on walking trips in 1916 and 1918, and then came to know intimately after his move to Montagnola in 1919, fired his imagination and further strengthened his will to express himself with pencil, brush, and paints.

In 1918, Hesse started to offer for sale manuscripts of poems accompanied by colored drawings; and in 1920, he published his first book incorporating his own watercolors. It was a slim volume with the title *Wanderung,* a collection of short prose texts — mostly contemplations of landscape, self- and artistic representation — and watercolors, both resulting from his walks in Tessin in 1918 and 1919, as well as ten poems written between 1912 and 1920.

The watercolors in *Wanderung* possess the quality of sketches rather than definitive depictions, and the openness of their form leaves room for a subjective reception by the beholder. With their faint colors and simple shapes, they express a certain tentativeness and passivity on the part of the painter, rather than emphasizing the activity and invention of the artist as creator. The texts accompanying the pictures reflect the same theme and develop it in various ways.

Hermann Goern sees in Hesse's *Wanderung* the author's self-confession as a "Doppeltalent," calling it "one of the most delightful and precious books by any German writer."[9] Perhaps Goern overstates his claim, but he makes another very apt observation: that Hesse's "undemanding little pictures stand . . . like initials before a text like a key signature before the following lines, and are much more than just incidental decoration or illustration."[10] The pictures provide the musical key for the text; they are indications of mood, not sophisticated and detailed representations to be taken up and transformed into the medium of writing. In that respect, they are similar to the pictures in the manuscripts Hesse was selling at the time. As Hesse himself wrote: "Ihr Wert ist kein artistischer, er liegt einzig darin, daß Gedicht und Bild hier völlig aus einer Hand und Handschrift kommen, aus demselben Empfinden her, also eine Einheit bilden, wie sie sonst zwischen Text und 'Illustration' nie da ist"[11] (Their worth is not artistic; it lies only in the fact that poem and picture here come from one hand and from one personal style, from the same mood, and thus form a unity such as otherwise is never there between text and "illustration"). Indeed, the unity of "Empfindung," of mood, throughout the texts and pictures of *Wanderung* is striking. This may be due to its personal nature: the expression of the artist's feeling, or mood, is less obscured by the conscious process of finding a literary form as is the case in more polished and ambitious texts.[12]

The section "Bergpaß," Mountain Pass, a reflection on the experience of nature, the change of this experience with time, and about its communication, may serve as an example here. The watercolor that precedes the text is not much more than an atmospheric sketch. In the careful coloring-in of the simple outlines it is easy to see a certain awkwardness, regarded by Michels as characteristic of the earliest of Hesse's attempts at painting.[13] Here, as in most of the *Wanderung* pictures, Hesse works with shades of color that flow into one another. Against an almost transparent chain of summits in the background, a mountain pass is depicted in natural hues of green and red. A curving pale yellow road draws the observer's eye from near the lower left corner into the center of the picture, to the top of the pass, and on into the distance beyond.

The simplicity of the text mirrors that of the image. The first paragraph, for instance, consists of short sentences, most of which follow the same paratactic pattern, building up a calm rythm, underpinned by the repetitions at the beginning of clauses: "Niemand hat hier etwas zu suchen, niemand hat hier Besitz [. . .]"[14] ("Nobody has anything to look for here, no one here owns anything," 15). When it comes to the description of the road, the sentence pattern changes to a winding hypotactical structure and, in analogy to the yellow arch of the curving road in the picture, brings movement into the calm, slightly monotonous text

Bergpaß (Mountain Pass). From Hesse,
Wanderung (Berlin: Fischer, 1920), 19.

rhythm, drawing the reader on — "zu anderen Tälern, anderen Häusern,
zu anderen Sprachen und Menschen" (*W* 9; to other valleys, other
houses, to other languages and other men," 15). The unity of mood
between the representations in the two media is built on thematical as
well as structural analogy.

The landscape description in the first paragraph is taken as a starting
point, a springboard for further observations and reflections. Hesse juxta-
poses two experiences of landscape. The traveler's journey on foot across
a mountain pass evokes memories of his first journey south, undertaken in
his youth. Instead of the desire of the youth to heighten the expression of
his experience by overlaying his descriptions with his own "Traumfarben,"
dream colors, he — and the writer and painter Hesse — has learnt to be receptive to what he sees. Instead of imposing his own viewpoint or artistic
aims, he is striving to capture it with calm, quiet, and grateful senses.

This does not mean, however, that art should be a mere reflection, a
mimetic mirror image of nature. Rather, the artist's work is an *answer* to
nature. This definition of art is made explicit in another of the sections in
Wanderung, entitled "See, Baum, Berg," in which the wanderer hears the
song of God, the song of nature, and answers it:

> Da fing er selber an zu singen, langsam und gedehnt. Sein Lied war
> ohne Kunst, es war wie Luft und Wellenschlag, es war nur ein Sum-
> men und bienenhaftes Brummsen. Das Lied gab dem singenden Gott
> in der Ferne Antwort, und dem singenden Strom im Baum, und dem
> rinnenden Gesang im Blut. (*W* 30)

[Then he himself started to sing, slowly and lingeringly. His song was artless, it was like air and the beating of waves, it was only a humming and buzzing like that of a bee. The song gave answer to the singing God in the distance, and to the singing stream in the tree, and to the running song in the blood. (90)]

The wanderer's answer to the song — and the creation — of God is one of simplicity, of artlessness and spontaneity. Read as a characterization of Hesse's work as an artist, it indicates the abandonment of all deliberate, willful creation that is guided by purpose and intellect.[15] Emphasized instead is the deep connection between nature and the artist's inner world, in other words the "poetic truth" to which Hesse referred in his letter to the Basel *National-Zeitung* quoted above.

The combination of paintings and text allows a multi-layered representation of exterior and interior world. In his contemporary review of *Wanderung,* Oscar Bie pointed out that the different media denote different levels of abstraction. Whereas, Bie claims, the pictures are a naïve and loving direct representation of a first impression, the prose texts build on this, taking a more distanced stance of observation or reflection resulting from the initial impression. The poems, finally, are yet one more step removed from the directness of the first impression: "The poems are the third form, flowers of this wandering."[16]

While not a cover-all description of all sections of the book, this description of the relationship between the different media certainly applies to the section "See, Baum, Berg." The picture here is very simple: a tree with lightly sketched foliage, dabbed with yellow paint swirls, fills almost the entire scene; behind it, we see a range of purple-colored hills across a stretch of light blue water. The faintness of the sketched outlines creates the impression of lightness, insubstantiality; only the tree trunk, defined by thicker lines, seems to be solid, tangible. The impression of vagueness is enhanced by the faded colors used.

The text thematically corresponds to the picture, but goes further, as it also expresses subjective reflection and imaginative content. A first indication of this is that the text accords color a much greater importance. The beginning reads: "Es war einmal ein See. Über den blauen See und den blauen Himmel hinweg ragte grün und gelb ein Frühlingsbaum" (*W* 29; "Once there was a lake. Above the blue lake and into the blue sky towered a spring tree, green and yellow. Beyond it the sky rested quietly on the arched mountain," 89). Not only is every noun qualified by a color, but the construction of the second sentence encourages the reading of "grün" as a noun, and thus accords it a certain independence. The imagined landscape thus has a greater intensity than the one represented in the picture. As the formula "Es war einmal" indicates, the text — and the color epithets that appear in it — does not strive for a representation in writing of what

See, Baum, Berg (Lake, Tree, Mountain).
From Hesse, *Wanderung,* 91.

has been seen, but is an imaginative reflection, a fairy tale — and, later in the text, a dream within this fairy tale.

The poem "Magie der Farben" ("Magic of Colors"), which follows this text, takes up the theme of answering divine creation by the creative activity of the artist: "Licht singt tausendfache Lieder, / Gott wird Welt im farbig Bunten" (*W* 30; "Light sings its songs a thousand times, / God becomes the world in so many colors," 92). The formulation of the praise of painting in the form of a poem ensures that both arts, painting and poetry, are celebrated at the same time.

Klingsors letzter Sommer

Some months after he had written the texts for *Wanderung,* but under very different circumstances, Hesse composed his prose narrative *Klingsors letzter Sommer.*[17] He had made the Casa Camuzzi in Montagnola his new home, and dedicated much time to developing his skills and expressivity in painting. Building on the intensity of the experience of his first summer there, he abandoned the pale, natural hues of the *Wanderung* watercolors, and instead used intense, strong, bright colors, concentrating on their abstract interplay.

The novella about the ecstasy and intoxication of the last summer in the life of the painter Klingsor gives insight into Hesse's own intensity of experience during that summer. That he saw the narrative as bearing witness on his own painting is evident from a letter on the subject to Walter Ueber Wasser, which he closes with the words: "Jetzt aber genug. Ich hoffe, der 'Klingsor' werde Ihnen mehr sagen als ein Brief es kann"[18] (But enough now. I hope "Klingsor" will say more to you than a letter can).

Even though Hesse does not manifestly combine the two media of painting and writing in this work, his intense pursuit of painting had an influence on the narrative that can hardly be overestimated.

Most immediately striking is how Hesse's work with paint, his exploration of colors and shapes, enriched the eidetic quality and the linguistic richness of his writing; the writing often reflects the abstracting vision of the painter. In the section "Der Kareno-Tag," for instance, Hesse describes how Klingsor hangs back from his friends in order to see them as "farbige Konstellationen"[19] (colored combinations, 169). The landscape descriptions in this chapter attain their sensual intensity through the application of three techniques that are analogous to painting techniques: firstly, through the number and variety of colors referred to and the exact definition of finely nuanced shades of color ("veronesergrün"/ "Verona green" [K 296/165], "smaragden"/ "emerald" [K 297/167], "rosig gelb"/ pinkish yellow [K 302]); secondly, through the emphasis on the independent expressive value of abstract color, the guiding aesthetic principle behind Expressionism ("Licht floß senkrecht herab, Farbe dampfte hundertfältig aus der Tiefe herauf" [K 299; "Light poured vertically down. Color steamed multifold out of the depths," 169]); thirdly, the intensity and memorability of the landscape descriptions, in this section more than in any other, rely on the evocation of paintings, both real and fictional, in the reader's imagination. Gauguin is named, for example, and this reference influences the reader's view of the colorful and fertile Tessin landscape, overlaying it with the jungle worlds of the painter of the Pacific.

Taking into account that one of the characters in *Klingsors letzter Sommer,* "Louis der Grausame" is the alter ego of one of Hesse's friends, the Swiss painter and stained-glass designer Louis Moilliet (1880–1962), Hesse's description of the village Kareno as "uralt, eng, finster, sarazenisch" (K 301; "ancient, narrow, densely dark, Saracen," 172) and of Klingsor and his friends as "Karawane" (K 302), his designation of their arrival at the "Königin der Gebirge" as "Ankunft in Damaskus" (ibid.; "Queen of the Mountains" [173]; "Arrival in Damascus" [174]), and his references to the intensity of the light evoke, among other mental images, the paintings by Moilliet, Paul Klee, and August Macke produced in Tunis in 1914.[20]

But the importance of painting for Hesse's *Klingsor* novella goes beyond the boost to the eidetic quality of his writing. Significantly, it is by painting that Klingsor fights death in the chapter "Die Musik des Untergangs" ("The Music of Doom"). With reference to Expressionist art, and more specifically, to the driven nature of the work of van Gogh — though he is not explicitly named[21] — Hesse's description of Klingsor's painting in the face of the recognition of his own mortality shows no interest in the finished works of art, or even in their different stages of development, but only in the act of painting itself, in the desperate frenzy of the attempt to fight death through creative activity.

But most interesting in the context of this essay is Klingsor's struggle for the means of expressing poetic truth through artistic creation. On the one hand, he rebels against the limitations of sequential experience: "Warum gab es Zeit?," he asks. "Warum immer nur dies idiotische Nacheinander und kein brausendes, sättigendes Zugleich?" (*K* 289; "Why did time exist? Why always this idiotic succession of one thing after another, and not a roaring, sating simultaneity?," 154, translation modified). In this frustration lies a lament over the limitations of the written word and a longing for the ability to create a work of art that would allow the observer to perceive a multiplicity of details and impressions (almost) simultaneously. Painting can do this; but painting alone cannot fulfill the creative demands of the artist, either. Hesse's depiction of Klingsor's self-portrait in the narrative's last chapter makes this clear. This section can be described, to use a term coined by J. Hollander, as "notional ekphrasis" — that is, the representation in writing of a *fictional* work of art.[22] As an actual painting, this self-portrait is an impossibility. Hesse does not describe it in terms of its colors, but as a repository of emotions, reflections, and associations; and as simultaneously containing a multiplicity of faces — among them that of an "Urwaldgötzen" ("jungle idol") and "des Verfallenden, des Untergehenden, des mit seinem Untergang Einverstandenen" (*K* 330; "the doomed and decaying man who accepted his fate," 213). Adding a strong element of temporality, he refers to the portrait as encompassing previous life stages and adding up to the sum of a life. Thus balancing various possibilities of visual interpretation, the text is not so much a description but rather the *creation* of a picture, and writing is the only possible medium in which it could possibly be created. Recognizing the irreconcilability of time and space, Hesse makes them collide in the illusion of a painting that cannot materially exist.

Klingsors letzter Sommer leaves no doubt that Hesse is striving for an ideal representation of poetic truth, but in order to capture the world of exterior appearances in their plentiful simultaneity and the expression of individual feelings and reflections at the same time, the constraints of time and space would need to be overcome. The adjective that Hesse uses to describe this liberation through art is "magisch"[23] (magic) — and neither writing, which is bound to time, nor painting, which is bound to space, can achieve it alone. But the combination of the two complementary media allows the artist to approach this creation of a "magic" space outside space and time.

Gedichte des Malers

Having experimented in *Wanderung* with the combination of picture and word and in *Klingsors letzter Sommer* with an attempt to render the vision of the painter and the act of painting through the medium of writing, Hesse returned to juxtaposing and complementing the two media in *Gedichte des Malers* (Poems of the Painter, 1920). The volume contains ten poems accompanied by watercolors painted in 1919.

In the short space of time since his early attempts of the *Wanderung* watercolors, Hesse's style of painting had evolved dramatically. Still taking the visual impression as a basis, he now eschewed their fluidity for an emphasis on the independent value of colors and forms, their combinations and contrasts. This interest in creating structures governed by rhythmical relationships between individual fields of color, is reminiscent of the French painter Robert Delaunay's experiments with Orphic cubism. Delaunay (1885–1941), as well as Macke (1887–1914) and Moilliet, who were influenced by him, aimed to create a style of painting equivalent to music, built on the abstraction of nature and light, structured by rhythmical harmonies of color and form.[24] That Hesse too built his understanding of the structural harmonies of painting on musical analogies is borne out by many remarks, among them the description of painting in his short text "Ohne Krapplack" (Without Madder Paint) as "Kampf mit diesen paar Farbflächen, die miteinander eine ganz bestimmte Musik ergeben mussten"[25] (struggle with these few blocks of color, which together had to result in a very particular music).

Hesse had already expressed this interest in structuring and rearranging the world through his painting in the poem "Malerfreude" (Painting Joy) published in *Wanderung*. Stressing the transformative power of the artist, he had claimed the superiority of the painted world over reality: "Aber hier in meinem Auge wohnt / Eine andre Ordnung aller Dinge, [. . .] / Neu und sinnvoll wird die Welt verteilt, / Und im Herzen wird es froh und helle" (*W* 30; "Here in my eye another order of things / Goes on living [. . .] / The world will share in freshness and meaning, / and hearts grow glad and light," 60).[26] In the *Gedichte des Malers*, he deepened this reflection on the artist's power to transform reality.

Der Maler malt eine Gärtnerei (The Poet Paints a Nursery).
From Hesse, *Gedichte des Malers* (Bern: Seldwyla, 1920).

Some of the watercolors included in this volume are similar in style to those published in *Wanderung,* showing a similar emphasis on atmosphere and mood. But the majority reflect Hesse's new style of painting, with its clearly defined contours and contrasts. The writing too reflects the new emphasis on form, rhythm, and structure. Thoughts and impressions are no longer expressed in flowing prose, as in *Wanderung,* but are transformed to find expression in the form of poems. What was only addition in *Wanderung,*[27] "dritte Form" in Oscar Bie's term, is central to this book. This change of poetic form may mean a loss of intimacy and spontaneity, but it accords the texts a higher level of sophistication.

The relationship between the two media in *Gedichte des Malers* may be exemplified by a closer look at the picture and text for "Der Maler malt eine Gärtnerei" (The Painter Paints a Nursery). The painting consists of simplified shapes, abstracted from nature: spherical hilltops, rectangular houses, a garden designed in circular and rectangular shapes. In this simplified, cubic representation, Hesse has gone a long way toward transforming the three-dimensional space of the landscape into the two-dimensional surface of the canvas. Through the use of this technique, the painting acquires a certain double-layered quality: on the one hand, the combinations of form and color constituting the picture allow the observer to recognize particular objects, but on the other hand they are integrated in an abstract system of relationships between colors and shapes. Through the use of contrasts and clear delineations of shape contours, Hesse emphasizes the independent and abstract value of color.

The corresponding poem not only names particular elements of the watercolor — such as the pink house and the color blue — but it is also an invitation to look beyond the world of objects and beyond the confines of representational art. Instead, the relish of color in its own right and the joy of painting are celebrated as "[. . .] Geistergruß / Aus jenem Paradies, / Das ich wie ihr verließ"[28] (Greeting of the spirits / From that paradise / That I like they left behind). The poem reads like a commentary on the painting, elucidating its technique and the way it should be viewed.[29] Only when we free ourselves from the interpretation of sensual information can we appreciate the power and attraction of the colors, overcome the distance between self and world, and approach the view of the "Gärtnerei" as a "greeting from paradise." In the poem, this exhortation to transcend reality and enter the magical world of color is explicit; and it helps us recognize that the picture achieves a similar effect. The leaves of the trees in the foreground overlay and extend into the simple and somewhat rigid rectangular and circular shapes of garden and buildings. They bring a dynamic force into an otherwise very static picture and guide the onlooker's gaze, through adjacent areas of color, into the painting. In this way, they help the viewer to refute the interpretation of the visual impression and to appreciate the pattern of colors and shapes and their harmonies and contrasts.

But the intermedial relationship is even closer than the purely thematical one of picture and commentary: it rests on structural correspondences, too. The painter's perspective, for instance, is the same in picture and text. The distance between artist and world, which is expressed in the painter's raised point of view in the picture, is reflected in the first line of the poem: "Was geht die Gärtnerei mich an?" (What does the nursery have to do with me?) And the personification of colors in the poem ("Lila singt einen zarten Ton, / Blau blickt herüber zum verlorenen Sohn" [Purple sings a tender tone / Blue looks over at the lost son]) corresponds to the emphasis on the independent values of the individual color surfaces.

In the combination of picture and poem with the title "Der Maler malt eine Fabrik im Tal" (The Painter Paints a Factory in the Valley), the relationship between the two media is just as close. Again, the subject of both painting and poem is the liberation from the tangible realities of this world and from representational art. Again, Hesse emphasizes the joy of the painter, who is able to transcend the world of objects to see and represent it as a rhythmic pattern.

Der Maler malt eine Fabrik (The Poet Paints a Factory).
From Hesse, *Gedichte des Malers,* 14.

In the watercolor, this pattern takes the form of a mosaic of colors and shapes. In particular, the fields in the upper half of the painting are represented as more or less rectangular and rhombic patches of color subordinated into a greater pattern reminiscent of a patchwork quilt. Light and joyful pastel colors — delicate greens, oranges, and yellows, interspersed with combinations of light shades of purple and pink — dominate. This lightening of the palette in the top half and the dynamic rhythm of the fan-like opening of the fields towards the sides and the top of the picture suggest the sense of liberation.[30]

The liberation from the object reference also finds expression in the juxtaposition of tree and factory chimney in the picture's foreground. In his 1920 article on Hesse's painting, Walter Ueber Wasser remarked on the incongruity of the "tote Mechanismus" (dead mechanism) of factories in Hesse's watercolors,[31] thereby indicating that he had not understood the abstracting purpose behind Hesse's landscape depictions. In this painting, Hesse positioned tree and factory chimney side by side and accorded them equal height in order to stress their equal beauty — not as objects, but as signifiers: as manifestations of color and form. The poem makes clear that he was interested in the color and shape of the chimney, in its formal relationship to its surroundings: "Aber schöner als alles leuchtet das rote

Kamin, / Senkrecht in diese törichte Welt gestellt" (But more beautiful than anything glows the red chimney / Standing vertically in this foolish world).[32]

These two examples may suffice here to demonstrate the close relationship between pictures and texts in *Gedichte des Malers*. It is an intermedial relationship that goes far beyond the atmospheric correspondences in *Wanderung*. Here, the two media support and interpret each other, and their combination crystallizes and intensifies the impact of the artistic statement.

Piktors Verwandlungen

For a brief period after *Gedichte des Malers,* Hesse gave more prominence to the production and re-production of his watercolors than his writings. In 1921, the album *Elf Aquarelle aus dem Tessin* (Twelve Watercolors from Tessin) was published, and a year later he painted a *Tessiner Bilderbuch* (Tessin Picture Book) for his friends Lisa and Theo Wenger. His watercolors of the early 1920s developed further towards greater proficiency in the treatment of color, light, and contrasts, and towards an ever more confident handling of the cubist understanding of form. He also started to experiment with what he called "Traumlandschaften,"[33] dream landscapes, further increasing the abstraction from nature by endowing all objects with sharp, crystalline forms.

In 1922, Hesse combined his painting with his writing once more, creating the first version of his "Bilderhandschrift" (picture manuscript) *Piktors Verwandlungen*. This tale, which can be read as an autobiographical reflection, was inspired by his love for Ruth Wenger, whom he had met in 1919 and who was to become his second wife in 1924. Hesse returns here to two themes already developed in his earlier work: the perpetual longing for change and self-transformation, and the recognition of the interdependence of antagonistic forces, which through their tension create a complex whole. Piktor, entering paradise, seeks happiness. He asks to be transformed into a tree, attracted by its seeming peace, strength, and dignity, and is happy in this guise until he meets a young girl. In his longing for her, he realizes his mistake, his loneliness and sadness. When she uses a magic stone to unite with him and thereby make him whole, he is freed from the rigidity of his existence as tree and finds true happiness:

> Er wurde Reh, er wurde Fisch, er wurde Mensch und Schlange, Wolke und Vogel. In jeder Gestalt aber war er ganz, war ein Paar, hatte Mond und Sonne, hatte Mann und Weib in sich, floß als Zwillingsfluß durch die Länder, stand als Doppelstern am Himmel.[34]

[He became deer, he became fish, he became human and Serpent, cloud and bird. In each new shape he was whole, was a pair, held moon and sun, man and wife inside him. He flowed as a twin river through the lands, shone as a double star in the firmament.]

In the pictures, the free interplay of bright colors and shapes, with which Hesse had been experimenting in the past years, is brought to a culmination; in some copies of the *Piktor* manuscripts, especially in the 1923 manuscript for Ruth Wenger, great care and attention is given to patterned and exuberantly decorated frames.

G. Wallis Field has stressed how much the *Piktor* watercolors differ from Hesse's other paintings, emphasizing their closeness to children's art work.[35] However, if we see the childlike character of the pictures as part of the magical abstraction that Hesse was aiming for, and therefore as a style that is related to the choice of the genre of the *Kunstmärchen,* the differences from Hesse's other contemporary paintings are minimal. We find in *Piktors Verwandlungen* the same cubist experiments with color and shape, the same crystalline landscapes that we encounter in his other work.

Enquiring into the nature of the relationship between the two media in *Piktors Verwandlungen,* it is worth raising the question whether it ought to be considered as an illustrated text or as the literary "Umdichtung"[36] of paintings. The advertisement in which Hesse announced the sale of his "Bilderhandschriften" seems to answer this question in an unequivocal manner: "Dies bisher nicht veröffentlichte Liebesmärchen," it claims, "ist aus den Bildern heraus entstanden, welche daher notwendig dazu gehören"[37] (This until-now-unpublished love story came to be out of the pictures, which therefore necessarily belong to it). Accordingly, Wolfgang Wildgen's semiotic interpretation of *Piktors Verwandlungen* builds on this understanding of the primacy of the picture.[38]

However, the same advertisement also characterizes *Piktors Verwandlungen* as "[e]in Märchen [. . .] [m]it vielen farbigen Bildern" (a fairy tale with many colorful pictures); and in the majority of Hesse criticism, the primacy of the text has been tacitly assumed: the pictures are regarded as mere addition to the text.[39] The truth — as so often — seems to lie somewhere between these two assumptions, for, as I will show in the following paragraphs, the influence flows both ways from one medium into the other: in other words, the primacy of one or the other medium shifts. What is a given, though, is the importance of the paintings to the book as a whole, and the inseparability of picture and word. Indeed, Volker Michels has interpreted the close alliance between the media as part of the message of this tale: ". . . in *Piktors Verwandlungen* the expression, in a very unusual way, becomes one with the form, because only in the tension between image and word does a whole arise, and in so doing repeats outwardly the experience of bipolarity in unity.[40]

The text offers information and hints at associations that cannot be made visible in pictorial form. Hesse intersperses the text liberally with synaesthetic combinations. With language, he can describe multi-layered sensual experiences, he can transcend time and space by calling upon memory and imagination, where the picture in its defined and delimited material inflexibility is powerless: "Eine von den Blumen [. . .] erinnerte ihn an seine erste Liebe. Eine roch nach dem Garten der Kindheit, wie die Stimme der Mutter klang ihr süßer Duft" (*P* 188; "one resembled his first love. The scent of another sang in his mother's voice, made him recall how they'd walked in the gardens when Pictor was still a little boy," 115).

The pictures are in some cases not much more than illustrations following the text, as in the case of the 1922 manuscript, which shows a little figure consisting of legs, a big eye for a body, and a hat, next to the sentence "Er war ganz Auge" (he was all eyes).[41]

In other cases, the watercolors enrich and complement the text far more significantly. In the picture from the 1923 version of the tale that Hesse produced for Ruth Wenger,[42] he paints the "Zauberstrom ewiger Verwandlung" (magic stream of eternal metamorphosis) as a bustling whirl of bright colors and clearly delineated shapes. The immediate overall impression, almost overwhelming in its vitality, is that of life unleashed, of a scene almost bursting out of its frame.

The corresponding paragraph in the text cannot express quite the same sense of vitality as the picture, as it is unable to accord us the near-simultaneity of impressions that the picture can. Built on a string of enumerations, it emphasizes a different aspect of the scene: it stresses the temporal element of the transformation of flowers, trees, elephants, or giraffes, into precious stones, birds, streams, crocodiles, or fishes. Hesse uses no color epithets in this paragraph, indeed only one expression, an imaginative combination of participle construction and composite noun, "blitzende Schwirrvögel" (*P* 190; flashing, whizzing birds), supplies a visual image at all. Text and picture, meaning and sensual impression, ideally complement each other.

Two further aspects contribute to the particular nature of the close relationship between text and picture in *Piktors Verwandlungen*. The first is the correspondence between the ornamental patterning in the pictures and the rhyme in the prose text. The ornamentation of the pictures, in particular the patterning in the frames of the 1923 manuscript for Ruth Wenger, which is created by repetition of shapes and color, is used in a purely decorative playful manner, independent of any spatial meaning. In analogy, the rhymes gain, especially through their playful repetition, a similar independence from the tale's content.[43] In both media, therefore, Hesse emphasizes the value of the signifiers: pure color and form, pure sound and rhythm; and further enhances their impact through their combination.

Zauberstrom ewiger Verwandlung (Magical Stream of Eternal Metamorphosis, 1923). From Hesse, *Piktors Verwandlungen,* facsimile of the manuscript version for Ruth Wenger, 1923. Printed in Hesse, *Piktors Verwandlungen,* ed. Volker Michels, Insel Taschenbuch 122 (Frankfurt am Main: Insel, 1977), no pagination.

The second aspect is demonstrated by the example of the picture and text relating to the transformation of the bird in the tale. The text describes how the bird metamorphoses into a "Vogelblume," "bird flower," and how this subsequently goes on to change into a "Vogelblumen-schmetterling," "bird flower butterfly" (*P* 189). In this playfully assembled designation, the previous stages of the bird's transformation remain included, the temporal element finds expression. And yet, at the same time, the simultaneity of possible embodiments of this imaginary creature is stressed by the use of the one compound word.

The text passage finds correspondence not in a single picture but in a sequence of three pictures. The process of transformation is expressed by the use of colors and shapes, which are repeated and gradually changed from frame to frame. The combination of the colors blue, red, and yellow in the bird's plumage in the first picture is taken up in the depiction of the "Vogelblume" in the second frame. Here, the red has gained dominance over blue and the floral element of the compound creature is attributed the color pink. The "Vogelblumenschmetterling," finally, is colored entirely in red, yellow, and pink, but the use of a strong, vibrant blue in the two flowers (which have no equivalent in the text) creates the visual link to the first picture and to the first incarnation of the changing creature.

A similar process can be observed in relation to the use of shapes in the three pictures. The rounded, beaked form of the bird's head is repeated, in a slightly transformed, more compact version in the second picture, to represent the head of the "Vogelblume." The rounded shape of the flower's body, lastly, is echoed in the butterfly's wings in the final picture.

Through their emphasis on the sequence of the transformation, which gives them an almost narrative quality, these pictures approach the structural characteristics of text. The text, on the other hand, achieves, through the unusual compound construction, an impact that, in its near-simultaneity, is close to that of a picture. Text and picture in *Piktors Verwandlungen* interpret each other, interlink, and even approach each other structurally. It is entirely appropriate here to speak of a "mutual illumination of the arts."[44]

Piktors Verwandlungen is, among other things, about the need for perpetual transformation as a means to save the soul from rigidity, ossification, and death. On a formal level, the many versions of the original 1922 *Piktor* manuscript, written by Hesse in the subsequent years, mirror this theme of constant flexibility and re-creation.

I have compared seven manuscripts of the tale — six of which are held by the manuscript department of the Deutsches Literaturarchiv in Marbach — ranging from the early, unpublished version of 1922, to the manuscript produced as a wedding gift for Charlotte Bodmer in 1935.[45] In their presentation, these versions vary from an informal draft in a well-

Verwandlung des Vogels (Metamorphosis of the Bird, 1923. Series of four pictures. From *Piktors Verwandlungen,* ed. Michels, no pagination.

thumbed exercise book to a handwritten and handpainted presentation copy that is bound and in its own individual sleeve.

Among the different versions, many changes and developments in the body of the text, the design of the pictures, and in the relationship between the two are discernible. As far as the text is concerned, Hesse constantly inserted words in one version, omitted other words in the next, and then returned to wordings previously discarded. Individual phrases, rhymes, and rhythmical repetitions appear and disappear from one version to the next. A linear development cannot be discerned. On the contrary, the work on this tale remains a playful testimony to Hesse's concern for flexibility.

There is a general development to be made out, however, concerning the use of pictures in the various versions of the *Piktor* manuscripts: namely one of gradual reduction. While Hesse painted twenty-nine watercolors for the 1922 version, he only included ten in the manuscript produced in 1935. Most noticeable in this respect is the difference between the earliest version from autumn 1922 and all the subsequent versions. In the 1922 manuscript, Hesse emphasizes the personal quality and the narrative element of the pictures. Time and again, the little figure of Piktor (Hesse) is shown making his way through paradise. A multitude of small vignettes is interspersed throughout the text, in many cases even breaking up the writing. This first manuscript contains what I would call the conceptual basis of the depictions, models that Hesse used later in different modifications. Indeed, the later versions each include selections of the range of motifs contained here — in different executions and with varying use of colors. While in 1922 he emphasized the abstract, conceptual character of the pictures in their simple, stylized forms, the watercolors of the later versions gradually approach a more detailed execution, striving for a closer representation of nature, a greater mimetic truth. In this, they reflect a general development in Hesse's style of painting, which, from the late 1920s, departed more and more from the dreamlike, abstract quality of his watercolors of the early years of the decade.

In the seven different versions of the *Piktor* manuscript I compared, the design of individual pages, that is, the relationship between text and pictures, is also continually changing: the distribution of text and pictures is never the same twice. A clear development can be seen from the highly integrated, intertwined combination of the two media in the earlier manuscripts towards a gradual weakening of this close connection and an ever stronger separation of text and pictures.

Overall, between 1922 and 1935 the text gradually gained priority over the watercolors in *Piktors Verwandlungen*. There may have been a number of reasons for this shift in the relationship between the two media. Practical considerations may have played a role; after all, manuscripts with fewer pictures could be produced faster. However, as Hesse complained re-

Doppelbaum (Double Tree, 1923). From *Piktors
Verwandlungen*, ed. Michels, no pagination.

Doppelbaum (Double Tree, 1935). From Hesse, *Piktors Verwandlungen,*
illustrated manuscript for Charlotte Bodmer, Manuscript Archive,
German Literature Archive, Marbach. Collection A: Hesse/Reber-Bodmer.

peatedly, he was not exactly inundated with commissions for his manuscripts.[46] Or should we see in this development a general weakening of his interest in the idea of the integrated intermedial work of art? Considering that the *Piktor* manuscripts constitute the last of his experiments in this art form, this is highly probable. Hesse's insight into his own limitations as a painter, which he repeatedly voiced in letters of these years,[47] may have played a role in this decline in his interest. The public reception of his experiments with the new medium was cool, too. When he showed some of his work in a joint exhibition with Emil Nolde in Winterthur in 1922, for instance, the press reaction was scathing and his paintings treated with contempt.[48]

But above all, it is worth remembering that the period considered here, the years 1918 to 1922, was one in which Hesse's belief in his own ability as a writer was deeply shaken. Painting and his experiments in combining the two arts helped him to overcome this crisis. A sign of his returning confidence is to be seen in the writing of *Klingsors letzter Sommer* — indeed, in a letter to Franz Karl Ginzkey of 5 August 1919, Hesse wrote: "Ich male viel, und das hilft mir den Weg auch für die Dichtung finden"[49] (I paint a lot, and that helps me find my way also in my writing). By the spring of 1922, he had largely defeated his doubts regarding his literary work: *Siddhartha,* the novel project that had been lying dormant for over a year, was completed in May.[50]

Conclusion

The development of the relationship between Hesse's writing and painting in the years 1918 to 1922 was one of ever-further-reaching correspondences and ever-more-fruitful mutually enhancing combinations. Learning to master the new medium of painting, he learned to respond creatively to the Tessin landscape, albeit tentatively at first, as his volume *Wanderung* shows. He intensified his painterly vision and skills and succeeded in transforming his experience of color that moved him so profoundly on his arrival in Montagnola — "dieser tolle flackernde Sommertraum" (*K* 286; this wild, flickering summer dream) — into art: first into his watercolors, then into a literary narrative, *Klingsors letzter Sommer.* Abstracting more and more from the landscape around him, he continued to transfer the structural innovations with which he experimented in painting to his literary production in *Gedichte des Malers.* Lastly, in the close interrelationship between the pictures and words of *Piktors Verwandlungen,* Hesse created the "magic" space beyond space and time that was most apt to represent his concept of poetic truth. He had, over a period of a few years, turned what had at first only been a therapeutic tool into a medium that supported, complemented, and ultimately transformed his writing. In this sense, it may be justified to consider *Piktors Verwandlungen* the culmination and completion of Hesse's exploration of the interrelationship between painting and writing — and its celebration, too; for the intermedial experiment had returned the writer to his writing.[51]

Notes

All illustrations in this essay are reproduced by kind permission of the Hermann-Hesse Editionsarchivs Volker Michels, Offenbach am Main, Germany.

[1] Erwin Panofsky, "Zum Problem der Beschreibung und Inhaltsdeutung von Werken der bildenden Kunst," *Logos* 21 (1932): 103–19.

[2] For an introduction to the methodology of intermedial analysis, see Ulrich Weisstein, "Einleitung. Literatur und bildende Kunstgeschichte, Systematik, Methoden," in *Literatur und bildende Kunst: Ein Handbuch zur Theorie und Praxis eines komparatistischen Grenzgebietes,* ed. Ulrich Weisstein (Berlin: Erich Schmidt, 1992), 11–31. See also: Thomas Eicher, "Kunst und Literatur," in *Intermedialität: Vom Bild zum Text,* ed. Thomas Eicher and Ulf Bleckmann (Bielefeld: Aisthesis, 1994), 356–57; Werner Wolf, "Intermedialität," in *Metzler Lexikon Literatur- und Kulturtheorie,* ed. Ansgar Nünning (Stuttgart and Weimar: Metzler, 2001), 284–85.

[3] For studies of "multiple talents," see, for example: Kent Hooper, *Ernst Barlach's Literary and Visual Art: The Issue of Multiple Talent* (Ann Arbor, MI: UMI Research Press, 1987); or Henry I. Schvey, "Doppelbegabte Künstler als Seher: O. Kokoschka, D. H. Lawrence and W. Blake," in *Literatur und bildende Kunst,* ed. Weisstein, 73–85. However, if the term of "multiple talent," as Kent Hooper suggests, should be restricted to artists who have produced works of undoubtedly equal quality in two media, the more modest term of "multiple creative activity" (or "Doppelbetätigung") might be more appropriate in the case of Hesse (see Hooper, 9).

[4] Hermann Hesse, letter of 13 January 1920 to the *National-Zeitung,* Basel (Hesse, *Gesammelte Briefe,* ed. Ursula Michels and Volker Michels, vol. 1: 1895–1921 [Frankfurt am Main: Suhrkamp, 1973], 439. Subsequent references to this source will be indicated by *GB* 1 and page number). Unless otherwise indicated, all English translations in this chapter are by Jim Walker and Ingo Cornils.

[5] In Hesse criticism before 1990, we find many vague references to similarities, but only few sustained analyses of the structural and thematic relationships between Hesse's works in the two media. Martin Pfeifer ("Hermann Hesse — Ein Dichter als Maler," *Literatur in Wissenschaft und Unterricht* 5 [1972]: 233–39) was one of the first to explore this area in some depth. By the end of the 1990s, however, the relatedness of Hesse's work to that of other more famous painters had been explored — among them van Gogh, the painters of the Expressionist groups "Der Blaue Reiter" and "Die Brücke" (see Volker Michels, "Vorwort," in *Hermann Hesse: Spiel mit Farben. Der Dichter als Maler,* ed. Volker Michels [Frankfurt am Main: Suhrkamp, 2005], 7–30) — and warnings were beginning to be expressed not to play off the painter Hesse against the author Hesse (see Volker Michels, "Farbe ist Leben. Hermann Hesse als Maler," in *Hermann Hesse: Farbe ist Leben,*

ed. Volker Michels [Frankfurt am Main and Leipzig: Insel, 1997], 9–38, here 35). In 1993, Reso Karalaschwili explored the use of color and painterly vision in Hesse's writing (*Hermann Hesse: Charakter und Weltbild* [Frankfurt am Main: Suhrkamp, 1993], especially 189–220 and 274–84). The comparative study of Hesse's painting and writing was then taken up in earnest by Volker Michels in "Farbe ist Leben. Hermann Hesse als Maler" and by Wolfgang Wildgen in "Image-texte, texte-images: Routes vers le chaos semiotique," in *Papers from the 1997 CISL Colloquium L'image dans le langage et dans les non-langages in Urbino, Italy* (http://www .hum.au.dk/semiotics/docs/epub/urb97WIL/Wildgen.htm), both in 1997; by Christian Immo Schneider in "Ut Pictura Poesis. Hermann Hesse as a Poet and Painter," http://www.gss.ucsb.edu/projects/hesse/papers/schnei.pdf (1998); by Giuseppe Curonici in "'Denn ohne diese Malerei wäre ich schon lange nicht mehr da.' Der Maler Hermann Hesse," in *"Höllenreise durch mich selbst": Hermann Hesse,* ed. Regina Bucher, Andres Furger, and Felix Graf (Zurich: Schweizerisches Landesmuseum, Zurich, and Verlag Neue Zürcher Zeitung, 2000), 27–42; and Sikander Singh in *Hermann Hesse* (Stuttgart: Reclam, 2006), especially 274–85.

[6] See Hermann Hesse, *Kurzgefaßter Lebenslauf,* in Hermann Hesse, *Sämtliche Werke,* ed. Volker Michels, vol. 12: *Autobiographische Schriften II. Selbstzeugnisse. Erinnerungen. Gedenkblätter und Rundbriefe* (Frankfurt am Main: Suhrkamp, 2003), 46–63. This volume will be cited subsequently as *SW* 12 and page number.

[7] In the autumn of 1920, for instance, Hesse wrote to Lisa Wenger: "Ich sehe den Weg, der mich tragen soll, noch nicht weiter, und habe zu dem mir gewohnten und gegebenen Wirkungsmittel, der Literatur, gar kein Vertrauen mehr" (*GB* 1:462; I don't yet see the further path that will carry me, and no longer have any confidence in my customary and given mode of action, literature).

[8] See, for example, Hesse's letter to Ludwig Finckh of 5 January 1920, in which he claims: "Ich [. . .] bin, alles in allem, durch das Malen in diesem letzten Jahr am Leben erhalten worden, das ich sonst nicht ausgehalten hätte" (*GB* 1:436; In the last year I have been, all in all, kept alive by painting, when I otherwise would not have survived). Similarly, he writes to Lisa Wenger on 2 May 1921: "Ein Stück Analyse und Auflockerung brauche ich, da mein Leben so wie jetzt nimmer lang zu ertragen ware, die Lähmung durch den vollkommenen Unglauben an den Wert unsrer ganzen Literatur ist für mich zu groß, und für stille angenehme Stunden habe ich das Malen, das hilft mir leben [. . .]" (*GB* 1:70–71; I need a bit of analysis and release, since I wouldn't long be able to bear my life as it is now; the paralysis due to complete lack of faith in the worth of our literature is for me too great, and for quiet, agreeable hours I have my painting, which helps me live . . .).

[9] Hermann Goern, "Der Maler Hermann Hesse," *Neue Schweizer Rundschau,* N.F. 20 (1952/53): 154–60, here 156.

[10] Goern, "Der Maler Hermann Hesse," 156.

[11] Hermann Hesse, letter to Cuno Amiet, 5 January 1919 (Hesse, *Gesammelte Briefe,* vol. 1, 386).

[12] See C. F. W. Behl, "Wanderung," *Das literarische Echo* 23 (1920/21): col. 816–17. He comments on the "Zwanglosigkeit" (informality, casual manner) which had in this book replaced Hesse's analytical tendencies.

[13] Volker Michels, "Vorwort," *Hermann Hesse: Spiel mit Farben,* 9. Referring to this technique, Giuseppe Curonici highlights the influence of Hesse's painter friend Hans Sturzenegger (Curonici, "'Denn ohne diese Malerei wäre ich schon lange nicht mehr da,'" 35).

[14] Hermann Hesse, *Wanderung,* in Hesse, *Sämtliche Werke,* ed. Volker Michels, vol. 11: *Autobiographische Schriften I: Wanderung. Kurgast. Die Nürnberger Reise. Tagebücher* (Frankfurt am Main: Suhrkamp, 2003), 5–35, here 9. Subsequent references to *Wanderung* are cited in the text with the abbreviation *W* and page number. English translations are from *Wandering: Notes and Sketches by Hermann Hesse,* trans. James Wright (New York: Farrar, Straus & Giroux, 1972) and follow the German in parentheses with page number.

[15] Already in 1917, Hesse expressed this understanding of the experience and the painting of landscape as a liberation "von der verfluchten Willenswelt" (Hermann Hesse, letter to Walter Schädelin, 21 April 1917, in Hesse, *Gesammelte Briefe,* vol. 1, 346).

[16] Oscar Bie, "*Wanderung* von Hermann Hesse," *Die neue Rundschau* 32:1 (1921): 670.

[17] *Klingsors letzter Sommer* was written in July and August 1919. Since the *Klingsor* narrative is extensively treated in Ralph Freedman's chapter in this volume, I am here exclusively concentrating on the relationship between the work and Hesse's painting.

[18] Hermann Hesse, letter to Walter Ueber Wasser, 26 January 1920, reproduced in Michels, "Vorwort," *Hermann Hesse: Spiel mit Farben,* 27.

[19] Hermann Hesse, *Klingsors letzter Sommer,* in Hesse, *Sämtliche Werke,* ed. Volker Michels, vol. 8: *Die Erzählungen 3. 1911–1954* (Frankfurt am Main: Suhrkamp, 2001), 284–333, here 299. Further references to the novella appear in the text as *K* and page number. English translations are from "Klingsor's Last Summer," in the volume *Klingsor's Last Summer,* trans. Richard and Clara Winston (New York: Farrar, Straus & Giroux, 1970) {PAGE NOS?} and follow the German quotations in parentheses with page number.

[20] For reproductions and analyses of the works resulting from the three painters' 1914 study trip to Tunis, see *Die Tunisreise: Klee, Macke, Moilliet,* ed. Ernst-Gerhard Güse, exhibition catalogue Westfälisches Landesmuseum für Kunst und Kulturgeschichte Münster (Stuttgart: G. Hatje, 1982).

[21] The relatedness of Klingsor's art to that of van Gogh's as well as the kinship between van Gogh and Hesse were already pointed out by Hugo Ball in 1927 (Hugo Ball, *Hermann Hesse: Sein Leben und sein Werk* [1927; Frankfurt am Main: Suhrkamp, 1947], 198). Michels extends the comparison to Hesse's own painting (Michels, "Vorwort," *Hermann Hesse: Spiel mit Farben,* 12–14).

[22] J. Hollander, "The Poetics of Ekphrasis," *Word and Image* 4:1 (1988): 209–19.

[23] Hesse, *Kurzgefaßter Lebenslauf, SW* 12:58.

[24] On Orphic cubism, see Adrian Hicken, *Apollinaire, Cubism and Orphism* (Aldershot: Ashgate, 2000).

[25] Hermann Hesse, "Ohne Krapplack," in Hesse, *Magie der Farben Aquarelle aus dem Tessin* (Frankfurt am Main: Suhrkamp, 1980), 31–38, here 36.

[26] Fritz Böttger's interpretation of this "Neu-Verteilung" of the world as relating to social conditions and relationships in his *Hermann Hesse: Leben, Werk, Zeit* (Berlin: Verlag der Nation, 1974), 286–94, is misleading in this context.

[27] Regarding the re-edition of his works, Hesse wrote to Peter Suhrkamp on 20 May 1951: "Was die Frage nach Gedichten innerhalb geschlossener Werke betrifft, so könnten nach meiner Meinung die Gedichte der *Wanderung* ruhig wegbleiben" (*GB* 4:112; Regarding the question of poems within distinct works, in my opinion the poems in *Wandering* could easily be left out).

[28] Hermann Hesse, *Der Maler malt eine Gärtnerei*, in Hesse, *Sämtliche Werke,* ed. Volker Michels, vol. 10: *Die Gedichte,* compiled by Peter Huber (Frankfurt am Main: Suhrkamp, 2002), 265. Subsequent references to this volume will be indicated as *SW* 10 and volume and page number.

[29] See Peter Spycher, *Eine Wanderung durch Hermann Hesses Lyrik: Dokumentationen und Interpretationen* (Bern: Peter Lang, 1990), 263: "The poet . . . explains what he has painted, why and wherefore he has painted his subject, and finally, how, why, and wherefore he paints. He writes therefore observations, meditations about his painterly experience, representation, and formation of a reality."

[30] In comparison to another painting of this scene by Hesse, *Fabrik im Tal (Noranco),* 1919, this aspect is especially clear. In that version, the colors are more naturalistic and the structure of the field pattern is not as developed. For a reproduction of the painting, see *Hermann Hesse als Maler in der Natur,* ed. Volker Michels and Ambrogio Pellegrini (Milan: Mazzotta, 1999), 66.

[31] Walter Ueber Wasser, "Der Maler Hermann Hesse," *Die Schweiz* 24:9 (1920): 1–5, here 5.

[32] Hermann Hesse, *Der Maler malt eine Fabrik im Tal,* in *SW* 10:268.

[33] This intention had already been expressed in *Klingsors letzter Sommer:* "Ich habe im Sinn," Klingsor writes to Louis, "sobald dieser Sommer herum ist, eine Zeitlang nur noch Phantasien zu malen, namentlich Träume (*K* 325; My plan is this: as soon as this summer is gone, to paint fantasies exclusively, namely dreams). For a reproduction of one of these "Traumgarten" or "Traumlandschaft" paintings, see Hans-Dieter Mück, *Hermann Hesse (1877–1962). Der Schriftsteller als Zeichner und Maler,* exhibition catalogue Kunsthaus Apolda Avantgarde (Stuttgart and Frankfurt am Main: ARTeFACT, 2001), front cover. The painting reproduced here is untitled and dates from 1920.

[34] Hermann Hesse, *Piktors Verwandlungen,* in Hesse, *Sämtliche Werke,* ed. Volker Michels, vol. 9: *Die Märchen. Legenden. Übertragungen. Dramatisches. Idyllen* (Frankfurt: Suhrkamp, 2002), 188–92, here 192. References to this work in the following paragraphs are to the text of this edition and appear, with the abbreviation *P* and page numbers, in brackets in the text. English translations are from *Pictor's Metamorphoses and Other Fantasies,* ed. with an introduction by Theodore Ziolkowski, trans. Rika Lesser (New York: Farrar, Straus & Giroux, 1982) and will follow the original quotations with page number.

[35] G. Wallis Field, "Hermann Hesses moderne Märchen," in *Hermann Hesse heute,* ed. Adrian Hsia (Bonn: Bouvier, 1980), 204–32, here 226.

[36] The term is Hesse's. He uses it in *Klingsors letzter Sommer* to describe the transformation of landscape views into paintings (*K* 288).

[37] Advertisement of Hesse's picture manuscripts, reprinted in Hesse, *Sämtliche Werke,* 12:214.

[38] See Wildgen, "Image-texte, texte-images."

[39] See for example Joseph Mileck, who considers *Piktors Verwandlungen* as an "Erzählung" and mentions the watercolors only in passing (Joseph Mileck, *Hermann Hesse: Dichter, Sucher, Bekenner* [Frankfurt am Main: Suhrkamp, 1987], 130–32). Similarly: Otto Basler, "Piktors Verwandlungen. Ein Märchen von Hermann Hesse," *Neue Schweizer Rundschau,* N.F. 22 (1954/55): 575–76.

[40] Volker Michels, "Nachwort," in Hermann Hesse, *Piktors Verwandlungen* (Frankfurt am Main: Insel, 1977), 63–91, here 89.

[41] Hermann Hesse, *Piktors Verwandlungen,* early manuscript version from autumn 1922, Handschriftenabteilung, Deutsches Literaturarchiv Marbach (Bestand: D: Hesse).

[42] Unless otherwise stated, all further references to the pictures in *Piktors Verwandlungen* are to the facsimile reprint of this 1923 version, published in Hermann Hesse, *Piktors Verwandlungen* (Frankfurt am Main: Suhrkamp, 1977), no page numbers.

[43] See the following example from the 1922 manuscript of *Piktors Verwandlungen* (cf. note 41 above): "Einen Vogel sah er sitzen, sah ihn im Grase sitzen und von Farben blitzen, alle Farben schien er zu besitzen. Den Vogel, den blitzenden, den alle Glanzfarben besitzenden, fragte er" (He saw a bird sitting, saw it sitting in the grass and colorfully flashing; it seemed to possess all colors. He asked the bird, the flashing one, the one possessing all brilliant colors:. . .).

[44] The phrase derives from Oskar Walzel's seminal essay on intermedial comparison, *Wechselseitige Erhellung der Künste: Ein Beitrag zur Würdigung kunstgeschichtlicher Begriffe* (Berlin: Reuther und Reichard, 1917).

[45] Apart from these two versions, the manuscript department in the Literaturarchiv Marbach holds three versions from 1923 and one from 1931, which is dedicated to Ninon Hesse. The seventh version used in my comparison is the published 1923 manuscript dedicated to Ruth Wenger (cf. note 42 above).

[46] See, for example, Hesse's letter to Ninon Dolbin from April 1928, in which he complains: "[. . .] aber von all den Tausenden, die sich vier- bis fünfmal im Jahr einen Anzug schneidern lassen, sind kaum ein halbes Dutzend wirklich so reich und auf das schöne und Aparte versessen, daß sie auf die Idee kommen, bei einem Dichter eigenhändige Gedichthandschriften mit eigenhändigen, farbigen Bildchen zu bestellen" (cited in Mück, *Hermann Hesse,* 21; . . . but out of all the thousands who have themselves a dress suit made four or five times a year there are hardly a dozen who are really so rich and so keen on beautiful and unique things that they think to commission from a poet handwritten manuscript poems with color pictures also in his own hand).

[47] In 1922, Hesse wrote to Cuno Amiet: "Es bleibt bei ganz einfachen landschaftlichen Motiven, weiter scheine ich nicht zu kommen. Wie schön das andere alles ist, Lüfte und Tiere, bewegtes Leben und gar das Schönste, die Menschen, das sehe ich

wohl, oft ergriffen und fast bestürzt, aber malen kann ich es nicht" (cited in Michels, "Vorwort," *Hermann Hesse: Spiel mit Farben,* 18; It remains at the level of very simple landscape motifs; further than that I don't seem to be able to progress. How beautiful all the rest is, atmospheres and animals, the motion of life and the most beautiful of all, human beings, that I can see, often moved and almost dismayed, but I cannot paint them). Similarly, in 1926, he called himself a "Dilettant" (Hermann Hesse, "Aquarell," *Frankfurter Zeitung,* 4 January 1926, quoted in Siegfried Unseld, *Hermann Hesse: Werk und Wirkungsgeschichte* (Frankfurt am Main: Suhrkamp, 1985), 84.

[48] See the review quoted (without reference) in Michels, "Vorwort," *Hermann Hesse: Spiel mit Farben,* 22: "If Hermann Hesse's writings were not better than his painting, one could feel sorry for him. . . . like this poet-painter, we create things such as this ourselves and dozens of our secondary school students do too."

[49] Hesse, *GB* 1:410. See in this context Kurt Wais's reference to a number of other famous writers who have found their way back to writing via painting, because, as Wais puts it, the painter is closer to the "vital source of art, to the beautiful beyond words." Kurt Wais, "Symbiose der Künste: Forschungsgrundlagen zur Wechselberührung zwischen Dichtung, Bild- und Tonkunst," in *Literatur und bildende Kunst,* ed. Weisstein, 34–53, here 51.

[50] Hesse started writing *Siddhartha* in December 1919, then paused and did not pick up his work on the novel again until March 1922 (see Unseld, *Hermann Hesse,* 89).

[51] Hesse continued to paint in later years. His weakening eyes did not allow him to persevere with the pursuit of watercoloring in the open air beyond the late 1930s, but he went on painting and selling manuscripts with pictures, which he produced at his desk. However, he published only very few more works that combined writing and painting; among them is *Sinclairs Notizbuch* (1923), which contains four watercolor illustrations.

15: Hermann Hesse and Music

C. Immo Schneider

H ERMANN HESSE'S RELATIONSHIP TO MUSIC is as many-faceted as the man and poet himself, and cannot be reduced to a common denominator. Even today, it is the topic of numerous essays, articles, and entire dissertations.[1] Thus, only selected aspects of Hesse's ideas on music can be discussed here: I. Hesse's Musical Influences; II. Hesse's Poetry as Musical Expression; III. Musical Forms in Hesse's Prose Works; IV. Hesse's Opinions on Music; and — an extended summary — V. Hesse's Musical Development.

I. Hesse's Musical Influences

Ich bin nicht mit Virtuosen und in Konzertsälen aufgewachsen, sondern mit Hausmusik, und das schönste war immer die, bei der man selbst mittätig sein konnte; mit der Geige und ein wenig Singen habe ich in den Knabenjahren die ersten Schritte ins Reich der Musik getan. (*SW* 12:606)

[I did not grow up knowing virtuosi in concert halls, but with "Hausmusik," music played at home, and that was at its best when I could play along; with the violin and a little singing I took my first steps into the world of music as a boy.]

This statement of Hesse's suggests that he never progressed musically beyond the dilettantism of *Hausmusik*. The question is not that simple. Hesse's fundamentally verbal talents were linked even in early life with a highly developed sense for the language of music, which he inherited from his mother and her family, especially from his grandfather, Dr. Hermann Gundert (1814–93), the noted philologist, lexicographer, and expert on Indian culture and Sanskrit. Gundert not only knew numerous languages of India and Europe, but also composed over 200 hymns, mainly in the Malayalam language, including the instrumental accompaniments. Hesse's mother, Marie, who wrote remarkable religious poetry, enjoyed singing and playing music with her family frequently.[2] Both of Marie's sons from her first marriage were fine singers and first acquainted Hermann with the songs of Schubert and Schumann. One half-brother, Theodor Isenberg, in fact, strove to become an opera singer before he became a pharmacist. Hesse's uncle, Friedrich Gundert, who directed the association of church choirs in Calw, made a lasting impression with performances of the great classical oratorios, in particular J. S. Bach's Passions according to St. John and St. Matthew.[3] Hesse corresponded with his nephew, Carlo Isenberg, a philologist, musician, and musicologist, on musical matters, and consulted him while preparing to write *Das Glasperlenspiel* (The Glass Bead Game), in which Isenberg's name appears in Latinized form as "Carlo Ferromonte" (*HM* 159–60). Hesse's fondness for music also played a role when he chose his three wives. Maria Hesse, née Bernoulli (1869–1963), the mother of his three sons, was a professional photographer, but also an accomplished pianist with conservative musical tastes: "She is shocked by any new chord or rhythm," Romain Rolland noted in his diary after visiting the Hesse family in Bern.[4] Hesse's second wife, Ruth, née Wenger (1897–1994), a trained singer.[5] His third wife, Ninon, née Ausländer (1895–1966), though a dedicated archeologist, shared, as had her predecessors, her husband's love for music, as many of her letters reveal.[6]

Hesse became acquainted with many musicians through concerts, personal encounters, or correspondence. In his youth he had heard the famous violinists Josef Joachim and Pablo de Sarasate perform. Some musicians were close friends, especially Othmar Schoeck (1886–1957), one of the most distinguished Swiss composers of the first half of the twentieth century. In his early years, Hesse repeatedly took walking tours in Italy with Schoeck, as well as with Fritz Brun, the director of the Symphony Orchestra of Bern. Another friend was Volkmar Andreä, the Director of the Zurich Conservatory of Music and of musical affairs at the university. Hesse knew and esteemed the pianists Ferruccio Busoni, Edwin Fischer, and Clara Haskil, the cellist Pierre Fournier, the singer Ilona Durigo, and Elaine Shaffer, the American flutist. A detailed analysis would be required to differentiate Hesse's own ideas about music from those of the professional musicians and friends with musical interests with whom he associated. In addition, Hesse read and occasionally reviewed books about music. Though never a practicing musician himself — he did not count singing and whistling — Hesse had been given a violin when he was twelve and had dreamed of becoming a virtuoso standing "vor überfüllten Riesensälen" (before overflowing audiences in gigantic concert halls) and "von Kaisern empfangen und mit goldenen Medaillen dekoriert worden" (being received by emperors to be decorated with golden medals) (*SW* 14:95) Later, he apparently took the advice of Aristotle: to cease performing music and to content himself with the skills learned in his youth, to judge what is beautiful and find a suitable happiness.[7]

II. Hesse's Poetry as Musical Expression

Introducing Hermann Hesse at the Nobel Prize award ceremonies in 1946, Anders Österling declared: "If Hesse's reputation as a prose writer fluctuates, there has never been any doubt about his stature as a poet. [. . .] his musical form is unsurpassed in our time."[8] During his long life, Hesse wrote some 1,400 poems (*SW* 10:624). As he wrote in 1921, "Lyrik ist nicht bloß Versbauen, Lyrik ist vor allem auch Musikmachen" (*SW* 12:189; Writing lyrical poetry is more than constructing verses; it is above all music-making). Hesse's conception of musical speech is defined, according to Peter Spycher, by "tempo, flow, rhythm, pleasant melodic and harmonic effects, rhyme, meter, and certain structural elements."[9] In music and poetry alike, meter signifies regular alternations between accented and unaccented elements. In both arts, rhythm, patterns of varied sound durations, comes about when the accentuation of certain notes or syllables does not coincide consistently with the limits of the metrical unit. Pleasing melodic-harmonic effects are achieved largely through rhyme, whose bright and dark vowels, diphthongs, and sound clusters function as higher and lower notes within the admittedly limited range of a voice heard reading a poem aloud, the changes in volume evoking musical dynamics. Aside from tempo and flow, contemporary poetry generally no longer observes specific metric or rhyming schemes. Some poets, however, like Hesse, continued to cultivate such forms, following traditions reaching from the Middle Ages and Renaissance to the mid-twentieth cetury. This is comparable to the development of tonality in Western music up to Arnold Schönberg's twelve-tone music on the one hand, and the introduction of the tonal systems of Asiatic cultures, as in the case of Olivier Messiaen, on the other. Hesse's use of meter and rhyme in most poems was not oldfashioned by any means, as both Gottfried Benn and Bertolt Brecht did the same. One important difference, among others, between these three poets is that, while Brecht often emulates the balladesque tone of François Villon, and Benn's unconventional rhymes recall Stefan George, Hesse felt drawn since childhood to "der quellenden Fülle Brentanos, dem spielenden Überschwang Arnims, der geistreichen Musik Tiecks und der stillen goldenen Tiefe des Novalis," to the "noch ganz romantischen, unerschöpflichen Eichendorff, dem vielfarbig funkelnden Heine," and finally to the two "großen Musiker(n) der deutschen Lyrik, Lenau und Mörike" (*SW* 17:247–48; the overflowing bounty of Brentano, the playful exuberance of Arnim, Tieck's ingenious musicality, and the quiet, golden depths of Novalis; to Eichendorff, inexhaustibly and genuinely Romantic, to Heine, sparkling in many hues, and finally to the two great musicians of German poetry, Lenau and Mörike). The music and poetry of folksongs as presented in Arnim's collection *Des Knaben Wunderhorn* (Youth's Magic Horn) set a standard for Hesse's lyrical practice. He always sought a "musikalisches Gesetz" (musical principle) in poems. By that he did not mean that " Gedichte nach einem festen Schema gebaut sein müssten und nirgends Silben fehlen dürften. Aber auch die Abweichungen sollten musikalisch-sprachlich begründet sein.[. . .]" (*GB* 1:233–34; poems must be constructed according to a certain scheme and never miss a syllable. But even departures from a form must be musically justified). Hesse's poetics by no means rest solely on his preference for German poetry of the early nineteenth century. Hesse scholars have largely overlooked the influence of the "dolce stil nuovo" of Dante Alighieri (1265–1321). In *Romantische Lieder* (Romantic Songs), Hesse's first publication, the poem "Ich habe den Fuß gesetzt" (I Have Set My Foot) is based on a passage from the *Vita Nuova* (*SW* 10:37–38). In the poems dedicated to them, Gertrud and Maria are said to have "something of the beauty and distinction of Dante's Beatrice" (*GB* 1:37–38). Hesse's affinity with the musical style of the folksong corresponds astonishingly to a passage in Dante's treatise on vernacular poetry, *De vulgari eloquentia,* describing a kind of poetry that is "a fiction expressed through rhetorical-musical forms."[10] Many of Hesse's poems have musical themes: "Barcarole," "Berceuse," "Dreistimmige Musik" (Music for Three Voices), "Flötenspiel" (Flute Music), "Gavotte," "Grande Valse," "Konzert," "Meiner Geige" (To My Violin), "Melodie," "Orgelspiel" (Organ Music), "Zu einer Toccata von Bach" (On a Toccata by Bach). It appears to be of no importance to him that Chopin's "Valse brillante" is expressed in an iambic meter rather than in the three-four dactylic beat that Novalis used more "musically" in his poem "Walzer" (Waltz).[11]

Hesse's poems on music, and not only those, consist of a rhythmically modulated melodic verse that expresses psychic feelings and changing moods through images. Among Hesse's poems that refer to abstract notations of tempi is the poem cycle "Feierliche Abendmusik" (Solemn Evening Music, 1911), comprising the poems "Allegro," "Andante," and "Adagio" (*SW* 10:218–19). Examples from this cycle follow:

From "Allegro":

Mitgeweht vom föhnigen Sturm	[Swept along by the storming foehn
Flieh ich mit unermüdetem Schritt	I flee at a tireless pace
Durch ein bewölktes Leben.	Through a life decked in clouds]

From "Andante":

Immer wieder ist Stern und Baum,	[Ever again star and tree
ist mir Wolke und Vogel nahe verwandt,	Cloud and bird are one with me
Grüßt mich als Bruder der Fels.	A boulder greets me as brother.]

And from "Adagio":

Traum gibt, was Tag verschloß;	[The dream reveals what the day concealed;
Nachts, wenn der Wille erliegt,	At night, when the will must yield,
Streben befreite Kräfte empor.	Powers now freed can arise.][12]

In reading these poems aloud, one should observe more than the indications of tempo; the occurrences of enjambment suggest more rapid movement, the commas at the end of a verse indicate a more leisurely pace, and the caesuras within a line retard the melodic flow. In the poetry of every epoch and nation, metaphoric language transposes associated ideas into images. Hesse, for whom "neben dem Sehen von Farben der höchste Genuß [. . .] die Musik [war]" (*GB* 2:22; together with beholding colors [. . .] music [was] the greatest delight) also makes the images "sound" audibly. A composer who has set a poem of Hesse's to music would be especially sensitive to this. But other readers too can experience synaesthesia in the way Hesse visualizes — for instance — earth, air, fire, and water metaphorically and makes them musical. Thus, in the poem "Orgelspiel": "fließt im Unterirdisch Dunkeln / Ewig fort der heilige Strom" (*SW* 10:346; in the subterranean dark / the sacred stream eternal flows). Air and fire combine in "Symphonie" as "der Feuerlüfte [. . .] Brand" (*SW* 10:192; the blaze of air on fire). In "Flötenspiel," the line "Als wäre Heimat jedes Land" (As though each land were home) brings the flutist's song back down to earth (*SW* 10:364).

While listening to music, Hesse visualized "Menschen, Meere, Gewitter, Tages- und Jahreszeiten" (people, oceans, storms, times of day and seasons of the year). Although some musical experts declare such visualization erroneous and dilettantish, Hesse knew professional musicians who experienced music similarly. Obviously, all members of a concert audience did not necessarily see what he saw, but similar ideas must have arisen in each of them upon hearing a certain piece (*SW* 13:344). Intuitively, Hesse the layman was stating what the musicologist Deryck Cook demonstrated in his treatises on the elements of musical communication and the principles of the history and psychology of the musical vocabulary.[13]

Listening to a toccata by Bach (probably BWV 565), Hesse saw or felt "den Vorgang der Schöpfung, und zwar den Moment der Lichtwerdung" (*HM* 169; the process of the world's creation, at the moment when first there was light). This is also how he describes the poem "Zu einer Toccata von Bach," which he attributes to Josef Knecht in *Das Glasperlenspiel* (*SW* 5:401). Was this a subjective speculation? In 2000, the church musician and theologian, Ernst Wacker, after a lifetime spent studying Bach's art of composition in minute detail, demonstrated that Bach's works for the organ as well as "The Well-Tempered Clavier" are devoted to transposing scenes from the Bible into music. For Wacker, the toccata in D Minor, including the fugue, symbolizes the Deluge. Hesse's impression of the piece as representing the Creation thus seems appropriate.[14]

An example of musical structure should be pointed out briefly: In his essay "The Sense of Lateness in Time and the Language of Hermann Hesse's Poetry" Rüdiger Görner emphasizes that there are "countless" references in Hesse's poetry to "the end," to autumn, illness, and death.[15] Earlier, in analogy to a musical composition, I had named this phenomenon, when it appears at the end of a poem "Todeskadenz," the cadence of death.[16] We also encounter it in many of Hesse's prose works as a natural or abrupt conclusion. But this "cadence" may also be seen in a positive light as commending acceptance of the inevitable, as in the famous poem, "Stufen":

Wohlan denn, Herz, nimm Abschied und gesunde! (*SW* 10:366)

[Well then, my heart, take your leave now and be healed!]

There is an unexpected sociological aspect to Hesse's musical techniques in his poetry. He responded to a survey conducted by the University of Vienna in 1930 with a single sentence to the effect that poetry would be "umso besser [. . .] je weniger Universitäten sich mit ihr beschäftigen" (*SW* 12:264; the better off the less universities concern themselves with it). Hesse later noted that this laconic barb did not apply to "allem und jedem Analysieren und Denken" (any and every analysis and critical thought), but only to the "Erstickung und Verdrängung des naiven durch das rationale Verhalten" (suffocation and repression of naive spontaneity by hyper-rationality; *GB* 4:268). Were such comments a reason for academic literary scholars to take so little interest in Hesse's poetry, at least until the end of the twentieth century? In any case, given the less rational than naive transformation of his poetry into music, his wish was fulfilled to an unexpectedly high degree; this was ironic, for, like Goethe, such things made little difference to him: "Ich bin froh, wenn ich unvertont bleibe" (*GB* 4:163; I am happy when I'm not set to music).

In 1950, Hesse wrote to the composer Justus Hermann Wetzel that there must be some 2,000 musical settings of his poems, "vom Wandervogel-Dilettantenlied mit Gitarre bis zu pompösen Vertonungen mit Orchester" (*HM* 188–89; from dilettantish Wandervogel songs for guitar to pompous settings for orchestral accompaniment). More recently, in 2004, Georg Günther published a 590-page catalogue of the printed scores and song manuscripts of settings of Hesse's poetry in the German Literature Archive in Marbach. Though not necessarily exhaustive, it contains some 2,100 titles by about 500 composers, male and female, each of whom has set between one and one hundred or more Hesse texts to music. The famous "Im Nebel" (In the Fog) alone has received 102 settings so far, and others have been similarly favored. We may safely conclude that Hesse is among the German poets most frequently set to music. Composers of Hesse songs, almost exclusively German, include the famous Richard Strauss and Othmar Schoeck, such noted ones as Gottfried von Einem, Paul Graener, Joseph Haas, Mark Lothar, Günther Raphael, Rudolf Mauersberger, Wilhelm Weismann, as well as others such as Edwin Fischer and Anton Heiller, who are better known as virtuosi of the piano or organ. Most of these compositions have been presented only sporadically in concert. The editor of the newest catalogue hopes that "from the abundance of material works previously unknown ones will come to light and that their discovery will be worthwhile."[17]

III. Musical Forms in Hesse's Prose Works

Prose works do not exhibit musical and metrical features to the degree lyric poetry does, even considering such "lyrical" devices as rhythmic or rhymed prose as in Rilke's *Cornet,* Rolland's *Colas Breugnon,* and in Hesse's own *Steppenwolf.* As is the case with writers of every epoch, Hesse occasionally relaxes the flow of a narrative by inserting verses or entire poems. In principle, the difference between poetry and music consists in the fact that, in the former, ideas must be presented sequentially, whereas they may appear simultaneously in the latter. In other words, there is no poetry for two voices, much less for polyphony. (Speakers assigned different rhythms, voices speaking in chorus, etc. are irrelevant here.) Novels and other narratives can only relate to musical forms through metaphorical analogies, conversely to the way one speaks of Bach's "painterly music," Chopin's "poetic effects," or Bruckner's "architectonic" structures. But the equation never quite works out. Hesse scholars have compared *Der Steppenwolf* and *Das Glasperlenspiel* with specific musical forms. The author himself gave hints encouraging such approaches, as will be discussed below.

Examples of musical structures are already present in Hesse's early prose, in the novel *Gertrud,* and in *Klingsors letzter Sommer* (Klingsor's Last Summer) as well as in *Kurgast* (The Guest at a Spa). *Eine Stunde hinter Mitternacht* (An Hour beyond Midnight), the *Notturni,* the "Lulu" chapter in *Hermann Lauscher,* and *Der Dichter* (The Poet), a novel first published in Hesse's *Sämtliche Werke,* could all be taken as variations on the theme of "Dichterliebe" (a poet's love).

> Dichterliebe! [. . .] die Menschen achten sie nicht hoch [. . .] Daß einer liebt und vom ersten Tag seiner Liebe verzichtet und sie, ihm selbst unerreichbar, bekränzt zu Sehnsucht und Traum in den Kreis der Sterne erhebt — wie sollten sie es verstehen? (*SW* 1:301)

> [A poet's love! [. . .] is held in low esteem [. . .] That someone can love and yet renounce that love from the very first day, which he then, though he cannot achieve it, crowns in his longing and his dreams and elevates to the stars — how can people understand that?]

This sounds like medieval minstrelsy, reinforced by a reminiscence of Dante's muse: "Daß du Maria, Elise, Lilia und Elinor hießest. Daß du Beatrice bist!" (*SW* 1:302; That you were named Maria, Elise, Lilia, and Elinor. That you are Beatrice!). For Hesse, all the women's names signify "Beatrice" and inspire his poetic imagination to new life: one of the "Variations" has the title "Incipit Vita Nova," a clear reference to Dante (*SW* 1:191) Even when a character is based on a real person, as in the case of "Lulu," alias Julie Hellmann, who enchanted Hesse and his friends in Tübingen for a time, she appears as a fairy princess in the style of E. T. A. Hoffmann, as in *Kranz für die schöne*

Lulu (*SW* 1:253–87; A Wreath for Lovely Lulu), in which poetry and prose are musically commingled. The *Notturni,* written between 1900 and 1902 and unpublished until they appeared in the *Sämtliche Werke,* "offer another example of Hesse's fascination with musical form and theme," as Richard C. Helt writes in his study of the young Hesse.[18] The *Notturni,* lyrical and prose variations in the spirit of medieval courtly love, "hohe Minne," proclaim that "Musik, das heißt Farbe, heißt Schwung, heißt Takt und Glut" (Music means color, vivacity, rhythm, and warmth); tellingly, they include four fictional "Marienlieder des Ritters Tannhäuser" (Hymns to Mary by Tannhäuser the Knight, *SW* 1:142–43). C. G. Jung's psychology would identify this as an "anima projection." The poet's love for "Elisabeth," whose name appears frequently in Hesse's poetry and prose prior to *Peter Camenzind,* has a special status. This figure is based on Elisabeth La Roche (1876–1965), whom he first met as a child in Basel in 1883, once more in 1899, and finally, "grown old and grey" in 1930 at the Mozart Festival (*HM* 153). The daughter of a pastor, she played the piano, taught music, danced, choreographed, and was, in fact, Hesse's "unattainable beloved," as Volker Michels has demonstrated.[19] The novel *Der Dichter* (The Poet), written around 1900 with the eloquent subtitle, "Ein Buch der Sehnsucht" (A Book of Longing) casts a new light on this tense and repressed love affair. As a psychological compensation for the longing that was unfulfilled in real life, the pianist Elisabeth in *Der Dichter* gives in to the poet Martin, who has wooed her tirelessly. However, this leads them to part by mutual consent. Elisabeth comes to realize that love has made her a more mature person and artist. Her concert is reviewed favorably: "An Stelle der fast herben Klassizität ist ein lebendig bewegter, hinreißender Vortrag getreten" (Her former severely classical manner has given way to a lively, emotional, exciting performance). The poet, on the other hand, must behold in his mirror "das Gesicht eines gebrochenen und vom Dämon gezeichneten Mannes" (the face of a broken man, marked by the demon). His "entartete Liebeslust" (degenerate lust) has cost him his self-esteem as a man and as an artist. He destroys his manuscripts and disappears into the mountains without a trace (*SW* 1:480–83). Reversing Shakespeare's notion, love has been the food of music, at least for Elisabeth. In *Gertrud,* a novel about musicians, however, a man, the composer Kuhn, is inspired artistically by his unfulfilled love for the wife of his friend, the singer Muoth.

Theodore Ziolkowski's description of *Der Steppenwolf* as a "sonata in prose" remains the best attempt so far to interpret a work by Hesse in analogy to a musical form.[20] Ziolkowski takes Hesse at his word when, defending his novel against the reproach of formlessness, he described it as being "um das Intermezzo des Traktats herum so streng [. . .] gebaut ist wie eine Sonate" (as strictly constructed as a sonata around the intermezzo of the Treatise).[21] Ziolkowski relates the novel's three main segments to the classical structure of the sonata in three movements. In the exposition of the first movement, two contrasting themes are established in the tonic and the dominant. This corresponds to the contrast between the Steppenwolf and the bourgeois in the "Vorwort des Herausgebers" (Editor's Preface). In the development, "Harry Hallers Aufzeichnungen" (Harry Haller's Diary), the significance of both themes is interpreted. The Treatise represents the reprise, where the themes are treated more theoretically and suggest a resolution of the conflict. Does the second part of the novel — from the end of the Treatise to the beginning of the "Magic Theater" — then correspond to the sonata's second movement, with individual scenes from the Magic Theater forming a "Finale with Variations" as the third movement? The analogy can only be accepted with reservations, as Ziolkowski concedes.

Because of the novel's complexities, it is much more difficult to relate *Das Glasperlenspiel* to any musical form. The concept of the sonata clearly does not suffice here, and comparison with a symphony would be too vague. Recently, Dominique Lingens has attempted to compare Hesse's magnum opus with a fugue, preferably from the Baroque, doubtless the musical form that makes the highest demands on a composer's inventiveness and skill.[22] Such an approach is suggested in the text itself; in the "allgemeinverständlichen Einführung" (introduction for the layman) it is stated expressly that a glass bead game could begin on the basis of the "Thema einer Bachfuge" (*SW* 5:34; the theme of a fugue by Bach). Bach's name appears frequently in the ensuing chapters. The esteem in which the community of glass bead game players holds Bach is emphasized in the biography of the theologian Knecht, a master from the eighteenth century, who became acquainted with Bach's works and resigned his office to become a "stiller Organist" (*SW* 5:616; a quiet organist). Hesse considered Bach's "Art of the Fugue" "das Höchste und Vollkommenste, was die abendländische Musik aller Zeiten hervorgebracht" (the highest and most perfect composition that Western music had produced).[23] In the chapter "Die Berufung" (The Calling), the old music master introduces young Knecht to the art of music by gradually developing a fugue, a technique that Hesse had noted while preparing to write the novel (*SW* 5:46; *HM* 162–63). Basing her arguments on those of Manfred Bukofzer, Lingens points out that for Bach, counterpoint is fundamental, never the melody alone. In a fugue, therefore, countermelodies and interludes always appear, creating in the aggregate a balance between polyphony and harmony. So too in *Das Glasperlenspiel* itself, which brings conflicting elements into confrontation and resolves their differences into harmony, to a "Unio Mystica aller getrennten Glieder der Universitas litterarum" (*SW* 5:32; Unio Mystica of all of the separated members of the Universitas litterarum). Characteristics of Baroque art are ambivalence and metamorphosis, multiplicity and polar oppositions, as well as a strong preference for symmetry under the influence of ideas from mathematics and geometry. Thus, a fugue by Bach symbolizes as can hardly another composition the progression and liberating metamorphosis of contradictory ideas in space and time.

Two lines from Hesse's poem "Stufen" (Stages), which Josef Knecht wanted to call "Transzendieren" (Transcend), but that his friend Tegularius would have preferred to call "Wesen der Musik," "stete Gegenwärtigkeit," and "Bereitschaft zum Weitereilen" (*SW* 5:343–44; the essence of music; permanence of the present moment; and readiness to hasten forward) reinforce the idea that the Latin "fuga" (flight) expresses in the original meaning of the word:

> Wir sollen heiter Raum um Raum durchschreiten,
> An keinem wie an einer Heimat hängen
>
> [Serenely let us move to distant places
> And let no sentiments of home detain us.[24]]

Associations also arise, of course, with the German word "fügen," to join in the sense of joining together elements that are disparate yet mutually complementary. That the structuring of a fugue involves "several sciences and arts," especially mathematics, is essential to the "symbolic language and grammar of the game" (*SW* 5:11). While Castalians, according to Lingens, emphasize *musica theoretica et speculativa,* theoretical and speculative music, Knecht is concerned above all with *musica instrumentalis (et vocalis),* instrumental and vocal music, as evidenced towards the close by the Magister playing the flute, in the symbolism of music as a return to monody, to unity, after he has left the Order's province and is about to dedicate himself to educating a single young man, the son of his exact opposite and friend, Plinio Designori; here too we find a resolution of opposites. Such a resolution becomes possible for Magister Ludi, whose life within and outside of Castalia the novel has represented, only at the end of his development. According to Lingens, he enters upon *musica mundana,* the harmony of all the spheres, only through his death in the lake high in the mountains, an allegory of the world of Bach. When the cellist Pierre Fournier played a solo suite by Bach for him, Hesse, as he noted in his *Engadiner Erlebnisse* (Experiences in the Engadine), felt enveloped in "die reine und strenge Luft Bachs" (Bach's pure, austere atmosphere), as though he had been elevated into "noch viel höhere, klarere, kristallenere Bergwelt" (a still higher, clearer, more crystalline mountain world), which reminded him of Castalia (*SW* 12: 605). Summarizing, Lingens argues that *Das Glasperlenspiel* is "like a great fugue, with its counterpoints and modulations, its themes and counter-themes, its expositions developed and redeveloped, presenting the image of a composition based on the interchange of the spirit and the world." But she adds knowingly that it is "[a] fugue that Josef Knecht brought to its conclusion, and at whose end, nonetheless, there also appeared a melody for a single voice."[25] Representing a discourse that leads to a unison of ideas was always, says Lingens, Hesse's "dilemma and problem." In *Kurgast,* he had stated already that, if he were a musician, he could "ohne Schwierigkeit" (without difficulty) write a melody for two voices that would express the series of notes in the "Lebensmelodie" (melody of life) and how they bring one another to a harmony despite their dissonances. Although, like the Chinese sage Lao Tse in many of his proverbs, Hesse himself could never bend "die beiden Pole des Lebens zueinander" (the two poles of life together), he constantly made the attempt (*SW* 11:126–27).

Hesse's *Ein Satz über die Kadenz* (A Sentence about Cadences) is a light-hearted imitation of a musical form through language. In a way similar to Kafka's story *Auf der Galerie* (On the Balcony), which depicts in two sentences how a woman rides in a circus ride around the ring, Hesse, in the 220 words of a single sentence, "plays," as a virtuoso a solo instrument, a single cadence until its final chord — the period (*SW* 10:573–74; *HM* 110).

IV. Hesse's Opinions on Music

> Was ich im Bereich der Künste ablehnen oder doch mit Mißtrauen betrachten, was ich dagegen verehren und lieben soll, wird mir nicht von objektiven, irgendwo genormten Begriffen von Wert und Schönheit diktiert, sondern von einer Art von Gewissen, das moralischer und nicht ästhetischer Natur ist. (*SW* 14:240)

> [What I reject in the arts or regard with mistrust, and what I am to revere and love, is not dictated to me by objective or theoretically formed ideas of value or beauty, but rather by a kind of conscience that is moral rather than aesthetic in nature.]

It was in this sense that Hesse, regarded himself as a "Musikfreund," or music lover, and considered himself in matters of musical criticism to be "Laie und Moralist," a layman and moralist (*HM* 192, 222). Nonetheless, he frequently touched upon musical topics in his works, and wrote essays titled "Alte Musik," "Ein Virtuosen-Konzert," "Mozarts Opern," "An einen Musiker" and "Nicht abgesandter Brief an eine Sängerin" (Ancient Music; A Virtuoso Concert; Mozart's Operas; To a Musician; and Unsent Letter to a Female Singer). The latter two in particular contain substantial opinions on musical ethics and the practice of interpretation. Innumerable remarks about music occur throughout Hesse's voluminous correspondence, sometimes offhand, sometimes sharply formulated insights. In his youth, Hesse's relation to music was entirely spontaneous. He loved and admired works by "serious" composers like Bach, Mozart, Beethoven, Schubert, Schumann, and Chopin almost uncritically. To Hesse, Chopin meant what Wagner had meant to Nietzsche — "oder noch mehr" (or still more). As he wrote to his parents in 1897, "mit diesen warmen, lebendigen Melodien, mit dieser pikanten, lasziven, nervösen Harmonie hängt alles Wesentliche meines geistigen und seelischen Wesens zusammen" (*HM* 127; Everything essential to my spiritual and intellectual being is linked to these warm, vivacious melodies, this piquant, lascivious, nervous harmony).

In an early prose piece, Hesse declares that he feels close to Chopin through the "Unstillbarkeit dieses Heimwehs," "das . . . nicht nur der Heimat (gilt), sondern allem Traum, allem zugleich Ersehnten und Erreichbaren" (*SW* 1:161; this insuperable homesickness [. . .] that longs not only for home, but for all dreams, for everything desired and fulfilled at once). With John Ruskin, one could easily associate such reflections with the "pathetic fallacy," a projection of subjective feelings upon music. However, it is thought-provoking that the pianist and Chopin scholar, Alfred Cortot, Hesse's exact contemporary (1877–1962), in describing the character of the "poet-musician," discusses how such a person had no other home than "his fervent thoughts" and "all the dreams and nostalgias of a limitless human heart."[26] Did Hesse develop a true spiritual empathy with Chopin, or did larger artistic and cultural impulses cause him to adopt a common, popular image of Chopin? Changing fashions shape interpretive approaches anew. Even in old age, a piece by Chopin moved Hesse to use the title "Der Trauermarsch" (Funeral March) on a souvenir note to a boyhood friend (*SW* 12:497–504). But that is an exception. Even at nineteen, Hesse had assured his teacher, Dr. Kapff, that he was "alles [. . .], nur kein Romantiker" (*GB* 1:20; all sorts of things, but not a Romantic). In "Notizen" (Notes) written in 1912, Hesse formulated his ideas on music definitively:

> Es gibt zweierlei Musik. Die eine ist klassisch, die andere romantisch. [. . .] Die eine ist kontrapunktisch, die andere koloristisch. Wer wenig von Musik versteht, genießt meistens die romantische leichter. Die klassische hat keine solche Orgien und Räusche zu bieten wie jene, sie bringt aber auch nie Dégout, schlechtes Gewissen und Katzenjammer. (*HM* 142)

> [There are two kinds of music. One is classical, the other Romantic. [. . .] One is contrapuntal, the other "coloristic." People who know little about music find the Romantic kind easier to enjoy. Classical music cannot offer the same orgies and ecstasies, but it never produces revulsion, a bad conscience, or a hangover.]

This dualistic conception determined Hesse's opinions regarding certain composers, works, and performances.

From this point on, Hesse emphatically turned away from Richard Wagner, whose music he had always found suspect. He felt that it did not belong in that region where — as he was later to formulate in *Das Glasperlenspiel* — "Ratio und Magie eins werden" (*HM* 212; the intellectual and the magical become one). Like Mark Twain, Hesse would have preferred Wagner's operas without the singing, but that was not why he disliked them. He described Wagner's fascinating effect on musicians, and especially on Hitler, as "schwarze Magie" (black magic), for at the end of these fascinations came "die Kriege und Kanonen, und alles andre was Gott verboten hat" (the wars and cannons, and everything else forbidden by God). As early as 1934, shortly after the Nazis' rise to power, Hesse wrote to Thomas Mann, a life-long devotee of Wagner, that Wagner, "dieser gerissene und gewissenlose Erfolgmacher" (this cunning, ruthless manipulator) was "genau der Götze, der ins jetzige Deutschland paßt" (exactly the idol that suits present-day Germany; *HM* 159). Hesse had a similarly low opinion of his contemporary, Richard Strauss (1864–1949), the most famous composer to set his poems to music. Hesse found Strauss's "Vier letzten Lieder" (Four Last Songs), a setting of three of his poems together with one by Eichendorff, to be like all music by that composer: "virtuos, raffiniert, voll handwerklicher Schönheit, aber ohne Zentrum, nur Selbstzweck" (*HM* 208; masterful, subtle, full of artistic beauty, but without a center, merely there for its own sake). Hesse rejected the cycle not only because of his distaste for "tempestuous music" or because Strauss was the last great late Romantic composer.[27] Hesse could not forgive Strauss for accepting "Vorteile und Huldigungen" (favors and honors) from the Nazis despite the fact that he had Jewish relatives (*GB* 3:325). Here, Hesse was mixing music with politics and morality, demanding political and moral integrity from the artist, above all others, if his works are to be seen as "weiße Magie" (white magic). Here Hesse defines "Magie" as the ability to become "sich von der Zeit und vom Außen unabhängig [. . .] und mit der Seele in dem zu leben, was uns schön, lebendig und heilig scheint, sei das nun Buddha, Jesus, Sokrates oder Goethe oder Musik oder Natur" (*GB* 2:88; independent of time and external things, letting the soul dwell in what is for us beautiful, vital, and sacred, whether that be Buddha, Jesus, Socrates, or Goethe, or music, or nature). His rejection of "Rauschmusik" (intoxicating music) has evident political and sociological ramifications. He believed that such music led from "Massenpsychose" to "Verbrüderungsszenen mit Rührung und Tränen" and finally to "Wahnsinn und Blutströmen" (from mass psychoses to tearful, emotional avowals of friendship to madness and bloodshed). He was referring here to the ambivalent effect of music, which can be positive, therapeutic, aiding meditation or in religious services, or negative, stimulating base desires or aiding the manipulations of unscrupulous rulers. In formulating the concept of a "Musik des Untergangs" (music of decline), he attributed to it the ability to reflect the fates of whole cultures.

This idea is at the center of a whole chapter of *Klingsors letzter Sommer* (*SW* 8:311–19). In this story, which transposes Van Gogh's expressionism into a poetic form, there are more than fifty different tonalities of color, as

Reso Karalaschwili has pointed out.[28] In addition, the story — anticipating *Das Glasperlenspiel* — is full of Chinese motifs, including some names and frequent references to Li Tai Pe (701–62), who wrote drinking songs and verses celebrating nature and with whom the painter Klingsor identifies when he is intoxicated. Klingsor's music of decline seems to correspond to the European sense of decline following the First World War, most forcibly expressed by Oswald Spengler in his epoch-making work, *Der Untergang des Abendlandes* (The Decline of the West, 1918–22). The phrase "die Musik des Untergangs" appears again in the introduction to *Das Glasperlenspiel*, but now as a universally valid principle of cultural history. It is symbolized in the tonal mode of Tsing Tse and is discussed as speculative theory in the lengthy quotation from "Springtime and Fall," a treatise on music by the Chinese statesman Lü Bu We (300–235 BCE). Lü believed that the downfall of the Chu state was caused by the "rauschende Musik," tempestuous music, that the tyrants Giae and Jou Sin had created, which was no longer based on "Harmonie zwischen Himmel und Erde" (*SW* 5:24–25; harmony between heaven and earth). Hesse's "Musik des Untergangs" in *Das Glasperlenspiel* could be seen as latent criticism, in the guise of ancient Chinese history, of his own time, specifically of the Nazi era, to which Castalia, which holds that "klassische Musik [ist] Extrakt und Inbegriff unserer Kultur" (classical music [is] the concentrated quintessence of our culture), stands in diametric opposition.[29] Hesse also believed that the ancient Chinese knew and understood more about the "Geist der echten Musik, ihre Moral" (*HM* 164; the spirit and morality of genuine music) than western music critics of his own time.

Regarding his preferences in music and styles of performing, Hesse adopted "ein wenig puritanische Kunstmoral" (*SW* 14:241; a somewhat puritanical artistic morality). According to Hermann Kasack, "Hesse's creativity was driven not by his intellect, but by his heart" (*HM* 9). That is not, however, true of his musical criticism, as can be seen in his "Nicht abgesandter Brief an eine Sängerin," in which Hesse writes ironically of her celebrated "goldenes Herz," heart of gold. That interests him as little as her "mehr oder minder hübsche Gestalt oder Toilette (more or less attractive appearance or her gown). He does not wish to hear about her "nahes Verhältnis zum Gesungenen und Ergriffenheit vom Kunstwerk" (her close relationship to the songs and how close she feels to the music), but rather is looking for "die möglichst genaue und vollkommene Widergabe dessen, was auf ihren Notenblättern geschrieben steht" (*SW* 14:237–38; the optimally precise and comprehensive reproduction of a song's words and music as written). In short, he expected performers to exercise self-discipline and do justice to the music. Hesse also did not have a high opinion of concerts by virtuosi, which he saw as "vor allem sportliche und [. . .] gesellschaftliche Angelegenheit[en]" (social and sporting events). Hesse had nothing against virtuosi, as long as they used their skills in the service of "good music." When such virtuosity degenerates into a star cult, however, Hesse's tolerance is at an end, especially when virtuosi use mawkish music to tickle audiences at "jener heiklen Stelle zwischen Tränendrüse und Geldbeutel" (that sensitive spot between tear duct and wallet). Light music, even of high quality, meant little to Hesse. Music was "etwas völlig anderes, etwas, das mit Virtuosentum nichts zu tun hatte, was der Anonymität, der Frömmigkeit bedurfte, um zum Blühen kommen" (*SW* 14:94–99; something entirely different for him, something that had nothing to do with virtuosity, something that required anonymity, piety, in order to flourish). The inscription on the Gewandhaus in Leipzig, "Res severa verum gaudium" (True joy is serious), expresses Hesse's conception of music. Thus, he praised a concert by the "gediegensten aller Cellisten," Pierre Fournier, for its "Reinheit und Konzessionslosigkeit" (purity and lack of compromise) but found fault with Pablo Casals because, in addition to serious pieces, he played light, showy ones (*SW* 12:604). Bach and Mozart, whom Hesse regarded most highly, were also masterful performers, but that did not trouble him, as he felt that virtuosity never became an end in itself for them or degenerated into showmanship, but rather served the work itself.

Mozart exerted the strongest musical influence on Hesse throughout his life, and references to him are to be found everywhere in his writings. Beginning a review of Annette Kolb's book on Mozart, Hesse begins: "Mozart gehört zu jenen paar größten Künstlern, welche eigentlich keine Biographie und keine Psychologie [*sic*] haben, welche dadurch so vollkommen unbegreiflich und zauberhaft geheimnisvoll werden, weil sie von der Kunst, vom Überpersönlichen und Überzeitlichen, mehr als zur Hälfte aufgesogen wird" (*SW* 20:237; Mozart is an artist of that very greatest kind that have no life story or spiritual life of their own, who become so incomprehensible and magical because they disappear more than halfway into art itself, transcending the personal and temporal). Hesse was irritated when he reviewed Arthur Schurig's critical biography of Mozart in 1914. He disliked the book's "Pietätlosigkeit" (lack of reverence); he would have preferred the author to have had the courage simply to forego the use of all letters, quotations, documents of the time about Mozart and historical assessments of his stature (*SW* 17:285–87). Such factual matters did not correspond to Hesse's image of the "geliebtesten Meister" (dearly beloved master) and "strahlenden Götterliebling" (radiant darling of the gods). He would have preferred a hagiographic approach similar to that in his own monographs on St. Francis of Assisi and Boccaccio (*SW* 1:593–660). Mozart appears in *Steppenwolf* as a perfect genius, not necessarily one whom we today would find likeable for his human foibles. Hesse imitates the witty language of Mozart's letters but omits the obscenities, contenting himself with quasi-humorous, rhymed prose: "O du gläubiges Herze, mit deiner Druckerschwärze, mit deinem Seelenschmerze, ich stifte dir eine Kerze, nur zum Scherze" (*SW* 4:194: "O heart of a gull, with printer's ink dull, and soul sorrow-full. A candle I'll leave you, if that'll relieve you"[30]). In a surrealistic anachronism, Hesse lets Mozart express his distaste for Brahms and Wagner, condemning the "zu dicke(n) Instrumentierung" (overly dense instrumentation) and "Materialvergeudung" (waste of good material) that he alleges characterized the style of both (*SW* 4:192–93).

"Mozart is Pablo," Joachim-Ernst Berendt asserts in his interpretation of *Der Steppenwolf*.[31] That would mean that Mozart, like Pablo, the saxophone player, also embodied jazz, which Hesse includes in his experimental novel as a complement to what is referred to as the "classical" music of the years 1500 to 1800. But for Hesse, jazz, like his "Krisis" poems, represented only an episode. The name "Pablo" seems associated more closely with such virtuosi as Sarasate and Casals, who shared that first name and — like jazz — did not entirely meet Hesse's standards of classical, ethical musicianship, of which Mozart was the supreme representative.[32] In settings other than the novel, too, Mozart and his music appear as quintessential expressions of cheerful serenity that triumphs over the world, the best remedy for suicidal moods. Hesse clearly would not have accepted the remark about the Adagio in B minor (KV 540) that Romain Rolland, in his novel *Le voyage intérieur*, has Olivier say to his friend Jean-Christoph while playing the piece for him: "Mozart is playing with his sorrows."[33]

While Hesse was "not interested in the theater," claiming never to have seen *Hamlet, King Lear,* or *Faust* on the stage, he enjoyed going to operas, provided that they were by Mozart. For him, they were "der Inbegriff von Theater," the quintessence of theater (*HM* 153). He had heard Mozart's *Die Zauberflöte* (The Magic Flute) countless times, three times in the winter of 1936 alone, and the opera inspired several of his poems (*SW* 10:356–57; *HM* 51). Their common love for Mozart runs like a golden path through Hesse's correspondence with his second wife, Ruth, a love that links them both to many other people — the letters of a writer of the *Steppenwolf* period, at the mercy of "the crisis of the man of fifty" and the young singer who was still learning her art.

Hesse's remark that he "needed music," that it was "the only form of art" that he found absolutely indispensable, provides a significant insight (*HM* 142). In *Der Dichter,* Hesse's early novel, Martin tells the pianist Elisabeth about King Saul, whose melancholy in his hours of torment only the music of the young David's harp could drive away.[34] "Ich wollte Sie bitten, mir diesen Davidsdienst zu tun" (I wanted to ask you to perform this service of David for me) says Martin to his "schöne Muse" (lovely muse; *SW* 1:456). In *Demian,* mutatis mutandis, the organist grants this favor to Emil Sinclair by repeatedly performing a "Passacaglia des alten Buxtehude" (a passacaglia by old Buxtehude) for him (*SW* 3:320). What Hesse describes here indirectly is his own suffering from "körperlicher und seelischer Melancholie" (physical and spiritual melancholy), a topic that Walter Benjamin (who esteemed Hesse greatly) discusses toward the end of his essay on the origins of tragedy in Germany. Benjamin points out that in Albrecht Dürer's engraving "Melancholia," a dog figures as a symbol of melancholy, in addition to a sphere and a stone, and that Aegidius Albertinus compares the mood of a melancholic person to that of that dog when he is rabid.[35] The dog's kinship with a coyote or a wolf of the steppes — "Steppenwolf" — is obvious. In his study of *Der Steppenwolf,* Peter Huber points out that the "Abendmensch," evening person, Harry Haller, inherently suicidal, is one of those "souls afflicted with feelings of guilt for being individuals"; who, as the Treatise states, see their liberator "im Tod, nicht im Leben" (*SW* 4:51; in death, not in life). The harmonious serenity of Mozart, which the "wolf" has still not achieved at the novel's close, acts as a palliative for Harry Haller's melancholy; appropriately, the last sentence asserts: "Mozart wartete auf mich" (Mozart was waiting for me).[36] That is why music continued to play a decisive role in Hesse's life and work. Neither his marriage to Ruth nor the years of psychotherapeutic discussions with Dr. Josef Bernhard Lang, a student of C. G. Jung, could compensate permanently for Hesse's — not exclusively, but often — melancholy disposition.[37] Music was indispensable to his creativity. Hesse mentioned Mozart in the very last letter he wrote (to Gertrud von Le Fort). And on the eve of his death he heard — a kind of viaticum — a radio performance of Mozart's Piano Sonata No. 7 in C Major (KV 309).

V. Hesse's Musical Development

Notes made in 1957 by the Canadian scholar G. Wallis Field, following a visit to Hesse, read like a summing-up of the writer's ideas on music. They reveal how clearly Hesse perceived the limits of his conceptions about music, especially in comparison with Thomas Mann. Hesse, says Field, believed that his nature and Mann's were diametrically opposed. In his youth, like Mann, he had preferred Romantic music, especially Chopin, Schumann, and Schubert. As time passed, however, he had increasingly looked backward, first to Mozart and Bach, then to Purcell and the great Italian composers. In contrast, Mann had gone steadily forward in time, finally reaching the realm of atonality. Despite their differences, they had built a "herzliche Freundschaft," a cordial friendship.[38] It would be mistaken to believe, however, that Hesse understood no music later than that of Robert Schumann. Even in old age, he called Bartók's Concerto for Orchestra "meisterhaft," masterful, although, contrasting it with a concerto by Handel, he found it expressed "statt Kosmos Chaos, statt Ordnung Wirrnis, statt Klarheit und Kontur zerflatternde Wogen klanglicher Sensationen, statt Aufbau und beherrschten Ablauf Zufälligkeit der Proportionen und Verzicht auf Architektur" (*HM*

202–3; not a cosmos, but chaos; not order, but confusion; not clarity and shapeliness, but fleeting waves of sonic sensations; not structure and a disciplined development, but arbitrary proportions and renunciation of architecture). He also enjoyed listening to Stravinsky, he wrote in 1953, "besonders wenn er mit alten Formen spielt" (*HM* 197; especially when he plays with older musical forms). Yet Hesse believed that in principle, however much he respected later great composers, music began its decline with Beethoven, reaching its final low point with twelve-tone music (*HM* 157). As he wrote in a poem entitled *Antwort an Freunde:*

Mancher versteht	[Some people understand
Zwölfergesang	Songs in twelve tones
Mit oder ohne Adorno	With or without Adorno
Nicht aber	But not
Unterzeichneter,	The undersigned
Dessen Augen	Whose eyes
Erstaunen blendet.	Astonishment dazzles.]

(*SW* 10:579–80)

Hermann Kasack's assertion that "music was not a central theme in any of Hesse's works" does not hold true (*HM* 10). Strictly speaking, most of his poems whose titles have to do with music deal with one of its aspects. Hesse transposes these aspects metaphorically into his own imagery. It is possible to divine Hesse's entire philosophy of music *in nuce* from the poem "Orgelspiel," for instance.[39] Reflections such as "An einen Musiker" (*SW* 12:676–81), "Alte Musik" (*SW* 13:335–39), "Nicht abgesandter Brief an eine Sängerin" (*SW* 15:237–44), "Mozarts Opern" (*SW* 14:170–71), "Musik" (*SW* 13 342–47), or "Virtuosen-Konzert" (*SW* 14:94–98) are concerned, like those of professional critics, with problems of musical style, interpretation, and the sociology of musical tastes. The novel *Gertrud* also presents, if we read closely, the story of an opera's composition, with its psychological and logistical prerequisites. (*SW* 2:352–70). However, Hesse never found himself in the situation of Thomas Mann, who was obliged to inform his readers that the compositional style depicted in chapter 21 of his *Doktor Faustus* was the intellectual property of Arnold Schönberg.

In an earlier article, I have pointed out how Hesse's musical criticism agrees, sometimes very precisely, with the ideas of British and American writers such as Charles Burney, Virgil Thomson, and Roger Sessions.[40] Yet he apparently did not consider significant such contemporary musicological studies as Albert Schweitzer's analysis of Bach's musical motifs, Arnold Schering's monograph on symbolism in music, or Deryck Cooke's deciphering of the vocabulary of music, because music, like poetry, was not an exact science, "sondern eben eine Kunst" (but instead an art), whose aspects of "Magie" or magic can never be exhaustively explained (*HM* 169). For similar reasons, he found psychological and especially psychoanalytical analyses of music suspect.[41] As he grew older, the moral-ethical function of music took on ever more importance for Hesse. "Wenn Lehár gleich Mozart ist," he wrote, "warum soll dann nicht Hitler gleich Jesus oder Sartre gleich Sokrates sein. Die Welt braucht [. . .] Moral nötiger als Gescheitheit, und Ordnung der Werte nötiger als Psychologie" (HM 184; If Lehár is equal to Mozart, then why isn't Hitler equal to Jesus or Sartre to Socrates? The world needs morality more urgently than cleverness, and giving order to our values more than psychology).

Such ideas recall the philosophy of values propounded by Rickert, Windelband, and other neo-Kantian thinkers, primarily of the Baden School, from which Martin Heidegger, resisting and subverting materialism, later developed his existential philosophy. The final line of Hesse's poem "Flötenspiel" — "Und alle Zeit ward Gegenwart" (SW 10:364; And all of time became the present) — which recurs in prose in the conversation between Knecht and Designori (SW 5:290) was for Hesse "das Endergebnis vieljähriger Spekulation über das Wesen der Musik" (the fruit of speculation about the essence of music over many years). The experience of music seemed to him, in terms of philosophy, "ästhetisch wahrnehmbar gemachte Zeit. Und zwar Gegenwart. Und dabei fällt einem die Identität von Augenblick und Ewigkeit ein" (HM 177; [a moment in] time rendered in an aesthetically perceptible form. Indeed, a present moment, in which one perceives the unity of the instant with eternity). Read adeptly, such remarks could lead one finally to associate Hesse's ideas on music with the existential mode of Heidegger's Sein und Zeit (Being and Time, 1927). That would be an illegitimate "glass bead game" gambit, however, especially as Hesse tended to make fun of Heidegger's philosophical language (GB 4:403).

Hesse's ideas on the sociology of music are sometimes contradictory. Thus, he saw it as positive that "was das Deutschland nach dem Mittelalter der Welt gegeben hatte, gab es in der Musik" (what Germany gave to the world after the Middle Ages, it gave in the form of music). And more emphatically, he wrote that it was in the music of Bach, not in literature, that Christianity took on artistic form for the last time (HM 157). Yet in Der Steppenwolf, he reproaches "de[n] deutschen Geist," the German spirit, for having luxuriated "in wunderbaren seligen Tongebilden [. . .] und die Mehrzahl seiner tatsächlichen Aufgaben versäumt" (SW 4:130; in wonderful, blissful music and having neglected its actual obligations). We could, however, regard such seemingly contradictory statements as prime examples of the development of Hesse's musical ideas, which was always open to new impulses and to change, especially since the negative opinion appeared in a work of fiction, while the positive one was contained in a later letter, expressing a serious opinion. Hesse remained open to new ideas all his life, readily amending old ones, to an amazing degree. How much further would his love for music have taken him if he had lived longer?

If the music of Bach was "painterly," as Albert Schweitzer believed, and Chopin was a "poète musicien," for Alfred Cortot, then Hesse's writings could rightly be called "musical." His last poem, "Knarren eines geknickten Astes" (Creaking of a Cracked Branch) is at once a song and an auditory experience. Hesse finished the third draft one day before he died.[42] He left as his legacy the musicality of his poetic language, whose tonalities in the original cannot be translated into any other language. In whatever languages we read his works, however, Hesse, and especially his conception of music, means to remind us "an das Licht, an die Idee der Ordnung, der Harmonie, des 'Sinnes' im Chaos" — "of life's radiance, of the idea of order, of harmony, and to seek 'meaning,' even in chaos."[43]

— *Translated by Michael M. Metzger*

Notes

[1] Among the most important Hesse bibliographies of the twentieth century in which primary and secondary literature about music can be found are: Otto Bareiss, *H. H. Eine Bibliographie* (Basel: Karl Maier-Bader, part 1: 1962, part 2: 1964) and Joseph Mileck, *Biography and Bibliography,* 2 vols. (Berkeley: U of California P, 1977). The yearly directories of Hesse research, started by Martin Pfeifer in 1964, have been continued since 1994 by Michael Limberg (Deschenweg 1, D-40591 Düsseldorf). Important for the twenty-first century are volumes 6–15 (2000–2008). Hesse's works will be cited in this article from the following sources: *SW = Sämtliche Werke in 20 Bänden,* ed. Volker Michels (Frankfurt am Main: Suhrkamp, 2001–5), volume and page numbers in arabic numerals; *GB = Gesammelte Briefe,* 4 vols., ed. Volker Michels in collaboration with Heiner Hesse and Ursula Michels (Frankfurt am Main: Suhrkamp Verlag, 1973–86); *HM = Hermann Hesse Musik: Betrachtungen, Gedichte, Rezensionen und Briefe,* ed. Volker Michels with an essay by Hermann Kasack (Frankfurt am Main: Suhrkamp, 1986).

[2] Hermann Gundert, *Quellen zu seinem Leben und Werk,* compiled and with commentary by Albert Frenz (Ulm: Süddeutsche Verlagsgesellschaft, 1991) vol. 3.1:113–14; Marie Hesse, *Ein Lebensbild in Briefen und Tagebüchern von Adele Gundert* (Stuttgart: D. Gundert, 1955), 164. Here it is noted that Johannes Hesse, the father of the poet, although he had "his greatest joy in song," nevertheless "could hardly sing a melody by himself" — or was, as it is said in German, artistic but not musical.

[3] *Kindheit und Jugend vor Neunzehnhundert: Hermann Hesse in Briefen und Lebenszeugnissen 1877–1895,* ed. Ninon Hesse (Frankfurt am Main: Suhrkamp, 1966), 214; *GB* 4:15.

[4] *Hermann Hesse in Augenzeugenberichten,* ed. Volker Michels (Frankfurt am Main: Suhrkamp, 1987), 71.

[5] *Hermann Hesse "Liebes Herz!": Briefwechsel mit seiner zweiten Frau Ruth,* ed. Ursula and Volker Michels (Frankfurt am Main: Suhrkamp Verlag, 2005), 564.

[6] Ninon Hesse, *Lieber, lieber Vogel: Briefe an Hermann Hesse,* ed. Gisela Kleine (Frankfurt am Main: Suhrkamp, 2002), 101, 114, 132, 140, 174, 276, 322, 364, 374, 482–83.

[7] Aristotle, *Politics* (Cambridge, MA: Harvard UP, 1959), 660 (1340b).

[8] Anders Österling, "Hermann Hesse, Presentation Address," in *Nobel Prize Library* (New York: Alexis Gregory, 1971), 235–36.

[9] Peter Spycher, *Eine Wanderung durch H. Hesses Lyrik: Dokumentation und Interpretation* (Bern: Peter Lang, 1990), 38.

[10] *Le Opere di Dante Alighieri,* ed. Dr. E. Moore (Oxford, UK: Oxford UP, 1924), 393.

[11] Novalis, *Werke,* ed. with commentary by Gerhard Schulz (Munich: C. H. Beck, 1969), 21.

[12] The three poems of "Feierliche Abendmusik," like this entire chapter, were translated by Michael M. Metzger.

[13] Deryck Cooke, *The Language of Music* (1959; Oxford, New York: Oxford UP, 1989).

[14] Ernst Wacker, *Johann Sebastian Bach: Das Wohltemperierte Klavier* (Lahr: Verlag Graffiti, 2000).

[15] Rüdiger Görner, "Letzte Lieder: Zur Sprache des Späten in der Lyrik Hermann Hesses," in *Hermann Hesse Today — Hermann Hesse heute,* ed. Ingo Cornils and Osman Durrani (Amsterdam, New York: Rodopi), 215.

[16] C. Immo Schneider, *Das Todesproblem bei Hermann Hesse* (Marburg: N. G. Elwert, 1973), 68–70.

[17] Georg Günther, *Hesse-Vertonungen: Verzeichnis der Drucke und Handschriften* (Marbach am Neckar: Deutsche Schillergesellschaft, 2004), 7.

[18] Richard C. Helt, *". . . A Poet or Nothing at all: The Tübingen and Basel Years of Hermann Hesse* (Oxford, UK: Berghahn, 1996), 56–57 n. 36.

[19] *Hermann Hesse: Sein Leben in Bildern und Texten,* ed. Volker Michels (Frankfurt am Main: Suhrkamp, 1979), 72.

[20] Theodore Ziolkowski, "Der Steppenwolf. Eine Sonate in Prosa," in *Materialien zu Hermann Hesses "Der Steppenwolf,"* ed. Volker Michels (Frankfurt am Main: Suhrkamp, 1972), 353–77. Longer English version in Ziolkowski, *The Novels of Hermann Hesse* (Princeton, NJ: Princeton UP, 1965), 178–228.

[21] H. Hesse, *Briefe.* Expanded edition (Frankfurt am Main: Suhrkamp, 1965), 37.

[22] Dominique Lingens, *Hermann Hesse et la musique* (Bern: Peter Lang, 2001), 311–73.

[23] *H. Hesse in Augenzeugenberichten,* 310. That he compared Bach's music with "Tao" is, considering Hesse's predilection for ancient Chinese musical thought, an extraordinary mark of favor.

[24] Trans. Richard and Clara Winston.

[25] Lingens, *H. Hesse et la musique,* 338.

[26] Alfred Cortot, *Aspects de Chopin* (Paris: Albin Michel, 1949), 323–24.

[27] This was a distinction held, within Switzerland and with qualifications, also by Hesse's friend Othmar Schoeck. Hesse thought highly of his friend's settings, and considered Schoeck the "bedeutendste(n) Liederkomponist(en) dieser Zeit" (the most significant contemporary composer of "Lieder" (*GB* 3:174).

[28] Reso Karalaschwili, "Die 'Taten des Lichts' — Zur Farbgebung in *Klein und Wagner* und *Klingsors letzter Sommer,*" in *Hermann Hesse: Charakter und Weltbild: Studien* (Frankfurt am Main: Suhrkamp, 1993), 174–84.

[29] Hesse's letter of January 1955 to Rudolf Pannwitz in *Materialien zu Hermann Hesses "Das Glasperlenspiel,"* ed. Volker Michels (Frankfurt am Main: Suhrkamp, 1973), 1:295–96.

[30] Trans. Basil Creighton.

[31] Joachim-Ernst Berendt, "Mozart ist Pablo," in *Über Hermann Hesse,* ed. Volker Michels (Frankfurt am Main: Suhrkamp, 1977), 2:276–85.

[32] It would be interesting to investigate the extent to which Hesse, when he used the term "Untergangsmusik," was thinking specifically of jazz, which began to spread around Europe in the 1920s. See David Tame, *The Secret Power of Music: The Transformation of Self and Society through Musical Energy* (Rochester, VT: Destiny Books, 1984), 187–204. Tame represents moralistic-psychotherapeutic viewpoints and, like Hesse, considers ancient Chinese musical thought to be timelessly valid.

[33] Romain Rolland, *Le voyage intérieur* (Paris: Albin Michel, 1942), 215.

[34] 1 Samuel 16:14–23.

[35] Walter Benjamin, *Gesammelte Schriften: Abhandlungen,* ed. Rolf Tiedemann and Hermann Schweppenhäuser (Frankfurt am Main: Suhrkamp, 1980), I.1:329–35.

[36] Peter Huber, "Der Steppenwolf," in *Interpretationen: Hermann Hesse — Romane* (Stuttgart: Reclam, 1994), 86–87.

[37] Hermann Hesse, *"Die dunkle und wilde Seite der Seele": Briefwechsel mit seinem Psychoanalytiker Josef Bernhard Lang 1916–44,* ed. Thomas Feitknecht (Frankfurt am Main: Suhrkamp, 2006).

[38] *H. Hesse in Augenzeugenberichten,* 437.

[39] As I tried to show on 14 July 2002 in the Stadtkirche in Calw, when I held a lecture and performed my organ fantasy based on the poem.

[40] C. Immo Schneider, "Hermann Hesses Musik-Kritik," in *Hermann Hesse heute,* ed. Adrian Hsia (Bonn: Bouvier Verlag Herbert Grundmann, 1980), esp. 107–12.

[41] See in this connection the individual reports and presentations given at the ninth international Hermann Hesse Colloquium in Calw in 1997: *Hermann Hesse und die Psychoanalyse: "Kunst als Therapie,"* ed. Michael Limberg (Bad Liebenzell/Calw: Verlag Bernhard Gengenbach, 1997).

[42] The first draft is found in *SW* 10:580–81. All three drafts are included in *Hermann Hesse zum Gedächtnis,* ed. Siegfried Unseld (Frankfurt am Main: Suhrkamp, 1962), n.p.

[43] Hermann Hesse, *Briefe,* expanded edition, 294–96 (Letter to P.H., 1950).

16: Hermann Hesse's Goethe

Hans-Joachim Hahn

G OETHE IS GENERALLY RECOGNIZED as Germany's greatest writer and
the leading figure during the late eighteenth and early nineteenth
century period of literary and cultural achievement — often referred to as
the *Goethezeit* or Age of Goethe — which established German neoclassicism and reaffirmed Germany's long humanist tradition. Hesse sought to
continue this tradition, especially its humanist ethical aspects, but during an
age that was preoccupied, first with an imperialist war and then with fascist barbarism. This made Hesse's position within Germany's literary tradition considerably more difficult; it also meant that Hesse had to invoke
Goethe's legacy on many occasions to provide support for his own literary
and cultural ambitions.[1] While Goethe was a significant factor in Hesse's
work, two important caveats have to preface any serious debate on this
topic: (1) A careful distinction has to be observed between any clearly
documented influence of Goethe on Hesse and other cases where themes
and styles are found to be common to the works of both authors,[2] referred to here as "correspondences"; (2) Since Goethe is the most important and influential author in the German language, his ideas may have
influenced Hesse via a number of different authors and often in a manner
which is no longer directly traceable.[3]

A simple statistical survey of Hesse's references to persons and key
figures would indicate that Goethe is by far the most prominent historical
figure in Hesse's oeuvre, more important than Nietzsche, the much-
admired Mozart, or even Novalis.[4] And while such positivist facts may be
open to misinterpretation, Hesse repeatedly affirms his great admiration
for and indebtedness to Goethe and to the literature and thought of the
period from 1740 to 1850. Hesse felt that the upheavals of the twentieth
century had caused us to discard the period of Goethe as merely a historic
past and to question the intellectual values of a time when "der deutsche
Geist zum letzten Male sich einen klassischen Ausdruck geschaffen hat"
(the German mind last came to a classical expression).[5]

The title of my essay seeks to take these cautionary remarks into consideration; it indicates a certain subjectivity on Hesse's part, implying that
his Goethe may not correspond to the received image developed by generations of Goethe scholars. While explicit references to Goethe are rare

in Hesse's narrative work, his essays frequently allude to Goethe, often discussing his personality or his work in considerable detail. Even with regard to Hesse's essays, one must distinguish between the earlier and later publications. The early essays are often very short, sometimes even bland and uninspiring, usually written out of financial necessity, when Hesse's slim narrative work could not sustain his material needs. Other essays were written during the period of hyperinflation and economic depression, when his income from royalties in Germany was virtually worthless.[6] The essay "Goethebücher" from 1911, for instance, reviews books on Goethe's life in Leipzig and Strasbourg, but produces little more than some general personal impressions: "Es ist ein eigener und großer Genuß, Goethes Leben so im Spiegel seiner jeweiligen Umgebung zu lesen, wo auch die kritischen und tadelnden Stimmen nicht fehlen" (It is a true and great pleasure to read Goethe's life in the mirror of his own milieu at the time, where there was no lack of critical and reproaching voices). Apart from Goethe's own correspondence, Hesse is not aware of any book on Goethe "das so unmittelbar die persönliche Ausstrahlung dieses Menschen wiedergäbe" (SW 17:39; that so directly communicates the charisma of this man).

From Dostoevsky to Goethe

The First World War and its immediate aftermath saw Hesse gripped by a general feeling of crisis, a belief in the decline of the Western world, so acutely expressed by Oswald Spengler, but recognized by a wide circle of writers and philosophers. Hesse's essay "Die Brüder Karamasoff oder der Untergang Europas," published in 1920, dramatically expresses such thoughts. Europe's young generation, Hesse proclaims, sees Dostoevsky as its model, rather than Goethe or even Nietzsche (SW 18:126). Unlike Spengler, Hesse views the decline of Europe not as a tragic finality, but as "eine Heimkehr zur Mutter," a return home to mother, a yearning towards Asia, where he perceives the sources of the Faustian "Mütter" to be; he expects this will naturally lead to a new birth, a kind of reincarnation (SW 18:126).

This needs some further explanation. The belief in an "eternal recurrence of the same" is reminiscent of Nietzsche's Dionysian cosmology, itself part of the tradition of the Heraclitian *palingenesis* or renewal of everything in existence. Such views enjoyed new popularity at the turn of the century. The Polish philosopher Count August Cieskowski, for instance, believed that the European peoples would experience their spiritual rebirth within a Slavonic culture.[7] Hesse's reference to the Faustian mothers is obviously a reference to Goethe's great drama, where the concept of motherhood plays a pivotal role. While this is not the place for a detailed discussion of Goethe's concept of "das ewig Weibliche," the eternal feminine, it is astonishing how profoundly Hesse comprehended Goethe's complex concept.[8] The female principle represents here the origin of all life; it leads to a return and a renaissance of an earlier civilization, specifically of antiquity and the beauty of the Hellenic world.[9] Hesse is therefore close to Goethe when he views such a return as "Abkehr von jeder festgelegten Ethik und Moral zugunsten eines Allesverstehens, Allesgeltenlassens, einer neuen gefährlichen, grausigen Heiligkeit" (*SW* 18:126; turning away from all fixed ethics and morality in favor of an understanding of everything, an acceptance of everything, a new, dangerous, horrifying holiness), which he sees as evident in the lives and conversations of the Karamazov brothers. Like Goethe's Faust, Hesse finds no salvation "im Erstarren,"[10] that is, in rigidity, ossification; he instead welcomes the terrifying "Schauder," shudder, traditionally associated with man's vision of the divine, of the origin of life.

Hesse believed that the rigidity of European civilization was particularly problematic among the bourgeoisie, who had adopted a philistine, superficial, and valueless lifestyle. "Der russische Mensch" by contrast, with his apparently completely amoral way of thinking and feeling, is capable of sensing "das Göttliche, Notwendige, Schicksalhafte auch noch im Bösesten, auch noch im Häßlichsten [um . . .] auch vor ihm noch Hochachtung und Gottesdienst darzubringen" (*SW* 18:127; the divine, the essential, the fateful even in the most evil and the most ugly [so as to] offer it reverence and praise, as to a divine being). Such a concept of amorality, of a Nietzschean morality beyond Good and Evil is already evident in Hesse's *Demian* (1917), hailed by his generation, according to Thomas Mann, as emitting an "elektrisierende, hoch sensationelle Wirkung," by which the novel influenced "den Nerv der Zeit [. . .] und eine[r] ganzen Jugend" (electrifying, highly sensational effect . . . the nerve of the time [. . .] and an entire [generation of] youth).[11] The Russian model, Hesse argued, was well on the way to producing a European solution, its essence providing a complete union of "Außen und Innen, Gut und Böse, Gott und Satan" (*SW* 18:128; Exterior and interior, good and evil, God and Satan). The god Abraxas in Hesse's *Demian,* though originating in Graeco-Oriental Gnosticism, anticipates such a development.[12] Goethe also refers to this god in his *West-Östliche Divan,*[13] but it is uncertain whether Hesse knew of this connection. Later on Hesse describes this new form of life in philosophical terms as "der Mensch, der im Begriff ist, sich aufzulösen und jenseits hinter den Vorhang, hinter das principium individuationis zurückzukehren" (*SW* 18:129; the human being who is about to dissolve and return to the other side of the curtain, behind the *principium individuationis*). The problem of a dissolution of individualism was pivotal to Hesse's generation; it is a central theme in Hofmannsthal's famous letter to Lord Chandos and in Brecht's early plays, but — as will be discussed later — Hesse relates it specifically to a fundamental feature that he discovers in the later Goethe.

Goethe's Liberation from a Bourgeois Prison — The Goethe of *Steppenwolf*

This leads us to a discussion of the Goethe figure in *Steppenwolf,* the novel where Goethe figures most prominently. Critically reflecting Hesse's personal development, *Steppenwolf* encompasses this European crisis of individuation as its central theme. As indicated in the fictional editor's preface, Harry Haller, the actual Steppenwolf character, suffers from "Heimweh" and "Heimatlosigkeit" — homesickness and lack of a home — in the same manner in which this experience was proclaimed by a whole generation of modernists and manifested in Nietzsche's famous poem *Vereinsamt.*[14] Haller belongs to the circle of "Verrückte," a term that does not refer solely to madness, but signifies some general form of dysfunction, a detachment from the norm, possibly even "Entrückung," transportation into another world, here the mad world of the Magic Theater. Remembering the experiences of the life he had once led, Haller confesses to a sentimental affection for the "hochanständigen, hochlangweiligen, tadellos gehaltenen Kleinbürgernestern" (*SW* 4:29 (highly respectable, extremely boring, meticulously maintained residences of the petit bourgeoisie). Haller's inner turmoil not only reflects a dichotomy between this orderly lifestyle with its rational norms and his own destructive, anarchic existence, but also reveals a fragmentation of his self "zwischen tausenden, zwischen unzählbaren Polpaaren" (*SW* 4:60: between thousands, indeed countless polarities). This turmoil also affects Haller's attitude to Goethe. The "editor" informs us that Haller's library contained a much-used edition of Goethe's complete works, but his appreciation of Goethe differs widely from the bourgeois, conventional attitude of Goethe readers: for the mainstream readership Goethe was the favorite author in *Geflügelte Worte,* a volume of literary quotations that first appeared in 1864 and intended to contain the essence of what had been achieved by "deutscher Geist und deutscher Fleiß" (German intellect and German industriousness).[15] In a history of literature written towards the end of the nineteenth century and still widely used in Hesse's time, Goethe was described as an author who had progressed beyond the "Flegeljahre der deutschen Dichtung" (uncouth adolescent phase of German poetry) and had created through "männlich feste[s] Leben [. . .] eine neue Blütezeit unserer Literatur" (his strong and masculine life . . . a new flowering of our literature).[16] This Goethe reception, in Hesse's view, had transformed the poet into a national icon, claimed by the educated middle classes as one of their own, while they remained oblivious to Goethe's cosmopolitan humanism, which was so vital for Hesse.

At the depth of his inner crisis Haller reflects on the graveyard of our cultural heritage and the demise of his idols Jesus, Socrates, Mozart, Haydn, Dante, and Goethe. They have become nothing but "erblindete Namen auf rostenden Blechtafeln, umstanden von verlegenen und verlogenen Trauernden" (*SW* 4:78; faded names on rusting plaques, surrounded by embarrassed and insincere mourners). Small wonder then at the debacle of Haller's visit to the professor's house: the professor, described as stiff and short-sighted, oozing a superficial civility, is in fact absorbed in his own, highly specialized scholarship; a typical "mandarin"[17] whose hysterical patriotism and support for the conservative nationalist policies of the "Kriegshetzepartei" (*SW* 4:81: party of warmongers) displays his political naivety. This passage reflects Hesse's early criticism of the intellectual climate in November 1914, when the "Nurpatrioten" (Only Patriots) condemned Goethe for his detachment during the 1813–1814 Wars of Liberation against Napoleon. Hesse was shocked that so many German intellectuals failed to appreciate that universal humanity is more important than patriotism.[18] While in the professor's house Haller looks at a postcard-size portrait of Goethe,

> einen charaktervollen, genial frisierten Greis mit schön modelliertem Gesicht, in welchem weder das berühmte Feuerauge fehlte noch der Zug von leicht hofmännisch übertünchter Einsamkeit und Tragik, auf welche der Künstler ganz besondere Mühe verwandt hatte. (*SW* 4:80)[19]

> [the striking head of an elderly, elaborately coiffured individual with a beautifully modeled face, omitting neither the famously fiery eye nor the cosmetic element of the tragic loneliness of a courtier, on which the painter had expended a great deal of effort.]

The narrator's description of the picture reflects the Goethe reception of the time. Goethe's image here is one that not only sits uncomfortably with Goethe as a poetic genius but also contradicts Hesse's observations on Goethe elsewhere in his various essays. The adjective "genial" refers to the figure's hairstyle and finely modeled face, while the fiery eye is a conventional attribution, suggesting dominance and willpower. The reference to "Einsamkeit und Tragik" imposes some over-theatrical, quasi-Wagnerian features onto Goethe, associated by the narrator with professors and actors, thus adding to the picture's general "Biederkeit," or stolid uprightness (*SW* 4:80). The Steppenwolf part of Haller is provoked; it derides the portrait as that of a vain *poseur,* a sentimental pompous ass (*SW* 4:82). This provocation achieves its aim; the professor's wife, who cherished the portrait as her favorite picture, is deeply insulted. Retreating rapidly, Haller compares himself with the "real" Goethe who occasionally also opted for rather crass expressions, unlike the "spießige Salongoethe" — bourgeois salon-Goethe — of the picture (*SW* 4:83). It is important to recognize that the professor represents the party of German warmongers that was keen to integrate the "Salongoethe" into German culture as part of their imperialist program.[20]

The incident at the professor's house causes a deep depression in Haller, driving him to the Schwarze Adler tavern and its demimonde. He meets the *dame aux camelias* Hermine, who gives him the peace of mind the professor had failed to provide. Her honest and uncomplicated criticism of his schoolboy behavior reconciles him with the genuine Goethe and affords him a new access to a deeper understanding. But to achieve this, Haller has to learn how to acquire Hermine's *joi de vivre*. Falling into a dream, he is visited by a mysterious Goethe, who takes on many different guises, initially appearing as the Goethe from the portrait, with a pompous "Ordensstern," or order of merit, on his chest, a showpiece of "Weimar culture." Haller attacks this insincere, pretentious figure who fails to live up to his Faust character and instead radiates false optimism: "Sie sind uns zu feierlich, Exzellenz, und zu eitel und wichtigtuerisch und zu wenig aufrichtig" (*SW* 4:94; Your excellency, you are too solemn for us, too vain and pompous and not honest enough). The sage of Weimar responds with a youthful smile and suggests that Haller should also condemn Mozart's *Magic Flute,* since it too radiates optimism and faith in the normative truth values of mankind. Haller is thrown by this reaction and subsequently accuses Goethe of resting on the laurels of his venerable old age and public esteem. Goethe's second response completely disarms Haller: Goethe admits to his love of life and detestation of death, adding that his whole nature was characterized by a childlike naivety, full of "Neugierde und Spieltrieb" (*SW* 4:96; curiosity and playfulness). With this confession, the Goethe figure seems to grow taller, and his "Ordensstern" changes into a bunch of wildflowers, while his most charming lyrics accompany this transformation. He converses with Haller as with an old friend, advising him not to take life or himself too seriously, to ignore the imperfections of the here and now and to open himself up to life's great joy, for "die Ewigkeit ist bloß ein Augenblick, gerade lange genug für einen Spaß" (*SW* 4:97; eternity only lasts for a moment, just long enough for some fun). Such sentiments are, according to Theodore Ziolkowski, part of Hesse's wider "chiliastic realm [. . .] in which the individual can actually participate through momentary visions and dreams."[21] The image of the scorpion illustrates these ideas: initially a symbol of death that troubles Haller at the beginning of his dream, it is magically changed by Goethe into a woman's tiny leg, now representing life and sensuality. The transformed Goethe shares many features with Hermine and Pablo and eventually even merges into the Mozart figure; all enjoy music and dancing, cultivating their "Spieltrieb," instinct for play, and indulging in a life of "Heiterkeit," serenity,[22] and indulging in a life of "Zufriedenheit," contentment, terms closely associated with Weimar culture that will be discussed in more detail later in this chapter.

This dream anticipates Haller's experiences in the Magic Theater, a place "Nur für Verrückte" (*SW* 4:34; For Madmen Only). Like Goethe, Haller is "weit abgerückt von 'jedermann'" (*SW* 4:73; far removed from "everyman"), far removed from the contemporary image of a professor and from university life in the Weimar Republic, where "patriotic" rightwing students proclaimed their continuing war fever, allegedly in the tradition of Kant, Fichte, Hegel, and Wagner and oblivious to the cosmopolitan humanism of Goethe, Hölderlin, Nietzsche, Mozart, Bach, and Schubert.[23] The Magic Theater, though apparently invoking an image of "les paradis artificiels," is not primarily accessed through Mescaline or other drugs, but is Hesse's attempt to create a "Gegenmagie," a counterculture, directed against the bourgeois antecedents of Nazi Germany and against the cliché of a German super-culture intent on destroying or perverting the values that German humanism and Romanticism had striven for.[24] This dream episode is therefore an attempt to "deconstruct" the conventional Goethe image, liberating Hesse's Goethe from its imprisonment by Germany's educated elite and from a rationalist *principium individuationis* that is confined within the categories of time and space, categories that have been shaken by Einstein's "Erschütterung der bisherigen Denkgrundlagen" (*SW* 4:79–80; shattering of all hitherto known intellectual foundations).

The traditional concept of individuality and, with it, our conventional notion of the genius figure, has become deeply problematic. It has lost its significance in Hermine's *demi monde,* in Pablo's Magic Theater with Marie's eroticism and the mirror room. Here Haller makes the acquaintance of a new Goethe, Hermine's Goethe, who is elevated to the rank of saints and divine beings. Homage to Goethe becomes a kind of "Frommsein" (*SW* 4:99; pious devotion), which has to be practiced outside the confines of time and reality. Hermine's image of the Savior corresponds to Haller's "Goethebild": stripped of their masks of intellect and idealism, both are "dumm und unzulänglich" (*SW* 4:99; stupid and inaccessible). Hermine's lesson helps Haller to confront his own failings: as long as he still wears a mask of "Idealität und Weltverächter" he must remain "im Grunde [. . .] ein Bourgeois" (*SW* 4:125; idealism and world hatred . . . a bourgeois at heart). As the progressive dissolution of his old ego continues, however, he discovers and rejects in himself the false features that had earlier provoked him in the Goethe portrait:

> Er selbst, der alte Harry, war genau solch ein bürgerlich idealisierter
> Goethe gewesen, so ein Geistesheld mit allzu edlem Blick, von Erha-

benheit, Geist und Menschlichkeit strahlend wie von Brillantine und beinahe über den eigenen Seelenadel gerührt. (*SW* 4:126)

[Old Harry himself had been just such a bourgeois, idealized Goethe, such an intellectual hero with the all-too-noble gaze of grandeur, *Geist* and humanity, gleaming like brilliantine and almost moved by the no-bility of his own mind.]

Haller's old Goethe is no more "real" than the professor's Goethe, and the new Goethe image now becomes Haller's alter ego; at one with Mozart and the saints, within the circle of "Unsterblichen," the Immortals (*SW* 4:148). Haller accepts Hermine's cosmology, a world of saints in a realm beyond time and space, where the arts become part of the "Reich Gottes" (*SW* 4:145; Kingdom of God). This realm incorporates "das Bild jeder echten Tat, die Kraft jedes echten Gefühls, auch wenn niemand davon weiß und es sich aufschreibt und für die Nachwelt aufbewahrt" (*SW* 4:146; the image of every genuine action, the strength of every true feeling, even if nobody knows of it and records it for posterity). Here Haller and Hermine have found their true "Heimat," together with Goethe, Novalis, Mozart, and the saints. Haller can now understand Goethe's laughter, a laughter derived from "übermenschliche Heiterkeit" (*SW* 4:147; superhuman ser-enity), and it will inspire him to compose his poem to the Immortals.

The poem itself consists of two parts: its first section describes the de-sire of mortals to escape the existing world, where we are imprisoned by time, and where space and eternity are beyond reach. Even Pablo's Magic Theater, where psychedelic experiences transport one above the "waves" of everyday reality, can achieve this only for a short duration: it cannot propel us into genuine immortality. The second part of the poem has overcome the constraints of the *principium individuationis* — the German adverb "dagegen" (against it) indicates this clearly — man is no longer constrained by a persona, the achieved eternity is "kühl und wandellos" (*SW* 4:148; cold and immobile), a world of perfect serenity.

Harry Haller, the Steppenwolf, can only approximate this state of eternal serenity; he is still bound up in the first section of the poem, still needing the Magic Theater's artificial dream experiences, induced by Pablo's opiate liquor and mescaline-enhanced cigarettes. Timothy Leary has argued that Hesse's Magic Theater is based on a psychedelic dream, and it is said that Aldous Huxley introduced the hippie generation of the 1960s to Hesse's dream world.[25] German literary critics, however, have frequently argued against such an interpretation, and this essay seeks to accommodate both schools of thought. A great many artists have sought to extend their poetic experiences with the help of narcotics, and Hesse himself experienced psychedelic dreams during his years of crisis between 1919 and 1931. His poem "Der Mann von fünfzig Jahren" (The Man of

Fifty Years) echoes Haller's experience inside the Magic Theater and the poem's title is an obvious reference to Goethe's *Wilhelm Meisters Wanderjahre* (Wilhelm Meister's Journeymanship, 1821, final version 1829), with its embedded novella of the same title.[26] Like Goethe's hero, Hesse's "Mann" desires the love of a young girl, but in a new twist, he feels that he has to read "ein Buch von Goethen," a book by Goethe, instead.[27] The poem's last stanza seeks an escape into complete eroticism; the final couplet is reminiscent of the Faustian pact: "Nachher dann in Gottes Namen / Soll der Tod mich Armen haben"[28] (In God's name then, / death can have me later, poor wretch). Further indirect correspondences between Faust and the Steppenwolf can be found, topics that transcend the work of both Hesse and Goethe, relating in general terms to man's Adamic aspirations for ultimate knowledge.

Haller, like Faust, undergoes a process of rejuvenation in Pablo's Magic Theater (*SW* 4:185) which itself is reminiscent of Goethe's "Hexenküche" (Witches' Kitchen). While Faust's experience of the "höchste Augenblick," the supreme moment,[29] ends his life on earth and promotes him, ever striving for higher aims, into the angelic world of the "ewig Weibliche," the eternal feminine, Haller experiences the artificial paradise only temporarily. The Magic Theater offers him an infinite number of possibilities whereby the Immortals become interchangeable: Goethe becomes one with Mozart (*SW* 4:195), just as the murdered Hermine becomes one with Haller and his own "Scheinselbstmord" (*SW* 4:167; apparent suicide) gives him the freedom to partake in the world of the Immortals.[30] Countless variations of metamorphoses are possible; life becomes seriously unserious and turns into a "Spiel," or game (*SW* 4:182). The music from Mozart's *Don Giovanni* anticipates Hermine's murder but, instead of the Commendatore, Mozart himself appears and laughs the ice-cold laughter "aus einem den Menschen unerhörten Jenseits von Gelittenhaben, von Götterhumor geboren" (*SW* 4:191; from the beyond, out of man's reach, [a laughter] born from the experience of suffering, from divine humor). In the hall of mirrors, Haller's previous life flashes past him while his thoughts are with Goethe and Mozart. He escapes the confines of his own individuality, smashes up his own mirror-image, and then kills Hermine, his alter ego. As he contemplates his victim, Haller once again recites his poem to the Immortals, but this time only its second part. As he finishes, Mozart enters the scene, by now seeming to have taken over from the immortal Goethe.

Much to Haller's disgust, Mozart plays a Handel concerto on the radio, for Haller an aesthetic crime, a mixture of "Bronchialschleim und zerkautem Gummi" (*SW* 4:198; bronchial phlegm and chewed gum), through which the radio becomes the ultimate weapon in a "Vernichtungskampf gegen die Kunst" (*SW* 4:198; battle of destruction against art). Mozart defends modern technology with arguments reminiscent of Walter

Benjamin's concept of the technical reproducibility of art.[31] While the radio — and one must think here of receivers from the 1920s — will disfigure Handel's music, it cannot destroy its "Urgeist," original spirit (*SW* 4:199), but instead radiates it into new environments, winning over new audiences. The immortal music and its imperfect technical rendition become an allegory for life, for the manner by which "die sogenannte Wirklichkeit mit dem herrlichen Bilderspiel der Welt um sich [schmeißt]" (*SW* 4:199; so-called reality with its splendid game of images of the world tossed about), a reality in which we have to learn to live. Mozart admonishes Haller to abandon his pathetic skepticism in favor of a new sense of humor that is the prerequisite for the serene life of the Immortals. Haller's mock-execution "condemns" him to eternal life and to a temporary exclusion from the Magic Theater. Mozart compounds this punishment by condemning Haller to listen to radio music for the rest of his life. Mozart then changes back into the figure of Pablo, who offers Haller one of his "magic" cigarettes, hoping that he will learn how to laugh and to join his and the Immortals' company.

The novel's ending is inconclusive. In a postscript from 1941 Hesse maintains that the book stakes out his own personal crisis, but that it is "keineswegs das Buch eines Verzweifelten, sondern das eines Gläubigen" (by no means the book of a desperate man, but that of a believer), one who has seen the light (*SW* 4:207–8). Perhaps we can best comprehend Haller if we see him as an "integrierter Außenseiter,"[32] a character who, though opposed to the normative values of his society, will ultimately accept the bourgeois reality of his time. His art elevates him into a world beyond Good and Evil, but daily life condemns him to live within given norms. In a strange, but probably unconnected, manner Haller/Hesse approximates the worldview of the aged Goethe, who also sought to reject the normative values of historical progression but who remained pragmatic enough to accept a social and political order that strove towards stability and thus affirmed the basis of civilization.

A Return to Goethe's Cosmopolitanism

A brief encounter with Hesse's later essays will demonstrate how this conflict between the ideal, mystical world and everyday reality, which Hesse had diagnosed in Goethe's work, became central to his understanding of Goethe. Hesse's essay "Dank an Goethe" (Tribute to Goethe), commissioned in 1932 by Romain Rolland[33] for the journal *Europe,* deserves close attention. The essay, obviously influenced by the advance of National Socialism in Germany, was written for a wider audience. Paying tribute to Goethe, "dem ich am meisten verdanke, der mich am meisten beschäftigt, bedrängt, ermuntert, zu Nachfolge oder Widerspruch gezwungen hat"

(*SW* 14:452; to whom I am most in debt, who occupies, challenges and encourages me the most and who has forced me both to follow and to contradict him), Hesse continues not only to acknowledge his great debt to Goethe, but also to explain his own critical distance to him. He reserves his more negative response for Goethe the august literary figure and educator, the illustrious Weimar "Salongoethe," and we recognize here the Goethe image that provoked Haller's outrage at the professor's house. The essay then expands on the more positive aspects of Haller's dream, discussing these in more general terms than was the case in the *Steppenwolf* passage. It focuses on Goethe's attempt to achieve a synthesis between spirit and nature, to bridge the divide between the naïve "Dichter" and the clever "Weltmann" (*SW* 14:454).

The essay also highlights the conflict between "Geist," the mind, and "Vaterlandsliebe," patriotism, a theme that occupied Hesse from as early as 1914 to the end of his life. Hesse recognized that this fissure was not just Goethe's problem, but remained the predicament of the German bourgeoisie. This meant that Goethe remained of the highest relevance for Hesse's generation. In yet another side-swipe at the nationalist representatives of Germany's mandarins, Hesse deplores the fact that the war generation of German intellectuals ignored Goethe, despite the fact that his life and work presented "die Regierung des Menschenlebens durch den Geist," the governing of human life by the intellect, as its greatest challenge (*SW* 14:456).

Hesse discovers Goethe's wisdom embedded in a universal world that had distanced itself from neoclassicism and its narrowly German environment and had reached out to the wisdom of India, China, and ancient Greece. It was a world beyond willpower and intellect, a world dedicated to "Frömmigkeit, Ehrfurcht, Dienenwollen: Tao" (*SW* 14:458; piety, reverence, the desire to serve: Tao). Like Goethe, Hesse was drawn more to the wisdom of China than to India.[34] Goethe's interest in Chinese and Indian literature and philosophy is well documented[35] and the later Goethe seemed more interested in Chinese literature than in Indian culture, probably since the latter had been interpreted by the late Romantic generation in a Christian-conservative spirit. It is possible that Goethe gained inspiration for his novella "Der Mann von fünfzig Jahren," which, as mentioned above, is included in *Wilhelm Meisters Wanderjahre,* from an English translation of the Chinese novel *Haoh Kjöh Tschwen,*[36] although echoes of the Chinese novel are much stronger in Goethe's *Wahlverwandtschaften.*[37] Furthermore, it seems likely that Hesse's interest in and knowledge of the Far East were related primarily to his own journey to the East in 1911, to recollections of his grandfather Gundert's missionary activities in India, and to the general interest in Oriental wisdom that was so topical in Hesse's lifetime.[38] Hesse acknowledges his debt to Romain Rolland, who had encouraged him to re-examine this new and mysterious Goethe, this writer full of contradictions who became more fascinating through his later works. He celebrates Goethe's striving for the highest principles of life, which enabled him to escape the confines of the *principium individuationis.*

Hesse's 1924 essay "Goethe und Bettina" covers a similar theme. Once again Hesse is fascinated by the older Goethe, in particular Goethe's strange relationship with the youthful Bettina von Arnim (1785–1859), who admired Goethe to the point of actual love. Bettina cherished the Goethe of the *Werther* years, oblivious to the fact that the old Goethe, having shed much of his previous persona, had by now become an institution. Hesse found this incongruent relationship fascinating; he himself became increasingly more interested in the older Goethe and in particular in Goethe's process of aging, his "zunehmende[r] Versteifung und Vereinsamung und seinem ganzen Absterben" (*SW* 14:381; increasing inflexibility and loneliness and his whole process of decay). He imagines Goethe's physical stature in his later Weimar years in images similar to those which appear in Harry Haller's dream: "ein etwas klein und brummig gewordener Greis" (*SW* 14:382; an old man who has become rather small and grumpy), whose physical existence is in a process of de-personalization, having become noumenal, mere intellectual energy devoid of any phenomenal attributes. This de-personalization has a profound effect on all those who belong to Goethe's circle; they all become part of his aura, gaining a new creativity through their affinity with the poet.

This process is analogous to T. S. Eliot's description of the relationship of a poem to its author: the poet's mind becomes detached from its work; a catalyst that transforms the world around him; "the more perfect the artist, the more completely separate in him will be the man who suffers and the mind which creates."[39] Eliot's observation seems indicative of the spirit of his time, as similar developments are to be found in the works of Hofmannsthal, Brecht, Hermann Broch and others; they indicate that writers of the early twentieth century experienced a general breaking up of individualism. Hesse analyzes this process of de-individualization in his Bettina essay and applies it to the genius in general. A genius will either perish in his environment or will assume total control over it. In either case the process illustrates "eine Tendenz zur Selbstaufgabe [. . .] diese Tendenz zur Entpersönlichung, welche ebensowohl das Gesicht einer Vergöttlichung wie einer Selbstzerfleischung annehmen kann" (*SW* 14:385; a tendency toward giving up the self . . . this tendency toward de-personalization, which can just as well take on the face of deification as it can that of self-mutilation). In *Steppenwolf* Haller undergoes such a transformation; in the case of Hesse's Goethe it meant that Goethe's depersonalization could acquire an aura of immortality, could become one with Mozart and Handel.

From the Individual to the Universal

The process of de-individualization is particularly vividly developed in *Das Glasperlenspiel,* especially in the figure of the Alt-Musikmeister. While Hesse himself fed speculations on the origins of the novel's main characters and their relationship to the author's contemporaries, it would be misleading to read the novel as a *roman à clef.*[40] Hesse himself suggested that the figure of Pater Jakobus was modeled on the Basel historian Jacob Burckhardt, and Thomas Mann thought he recognized himself in the Altmeister Thomas von Trave. However, in view of Hesse's own conception of the de-personalization of the genius, such considerations should not be taken too seriously. The most that can be suggested here is that the Alt-Musikmeister shares certain features with Goethe, as are discussed in Hesse's essay "Goethe und Bettina." Goethe's own observations on such a process of de-personalization, made in his posthumously published notes *Maximen und Reflexionen*(Maxims and Reflections), point in a similar direction.

Speculating on the possibility of a beautiful old age, Goethe suggested that age requires a "stufenweises Zurücktreten aus der Erscheinung,"[41] a gradual retreat from the phenomenal world. Haller's dream provides further similarities; in both instances the reader is introduced to a wise, venerable and friendly old man, whose rosy face suggests eternal youth, radiating serenity and an almost childlike smile.[42] Correspondences between the fictitious Alt-Musikmeister and Goethe can certainly be found, but they are by no means definitive and could easily be transposed onto other historical figures.[43] In its final stages the Alt-Musikmeister's aging process bears similarities to Goethe's, as described in Hesse's Goethe and Bettina essay. Particularly important are the stages of "Abseitigkeit," remoteness, and "Nichtmehrhiersein," absence, which have their reflection in the music master's tender and "thin" music and in his intense serenity (*SW* 5:229–30). Visiting his former teacher, Knecht is greeted with a welcoming smile that radiates a serenity that is "kindlich offen," innocent as a child (*SW* 5:230). Their conversation has much in common with the discourse between Goethe and Bettina in that Knecht does all the talking, while the master responds with a simple smile or a brief glance. The master admonishes Knecht not to tire himself, thereby reminding him of the art of meditation, which he had taught him in earlier years. The Alt-Musikmeister's transformation, however, goes well beyond anything that Hesse had observed in Goethe's aging process, it is a transformation into a state of saintliness: "weg von den Menschen und hin zur Stille, weg von den Worten und hin zur Musik, weg von den Gedanken und hin zur Einheit" (*SW* 5:233–34; away from people and into the quiet, away from the words and into the music, away from thoughts and into unity). Such a process comes close to transubstantiation, having more in common with Hesse's interest in Confucian philosophy than with his affinity to Goethe, though one does not cancel out the other. This process is reflected in the figure of the "ältere Bruder" and his interest in the philosophy of the *I Ching,* or *Book of Changes* (*SW* 5:111). However, the development of the Alt-Musikmeister is probably more akin to Chinese wisdom than to Goethe's aging process, a case of one of the 'correspondences' referred to at the beginning of this chapter.[44] The Alt-Musikmeister has achieved an aura of "Gnade, Vollendung, Altersweisheit, Seligkeit" (*SW* 5:236; grace, perfection, the wisdom of old age, bliss) and he transmits his saintliness to Knecht, who feels his inner resistance broken and is accepted into the master's "Frieden und seine Helligkeit," embraced by "Heiterkeit und wunderbare[r] Ruhe" (*SW* 5:237; peace and brightness [embraced by] serenity and a miraculous calm). Knecht experiences this miraculous state of bliss as music, "als eine völlig unmateriell gewordene, esoterische Musik, welche jeden in den Zauberkreis Eintretenden mit aufnimmt wie ein mehrstimmiges Lied eine neu einfallende Stimme" (*SW* 5:237; as wholly spiritual, esoteric music, which accepts everybody into its magic circle just as a part song will accept a new voice). The Alt-Musikmeister's dying is described as a progressive "Entstofflichung," the fading away of his physical substance, his essence concentrated in the glance of his eyes and his radiant face (*SW* 5:255).

Hesse's Pedagogy and Goethe's "Pedagogic Province"

Before we continue our discussion of *Das Glasperlenspiel,* a few observations on previous research concerning Goethe's possible influence on this novel seem pertinent. Literature on this topic is immense; we have to restrict ourselves to the more important contributions. Opinion on Hesse's indebtedness to Goethe varies considerably; while some critics seek to establish a very close relationship between the two writers, others warn against overstating this connection, since it could easily overshadow the more relevant links between Hesse and his contemporaries. Goethe's concept of the Bildungsroman is a particular case in point. Sikander Singh has recently explored links between Goethe's *Wilhelm Meister* and Hesse's novels, applying the term even to such early Hesse narratives as *Gertrud* and *Demian,* but particularly to *Steppenwolf, Morgenlandfahrt,* and *Glasperlenspiel.*[45] He points to parallels between Goethe's Turmgesellschaft or Tower Society and the Magic Theater, to the secret society of the *Morgenlandfahrer,* to the Castalian order, and views Knecht's name as an antithesis of Goethe's "Meister." Hesse may have encouraged this search for correspondences, frequently referring to Castalia as a "pädagogische

Provinz," a phrase coined by Goethe in the *Wanderjahre,* where the co-cept plays an important role (*SW* 5:53, 132). However, as pointed out by Joseph Mileck, "Goethe's hero lives in, and is fashioned by, the activity of the greater world; Hesse's, like a greenhouse flower, dwells in an isolated pedagogical province, the protégé of an esoteric hierarchy of epigon intellectuals devoted to their glass beads."[46] George Wallis Field explored the work of both writers under the category of "Erlebnisdichtung," a poetry that, according to Field, focuses on a life dominated by the spirit. He establishes many similarities between Hesse's *Glasperlenspiel* and Goethe's *Faust,* rejecting the theory that the Alt-Musikmeister is a personification of Goethe, since the former is too passive and saintly and "seems never to have been troubled by the dualisms characteristic of Goethe."[47] Theodore Ziolkowski introduces the concept of the "Bundesroman," the novel of orders or societies, into the debate, a term borrowed from Marianne Thalmann's study of the "Trivialroman" or popular novel. Ziolkowski alerts us to the fact that "most of the important men of [Goethe's] age [. . .] belonged to one order or the other."[48] He also acknowledges similarities between Goethe's pedagogical province and Hesse's Castalia and refers to an intentioned contrast between "Knecht" and "Meister," but concludes: "in general the results have shown that the resemblances are often superficial. Goethe's conception of 'Doing and Thinking' for instance, turns out to be quite different from Hesse's idea of 'vita activa and vita contemplativa.'"[49]

This brief survey of research on Goethe's apparent influence on Hesse's *Glasperlenspiel* will have demonstrated that it is problematic to establish direct links between Hesse and Goethe. It is far better to view the Bildungsroman, both as a genre and in this instance, Hesse's *Glasperlenspiel,* in a very general manner as "a humanistic project [. . .] for a vindication of the human subject in his or her wholeness."[50] Such an attitude will open our minds to a discussion of the novel's more political and cultural dimensions, where, once again, this novel represents Hesse's spiritual and intellectual resistance to fascism.[51] Nevertheless, correspondences between Hesse and Goethe do exist, but they are of a more subtle and at the same time more profound nature than has been observed so far.

Before discussing these in greater detail, it may be helpful to refer to Hesse's essay on Goethe's *Wilhelm Meister,* an essay which is confined to the *Lehrjahre* (Wilhelm Meister's Apprenticeship, 1795–96). (This does not imply that Hesse was not also familiar with the *Wanderjahre,* and some of his observations here are equally applicable to the *Wanderjahre.*) Hesse defines the main theme of the essay as an all-embracing humanism, with special concern for "Ehrfurcht" (reverence) for human nature and faith in the future of civilization, and he sees the general ambience of Goethe's novel as integral to the period of 1750 to 1850. The legacy of Kant, Mo-

zart, Frederick the Great, and Lessing culminates in Goethe as their heir
and the epitome of this age. Referring briefly to the origins of the novel
genre, Hesse describes *Robinson Crusoe* and *Wilhelm Meister* as its arche-
typical models. He focuses on *Wilhelm Meister* as Germany's typical form
of romance which dominated the literary scene until the end of the nineteenth century, defining as its essence its universal and holistic nature,
which is "über das Persönliche hinausgerückt" (*SW* 18:376; extends beyond the personal). *Wilhelm Meister* and *Faust*, says Hesse, each contain the
totality of Goethe's philosophy of life, representing at the same time the
cultural ideal of their age in its most perfect and conscious manner. Hesse
continues with what at first looks like an element of criticism when he
suggests that Goethe was not an accomplished master of prose fiction, but
remained a dilettante in the art of narration. In this criticism, Hesse was
following Schiller, and was probably also influenced by contemporary critics who considered Goethe's *Wilhelm Meister* too fragmented, a book of
wisdom but a failed novel.[52] Like Schiller, Hesse concludes that Goethe's
novel in its universality has managed to reveal "die Weisheit seines Inne-
ren, um seine tausendfach erlebte Lehre der Liebe auszusprechen und
mitzuteilen" (*SW* 18:379; his inner wisdom, in order to express and share
his lesson of love, experienced thousands of times over). This universality
drives its protagonist to achieve "Wachstum und Bildung zum immer Voll-
kommeneren" (*SW* 18:380; growth and development toward the always
more perfect), thereby revealing its three ethical constituents, "Dankbar-
keit, Ehrfurcht, Gerechtigkeit" (*SW* 18:381; thankfulness, reverence, justice), humanity's most valuable qualities, qualities that Hesse also traces in
the aesthetic letters of Schiller and in Mozart's *Magic Flute*.

It would be wrong to use the Wilhelm Meister essay as a key with
which to interpret *Das Glasperlenspiel*, though some important features are
common to both novels. Both works share a utopian vision in their depiction of the beauty of human order, through which their authors sought to
repel the forces of barbarism in their own time.[53] Hesse's *Glasperlenspiel* owes at least as much to Goethe's second part of *Wilhelm Meister*, the
Wanderjahre, which bears the subtitle *Die Entsagenden*, suggesting an
element of renunciation, referring here to the love of Wilhelm and Natalie,
their "Liebe ohne Besitz," love without possession.[54] For Goethe, "Entsagung" means recognizing human limitations: by relinquishing the category
of time, concerns of the past and fears of the future, man is no longer dis-
tracted by present-day matters, by the anxieties of the here and now.[55]
With this definition Goethe moves into the vicinity of spiritual meditation, an exercise that helps to recognize the relative unimportance of the
personal self. Taken in a wider context, the subtitle therefore refers to the
renunciation of subjectivity. Wilhelm is no longer the unchallenged protagonist from the *Lehrjahre*, but has instead become part of a group of

characters, associated either with the Turmgesellschaft or with a circle of emigrants intending to settle in America.

In Hesse's novel the theme of "Entsagung" relates to Knecht's subordination to the rules of Castalia, to his eventual resignation from this order, and ultimately to his death and his enduring presence in the character of Tito. The parallels between the two stories are not immediately obvious, yet they contain elements that make comparison possible. Knecht's renunciation becomes part of his "Dienst," his service, a theme that is also prominent in Goethe's novel in the form of Wilhelm's service to society and a gradual renunciation of his personality.[56] Knecht's own devotion to service is already indicated in his name: though a "Meister," a Magister Ludi, he serves Castalia to the extent of renouncing his private life. When Knecht realizes that this service excludes service to the wider world (*SW* 5:88), he abandons his elevated position in order to serve society in a more practical manner. His letter of resignation criticizes Castalia for its elitism, its aloofness from the "Volksgefüge," the fabric of the nation, from the world and its history (*SW* 5:319). He considers Castalia an apolitical and essentially selfish organization that, in cultivating scholarship for its own sake, has become a kind of "Spazierengehen im Garten einer Bildung" (*SW* 5:320; strolling around in the garden of learning).

Many critics have referred to the relationship between Castalia and Goethe's "pädagogischer Provinz." However, the attempt to see in the *Glasperlenspiel* a kind of "reconciliation of human individuality with the requirements of daily life imposed by society"[57] is inappropriate, just as misleading as to view Goethe's pedagogical province as some educational utopia. Differences between the two "provinces" are numerous: in Goethe's novel the "Provinz" occupies a minor part; its presentation is by no means entirely positive. Adolf Muschg compares it to a Soviet Gulag, and Thomas Degering describes the province as Goethe's vision of a society, "that allows its members no room for free play, to say nothing of room for development."[58] The two provinces differ also with regard to their purpose. Goethe's establishment seems modeled on Rousseau's pedagogy in the sense that music is simply a conduit for the acquisition of writing and arithmetic, whereas Castalia uses music in a holistic manner, whereby a pupil achieves self-perfection (*SW* 5:32). A more comprehensive search for parallels between the two novels would find perhaps some implicit criticism of the German concept of *Bildung* as represented in both Castalia and the province. Such an interpretation would indicate that Hesse's views on education have remained consistent from the time of writing *Unterm Rad*.

Similar observations apply to the treatment of "Ehrfurcht" in both novels. In the pedagogical province reverence is initially divided into four different categories, culminating in reverence for one's own life.[59] General religious and neoclassical aspects complement this concept, which has much in common with the humanist ideas of Lessing, freemasonry, and eighteenth-century philosophy. Goethe executed this in a rather mechanical and forced manner, religion being merely one element in his complex definition of "Ehrfurcht." While religion alleviates "Furcht," fear, it does not lead to the reverence for one's own existence that allows us to achieve our highest ambitions, enabling us to appreciate ourselves as the best "was Gott und Natur hervorgebracht haben" (that God and nature have brought forth).[60] Hesse is not only less specific in his novel, he also does not raise humankind to that high level that all but removes the difference between God and man. Knecht's visit to Mariafels and his conversations with Pater Jakobus introduce us to a form of reverence that shows greater commitment. Jakobus views Castalia as a blasphemous imitation of his own Benedictine order (*SW* 5:146) in that it fails to recognize the essential union between church and religion. Hesse gained inspiration for Knecht and Jakobus from the little-known Swabian pietist Johann Albrecht Bengel, whose work he had studied while writing his novel and whom he described as a true sage who succeeded in transforming enlightened ideas into the "Unzerstörbarkeit des Geistes" (indestructibility of the mind).[61] By strange coincidence Goethe had also read Bengel during his Leipzig years, admiring his interconfessional, mystical piety that maintained a healthy distance from religious dogma.[62] Knecht and Jakobus admire the manner in which Bengel sought to establish an encyclopedia of all knowledge, which he managed to forge into a new totality. While Knecht still feels that Castalia achieves a similar synthesis, Jakobus finds that Bengel's work is more closely related to his own order, believing it to be superior to Castalia's "intellektuell-aesthetische Geistigkeit" (*SW* 5:149; intellectual and aesthetic spirituality).

Within the Castalian tradition, the "Spiel," or game, takes on the significance of a "Festspiel," or festival, a very popular concept towards the end of the nineteenth century. In the novel it is both an intellectual and an aesthetic exercise of the highest spiritual and ethical significance, reconciling the order's various disciplines and, as "Gleichnis der Harmonie" (*SW* 5:184; allegory of harmony), assuming a quasi-religious function. For the members of Castalia the game acquires the significance of holy sacrament, others view it as a kind of "Religionsersatz," substitute for religion. Hesse wanted his readers to compare the game to a musical performance; its insistence on a set of firm rules turns it into a "Schule des Gehorsams," school of obedience.[63] "Spielen," to play, is contrasted with political engagement, an activity that lacks "die Demut des Wissens," the humility of knowledge, and thereby leads to an exaggerated estimation of one's own ego.

Hesse's definition of a "Spiel" probably owes more to Schiller than to Goethe, though Schiller's famous essays "Über die ästhetische Erziehung des Menschen in einer Reihe von Briefen" (1795), known as the Aesthetic Essays, were inspired by Goethe's *Meister*, a fact of which Hesse was aware (*SW* 18:376). A game in Schiller's sense unites man's two driving forces, one sensuous, the other aesthetic-formal, into a synthesis and thus affords us complete freedom and perfection. Knecht, like Schiller, recognizes that in the game we can only approximate an ideal, never achieving reality, and this dilemma persuades Knecht to leave Castalia. The essence of every game is "Heiterkeit," serenity, another integral element of neo-classicism, and again better known through Schiller's philosophy than through Goethe. However, it is quite possible that Hesse was also influenced by Buddhist mysticism. Knecht defines Castalia's serenity in discussion with Designori, who, having undergone some form of personal crisis, seeks spiritual help. Castalia produces the highest form of "Heiterkeit" by uniting the three principles of scholarship, reverence for beauty, and meditation (*SW* 5:291). The Alt-Musikmeister finds true serenity, defined here as the highest form of knowledge and love (*SW* 5:289). Once again the key to the highest secrets of knowledge and life is associated with a process of de-personalization, an act of meditation that helps us overcome our selfishness.

The Death of the Narrator?

One last aspect where Goethe's influence may be discerned, though concrete evidence cannot be provided, concerns the narrative technique of *Das Glasperlenspiel*. Already in *Der Steppenwolf*, Hesse had abandoned the conventional technique of the omniscient narrator when he introduced the figure of an editor, followed by the "Traktat vom Steppenwolf" as a free-standing, independent treatise. *Das Glasperlenspiel* goes even further. While also beginning with a general introduction by an editor or historian, followed by Knecht's biography and some putative speculations on his end, we are given a set of Knecht's poems as well as three self-contained biographies, allegedly written by Knecht but not directly related to his life. While the posthumously published "Gedichte des Schülers und Studenten" (Poems of the Pupil and Student) explore the nature and cultural possibilities of the game, the three biographies serve to expand the novel's perspective, reaching into prehistory ("Regenmacher," Rainmaker), spiritual life in early Middle Eastern Christianity ("Der Beichtvater," Father Confessor) and finally Indian religion and philosophy ("Indischer Lebenslauf," Indian Biography). All these compilations serve as broad variations on the main theme of the novel, which is that a spiritual life can be rewarding and socially fulfilling.

Such a technique can be found in many modern novels; references to Herman Broch's trilogy of novels *Die Schlafwandler* (The Sleepwalkers, 1930/32) are significant, since Hesse actually reviewed this work (*SW* 19:296–98). Hesse was enthusiastic about the trilogy's content, but was critical of Broch's narrative style, in particular of what he saw as a dissolution of form caused by the absence of a conventional hero. Hesse's review of Broch, together with his study of Goethe's *Wilhelm Meister*, suggests that his own narrative technique may have been influenced by a number of sources. A comparison with Goethe's *Wanderjahre* is once again intriguing, since it reveals the repeatedly observed dissolution of the individuality principle. Goethe referred to his novel's "Aggregatstruktur," aggregate structure, which renders any systematic analysis impossible.[64] Modern critics define the *Wanderjahre* as an "Archivroman,"[65] referring here to Makarien's archive and to the fact that the narrator's role has been subverted by an editor who is anything but omniscient. In addition, other characters provide their own self-contained novellas. Adolf Muschg refers to the novel as a "Gesellschaftsroman," novel of a society, since the society rather than an individual determines the narrative, while the "editor" declares himself insufficiently competent in explaining the novel's overall pattern.[66] The openness and unpredictable nature of the *Wanderjahre* suggests that it cannot be subsumed within the narrower concept of the Bildungsroman, no longer referring to a distinctive form of education or having a protagonist whose education is a central theme within the novel.

It remains uncertain whether Hesse was consciously following the "archival" structure of Goethe's novel. Apparent similarities in the narrative structures of the two novels may be traced back to a belief, held by both authors, in the development of life through a series of individual steps ("Stufenfolgen"). Hesse may have taken up the essence of Goethe's morphology in his poem "Stufen" (*SW* 5:407), though mention of a "Weltgeist" may also suggest a reference to Hegel's philosophy.[67] In addition, Hesse may also have had in mind the popular concept of reincarnation. With explicit reference to the composition of *Das Glasperlenspiel*, Hesse stated, in a letter to Rudolf Pannwitz, that he was thinking of reincarnation as a form of expression "für das Stabile im Fließenden" (for what is stable in the flow). In the same letter he also cites his "Vision eines individuellen, aber überzeitlichen Lebenslaufes" (vision of an individual but timeless life), envisaging a person who witnesses "in mehreren Wiedergeburten die großen Epochen der Menschheitsgeschichte" (in several reincarnations the great epochs of human history).[68] The concept of reincarnation or *palingenesis* would also provide the inspiration for Knecht's death and his re-emergence in Tito as well as for the composition of the three biographies in which Knecht emerges in different epochs.

Conclusion

In the course of this article a number of connections to Goethe have been established which significantly influenced Hesse's literary work. The earliest significant references surfaced during the First World War and its immediate aftermath; they are usually of a broadly political nature, critical of Wilhelmine society that had abandoned Goethe in favor of minor, nationalist writers. Hesse's comments amount to a fundamental critique of the German bourgeoisie, in particular of its academic strata. Hesse is at pains to establish an image of Goethe that was removed from nineteenth-century stereotypes, a cosmopolitan Goethe who had benefited from his encounters with Eastern philosophy and literature. Furthermore, Goethe is no longer portrayed as the genius of the Strasbourg years but as the aged Goethe who experienced a "stufenweises Zurücktreten aus der Erscheinung." This kind of de-personalization became a central theme for many writers of the early twentieth century; it can be traced back to the philosophical and scientific discoveries of the time, which had led to a general crisis of individuality. By dislodging Goethe from his pillar of respectability, Hesse contributes to a modern perception of Goethe as a figure of the Magic Theater, a place "for madmen only," which itself is a precursor of Castalia. Castalia is a place "für Entrückte," people who are removed from the "real world." In this Theater, detached from the hectic political and social rush of time, Goethe can be seen as seriously unserious, having acquired the serenity of the Immortals. Hesse's transformed Goethe becomes accessible to the Steppenwolf character; he turns into a persona that is interchangeable with Mozart and other great figures and can even be a potential model for Haller/Hesse. Hesse repeatedly referred to the Faustian component in Goethe's work, though he was less concerned with Faust's pursuit of knowledge, which is predominantly concerned with *Erkenntnis*, scientific knowledge, and instead emphasizes the power of intuition and Faust's search for "das ewig Weibliche," a mystical experience that also draws on a Far-Eastern mystical tradition.

Some Hesse experts have been concerned that such a view may not be in accordance with Goethe's humanist concept of *Bildung*. A particularly vexed issue concerns Hesse's alleged indebtedness to the Goethean Bildungsroman. Some modern Goethe scholars no longer consider the "pädagogische Provinz" in positive terms, as a model for education, but interpret it instead as a somewhat surreal critique of the Humboldtian ideal of *Bildung*.[69] Such a reading could serve to establish a new link between Goethe's pedagogical province and Hesse's Castalia: neither achieves a genuine reconciliation between a person's individual development and the realization of one's social responsibilities. Such an understanding of *Das Glasperlenspiel* would emphasize Hesse's consistent views on education, reaching back to his earliest works. Our discussions have illustrated that a narrow comparison of Hesse's *Das Glasperlenspiel* with Goethe's *Wilhelm Meisters Wanderjahre* can be problematic. While no one would wish to ignore their many similarities, some of which were explicitly mentioned by Hesse, direct links between the two novels cannot be established. There are only "correspondences," similarities in approach, usually of a thematic nature.

The search for individual themes would indicate similar correspondences. While the theme of "Entsagung" figures prominently in both novels, where individual characters renounce personal ambition in favor of higher social aims, *Das Glasperlenspiel* has probably as much in common with Buddhist philosophy and Indian mysticism as with Goethe's *Wanderjahre*. The theme of "Ehrfurcht" as a discipline in the pedagogical province appears instrumentalized and mechanical, whereas Hesse's novel develops it into a quasi-religious theme, an intellectual variation of a highly aestheticized spirituality. The use of the word "Spiel" in Hesse's novel may be closer to the nineteenth-century concept of "Festspiel," than to its neoclassical notion, though both exhibit strong social and cultural components. Correspondences in the narrative technique of the two novels can be traced, and it is possible that Goethe's concept of an "Aggregatstruktur" became an antecedent to the modern novel of the early twentieth century. On the other hand, Hesse's narrative technique seems more inspired by Far-Eastern theories of reincarnation, thereby giving emphasis to the "Überzeitlichkeit" (the theme of timelessness) in his work.

These rather cautious remarks on the relationship between Hesse and Goethe should not be seen as an attempt to lessen Goethe's importance for Hesse. As the title of this article indicates, we have attempted to look at Hesse's Goethe, at a revitalized Goethe who has been liberated from the dusty conservatism of the nineteenth century and from a society that sought to employ him for its own cultural and political aims. Alongside similar movements, such as that of Rudolf Steiner and his Goethe Circles, which itself can be traced back to the German youth culture of the turn of the century, Hesse's new Goethe was to prove a great source of comfort and inspiration to a whole generation weary of nationalism and warmongering.

Notes

[1] Numerous connections between Hesse's work and Goethe have been attempted, especially in postwar Germany, where critics sought to establish a tradition of German humanism to counter the fascist perversion of German culture. See Inge Meidinger-Geise, "Zum Wortschatz Utopiens. Zur sprachlichen Anschaulichkeit des Erziehungsstaates in Goethes *Wilhelm Meister* und Hermann Hesse's *Glasperlen-*

spiel," *Muttersprache* 1 (1949): 245–52; Otto Engel, *Hermann Hesse: Dichtung und Gedanke* (Stuttgart: Frommann, 1948); Christa M. Konheiser-Barwanietz, *Hermann Hesse und Goethe* (Bern: von Holten, 1954); and Inge David Halpert, "The Alt-Musikmeister and Goethe," *Monatshefte für deutschen Unterricht, deutsche Sprache und Literatur* 52 (1960): 19–25.

[2] Joseph Mileck, *Hermann Hesse and His Critics: The Criticism and Bibliography of Half a Century* (Chapel Hill: U of North Carolina P, 1958), 98.

[3] This is the case with reference to the genre of the Bildungsroman (novel of development), a form of novel used by many German authors throughout the nineteenth century.

[4] See Ursula Apel, ed., *Hermann Hesse, Personen und Schlüsselfiguren in seinem Werk*. 2 vols. (Munich, London: Saur, 1989), in which ten pages are taken up by references to Goethe, five to Nietzsche, four to Mozart and three to Novalis.

[5] Hesse, "Das klassische Jahrhundert deutschen Geistes," in Hermann Hesse, *Sämtliche Werke*, ed. Volker Michels, vol. 18: *Die Welt im Buch III: Rezensionen und Aufsätze aus den Jahren 1917–1925* (Frankfurt am Main: Suhrkamp, 2001), 483. All further quotations from Hesse are taken from this edition. They will appear in the text in parenthesis with *SW* and volume and page number. English translations are by the author.

[6] See Egon Schwarz, "Hermann Hesses Buchbesprechungen. Reaktionen auf ihre Form, Ästhetik und Geschichtlichkeit," in Schwarz, *Dichtung, Kritik, Geschichte: Essays zur Literatur 1900–1930* (Göttingen: Vandenhoeck & Ruprecht, 1983), 177.

[7] See André Liebich, ed., *Selected Writings of August Cieszkowski*, trans. and with introduction by Liebich (Cambridge: Cambridge UP, 1979), see also August Cieszkowski, *Gott und Palingenesie* (Berlin, 1842).

[8] See in particular the chapter by Frederick A. Lubich on *Narziss und Goldmund* in this volume.

[9] See Erich Trunz, ed., *Goethe Faust, Der Tragödie erster und zweiter Teil, Urfaust* (Munich: C. H. Beck, 1972), 547: "Zu den Müttern gehen heißt etwa: Urbilder des Lebens schauen." (To go to the Mothers means approximately: to see the archetypes of life.)

[10] Goethe's *Faust*, Part Two, verse 6271.

[11] Thomas Mann, preface to the American edition of *Demian* (1948), quoted from Siegfried Unseld, *Hermann Hesse — eine Werkgeschichte* (Frankfurt am Main: Suhrkamp, 1973), 168.

[12] Manfred Lurker, *Dictionary of Gods and Goddesses, Devils and Demons* (London, New York: Routledge & Kegan Paul, 1987), 10.

[13] Johann Wolfgang Goethe, "Segenspfänder," in *West-Östlicher Divan, Sämtliche Werke, Briefe, Tagebücher und Gespräche*, ed. F. Apel et al., vol. 3/1 (Frankfurt am Main: Deutscher Klassiker Verlag, 1994), 14.

[14] Hesse refers to the poem in *SW 4:70* as "*Herbstlied*" *(Autumn Song). It is more commonly known as "Vereinsamt," which might be translated as "Left Alone" or "Isolated."*

[15] *Georg Büchmann, ed., Geflügelte Worte: Der Zitatenschatz des deutschen Volkes,* 25th edn. (Berlin: Haude & Spenersche Buchhandlung, 1912), vii.

[16] Robert König. *Deutsche Literaturgeschichte,* 12th edn. (Bielefeld and Leipzig: Velhagen & Klasing, 1882), 423.

[17] The term is used here in the sense in which Fritz Karl Ringer employs it in his book *The Decline of the German Mandarins: The German Academic Community 1890–1933* (Cambridge, MA: Harvard UP, 1969).

[18] Hesse, "O Freunde, nicht diese Töne," *Neue Züricher Zeitung,* 3 November 1914, in *SW* 15:12.

[19] A copy of the presumptive portrait is illustrated in Volker Michels, ed., *Materialien zu Hermann Hesses Steppenwolf* (Frankfurt am Main: Suhrkamp, 1972), 75.

[20] See Erich Marcks, *Wo stehen wir? Eine Rede* (Stuttgart, 1914).

[21] Theodore Ziolkowski, *The Novels of Hermann Hesse* (Princeton, NJ: Princeton UP, 1965), 37.

[22] The term "Heiterkeit," a key word in the Age of Goethe, refers here to Winckelmann's concept of Greek serenity.

[23] See Michels, ed., *Materialien zu Hermann Hesses Steppenwolf,* 224–28.

[24] Hans Mayer, "Hermann Hesse und das Magische Theater," in *Zutrauen zur Wahrheit: Große Tübinger Reden aus fünf Jahrzehnten,* ed. Gert Ueding (Tübingen: Attempto, 1993), 227.

[25] See Mayer, "Hermann Hesse und das Magische Theater" or Horst Dieter Kreidler, "Pablo und die Unsterblichen," in *Materialien zu Hermann Hesses Steppenwolf,* ed. Michels, 381–88.

[26] See Goethe, "Der Mann von fünfzig Jahren," *Wilhelm Meisters Wanderjahre,* book 2, chapters 3, 4, and 5.

[27] Michels, ed., *Materialien zu Hermann Hesses Steppenwolf,* 197.

[28] Michels, ed., *Materialien zu Hermann Hesses Steppenwolf,* 198.

[29] Goethe's *Faust* (Part Two), verse 11586.

[30] See also Sikander Singh, *Hermann Hesse* (Stuttgart: Reclam, 2006), 180. Immortality is here seen under the aspect of timelessness.

[31] Walter Benjamin, "The Work of Art in the Age of Mechanical Reproduction," in Walter Benjamin, *Illuminations,* ed. Hannah Arendt, trans. Harry Zohn (London: Pimlico, 1999), 211–45.

[32] See Karl-Heinz Hucke, *Der integrierte Außenseiter: Hesses frühe Helden* (Frankfurt am Main: P. Lang, 1983), 12.

[33] Rolland (1866–1944), the French dramatist, essayist, art historian, and winner of the Nobel Prize for Literature in 1915, was a friend and longtime correspondent of Hesse's.

[34] See Hermann Hesse, *Gesammelte Briefe,* ed. Ursula and Volker Michels, vol. 1 (Frankfurt am Main: Suhrkamp, 1973), 201. See also Siddhartha's attempt to find his own approach to Indian wisdom.

[35] See Yan Baoyu, "China," and Johannes Mehlig, "Indien," in *Goethe Handbuch,* ed. Bernd Witte et al., vol. 4/1 (Stuttgart, Weimar: Metzler, 1998), 163–65 and

521–24. See also Johann Peter Eckermann, *Gespräche mit Goethe in den letzten Jahren seines Lebens,* ed. Christoph Michel and Hans Grüters (Frankfurt am Main: Deutscher Klassiker Verlag, 1999), 223–24.

[36] *Goethe Handbuch,* ed. Witte, vol. 4/1, 164. Cf. Brief Schillers an Goethe, 24 January 1796, in, *Briefwechsel zwischen Schiller und Goethe in den Jahren 1794–1805,* in *Sämtliche Werke* Münchener Ausgabe, vol. 8.1, ed. Karl Richter et al. (Munich: Hanser, 1990), 154–55.

[37] A detailed synopsis of *Hao-chiu chuan* is found in *The Indiana Companion to Traditional Chinese Literature,* ed. William H. Nienhauser Jr. (Bloomington: Indiana UP, 1986–98), 400–401.

[38] See Ziolkowski, *The Novels of Hermann Hesse,* 146–47.

[39] T. S. Eliot, "Tradition and the Individual Talent," in T. S. Eliot, *Selected Prose,* ed. John Hayward (Harmondsworth: Penguin, 1958), 26.

[40] As do Inge D. Halpert in "The Alt-Musikmeister and Goethe" and Christian Immo Schneider in *Hermann Hesse,* 98.

[41] Goethe, *Sämtliche Werke, Briefe, Tagebücher und Gespräche,* Frankfurter Ausgabe (Frankfurt am Main: Deutscher Klassiker Verlag, 1997), vol. 1/13, 270.

[42] Halpert, "The Alt-Musikmeister and Goethe," 21, here quoting from a translation of *Steppenwolf.*

[43] See for instance "Josef Knechts hinterlassene Schriften," in *SW* 5:399–400, 403, 407–8.

[44] See my references to Goethe's and Hesse's "Stufen," later on in this essay.

[45] Singh, *Hermann Hesse,* 93, 117, 167, 172, 204, 213.

[46] Mileck, *Hermann Hesse's Glasperlenspiel* (Berkeley: U of California P, 1952), 256. Inge Meidinger-Geise draws similar conclusions; see "Zum Wortschatz Utopiens," 246–47.

[47] George Wallis Field, "Goethe and *Das Glasperlenspiel,*" *German Life and Letters* 23 (1969), 96.

[48] Ziolkowski, *The Novels of Hermann Hesse,* 255.

[49] Ziolkowski, *The Novels of Hermann Hesse,* 258–59.

[50] Martin Swales, "New Media, Virtual Reality, Flawed Utopia? Reflections on Thomas Mann's *Der Zauberberg* and Hermann Hesse's *Der Steppenwolf,*" in *Hermann Hesse Today / Hermann Hesse heute,* ed. Ingo Cornils and Osman Durrani (Amsterdam, New York: Rodopi, 2005), 33.

[51] See Hesse's letter to Alice Leuthold, in, *Materialien zu Hermann Hesses Das Glasperlenspiel,* ed. Volker Michels (Frankfurt am Main: Suhrkamp, 1973), 90. See also Willy Michel and Edith Michel, "*Das Glasperlenspiel.* Pädagogische Utopie, dialektische Entwicklung und hermeneutische Erinnerung," in *Hermann Hesse — Romane* (Stuttgart: Reclam, 1994), 135 and Rätus Luck, "*Das Glasperlenspiel* in den Briefen Hermann Hesses," in *Der Dichter sucht Verständnis und Erkanntwerden: Neue Arbeiten zu Hermann Hesse und seinem Roman Das Glasperlenspiel,* ed. Eva Zimmermann (Bern, Oxford: P. Lang, 2002), 11–12.

[52] See diverse references by Wilhelm Scherer, Friedrich Gundolf, and Eduard Spranger in their various histories of German literature of the nineteenth century.

[53] In Goethe's case the French Revolution. See Helmut Brandt, "Entsagung und Französische Revolution: Goethes Prokurator- und Ferdinand-Novelle in weiterführender Betrachtung," in *Deutsche Klassik und Revolution,* ed. Paolo Chiarini (Rome: Edizioni dell'Ateneo, 1981), 198.

[54] Arthur Henkel, *Entsagung, eine Studie zu Goethes Altersroman* (Tübingen: Niemeyer, 1954), 31.

[55] See Goethe, *Sämtliche Werke, Briefe, Tagebücher und Gespräche,* vol. 1/10, 295 and 345.

[56] Eberhard Lämmert, "Goethes empirischer Beitrag zur Romantheorie," in *Goethes Erzählwerk, Interpretationen,* ed. Paul Michael Lützeler (Stuttgart: Reclam, 1985), 30.

[57] Singh, *Hermann Hesse,* 222. See also Ziolkowski, *The Novels of Hermann Hesse,* 285–86 and W. and E. Michel, *"Das Glasperlenspiel,"* 134.

[58] Adolf Muschg, *Goethe als Emigrant: Auf der Suche nach dem Grünen bei einem alten Dichter* (Frankfurt am Main: Suhrkamp, 1986), 114, and Thomas Degering, *Das Elend der Entsagung: Goethes Wilhelm Meisters Wanderjahre* (Bonn: Bouvier, 1982), 312.

[59] The four forms of reverence are: reverence for the things above us (God), for that which is beneath us (nature), for what is among us (other people), and for oneself, the highest form of reverence.

[60] Goethe, *Sämtliche Werke, Briefe, Tagebücher und Gespräche,* vol. 1/10, 423.

[61] See Michels, ed., *Materialien zu Hermann Hesses Das Glasperlenspiel,* 78–79, letter to Fanny Schiler, January 1934.

[62] See *Goethe Handbuch,* ed. Witte, vol. 4/1, 113.

[63] Michels, ed., *Materialien zu Hermann Hesses Das Glasperlenspiel,* 315.

[64] 18 February 1830. Kanzler von Müller, *Unterhaltungen mit Goethe,* ed. Ernst Grumach (Weimar: Hermann Böhlau Nachfolger, 1956), 183.

[65] See Ehrhard Bahr, "Wilhelm Meisters Wanderjahre oder die Entsagenden," in *Goethe Handbuch,* ed. Witte, vol. 3, 206.

[66] Muschg, *Goethe als Emigrant,* 110.

[67] W. and E. Michel, *"Das Glasperlenspiel,"* 163.

[68] Hermann Hesse, *Briefe,* new, expanded edition (Frankfurt am Main: Suhrkamp, 1959), 462.

[69] In particular Thomas Degering, *Das Elend der Entsagung,* and Adolf Muschg, *Goethe als Emigrant.*

Selected English Translations of Hesse's Works Discussed

(In order of the essays in this book; multiple translations listed chronologically.)

Beneath the Wheel. Translated by Michael Roloff. New York: Farrar, Straus and Giroux, 1968.

Rosshalde. Translated by Ralph Manheim. New York: Farrar, Straus and Giroux, 1970.

Demian: The Story of Emil Sinclair's Youth. Translated by Michael Roloff and Michael Lebeck. Introduction by Thomas Mann. New York: Harper & Row, 1965; reprint, New York: Bantam, 1968.

"Klingsor's Last Summer." In *Klingsor's Last Summer*. Translated by Richard and Clara Winston. New York: Farrar, Straus and Giroux, 1970.

Siddhartha. Translated by Hilda Rosner. New York: New Directions, 1951. Reprint, New York: Bantam, 1971.

Siddhartha: A New Translation. Translated by Joachim Neugroschel. Introduction by Ralph Freedman. New York: Penguin, 1999.

Siddhartha: A New Translation. Translated by Sherab Chodzin Kohn. Introduction by Paul W. Morris. Boston: Shambala, 2000.

Siddhartha: An Indian Poem. Translated by Susan Bernofsky. Introduction by Tom Robbins. New York: Modern Library, 2006.

"Klein and Wagner." In *Klingsor's Last Summer*. Translated by Richard and Clara Winston. New York: Farrar, Straus and Giroux, 1970. 45-144.

Steppenwolf. Translated by Basil Creighton. New York: Bantam Books, 1969.

Narcissus and Goldmund. Translated by Ursule Molinaro. New York: Farrar, Straus and Giroux, 1969. Reprint, New York: Bantam, 1971. Reprint New York: Macmillan, 2003.

Magister Ludi: The Glass Bead Game. Translated by Richard and Clara Winston. Introduction by Theodore Ziolkowski. New York: Holt, Rinehart, and Winston, 1969. Reprint, New York: Bantam, 1970.

Poems. Translated by James Wright. New York: Farrar, Straus and Giroux, 1970.

If the War Goes on ...Reflections on War and Politics. Trans. Ralph Manheim. New York: Farrar, Straus and Giroux, 1971.

"Pictor's Metamorphoses." In *Pictor's Metamorphoses and Other Fantasies.* Ed. and with an introduction by Theodore Ziolkowski. Translated by Rika Lesser. New York: Farrar, Straus and Giroux, 1982.

Wandering: Notes and Sketches. Translated by James Wright. New York: Farrar, Straus, and Giroux, 1972.

Select Bibliography

(Listed chronologically within each rubric.)

Hesse's Works

Sämtliche Werke. Ed. Volker Michels. 20 volumes plus index. Frankfurt: Suhr-kamp 2001-2007. Abbreviated as *SW*.

Hesse's Letters

Gesammelte Briefe. Ed. Ursula and Volker Michels. 4 volumes. Frankfurt: Suhr-kamp 1973-1986. Abbreviated as *GB*.

Ausgewählte Briefe. Frankfurt: Suhrkamp, 1974. Abbreviated as *AB*.

The Hesse/Mann Letters. The Correspondence of Hermann Hesse and Thomas Mann. Ed. Anni Carlsson and Volker Michels. London: Peter Owen, 1976.

Briefe an Freunde. Ed. Volker Michels. Frankfurt: Insel, 2000.

"Die dunkle und die wilde Seite der Seele": Briefwechsel mit seinem Psychoan-alytiker Josef Bernhard Lang. Ed. Thomas Feitknecht. Frankfurt: Suhrkamp, 2006.

Other Correspondence

Ninon Hesse. *Lieber, lieber Vogel: Briefe an Hermann Hesse*. Ed. Gisela Kleine. Frankfurt: Suhrkamp, 2000.

Bibliography of Secondary Literature on Hermann Hesse

Jürgen Below. *Hermann Hesse Bibliographie: Sekundärliteratur 1899-2007*. 5 volumes. Berlin / New York: de Gruyter, 2007.

Internet Resources

Hermann Hesse Homepage. Ed. Günther Gottschalk. University of California at Santa Barbara, http://www.gss.ucsb.edu/projects/hesse/.

Biographies

Hugo Ball. *Hermann Hesse: Sein Leben und sein Werk*. Ed. Volker Michels. Göttingen: Wallstein 2006 (first published 1927).

Bernhard Zeller. *Hermann Hesse*. Reinbek: Rowohlt, 1963.

Hermann Hesse. *Kindheit und Jugend vor Neunzehnhundert*. Ed. Ninon Hesse. 2 volumes. Frankfurt: Suhrkamp, 1966.

Ralph Freedman. *Hermann Hesse: Pilgrim of Crisis*. New York: Pantheon, 1978.

Joseph Mileck. *Hermann Hesse: Life and Art*. U of California P, 1978.

Hermann Hesse. *Sein Leben in Bildern und Texten*. Ed. Volker Michels. Frankfurt: Insel, 1987.

Hermann Hesse. *Werk und Wirkungsgeschichte*. Ed. Siegfried Unseld. Frankfurt: Insel, 1987.

Hermann Hesse in Augenzeugenberichten. Ed. Volker Michels. Frankfurt: Suhrkamp, 1991.

Klaus Walther. *Hermann Hesse*. Munich: dtv, 2002.

Michael Limberg. *Hermann Hesse: Leben, Werk, Wirkung*. Frankfurt: Suhrkamp, 2005.

Interpretations

Hermann Hesse Jahrbuch. Ed. Mauro Ponzi. Tübingen: Niemeyer, 2004-.

Colin Wilson. *The Outsider*. London: Gollancz, 1956.

Theodore Ziolkowski. *The Novels of Hermann Hesse: A Study in Theme and Structure*. Princeton UP, 1965.

Hesse Companion. Ed. Anna Otten. Albuquerque: U of New Mexico P, 1977.

Klaus von Seckendorff. *Hermann Hesses propagandistische Prosa*. Bonn: Bouvier Verlag, 1982.

Text und Kritik: Hermann Hesse. Ed. Heinz Ludwig Arnold. No.10/11. Munich: Text und Kritik, 1983.

Reso Karalaschwili. *Hermann Hesses Romanwelt*. Cologne: Böhlau, 1986.

Martin Pfeifer. *Hesse Kommentar zu sämtlichen Werken*. Frankfurt: Suhrkamp, 1990.

Christian Immo Schneider. *Hermann Hesse*. Munich: Beck, 1991.

Interpretationen: Hermann Hesses Romane. Stuttgart: Reclam, 1994.

Helga Esselborn-Krumbiegel. *Hermann Hesse: Literaturwissen für Schule und Studium*. Stuttgart: Reclam, 1996.

Erich Valentin. *Die goldene Spur: Mozart in der Dichtung Hermann Hesses*. Munich: A1 Verlag, 1998.

Lewis W. Tusken. *Hermann Hesse: The Man, His Myth, His Metaphor*. Columbia, SC: U of South Carolina P, 1998.

"Der Dichter sucht Verständnis und Erkanntwerden": Neue Arbeiten zu Hermann Hesse und seinem Roman Das Glasperlenspiel. Ed. Eva Zimmermann. Bern: Peter Lang, 2002.

Hermann Hesse: 1877–1962–2002. Ed. Cornelia Blasberg. Tübingen: Attempto, 2003.

Hermann Hesse. Ed. Harold Bloom. Philadelphia: Chelsea House, 2003.

Hermann Hesse und die literarische Moderne: Aufsätze und Materialien. Ed. Andreas Solbach. Frankfurt: Suhrkamp, 2004.

Hermann Hesse Heute / Hermann Hesse Today. Ed. Ingo Cornils and Osman Durrani. Amsterdam: Rodopi, 2005.

Marco Schickling, *Hermann Hesse als Literaturkritiker*, Heidelberg: Winter 2005.

"Im Dienste der gemeinsamen Sache" — Hermann Hesse und der Suhrkamp Verlag. Ed. Regina Bucher, Wolfgang Schopf, Volker Michels, and Harry Joelson-Strohbach. Montagnola: Fondazione Hermann Hesse Montagnola, 2005. Catalogue to exhibition in Hermann Hesse Museum Montagnola.

Sikander Singh. *Hermann Hesse*. Stuttgart: Reclam, 2006.

Laszlo V. Szabo. *Der Einfluss Friedrich Nietzsches auf Hermann Hesse*. Vienna: Praesens Verlag, 2007.

"Die gefährliche Lust, unerschrocken zu denken": Das Menschenbild bei Hermann Hesse. Ed. Michael Limberg. Stuttgart: Klett, 2008.

Barry Stephenson. *Veneration and Revolt: Hermann Hesse and Swabian Pietism*. Waterloo, Ontario: Wilfried Laurier UP, 2009.

Contributors

OLAF BERWALD is Chair of Modern and Classical Languages and Literatures and Associate Professor of German at the University of North Dakota. His publications include the monographs *Philipp Melanchthons Sicht der Rhetorik* (1994) and *An Introduction to the Works of Peter Weiss* (2003), the edited volume *Der untote Gott: Ästhetik und Religion in der deutschen und österreichischen Literatur des 20. Jahrhunderts* (with Gregor Thuswaldner, 2007), as well as articles and book chapters on Kafka, Broch, Canetti, Weiss, Carl Einstein, and literary theory.

PAUL BISHOP is Professor of German at the University of Glasgow. His research interests include Goethe, Schiller, Nietzsche, Thomas Mann, Ernst Cassirer, Hermann Hesse, psychoanalysis, and *Lebensphilosophie*. His most recent publication is *Analytical Psychology and German Classical Aesthetics: Goethe, Schiller, and Jung* (2 vols., 2007-2008).

INGO CORNILS is Senior Lecturer in German and Head of the Department of German, Russian and Slavonic Studies at the University of Leeds, UK. Among his publications are the volumes *Hermann Hesse Today / Hermann Hesse heute* (co-edited with Osman Durrani, 2005), *(Un-)erfüllte Wirklichkeit: Neue Studien zu Uwe Timms Werk* (co-edited with Frank Finlay, 2006), and *Baader-Meinhof Returns: History and Cultural Memory of German Left-Wing Terrorism* (co-edited with Gerrit-Jan Berendse, 2008).

OSMAN DURRANI was a Lecturer in Durham between 1972 and 1995, and has been Professor of German at the University of Kent in Canterbury, UK, since 1995. His research interests range from literary studies (mid-eighteenth century to the present day) to popular culture, and include several humanities computing and artificial intelligence projects. Among his publications are *Fictions of Germany* (1994), *The New Germany* (1995), and *Faust: Icon of Modern Culture* (2004).

RALPH FREEDMAN taught Comparative Literature at the University of Iowa for twelve years and at Princeton for twenty-two years, retiring from Princeton in 1988. From 1988 to 1990 he was Visiting Augustus B. Longstreet Professor at Emory University. He also served as a Senior Fellow of the School of Criticism and Theory from 1975 to 1988. His publications include *The Lyrical Novel: Studies in Hermann Hesse, Andre Gide, and Virginia Woolf* (1963), which has been translated into Spanish and Korean; *Hermann Hesse: Pilgrim of Crisis* (1978), which has been translated into German, Italian, and Japanese; and *Life of A Poet: Rainer Maria Rilke*

(1996), which has been translated into German, French, and Chinese; as well as many essays. His work includes fiction: two original novels, *Divided* (1948) and *Rue the Day* (2009); and a translation into English of Sten Nadolny's 1987 novel *Die Entdeckung der Langsamkeit* (as *The Discovery of Slowness*, 2003).

HANS-JOACHIM HAHN is Emeritus Professor at Oxford Brookes University. His publications include *German Thought and Culture* (1995), *German Education and Society* (1998), *The 1848 Revolutions in German-Speaking Europe* (2001), and numerous essays on German literature in the nineteenth and twentieth centuries, especially on Novalis, Eichendorff, Heine, Freytag, Benn, and Hesse.

STEFAN HÖPPNER is Assistant Professor of German Literature at the University of Freiburg, Germany. He is the author of *Zwischen Utopia und Neuer Welt* (2005), a study of the image of the United States in the writings of Arno Schmidt. In addition, he has published on utopian literature, Romanticism, as well as on contemporary German literature and pop culture, particularly comics and pop music. He is currently preparing a book on cross-currents between literature and science in German Romanticism. In addition to his academic pursuits, Höppner is a poet and musician.

ADRIAN HSIA is retired as Professor of German Studies at McGill University. He was also Honorary Professor of Chinese Studies at the University of Hong Kong and Editor of the Monograph Series Euro-Sinica. His publications include the monographs *Hermann Hesse und China, Chinesia: The European Construction of China in Literature of the 17th and 18th Centuries,* and *Orient und Okzident: Zur Faustrezeption in nicht-christlichen Kulturen,* and the edited volumes *The Vision of China in the English Literature of the 17th and 18th Centuries* and *Mission und Theater: China und Japan auf den deutschen Bühnen der Gesellschaft Jesu* (co-edited with Ruprecht Wimmer), as well as about 100 articles on transcultural studies.

FREDERICK A. LUBICH is Professor of German at Old Dominion University in Norfolk, Virginia, and President of the Society of Contemporary American Literature in German. He is the author and editor of five books on modern German literature and culture (including books on Thomas Mann and Max Frisch), numerous scholarly articles and journalistic essays, as well as poetry. He has lectured widely in over thirty countries around the world.

VOLKER MICHELS is the editor of Hermann Hesse's collected works (20 volumes plus index) and letters (4 volumes, with Ursula Michels and Heiner Hesse) at Suhrkamp Verlag, Frankfurt. He maintains the Hesse Editions Archive in Offenbach am Main and has published numerous collections of secondary literature on Hesse's main works.

KAMAKSHI PAPPU MURTI is Professor of German at Middlebury College. She has published on German Orientalism and discourse of minorities, including two books: *Die Reinkarnation des Lesers als Autor: ein rezeptionsgeschichtlicher Versuch über den Einfluß der altindischen Literatur auf deutsche Schriftsteller um 1900* (1990) and *India: The Seductive and Seduced 'Other' of German Orientalism* (2000). Currently, she is working on a book-length manuscript about the Muslim headscarf entitled "Turkey, Germany, and the Shifting Boundaries of Identity."

MARCO SCHICKLING is German Teacher and Head of Lower Secondary German at the Internationale Schule Frankfurt/Rhein-Main (ISF). From 1998 until 2003 he was Co-Editor of Hermann Hesse's Literary Criticism at Suhrkamp Verlag, Frankfurt. His publications include his doctorate, *Hermann Hesse als Literaturkritiker* (2005), as well as several essays and lectures on Hesse and Robert Walser.

C. IMMO SCHNEIDER is Professor Emeritus of Foreign Languages at Central Washington University, a former member of the Thomanerchor, Leipzig, and a concert organist and composer. His publications include *Das Todesproblem bei Hermann Hesse* (1973), *Hermann Hesse* (1994, translated into Italian), *Zwölf Vignetten zu alten deutschen Weihnachtsliedern* (1988), and *Twelve Short Organ Pieces* (1991). His Compact Disc recording *Orgelmusik aus fünf Jahrhunderten* appeared in 1997.

ANDREAS SOLBACH, University Professor of German at the Johannes Gutenberg University, Mainz, studied German, English, and Philosophy in Marburg, Berlin, New Orleans, and at Harvard, where he received his doctorate in 1990 with a dissertation on societal ethics and the theory of the novel in the early modern period. He submitted his *Habilitationsarbeit* in 1994 at the Free University of Berlin, a monograph on the Baroque author Johann Beer. He is a founder and was first president of the International Andreas Gryphius Society and the Heimito von Doderer Society. He has written three books and approximately seventy articles, and has edited half a dozen collected volumes. His interests include the literature of the early modern period and the twentieth century, as well as rhetoric and narratology. For some time he has been pursuing a further concentration in the realm of popular literature and culture.

MARTIN SWALES is Emeritus Professor of German at University College London and a Fellow of the British Academy. His publications include studies of Arthur Schnitzler, the German Novelle, the German Bildungsroman, Adalbert Stifter, Thomas Mann, Goethe, German Realism, Goethe's *Werther,* and Thomas Mann's *Buddenbrooks.*

JEFFORD VAHLBUSCH, Associate Professor of German and Director of the University Honors Program at the University of Wisconsin-Eau Claire, received his PhD from the University of Michigan in 1998 with a two-volume dissertation on the Marxist critique of Nietzsche. He is particularly interested in the popular and scholarly reception of literary works, and is currently working on a study of the so-called Hesse boom of the 1960s and 1970s.

Godela Weiss-Sussex is Senior Lecturer in Modern German Literature at the Institute of Germanic and Romance Studies, University of London. Her main research interests lie in nineteenth- and twentieth-century literature and the visual arts and in the works of German-Jewish writers. Her publications include *"Not an Essence but a Positioning": German-Jewish Women Writers, 1900-1938* (co-edited, 2009); *"Verwisch die Spuren!" Bertolt Brecht's Work and Legacy: A Reassessment* (co-edited, 2008); and *Metropolitan Chronicles: Georg Hermann's Berlin Novels 1897 to 1912* (2000).

Index

Abel, 90, 91, 95. *See also* Cain
Abelard, Peter, 219
Abraxas, 99–100, 397
Adorno, Theodor, 187
Age of Enlightenment, 198, 201,
    208
AIDS, 205
Albertson, David, 265
allegory, 49, 141
Andreä, Volkmar, 374
Apollo, 217
Aristotle, 374
Arles, 140
Arnim, Bettina von, 406
Arnim, Ludwig Achim von, 375
Art Nouveau, 192–93, 201
Atman, 150, 153; in Zen Buddhism,
    166–68
Auschwitz, 208

Bach, Johann Sebastian, 245, 374,
    376–77, 381–83, 387, 389, 391,
    401
Bachofen, Johann Jacob, 81, 188,
    201, 205, 223, 269
Ball, Hugo, 17, 22, 35, 120, 254,
    307, 342
Ball-Hennings, Emmy, 243
Basel, 2, 3, 345
Beckett, Samuel, 208
Beethoven, Ludwig van, 339, 383
Behrendt, Joachim-Ernst, 388
Belhalfaoui, Barbara, 217
Below, Jürgen, 12
Bengel, Johann Albrecht, 227, 412
Benjamin, Walter, 176, 389
Benjamin, Walter, works by:
    *Das Kunstwerk im Zeitalter seiner
    Reproduzierbarkeit*, 175

Benn, Gottfried, 311, 375
Bercholz, Samuel, 158
Bermann Fischer, Gottfried, 217,
    316
Bern, 3, 59, 81, 120–21, 140, 144,
    163, 304, 306, 310, 331–32, 374
Bernoulli, Fritz, 121
Bernovsky, Susan, 161, 163
Best, Werner, 314
Bie, Oscar, 349, 354
Bieder, Werner, 276
Bildungsroman, 8, 60, 181–83, 272,
    415
Bismarck, Otto von, 308
Black Forest, 140
Bloch, Ernst, 307
Bloom, Harold, 13
Boccaccio, Giovanni, 387
Böcklin, Arnold, 3, 326
Bodmer, Charlotte, 361
Bogner, Rolf Georg, 121
Böhmer, Gunter, 314
Böll, Heinrich, 12
Bollnow, Otto F., 217, 232
Bonniers Litterära Magasin, 315
Bosch, Hieronymus, 204
Böttger, Fritz, 35
Boulby, Mark, 11, 43, 227
Brahman, 149, 168; concept of,
    151–53
Brahms, Johannes, 123, 388
Brecht, Bertolt, 243, 314, 375, 397,
    406
Brentano, Bernhard von, 314
Broch, Hermann, 171, 406
Broch, Hermann, works by:
    Der Schlafwandler, 233, 414
Bruckner, Anton, 379
Brueghel, Pieter, 204

Brun, Fritz, 374
Buber, Martin, 328
Büchner, Georg, 247
Buddha, 160, 166, 282, 385;
  historical, 268; in *Siddhartha*,
  154–55; teaching, 149–50
Bukofzer, Manfred, 381
Bülow, Bernhard von, 305
Burckhardt, Jacob, 3, 229, 231, 407
Butler, William, 276

Cain, 90–92, 95. *See also* Abel
Calw, 2–3, 23
Cardinal, Agnes, 265
Casa Carmuzzi, 141–42, 350
Castalia/Kastalien, 5, 217, 227,
  291, 386, 408, 411–13, 415
Castiglione, 119
Catholic Church, 187, 206, 318
Celan, Paul, 204, 243
Ceylon, 3
Chamberlain, Neville, 316
Chögyam Trungpa, 158
Chopin, Frederic, 379, 383–84, 389
Christ, 85, 94, 131, 166, 202, 206,
  385, 399
Chuang Zi, 155, 341
Cieskowski, Count August, 396
Cixous, Helene, 195–97
Clement, Catherine, 195, 197
Cohn, Hilde, 232
Cold War, 319
Communism, 176, 313, 318–19
Confucius, 149
Conor, Liz, 284
Cook, Deryck, 377, 390
Cornils, Ingo, 265, 269
Cortot, Alfred, 384, 392
Cremerius, Johannes, 131
Cusa, Nicholas of, 219

Dada, 254
Dalai Lama, 319
Dante Alighieri, 97, 326, 376, 379,
  399

Dao De Jing, 150–51
Decker, Eduard Douwes, 303
Deep Purple, 192
Degering, Thomas, 411
Delaunay, Robert, 353
Dickens, Charles, 75
Döblin, Alfred, 171
Dolbin, Ninon, 5
Don Quixote, 265
Dostoevsky, Fyodor, 75, 163, 396
Douglas, Mary, 87
dreams, 267, 323
Drews, Jörg, 264–65
Dunlop, Geoffrey, 287
Dürer, Albrecht, 389
Durrani, Osman, 265, 269
Dylan, Bob, 193

East Indies, 161, 303
Eichendorf, Joseph Freiherr von,
  375, 385
Einstein, Albert, 401
Eisner, Kurt, 307
Eliot, T. S., 406
Englert, Josef, 143–44
Enright, D. J., 17–19, 45
Eros, 200
Eschenbach, Wolfram von, 139
Esselborn-Krumbiegel, Helga, 9, 38
Europe, 106, 171, 190, 302, 307
Expressionism, 121, 351, 385

Faber du Faur, Curt von, 224
Faust, 68, 93, 183, 222, 224, 227,
  403, 415
Fichte, Johann Gottlieb, 401
Field, George Wallis, 76, 231, 358,
  389, 409
First World War, 3–4, 10–12, 121,
  132, 139, 157, 163, 188, 248,
  280, 302, 304, 311, 314, 318,
  320, 346, 386, 415
Flaubert, Gustave, 58
Fontane, Theodor, 58
Foucault, Michel, 201, 287, 289

Fournier, Pierre, 382, 387
Frankfurter Zeitung, 306, 329
Freedman, Ralph, 11, 120, 156–59, 161, 184
Freud, Sigmund, 127–28, 144, 188–89, 303, 328, 331
Fricke, Petra, 272
Frisch, Max, 318
Fried, Alfred H., 307

Gaia, 199
Gaienhofen, 3, 81, 302
Ganeshan, Vridhagiri, 164–65
Gauguin, Paul, 140
Gaupp, Robert, 124
Gellner, Christoph, 165
Geneva, 143
Gennep, Arnold von, 84, 90, 108
George, Stefan, 229, 375
German classical aesthetics, 223
German High Modernism, 173
German Romanticism, 139, 191, 265, 278, 401
German Student Movement, 291
Gilbert, Sandra, 196
Giles, James, 274
Ginzkey, Franz Karl, 366
God, 168, 192, 199, 349; absence of, 207–9; concept of, 151–52
Goethe, Johann Wolfgang von, 93, 178, 181–85, 196, 216, 227, 242, 256, 336–37, 340, 385, 395–402, 404–7, 409, 411
Goethe, Johann Wolfgang von, works by:
    Faust I, 183, 213, 397, 403
    Die Leiden des jungen Werther, 182, 185, 263, 406
    Die Wahlverwandtschaften, 59, 405
    West-Östlicher Divan, 397
    Wilhelm Meisters Lehrjahre, 181–82, 408–10, 413–15
    Wilhelm Meisters Wanderjahre, 403, 405, 409, 414, 416

Goethe Prize, 6
Goern, Hermann, 347
Görner, Rüdiger, 241, 377
Gottschalk, Günther, 11
Götz, Ignacio, 224
Grass, Günter, 12, 186
Groves, Anthony Norris, 276
Gundert, Friedrich, 373
Gundert, Hermann, 2, 276–78, 373
Gundert, Wilhelm, 162–63
Günther, Georg, 378

Hahn, Hans-Joachim, 45
Halpert, Inge, 227
Handel, George Frideric, 389, 403, 406
Harlow, Jean, 195
Hartmann, Otto, 125
Hauptmann, Gerhart, 75
Haußmann, Conrad, 301–2, 306, 310
Hegel, Georg Wilhelm Friedrich, 123, 219, 222, 230–31, 319, 401, 414
Heidegger, Martin, 391
Heilbronn, 23
Heine, Heinrich, 21
Heiney, Donald, 19
Hellmann, Julie, 379
Helt, Richard, 22, 380
Herder, Johann Gottfried, 340
Herrmann-Neisse, Max, 250
Hesse, Bruno, 121, 232
Hesse, Heiner, 121
Hesse, Hermann, works by:
    Dank an Goethe, 404
    Eine Stunde hinter Mitternacht, 3, 325, 327, 379
    Gertrud, 3, 81, 326–27, 376, 379–80, 389–90, 408
    Hermann Lauscher, 327, 379
    Kinderseele, 85, 88, 120
    Kindheit des Zauberers, 324
    Klingsors letzter Sommer, 350–51, 353, 366, 379

Hesse, Hermann, works by :
 (continued)
 Krieg und Frieden, 318
 Krisis: Ein Stück Tagebuch, 178,
  254–55
 Künstler und Psychoanalyse, 127,
  144, 329, 335
 Kurgast, 337, 379, 383
 Kurzgefaßter Lebenslauf, 10, 126,
  341
 Die Morgenlandfahrt, 5, 140, 335
 Peter Camenzind, 3, 6, 60, 70, 81,
  123, 302–3, 327
 Piktors Verwandlungen, 357, 361,
  363, 366–67
 Robert Aghion, 328
 *Zarathustras Wiederkehr: Ein Wort
  an die deutsche Jugend,* 307
Hesse, Johannes, 2, 81
Hesse, Maria (née Bernoulli), 3, 59,
 81, 121, 157, 302, 374
Hesse, Marie, 2, 373
Hesse, Martin, 57, 81, 121, 280
Hesse, Ninon (née Ausländer), 2,
 316, 333
Heuss, Theodor, 6
Heym, Georg, 128
Hildebrandt, Kurt, 229
Hindenburg, Paul von, 311, 313–14
Hinduism, 226, 263, 282
Hitler, Adolf, 5, 7, 249, 313, 318
Hoerschelmann, Rolf von, 219
Hoffmann, E. T. A., 379
Hofmann, Ludwig von, 303
Hofmannsthal, Hugo von, 397, 406
Hölderlin, Friedrich, 81, 123, 244,
 255–56, 339, 401
Hollander, John, 352
Hollywood cinema, 195
Holocaust, 203–6, 208
Holz, Arno, 75, 243
Homer, 324, 329
homoeroticism, 265, 293
homosexuality, 201
Horkheimer, Max, 187

Hotz, Heinrich Ferdinand, 330
Huber, Peter, 241, 389
Hugenberg, Alfred, 313
Huxley, Aldous, 402

I Ching, 232, 408
Ibsen, Henrik, 75
India, 76, 263, 276, 278, 280–83,
 296; Hesse's trip to, 298
industrialization, 9
Isenberg, Carlo, 374
Isenberg, Karl, 22–25, 34, 39
Isenberg, Theodor, 373
Iser, Wolfgang, 265

Jauss, Hans Robert, 265
Jews, 157, 202–3, 205–6, 208, 310,
 315, 317, 322
Johann, Klaus, 20, 37
Jones, William, 277
Jong, Erica, 197
Jung, Carl Gustav, 4, 81, 117, 127–
 28, 131, 144, 149, 157, 160,
 162, 188, 233, 331, 333–34, 339,
 380, 389

Kafka, Franz, 123, 157, 171, 216,
 383
Kaiser, Georg, 128
Kama Sutra, 278, 282
Kant, Immanuel, 219, 401, 409
Karalaschwili, Reso, 8, 151–53, 386
Kasack, Hermann, 386, 390
Kaufman, Rene, 285
Kayser, Rudolf, 83
Keller, Gottfried, 81, 338
Kerouac, Jack, 162–63
Kläber, Kurt, 314
Kleist, Heinrich von, 202
Kohn, Sherab Chödzin, 158–59,
 162, 164–65
Kolb, Annette, 307, 387
Klabund (pseud. Alfred Henschke),
 128
Klaiber, Reinhold, 220

Klee, Paul, 352
Klein, Melanie, 188, 198
Koester, Rudolf, 131
Kohlrausch, Martin, 301
Kreidolf, Ernst, 330
Kristeva, Julia, 274, 289
Kuhn, Heribert, 19–20, 38
Küsnacht, 149

Landauer, Gustav, 203
Lang, Josef Bernhard, 4, 81, 127,
    389; on marriage, 121–22;
    treatment of Hesse, 331–33
Langen, Albert, 301–2
Lao Zi (Lao Tse), 149–50, 155,
    160, 383
League of Nations, 310
Leary, Timothy, 184–85, 192–93,
    402
Lebensreform, 302–3, 305, 320
Led Zeppelin, 192
Lehmann, Wilhelm, 243
Leibniz, Gottfried, 219
Lenau, Nikolaus, 375
Lenin, Vladimir, 306
Lessing, Gotthold Ephraim, 410,
    412
Levinas, Emanuel, 208
Lewis, Matthew, 287
Li Tai Pe, 144
Lie Zi, 151
Liebknecht, Karl, 203, 307
Lingens, Dominique, 381–83
Loerke, Oskar, 243, 311
London, 12
Loos, Adolf, 201
Löwenstein, Richard, 328
Lü Bu We, 386
Lubich, Frederick A., 265, 269
Lucerne, 330–32, 346
Luther, Martin, 94
Luxemburg, Rosa, 203, 307

Maas, Joachim, 314
Macke, August, 352–53

Maeterlinck, Maurice, 327
Magic Theater, 132, 178–80, 182,
    184, 381, 398, 401–4, 408, 415
magical realism, 186
Magnus, Albertus, 219
Mainz, 12
Mann, Heinrich, 329
Mann, Thomas, 1, 12–13, 75–76,
    157, 161, 220, 224, 228, 233,
    242, 311, 314, 323–24, 385, 389,
    397, 407
Mann, Thomas, works by:
    Doktor Faustus, 228, 390
    Felix Krull, 28, 281, 324
    Josef und seine Brüder, 233
    Tonio Kröger, 324
    Der Zauberberg, 171
Mansfield, Jayne, 195
Marbach, 162
Marcuse, Herbert, 205
Marquez, Gabriel Garcia, 186
Marti, Fritz, 338
Marxism, 230, 249, 313
März, 301–2
Maugham, William Somerset, 162–
    63
Maulbronn, 21–22, 29–31, 40, 45–
    46, 48, 50
Maya, 167, 168
Meister, Rolf, 44
Mephisto, 93, 227
Messiaen, Olivier, 375
Meyer, Agnes E., 228
Michel, Edith, 217
Michel, Willy, 217
Michels, Volker, 12, 17, 26, 51,
    127, 140, 380
Middle Ages, 187–88, 194, 207–8,
    375
Middleton, J. C., 233
Mileck, Joseph, 11, 17, 117, 121,
    184, 271
Mill, James, 277
Minnesang, 192
Mog, Paul, 39

Moillet, Louis, 143, 351, 353
Montagnola, 4–5, 117, 120–21,
    184, 215, 350, 366
Monte Verita, 11, 165, 303
Morgenthaler, Ernst, 227
Mörike, Eduard, 375
Morris, Paul W., 159–61
Mozart, Wolfgang Amadeus, 178,
    184–85, 380, 383, 387–89, 395,
    400–404, 406, 409–10, 415
Muehlon, Johann Wilhelm, 307
Mühlhausen, 125
Müller, Friedrich Max, 264, 268,
    278
Müller, Michael, 35, 39, 47
Munch, Edward, 200
Münchner Zeitung, 328
Munich, 4
Murti, Kamakshi P., 164
Muschg, Adolf, 11, 411, 414
Musil, Robert, 171

Napoleon, 399
National Socialism, 36, 203–4, 206,
    215, 313, 404, 309, 313
National-Zeitung, 346
Negus, Kenneth, 232
Neng, Hui, 166, 167
Neue Zürcher Zeitung, 26–27, 304,
    306, 328
Neugroschel, Joachim, 156–58, 161,
    164
New Age, 158, 163, 199, 209
New Testament, 29–30, 149, 209,
    227
Niemöller, Martin, 318
Nietzsche, Friedrich, 3, 9, 81, 92,
    94, 123–24, 176, 187, 208, 222,
    229, 267, 284, 339, 384, 395–96,
    398, 401
nirvana, 155, 290
Nobel Prize for Literature, 184, 374
Nolde, Emil, 366
Noob, Joachim, 46

Novalis, 81, 98, 123, 140, 219, 267,
    339, 375–76, 395, 402
Novelle/novella, 57, 139
Nußbaum, Felix, 204

Oetinger, F. C., 227
Orme, Robert, 281
Österling, Anders, 374
Otten, Anna, 1
Ovid, 287

Palm, August, 20–22
Palmer, Craig Bernard, 272–73, 284
Pannwitz, Rudolf, 224, 414
Panofsky, Erwin, 345
Petropoulou, Evi, 270
Pfeifer, Martin, 35
Philippi, Klaus-Peter, 7
pietism, 2, 181
Pink Floyd, 192
Pinsky, Robert, 243
Plato, 92, 229, 269
Pope Benedict XVI, 208
Pope Pius XII, 206
Potoker, Edward M., 45
Prakash, Gyan, 268, 277–78
Protestant Reformation, 208
psychoanalysis, 14, 83, 117, 127–28,
    131, 157, 159–60, 179, 188
Puppe, Heinz W., 129
Purcell, Henry, 389

Raphael, Lev, 285
Rathenau, Walther, 203
Rauch-Rapaport, Angelika, 271–72
Red Cross, 305
Reich-Ranicki, Marcel, 7–8
Reichskristallnacht, 251
Reinhard, Hans, 326
Renaissance, 200, 375
Rilke, Rainer Maria, 247, 340, 379
Rinser, Louise, 318
Robbins, Tom, 161–65
Rolland, Romain, 374, 379, 388,
    404–5

Rooks, Conrad, 264
Rops, Felicien, 200
Rosenberg, Alfred, 233
Rosner, Hilda, 156, 158, 16
Rousseau, Jean-Jacques, 411
Rupp, Elisabeth, 143
Rushdie, Salman, 186

S. Fischer Verlag, 215, 316
Said, Edward, 282
Sansara, 152
Sanskrit, 164, 277, 373
Schädelin, Walter, 330
Schäfer, Wilhelm, 311
Schering, Arnold, 390
Schickele, Rene, 307
Schiller, Friedrich, 123, 126, 220, 310, 410, 413
Schlaf, Johannes, 75
Schmidt, Carl, 95
Schmidt, Hans Rudolf, 43
Schnittkin, Theodor, 339
Schoeck, Othmar, 374
Schönberg, Arnold, 375
Schopenhauer, Arthur, 229, 267
Schrempf, Christoph, 125–27, 336
Schubert, Franz, 219, 374, 383, 389, 401
Schumann, Robert, 374, 383, 389
Schussen, Wilhelm, 317
Schweckendieck, Adolf, 44–45
Schweitzer, Albert, 390, 392
Second World War, 204, 313, 316–17
Secundus, Johannes, 219
Seelig, Carl, 140
Seghers, Anna, 314
Seidlin, Oskar, 216, 222–23, 227, 232
Serrano, Miguel, 270
Servais, Franz, 35
sexuality, 194
Shaw, Leroy, 150
Sieveking, Gerhart, 83
Simplizissimus, 301

Sinclair, Emil, 4, 309
Singh, Sikander, 12, 36, 38, 70, 74, 131
Socrates, 92, 229, 269, 385
Solbach, Andreas, 42–43, 127
Solothurn, 11
Soutter, Louis, 246
Spengler, Oswald, 9, 386, 396
Spinoza, Baruch, 229
Sri Lanka, 3, 160–61
St. Francis of Assisi, 387
St. Hilarion, 225
St. Ignatius, 221
St. Jerome, 215
St. John, 288
Stalin, Joseph, 249, 318
Steiner, Rudolf, 416
Stelzig, Eugene L., 51
Steudel, Fr., 35, 42, 49
Stingelin, Martin, 121
Stoler, Ann Laura, 276, 283
Stolte, Heinz, 17, 45
Strauss, Richard, 378, 385
Strauß und Torney, Lulu von, 82
Stravinsky, Igor, 390
Strohmayer, Wilhelm, 43–44, 49
Stuttgart, 23
Suhrkamp, Peter, 6, 12, 243, 316
Suhrkamp Verlag, 6, 12, 18, 20, 318
Suzuki, Daisetz Teitaro, 162
Swabia, 2, 23, 126, 227

Tao, 150–54, 166, 168
technology, 176
Tertullian, 215
Thalmann, Marianne, 409
The Doors, 192
Theresienstadt, 204
Theweleit, Klaus, 195
Third Reich, 6, 203, 314
Thoma, Ludwig, 301–2
Thu Fu, 144
Ticino/Tessin, 117, 121, 140–41, 145, 184, 314, 366
Tieck, Ludwig, 375

Tolstoy, Leo, 58
Tönnies, Ferdinand, 104
Trotsky, Leon, 306
Tübingen, 2–3, 24, 326, 379
Tucholsky, Kurt, 14, 78
Tuite, Clara, 287
Turner, Victor, 84, 108–9
Tusken, Lewis W., 11, 45, 61, 70, 73, 76
Twain, Mark, 385

Uhland, Ludwig, 219
Ulm, 23
Unseld, Siegfried, 12
Upanishads, 149
Utopie/utopia, 227, 265

van de Velde, Henry, 303
van Gogh, Vincent, 140, 352, 385
Varges Llosa, Mario, 186
Vasquez, Manuel, 280
Versailles, 306
Vesper, Will, 5
Villon, Francois, 375
Vischer, Friedrich Theodor, 126
Vivos voco, 120, 310

Wackenroder, Wilhelm Heinrich, 81
Wagner, Ernst, 121, 123–26
Wagner, Richard, 117–18, 123–24, 205, 383–85, 388, 401
Walser, Martin, 334
Walther, Klaus, 57
Wasser, Walter Ueber, 351, 356
Weber, Alfred, 122
Wedekind, Frank, 303
Weimar Republic, 4–5, 11, 203, 311, 313, 315, 401
Weiss, Peter, 314
Welti, Albert, 59
Wenger, Lisa, 357
Wenger, Ruth, 4, 143, 145, 359, 374, 388
Wenger, Theo, 357
West, Mae, 195

Wetzel, Justus Hermann, 378
White, Ann, 227
White, John, 227
Wiegand, Heinrich, 314
Wieland, Christoph Martin, 181
Wildgen, Wolfgang, 358
Wilhelm, Richard, 163, 233
Wilhelm II, 3, 301–2
Wilson, Colin, 11, 184
Winterthur, 366
Wohmann, Gabriele, 35
Woltereck, Richard, 120, 304, 310
Woodstock Festival, 190–91

Zen Buddhism, 159, 162, 166
Ziolkowski, Theodore, 11, 13, 17, 70, 151–52, 184, 217, 224, 227–28, 231–32, 264, 380, 409
Zurich, 149, 215
Zweig, Stefan, 140, 150